THE DOCUMENTARY HISTORY OF THE RATIFICATION OF THE CONSTITUTION

VOLUME XIX

Ratification of the Constitution by the States

NEW YORK

[1]

D0780278

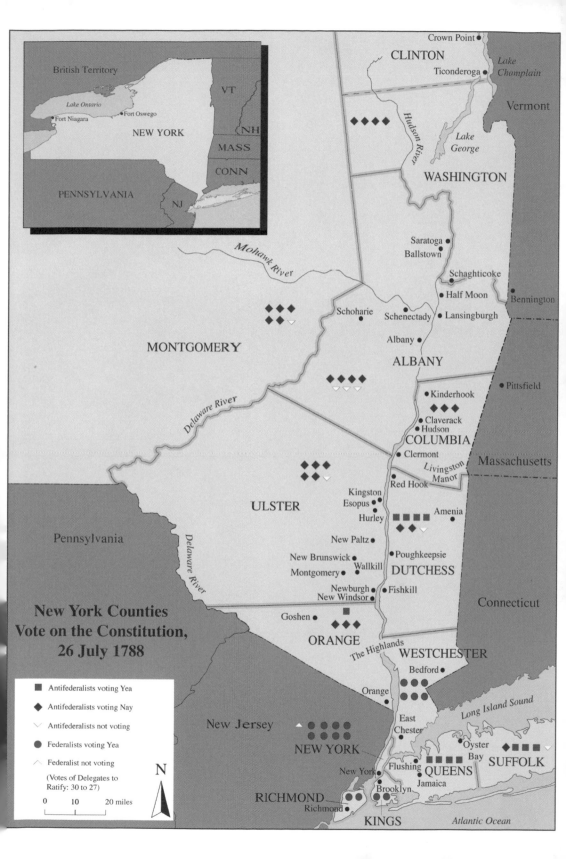

**New York Counties
Vote on the Constitution,
26 July 1788**

Legend:
- ■ Antifederalists voting Yea
- ◆ Antifederalists voting Nay
- ∨ Antifederalists not voting
- ● Federalists voting Yea
- ∧ Federalist not voting

(Votes of Delegates to
Ratify: 30 to 27)

0   10   20 miles

N

Inset map labels: British Territory, Lake Ontario, Fort Niagara, Fort Oswego, NEW YORK, PENNSYLVANIA, VT, NH, MASS, CONN, NJ

Main map labels: CLINTON, Crown Point, Ticonderoga, Lake Champlain, Vermont, Hudson River, Lake George, WASHINGTON, Saratoga, Ballstown, Schaghticoke, Half Moon, Bennington, Schoharie, Schenectady, Lansingburgh, Albany, ALBANY, MONTGOMERY, Kinderhook, Pittsfield, Claverack, Hudson, COLUMBIA, Clermont, Massachusetts, Delaware River, Livingston Manor, Red Hook, Kingston, Esopus, Hurley, Amenia, ULSTER, New Paltz, New Brunswick, Wallkill, Poughkeepsie, Montgomery, DUTCHESS, Newburgh, New Windsor, Fishkill, Connecticut, Pennsylvania, Goshen, ORANGE, WESTCHESTER, The Highlands, Bedford, Orange, East Chester, Long Island Sound, New Jersey, Oyster Bay, SUFFOLK, NEW YORK, Flushing, QUEENS, New York, Jamaica, Brooklyn, RICHMOND, Richmond, KINGS, Atlantic Ocean

THE DOCUMENTARY HISTORY OF THE RATIFICATION OF THE CONSTITUTION

Volume XIX

Ratification of the Constitution

by the States

NEW YORK

[1]

Editors

JOHN P. KAMINSKI   GASPARE J. SALADINO

RICHARD LEFFLER   CHARLES H. SCHOENLEBER

Assistant Editor   Editorial Assistant
MARGARET A. HOGAN   SARAH K. DANFORTH

MADISON
WISCONSIN HISTORICAL SOCIETY PRESS
2 0 0 3

The Documentary History of the Ratification of the Constitution is sponsored by the National Historical Publications and Records Commission and the University of Wisconsin-Madison. Preparation of this volume was made possible by grants from the National Historical Publications and Records Commission; the Division of Research and Education Programs of the National Endowment for the Humanities, an independent federal agency; the Lynde and Harry Bradley Foundation; and the E. Gordon Fox Fund. Publication was made possible in part by a grant from the National Historical Publications and Records Commission.

Copyright © 2003 by
THE STATE HISTORICAL SOCIETY OF WISCONSIN
All rights reserved

Manufactured in the United States of America

♾ This paper meets the requirements of ANSI/NISO Z39.48-1992 (Performance of Paper).

LIBRARY OF CONGRESS CATALOGING IN PUBLICATION DATA [REVISED]
Main entry under title:
The Documentary history of the ratification
    of the Constitution.
    Editors for v. 19: John P. Kaminski, Gaspare J. Saladino, Richard Leffler, Charles H. Schoenleber.
    CONTENTS: v. 1. Constitutional documents and records, 1776–1787.—v. 2. Ratification of the Constitution by the States: Pennsylvania.—v. 3. Ratification of the Constitution by the States: Delaware, New Jersey, Georgia, Connecticut.—v. 4. Ratification of the Constitution by the States: Massachusetts (1).—v. 5. Ratification of the Constitution by the States: Massachusetts (2).—v. 6. Ratification of the Constitution by the States: Massachusetts (3).—v. 7. Ratification of the Constitution by the States: Massachusetts (4).—v. 8. Ratification of the Constitution by the States: Virginia (1).—v. 9. Ratification of the Constitution by the States: Virginia (2).—v. 10. Ratification of the Constitution by the States: Virginia (3).—v. 13. Commentaries on the Constitution, public and private (1).—v. 14. Commentaries on the Constitution, public and private (2).—v. 15. Commentaries on the Constitution, public and private (3).—v. 16. Commentaries on the Constitution, public and private (4).—v. 17. Commentaries on the Constitution, public and private (5).—v. 18. Commentaries on the Constitution, public and private (6).—v. 19. Ratification of the Constitution by the States: New York (1).
    1. United States—Constitutional history—Sources.
    I. Jensen, Merrill. II. Kaminski, John P. III. Saladino,
    Gaspare J. IV. Leffler, Richard. V. Schoenleber, Charles H.
KF4502.D63   342'.73'029   75–14149
ISBN 0–87020–342-8   347.30229   AACR2

To

JOHN Y. SIMON

Dean of Documentary Editors

EDITORIAL ADVISORY COMMITTEE

Whitfield J. Bell, Jr.
Charlene N. Bickford
Jackson Turner Main
Leonard Rapport
James Morton Smith
Robert J. Taylor
Dorothy Twohig

Contents

I. THE DEBATE OVER THE CONSTITUTION IN NEW YORK
21 July 1787–31 January 1788

CONTENTS ix

Americanus IV, New York Daily Advertiser, 5–6 December 354
Don Diego de Gardoqui to Conde de Floridablanca, New York, 6 December 360
P. Valerius Agricola, Albany Gazette, 6 December 361
Cincinnatus VI: To James Wilson, Esquire, New York Journal, 6 December 367
A Countryman I (DeWitt Clinton), New York Journal, 6 December 372
New York Journal, 6 December 378
Publius: The Federalist 18, New York Packet, 7 December 379
   See CC:330
James Kent to Nathaniel Lawrence, Poughkeepsie, 8 December 379
Robert R. Livingston to John Stevens, Sr., New York, 8 December 380
Publius: The Federalist 19, New York Independent Journal, 8 December 381
   See CC:333
William Constable to William Chambers, New York, 10 December 381
Roderick Razor, New York Daily Advertiser, 11 December 382
Examiner I, New York Journal, 11 December 388
Publius: The Federalist 20, New York Packet, 11 December 390
   See CC:340
One of Your Constant Readers, Lansingburgh Northern Centinel, 11 December 390
Lansingburgh Northern Centinel, 11 December 392
Cato, Poughkeepsie Country Journal, 12 December 394
Americanus V, New York Daily Advertiser, 12 December 397
D——, New York Daily Advertiser, 12 December 402
Publius: The Federalist 21, New York Independent Journal, 12 December 403
   See CC:341
One of the Nobility, New York Journal, 12 December 403
A Countryman II (DeWitt Clinton), New York Journal, 13 December 406
Brutus V, New York Journal, 13 December 410
Cato VI, New York Journal, 13 December 416
New York Daily Advertiser, 14 December 420
Democritus, New York Journal, 14 December 421
Examiner II, New York Journal, 14 December 423
Publius: The Federalist 22, New York Packet, 14 December 424
   See CC:347
Antoine de La Forest to Comte de Montmorin, New York, 15 December 424
A Countryman IV (Hugh Hughes), New York Journal, 15 December 424
New York Journal, 17 December 428
Publius: The Federalist 23, New York Packet, 18 December 428
   See CC:352
Lansingburgh Northern Centinel, 18 December 429
A Country Federalist, Poughkeepsie Country Journal, 19 December
   (supplement) 430
Cato, Poughkeepsie Country Journal, 19 December (supplement) 438
Publius: The Federalist 24, New York Independent Journal, 19 December 440
   See CC:355
Examiner III, New York Journal, 19 December 441
A Friend to Common Sense, New York Journal, 19 December 442
Pennsylvania Journal, 19 December 444
Albany Gazette, 20 December 444
Albany Gazette, 20 December 444
Albany Gazette, 20 December 445

Acknowledgments

This volume was supported principally by grants from the National Historical Publications and Records Commission, the National Endowment for the Humanities, and the E. Gordon Fox Fund. Substantial aid was provided also by the Lynde and Harry Bradley Foundation.

We extend our thanks and appreciation to Ann C. Newhall, Roger A. Bruns, Timothy D. W. Connelly, and Mary A. Giunta of the NHPRC; Bruce Cole, James Herbert, Elizabeth Arndt, and Michael Hall of the NEH; and Dianne J. Sehler of the Bradley Foundation.

A continuing debt of gratitude is owed to the administration, faculty, and staff of the University of Wisconsin-Madison, especially Chancellor John D. Wiley; Dean Phillip R. Certain, Associate Dean David Horvath, Assistant Dean Margaret M. Sullivan, and Linda J. Johnson of the College of Letters and Sciences; Charles L. Hoffman, August P. Hackbart, and Thomas G. Handland of Research and Sponsored Programs; and Chair Thomas Spear, Michael R. Burmeister, Jessica S. Hansey, Sandra J. Heitzkey, Mark A. Hull, Mary L. Lybeck, Mary J. Nuzzo, John J. Persike, Theresa K. Tobias, Judith A. Vezzetti, and Jeffrey P. Ziarnik of the Department of History.

For aid in fund raising, we are indebted to the University of Wisconsin Foundation, especially to President Andrew A. Wilcox, Marion F. Brown, Martha A. Taylor, and Jennifer Kidon-DeKrey.

The Wisconsin Historical Society has been our primary research library and our publisher for many years. The Society's staff continues its invaluable and splendid support. We thank Lori B. Bessler, Carol A. Crossan, James P. Danky, Susan J. Dorst, Michael I. Edmonds, Peter Gottlieb, James L. Hansen, Laura K. Hemming, Harold L. Miller, Charlotte M. Mullen, Keith W. Rabiola, Geraldine E. Strey, and Lloyd F. Velicer. The staffs of the reference, circulation, catalog, interlibrary loan, rare books, and acquisitions departments of the Memorial and Law libraries of the University of Wisconsin-Madison continue to be most important to our work.

Others have provided essential information: Kenneth R. Bowling, Documentary History of the First Federal Congress; Douglas E. Clanin, Indiana Historical Society; Frank M. Clover and Johann Sommerville, Department of History, University of Wisconsin-Madison; James G. McKeown, Department of Classics, University of Wisconsin-Madison; and Leonard Rapport, Washington, D.C.

We thank Marieka Brouwer, who, under the direction of Onno Brouwer of the University of Wisconsin-Madison Cartographic Laboratory, prepared the New York map found on the end papers.

This volume is dedicated to Professor John Y. Simon of Southern Illinois University. For forty years John has edited The Papers of Ulysses S. Grant. An expert on the Civil War, Illinois history, Abraham Lincoln, and Grant, John has written and spoken innumerable times on these subjects. As America's senior editor of historical documents, John regularly testifies before the U.S. Congress when documentary editing is being considered. John was also the driving force behind the creation of The Association for Documentary Editing founded in 1978. He was one of its first presidents.

Organization

The Documentary History of the Ratification of the Constitution is divided
into:
  (1) *Constitutional Documents and Records, 1776–1787* (1 volume),
  (2) *Ratification of the Constitution by the States* (18 volumes),
  (3) *Commentaries on the Constitution: Public and Private* (6 volumes),
  (4) *The Bill of Rights* (1 or 2 volumes).

Constitutional Documents and Records, 1776–1787.
  This introductory volume, a companion to all of the other volumes,
traces the constitutional development of the United States during its
first twelve years. Cross-references to it appear frequently in other volumes when contemporaries refer to events and proposals from 1776 to
1787. The documents include: (1) the Declaration of Independence,
(2) the Articles of Confederation, (3) ratification of the Articles, (4)
proposed amendments to the Articles, proposed grants of power to
Congress, and ordinances for the Western Territory, (5) the calling of
the Constitutional Convention, (6) the appointment of Convention delegates, (7) the resolutions and draft constitutions of the Convention,
(8) the report of the Convention, and (9) the Confederation Congress
and the Constitution.

Ratification of the Constitution by the States.
  The volumes are arranged in the order in which the states considered the Constitution. Although there are variations, the documents
for each state are organized into the following groups: (1) commentaries from the adjournment of the Constitutional Convention to the
meeting of the state legislature that called the state convention, (2) the
proceedings of the legislature in calling the convention, (3) commentaries from the call of the convention until its meeting, (4) the election
of convention delegates, (5) the proceedings of the convention, and
(6) post-convention documents.

Microfiche Supplements to Ratification of the Constitution by the States.
  With the publication of the New York and Massachusetts volumes
separate microfiche supplements will no longer be produced. Instead,
all documents in Mfm:N.Y. and Mfm:Mass. (as well as all past microfiche
supplements—Mfm:Pa., Del., N.J., Ga., Conn., and Va.) have been
placed on the publisher's website: www.wisconsinhistory.org/ratifica-
tion. This new method of publication should make the supplemental
documents more easily accessible.

Much of the material for each state is repetitious or peripheral but still valuable. Literal transcripts of this material are placed on microfiche supplements. Occasionally, photographic copies of significant manuscripts are also included.

The types of documents in the supplements are:

(1) newspaper items that repeat arguments, examples of which are printed in the state volumes,

(2) pamphlets that circulated primarily within one state and that are not printed in the state volumes or in *Commentaries,*

(3) letters that contain supplementary material about politics and social relationships,

(4) photographic copies of petitions with the names of signers,

(5) photographic copies of manuscripts such as notes of debates, and

(6) miscellaneous documents such as election certificates, attendance records, pay vouchers and other financial records, etc.

Commentaries on the Constitution: Public and Private.

This series contains newspaper items, pamphlets, and broadsides that circulated regionally or nationally. It also includes some private letters that give the writers' opinions of the Constitution in general or that report on the prospects for ratification in several states. Except for some grouped items, documents are arranged chronologically and are numbered consecutively throughout the six volumes. There are frequent cross-references between *Commentaries* and the state series.

The Bill of Rights.

The public and private debate on the Constitution continued in several states after ratification. It was centered on the issue of whether there should be amendments to the Constitution and the manner in which amendments should be proposed—by a second constitutional convention or by the new U.S. Congress. A bill of rights was proposed in the U.S. Congress on 8 June 1789. Twelve amendments were adopted on 25 September and were sent to the states on 2 October. This volume(s) will contain the documents related to the public and private debate over amendments, to the proposal of amendments by Congress, and to the ratification of the Bill of Rights by the states.

Editorial Procedures

With a few exceptions all documents are transcribed literally. Obvious slips of the pen and errors in typesetting are silently corrected. When spelling or capitalization is unclear, modern usage is followed. Superscripts and interlineated material are lowered to the line. Thorns are spelled out (i.e., "ye" becomes "the"). Crossed-out words are retained when significant and legible.

Brackets are used for editorial insertions. Conjectural readings are enclosed in brackets with a question mark. Illegible and missing words are indicated by dashes enclosed in brackets. However, when the author's intent is obvious, illegible or missing material, up to five characters in length, has been silently provided.

All headings are supplied by the editors. Headings for letters contain the names of the writer and the recipient and the place and date of writing. Headings for newspapers contain the pseudonym, if any, and the name and date of the newspaper. Headings for broadsides and pamphlets contain the pseudonym and a shortened form of the title. Full titles of broadsides and pamphlets and information on authorship are given in editorial notes. Headings for public meetings contain the place and date of the meeting.

Salutations, closings of letters, addresses, endorsements, and docketings are deleted unless they provide important information, which is then either retained in the document or placed in editorial notes.

Contemporary footnotes and marginal notes are printed after the text of the document and immediately preceding editorial footnotes. Symbols, such as stars, asterisks, and daggers have been replaced by superscripts (a), (b), (c), etc.

Many documents, particularly letters, are excerpted when they contain material that is not directly relevant to ratification. When longer excerpts or entire documents have been printed elsewhere, or are included in the microfiche supplements, this fact is noted.

General Ratification Chronology, 1786–1791

1786

21 January	Virginia calls meeting to consider granting Congress power to regulate trade.
11–14 September	Annapolis Convention.
20 September	Congress receives Annapolis Convention report recommending that states elect delegates to a convention at Philadelphia in May 1787.
11 October	Congress appoints committee to consider Annapolis Convention report.
23 November	Virginia authorizes election of delegates to Convention at Philadelphia.
23 November	New Jersey elects delegates.
4 December	Virginia elects delegates.
30 December	Pennsylvania elects delegates.

1787

6 January	North Carolina elects delegates.
17 January	New Hampshire elects delegates.
3 February	Delaware elects delegates.
10 February	Georgia elects delegates.
21 February	Congress calls Constitutional Convention.
22 February	Massachusetts authorizes election of delegates.
28 February	New York authorizes election of delegates.
3 March	Massachusetts elects delegates.
6 March	New York elects delegates.
8 March	South Carolina elects delegates.
14 March	Rhode Island refuses to elect delegates.
23 April–26 May	Maryland elects delegates.
5 May	Rhode Island again refuses to elect delegates.
14 May	Convention meets; quorum not present.
14–17 May	Connecticut elects delegates.
25 May	Convention begins with quorum of seven states.
16 June	Rhode Island again refuses to elect delegates.
27 June	New Hampshire renews election of delegates.
13 July	Congress adopts Northwest Ordinance.
6 August	Committee of Detail submits draft constitution to Convention.
12 September	Committee of Style submits draft constitution to Convention.
17 September	Constitution signed and Convention adjourns *sine die*.
20 September	Congress reads Constitution.
26–28 September	Congress debates Constitution.
28 September	Congress transmits Constitution to the states.
28–29 September	Pennsylvania calls state convention.

17 October	Connecticut calls state convention.
25 October	Massachusetts calls state convention.
26 October	Georgia calls state convention.
31 October	Virginia calls state convention.
1 November	New Jersey calls state convention.
6 November	Pennsylvania elects delegates to state convention.
10 November	Delaware calls state convention.
12 November	Connecticut elects delegates to state convention.
19 November– 7 January 1788	Massachusetts elects delegates to state convention.
20 November– 15 December	Pennsylvania Convention.
26 November	Delaware elects delegates to state convention.
27 November– 1 December	Maryland calls state convention.
27 November– 1 December	New Jersey elects delegates to state convention.
3–7 December	Delaware Convention.
4–5 December	Georgia elects delegates to state convention.
6 December	North Carolina calls state convention.
7 December	Delaware Convention ratifies Constitution, 30 to 0.
11–20 December	New Jersey Convention.
12 December	Pennsylvania Convention ratifies Constitution, 46 to 23.
14 December	New Hampshire calls state convention.
18 December	New Jersey Convention ratifies Constitution, 38 to 0.
25 December– 5 January 1788	Georgia Convention.
31 December	Georgia Convention ratifies Constitution, 26 to 0.
31 December– 12 February 1788	New Hampshire elects delegates to state convention.

1788

3–9 January	Connecticut Convention.
9 January	Connecticut Convention ratifies Constitution, 128 to 40.
9 January–7 February	Massachusetts Convention.
19 January	South Carolina calls state convention.
1 February	New York calls state convention.
6 February	Massachusetts Convention ratifies Constitution, 187 to 168, and proposes amendments.
13–22 February	New Hampshire Convention: first session.
1 March	Rhode Island calls statewide referendum on Constitution.
3–27 March	Virginia elects delegates to state convention.
24 March	Rhode Island referendum: voters reject Constitution, 2,711 to 239.
28–29 March	North Carolina elects delegates to state convention.
7 April	Maryland elects delegates to state convention.
11–12 April	South Carolina elects delegates to state convention.
21–29 April	Maryland Convention.

26 April	Maryland Convention ratifies Constitution, 63 to 11.
29 April–3 May	New York elects delegates to state convention.
12–24 May	South Carolina Convention.
23 May	South Carolina Convention ratifies Constitution, 149 to 73, and proposes amendments.
2–27 June	Virginia Convention.
17 June–26 July	New York Convention.
18–21 June	New Hampshire Convention: second session.
21 June	New Hampshire Convention ratifies Constitution, 57 to 47, and proposes amendments.
25 June	Virginia Convention ratifies Constitution, 89 to 79.
27 June	Virginia Convention proposes amendments.
2 July	New Hampshire ratification read in Congress; Congress appoints committee to report an act for putting the Constitution into operation.
21 July–4 August	First North Carolina Convention.
26 July	New York Convention Circular Letter calls for second constitutional convention.
26 July	New York Convention ratifies Constitution, 30 to 27, and proposes amendments.
2 August	North Carolina Convention proposes amendments and refuses to ratify until amendments are submitted to Congress and to a second constitutional convention.
13 September	Congress sets dates for election of President and meeting of new government under the Constitution.
20 November	Virginia requests Congress under the Constitution to call a second constitutional convention.
30 November	North Carolina calls second state convention.

1789

4 March	First Federal Congress convenes.
1 April	House of Representatives attains quorum.
6 April	Senate attains quorum.
30 April	George Washington inaugurated first President.
8 June	James Madison proposes Bill of Rights in Congress.
21–22 August	North Carolina elects delegates to second state convention.
25 September	Congress adopts twelve amendments to Constitution to be submitted to the states.
16–23 November	Second North Carolina Convention.
21 November	Second North Carolina Convention ratifies Constitution, 194 to 77, and proposes amendments.

1790

17 January	Rhode Island calls state convention.
8 February	Rhode Island elects delegates to state convention.
1–6 March	Rhode Island Convention: first session.
24–29 May	Rhode Island Convention: second session.
29 May	Rhode Island Convention ratifies Constitution, 34 to 32, and proposes amendments.

1791

15 December	Bill of Rights adopted.

Calendar for the Years
1787–1788

1787

S	M	T	W	T	F	S
JANUARY						
	1	2	3	4	5	6
7	8	9	10	11	12	13
14	15	16	17	18	19	20
21	22	23	24	25	26	27
28	29	30	31			

S	M	T	W	T	F	S
FEBRUARY						
				1	2	3
4	5	6	7	8	9	10
11	12	13	14	15	16	17
18	19	20	21	22	23	24
25	26	27	28			

S	M	T	W	T	F	S
MARCH						
				1	2	3
4	5	6	7	8	9	10
11	12	13	14	15	16	17
18	19	20	21	22	23	24
25	26	27	28	29	30	31

S	M	T	W	T	F	S
APRIL						
1	2	3	4	5	6	7
8	9	10	11	12	13	14
15	16	17	18	19	20	21
22	23	24	25	26	27	28
29	30					

S	M	T	W	T	F	S
MAY						
	1	2	3	4	5	
6	7	8	9	10	11	12
13	14	15	16	17	18	19
20	21	22	23	24	25	26
27	28	29	30	31		

S	M	T	W	T	F	S
JUNE						
					1	2
3	4	5	6	7	8	9
10	11	12	13	14	15	16
17	18	19	20	21	22	23
24	25	26	27	28	29	30

S	M	T	W	T	F	S
JULY						
1	2	3	4	5	6	7
8	9	10	11	12	13	14
15	16	17	18	19	20	21
22	23	24	25	26	27	28
29	30	31				

S	M	T	W	T	F	S
AUGUST						
			1	2	3	4
5	6	7	8	9	10	11
12	13	14	15	16	17	18
19	20	21	22	23	24	25
26	27	28	29	30	31	

S	M	T	W	T	F	S
SEPTEMBER						1
2	3	4	5	6	7	8
9	10	11	12	13	14	15
16	17	18	19	20	21	22
23	24	25	26	27	28	29
30						

S	M	T	W	T	F	S
OCTOBER						
	1	2	3	4	5	6
7	8	9	10	11	12	13
14	15	16	17	18	19	20
21	22	23	24	25	26	27
28	29	30	31			

S	M	T	W	T	F	S
NOVEMBER						
				1	2	3
4	5	6	7	8	9	10
11	12	13	14	15	16	17
18	19	20	21	22	23	24
25	26	27	28	29	30	

S	M	T	W	T	F	S
DECEMBER						1
2	3	4	5	6	7	8
9	10	11	12	13	14	15
16	17	18	19	20	21	22
23	24	25	26	27	28	29
30	31					

1788

S	M	T	W	T	F	S
JANUARY						
		1	2	3	4	5
6	7	8	9	10	11	12
13	14	15	16	17	18	19
20	21	22	23	24	25	26
27	28	29	30	31		

S	M	T	W	T	F	S
FEBRUARY						
					1	2
3	4	5	6	7	8	9
10	11	12	13	14	15	16
17	18	19	20	21	22	23
24	25	26	27	28	29	

S	M	T	W	T	F	S
MARCH						1
2	3	4	5	6	7	8
9	10	11	12	13	14	15
16	17	18	19	20	21	22
23	24	25	26	27	28	29
30	31					

S	M	T	W	T	F	S
APRIL						
		1	2	3	4	5
6	7	8	9	10	11	12
13	14	15	16	17	18	19
20	21	22	23	24	25	26
27	28	29	30			

S	M	T	W	T	F	S
MAY						
				1	2	3
4	5	6	7	8	9	10
11	12	13	14	15	16	17
18	19	20	21	22	23	24
25	26	27	28	29	30	31

S	M	T	W	T	F	S
JUNE						
1	2	3	4	5	6	7
8	9	10	11	12	13	14
15	16	17	18	19	20	21
22	23	24	25	26	27	28
29	30					

S	M	T	W	T	F	S
JULY						
		1	2	3	4	5
6	7	8	9	10	11	12
13	14	15	16	17	18	19
20	21	22	23	24	25	26
27	28	29	30	31		

S	M	T	W	T	F	S
AUGUST					1	2
3	4	5	6	7	8	9
10	11	12	13	14	15	16
17	18	19	20	21	22	23
24	25	26	27	28	29	30
31						

S	M	T	W	T	F	S
SEPTEMBER						
	1	2	3	4	5	6
7	8	9	10	11	12	13
14	15	16	17	18	19	20
21	22	23	24	25	26	27
28	29	30				

S	M	T	W	T	F	S
OCTOBER						
			1	2	3	4
5	6	7	8	9	10	11
12	13	14	15	16	17	18
19	20	21	22	23	24	25
26	27	28	29	30	31	

S	M	T	W	T	F	S
NOVEMBER						1
2	3	4	5	6	7	8
9	10	11	12	13	14	15
16	17	18	19	20	21	22
23	24	25	26	27	28	29
30						

S	M	T	W	T	F	S
DECEMBER						
	1	2	3	4	5	6
7	8	9	10	11	12	13
14	15	16	17	18	19	20
21	22	23	24	25	26	27
28	29	30	31			

New York Introduction

A New State Constitution

During the decade preceding the War for Independence, New York was divided into two large provincial factions—the Delanceys and the Livingstons. When independence neared, the Delanceys were in power and they remained loyal to the king. The opposition to British imperial policy consisted of three groups—the radical elements led by New York City mechanics who advocated independence from Great Britain, a very conservative group that wanted reconciliation, and another conservative group that wanted to delay independence but would not give up key colonial rights. Because conservatives controlled the third Provincial Congress, that body gave no instructions on the question of independence to New York's delegates to the Second Continental Congress meeting in Philadelphia. Not being instructed, the New York delegation, standing alone, did not vote on independence on 2 July 1776. Earlier, in response to the Continental Congress' resolution of 15 May 1776, the third Provincial Congress had called on the electors in the different counties to elect a fourth provincial congress which might draft a constitution creating a state government. The election took place and the new Provincial Congress on 9 July resolved unanimously to join the other colonies in declaring independence. The next day it renamed itself the Provincial Convention. On 1 August the Convention appointed a committee of thirteen to draft a state constitution and to report by 26 August. The committee did not report until 12 March 1777. After almost six weeks of debate, the Convention on 20 April voted "in the name and by the authority of the good people of this State" to adopt the constitution.

The new constitution provided the framework for one of the most conservative state governments in the Union. Among the leading architects were John Jay, James Duane, Robert R. Livingston, Gouverneur Morris, and Abraham Yates, Jr. (chair). The first article provided "that no authority shall on any pretence whatever be exercised over the people or members of this State, but such as shall be derived from and granted by them."

"The supreme legislative power" was vested in a legislature consisting of an Assembly "of at least seventy members" and a Senate of at least twenty-four. The legislature was required to meet at least once each year. Each house could judge of its own members and each needed a majority for a quorum. The Assembly could elect its own speaker; the lieutenant governor would serve as the president of the Senate with a casting vote in case of ties. The doors of both houses were to be open, "except when the welfare of the State" required secrecy. Bills could originate in either house. A conference committee would resolve differences between the two houses.

The Assembly was elected annually by adult male inhabitants who had resided in a county for six months and who were freeholders owning land worth at least £20 (half the colonial requirement) or tenants paying annual rents of at least £2 and who had "been rated and actually paid taxes to this State." All freemen as of 14 October 1775 in New York City and Albany could also vote. As the population increased (determined by a septennial census), a county's representation could be increased or the legislature could create new counties until the Assembly grew to a maximum of 300 members. Because of a demand for switching from *viva voce* to balloting, it was decided that "as soon as may be" after the war, an experiment with balloting for both houses of the legislature should be tried. If, however, "after a full and fair experiment" balloting should "be found less conducive to the safety or interest of the State, than the method of voting *viva voce*, it shall be lawful and constitutional for the legislature" by a two-thirds vote of those present in each house to restore voice voting.

The Senate was to be chosen by freeholders possessed of net property worth £100. Immediately after the first election, the twenty-four senators would be divided by lot into four classes of six senators each. Those in the first class would have a one-year term, in the second class two years, etc. In this way after the first four years all senators would have a four-year term with one-quarter of the senators being elected in any given year. The state's senators were to be grouped into four districts— southern, eastern, western, and middle districts. The constitution initially allotted nine senators to the southern district, three to the eastern district (which included Vermont), and six each to the middle and western districts. When a septennial census indicated a sufficient population growth, the legislature could increase the number of senators to a maximum of 100 and increase the number of counties and districts.

The "supreme executive power, and authority" was lodged in a governor elected by ballot by those freeholders qualified to vote for the Senate. The governor had a three-year term, the longest of any state executive in the Union. No reeligibility restrictions were placed upon him. The governor was general and commander-in-chief of the state militia and admiral of the state navy. He could call the legislature into special session "on extraordinary occasions" and could prorogue it but for no more than sixty days within a year. A lieutenant governor was elected in the same manner as the governor. The lieutenant governor would serve as president of the Senate.

The constitution provided for two unique councils—the Council of Revision and the Council of Appointment—to handle certain executive functions. The Council of Revision consisted of the governor, the chancellor, and the three justices of the Supreme Court. A quorum of the Council consisted of the governor and any two of the four other members. Every bill passed by the legislature had to be submitted to the Council of Revision for its "revisal and consideration." The Council had to act within ten days, otherwise the bill automatically became law. If the majority of the Council agreed on a report objecting to the bill, the bill and the objections would be returned to the originating house, which could override the Council's objection by a two-thirds vote. The bill and objections would then be sent to the other house, and, if it overrode the objections by a two-thirds vote of the members present, the bill became law. (See Appendix I.)

The Council of Appointment made all appointments not otherwise provided for by the constitution. All Council appointees, whose tenures were not otherwise fixed by the constitution, served at the pleasure of the Council. The Assembly annually appointed one senator from each senatorial district to the Council. The Assembly usually selected the new Council well into the first legislative session after the previous Council had served one full year. Senators could not serve two consecutive terms on the Council. The Governor was president of the Council but could only vote in case of a tie. (See Appendix I.)

The constitution referred to a Supreme Court but never specified its composition. The justices of the Supreme Court were first appointed by the Provincial Convention early in May 1777; they were John Jay (chief justice), Robert Yates, and John Sloss Hobart. These men refused to exercise their duties until the Council of Appointment reappointed them. Equity cases were under the jurisdiction of the chancellor in a court of chancery. The chancellor, Supreme Court justices, and the first judge of each of the county courts (all appointed by the Council of Appointment) served during good behavior or until they reached the age of sixty. The other county judges and justices of the peace served at the pleasure of the Council of Appointment, but their commissions had to be issued at least once every three years. Judges appointed the officers of their courts. Sheriffs and coroners served one-year terms, but not for more than four consecutive years. Sheriffs could hold no other offices concurrently. The Assembly alone, by a two-thirds vote of those present, had the power to impeach government officials.

The constitution provided for a unique court for the trial of impeachments and the correction of errors. It consisted of the president
of the Senate, the senators, the chancellor, and the justices of the Supreme Court. The chancellor or the justices of the Supreme Court were
ineligible to sit on cases appealed from their courts. The court, based
to a certain extent on the British House of Lords, was created by law
in November 1784.

The legislature elected members of Congress annually. Each house
would nominate the number of delegates to be elected. At a joint session those nominated by both houses were declared elected. Half of
the remaining nominees were to be chosen by joint ballot. (The Articles of Confederation provided that each state could have between two
and seven delegates; New York usually elected five or six delegates.)

The constitution provided that the English common law and the statute law of England and the colony of New York as of 19 April 1775
(the date of the Battles of Lexington and Concord) should continue
as law unless altered by the legislature. Unlike some other states, New
York had no separate bill of rights prefacing its constitution. Within
the body of the constitution, a number of rights were protected. No
New Yorker could be disfranchised or deprived of his rights or privileges unless by the law of the land or judgment of his peers. The Anglican Church and the Dutch Reformed Church were disestablished,
and the constitution provided that "the free exercise and enjoyment
of religious profession and worship, without discrimination or preference, shall for ever hereafter be allowed within this State to all mankind. Provided that the liberty of conscience hereby granted, shall not
be so construed, as to excuse acts of licentiousness, or justify practices
inconsistent with the peace or safety of this State." Ministers could not
hold civil or military office, and Quakers could be granted conscientious objector status. The trial by jury as formerly practiced in New
York was to "remain inviolate forever," bills of attainder were forbidden
for crimes committed after the war, the right to counsel was guaranteed
in criminal and civil cases, and no new courts could be established but
that "shall proceed according to the course of the common law." The
legislature was given authority over naturalization. (See Appendix I.)

The Revolution and a Strengthened Congress

Conservative Whigs were pleased with New York's constitution. John
Jay wrote that "Our Constitution is universally approved, even in New
England, where few New York productions have credit. But, unless the
government be committed to proper hands, it will be weak and unsta-
ble at home, and contemptible abroad."[1] Men like Jay hoped and expected to fill the offices with wealthy conservatives. To their chagrin

militia and Continental Army General George Clinton, an Ulster County farmer-lawyer, defeated the aristocratic Philip Schuyler in the gubernatorial election in June 1777. Schuyler lamented his loss to Clinton, a man who was by "family and connections" not entitled to "so distinguished a predominance."[2] Clinton was also elected lieutenant governor, but resigned the post allowing runner-up Pierre Van Cortlandt, a wealthy Westchester manor lord, to assume the office. Both Clinton and Van Cortlandt were reelected continuously five additional times before Clinton retired in 1795. Much of the politics of New York during and after the Revolution centered around the disagreements between the Clintonians and Anti-Clintonians over both state and continental matters.

New York suffered greatly during the Revolution. Throughout most of the war years New York City and parts of the lower six counties were occupied by British troops. The state was thus unable to derive revenue from the trade normally flowing through the port of New York. New York was often the theater of military action as the British attempted to cut off New England from the other states at the Hudson River. Even after Burgoyne's surrender at Saratoga in October 1777, Loyalists, assisted by British regulars and their Indian allies, attacked throughout the Mohawk and Hudson River valleys. New York constantly sought assistance from General George Washington and Congress; but the commander-in-chief never had sufficient forces to meet all the requests and Congress, without coercive power over the states, could provide little aid.

Since Congress was weak, New York (and a few other states) tried to strengthen it. On 6 February 1778 the New York legislature (without amendments) nearly unanimously ratified the Articles of Confederation, proposed by Congress and sent to the states for their approval in November 1777. Governor Clinton signed the act adopting the Articles on 16 February. If Congress were strengthened, he wrote Alexander Hamilton, beyond the provisions of the Articles, "Even their Want of Wisdom but too Evident in most of their Measures woud in that Case be less Injurious."[3] Hamilton agreed that Congress' lack of powers "will, in all probability, ruin us."[4]

George Washington appreciated Clinton's efforts to strengthen Congress and assist the army. "In the confidence of friendship," the commander-in-chief thanked the governor for his support. The weakness of Congress and the lack of support from the states, declared Washington, "have uniformly appeared to me to threaten the subversion of our independence. . . . I should acknowledge, to the honor of your State, that the pernicious system I have complained of has not influenced your councils; but that New York is among the few that has felt the necessity of energy, and considering its situation, has done everything that could be expected from it."⁵

In August 1780 delegates from New Hampshire, Massachusetts, and Connecticut met in Boston to discuss efforts to coordinate activities and to strengthen Congress. The delegates called another convention to meet in Hartford in November 1780 and New York was invited to participate. In transmitting this invitation to the legislature on 7 September, Governor Clinton declared that the powers of Congress had to be increased: "When we reflect upon the present situation of our public affairs, it is evident our embarrassments in the prosecution of the war are chiefly to be attributed to a defect in power in those who ought to exercise a supreme direction, for while congress only recommend and the different States deliberate upon the propriety of the recommendation, we cannot expect a union of force or counsel." He believed that Congress should be vested "with such authority as that in all matters which relate to the war, their requisitions may be peremptory."⁶

The legislature on 23 September agreed to appoint delegates to attend the Hartford Convention "to propose and agree to . . . all such Measures as shall appear calculated to give a Vigour to the governing Powers, equal to the present Crisis."⁷ Schuyler wrote to his soon to be son-in-law Alexander Hamilton that "A Spirit favorable to the common cause has pervaded almost both houses, they begin to talk of a dictator and vice dictators, as if it was a thing that was already determined on. To the Convention to be held at Hartford I believe I shall be sent with Instructions to propose that a Dictator should be appointed."⁸ On 10 October, the legislature instructed its delegates to Congress to declare New York's earnest wish that throughout the war or until a confederation government was adopted, Congress should "exercise every Power which they may deem necessary for an effectual Prosecution of the War," and that whenever a state failed to provide its quota of men, money, or provisions, "that Congress direct the Commander in Chief without Delay to march the Army, or such Part of it as may be requisite, into such State, and by a Military Force, compel it to furnish its Deficiency."⁹ New York Congressman James Duane told the governor that the resolution "does Honour" to the legislature's "Zeal and publick Spirit."¹⁰

The Hartford Convention, meeting in November 1780, proposed that George Washington be given dictatorial powers and that Congress be given the power to levy tariffs to pay the interest on the public debt and a coercive power to force the states to comply with its requisitions. Furthermore, the delegates advocated that Congress be vested with broad implied powers in addition to the powers specified in the Articles of Confederation. By the end of March 1781, the New York legislature and the governor had endorsed the convention's proposals.

On 5 February 1781, Governor Clinton writing to President of Congress Samuel Huntington challenged what he and the legislature thought was an unfair congressional requisition on the state. In this lengthy letter, he detailed the pain and anguish New Yorkers had endured for the previous five years. Clinton warned Congress that New York could not be expected to withstand the combined attacks of British regulars, Hessians, Loyalists, hostile Indians, and rebellious Vermonters (see below for Vermont) if Congress sapped the state's strength to compensate for the lack of support from other states. Clinton also suggested that Congress either did not have the power to enforce its laws and compel each state to do its duty, or that Congress neglected to exert the coercive power that it did have. New York would not presume to say "whether Congress has *adequate* Powers or not? But we will without hesitation declare that if it has them not, it ought to have them, and that we stand ready on our Part to confer them." But the governor argued that Congress had already exercised "extensive Powers." It had waged war, absolved its citizens of allegiance to the British Crown, emitted money, entered into treaties, sent and received ambassadors, and given dictatorial powers to the commander-in-chief. No state had objected. "Hence we venture to conclude," declared Clinton, "that other States are in Sentiment with us, that these were Powers that necessarily existed in Congress, and we cannot suppose that they should want the Power of compelling the several States to their Duty and thereby enabling the Confederacy to expel the common Enemy."[11] Congress needed to assert itself.

On 1 March 1781, Maryland became the last state to ratify the Articles of Confederation. Congress immediately notified the states that the first federal constitution had been adopted. Governor Clinton relayed the message to the state legislature on 19 March, declaring that "This important event, as it establishes our union, and defeats the first hope of our enemy, cannot but afford the highest satisfaction."[12]

The financial and military difficulties facing the country prompted Congress on 3 February to propose a federal tariff of five percent on all foreign imports—the Impost of 1781—earmarked to pay the interest and principal on the war debt. New York acted swiftly and ratified the impost on 19 March. Eleven other states adopted the impost, but Rhode Island refused. Because the Articles of Confederation required that amendments be adopted by all thirteen state legislatures, the impost died.

Although America's overall military prospects had brightened after Yorktown in October 1781, its finances had worsened. New York still remained occupied, whereby its commerce was disrupted. Governor Clinton wrote John Hanson, President of Congress, in November 1781 expressing his concern "that there is more than a Hazard that we shall not be able, without a Change in our Circumstances, long to maintain our civil Government." Alluding to his letter of 5 February (above) and to various resolutions passed by the legislature at its last session, he assured Hanson that New York was completely federal: "I trust there can be no higher Evidence of a sincere Disposition in the State to promote the common Interest than the alacrity with which they passed the Law for granting to Congress a Duty on Imports and their present proffer to accede to any Propositions which may be made for rendering the Union among the States more intimate and for enabling Congress to draw forth and employ the Resources of the whole Empire with the utmost Vigor." The governor admitted that the state had few resources at present to pay its federal requisitions, but, he predicted, when the British evacuated New York City and peace was established, New York would prosper. Clinton assured Hanson that the state would "chearfully consent to vest" Congress "with every Power requisite to an effectual Defence against foreign Invasion and for the Preservation of internal Peace and Harmony."[13]

Concurring with Governor Clinton's opinion, the New York legislature, meeting in special session in July 1782, resolved that Congress ought to be given additional taxing authority and that a general convention be called to revise the Articles of Confederation. These resolutions were forwarded to Congress, but New York Congressman Ezra L'Hommedieu informed Clinton that they would not have the desired consequences because "very few States seem disposed to grant further Powers to Congress."[14] By mid-January 1783, however, Congressman Alexander Hamilton, who in September 1780 had called for a national convention to strengthen Congress, felt more optimistic. "Every day proves more & more the insufficiency of the confederation. The proselytes to this opinion are increasing fast, . . . and I am not without hope it may ere long take place. But I am far from being sanguine."[15]

Hamilton's optimism was not borne out. The reduced British threat made states less willing to increase the powers of Congress. The New York resolutions were considered by various congressional committees, but in September 1783 a committee recommended that action be postponed. The following month, Clinton wrote to Washington that he was "fully persuaded unless the Powers of the national Council are enlarged and that Body better supported than it is at present, all their Measures will discover such feebleness and want of Energy as will stain us with Disgrace and expose us to the worst of Evils."[16]

A New State Perspective

With the end of hostilities and the evacuation of British troops, the military justification for a strong Union with increased congressional powers ended. Consequently, New Yorkers reassessed their state's position within the Union. Alexander Hamilton reported from Congress that "There are two classes of men [in Congress] . . . one attached to state, the other to Continental politics."[17] In postwar New York two political parties developed—the followers of Governor Clinton opted to address the state's problems, while the followers of Philip Schuyler favored a more Continental program.

Hamilton described his father-in-law as the second most influential man in the state—second only to the governor. Schuyler, however, according to Hamilton, had "more weight in the Legislature than the Governor; but not so much as not to be exposed to the mortification of seeing important measures patronised by him frequently miscarry."[18] In a candid characterization of Schuyler's role in the state Senate, the governor wrote "in special Confidence" in January 1787 that "Genl Schuyler arrived last Night & now I suppose the Senate Room will ring with incoherent Rhapsody and feigned Patriotism, hitherto it has been blessed with singular Harmony—So much for Politics."[19] By the end of 1786, the mantle had shifted to Hamilton.

Party structure and hierarchy were not as clear on the other side. Everyone knew that George Clinton controlled a large number of legislative votes, and that he was the titular head of a party composed of several factions led by different men. The aristocratic Schuylerites— later to be Hamiltonians—did not want the popular governor as an avowed, personal enemy. Far better to oppose some of the more radical factions led by Abraham Yates, Jr., John Lansing, Jr., Ephraim Paine, and "the levellers" Mathew Adgate and Jacob Ford. Yates served especially well as the aristocrats' whipping boy. According to Hamilton, he "is a man whose ignorance and perverseness are only surpassed by his pertinacity and conceit. He hates all high-flyers, which is the appellation he gives to men of genius."[20]

George Clinton was satisfied to exert his influence behind the scenes and was not eager to be publicly acclaimed as the leader of a political party. He believed that he could be more effective above the fray of partisan politics. Furthermore the majority in the legislature was composed of various elements, some of which were too radical for the governor's taste. By staying publicly aloof, the governor stayed out of the rough and tumble political battles, yet he could usually win support for or kill legislative proposals at will.[21]

Clintonians felt that New York had contributed more than its fair share of men and money toward the war effort. Since both the state and federal financial crises could probably not be solved simultaneously, and since it appeared that other states would not contribute significantly to alleviate the federal financial problem, Clintonians decided to concentrate on New York's problems. Therefore, they developed an economic program calling for (1) a state impost, (2) sale of confiscated Loyalist estates and unsettled state lands, (3) a moderate real estate and personal property tax, (4) the issuance of paper money on loan to farmers, (5) the funding of the state debt, and (6) the state assumption of a portion of the federal debt owned by New Yorkers. Schuylerites strenuously opposed this program.

The Clintonian program began on 15 March 1783 with the repeal of New York's earlier approval of the Impost of 1781, the British evacuation of New York City in late November 1783, and the passage in March 1784 of a state impost that was revised in November 1784. The state impost was to be the cornerstone of the new financial system, and as such Clintonians refused to support a continental impost. Annual income from the state impost during the Confederation years ranged between $100,000 and $225,000, and represented between one-third to over one-half the state's annual income. This income was especially significant because much of it was paid by non-New Yorkers. Although the impost was initially paid by importing merchants resident in New York, much of it was passed along to consumers in other states in the form of higher prices for imported goods that were reexported and sold in other states. Half of the foreign goods consumed in Connecticut and New Jersey were originally imported into New York City. Thus, when consumers in other states paid higher prices for imported goods, the additional cost was paid into the treasury of New York. The impost also acted as an invisible tax on New Yorkers to be collected by merchants—a group not well represented among Clintonians. The income from this hidden tax was so substantial that other taxes were kept very low.

Confiscated Loyalist Property

Land sales were expected to contribute significantly to the state's financial recovery. Almost $4,000,000 was raised from the sale of confiscated Loyalist estates. Some Whig manor lords felt uncomfortable about the confiscation of these estates and the creation of moderate-sized parcels from them. Nationalists (those who still wanted to newly created land office to start selling land in the disputed territory. Sensing that Congress could not resolve the matter, both states appointed agents in 1786[31] who met in Hartford, Conn., between 30 November and 16 December and negotiated a compromise. New York was to retain the jurisdictional control over the land but Massachusetts would retain property rights. Although New York retained control over the territory, it lost the vast revenue expected from the sale of the land.

The Northwest Forts

Another point of contention between New York and Congress concerned the northwest forts that the British continued to occupy after the war in violation of the 1783 Treaty of Peace. Of the seven forts in question, five were within the boundaries of New York. As the end of the war neared, New York was eager to occupy the forts to regain control of the lucrative fur trade, assert hegemony over the Indians, and assure its claim to the region. On 27 March 1783 the state legislature passed concurrent resolutions calling for the state to occupy the forts immediately upon the British evacuation. To leave the forts vacant would risk their destruction by Indians. To have the forts garrisoned with Continental troops would encourage those states and individuals who wanted to divest New York of its western lands.

Because the Articles of Confederation forbade states to maintain an army in peacetime "except such number only, as in the judgment of the united states, in congress assembled, shall be deemed requisite to garrison the forts necessary for the defence of such state,"[32] New York requested that Congress allow it to occupy the forts with up to 500 soldiers to be taken from New York troops already under Continental command, who had enlisted for three years' service beginning in April 1781. The legislature asked Congress to declare that these soldiers henceforth would be "in the immediate Service of this State, and not in the Pay or Service of the United States." Since New York was bereft of funds, however, the legislature requested that Congress provide "immediate Subsistence" and munitions for the units and charge these expenses against New York's account with the Confederation.[33] On 1 April 1783, Governor Clinton sent the resolutions to Alexander Hamilton and William Floyd, the state's delegates to Congress. They did not submit the resolutions to Congress. Instead Hamilton committed them to his own committee to prepare a report on a military establishment and then did not pursue the New York resolutions. In effect, he buried the resolutions. A week later the New York delegates reported that the resolutions were sent to committee, but that they thought "it improbable Congress will accede to the idea."[34] On 1 June Hamilton informed

the governor that Congress had agreed to a temporary provision instructing General Washington to garrison the evacuated forts with
three-year Continental soldiers, which Hamilton endorsed as "more for
the interest of the state than to have them garrisoned at" New York's
expense.[35]

Congress reconsidered the garrisoning problem in the spring of
1784. Congressman Ephraim Paine wrote the governor that Congress
would not give New York an estimate of the number of soldiers needed
to garrison the forts until it had decided upon the measures necessary
to take possession of the forts. Paine asked the governor if New York
was likely to raise soldiers to occupy the forts. If so, the state's delegates
would "Endeavour to protract the Determination of Congress upon the
Subject of arangements in order to give an opportunity to our troops
first to get Possession." Paine felt it was important for New York troops
to occupy at least Forts Niagara and Oswego because "it appears to be
the general Sense of the Delegates that the western Country ought to
be Considered as belonging to the united States in Common."[36]

Frustrated with Congress, on 19 March 1784 Governor Clinton (in
violation of the sixth article of the Articles of Confederation) had commissioned a secret envoy to meet with Sir Frederick Haldimand, governor general of Canada, to determine when the British would evacuate
the forts. Haldimand informed New York's envoy that when the forts
were evacuated they would be turned over to Congress. Meanwhile,
however, Great Britain would not evacuate the forts until Americans
compensated Loyalists and removed state impediments hampering British creditors from collecting prewar debts from Americans.

Congressman Paine objected to Congress' "utmost Chicanery." He
believed that Massachusetts had offered to turn over some of the western lands to Congress and retain the rest. Soon, Paine wrote, Congress
would order Massachusetts Continental troops stationed at West Point
to garrison the posts when evacuated by the British. The delegates'
"Chagrin was very visible when Congress were tould plainly that New
York would not Suffer the Massachusets troops to march into that
Country."[37]

A compromise was reached on 3 June 1784—the very day Massachusetts delegates petitioned Congress claiming western New York as Massachusetts property. New York would not be allowed to raise troops for
garrison duty, nor would Congress send Continental soldiers to occupy
the forts. When needed, Congress would call for a regiment of 700
men to be drawn from the militias of four states—New Jersey would
supply 110 soldiers, New York and Connecticut 165 each, and Pennsylvania 260. Pennsylvania would supply the commanding officer.[38]

The Impost of 1783

In April 1783 Congress proposed to the states an economic program to help pay the war debt. Among other things, Congress requested that the method of apportioning federal expenses among the states be changed from the value of land to population. New York adopted this amendment on 9 April 1785. Congress also asked the states to give it the power to levy a five percent tariff for twenty-five years with revenue earmarked exclusively to pay the war debt. New Yorkers divided over the wisdom of granting such a power to Congress. The state's two delegates to Congress—Alexander Hamilton and William Floyd—split their vote on the proposed plan. Floyd supported the measure, but Hamilton opposed it because it was too weak. Despite his opposition, Hamilton urged Governor Clinton to support the impost, but by this time, the governor and his followers had become disenchanted with Congress. They now looked to strengthen the state of New York so that it could stand up to incursions from its neighbors.

Some New Yorkers had ideological reasons for opposing the federal impost. Abraham Yates, Jr., led the opposition in a series of newspaper essays expounding upon the danger of giving Congress the power to levy taxes and to collect revenue independent of the states. These ideologues called for Congress to have the means to pay the public debt, but they demanded that the states should retain the power of the purse and grant Congress the funds it needed.

Yates and others feared that Congress would misuse its taxing power to create a powerful and oppressive bureaucracy reminiscent of prewar imperial harassment. It would appoint "collectors, deputy-collectors, comptrollers, clerks, tide-waiters, and searchers." Ships and soldiers would be maintained in port towns to enforce the tariff. Special courts would be created to try offenders. Opponents of the impost also argued that when the federal government augmented its power, Congress' voracious appetite for authority would be satiated only when it had "swallowed entirely *the sovereignty of the particular states.*"[39] Similar fears surfaced in other states. Consequently, when some states ratified the Impost of 1783, they provided in their acts of ratification that the state constitutional protections accorded their citizens would not be violated by despotic federal prosecutions. Instead of taking such a halfway measure, the New York Senate defeated the impost eleven to seven on 14 April 1785.

On 15 February 1786, Congress asked New York to reconsider its rejection. State Senator Philip Schuyler, in a letter to his political lieutenants in Albany County, held out little hope, but vowed to do his best to obtain the adoption of the impost "for the honor, for the interest and *for the security of the peace* of the state." He was not at liberty to tell them what he meant by the "security of the peace of the state." All he could say at that time was "that we have it in our power by *our prudence*, not by our *strength* to avert disagreeable consequences—we may be driven to do by compulsion that which ought to flow spontaneously from our Justice and from neighbourly considerations."[40] A month later, Schuyler elaborated on his fears. If the legislature refused to pass the impost, "the consequences are seriously to be apprehended." Connecticut had already sent emissaries to Vermont and to western Massachusetts to seek their cooperation in compelling New York's compliance. Such a combination, Schuyler asserted, "will be powerful, and if once hostile disturbances arise, heaven only knows where they will end."[41] Schuyler was not alone in predicting violence. Nathaniel Gorham, a Massachusetts delegate to Congress, believed that it was only "the restraining hand of Congress (weak as it is) that prevents NJ and Conne. from entering the lists very seriously with NY & blood shed would very quickly be the consequence."[42]

Animosity toward New York raged throughout New Jersey and Connecticut. Half of all foreign goods imported into these states came through the Port of New York. In effect, New Jersey and Connecticut consumers, and to a lesser extent those in Massachusetts and Vermont, paid New York's state impost in the form of higher prices. They subsidized New York's low real estate and personal property taxes. This hidden tax cost New Jersey and Connecticut approximately £30,000 and £50,000 per year, respectively. Gorham believed that the discontent fostered by this economic domination would "greatly weaken if not destroy the Union." New Jersey's legislature fought back by resolving not to pay its congressional requisitions until New York gave up its state impost or applied its revenue "for the general purposes of the Union."[43] "Gustavus," writing in the *New York Journal*, 2 March 1786, chided his fellow New Yorkers: "That by our own impost we actually lay two states under contributions, and thereby pay our debt with monies which properly belong to the treasuries of Jersey and Connecticut." But most New Yorkers were not embarrassed; they understood the economics of their port and appreciated its benefits. "Let our imposts and advantages be taken from us, shall we not be obliged to lay as heavy taxes as Connecticut, Boston, &c." The bountiful revenue from the Port of New York was "a privilege Providence hath endowed us with," and New Yorkers were not about to surrender it to Congress.[44]

Attention focused on the New York legislature in April 1786 as it reconsidered the impost. To some the stakes were high—perhaps the very existence of the Union. Some delegates in Congress felt that New

York would accept the impost rather than risk the consequences. Clintonians, however, aware of the attention their state was receiving, chose
to adopt the impost with important restrictions. On 4 May New York
acceded to the principle that revenue from imports should accrue to
Congress for the next twenty-five years to pay the interest and principal
on the public debt. But New York would use the mechanism and bureaucracy of the state impost to collect the revenue. Furthermore, the
state reserved the right to pay Congress the impost revenue with its
paper money.

Congress, now meeting in New York City, received New York's act on
12 May 1786 and appointed a committee to consider it. On 16 June,
the committee's report was read. The committee proposed a resolution
asserting that New York's act "so essentially varies" from Congress' system, that it could not "be considered as a compliance."[45]

Not all congressmen wanted to reject New York's adoption. When
Congress debated the report on 27 July Melancton Smith, one of Clinton's closest advisers, argued that most of the states had "restrictions
& limitations" in their ratification acts so that Congress could not "exercise, appoint or controul any judicial power at all. The Courts of the
diff. States are only competent, and not accountable or controulable
by the U.S." The states, Smith persisted, "generally have not given the
powers asked, yet Cong. have determined these Laws are a compliance—a strict compliance they cannot be—it must be meant then that
they are a substantial compliance—and so a sub[stantial] comp[liance]
is suffi[cient]." Congress would receive the revenue it needed.[46]

James Monroe wrote Clinton that the Virginia congressional delegation wanted to avoid irritating New York. In their judgment, "the
best plan" was for Congress to draft an ordinance implementing the
impost that would show the New York legislature that the new revenue
plan would not be "a system of oppression, but in conformity with the
laws & constitution of the state itself." With this assurance, the legislature would be induced "to grant powers in such conformity with the
acts of other states as to enable them [i.e., Congress] to carry it into
effect." Congress, according to the Virginians, should "proceed with
temper in this business . . . to conciliate & gain the confidence of the
state & all its citizens."[47] Other congressmen, such as Stephen Mix
Mitchell of Connecticut, hoped that Clinton would see "the Precipice
on which the united States as a collective body stand, by reason of
withholding the necessary Means for the preservation of our Union."[48]

The majority of Congress, however, disagreed, and, on 11 August,
Congress asked Governor Clinton to call a special session of the legislature to reconsider the impost. Five days later the governor rejected

the request, referring to the state's constitutional provision that allowed the governor to call special sessions only on "extraordinary Occasions." "I cannot yield a Compliance," Clinton explained, "without breaking through one of those Checks which the Wisdom of our Constitution has provided against the Abuse of Office."[49] On 23 August, Congress again debated and rejected New York's ratification of the impost. For a second time, it requested the governor to call an early session, but Clinton again rejected the request.

Several members of Congress opposed this second request. New York Congressman Melancton Smith unsuccessfully offered a motion opposing a second request to the governor because "it would be inexpedient."[50] North Carolina Congressman Timothy Bloodworth thought this second request to Governor Clinton "improper as there is not the least probabil[it]y of his complying, deeming the measure unwarrantable by the constitution."[51]

Massachusetts Congressman Rufus King had a different perspective. Suggesting that Congress was "as the lawyers say, at issue with New York," King observed that Clinton "is the only one of the thirteen [state governors] who would under similar circumstances refuse" to call the legislature into special session. But King welcomed Clinton's adamant stance and New York's refusal to alter its act adopting the impost. Without a revenue from the impost, King believed that Congress would be justified in doing "every thing in their power for the public Good."[52] Clinton's actions and New York's obstinacy, consequently, would help those nationalists who wanted more power for Congress.

When the legislature convened for its regular session in January 1787, the nationalist forces in the Assembly were mobilized by a new leader. Alexander Hamilton had been elected to the Assembly. On 13 January 1787, Clinton delivered his opening address to the legislature, in which he transmitted Congress' request for a reconsideration of the impost. The governor justified his refusal to call a special session of the legislature and said that he would "forbear making any remarks on a subject which hath been so repeatedly submitted to the consideration of the legislature, and must be well understood."[53] Hamiltonians tried to censure Clinton for not calling the early session. The Assembly, however, approved the governor's inaction, 36 to 9. Connecticut Congressman Stephen Mix Mitchell wrote that the Assembly, in approving Clinton's inaction, "stepd. as twere out of their way to give Congress a Slap in the face."[54]

The Assembly submitted the impost to a three-man committee composed of two Hamiltonians and one Clintonian. On 9 February, the committee recommended a bill that would meet Congress' standards, but Clintonian assemblymen—described by one partisan as "mere machines" under the control of the governor—amended the bill so that it would still remain unacceptable to Congress. On 15 February Hamilton delivered a lengthy, impassioned speech in favor of the federal impost that, according to "Rough Carver" was followed by "a contemptuous silence. . . . The members appeared pre-determined, having . . . *made up their minds on the subject.*"[55] The Assembly then voted 38 to 19 for the amended impost bill—the Clintonian-dominated Assembly had succeeded in retaining the impost and its revenue for state use. The Assembly's actions, according to Virginia Congressman James Madison, "put a definitive veto on the Impost."[56]

Opposition to the impost came from Abraham Yates, Jr., in the Senate and John Lansing, Jr., in the Assembly, whom Hamiltonians attacked as demagogues, pandering to the "little folks." They were also accused, for the love of "power and office," of daily paying "homage to the G——r." As for Clinton, it was "whispered that he also is in secret an anti-impost man." It seemed clear that Clinton had sufficient influence in the Assembly to exert his will, and "a distant hint only from" him could have adopted the impost for Congress.[57] A month after the vote, Philip Schuyler charged that the delegates against the impost were led "by promises, and the influence of a certain great man."[58]

A Devastated Economy

The end of the Revolution in New York brought a short period of prosperity followed by a swift deflation that soon deepened into the "bad times" of 1785–86. These years of severe economic distress were marked by extensive public and private indebtedness, disorganization of trade, contraction of the circulating currency, and drastically reduced agricultural prices. Distressed New Yorkers demanded some sort of relief. Twice in 1784 the Assembly yielded to public demand and passed paper-money proposals, only to have the Senate reject them.

The New York City Chamber of Commerce opposed paper money because it "would not promote the general interest of the State; and that 'till such time as the Public confidence is restored, by a faithful performance of all Contracts Public and Private, it must inevitably depreciate to the Ultimate injury of the Merchants and Inhabitants of this City." But if the legislature did issue paper money, the chamber hoped that it would not be legal tender.[59] Most members of the Chamber admitted that a scarcity of specie existed and that the poor were suffering, but they were afraid that paper money would be issued to excess, leading to an unbridled depreciation, such as had happened to the

Continental currency during the war. To alleviate the distress, petitions submitted to the legislature recommended that the general form of taxation be altered and that the collection of tax arrears be postponed thus lightening the tax burden on those least able to pay.[60]

Some influential men who denounced state paper money believed that a private commercial bank was required. In March 1784 the Bank of New York had been chartered, with some of the leading conservatives as stockholders, including such men as Alexander Hamilton and Philip Schuyler, who steadfastly opposed state currency. The policies of the bank aroused intense opposition from the yeomanry because it concentered capital from the state's monied men and refused loans to farmers, even to those who owned substantial quantities of land, while a merchant, "whose property is of the most precarious and delusive nature, may readily procure a fictitious capital to facilitate his importation of foreign merchandize."[61] The only people who benefited from a bank were those who had connections with the institution. Some, in fact, believed that the bank's policies had contributed to the hard times of the mid-1780s.

Hamiltonians had their own economic agenda. In their opinion, America's economic crisis could be solved only by granting Congress the impost, vesting it with the power to regulate commerce, and eradicating the spirit of luxury that existed throughout the country.[62]

The legislative struggle over paper money began in February 1784, when the Assembly passed a bill authorizing £100,000 of paper, but the bill was defeated in the Senate. Late in October, the house approved £150,000. The Senate again defeated this measure. The following year the lower house, by a vote of 22 to 18, authorized £100,000 in paper. The Senate, in mid-April, tenaciously adhered to its hard-money principles and again rejected the Assembly's handiwork. By 1786, the Senate admitted that a scarcity of specie existed and that yeomen were being ruined by forced sales in which their farms sold for only a fraction of their real value. Despite this admission, the Senate still opposed state paper money. The Assembly, however, was more resolute than ever.

Early in January 1786, a joint committee was appointed to consider financial matters. Deliberations were "conducted with unusual Harmony."[63] After several meetings, the "prevailing sentiment" favored a paper-money loan office modelled on colonial experience. Furthermore, paper-money adherents on the committee stressed the need for the state to pay public creditors the interest on their securities. Hardmoney committeemen warned that New Yorkers would pay their taxes in this newly proposed paper currency, thereby reducing specie revenue enough so that the state would be unable to pay its congressional requisitions. New York would have to break faith with Congress. To prevent this, paper-money committeemen proposed that the state "assume" and "fund" the national debt held by New Yorkers. All national securities would be exchanged for new state securities that would receive interest paid in paper money. The paper currency would be backed by import duties and other taxes. By accepting paper money for taxes, the state would ensure that the bills would remain buoyant. After consideration, the committee recommended that £200,000 be emitted—one-quarter to pay the interest on the state and the assumed Continental debts and the other three-quarters to be loaned on real estate mortgages.

Acting on the joint committee's recommendation, the Assembly appointed a committee on 21 January 1786, consisting of one member from each county, to consider the best method for emitting paper money and for redeeming public securities. On 23 February, the committee reported a bill providing for the emission of £200,000. "The grand question" of whether or not the money should be legal tender was put to an initial vote on 23 February, when the Assembly overwhelmingly defeated the tender provision by a vote of 47 to 12. Realizing that a tender provision jeopardized the entire bill, paper-money advocates proposed a compromise, making the currency legal tender only in law suits, thus protecting hard-pressed debtors. The compromise satisfied most assemblymen, and the bill passed on 6 March by a sizable margin of 43 to 9.

To gain the governor's endorsement, and thus to assure passage of the bill, several funding proposals were added. The entire state debt was funded, while Continental loan-office certificates and "Barber's Notes" (certificates issued for supplies furnished to the Continental Army) owned by New Yorkers were also assumed by the state. Some people wanted either a complete assumption or a complete separation from the Continental debt. Clinton and the paper-money advocates, however, realized the political potency of the partial assumption of the federal debt. The state assumed only twenty-eight percent, or $1,400,000 out of a total federal debt of about $5,000,000 held by New Yorkers. The assumed federal debt was held by approximately half of the state's voters. The unassumed $3,600,000 was owned by several hundred wealthy New Yorkers, most of whom had little sympathy for Clinton.[64] The bill, in essence, converted large numbers of federal creditors into state creditors; in the process their economic welfare was tied to the state—not to the Confederation—and earned for the governor their political gratitude.

After the Assembly approved the bill, it went to the Senate where paper money had always foundered. On 29 March 1786, the Senate proposed twelve amendments—including a prohibition of the assumption of the federal debt. The Assembly rejected the amendments, and the Senate backed down on all but two minor amendments rather than killing a fourth paper-money bill.[65]

Before the bill became law it had one more hurdle—the Council of Revision. It was here that hard-money men placed their last hope. Within the council there was considerable dispute. John Sloss Hobart, Robert R. Livingston, and Lewis Morris struggled to defeat the bill, while Governor Clinton and Robert Yates favored it. From 6 to 15 April, the three opponents presented their reasons for vetoing the bill, but no one veto report received the endorsement of more than two councillors; consequently the bill automatically became law after ten days.

The act authorized £200,000 of paper money—three-quarters earmarked for mortgages on real estate and the remainder to be paid to New York's public creditors as interest on both state and Continental securities. The paper money could be used to pay taxes and other governmental fees. Mortgages had a fourteen-year term at five percent annual interest.

The paper money came from the presses in July 1786. The fear of depreciation proved unwarranted. The state's money passed "universally equal with gold and silver, and is catched at with avidity even by strangers."[66] Even fiscally conservative Alexander Hamilton assured the Assembly that "there need be no apprehension of" the paper currency's future fate. Largely because the scarcity of specie still existed, the demand for paper money "had not lessened," and the whole populace seemed satisfied with the currency.[67]

Paper-money men predicted that the state's domestic and foreign trade would immediately increase when paper was issued. Beginning in late 1786 and early 1787, American commerce grew rapidly; and, by 1788, New York had regained much of its prewar commercial vitality. By the end of 1788, New York City, a broken port in 1783, was importing and exporting more than before the war; and about two-thirds of this trade was carried in New York ships. The revenue obtained from the state impost did much to stabilize the state's finances.[68] Paper money had played an important role in restoring New York's prosperity.

The debt-funding aspect of the paper-money program succeeded beyond anyone's expectations. Paper money coupled with the state's other revenue was used to purchase large quantities of Continental securities, replacing them with state securities until, by 1790, the state of New

York owned federal securities worth over $2,880,000 in specie. The interest due New York on these securities more than equalled the annual requisitions on the state by Congress. Had this process continued a few more years, New York, along with some of the other states, would have assumed the entire domestic federal debt.[69] To a considerable degree, the paper money made these purchases possible, but New York's funding and assumption programs also contributed to maintaining the paper money's value.

Commerce and the Annapolis Convention

Many New Yorkers favored empowering Congress to deal with the postwar British trade restrictions.[70] On 4 May 1784, five days after Congress' request, New York's legislature granted Congress authority for fifteen years to curtail trade with foreign countries that had no commercial treaty with the United States. New Yorkers agreed with Congress that "The fortune of every citizen is interested" in commerce; "for it is the constant source of wealth and incentive to industry; and the value of our produce and our land must ever rise or fall in proportion to the prosperous or adverse state of trade."[71] After the enactment of New York's comprehensive impost act in November 1784, Clintonians' support of efforts to defend American commerce intensified. Although merchants generally opposed the governor, Clintonians supported efforts to increase commerce because more foreign trade meant more revenue for the state treasury.

This desire to stimulate commerce explains why New York endorsed Virginia's call on 21 January 1786 for a commercial convention of the states. On 14 March, Clinton submitted Virginia's proposal to the Assembly, which the following day resolved that five commissioners be appointed to attend the convention at Annapolis. Three days later, the Senate by a 14 to 4 margin concurred. On 20 April, the Assembly appointed Alexander Hamilton, Robert C. Livingston, and Leonard Gansevoort as commissioners. On the last day of the session (5 May), the Senate added three more commissioners—Robert R. Livingston, James Duane, and Egbert Benson—and the Assembly agreed. All six non-Clintonians supported strengthening the powers of Congress.

The legislature authorized the commissioners "to take into consideration the trade and commerce of the United States, to consider how far an uniform system in their commercial intercourse and regulations, may be necessary to their common interest and permanent harmony."[72] Before any power could be conferred on Congress, however, any proposal of the convention had to receive the unanimous approval of the state legislatures. Such unanimous approval would give the legislature the right to reject any plan that might be detrimental to New York.

In September 1786 only Hamilton and Benson attended the Annapolis Convention, where they met with commissioners from Delaware, New Jersey, Pennsylvania, and Virginia. The commissioners quickly adopted a report, drafted by Hamilton, that acknowledged the poor attendance at the convention and the diversity of the commissioners' instructions. Rather than deliberate under these conditions, the commissioners called for a general convention of all the states to meet in Philadelphia the following May to revise the Articles of Confederation.

The Constitutional Convention

On 13 January 1787, Governor Clinton addressed the opening session of the legislature meeting in New York City and delivered a copy of the Annapolis Convention report to the Assembly. Two days later the Assembly submitted to a committee the Annapolis report and Virginia's act of 23 November 1786 authorizing the appointment of delegates to a general convention.

On 15 February 1787, the Assembly rejected an unconditional ratification of the congressional impost, thus effectively killing the impost. (See above.) Then, on 17 February, without any reference to the Annapolis Convention report, the Hamiltonian forces in the Assembly proposed and the Assembly adopted a resolution instructing the state's delegates in Congress to move for the calling of a convention "for the purpose of revising the Articles of Confederation." On 20 February, Philip Schuyler led the Senate in a 10 to 9 vote concurring. The call for a convention could not have succeeded without support from Clintonians. They supported it to demonstrate that they were not entirely antifederal; they saw the necessity of strengthening Congress in areas other than granting it an independent source of income, and they were confident that they could prevent the ratification of any unacceptable convention proposal.

Philip Schuyler believed that New York called for a constitutional convention because several members of Congress had indicated a preference for the call of a convention to emanate from a state rather than from the ad hoc Annapolis delegates. An opportunity for such a state call had arisen in the New York legislature after the defeat of the impost despite Hamilton's speech of 15 February. Many delegates voted against the impost because of pressure exerted by the governor. According to Schuyler, some of these delegates felt "ashamed of their conduct, and wished an opportunity to make some atonement." Seizing this opportunity, Hamilton and Schuyler's forces introduced the call of a convention in the Assembly, which was "violently opposed" by the governor's friends, "but as many of those, who are at his beck, had committed themselves too far in private conversation, they voted (tho perhaps) reluctantly, for It."[73]

Despite the legislature's call for a convention, Schuyler was pessimistic about New York's and the Union's political future. The Clintonians—whose principles, stated Schuyler, included "a state impost, no direct taxation, keep all power in the hands of the legislature, give none to Congress which may destroy our influence, and cast a shade over that plenitude of power which we now enjoy"—were willing that a constitutional convention meet and propose alterations "confering additional powers on Congress." Clintonians, however, according to Schuyler, would oppose these amendments as "destructive of Liberty, may [induce?] a King, an Aristocracy, or a despot."[74]

When Congress considered the Annapolis Convention report on 21 February, New York congressmen Melancton Smith and Egbert Benson submitted their legislature's call for a convention. Unaware that nationalists in both the New York Assembly and Senate had pushed this resolution through to adoption, congressmen looked upon the proposal with considerable skepticism. A state that less than a week earlier had killed the federal impost now seemed to advocate strengthening Congress. To some congressmen, it appeared as if New York was attempting to scuttle the convention called by the Annapolis commissioners by proposing an alternative to it. (By ignoring any reference to the convention called by the Annapolis commissioners, New York's resolutions seemed to invalidate the appointment of convention delegates that had already taken place in six states.)[75] Therefore, Congress refused to consider New York's resolution. Instead, it considered a proposal for a general convention submitted by the Massachusetts delegates even though this proposal did not refer either to the Annapolis Convention report or to the state appointments of delegates that had already occurred. Congress amended the Massachusetts proposal and acknowledged the validity of these appointments as well as any future appointments to the convention called to meet in Philadelphia.

On 23 February 1787, Governor Clinton sent the legislature the congressional resolution calling the Constitutional Convention. Three days later, the Assembly resolved that five delegates be appointed to the Convention by a joint ballot of both houses. On 27 February, the Senate disagreed, objecting to its inferior status in a joint ballot. The following day, the Senate voted on a straight party vote of 11 to 7 to reduce the number of delegates to three. The Clintonians supported the reduction. Then the Senate rejected 12 to 6 a motion to elect the delegates by joint ballot. After which, Senator Abraham Yates, Jr., proposed that the Convention limit its proposals to alterations and amendments "not repugnant to or inconsistent with the constitution of this State." The Senate narrowly defeated Yates's proposal when two Clintonians, Thomas Treadwell and John Williams, abandoned it and Lieutenant Governor Pierre Van Cortlandt, the president of the Senate, cast his vote against it, breaking the 9 to 9 tie. The Senate finally approved the resolution that provided for the election of three delegates by each house voting separately, the same manner specified in the state constitution for the election of delegates to Congress. The Assembly concurred later on 28 February.

On 6 March, the Assembly voted in open balloting for convention delegates. All fifty-two assemblymen voted for state Supreme Court Judge Robert Yates, while Alexander Hamilton received all but three votes (one being his own). The real contest centered on the third delegate—and with it, who would control the delegation. John Lansing, Jr., narrowly defeated New York City Mayor James Duane for the Assembly's nomination by a vote of 26 to 23. After the Senate also nominated Yates, Hamilton, and Lansing, the two houses compared their nominees, adjourned to their separate chambers, and passed resolutions officially appointing the three men.

On 16 April, the Assembly agreed to Hamilton's motion authorizing the appointment of two additional convention delegates, totalling five—the number of delegates usually elected to Congress. Two days later, however, the Senate rejected the increase. (See Appendix II, below.) By appointing a three-man delegation and weighting it in their favor, Clintonians felt that the Clintonian delegates could control their state's actions in the convention. In letters to fellow Convention delegates George Washington and Edmund Randolph, Virginia Congressman James Madison, writing from New York City, described Yates and Lansing as "pretty much linked to the antifederal party here, and are likely of course to be a clog on their Colleague." Madison believed that the two Clintonians "lean too much towards State considerations to be good members of an Assembly which will only be useful in proportion to its superiority to partial views & interests."[76] George Washington lamented that "It is somewhat singular that a State (New York) which used to be foremost in all foederal measures, should now turn her face against them in almost every instance."[77]

Yates and Hamilton first attended the Convention in Philadelphia on 25 May, the first day of a quorum. Lansing came a week later on 2 June. From the beginning the Clintonian delegates had "forebodings" about the Convention. On 30 May, Yates voted in the minority against Hamilton on a motion that called for the Convention to create a "national Governt." Two days later, Robert Yates wrote a confidential letter to his uncle, Abraham Yates, Jr., then serving in Congress in New York City, in which he indicated that his "forebodings . . . are too much realized." Because of the Convention's secrecy rule, Yates could not relate any of "its business until the final close of it. While I remain a sitting member these rules must be obligatory." He was uncertain how long he would remain in Philadelphia, but "in the mean while," he was keeping "an Exact journal of all its proceedings." With this letter Yates communicated important and sensitive information back to New York. Because of the dominance of nationalist sentiment in the Convention, Yates and Lansing might abandon the Convention. This would leave New York unrepresented in the Convention because a minimum of two delegates had to be present for a state's vote to count. Realizing the explosiveness of his letter, Yates warned his uncle that "This Communication is in the most perfect confidence, in which only one person [i.e., George Clinton] beside yourself can participate."[78]

Throughout their stay in the Convention, Yates and Lansing voted with a minority of delegates who favored amending the Articles of Confederation in order to invest Congress with limited additional powers that would not unduly shift sovereignty away from the states. They usually voted together against Hamilton. During the climactic debate over the choice of the Virginia Plan (29 May) which called for the abandonment of the Articles of Confederation in favor of a national government, or the New Jersey Plan (15 June) which proposed amendments to the Articles of Confederation, Lansing argued on 16 June that the mere consideration of a national government violated the resolution of Congress calling the Convention as well as the delegates' commissions from their state legislatures. New York, he told the Convention, "would never have concurred in sending deputies to the convention, if she had supposed the deliberations were to turn on a consolidation of the States, and a National Government." Furthermore, he asked "was it probable that the States would adopt & ratify a scheme, which they had never authorized us to propose? and which so far exceeded what they regarded as sufficient?" The states, according to Lansing, would "never sacrifice their essential rights to a national government." Both the states and the people wanted Congress strengthened, not a new government.[79]

Hamilton was silent for most of the first three weeks of the Convention, partly because he disagreed with both the Virginia and the New Jersey plans and "partly from his delicate situation with respect to his own State, to whose sentiments as expressed by his Colleagues, he could by no means accede." On 18 June, however, Hamilton expressed his opinion that "no amendment of the confederation . . . could possibly answer the purpose." The delegates, Hamilton suggested, "owed it to our Country, to do on this emergency whatever we should deem essential to its happiness."[80] Concluding his five-hour oration, Hamilton sketched an outline for a plan of government that called for a bicameral Congress composed of representatives with three-year terms elected by the people and senators with life-time terms selected by electors chosen by the people. Hamilton's single chief executive would also be selected by electors chosen by the people and he too would have life tenure and the veto power. A supreme court of twelve justices with life tenure would have final judicial authority, and Congress could create inferior courts. All state laws contrary to the constitution or federal laws would be void. State governors, according to Hamilton, would be appointed by the general government, and they would have veto power over their legislatures.

Hamilton knew that the Convention would never approve his plan. But he believed that there were "evils operating in the States which must soon cure the people of their fondness for democracies."[81] Once the people tired of democracy, he argued, they would be more receptive to his ideas. Many of the delegates admired Hamilton's forthrightness and some even agreed with his ideas, but few supported him. Connecticut delegate William Samuel Johnson said that Hamilton was "praised by every gentleman, but supported by no gentleman."[82] Frustrated with his minority position within the New York delegation, Hamilton left the Convention at the end of June. While in New York, Hamilton publicly criticized Governor Clinton for his alleged opposition to the Convention. Thinly disguising his authorship, Hamilton's attack was published in the *Daily Advertiser* on 21 July and provoked heated controversy for several weeks. (See "Alexander Hamilton Attacks Governor George Clinton," 21 July–30 October 1787 [I below].) Hamilton returned to the Convention briefly in mid-August and was in New York from 20 August until 2 September. On 8 September, he was appointed to the Committee of Style and signed the Constitution nine days later as the only delegate from New York.

Yates and Lansing also became increasingly convinced of the futility of their position as the Convention proceeded toward the creation of a national government. Finally, on 10 July, they too abandoned the Convention, never to return, leaving New York unrepresented.

For more than five months, Yates and Lansing remained publicly silent about their early departure from the Convention. As the New York legislative session approached in January 1788, they decided to write an "official" report, perhaps with some urging from the Governor Clinton.[83] On 21 December 1787, shortly before the legislature's scheduled meeting, Yates and Lansing wrote the governor, giving their reasons for opposing the Constitution and for their abandonment of the Convention. When the legislature attained a quorum, Clinton delivered the letter, the new Constitution, Congress' resolution of 28 September 1787, and the other public documents that he had received since the legislature's last session (II below).

Yates and Lansing justified their departure as a matter of principle. The Convention was creating "a system of consolidated Government" which was not "in the remotest degree . . . in contemplation of the Legislature of this State." The delegates—New York's in particular— had been commissioned to revise and amend the Articles of Confederation, not "to abrogate" them. Furthermore, the consolidated government proposed by the Convention "must unavoidably, in a short time, be productive of the destruction of the civil liberty of such citizens who could be effectually coerced by it." They were certain that the new Constitution would not "afford that security to equal and permanent liberty, which we wished to make an invariable object of our pursuit." The absentees justified their refusal to return to Philadelphia because the principles of the new Constitution "were so well established as to convince us that no alteration was to be expected, to conform it to our ideas of expediency and safety. A persuasion that our further attendance would be fruitless and unavailing, rendered us less solicitous to return."[84] Virginia Congressman Edward Carrington believed that the letter "is perfectly in conformity with the views of their Mission," which was to represent the interests of New York, a state marked by "her uniform opposition to every federal interest for several years."[85]

1. Jay to Leonard Gansevoort, 5 June 1777, Johnston, *Jay*, I, 141.
2. Philip Schuyler to John Jay, 14 July 1777, *ibid.*, 146–47.
3. George Clinton to Alexander Hamilton, 5 March 1778, Syrett, I, 436.
4. Hamilton to George Clinton, 12 March 1778, *ibid.*, 439.
5. George Washington to George Clinton, 27 June 1780, *Revolutionary Relics, or Clinton Correspondence* . . . (New York, 1842), 7.
6. *Messages from the Governors*, II, 107.

7. *Votes and Proceedings of the Assembly of the State of New-York* . . . [7 September–10 October 1780] [Poughkeepsie, 1780], 22 (Evans 16907). On 25–26 September the legislature appointed Philip Schuyler, John Sloss Hobart, and Egbert Benson as Convention delegates.

8. To Hamilton, 16 September 1780, Syrett, II, 433.

9. *Votes and Proceedings*, 43.

10. 14 November 1780, Smith, *Letters*, XVI, 333.

11. PCC, Item 67, New York State Papers, 1775–88, Vol. II, 344–59, DNA.

12. *Messages from the Governors*, II, 127.

13. 24 November 1781, PCC, Item 67, New York State Papers, 1775–88, Vol. II, 443–47, DNA; and Clinton, *Public Papers*, VII, 520–22.

14. 11 September 1782, Smith, *Letters*, XIX, 149.

15. Hamilton to Clinton, 12 January 1783, Syrett, III, 240.

16. 14 October 1783, Washington Papers, DLC.

17. Hamilton to George Washington, 8 April 1783, Syrett, III, 318.

18. Hamilton to Robert Morris, 13 August 1782, *ibid.*, 138.

19. George Clinton to Christopher Tappen, 26 January 1787, Lloyd W. Smith Collection, Morristown National Historical Park, Morristown, N.J.

20. Alexander Hamilton to Robert R. Livingston, 25 April 1785, and Hamilton to Robert Morris, 13 August 1782, Syrett, III, 608–9, 139.

21. Alexander Hamilton had previously criticized Clinton for secretly taking positions on public matters and then taking care "to propagate his sentiments, in the manner in which it could be done with most effect. This," Hamilton asserted, "appears to have been his practice" (*Daily Advertiser*, 15 September 1787, I below).

22. William Floyd to George Clinton, 17 March 1783, Smith, *Letters*, XX, 35.

23. PCC, Item 67, New York State Papers, 1775–88, Vol. II, 465–67, DNA.

24. Charles DeWitt and Ephraim Paine to George Clinton, 9 April 1784, Smith, *Letters*, XXI, 503–4.

25. Jay to George Clinton, 7 October 1779 and Livingston to Clinton, 30 November 1779, Smith, *Letters*, XIV, 38–41, 240–41.

26. Clinton to Robert R. Livingston, 7 January 1780, Clinton, *Public Papers*, V, 445–46.

27. *Ibid.*, 499–502, VI, 203–5.

28. Smith, *Letters*, XXI, 504.

29. Paine to Clinton, 29 April 1784, *ibid.*, 556–57.

30. DeWitt to Clinton, 4 June 1784, *ibid.*, 664.

31. On 28 April 1786 the New York legislature appointed James Duane, Robert R. Livingston, Egbert Benson, John Haring, Melancton Smith, Robert Yates, and John Lansing, Jr., as its agents. It authorized any five of them to settle the "Controversy" with Massachusetts "otherwise than by the said Fœderal Court" (*Laws of New-York* [31 January–5 May 1786] [New York, 1786], Chapter XLIX, 95 [Evans 19854]).

32. Article VI, CDR, 88.

33. Clinton, *Public Papers*, VIII, 108–9.

34. New York Delegates to George Clinton, 9 April 1783, Smith, *Letters*, XX, 157.

35. Hamilton to George Clinton, 1 June 1783, *ibid.*, 296. Clinton greatly objected to Hamilton's handling of this matter.

36. Paine to Clinton, 29 April 1784, Smith, *Letters*, XXI, 556.

37. Ephraim Paine to Robert R. Livingston, 24 May 1784, *ibid.*, 640.

38. JCC, XXVII, 530–40; Hugh Williamson to James Duane, 8 June 1784, Smith, *Letters*, XXI, 674–75.

39. "A Rough Hewer," *New York Journal*, 17 March 1785.

40. Schuyler to Abraham Ten Broeck et al., 19 February 1786, N.

41. Schuyler to Abraham Ten Broeck, 19 March 1786, N.
42. Gorham to James Warren, 6 March 1786, Smith, *Letters*, XXIII, 180.
43. *Ibid.*
44. From John Williams, 29 January 1788 (I below). An "Extract of a letter from a gentleman in New-York, to his friend in Connecticut," in the *Norwich Packet*, 8 November 1787, took the opposite position: "Tho' we are sensible, that the harbour of New-York is so commodiously situated for trade, that we might reap great profits from duties on articles which are exported from hence into other states. But we may not think too much of our own particular interest to the injury of the whole.—At the same time I must confess myself at last convinced by these patriots in this state who maintain; that the port of New-York, having been saved by the united arms of all the states, ought to be free for all" (Mfm:N.Y.).
45. JCC, XXX, 263, 345n, 439–41. Quoted text on p. 441.
46. 27 July 1786, Smith, *Letters*, XXIII, 416–20.
47. Monroe to Clinton, 16 August 1786, *ibid.*, 479–80.
48. Mitchell to William Samuel Johnson, 9 August 1786, *ibid.*, 525n.
49. Clinton to the President of Congress, 16 August 1786, PCC, Item 67, New York State Papers, 1775–88, Vol. II, 540, 541, DNA.
50. JCC, XXXI, 556n.
51. Bloodworth to Governor Richard Caswell, 24 August 1786, Smith, *Letters*, XXIII, 521.
52. King to Elbridge Gerry, 26 August 1786, *ibid.*, 529–30.
53. *Messages from the Governors*, II, 264.
54. Mitchell to Jeremiah Wadsworth, 24 January 1787, Smith, *Letters*, XXIV, 74.
55. "Rough Carver," *Daily Advertiser*, 3 September 1787 (I below).
56. Madison to George Washington, 21 February 1787, Rutland, *Madison*, IX, 285.
57. "Leo," *Daily Advertiser*, 27 February 1787.
58. Philip Schuyler to Henry Van Schaack, 13 March 1787 (Appendix II [below]). In the state ratifying convention on 28 June 1788, Governor Clinton professed that he had uniformly supported an impost for Congress. He confessed, however, "the manner in which that body proposed to exercise the power, I could not agree to. I firmly believed that if it were granted in the form recommended, it would prove unproductive, and would also lead to the establishment of dangerous principles." Clinton favored "granting the revenue" but opposed giving Congress the "power of collection or a controul over our state officers" (V below).

In March 1789, Alexander Hamilton resurrected the debate over the impost as a campaign issue in the hotly contested gubernatorial election and accused Clinton of duplicity. Hamilton discredited Clinton's statement in the ratifying convention "that he had always been a friend to the impost, but *could not agree to the manner in which Congress proposed to exercise the power.*" To oppose a specific plan and profess support for a general principle was sheer "hypocrisy." Hamilton claimed to have "unquestionable evidence" that the governor had used his "personal influence" with various legislators to "prejudice them against the granting of the impost." Clinton supposedly warned the legislators that Congress, as a single-house legislature with no effective checks on its power, ought not to be trusted with a revenue independent of state control. Hamilton questioned the propriety of this kind of executive interference with legislators. To him, it appeared "highly exceptionable" ("H. G." VII, *Daily Advertiser*, 20 March 1789, printed in Syrett, V, 277–78).
59. *New York Packet*, 13 February 1786.
60. Petitions from the City and County of Albany, 2 February 1785, and from the Inhabitants of Hillsdale in Albany County, 24 February, and 2 March, all in the New York State Library.

61. "Honestus," *New York Packet*, 27 March 1786. "Fictitious capital" referred to the insufficient collateral used by some merchants in obtaining loans.

62. *Daily Advertiser*, 1 August 1786.

63. John Lansing, Jr., to Abraham Ten Broeck, 28 January 1786, Ten Broeck Papers, Albany Institute of History and Art.

64. "Gustavus," *New York Packet*, 13 April 1786; Matthew Visscher to Abraham Yates, Jr., 6 March 1786, Abraham Yates Papers, NN.

65. Philip Schuyler to Abraham Ten Broeck, 19 March 1786, and Schuyler to Stephen Van Rensselaer, 22, 30 March 1786, Schuyler Papers, N; Schuyler to Leonard Gansevoort, 22 March 1786, de Coppet Collection, Princeton University.

66. *New York Journal*, 24 August 1786.

67. Hamilton Speech in Assembly, 15 February 1787, Syrett, IV, 90; Nicholas Hoffman to John Williams, 2 November 1787, John Williams Papers, N.

68. Merrill Jensen, *The New Nation: A History of the United States During the Confederation, 1781–1789* (New York, 1950), 215; *New York Packet*, 18 November 1788, 10 March 1789.

69. E. James Ferguson, "State Assumption of the Federal Debt During the Confederation," *Mississippi Valley Historical Review*, 38 (1951), 418; *Daily Advertiser*, 28 January, 2 February 1788.

70. For the postwar British trade policy, enunciated most strenuously by Lord Sheffield in his *Observations on the Commerce of the American States* (London, 1783), see Robert B. Bittner, "The Definition of Economic Independence and the New Nation" (Ph.D. diss., University of Wisconsin, 1970).

71. CDR, 153.

72. *Senate Journal* [16 January–5 May 1786] (New York, 1786), 103 (Evans 19853).

73. Philip Schuyler to Henry Van Schaack, 13 March 1787, Appendix II (below).

74. *Ibid.*

75. See James Madison's Notes on Debates in Congress, 21 February 1787, Rutland, *Madison*, IX, 290–91; CDR, 188–90.

76. Madison to Randolph and to Washington, 11 and 18 March 1787, Rutland, *Madison*, IX, 307, 315.

77. Washington to Madison, 31 March 1787, *ibid.*, 343.

78. Robert Yates to Abraham Yates, Jr., 1 June 1787, Abraham Yates Papers, NN. Robert Yates ended his letter by asking his uncle to communicate "My Respectful compliments to the Governor."

79. Farrand, I, 249–50, 257–58.

80. *Ibid.*, 282–83.

81. *Ibid.*, 291.

82. *Ibid.*, 363, 366.

83. Walter Rutherfurd believed that Clinton "had a hand" in convincing Yates and Lansing to write their letter (to John Rutherfurd, 8, 15 January 1788 [I below]).

84. For Yates and Lansing's letter, see I below.

85. Carrington to James Madison, 10 February 1788 (RCS:Va., 360).

Note on Sources

Legislative and Executive Records

The journals of the New York Assembly and Senate for the legislative session that adopted the resolution of 1 February 1788 calling a state convention to consider the Constitution were published by Samuel and John Loudon, printers to the state, as *Journal of the Assembly of the State of New-York, at Their Eleventh Session, Begun and Holden at Poughkeepsie in Dutchess County, the Ninth Day of January, 1788* (Poughkeepsie, 1788), and *Journal of the Senate of the State of New-York, at Their Eleventh Session, Begun and Holden at Poughkeepsie in Dutchess County, the Eleventh Day of January, 1788* (Poughkeepsie, 1788) (Evans 21314–15. The manuscript journals of the legislature do not exist.). The resolution calling the state ratifying convention was printed as a broadside by order of the legislature (Evans 45311).

A manuscript copy of Governor George Clinton's speech opening this session of the legislature is in the Clinton Papers at the New-York Historical Society. Other official gubernatorial papers were perhaps part of the once voluminous Clinton Papers at the New York State Library in Albany. In the disastrous 1911 fire at that library about three-fourths of this material was lost or severely damaged. Fortunately, a good part of the Clinton Papers, especially the revolutionary war correspondence, had already been printed. The surviving Clinton Papers are now housed in the records of the Office of Governor in the New York State Archives in Albany. Established by law in 1971, the Archives also holds other state records that were once in the New York State Library. (See *Guide to Records in the New York State Archives* [Albany, 1993].)

Some of the proceedings of both houses of the legislature on the resolution calling a state ratifying convention were published by Francis Childs in his *Daily Advertiser* and by Thomas Greenleaf in his *New York Journal.* Childs attended the legislature and also took shorthand notes of the debates, while Greenleaf arranged to have a correspondent send him reports. On 8 February 1788, the *Advertiser* printed the Senate's debates of 1 February, while on 12 February, it printed the Assembly's debates of 31 January.

Personal Papers

There are numerous collections of personal papers, representing both Antifederalist and Federalist points of view, dealing with the debate over the ratification of Constitution from September 1787 through

July 1788. The fewest letters are for the period September 1787 through
January 1788. The number of letters describing the election campaign
for state Convention delegates is unmatched by any other state. New
York also has a large number of letters dealing with the Convention
itself.

The New-York Historical Society, the New York Public Library, and
the Columbia University Libraries have valuable collections. The New-
York Historical Society has the papers of such Federalists as Abraham
and Evert Bancker (Bancker Family Papers), James Duane, Robert R.
Livingston, Walter Rutherfurd, and Richard Varick; and such Antifederalists as John Lamb, John Smith of Mastic, Long Island, and Abraham
B. Bancker. The Lamb Papers describe the interstate and intrastate
cooperation among Antifederalists and the work of Antifederalist committees in New York. The New York Public Library owns the papers of
such Antifederalists as Abraham Yates, Jr., Abraham G. Lansing, Gilbert
Livingston, and George Clinton. The Yates Papers, which are particularly rich, include letters from prominent Antifederalist politicians,
drafts of Yates's many pseudonymous newspaper essays, and a draft history of the movement for the Constitution. Federalists are represented
in the collections of Leonard Gansevoort and Philip Schuyler. There
are also some useful items in such business papers as the Constable-
Pierrepont Collection, the Collin McGregor Letterbooks, and the Lewis
Ogden Letterbook. Columbia University Libraries (Rare Book and
Manuscript Library) owns the De Witt Clinton Papers, including a brief
journal that this young Antifederalist kept at the state Convention. Most
importantly, Columbia has the largest collection of the papers of John
Jay. The Van Schaack Family Correspondence at Columbia contains the
letters of Federalist Peter Van Schaack. (For full details on the manuscripts of these libraries, see Evarts B. Greene and Richard B. Morris,
eds., *A Guide to the Principal Sources for Early American History (1600–1800)
in the City of New York* [1929; 2nd ed., New York, 1953]; Arthur J. Breton,
ed., *A Guide to the Manuscript Collections of The New-York Historical Society*
[2 vols., Westport, Conn., 1972]; and New York Public Library, *Dictionary Catalog of the Manuscript Division* [2 vols., Boston, 1967].)

Several libraries outside New York City also have important collections. The papers of Antifederalist Melancton Smith at the New York
State Library in Albany include Smith's superb notes of debates in the
Confederation Congress that transmitted the Constitution to the states
on 28 September 1787, a number of Smith's letters and speeches, and
a wide variety of material on the state Convention. The extensive correspondence of Antifederalist Peter Van Gaasbeek is divided between
the Senate House Museum in Kingston and the Franklin D. Roosevelt
Library in Hyde Park. (For an analysis of the papers at Kingston, see

Michael D'Innocenzo and John Turner, "The Peter Van Gaasbeek Papers: A Resource for Early New York History, 1771–1797," *New York History*, 47 [1966], 153–59.)

The Library of Congress has the papers of Antifederalist Hugh Hughes, which include several important letters and the drafts of his pseudonymous newspapers essays, and the largest and most varied collection of the papers of Alexander Hamilton. Some of Hamilton's letters are also in the papers of James Madison and George Washington. The papers of Hamilton and Madison are good in describing the writing and publication of *The Federalist*—the principal and most voluminous Federalist commentary on the Constitution. As a congressman resident in New York, Madison reported on New York politics; while Washington was one of those to whom he (and others) reported. The Webb Papers at Yale University include the letters of Federalist Samuel Blachley Webb, a commercial agent in New York City. The Henry Van Schaack Scrapbook at the Newberry Library in Chicago has a few letters of Peter Van Schaack and Philip Schuyler.

As the seat of the Confederation Congress, New York City was the residence of congressmen, members of the executive departments, and foreign diplomats—many of whom wrote letters about the Constitution. The Gilder Lehrman Collection on deposit at the Pierpont Morgan Library has Secretary at War Henry Knox's voluminous papers, while Postmaster General Ebenezer Hazard's letters are in the Jeremy Belknap Papers at the Massachusetts Historical Society. The letters and papers of all congressmen have been published in Paul H. Smith et al., eds., *Letters of Delegates to Congress, 1774–1789* (26 vols., Washington, D.C., 1976–2000). The Library of Congress has the correspondence of French, English, Spanish, and Dutch diplomats based in New York City.

Newspapers

From September 1787 through July 1788, twelve newspapers and a monthly magazine were published in New York at one time or another. Seven newspapers and the magazine were printed in New York City, two newspapers in Albany, and one newspaper each in Hudson and Poughkeepsie. The twelfth newspaper was printed first in Lansingburgh, then in Albany, finally returning to Lansingburgh.

The seven newspapers printed in New York City included three dailies, three semiweeklies, and one weekly. The dailies were *The Daily Advertiser*; *The New-York Morning Post, and Daily Advertiser*; and *The New-York Journal, and Daily Patriotic Register*.

The oldest daily in New York City was William Morton's *New York Morning Post*. Originally established as a semiweekly by Morton and Samuel Horner in April 1783, it became a daily on 23 February 1785.

(Horner died in January 1786, making Morton the sole owner.) The *Morning Post*, many issues of which are not extant, published both Federalist and Antifederalist pieces, many of them taken from out-of-state newspapers. Few original items appeared in the extant issues of the *Morning Post*. It seemed that this newspaper leaned slightly toward the Antifederalists.

The *Daily Advertiser*, founded by Francis Childs on 1 March 1785 with the assistance of Benjamin Franklin, was the first newspaper in the city to be established originally as a daily. The *Advertiser* published numerous Federalist essays, including the first fifty-one numbers of *The Federalist*. The *Advertiser's* motto, which was dropped with the issue of 17 October 1787, was: "The Noblest Motive is the Public Good." In January 1788 Childs, in response to "the very liberal and flattering Encouragement" he had received from his subscribers since beginning operation, went to Poughkeepsie, at *"considerable Expence,"* in order to take shorthand notes of the legislature's proceedings and debates so that they could be printed in the *Advertiser*. Childs hoped that the continued encouragement of his subscribers would permit him to continue such "Useful and Important Information" every year (*Daily Advertiser*, 14 January 1788. Childs had published extensive accounts of the debates of the January–April 1787 session of the legislature. See, for example his recording of the speeches of Alexander Hamilton in the New York Assembly as printed in Syrett, IV, passim.).

Thomas Greenleaf's daily *New York Journal* was a staunchly Antifederalist newspaper. Greenleaf, manager of the *Journal* since September 1785, purchased the weekly newspaper in January 1787 from Eleazer Oswald of the Philadelphia *Independent Gazetteer*. Oswald had taken over the publication of the *Journal* in March 1785 from his mother-in-law Elizabeth Holt, the widow of former patriot printer John Holt who had established the paper. Since Oswald resided in Philadelphia, he hired Greenleaf to manage the paper for him.

Greenleaf's belief in the importance of newspapers was expressed succinctly in his motto and in a statement he made in May 1788. Greenleaf's motto, taken from James Thomson's *Liberty* (1734–35), reads: "Here TRUTH Unlicens'd reigns; and dares accost—e'en KINGS themselves, or RULERS of the FREE!" On 29 May Greenleaf printed this statement from a "a correspondent": "NEWSPAPERS are the GUARDIANS OF FREEDOM; by NEWSPAPERS only are ye made acquainted with the *rise* and *fall* of empires: and, of the FREEDOM or the SLAVERY of your own species" (CC:Vol. 6, p. 375).

During the meeting of the Constitutional Convention, Greenleaf supported the establishment of a strong central government, but in early

September 1787 he began to print Antifederalist items. The *Journal,* published on Thursdays, became so biased, in the eyes of Federalists, that on 4 October Greenleaf defended his publication policy (I below). By 18 October the weekly *Journal* was so inundated with Antifederalist material that Greenleaf had to print an extra issue. The next week he noted that "want of room" caused him to postpone the publication of a piece signed "Timoleon," but he hoped that in a few weeks, as was "generally desired by his friends and customers," he would be able to publish his newspaper more often. In his next three issues, Greenleaf apologized that "want of room" prevented him from printing certain essays, although he published another extra issue on 1 November. Finally, on 15 November he announced that the *Journal* would become a daily because of "the solicitations of a respectable number of his present subscribers—and by means of the generous patronage of a few valued friends and the public. . . ." He declared that in this time of "CRISIS" people needed to be well informed about the new Constitution; he wanted to ensure that there would be "free discussion on that momentous topic." By publishing only once a week, Greenleaf claimed that he had "unavoidably neglected" half of the original essays that he had received. Although four other New York City newspapers published a total of sixteen separate issues a week during the fall of 1787, Greenleaf intimated that a "FREE and IMPARTIAL discussion" of the Constitution depended upon the daily publication of the *Journal.* Greenleaf charged $6.00 per annum for his new daily, the same price charged by the *Daily Advertiser,* which carried the largest number of advertisements of any New York City newspaper. However, since "the principal support of a Daily newspaper is derived from Advertisements," Greenleaf requested that "Gentlemen in the mercantile line, and all others who occasionally Advertise" place advertisements in the *Journal* (Mfm:N.Y.).

Despite the reasonable cost of the paper, at the beginning of the new year Greenleaf, like other printers, had to call upon his subscribers to pay their arrears. He had been to "great expence" in printing the newspaper (*New York Journal,* 3 January 1788, Mfm:NY.). Greenleaf continued to have financial problems because of the expense in publishing a daily newspaper and on 19 May 1788—the six-month anniversary of his daily newspaper—he requested that "those gentlemen who profess to be liberal supporters of 'THE FREEDOM OF THE PRESS,' will afford him a proportion of their advertisements, for which they will be entitled to his unfeigned thanks" (Mfm:N.Y.). Greenleaf was plainly calling upon those who did not agree with him on political matters to help support the publication of his newspaper. New York City was overwhelmingly Federalist so that he needed the support of some Federalists.

The first issue of the daily *New-York Journal, and Daily Patriotic Register* appeared on 19 November 1787. Greenleaf noted that, contrary to some insinuations, he was undertaking "the arduous task of a Daily Paper" from none "other than laudable motives." He informed the other newspaper publishers that he would not use "dishonorable means" in competing with them, and he hoped that they would harbor "no idea of unfriendliness" toward him (Mfm:N.Y.).

Despite Greenleaf's conciliatory attitude, his relations with his fellow printers were sometimes tense. For example, Greenleaf and the printers of the *New York Morning Post* and *New York Packet* exchanged scurrilous satirical articles after the *Morning Post* printed a spurious advertisement on 7 January 1788, satirizing Greenleaf as "a Gay, volatile ANTI-FEDERAL PRINTER." (See "Antifederalism of Thomas Greenleaf Satirized in the New York Morning Post and New York Packet," 7–11 January 1788, Mfm:N.Y.) In March 1788 Greenleaf was criticized as an Antifederalist partisan for printing an item stating that Virginian Arthur Lee, a member of the Confederation Board of Treasury and an Antifederalist, had asserted that four-fifths of the people of Virginia opposed the Constitution. (See "Arthur Lee's Report of Virginia Antifederalism," 7 March 1788, CC:602.) And in early May 1788, Greenleaf and Francis Childs of the *Daily Advertiser* were involved in a bitter exchange over a *New York Journal* item of 29 April that incorrectly referred to the appointment of Thomas Wooldridge as the new British vice consul for the New England states. According to Greenleaf, he had been given the item by a gentleman just as he was completing the printing of the issue for the day. Therefore, Greenleaf printed only 20 or 30 newspapers containing that item that he "left solely at the disposal" of Wooldridge. When Greenleaf's action was discovered, Greenleaf was forced to defend himself, but Childs dismissed his explanation as fraudulent. In turn, Greenleaf charged that Childs was trying to destroy his reputation and credit. Childs rejoindered that Greenleaf's had not adequately explained his behavior, and he reminded his readers of Greenleaf's role in printing the item regarding Arthur Lee and Virginia Antifederalism. (See "Thomas Greenleaf Erroneously Reports the Appointment of a New British Vice Consul for the New England States," 29 April–6 May 1788, Mfm:N.Y. For a fuller summary of the incident, see CC:Vol. 4, p. 593, note 9.)

Greenleaf's daily newspaper, however, did not entirely supplant his regular weekly issue. Greenleaf had announced on 15 November that his regular Thursday issue would continue with the title *The New-York Journal, and Weekly Register,* and that it would contain "the choicest pieces, and the fewest advertisements." The price for the Thursday issue was $2.00, the same that it had been before 15 November

(Mfm:N.Y.). The Thursday issue, which would have "a more *general Circulation in the Country*, than that of any other day in the Week," did indeed have "the choicest pieces." (See Charles Tillinghast to Hugh Hughes, 27–28 January 1788, I below.)

After becoming a daily, the *New York Journal* probably equaled Eleazer Oswald's Philadelphia *Independent Gazetteer* in the quantity and quality of Antifederalist material that it published. The *Journal* printed several important serialized essays, such as "Cato" (7 nos.), "Brutus" (16 nos.), "Cincinnatus" (6 nos.), "A Countryman" (Hugh Hughes, 6 nos.), and "A Countryman" (De Witt Clinton, 5 nos.). The *Journal* also reprinted many out-of-state Antifederalist articles, e.g., seventeen of eighteen essays of "Centinel," seven of eight numbers of "An Old Whig," and all twelve installments of Luther Martin's *Genuine Information*. ("Centinel" and "An Old Whig" first appeared in Philadelphia, and *Genuine Information* in Baltimore.)

However, to demonstrate that his newspaper was open to all parties, Greenleaf also published some original Federalist essays. Perhaps, the best examples of such an intent were his publication of numbers 23 to 39 of *The Federalist*, the most influential, voluminous, and prestigious Federalist publication, and the five scurrilous essays of "Examiner." When he printed *The Federalist* 23, he inserted this prefatory statement: "Yesterday the manuscript copy of the subsequent was communicated to the Editor, with an assurance, that his press should be preferred, in future, for the first ushering into public view, the succeeding numbers. If the public are pleased to stigmatize the Editor as a partial printer, in the face of his reiterated assertions of 'BEING INFLUENCED BY NONE,' what more can be said! This stigma he prefers, to that of slavish copiest; consequently, unless manuscripts are communicated, he will be constrained (however injudicious) still to crouch under the weighty charge of partiality." For publishing some numbers of *The Federalist* and all of the "Examiner," Greenleaf was criticized by some of his subscribers. "A Friend," however, praised Greenleaf for having "a just idea of the freedom of the press" and condemned those who censured him. (See the headnote to *The Federalist* 1, *Independent Journal*, 27 October; "Examiner" I–V, 11 December 1787–4 January 1788; and "Twenty-seven Subscribers," *New York Journal*, 1 January, all in I below; and "A Fœderalist" and "A Friend," *New York Journal*, 6 December, both in Mfm:N.Y.) Another good example of Greenleaf's impartiality was the reprinting of four of the five numbers of Connecticut Federalist Roger Sherman's "Countryman" essays that had first been printed in New Haven.

At the beginning of the new year in 1788, Greenleaf expressed pride in his publication record, when he called upon his subscribers to pay their arrears. The rubbing off of "all OLD SCORES," he wrote, would "give him new spirit, and enable him with greater perseverance to pursue the great objects of his vocation—to soar among the spirits of BRUTUS, CATO, PUBLIUS, LANDHOLDER, &c. to detect the *evil one* from amid (if there he be) and to place him upon the steep of a precipice, that he might tumble thence down headlong. Thus circumstanced, and being ever anxious to perform impossibilities, viz. to please every one, soliciting the continuation of public favors, &c. is the Editor ever devoted, &c. &c." (*New York Journal*, 3 January 1788, Mfm:N.Y. The widely circulated "Landholder" essays, written by Oliver Ellsworth of Connecticut and first published in Hartford, were not reprinted by Greenleaf.).

Even though Greenleaf published daily, he still had problems printing all that he wanted. On 7 January 1788, he printed this statement: "The Editor's Daily Receptacles for Communications, from his numerous and very attentive Correspondents, for the six ensuing Days, are so crowded, that he shall not have it in his Power to gratify them, all nor any one of them in particular, on either side of the GREAT LAKE NEW-CONSTITUTION. He shall, however, STRIVE; some Bread and some Cheese, says the Epicure, relish best, and should a little Mustard and Vinegar, be intermixed, our Readers in general would not disapprove."

Federalists bitterly attacked Greenleaf. Confederation Postmaster General Ebenezer Hazard—whom Greenleaf had accused of preventing Antifederalist newspapers from going through the mails—described Greenleaf as "brainless," an "Echo" of Eleazer Oswald, and "a poor thick-sculled Creature" (Hazard to Jeremy Belknap, 5 March, 12 April, and 10 May 1788, CC:Vol. 4, pp. 554, 583, 592). "Anarchy" charged Greenleaf with having "talents of misrepresentation" (*Country Journal*, 18 March, IV below, Dutchess County Election), while "Fed." asserted that Greenleaf had "a little mind" and "a sterile brain" (*New York Packet*, 25 July, Mfm:N.Y.). In disgust, some people cancelled their subscriptions to the *Journal*. Finally, after the news of the New York Convention's ratification of the Constitution arrived late on the night of 26 July 1788, a mob broke into Greenleaf's shop and destroyed much of his type. Because of these losses, the last daily issue of the *Journal* appeared on 26 July. Publication resumed five days later as a weekly.

New York City's three semiweeklies were *The New-York Packet*; *The Independent Journal: or, the General Advertiser*; and *The New-York Museum*. The *New York Packet* and the *New York Museum* appeared on Tuesdays and Fridays, while the *Independent Journal* was published on Wednesdays and Saturdays. The *New York Packet* and the *Independent Journal* were both Federalist newspapers, with each of them printing all eighty-five numbers of *The Federalist*. The *New York Packet* was owned by Samuel and John Loudon, who were also printers to the state of New York. The motto of the *Packet* was "*Tros Tyriusque Nobis Nullo Discrimine Agetur.* *Virg.*" (I shall act impartially toward all, Virgil, *The Aeneid*, Book I.). For more on Samuel Loudon, a strong supporter of American independence, who, despite hardships, kept his newspaper going during the Revolution, see A. J. Wall, "Samuel Loudon (1727–1813): Merchant, Printer and Patriot, With Some of His Letters," *Quarterly Bulletin of the New-York Historical Society*, VI (1922–1923), 75–92.

The *Independent Journal* was owned by J. M'Lean & Co. With the issue of 2 July 1788, Archibald M'Lean was admitted to the firm. In late September 1787 John M'Lean printed the four-page broadside of the Constitution that the Confederation Congress sent to the states for their ratification. In March and May 1788 J. and A. M'Lean also printed the two volumes of *The Federalist*. (At the same time that he was publishing the *Independent Journal*, John M'Lean also owned a Virginia newspaper, the *Norfolk and Portsmouth Journal.*) There are few extant issues of John Russell's *New York Museum*, the first issue of which appeared on 23 May 1788. Published on Tuesday and Friday, its motto was: "Multum in Parvo" (Much in little; a great deal in a small compass).

The only weekly printed in New York City in 1788 (before 26 July) was *The Impartial Gazetteer, and Saturday Evening's Post* which was established in May 1788 by John Harrisson and Stephen Purdy, Jr. It appeared on Saturday evenings at 5:00 P.M. In September 1788 it became *The New-York Weekly Museum.*

The state's only magazine—the monthly *The American Magazine. Containing a Miscellaneous Collection of Original and Other Valuable Essays, in Prose and Verse, and Calculated Both for Instruction and Amusement*—was published in New York City by Samuel Loudon, under the editorship of Connecticut native Noah Webster. Its motto was: "Science the guide, and truth the eternal goal." The first issue, that of December 1787, was advertised for sale on 1 January 1788; thereafter issues of the magazine would be advertised early in the month following the month that appeared on the title pages. Each issue was seventy-two pages and sold for a quarter dollar. Annual subscriptions cost $2.50. Webster, one of the most prolific Federalist propagandists, had been in Philadelphia before he left for New York City in the Fall of 1787 to edit the magazine. Webster included some of his own writings in the magazine. (See, for example, "Giles Hickory," *American Magazine*, 1 January 1788, and the headnote thereto, I below.)

Albany had two newspapers—*The Albany Gazette* and *The Albany Journal: or, the Montgomery, Washington and Columbia Intelligencer.* The weekly *Gazette,* which was established in 1784 and appeared on Thursdays, was published by Charles R. Webster. By December 1788, more than 800 copies of *Albany Gazette* were printed each week; it circulated in the New York counties of Albany, Clinton, Columbia, Montgomery, and Washington and in Bennington, Vermont, and Berkshire County, Massachusetts. It was also sent regularly to the principal towns from New Hampshire to Virginia (*Albany Gazette*, 26 December, Mfm:N.Y.). The *Albany Journal* was published by Charles R.Webster and his twin brother George. The *Journal* was established as a semiweekly on 26 January 1788, although it became a weekly with the issue of 31 March 1788. As a semiweekly the *Journal* appeared on Mondays and Saturdays, and as a weekly it appeared on Mondays. The newspapers were Federalist, and they often shared articles. Albany Antifederalists sharply criticized the Websters, especially Charles. A few days after the Websters established the *Journal*, Abraham G. Lansing wrote Abraham Yates, Jr., that "it is the sincere wish of our Friends that some Person would set himself down here and disconcert these White Livers by publishing an impartial paper." Lansing hoped that Melancton Smith would prevail "on [Thomas] Greenleaf [of the *New York Journal*] to send one of his Journeymen to set up a printing office" in Albany (31 January, I below). Aware of this strong opposition to them, the Websters reluctantly published a few Antifederalist items. Dissatisfied with the half-hearted actions of the Websters, Albany Antifederalists pressed harder to establish an impartial newspaper to be called the *Albany Register*, but with no assistance from Greenleaf and Antifederalist leaders in New York City, they abandoned their search by the end of March (John Lansing, Jr., et al. to Melancton Smith, 1 March; and Abraham G. Lansing to Abraham Yates, Jr., 2 March [both III below]; and John Lansing, Jr., and Abraham G. Lansing to John Lamb, 23 March [IV below, Albany County Election]. The *Albany Register* was finally established in October 1788; it appeared on Mondays.).

Printed in neighboring Lansingburgh, the weekly *Northern Centinel, and Lansingburgh Advertiser*, published by Thomas Claxton and John Babcock on Tuesdays, was a Federalist newspaper. Its motto was: "The PRESS is the CRADLE of SCIENCE, the NURSE of GENIUS, and the SHIELD of LIBERTY." "Dissatisfied with their situation" in Lansingburgh, Claxton and Babcock moved their newspaper to Albany in January 1788, and from 11 February to 14 April, they published on Mondays as the *Federal Herald* (Abraham G. Lansing to Abraham Yates, Jr., 31 January 1788, I below. Lansing described the newspaper as insignificant.). The paper was eventually returned to Lansingburgh, and, beginning with the issue of 28 April, it appeared on Mondays under the same name. Ezra Hickok, however, had replaced Claxton as Babcock's partner. When Antifederalists criticized the *Northern Centinel* for not printing articles against the Constitution, the editors replied on 8 January 1788 that "*in defence of their characters as printers . . . that not an original observation in opposition to federal measures hath yet been handed them for publication.* — Their Press IS *and* EVER HATH BEEN FREE" (Mfm:N.Y.).

Ashbel Stoddard's Federalist *The Hudson Weekly Gazette* printed both Federalist and Antifederalist material. The newspaper was established by Stoddard and Charles R. Webster in 1785 only two years after the town of Hudson was founded. (The rapidly growing town was incorporated as the state's third city in 1787.) Stoddard and Webster, both natives of Connecticut, had been apprentices together on the Hartford *Connecticut Courant.* In 1786 Webster, who was also publishing the *Albany Gazette,* left the firm. The *Hudson Weekly Gazette* was printed on Thursdays until 15 April 1788 when it began to appear on Tuesdays. In April 1788 Stoddard, proud of his impartiality, informed his readers that "All pieces written with decency, whether federal or antifederal, will be inserted without distinction." He refused to print an item signed "An Antifederalist" because "it contains nothing but private invectives." His newspaper would not be devoted "to scurrility from pecuniary motives" (*Hudson Weekly Gazette,* 22 April 1788, Mfm:N.Y.).

The Country Journal, and the Poughkeepsie Advertiser, another Federalist weekly, was owned by Nicholas Power. The *Country Journal* was printed on Wednesdays. On 11 March 1788 Power informed his customers that he would soon get new printing equipment and that he would probably "enlarge his paper to the size of the largest printed in the State" (Mfm:N.Y.) The *Country Journal* published both Federalist and Antifederalist material. Its motto was: "In my Free Page let different Works reside,/Tho' Party's hostile Lines whose Works divide;/Party! Whose murdering Spirit I abhor More subtly cruel, and less brave than war." (With the issue of 30 September 1788, Power changed the name to *The Country Journal, and Dutchess and Ulster County Farmer's Register* and added the motto, "Venerate the Plough.") The *Country Journal* was the only newspaper in America to print, in its entirety, the *Letters from the Federal Farmer to the Republican,* a major Antifederalist pamphlet.

Even though Power abhorred party spirit, he was accused by a correspondent of favoring "one particular party" over another. The correspondent threatened that "a considerable number of us" would cancel their subscriptions if Power did not print "what comes to hand from either party." Power denied that he favored one party over another (*Country Journal,* 17 June 1788, Mfm:N.Y.). Power was defended by an "Unprejudiced Person," who stated that the printer had indeed been impartial because he published articles filled with invectives from both parties (*ibid.*, 8 July 1788). (For Power's difficulties with a post rider who carried his newspaper, a not uncommon situation for printers, and for his resolution of the problem, see *Country Journal*, 22 January 1788, Mfm:N.Y.).

The *Albany Gazette, Northern Centinel,* and *Hudson Weekly Gazette* each demonstrated their Federalist bias by reprinting in consecutive weeks at least the first ten numbers of *The Federalist.* Beginning on 9 January 1788, the *Country Journal* reprinted, at the instigation of Federalist James Kent, *The Federalist* 14–21 in consecutive weeks, almost entirely in supplementary issues.

For general treatments of newspapers during the debate over the ratification of the Constitution in New York, see Linda Grant De Pauw, *The Eleventh Pillar: New York State and the Federal Constitution* (Ithaca, N.Y., 1966), 91–105; John P. Kaminski, "The Role of Newspapers in New York's Debate Over the Federal Constitution," in Stephen L. Schechter and Richard B. Bernstein, eds., *New York and the Union: Contributions to the American Constitutional Experience* (Albany, 1990), 280–92; Gaspare J. Saladino, "Newspapers and Magazines of New York State (1787–1788)," in *ibid.,* 293–97; and Saladino, "Pseudonyms Used in the Newspaper Debate over the Ratification of the United States Constitution in the State of New York, September 1787–July 1788," in *ibid.,* 298–325.

Pamphlets and Broadsides

New York printers published nine pamphlets and a two-volume edition of *The Federalist,* the principal Federalist commentary on the Constitution (see below). Three pamphlets were treatises on the Constitution by New Yorkers. One pamphlet was written by a South Carolina delegate to the Constitutional Convention, one by a resident of New Jersey, one was a reprint of a work written by an inhabitant of Massachusetts, and the last was a collection of out-of-state Antifederalist essays and letters. The authorship of the ninth pamphlet, *Letters from the Federal Farmer to the Republican,* is uncertain. *The Federalist* was written by two New Yorkers and a Virginian.

Some bibliographers believe that Thomas Greenleaf of the *New York Journal* published five Antifederalist pamphlets between November 1787 and May 1788. These were, in the order that they were published:

• *Observations Leading to a Fair Examination of the System of Government Proposed by the Late Convention; and to Several Essential and Necessary Alterations in It. In a Number of Letters from the Federal Farmer to the Republican* (1787) (Evans 20454–56; two of these three editions listed by Evans were probably printed by Greenleaf);

- "A Columbian Patriot" (Mercy Otis Warren), *Observations on the New Constitution, and on the Fœderal and State Conventions* (1788) (Evans 21112, reprint of a Boston pamphlet);
- *Observations on the Proposed Constitution for the United States of America, Clearly Shewing It to be a Complete System of Aristocracy and Tyranny, and Destructive of the Rights and Liberties of the People* (1788) (Evans 21344, a reprinting of out-of-state Antifederalist material);
- "A Plebeian" (Melancton Smith?), *An Address to the People of the State of New-York: Shewing the Necessity of Making Amendments to the Constitution, Proposed for the United States, Previous to Its Adoption* (1788) (Evans 21465); and
- *An Additional Number of Letters from the Federal Farmer to the Republican; Leading to a Fair Examination of the System of Government Proposed by the Late Convention; and to Several Essential and Necessary Alterations in It; and Calculated to Illustrate and Support the Principles and Positions Laid Down in the Preceding Letters* (1788) (Evans 21197).

In 1788 Samuel and John Loudon of the *New York Packet* published "A Citizen of New-York" (John Jay), *An Address to the People of the State of New-York, on the Subject of the Constitution, Agreed upon at Philadelphia, the 17th of September 1787* (Evans 21175). Charles R. Webster of the *Albany Gazette* and the *Albany Journal* also printed in 1788 "The Federal Committee, of the City of Albany," *An Impartial Address, to the Citizens of the City and County of Albany: or, the 35 Anti-Federal Objections Refuted* (Evans 21167). John and Archibald M'Lean of the *Independent Journal* struck off in two volumes entitled *The Federalist: A Collection of Essays, Written in Favour of the New Constitution, as Agreed upon by the Federal Convention, September 17, 1787* that contained the eighty-five essays written by Alexander Hamilton, John Jay, and James Madison, under the pseudonym "Publius" (Evans 21127, the first volume appeared in March 1788, the second in May of that year). The first seventy-seven of the eighty-five essays had first appeared in New York City newspapers, while the last eight appeared for the first time in the second volume before being reprinted in the city's newspapers. (For later editions of *The Federalist*, see the next section immediately below.)

In 1787 Francis Childs of the *Daily Advertiser* struck off *Observations on the Plan of Government Submitted to the Federal Convention, in Philadelphia, on the 28th of May, 1787. By Mr. Charles Pinckney, Delegate from the State of South-Carolina. Delivered at Different Times in the Course of Their Discussion* (Evans 20649–50). In the same year, New York City printer William Ross published "A Farmer, of New-Jersey" (John Stevens, Jr.), *Observations on Government, Including Some Animadversions on Mr. Adams's Defence of the Constitutions of Government of the United States of America: and on Mr. De Lolme's Constitution of England* (Evans 20465). (For the publication of the text of the Constitution in pamphlets and almanacs, see "The Publication of the Constitution in New York," 21 September 1787–June 1788, I below.)

New York printers published more than twenty-five Constitution-related broadsides (in addition to the text of the Constitution). For example, Thomas Greenleaf reprinted "Centinel" I–II (CC:133, 190, from Philadelphia) and Timoleon" (an original New York item) as a two-page broadside (Evans 45045), and Ashbel Stoddard of the *Hudson Weekly Gazette* reprinted "The Dissent of the Minority of the Pennsylvania Convention" (CC:353) as a four-page broadside (Evans 20620). During March and April 1788, at least a dozen handbills appeared in New York City and Albany as Antifederalists and Federalists campaigned for the elections of delegates to the state ratifying convention. In early July 1788, while the state ratifying convention was meeting in Poughkeepsie, two broadsides (one in New York City and the other in Poughkeepsie) were struck announcing Virginia's ratification of the Constitution (Evans 21559, 45393). (For the broadside printings of the Constitution, see "The Publication of the Constitution in New York," 21 September 1787–June 1788, I below.)

Although not directly related to the private and public debate over the ratification of the Constitution in New York, three additional New York imprints are useful for studying the debate in that they help to identify some of the debate's participants. These are the directories for New York City for the years 1786 and 1787 (both by city merchant David Franks) and for 1789 (Evans 19655, 20369 22021). The 1786 directory, the first of its kind for New York City, was reprinted several times in the nineteenth century. In 1905 the 1786 directory was reprinted by H. J. Sachs & Company, of New York City, prefixed with a description of the city by Noah Webster. In 1997 the Sachs edition was reprinted by Heritage Books, Inc., of Bowie, Maryland.

The Federalist

The Federalist has gone through scores of editions since it was first published in two volumes in 1788. The standard edition is Jacob E. Cooke, ed., *The Federalist* (Middletown, Conn., 1961). Thomas S. Engeman, Edward J. Erler, and Thomas B. Hofeller have keyed *The Federalist Concordance* (Middletown, Conn., 1980) to this edition. (In 1988 this 622-page concordance was reprinted by the University of Chicago Press.) *The Documentary History of the Ratification of the Constitution* has printed all eighty-five essays in its series *Commentaries on the Constitution:*

Public and Private, Vols. 1–6 (1981–1995). In these volumes, *The Feder-alist* essays appear in their original context, surrounded by other Fed-eralist and Antifederalist essays. The editors have provided editorial notes discussing the authorship and circulation of the essays and the commentaries upon them. Some editions of *The Federalist* have fine scholarly commentaries on the essays and on the authorship of some of the disputed numbers, or, for various other reasons, are worthwhile. Among the best are those edited by Charles A. Beard, Max Beloff, George W. Carey and James McClellan, Henry B. Dawson, Roy P. Fair-field, Isaac Kramnick, Clinton Rossiter, Robert Scigliano, Quentin P. Taylor, and Benjamin Fletcher Wright. (Some of these scholars have edited selected editions.) Scigliano's introduction has the most recent discussion on the disputed authorship of certain numbers of *The Fed-eralist*. In 1996 the Wright edition was reprinted with a foreword by R. B. Bernstein, and three years later the Rossiter volume was reissued with a new introduction and notes by Charles R. Kesler. (For scholarly commentaries on *The Federalist*, see the section on "Secondary Ac-counts" below.)

The Sources for the New York Convention

The sources for the New York Convention are extensive. Elections returns for the delegates are in the *Daily Advertiser*, 29 May–14 June 1788, and the *New York Journal*, 31 May–12 June. The *Journal* listed all of the elected delegates and their party affiliations, concluding that forty-six of the sixty-five delegates were Antifederalists. Together the two newspapers printed the vote totals for nine of the thirteen counties. On 7 June the *Advertiser* carried the vote totals for Queens County by towns. The papers of Convention secretary, John McKesson, at the New-York Historical Society, have all the election certificates except those for Columbia County and the City and County of New York. The latter's certificate is in the Historical Society's James Duane Papers.

The sources for the Convention consist of the Journal (manuscript and printed); notes of debates taken by delegates and private reporters or observers; drafts of manuscripts, such as resolutions and committee reports; newspaper summaries of proceedings and debates; private let-ters written by members of the Convention or by observers; and a brief journal by De Witt Clinton.

The manuscript Journal of the Convention is in the records of the Department of State located in the New York State Archives. Lengthy fragments of smooth and rough Journals, from which this Journal was apparently constructed, are in the McKesson Papers at the New-York

Historical Society. The McKesson Papers also include roll calls for in-sertion in the Journal. The manuscript Journal in the New York State Archives contains a twenty-page pamphlet of the Constitution printed for the use of the Convention delegates by Convention printer Nicholas Power of the *Country Journal.* At the end of the Journal is a copy of the circular letter, signed by the delegates, to be transmitted to the exec-utives of the other states in which the Convention strongly recom-mended the calling of a second constitutional convention to consider amendments to the Constitution proposed by the various state ratifying conventions. The names of the delegates do not appear in the official printed version of the Journal. The manuscript Journals, with the ex-ception of the copy of the circular letter, formed the basis for the Jour-nal printed by Nicholas Power. By order of the Convention, each del-egate was to receive a copy of the Journal and a copy was to be sent "to each city, town, district, and precinct" in the state.

The McKesson Papers also include drafts of resolutions in the hand-writing of such delegates as John Jay, Robert R. Livingston, Melancton Smith, and John Lansing, Jr. The McKesson papers contain drafts of committee reports, recommended amendments to the Constitution, a declaration of rights, forms of ratification, and the circular letter. More drafts of recommended amendments to the Constitution, forms of rat-ification, and the circular letter are in the Melancton Smith Papers at the New York State Library. These papers also include drafts of Smith's speeches. Drafts for speeches by other delegates are in the Robert R. Livingston Papers, New-York Historical Society; the George Clinton Pa-pers, New York Public Library; and the Alexander Hamilton Papers, Library of Congress.

The debates of the Convention can be reconstructed from a variety of sources. For the most part, the fullest sets of notes cover the debates for the month of June; most accounts fall off badly in July. The most complete account of the debates was printed by Francis Childs of the *Daily Advertiser,* who took shorthand notes and who published a pam-phlet entitled *The Debates and Proceedings of the Convention of the State of New-York, Assembled at Poughkeepsie, on the 17th June, 1788. To Deliberate and Decide on the Form of Federal Government Recommended by the General Convention at Philadelphia, on the 17th September, 1787. Taken in Short Hand* (Evans 21310. Childs first advertised the sale of this pamphlet in his *Daily Advertiser* on 16 December 1788.). Childs's version of the debates is the fullest through 2 July, but it then becomes a summary of the proceedings and must be supplemented by the Journal because Childs did not always give a full account of the proceedings. Despite Childs's denials, he was described by one Antifederalist as a "partyman" whose records of debates favored Federalist speakers (De Witt Clinton Journal, 19 July 1788, Columbia University Libraries, Rare Book and Manuscript Library).

In addition to Childs's *Daily Advertiser*, printed original accounts of the Convention's debates and proceedings appeared in Greenleaf's *New York Journal* and Power's *Country Journal*. The *Country Journal* carried the fullest reports for the first two days of the Convention and it was the first newspaper to carry the Form of Ratification and the circular letter. (Power also printed the circular letter as a broadside [Evans 21312].) The *Daily Advertiser*, perhaps with the intention of printing all of Childs's notes, published complete debates for 19 and 20 June but stopped such treatment in favor of summaries of debates and proceedings. The *New York Journal* published the fullest summaries of debates and proceedings for July.

Convention secretary John McKesson and several delegates took notes of debates. The most extensive notes for June were kept by McKesson and Melancton Smith. Gilbert Livingston's notes, in the New York Public Library, surpass any set of notes for the period 14 to 26 July. Other note takers, whose notes are meager and difficult to use, are Alexander Hamilton, Richard Harison, Robert R. Livingston, and Robert Yates. The Hamilton and Harison notes are in the Hamilton Papers and the Yates notes are in the Edmund C. Genêt Papers—all in the Library of Congress. Robert R. Livingston's notes are in his papers at the New-York Historical Society. De Witt Clinton's journal (15–19 July, in his papers at Columbia University, contains a brief account of speeches and Convention gossip. The Morris-Popham Papers at the Library of Congress has a notebook that includes delegate Richard Morris' general comments on the Constitution and Morris' replies to most of them. It is not clear if these notes were taken during the Convention. The copy of the Form of Ratification sent to the Confederation Congress is in the National Archives, Washington, D.C., and the copy retained by the state of New York is in the New York State Archives (Department of State records).

A last invaluable source for the study of the Convention is the many dozens of letters written by Convention delegates and spectators. More than a dozen delegates wrote letters commenting on the Convention, with at least two of them (Alexander Hamilton and John Jay) writing as many as ten letters. Abraham B. Bancker, one of the Convention's secretaries, also wrote at least ten letters.

Secondary Accounts

The secondary literature on colonial and revolutionary New York state is vast. An excellent synthesis of the entire colonial period, with a splendid bibliography, is Michael Kammen, *Colonial New York: A History* (New York, 1975). Still useful for much of the colonial period is Loyalist William Smith, Jr.'s, *The History of the Province of New York . . .* , ed. Michael Kammen (2 vols., Cambridge, Mass., 1972). Sound treatments of the history of the "revolutionary generation" (1763–89) are: Alexander C. Flick, ed., *History of the State of New York* (10 vols., New York, 1933–1937; see vols. 3 to 5); Edward Countryman, *A People in Revolution: The American Revolution and Political Society in New York, 1760–1790* (Baltimore, 1981); Paul A. Gilje and William Pencak, eds., *New York in the Age of the Constitution, 1775–1800* (Rutherford, N.J., 1992); Milton M. Klein, ed., *The Empire State: A History of New York* (Ithaca, N.Y., 2001; see parts 2 and 3); and Alfred F. Young, *The Democratic Republicans of New York: The Origins, 1763–1797* (Chapel Hill, N.C., 1967). The selected readings in Klein, ed., *The Empire State*, contain a host of scholarly journal articles that are too numerous to be listed here, although a few major articles are included in this "Note on Sources."

Some of the major published accounts on the government, politics, law, and economy for the period just prior to and during the Revolution are: Carl Lotus Becker, *The History of Political Parties in the Province of New York, 1760–1776* (Madison, Wis., 1909; numerous reprint editions); Patricia U. Bonomi, *A Factious People: Politics and Society in Colonial New York* (New York, 1971); Roger James Champagne, "The Sons of Liberty and the Aristocracy in New York Politics, 1765–1790" (Ph.D. diss., University of Wisconsin-Madison, 1960); Roger J. Champagne, *Alexander McDougall and the American Revolution in New York* (Schenectady, 1975); Robert A. East, *Business Enterprise in the American Revolutionary Era* (1938; reprint ed., Gloucester, Mass., 1964); Marc Egnal, *A Mighty Empire: The Origins of the American Revolution* (Ithaca, N.Y., 1988); Alexander C. Flick, *The American Revolution in New York: Its Political, Social and Economic Significance* (1926; reprint ed., Port Washington, N.Y., 1967); Julius Goebel, Jr., and T. Raymond Naughton, *Law Enforcement in Colonial New York: A Study in Criminal Procedure (1664–1776)* (1944; reprint ed., Montclair, N.J., 1970); Douglas Greenberg, *Crime and Law Enforcement in the Colony of New York, 1691–1776* (Ithaca, N.Y., 1976); Virginia D. Harrington, *The New York Merchant on the Eve of the Revolution* (1935; reprint ed., Gloucester, Mass., 1964); Leo Hershkowitz and Milton M. Klein, eds., *Courts and Law in Early New York: Selected Essays* (Port Washington, N.Y., 1978); Merrill Jensen, *The Founding of a Nation: A History of the American Revolution, 1763–1776* (New York, 1968); Jacob Judd and Irwin H. Polishook, eds., *Aspects of Early New York Society and Politics* (Tarrytown, N.Y., 1974); Stanley Nider Katz, *Newcastle's New York: Anglo-American Politics, 1732–1753* (Cambridge, Mass., 1968); Sung Bok

Kim, *Landlord and Tenant in Colonial New York: Manorial Society, 1664–1775* (Chapel Hill, N.C., 1978); Milton M. Klein, "Liberty as Nature's Gift: The Colonial Origins of the Bill of Rights in New York," in Patrick T. Conley and John P. Kaminski, eds., *The Bill of Rights and the States: The Colonial and Revolutionary Origins of American Liberties* (Madison, Wis., 1992), 215–45; Klein, *The Politics of Diversity: [Nine] Essays in the History of Colonial New York* (Port Washington, N.Y., 1974); Leopold S. Launitz-Schürer, Jr., *Loyal Whigs and Revolutionaries: The Making of the Revolution in New York, 1765–1776* (New York, 1980); Jesse Lemisch, *Jack Tar vs. John Bull: The Role of New York's Seamen in Precipitating the Revolution* (New York, 1997); Mary Lou Lustig, *Privilege and Prerogative: New York's Provincial Elite, 1710–1776* (Madison, N.J., 1995); Pauline Maier, *From Resistance to Revolution: Colonial Radicals and the Development of American Opposition to Britain, 1765–1776* (New York, 1972); Irving Mark, *Agrarian Conflicts in Colonial New York, 1711–1775* (1940; reprint ed., Port Washington, N.Y., 1965); Bernard Mason, *The Road to Independence: The Revolutionary Movement in New York, 1773–1777* (Lexington, Ky., 1966); Cathy Matson, *Merchants & Empire: Trading in Colonial New York* (Baltimore, 1998); Edmund S. Morgan and Helen M. Morgan, *The Stamp Crisis: Prologue to Revolution* (1953; 3rd ed., Chapel Hill, N.C., 1995); Benjamin H. Newcomb, *Political Partisanship in the American Middle Colonies, 1700–1776* (Baton Rouge, La., 1995); Thomas Elliot Norton, *The Fur Trade in Colonial New York, 1686–1776* (Madison, Wis., 1974); Deborah A. Rosen, *Courts and Commerce: Gender, Law, and the Market Economy in Colonial New York* (Columbus, Ohio, 1997); William S. Sachs, "Interurban Correspondents and the Development of a National Economy before the Revolution: New York as a Case Study," *New York History*, 36 (1955), 320–35; Philip J. Schwarz, *The Jarring Interests: New York's Boundary Makers, 1664–1776* (Albany, 1979); Joseph S. Tiedemann, *Reluctant Revolutionaries: New York City and the Road to Independence, 1763–1776* (Ithaca, N.Y., 1997); Alan Tully, *Forming American Politics: Ideals, Interests, and Institutions in Colonial New York and Pennsylvania* (Baltimore, 1994); and Philip L. White, *The Beekmans of New York in Politics and Commerce, 1647–1877* (New York, 1956).

Specialized monographs for studying the "revolutionary generation" are also useful. On the state constitution of 1777, see Willi Paul Adams, *The First American Constitutions: Republican Ideology and the Making of the State Constitutions in the Revolutionary Era* (1980; expanded ed., Lanham, Md., 2001); New York State Bicentennial Commission, *Essays on the Genesis of the Empire State* (Albany, 1979), reprinted in Stephen L. Schechter and Richard B. Bernstein, eds., *New York and the Union: Contributions to the American Constitutional Experience* (Albany, 1990), 148–82; Peter J.

Galie, *Ordered Liberty: A Constitutional History of New York* (New York, 1996); Donald S. Lutz, *Popular Consent and Popular Control: Whig Political Theory in the Early State Constitutions* (Baton Rouge, La., 1980); and William A. Polf, *1777: The Political Revolution and New York's First Constitution* (Albany, 1977).

On Loyalists, see Robert McCluer Calhoon, *The Loyalists in Revolutionary America, 1760–1781* (New York, 1965); Robert A. East and Jacob Judd, eds., *The Loyalist Americans: A Focus on Greater New York* (Tarrytown, N.Y., 1975); Alexander Clarence Flick, *Loyalism in New York During the American Revolution* (1901; reprint ed., New York, 1969); Michael Kammen, "The American Revolution as a *Crise de Conscience:* The Case of New York," in Richard M. Jellison, ed., *Society, Freedom, and Conscience: The American Revolution in Virginia, Massachusetts, and New York* (New York, 1976), 125–89; Janice Potter, *The Liberty We Seek: Loyalist Ideology in Colonial New York and Massachusetts* (Cambridge, Mass., 1983); Philip Ranlet, *The New York Loyalists* (Knoxville, Tenn., 1986); and Harry B. Yoshpe, *The Disposition of Loyalist Estates in the Southern District of the State of New York* (1939; reprint ed., New York, 1967).

On the role of religion, an important determinant in New York politics, see Sydney E. Ahlstrom, *A Religious History of the American People* (New Haven, 1972); Randall Balmer, *A Perfect Babel of Confusion: Dutch Religion and English Culture in the Middle Colonies* (New York, 1989); Patricia U. Bonomi, *Under the Cope of Heaven: Religion, Society, and Politics in Colonial America* (New York, 1986); Carl Bridenbaugh, *Mitre and Sceptre: Transatlantic Faiths, Ideas, Personalities, and Politics, 1689–1775* (New York, 1962); Arthur Lyon Cross, *The Anglican Episcopate and the American Colonies* (1902; reprint ed., Hamden, Conn., 1964); Paul Finkelman, "The Soul and the State: Religious Freedom in New York and the Origin of the First Amendment," in Stephen L. Schechter and Richard B. Bernstein, eds., *New York and the Union: Contributions to the American Constitutional Experience* (Albany, 1990), 78–105; David G. Hackett, *The Rude Hand of Innovation: Religion and Social Order in Albany, New York, 1652–1836* (New York, 1991); Richard W. Pointer, *Protestant Pluralism and the New York Experience: A Study of Eighteenth-Century Religious Diversity* (Bloomington, Ind., 1988); John Webb Pratt, *Religion, Politics, and Diversity: The Church-State Theme in New York History* (Ithaca, N.Y., 1967); and A. G. Roeber, *Palatines, Liberty, and Property: German Lutherans in Colonial British America* (Baltimore, 1993).

For Vermont, which declared its independence from New York in 1777, see Michael A. Bellesiles, *Revolutionary Outlaws: Ethan Allen and the Struggle for Independence on the Early American Frontier* (Charlottesville, Va., 1993); Dixon Ryan Fox, *Yankees and Yorkers* (New York, 1940); Matt

Bushnell Jones, *Vermont in the Making, 1750–1777* (1939; reprint ed., Hamden, Conn., 1968); Peter S. Onuf, *The Origins of the Federal Republic: Jurisdictional Controversies in the United States, 1775–1787* (Philadelphia, 1983); and Chilton Williamson, *Vermont in Quandary: 1763–1825* (Montpelier, Vt., 1949).

On the city of New York in the second half of the eighteenth century, see Wilbur C. Abbott, *New York in the American Revolution* (New York, 1929); Oscar Theodore Barck, Jr., *New York City During the War for Independence: With Special Reference to the Period of British Occupation* (1931; reprint ed., Port Washington, N.Y., 1966); Carl Bridenbaugh, *Cities in Revolt: Urban Life in America, 1743–1776* (New York, 1955); Edwin G. Burrows and Mike Wallace, *Gotham: A History of New York City to 1898* (New York, 1999; see parts 2 and 3); Robert E. Cray, Jr., *Paupers and Poor Relief in New York City and Its Rural Environs, 1700–1830* (Philadelphia, 1988); George William Edwards, *New York as an Eighteenth Century Municipality, 1731–1776* (New York, 1917); Paul A. Gilje and William Pencak, eds., *New York in the Age of the Constitution, 1775–1800* (Rutherford, N.J., 1992); Paul A. Gilje, *The Road to Mobocracy: Popular Disorder in New York City, 1763–1834* (Chapel Hill, N.C., 1987); J. T. Headley, *The Great Riots of New York, 1712–1873 . . .* (1873; reprint ed., Indianapolis, Ind., 1970); Graham Russell Hodges, *New York City Cartmen, 1667–1850* (New York, 1986); Gary B. Nash, *The Urban Crucible: Social Change, Political Consciousness, and the Origins of the American Revolution* (Cambridge, Mass., 1979); Sidney Irving Pomerantz, *New York, An American City, 1783–1803: A Study of Urban Life* (1938; 2nd ed., Port Washington, N.Y., 1968); Nan A. Rothschild, *New York City Neighborhoods: The 18th Century* (San Diego, Calif., 1990); Ira Rosenwaike, *Population History of New York City* (Syracuse, 1972); Thomas E. V. Smith, *The City of New York in the Year of Washington's Inauguration, 1789* (1889; reprint ed., Riverside, Conn., 1972); I. N. Phelps Stokes, *The Iconography of Manhattan Island, 1498–1909 . . .* (1915–1928; reprint ed., 6 vols., New York, 1967); Robert J. Swan, "Prelude and Aftermath of the Doctors' Riot of 1788: A Religious Interpretation of White and Black Reaction to Grave Robbing," *New York History*, 81 (2000), 417–56; Thomas Jefferson Wertenbaker, *Father Knickerbocker Rebels: New York City During the Revolution* (New York, 1948); Shane White, *Somewhat More Independent: The End of Slavery in New York City, 1770–1810* (Athens, Ga., 1991); Sean Wilentz, *Chants Democratic: New York City & the Rise of the American Working Class, 1788–1850* (New York, 1984); and Bruce Martin Wilkenfeld, *The Social and Economic Structure of the City of New York, 1695–1796* (New York, 1978). (Burrows and Wallace, *Gotham*, has an extensive bibliography and a comprehensive index. Smith's highly detailed study, however, lacks an index, but this should not dissuade one from using this invaluable work.) Also helpful is Kenneth T. Jackson, *The Encyclopedia of New York City* (New Haven, 1995). For New York City and several other New York communities after the Revolution, see Stephen L. Schechter and Wendell Tripp, eds., *World of the Founders: New York Communities in the Federal Period* (Albany, 1990).

For the state and city during the Confederation period, see Robert Greenhalgh Albion, "New York Port in the New Republic, 1783–1793," *New York History*, 21 (1940), 388–403; Kenneth R. Bowling, *The Creation of Washington, D.C.: The Idea and Location of the American Capital* (Fairfax, Va., 1991); Thomas C. Cochran, *New York in the Confederation: An Economic Study* (1932; reprint ed., Clifton, N.J., 1972); Merrill Jensen, *The New Nation: A History of the United States During the Confederation, 1781–1789* (1950; reprint ed., Boston, 1981); John P. Kaminski, *Paper Politics: The Northern State Loan-Offices During the Confederation, 1783–1790* (New York, 1989); Kaminski, *George Clinton: Yeoman Politician of the New Republic* (Madison, Wis., 1993); Charles Edward La Cerra, Jr., "The Role of Aristocracy in New York State Politics During the Period of the Confederation, 1783–1788" (Ph.D. diss., New York University, 1969); Jackson Turner Main, *Political Parties before the Constitution* (Chapel Hill, N.C., 1973), Main, *The Upper House in Revolutionary America, 1763–1788* (Madison, Wis., 1967); Cathy Matson, "Public Vices, Private Benefit: William Duer and His Circle, 1776–1792," in William Pencak and Conrad Edick Wright, eds., *New York and the Rise of American Capitalism: Economic Development and the Social and Political History of an American State, 1780–1870* (New York, 1989), 72–123; Samuel Duff McCoy, "The Port of New York (1783–1789): Lost Island of Sailing Ships," *New York History*, 17 (1936), 379–90; Richard B. Morris, *The Forging of the Union, 1781–1789* (New York, 1987); Curtis P. Nettels, *The Emergence of a National Economy, 1775–1815* (New York, 1962); Sidney Irving Pomerantz, *New York, An American City, 1783–1803: A Study of Urban Life* (1938; 2nd ed., Port Washington, N.Y., 1968); E. Wilder Spaulding, *New York in the Critical Period, 1783–1789* (1932; reprint ed., Port Washington, N.Y., 1963); Edmund Philip Willis, "Social Origins of Political Leadership in New York City from the Revolution to 1815" (Ph.D. diss., University of California, Berkeley, 1967); and William F. Zornow, "New York Tariff Policies, 1775–1789," *New York History*, 37 (1956), 40–63.

On New York's ratification of the Constitution, see the following which are arranged in chronological order: Clarence E. Miner, *The Ratification of the Federal Constitution by the State of New York* (New York, 1921); Staughton Lynd, *Anti-Federalism in Dutchess County, New York: A Study of Democracy and Class Conflict in the Revolutionary Era* (Chicago, 1962);

Linda Grant De Pauw, *The Eleventh Pillar: New York State and the Federal Constitution* (Ithaca, N.Y., 1966); several reprinted articles in Staughton Lynd, *Class Conflict, Slavery, and the United States Constitution, Ten Essays* (Indianapolis, 1967); Robin Brooks, "Alexander Hamilton, Melancton Smith, and the Ratification of the Constitution in New York," *William and Mary Quarterly*, 3rd ser., 24 (1967), 339–58; William Jeffrey, ed., "The Letters of 'Brutus'—A Neglected Element in the Ratification Campaign of 1787–88," *University of Cincinnati Law Review*, 40 (1971), 643–777; Theophilus Parsons, Jr., "The Old Conviction versus the New Realities: New York Antifederalist Leaders and the Radical Whig Tradition" (Ph.D. diss., Columbia University, 1974); Steven R. Boyd, "The Impact of the Constitution on State Politics: New York as a Test Case," in James Kirby Martin, ed., *The Human Dimensions of Nation Making: Essays on Colonial and Revolutionary America* (Madison, Wis., 1976), 270–303; Walter Hartwell Bennett, ed., *Letters from the Federal Farmer to the Republican* (University, Ala., 1978); Richard B. Morris, "John Jay and the Adoption of the Federal Constitution in New York: A New Reading of Persons and Events," *New York History*, 62 (1982), 132–64; John P. Kaminski, "New York: The Reluctant Pillar," in Stephen L. Schechter, ed., *The Reluctant Pillar: New York and the Adoption of the Federal Constitution* (Troy, N.Y., 1985), 48–117; David E. Narrett, "A Zeal for Liberty: The Anti-Federalist Case Against the Constitution in New York," in Narrett and Joyce S. Goldberg, eds., *Essays on Liberty and Federalism: The Shaping of the U.S. Constitution* (College Station, Tex., 1988), 48–87; Cecil L. Eubanks, "New York: Federalism and the Political Economy of Union," in Michael Allen Gillespie and Michael Lienesch, eds., *Ratifying the Constitution* (Lawrence, Kan., 1989), 300–340; Cathy Matson, "New York City Merchants and the Constitution: A Fragile Consensus," in Stephen L. Schechter and Richard B. Bernstein, eds., *New York and the Union: Contributions to the American Constitutional Experience* (Albany, 1990), 254–79; Gaspare J. Saladino, "The Federal Express," in *ibid.*, 326–41; and Saul Cornell, "Politics of the Middling Sort: The Bourgeois Radicalism of Abraham Yates, Melancton Smith, and the New York Antifederalists," in Paul A. Gilje and William Pencak, eds., *New York in the Age of the Constitution, 1775–1800* (New York, 1992), 151–75.

   Also useful are the well-known general studies of the debate over and the politics of the ratification of the Constitution by the following: Orin Grant Libby (1894), Charles A. Beard (1913), Robert E. Brown (1956), Forrest McDonald (1958), Jackson Turner Main (1961), Cecilia M. Kenyon (1966), Robert Allen Rutland (1966), Gordon S. Wood (1969), Stephen R. Boyd (1979), Herbert J. Storing (1981), Jack N. Rakove (1996), William H. Riker (1996), and Saul Cornell (1999). See also the new postscript, "Fulfillment: A Commentary on the Constitution," in Bernard Bailyn, *The Ideological Origins of the American Revolution* (1967; enlarged ed., Cambridge, Mass., 1992), 321–79.

On *The Federalist*—the most celebrated commentary on the Constitution—see the following: W. B. Allen with Kevin A. Cloonan, *The Federalist Papers: A Commentary, "The Baton Rouge Lectures"* (New York, 2000); George W. Carey, *The Federalist: Design for a Constitutional Republic* (Urbana, Ill., 1989); Gottfried Dietze, *The Federalist: A Classic on Federalism and Free Government* (Baltimore, 1960); David F. Epstein, *The Political Theory of "The Federalist"* (Chicago, 1984); Albert Furtwangler, *The Authority of Publius: A Reading of the Federalist Papers* (Ithaca, N.Y., 1984); Charles R. Kesler, ed., *Saving the Revolution: "The Federalist Papers" and The American Founding* (New York, 1987); Edward Millican, *One United People: The Federalist Papers and the National Idea* (Lexington, Ky., 1990); Richard B. Morris, *Witnesses at the Creation: Hamilton, Madison, Jay, and the Constitution* (New York, 1985); Morton White, *Philosophy, "The Federalist," and the Constitution* (New York, 1987); and Garry Wills, *Explaining America: The Federalist* (London, 1981). (The Allen-Cloonan volume has an appendix listing the Supreme Court cases that have referred to *The Federalist* arranged by the numbers of the essays.) A last worthwhile book on *The Federalist* is Frederick Mosteller and David L. Wallace, *Inference and Disputed Authorship: The Federalist* (Reading, Mass., 1964), which employs a statistical method to determine the authorship of the disputed essays. For a listing of many of the scholarly articles on *The Federalist*, especially those by Douglass Adair, Martin Diamond, Daniel W. Howe, and Alpheus T. Mason, published before 1988, see Patrick T. Conley's comprehensive bibliographic essay in Conley and John P. Kaminski, eds., *The Constitution and the States: The Role of the Original Thirteen in the Framing and Adoption of the Federal Constitution* (Madison, Wis., 1988), 320–22.

Many biographies exist for the major political figures of New York. Among the better ones are:

• Egbert Benson: by Wythe Holt and David A. Nourse (co-authors). See also Robert Ernst,"Egbert Benson, Forgotten Statesman of Revolutionary New York," *New York History*, 78 (1997), 5–32, and John D. Gordan III, "Egbert Benson: A Nationalist in Congress, 1789–1793," in Kenneth R. Bowling and Donald R. Kennon, eds., *Neither Separate nor Equal: Congress in the 1790s* (Athens, Ohio, 2000), 61–90.

• George Clinton: by John P. Kaminski and E. Wilder Spaulding. See also Harold Hastings and J. A. Holden, eds., *Public Papers of George Clinton* . . . (10 vols., New York and Albany, 1899–1914).

• James Duane: by Edward P. Alexander.

• William Duer: by Robert F. Jones. See also "William Duer, Entrepreneur, 1747–99," in Joseph Stancliffe Davis, *Essays in the Earlier History of American Corporations* (2 vols., Cambridge, Mass., 1917), I, 109–345; Robert F. Jones, "Economic Opportunism and the Constitution in New York State: The Example of William Duer," *New York History*, 68 (1987), 357–72; and Cathy Matson, "Public Vices, Private Benefit: William Duer and His Circle, 1776–1792," in William Pencak and Conrad Edick Wright, eds., *New York and the Rise of American Capitalism: Economic Development and the Social and Political History of an American State, 1780–1870* (New York, 1989), 72–123.

• Gansevoort Family: by Alice P. Kenney

• Alexander Hamilton: by Jacob Ernest Cooke, Forrest McDonald, John C. Miller, Broadus Mitchell, Clinton Rossiter, and Gerald Stourzh. See also James Willard Hurst, "Alexander Hamilton, Law Maker," *Columbia Law Review*, 78 (1978), 483–547; Julius Goebel, Jr., and Joseph H. Smith, eds., *The Law Practice of Alexander Hamilton: Documents and Commentary* (5 vols., New York, 1964–1981); and Harold C. Syrett, ed., *The Papers of Alexander Hamilton* (27 vols., New York, 1961–1987).

• John Sloss Hobart: by Mary Voyse

• Hugh Hughes: Bernard Friedman, "Hugh Hughes, A Study in Revolutionary Idealism," *New York History*, 64 (1983), 228–59.

• John Jay: by William Jay, Herbert A. Johnson, Richard B. Morris, and Frank Monaghan. See also the January 2000 issue (Vol. 81, no. 1) of *New York History*; Henry P. Johnston, ed., *The Correspondence and Public Papers of John Jay* . . . (4 vols., New York, 1890–1893); and Richard B. Morris, ed., *John Jay: The Making of A Revolutionary, Unpublished Papers, 1745–1780* (New York, 1975), and *John Jay: The Winning of the Peace, Unpublished Papers, 1780–1784* (New York, 1980).

• James Kent: by John Theodore Horton and William Kent.

• John Lamb: by Isaac Q. Leake.

• Robert R. Livingston: by George Dangerfield.

• Livingston Family: by Cynthia A. Kierner, Edwin Brockholst Livingston, and Richard T. Wiles (ed.)

• Gouverneur Morris: by Mary-Jo Kline and Max M. Mintz.

• Philip Schuyler: by Martin H. Bush, Don R. Gerlach, and Benson J. Lossing.

• Melancton Smith: by Robin Brooks (Ph.D. diss.).

• Marinus Willett: by Larry Lowenthal and Howard Thomas.

• Abraham Yates, Jr.: by Stefan Bielinski.

Research and Bibliographic Aids
Lastly, several research and bibliographic aids have facilitated our work. See Wayne Bodle, "Themes and Directions in Middle Colonies

Historiography, 1980–1994," *William and Mary Quarterly*, 3rd ser., 51 (1994), 355–88; Patricia U. Bonomi, "The Middle Colonies: Embryo of the New Political Order," in Alden T. Vaughan and George Athan Billias, eds., *Perspectives on Early American History: Essays in Honor of Richard B. Morris* (New York, 1973), 63–92; David Maldwyn Ellis, "Recent Historical Writings on New York Topics," *New York History*, 63 (1982), 74–96; Robert J. Gough, "The Myth of the 'Middle Colonies': An Analysis of Regionalization in Early America," *Pennsylvania Magazine of History and Biography*, 107 (1983), 393–419; Douglas Greenberg, "The Middle Colonies in Recent American Historiography," *William and Mary Quarterly*, 3rd ser., 36 (1979), 396–427; Jack P. Greene and J. R. Pole, eds., *Colonial British America: Essays in the New History of the Early Modern Era* (Baltimore, 1984); Milton M. Klein, comp., *New York in the American Revolution: A Bibliography* (Albany, 1974); John J. McCusker and Russell R. Menard, *The Economy of British America, 1607–1789. With Supplementary Bibliography* (Chapel Hill, N.C., 1991); Gaspare J. Saladino, "A Guide to Sources for Studying the Ratification of the Constitution by New York State," in Stephen L. Schechter, ed., *The Reluctant Pillar: New York and the Adoption of the Federal Constitution* (Troy, N.Y., 1985), 118–47; Saladino, "A Supplement to 'A Guide to Sources for Studying the Ratification of the Constitution by New York State,' " in Schechter and Richard B. Bernstein, eds., *New York and the Union: Contributions to the American Constitutional Experience* (Albany, 1990), 351–73; and, Saladino, "The Bill of Rights: A Bibliographic Essay," in Patrick T. Conley and John P. Kaminski, eds., *The Bill of Rights and the States: The Colonial and Revolutionary Origins of American Liberties* (Madison, Wis., 1992), 461–514.; Milton Halsey Thomas, comp., *Columbia University Officers and Alumni, 1754–1857* (New York, 1936); and Edgar A. Werner, comp., *Civil List and Constitutional History of the Colony and State of New York . . .* (Albany, 1889). The volumes of Milton M. Klein and Jack P. Greene and J. R. Pole, in particular, contain references to a host of scholarly journal articles and unpublished doctoral dissertations that are too numerous to be included in this note. Saladino's articles include summaries of the writings on the adoption and ratification of the Constitution and the origins, proposal, adoption, and ratification of the Bill of Rights.

Symbols

Manuscripts

FC	File Copy
MS	Manuscript
RC	Recipient's Copy
Tr	Translation from Foreign Language

Manuscript Depositories

DLC	Library of Congress
DNA	National Archives
MHi	Massachusetts Historical Society
N	New York State Library
NHi	New-York Historical Society
NN	New York Public Library
NjHi	New Jersey Historical Society
PHi	Historical Society of Pennsylvania

Short Titles

Adams, *Defence* — John Adams, *A Defence of the Constitutions of Government of the United States* . . . (3 vols., London, 1787–1788).

Assembly Journal — *Journal of the Assembly of the State of New-York* . . .

Blackstone, *Commentaries* — Sir William Blackstone, *Commentaries on the Laws of England. In Four Books.* (Re-printed from the British Copy, Page for Page with the Last Edition, 5 vols., Philadelphia, 1771–1772). Originally published in London from 1765 to 1769.

Boyd — Julian P. Boyd et al., eds., *The Papers of Thomas Jefferson* (Princeton, N.J., 1950—).

Clinton, *Public Papers* — Hugh Hastings and J. A. Holden, eds., *Public Papers of George Clinton, First Governor of New York* . . . (10 vols., New York and Albany, 1899–1914).

DHFFE	Merrill Jensen, Robert A. Becker, and Gordon DenBoer, eds., *The Documentary History of the First Federal Elections, 1788–1790* (4 vols., Madison, Wis., 1976–1989).
Evans	Charles Evans, *American Bibliography* (12 vols., Chicago, 1903–1934).
Farrand	Max Farrand, ed., *The Records of the Federal Convention of 1787* (3rd ed., 3 vols., New Haven, 1927).
Farrand, *Supplement*	James H. Hutson, ed., *Supplement to Max Farrand's The Records of the Federal Convention of 1787* (New Haven, 1987).
Ford, *Essays*	Paul Leicester Ford, ed., *Essays on the Constitution of the United States, Published during Its Discussion by the People 1787–1788* (Brooklyn, N.Y., 1888).
Ford, *Pamphlets*	Paul Leicester Ford, ed., *Pamphlets on the Constitution of the United States, Published during Its Discussion by the People 1787–1788* (Brooklyn, N.Y., 1888).
JCC	Worthington C. Ford et al., eds., *Journals of the Continental Congress, 1774–1789* . . . (34 vols., Washington, D.C., 1904–1937).
Johnston, *Jay*	Henry P. Johnston, ed., *The Correspondence and Public Papers of John Jay* . . . (4 vols., New York and London, 1890–1893).
Kaminski, *Clinton*	John P. Kaminski, *George Clinton: Yeoman Politician of the New Republic* (Madison, Wis., 1993).
Laws of New-York	*Laws of the State of New-York* . . .
Locke, *Two Treatises*	John Locke, *Two Treatises of Government: A Critical Edition with an Introduction and Apparatus Criticus*, ed. Peter Laslett (Cambridge, Eng., 1964). The first edition was printed in 1689.
Messages from the Governors	Charles Z. Lincoln, ed., *Messages from the Governors* . . . [1683–1906] (11 vols., Albany, 1909).
Montesquieu, *Spirit of Laws*	Charles, Baron de Montesquieu, *The Spirit of Laws* (Translated from the French by Thomas Nugent, 5th ed., 2 vols., London, 1773). Originally published in Geneva in 1748.
PCC	Papers of the Continental Congress, 1774–1789 (Record Group 360, National Archives).
Rutland, *Madison*	Robert A. Rutland et al., eds., *The Papers of James Madison*, Volumes VIII–XVII (Chicago and Charlottesville, 1973–1991).

Senate Journal	*Journal of the Senate of the State of New-York* . . .
Smith, *Letters*	Paul H. Smith, ed., *Letters of Delegates to Congress, 1774–1789* (26 vols., Washington, D.C., 1976–2000).
Storing, *Complete Anti-Federalist*	Herbert J. Storing, ed., With the Assistance of Murray Dry, *The Complete Anti-Federalist* (7 vols., Chicago, 1981).
Syrett	Harold C. Syrett, ed., *The Papers of Alexander Hamilton* (27 vols., New York, 1961–1987).
Thorpe	Francis N. Thorpe, ed., *The Federal and State Constitutions* . . . (7 vols., Washington, D.C., 1909).

Cross-references to Volumes of
The Documentary History of the Ratification of the Constitution

CC	References to *Commentaries on the Constitution* are cited as "CC" followed by the number of the document. For example: "CC:25."
CDR	References to the first volume, titled *Constitutional Documents and Records, 1776–1787*, are cited as "CDR" followed by the page number. For example: "CDR, 325."
RCS	References to the series of volumes titled, *Ratification of the Constitution by the States*, are cited as "RCS" followed by the abbreviation of the state and the page number. For example: "RCS:N.Y., 325."
Mfm	References to the microform supplements to the "RCS" volumes are cited as "Mfm" followed by the abbreviation of the state and the number of the document. For example: "Mfm:N.Y. 25." All documents in the microfiche supplements are now available on the publisher's website: www.wisconsinhistory.org.

New York Chronology, 1777–1790

1777

April 20	State constitution adopted
June	George Clinton elected first governor

1778

February 6	Legislature adopts Articles of Confederation

1780

September 3	Alexander Hamilton calls for national convention
September 7	Governor Clinton addresses legislature asking for more power for Congress
September 26	Legislature appoints commissioners to Hartford Convention
October 10	Legislature instructs delegates to Congress and Hartford Convention commissioners to give more power to Congress
November 8–22	Hartford Convention

1781

March 19	Legislature adopts Impost of 1781

1782

July 21	Legislature calls for national convention and increased powers for Congress
November 30	Preliminary Peace Treaty signed

1783

March 15	Legislature repeals its adoption of Impost of 1781
April 18	Congress proposes Impost of 1783
November 25	British evacuate New York City

1784

March 22	State impost enacted
March 31	Legislature refuses to compensate Loyalists for confiscated estates
May 4	Legislature invites Congress' request to counteract British commercial policy respecting America
June 3	Massachusetts petitions Congress claiming ownership of western New York
August 27	*Rutgers* v. *Waddington*
November 18	Legislature approves state impost

1785

April 4	Legislature approves 30 April 1784 grant of temporary power to Congress to regulate commerce

April 9	Legislature adopts amendment to Articles of Confederation changing method of apportioning expenses of government
April 14	Senate defeats Impost of 1783

1786

February 15	Congress asks New York to reconsider Impost of 1783
March 14	Legislature receives Virginia's call of Annapolis Convention
March 17	Legislature approves appointment of commissioners to Annapolis Convention
April 18	Paper money act becomes law
April 20	Assembly appoints commissioners to Annapolis Convention
May 4	Legislature conditionally adopts Impost of 1783
May 5	Senate agrees with appointment of commissioners to Annapolis Convention
August 11	Congress requests New York to reconsider its approval of Impost of 1783
August 23	Congress again requests New York to reconsider its approval of Impost of 1783
September 11–14	Annapolis Convention
December 16	Hartford agreement between New York and Massachusetts over land in western New York

1787

January 13	Legislature receives Annapolis Convention report
January 26	Legislature adopts state bill of rights
February 15	Assembly refuses to alter its approval of Impost of 1783
February 20	Legislature instructs delegates to Congress to move for appointment of a constitutional convention
February 21	Congress rejects New York's call for a convention and accepts amended motion by Massachusetts for a convention
February 23	Legislature receives congressional resolution of 21 February calling Constitutional Convention
February 28	Legislature authorizes election of delegates to Constitutional Convention
March 6	Legislature elects three delegates (Alexander Hamilton, John Lansing, Jr., and Robert Yates) to Constitutional Convention
April 18	Senate rejects Alexander Hamilton's motion for appointment of two additional delegates to Constitutional Convention
May 25	Robert Yates and Alexander Hamilton first attend Constitutional Convention
June 2	John Lansing, Jr., first attends Constitutional Convention
June 16	Lansing's speech in Constitutional Convention
June 18	Hamilton's "plan" submitted to Constitutional Convention
July 10	Yates and Lansing leave Constitutional Convention
July 21	Hamilton publicly attacks Governor Clinton for his opposition to Constitutional Convention

September 3	Hamilton, who had left in late June, returns to Constitutional Convention
September 17	Constitutional Convention signs Constitution with Hamilton signing for New York
September 21	Constitution first printed in New York (*Daily Advertiser* and *New York Packet*)
September 27	Cato series first printed
October 18	Brutus series first printed
October 27	Publius, The Federalist, first printed
November 1	Cincinnatus series first printed
November 2	Americanus series first printed
November c. 8	Federal Farmer pamphlet first printed
November 19	*New York Journal* becomes a daily
November 21	A Countryman (Hugh Hughes) series first printed
December 6	A Countryman (De Witt Clinton) series first printed
December 11	Examiner series first printed
December 21	Yates and Lansing write letter to Governor Clinton explaining why they left Constitutional Convention early

1788

January 11	Governor Clinton transmits Constitution and Yates-Lansing letter to legislature
January 14	Yates-Lansing letter first printed
January 31	Assembly adopts resolution calling state convention
February 1	Senates concurs with Assembly's resolution calling state convention
February 7	Constitution burned at Montgomery, Ulster County
March 22	Volume I of Publius, *The Federalist*, printed (36 essays)
April 13–14	Doctors' riots in New York City
April 15	John Jay's A Citizen of New-York pamphlet printed
April 17	A Plebeian pamphlet printed
April 29–May 3	Elections for state convention
May c. 18	Federal Republican Committee formed in New York City
May 27	Ballot boxes opened and votes counted for election to state convention
May 28	Volume II of Publius, *The Federalist*, printed (49 essays)
June 17	State Convention convenes in Poughkeepsie
June 17	George Clinton elected president of Convention
June 18	Convention reads Constitution
June 19	Henry Outhoudt elected chairman committee of the whole
June 24	News of New Hampshire's ratification of Constitution arrives in Poughkeepsie
July 2	News of Virginia's ratification of Constitution arrives in Poughkeepsie
July 7	Convention finishes discussion of Constitution, and John Lansing, Jr., presents a bill of rights to be prefixed to Constitution
July 10	Lansing presents plan of ratification with conditional amendments
July 11	John Jay proposes unconditional ratification

July 15	Melancton Smith proposes limited ratification of Constitution
July 16	John Sloss Hobart's motion to adjourn defeated
July 19	Lansing proposes conditional ratification with amendments
July 23	New York City Federal Procession
July 23	Samuel Jones's amendment to ratify "in full confidence" that amendments would be adopted
July 23	Convention's committee of the whole votes to ratify Constitution without conditional amendments 31 to 29
July 24	Lansing proposes limited-term ratification
July 25	Convention rejects Lansing's motion for limited-term ratification
July 26	Convention adopts Constitution 30 to 27 with proposed amendments
July 26	Circular Letter to states approved
July 27	Sacking of Thomas Greenleaf's print shop
October 30	Federal Republican Committee reorganizes in New York City to work for a second constitutional convention

1789

February 7	Legislature resolves to ask Congress to call a convention to draft amendments to the Constitution

1790

January 13	Legislature receives proposed twelve amendments to Constitution
February 26	Legislature adopts eleven of twelve proposed amendments to Constitution

Officers of the State of New York
1787–1788

Governor
George Clinton

Lieutenant Governor
Pierre Van Cortlandt

Chancellor
Robert R. Livingston

Justices of the Supreme Court
Richard Morris, Chief Justice
John Sloss Hobart
Robert Yates

Clerk of the Supreme Court
John McKesson

Judge of the Court of Admiralty
Lewis Graham

Secretary of State
Lewis A. Scott

Attorney General
Egbert Benson
Richard Varick
(appointed 14 May 1788)

Treasurer
Gerard Bancker

Auditor-General
Peter T. Curtenius

Surveyor General
Simeon DeWitt

Mayor of New York City
James Duane

Mayor of Albany
John Lansing, Jr.

Mayor of Hudson
Seth Jenkins

Council of Appointment
George Clinton
Appointed 18 January 1787
William Floyd
John Hathorn

Ebenezer Russell
Peter Schuyler
Appointed 18 January 1788
Anthony Hoffman
David Hopkins
Philip Schuyler
John Vanderbilt

Council of Revision
George Clinton
Robert R. Livingston
Richard Morris
John Sloss Hobart
Robert Yates

Annapolis Convention Delegates
Egbert Benson*
Alexander Hamilton*
Robert C. Livingston
Robert R. Livingston
James Duane
Leonard Gansevoort
*Attended

Delegates to Congress
Elected 26 January 1787
Abraham Yates, Jr.
John Lansing, Jr.
Melancton Smith
John Haring
Egbert Benson
Elected 22 January 1788
Abraham Yates, Jr.
Ezra L'Hommedieu
Egbert Benson
Leonard Gansevoort
Alexander Hamilton

Constitutional Convention
Alexander Hamilton*
Robert Yates**
John Lansing, Jr.**
*Signed Constitution
**Left Convention on 10 July 1787

Confederation Secretary for Foreign Affairs
John Jay

The New York Legislature
9 January–22 March 1788

ASSEMBLY

Speaker: Richard Varick   Clerk: John McKesson

City and County of New York
David Brooks
Nicholas Bayard
Richard Varick
Gulian Verplanck
Richard Harison
Nicholas Low
Comfort Sands
Daniel Niven
Evert Bancker

City and County of Albany
John Younglove
Leonard Gansevoort
Hezekiah Van Orden
John De Peyster Ten Eyck

Queens County
Samuel Jones
Whitehead Cornwell
Francis Lewis, Jr.
Stephen Carman

Kings County
Cornelius Wyckoff
Charles Doughty

Richmond County
John C. Dongan
Peter Winant

Westchester County
Ebenezer Lockwood
Jonathan G. Tompkins
Thomas Thomas
Abijah Gilbert
Joseph Strang
Samuel Drake

Orange County
William Thompson
Henry Wisner, Jr.
Jeremiah Clark
Peter Taulman

James Gordon
Dirck Van Ingen
Thomas Sickles

Suffolk County
Jonathan N. Havens
David Hedges
Daniel Osborn
John Smith

Ulster County
John Cantine
Cornelius C. Schoonmaker
Charles DeWitt
Nathan Smith
James Bruyn
James Clinton

Dutchess County
Egbert Benson
Peter Cantine, Jr.
Thomas Tillotson
Matthew Patterson
John DeWitt, Jr.
Morris Graham
Isaac Bloom

Montgomery County
James Livingston
John Frey
John Winn
Isaac Paris
Volkert Veeder
Abraham Arndt

Washington County
Alexander Webster
Peter B. Tearse
Albert Baker
Edward Savage

Columbia County
William Powers
Peter Silvester
John Livingston

lxxxviii

SENATE*

President: Pierre Van Cortlandt   Clerk: Abraham B. Bancker

Southern District
John Vanderbilt
Lewis Morris
Samuel Townsend
Ezra L'Hommedieu
Thomas Tredwell
James Duane
William Floyd
John Lawrence

Middle District
John Hathorn
Jacobus Swartwout
Anthony Hoffman
John Haring

Cornelius Humphrey
Arthur Parks

Western District
Abraham Yates, Jr.
Peter Schuyler
Jellis Fonda
Peter Van Ness
Philip Schuyler
Volkert P. Douw

Eastern District
John Williams
Ebenezer Russell
David Hopkins

Southern District: City and County of New York, and Kings, Queens, Richmond, Suffolk, and Westchester counties
Middle District: Columbia, Dutchess, Orange, and Ulster counties
Western District: City and County of Albany and Montgomery County
Eastern District: Washington and Clinton counties

The Ratification of the Constitution by the States

NEW YORK
[1]

I.
THE DEBATE OVER THE
CONSTITUTION IN NEW YORK
21 July 1787–31 January 1788

Introduction

Public Commentaries on the Constitution

Between 17 September 1787 and 31 January 1788, ten newspapers and a monthly magazine were printed in New York. Two newspapers were dailies; three were semiweeklies; and four were weeklies. The tenth newspaper, the *New York Journal,* was a weekly until 15 November, after which it became a daily. Nine newspapers printed the new Constitution between 21 September and 4 October. (The tenth newspaper, the *Albany Journal,* did not begin publication until 26 January 1788.) By the end of 1787, the Constitution had also appeared in several pamphlet and broadside editions and in almanacs. (See "The Publication of the Constitution in New York," 21 September 1787–June 1788, below.)

Newspapers reported on discontent, turmoil, and violence in Delaware, Georgia, New Hampshire, New York, Pennsylvania, South Carolina, and Virginia. Articles and squibs criticized the Rhode Island legislature for its radical financial policies and its refusal to send delegates to the Constitutional Convention. Items appeared regarding the navigation of the Mississippi River and the dangers of Shays's Rebellion, including the fate of Shaysite leaders. Newspapers printed reports of or the proceedings of public meetings in other states recommending the Constitution's ratification; the text of Congress' resolution of 28 September transmitting the Constitution to the states for their ratification; the texts or reports of speeches by state executives forwarding the Constitution to their state legislatures; squibs speculating about the prospects of ratification in New York and other states; reports of or the proceedings of the legislatures of every state on the calling of state conventions to consider the Constitution; reports of the refusal of the Rhode Island legislature to call a state convention; reports of the elections of delegates to state conventions; reports of instructions to state convention delegates; reports of or the proceedings of state conventions; reports of ratification by state conventions; and reports of celebrations of ratification. Numerous brief items appeared praising both George Washington, the president of the Constitutional Convention, and Benjamin Franklin, its elder statesman; while other items criticized

3

Elbridge Gerry of Massachusetts and George Mason of Virginia for refusing to sign the Constitution.

Most importantly, New York newspapers abounded with major essays, both original and reprinted, defending or criticizing the Constitution, as New York joined Philadelphia as primary centers for the national debate over the ratification of the Constitution. Newspapers also printed many essays filled with personal invective, with Alexander Hamilton being the favorite Antifederalist target and Abraham Yates, Jr., being the preferred Federalist target. Both sides of the question were well represented, although the Federalist viewpoint received wider coverage since the majority of New York's newspapers were Federalist. The number of original major essays produced by New York's newspapers was exceeded probably only by that in Pennsylvania. Although New York newspapers printed far fewer original squibs than those found in Philadelphia newspapers, New York printers reprinted many of the squibs originating in Philadelphia newspapers.

The major Federalist articles that originated in New York include: "Curtius" I–III, *Daily Advertiser*, 29 September, 18 October, and 3 November (supplement); "Caesar" I–II (Alexander Hamilton?), *Daily Advertiser*, 1, 17 October; "Publius," *The Federalist* 1–47 (Alexander Hamilton, John Jay, and James Madison), *Independent Journal, New York Packet, Daily Advertiser*, and *New York Journal*, 27 October–30 January 1788; "Americanus" I–VII (John Stevens, Jr.), *Daily Advertiser*, 2, 23, 30 November, 5–6, 12 December 1787, and 12, 21 January 1788; "A Farmer, of New-Jersey" (John Stevens, Jr.), *Observations on Government*, 3 November; "P. Valerius Agricola," *Albany Gazette*, 8 November and 6 December; "Roderick Razor," *Daily Advertiser*, 11 December; "Examiner" I–V (Charles McKnight), *New York Journal*, 11, 14, 19, 24 December 1787, and 4 January 1788; "Country Federalist" (James Kent), *Country Journal*, 19 December 1787 (supplement); "A Lunarian," *Daily Advertiser*, 20 December; "America" (Noah Webster), *Daily Advertiser*, 31 December; "Giles Hickory" (Noah Webster), *American Magazine*, 1 January 1788; and "Curtiopolis," *Daily Advertiser*, 18 January.

The Federalist position on the Constitution was buttressed by numerous major writings reprinted from out-of-state newspapers, particularly those in Pennsylvania, Massachusetts, and Connecticut. These writings include: "An American Citizen" I–IV (Tench Coxe), Philadelphia *Independent Gazetteer*, 26, 28, 29 September, and broadside, 21 October (CC:100–A, 109, 112, 183–A); "Foreign Spectator" (Nicholas Collin) Philadelphia *Independent Gazetteer*, 2 October (CC:124); "Social Compact," *New Haven Gazette*, 4 October (CC:130); "Foederal Constitution,"

Pennsylvania Gazette, 10 October (CC:150); "One of the People," *Massachusetts Centinel,* 17 October (CC:168); "A Political Dialogue," *Massachusetts Centinel,* 24 October (CC:189); "Landholder" I, VI, VIII (Oliver Ellsworth), *Connecticut Courant,* 5 November, and 10, 24 December (CC:230, 335, 371); "The Prayer of an American Citizen" (Mathew Carey), Philadelphia *American Museum,* 7 November (CC:235); "A Citizen of Philadelphia" (Pelatiah Webster), *The Weaknesses of Brutus Exposed,* 8 November (CC:244); "Plain Truth," Philadelphia *Independent Gazetteer,* 10 November (RCS:Pa., 216–23); "A Countryman" I–V (Roger Sherman), *New Haven Gazette,* 15, 22, 29 November, and 6, 20 December (CC:261, 284, 305, 322, 361); "Anti-Cincinnatus," Northampton, Mass., *Hampshire Gazette,* 19 December (CC:354); "New England," *Connecticut Courant,* 24 December (CC:372); "One of the People," *Maryland Journal,* 25 December (CC:377); "New Roof" (Francis Hopkinson), *Pennsylvania Packet,* 29 December (CC:395); "Philanthropos" (Tench Coxe), Philadelphia *Independent Gazetteer,* 16 January 1788 (CC:454); "A Citizen of Philadelphia" (Pelatiah Webster?), *Pennsylvania Gazette,* 23 January (RCS:Pa., 658–60); and a Spurious Centinel Letter (Francis Hopkinson), *Pennsylvania Gazette,* 23 January (CC:471). (See also "New York Reprinting of the Essays of An American Citizen," 6 October–29 November 1787; and "New York Reprinting of New England's Response to the Federal Farmer's Letters to the Republican," 4 January 1788, both below.)

New York newspapers also reprinted the most influential Federalist statement on the meaning of the Constitution—a speech by James Wilson, a Pennsylvania signer of the Constitution, which he delivered to a Philadelphia public meeting on 6 October. (See "New York Reprinting of James Wilson's 6 October Speech Before a Philadelphia Public Meeting," 13–25 October, below.) Lastly, New York newspapers reprinted Benjamin Franklin's last speech delivered to the Constitutional Convention on 17 September. This speech first appeared in the *Boston Gazette* on 3 December. (See CC:77; and RCS:Mass., 369–80.)

The major Antifederalist essays originating in New York were printed almost entirely in Thomas Greenleaf's *New York Journal.* The *Journal's* articles include: "Cato" I–VII (George Clinton?), 27 September, 11, 25 October, 8, 22 November, 13 December 1787, and 3 January 1788; "Brutus" I–XI (Melancton Smith?), 18 October, 1, 15, 29 November, 13, 27 December 1787, and 3, 10, 17, 24, 31 January 1788; "Sidney" (Abraham Yates, Jr.), 18 October (extraordinary); "A Republican" I, 25 October; "Cincinnatus" I–VI (Arthur Lee), 1, 8, 15, 22, 29 November, 6 December; "Timoleon," 1 November (extraordinary), and as a broadside, post-1 November (Thomas Greenleaf, Evans 45045); "Brutus, Junior," 8 November; "A Countryman" I–V (Hugh Hughes), 21, 23 November, 3, 15 December 1787, and 22 January 1788; "A Baptist," 30 November; "A Countryman" I–V (DeWitt Clinton), 6, 13, 20 December, 1787, and 10, 17 January 1788; "Democritus," 14, 21, 28 December; "A Republican," 27 December; and "Expositor" I (Hugh Hughes), 24, 31 January, 7 February. A last major Antifederalist pseudonymous piece, signed "Sidney" (Abraham Yates, Jr.), appeared in the *Albany Gazette* on 24 January 1788.

The most important Antifederalist item originating in New York, and perhaps in all of the United States, was the pamphlet, *Letters from the Federal Farmer to the Republican*, which went on sale in New York City on 8 November 1787 and which went through three, possibly four, editions. For months, the pamphlet circulated throughout the state and between 14 November and 2 January 1788 the *Country Journal* reprinted it in weekly installments. It was the only Antifederalist pamphlet to be printed in New York before 1 February 1788 when the state legislature called a convention to consider the Constitution.

New York newspapers, especially Thomas Greenleaf's *New York Journal*, also reprinted numerous major Antifederalist essays from out-of-state newspapers, most particularly from two Philadelphia Antifederalist newspapers—the *Independent Gazetteer* and the *Freeman's Journal*. These essays include "Strictures on the Proposed Constitution" (George Turner?), *Freeman's Journal*, 26 September (CC:97); "Centinel" I, III–V, VII–XI (Samuel Bryan), *Independent Gazetteer*, 5 October, 8, 30 November, 4, 29 December 1787, and 2, 8, 12, 16 January 1788 (CC:133, 243, 311, 318, 394, 410, 427, 443, 453); "Centinel" II (Samuel Bryan), *Freeman's Journal*, 24 October (CC:190); "Centinel" VI (Samuel Bryan), *Pennsylvania Packet*, 25 December (CC:379); "A Democratic Federalist," *Pennsylvania Herald*, 17 October (CC:167); "Cato Uticensis" (George Mason?), *Virginia Independent Chronicle*, 17 October (RCS:Va., 70–76); "An Old Whig" I–VII, *Independent Gazetteer*, 12, 17, 20, 27 October, and 1, 24, 28 November (CC:157, 170, 181, 202, 224, 292, 301); "An Officer of the Late Continental Army" (William Findley?), *Independent Gazetteer*, 6 November (RCS:Pa., 210–16); "Agrippa" I, VII (James Winthrop), *Massachusetts Gazette*, 23 November, and 18 December (RCS:Mass., 303–6, 483–86); "Many Customers," *Independent Gazetteer*, 1 December (RCS:Pa., 306–9); "One of the Common People," *Boston Gazette*, 3 December (RCS:Mass., 367–69); "Z," Boston *Independent Chronicle*, 6 December (RCS:Mass., 373–75); "Columbus," *Pennsylvania Herald*, 8 December (RCS:Pa., 313–15); "Poplicola," *Boston Gazette*, 24 December (CC:369); "Philadelphiensis" VI, VIII (Benjamin Workman), *Freeman's Journal*, 26 December 1787, and 23 January 1788 (CC:382, 473); "Helvidius Priscus" I–II (James Warren?), Boston *Independent Chronicle*,

27 December 1787, and 10 January 1788 (RCS:Mass., 534–39, 684–87); *Genuine Information* I–II (Luther Martin), Baltimore *Maryland Gazette,* 28 December 1787, and 1 January 1788 (CC:389, 401); and "The Republican Federalist" I (James Warren?), *Massachusetts Centinel,* 29 December (RCS:Mass., 549–54). Shortly after 1 November, Thomas Greenleaf reprinted "Centinel" I–II as a broadside, along with "Timoleon," an original New York item (Evans 45045). (See also "New York Reprinting of the Centinel Essays," 17 October 1787–12 April 1788; and "New York Reprinting of Luther Martin's *Genuine Information,*" 15 January–7 April 1788, both below.)

Other major Antifederalist items reprinted in New York were the address of the seceding members of the Pennsylvania Assembly, broadside, 2 October (RCS:Pa., 112–17, and CC:125–A); Virginian George Mason's objections to the Constitution, *Massachusetts Centinel,* 21 November (CC:276–A); Virginia congressman Richard Henry Lee's proposed amendments to the Constitution, Petersburg *Virginia Gazette,* 6 December (CC:325); the dissent of the minority of the Pennsylvania Convention, *Pennsylvania Packet,* 18 December (CC:353); and Virginia Governor Edmund Randolph's letter of 10 October explaining why he did not sign the Constitution, pamphlet, c. 27 December (CC:385). (See also "New York Reprinting of the Address of the Seceding Members of the Pennsylvania Assembly," 9–18 October; "New York Reprinting of George Mason's Objections to the Constitution," 30 November–13 December; "New York Reprinting of Richard Henry Lee's Proposed Amendments to the Constitution," 22 December 1787–24 January 1788; "New York Reprinting of the Dissent of the Minority of the Pennsylvania Convention," 27 December 1787–April 1788; and "New York Reprinting of Virginia Governor Edmund Randolph's 10 October 1787 Letter to the Speaker of the Virginia House of Delegates," 8 January–April 1788, all below.)

Private Commentaries on the Constitution
Private letters are critical to understanding the ratification debate. Letter writers analyzed, extolled, and attacked provisions of the Constitution; explained why it should be adopted, rejected, or amended; speculated on the chances for ratification in New York and other states; described and analyzed the newspaper literature on the Constitution; speculated about the authorship of newspaper essays; explained how the essays got into the hands of the newspaper printers; described the politics of New York state and the actions of the New York legislature on calling a ratifying convention; and closely watched the progress of ratifying conventions in other states, especially Massachusetts. John Jay,

to quash a rumor that he opposed the Constitution, wrote a letter (whose publication he encouraged) insisting that he supported the Constitution. Letters of Alexander Hamilton and James Madison reveal their roles in writing *The Federalist*. A letter by Melancton Smith suggests that he might have been the author of the Antifederalist essays of "Brutus." A letter from Constitutional Convention delegates Robert Yates and John Lansing, Jr., to Governor George Clinton explains why they left the Convention early and why they opposed the Constitution. Hugh Ledlie, an elderly Connecticut Son of Liberty, remembered his former allies among the New York Sons of Liberty, some of whom now opposed the Constitution, and decried the methods used by Federalists to ratify the Constitution. And a lengthy and informative letter of Charles Tillinghast, son-in-law of Antifederalist leader John Lamb, says much about the writing and publication of Antifederalist essays.

Alexander Hamilton Attacks Governor George Clinton
21 July–30 October 1787

In the spring and summer of 1787 the Constitutional Convention met in Philadelphia to revise and amend the Articles of Confederation. Three or four weeks after the Convention began its sessions on 25 May, it became known that, instead of amending the Articles, the Convention would establish a new government for the United States. Advocates of such a government in New York and Pennsylvania believed that the principal opposition to it would come from state officeholders who feared they would lose their power. The first-known public attack on these state officeholders was made by a correspondent in the *Pennsylvania Gazette* on 20 June, who warned officeholders to be quiet or else they would suffer the same fate suffered by Loyalists early in the American Revolution (CC:40–A). This brief item was reprinted in the *New York Journal*, 28 June, and *Northern Centinel*, 2 July.

The most important attack on any state officeholder was made against New York Governor George Clinton in the *Daily Advertiser* on 21 July by Alexander Hamilton, a New York delegate to the Constitutional Convention on leave from that body. Writing anonymously, Hamilton claimed that Clinton had opposed the appointment of delegates to the Constitutional Convention and had "predicted a mischievous issue of that measure." According to Hamilton, Clinton had stated publicly that the Convention was unnecessary and that the "evils" it intended to remedy were imaginary. Hamilton rejected Clinton's alleged analysis of the Confederation's political and economic condition and defended the appointment of a convention that would create a strong central government able to address the many "evils" that had befallen America. Hamilton accused Clinton of having a "greater attachment to his *own power* than to the *public good.*" New Yorkers were told to watch Clinton "with a jealous eye, and when he sounds the alarm of danger from another quarter, to examine whether they have not more to apprehend from *himself.*"

Support for Hamilton's position came swiftly. "An Admirer of Anti-Federal Men," *Daily Advertiser*, 26 July, decried "the conduct of several leading men" who had "given the friends to liberty much uneasiness." He praised the Convention delegates and called upon Americans to have confidence in them. On 1 August the *Pennsylvania Herald* heard from a New York gentleman that "the anti-fœderal disposition of a great officer" in New York had seriously alarmed the people with "anticipation of anarchy and division." An anonymous verse printed in the *Massachusetts Centinel*, 18 August, accused Clinton of seeking "to wreck" the Union. Other newspapers outside New York—in brief and widely circulated articles—did not identify Clinton by name but instead criticized self-interested and scheming officeholders in general for their opposition to a convention that promised to create a vigorous central government. (See *New Hampshire Spy* and *Salem Mercury*, 7 August, and *Pennsylvania Gazette*, 8 August [CC:62, 61, 40–D], all of which were reprinted in New York.) On 1 September, David Humphreys of Connecticut, who like Hamilton served as an aide-de-camp to George Washington during the Revolution, complimented Hamilton for the "honest boldness" of his public attack on Clinton's Antifederalist views.

Humphreys was disturbed by "popular Demagogues who are determined to keep themselves in office at the risque of every thing" (CC:51–F).

In early September the attack upon Clinton in New York was renewed, perhaps in anticipation of the completion of the Constitutional Convention's work. Soon after, Clinton and his supporters came to his defense, and, in turn, they were answered by Hamilton and his advocates. The debate lasted until mid-October. "Rough Carver," a parody of Antifederalist Abraham Yates, Jr.'s, use of the pseudonym "Rough Hewer," criticized those persons whose refusal to increase the powers of the Confederation Congress had endangered the Union to the point of its impending dissolution. According to "Rough Carver," opponents of a strong Union had "coolly" opposed all things that did "not bear the marks of *Self*"; they had "nothing in view but their own aggrandizement." He wanted Clinton—their "thick skulled and double-hearted Chief"— replaced as governor (*Daily Advertiser*, 3, 4 September).

Clinton's adherents responded slowly. On 6 September "A Republican" (possibly Clinton himself), writing in the *New York Journal*, answered Hamilton's initial 21 July attack. "A Republican" defended Clinton's right, as a "citizen of a free state" and a public officer, to speak "freely and unreservedly to express his sentiments on public measures, however serious the posture of our national affairs may be." Clinton's attacker, declared "A Republican," belonged to an "opulent and ambitious" party, a "lordly faction," that sought to undermine the state government so "that they may establish a system more favorable to their aristocratic views." "A Republican" concluded by quoting some verse from English poet Charles Churchill to suggest that Hamilton had penned the attack on Clinton. In the same issue of the *New York Journal*, "Adrastus" also hinted that he knew the identity of Clinton's attacker because the attacker's style was well known. He warned readers to guard against "so dangerous a member of society, who, with a smooth tongue and double face, is capable of concealing and executing the worst intentions beneath the mask of sincerity and friendship" (Mfm:N.Y.). "An Old Soldier," *Northern Centinel*, 10 September, and "Rusticus," *New York Journal*, 13 September, also defended Clinton.

While answering "A Republican" in the *Daily Advertiser* on 10 September, "Aristides" defended Hamilton, stating that no man was more "worthy of credit." When he attacked Clinton, Hamilton was "impelled, from pure principles." Hamilton, stated "Aristides," had not misrepresented Clinton's views and neither Clinton nor his defenders denied the charges. Clinton had definitely been hostile to all measures seeking to strengthen the central government. As governor, Clinton exercised too much power, while he and his "motley group" created a dangerous "system of *connections and dependencies*." On 20 September "Anti-Defamationis," writing in the *New York Journal*, denounced "Aristides" and others for attacking Clinton, whose duty it was to criticize the Convention if he thought "evil instead of good would result from their deliberations."

Defending himself in a lengthy article for the *Daily Advertiser* on 15 September, Hamilton admitted writing the 21 July attack upon Clinton, stating that he had left his name with the printer "to be disclosed to any person who should apply for it, on the part of the Governor." His denunciations of Clinton were well founded because the governor's wish to retain his power would come at the expense of the nation's peace and happiness. In a free country, declared Hamilton, citizens had every right to question their rulers' conduct. How could one voice injure a man who possessed "all the influence to be derived from long continuance in office." Finally, Hamilton insisted that his actions were consistent "with the strictest rules of integrity and honor."

After Hamilton publicly acknowledged his authorship of the 21 July attack on Clinton, he was lambasted by "Inspector" in three satirical articles printed in the *New York Journal*, 20 September, and 4 and 18 October (the latter two on Mfm:N.Y.). According to "Inspector," Hamilton (referred to as "Tom S**t") was "over-rated"; he was of low and illegitimate West Indian birth; he was an "upstart attorney" who advanced his military career by ingratiating himself with General George Washington, only to be summarily dismissed by Washington from his staff; he owed his position to his wealthy and influential father-in-law, Philip Schuyler (referred to, among other names, as Hamilton's "immaculate daddy, Justice Midas"); his vanity led him to attack Clinton whom he wanted to see replaced as governor by Schuyler; he expressed monarchical views in the Constitutional Convention; he despised the common people; and as a lawyer he grew rich defending Loyalists ("traitors").

"Inspector's" description of Hamilton's relationship to Washington distressed Hamilton so much that he wrote Washington, requesting that their relationship be put "in its true light." In his response, Washington described "Inspector's" charges as unfounded and told Hamilton that he held him in high esteem. However, Washington was dismayed that two such worthy characters as Hamilton and Clinton were at odds with one another. (See Hamilton to Washington, 8–10 October; Washington to Hamilton, 18 October; and Hamilton to Washington, 30 October.)

On 6 and 9 October, two writers defended Hamilton in the *Daily Advertiser*. "Aristides" criticized the printer of the *New York Journal* for his partiality in printing "Inspector," who should have signed himself "An Inquisitor" because of his "gross" and libelous attack on Hamilton, a man who was "invulnerable in *his own personal conduct*." Moreover, the nation owed "some weighty obligations" to Hamilton, who had always acted judiciously, patriotically, and honorably in his professional and public life (Mfm:N.Y.). "Philopolitis" noted that such "impotent and scurrilous" attacks on Hamilton would increase the public esteem for him since the charges against him were malignant and fabricated (Mfm:N.Y.). "A Customer" in the *New York Journal*, 11 October, criticized "Aristides" and "Philopolitis" for not "referring to particulars" and instead listed Hamilton's accomplishments (Mfm:N.Y.).

(Unless otherwise indicated, the documents cited in this editorial note are printed below.)

New York Daily Advertiser, 21 July 1787[1]

It is currently reported and believed, that his Excellency Governor CLINTON has, in public company, without reserve, reprobated the appointment of the Convention, and predicted a mischievous issue of that measure. His observations are said to be to this effect:—That the present confederation is, in itself, equal to the purposes of the union:—

That the appointment of a Convention is calculated to impress the people with an idea of evils which do not exist:—That if either nothing should be proposed by the Convention, or if what they should propose should not be agreed to, the one or the other would tend to beget despair in the public mind; and that, in all probability, the result of their deliberations, whatever it might be, would only serve to throw the community into confusion.

Upon this conduct of his Excellency, if he is not misrepresented, the following reflections will naturally occur to every considerate and impartial man:

First. That from the almost universal concurrence of the states in the measure of appointing a Convention, and from the powers given to their Deputies, "to devise and propose such alterations in the Federal Constitution as are necessary to *render it adequate* to the purposes of government, and to the exigencies of the union,"[2] it appears clearly to be the general sense of America, that the present confederation *is not* "equal to the purposes of the union," but requires material alterations.

Secondly. That the concurrence of the legislatures of twelve out of the thirteen states,[3] which compose the union (actuated as they are by a diversity of prejudices and supposed interests) in a measure of so extraordinary a complexion, the direct object of which is the abridgement of their own power, in favor of a general government, is of itself a strong presumptive proof that there exist real evils; and that these evils are of so extensive and cogent a nature, as to have been capable of giving an impulse from one extremity of the United States to the other.

Thirdly. That some of these evils are so obvious, that they do not seem to admit of doubt or equivocation;—of this description are,

1. The *defective* and *disproportionate* contributions of the several states to the common treasury, and, in consequence of this, the total want of means in the United States to pay their debts, foreign or domestic, or to support those establishments which are necessary to the public tranquillity.[4]

2. The general stagnation of commerce, occasioned no doubt, in a great degree, by the exclusions, and restraints with which foreign nations fetter our trade with them; while they enjoy in our ports unlimited freedom, and while our government is incapable of making those defensive regulations, which would be likely to produce a greater reciprocity of privileges.

3d. The degradation of our national character and consequence, to such an extreme of insignificance, that foreign powers in plain terms, refuse to treat with us, alledging, and alledging truly, that we have no government to ensure the performance of the stipulations on our part.

Fourthly. That these and many other facts and circumstances, prove to a demonstration, that the general government is fundamentally defective; that the very existence of the union is in imminent danger, and that there is great reason to dread, that without some speedy and radical alterations, these states may shortly become thirteen distinct and unconnected communities, exposed, without a common head, to all the hazard of foreign invasion, and intrigue, of hostility with each other, and of internal faction and insurrection.

Fifthly. That at this very instant the union is so far nominal, that it is not only destitute of the necessary powers to administer the common concerns of the nation, but is scarcely able to keep up the appearances of existence; sunk to so low an ebb that it can with difficulty engage the attendance of a sufficient number of members in Congress, even to *deliberate* upon any matter of importance.

Sixthly. That this state of our affairs called for the collective wisdom of the union to provide an effectual remedy; that there were only two ways of uniting its councils to that end, one through the medium of Congress, and the other through the medium of a body specially appointed for the purpose; that several reasons conspired to render the latter mode preferable. Congress, occupied in the ordinary administration of the government could not give so steady and undivided an attention to the national reform as the crisis demanded: The parties, which will always grow up in an established body, would render them less likely to agree in a proper plan. Any plan they should agree upon, would have greater prejudices to encounter in its progress through the states; for the mind is naturally prone to suspect the aims of men who propose the encrease of a power, of which they themselves have the present possession; and, in several of the states, industrious and wicked pains have been taken by the parties unfriendly to the measures of the union, to discredit and debase the authority and influence of Congress. In addition to these considerations, the states would have it in their power, in a special Convention, to avail themselves of the weight and abilities of men, who could not have been induced to accept an appointment to Congress; and whose aid, in a work of such magnitude, was on many accounts desirable. The late illustrious Commander in Chief stands foremost in this number.

Seventhly. That though it is too justly to be apprehended that local views, state prejudices, and personal interests, will frustrate the hope of any effectual plan from any body of men whatever, appointed by so many separate states, yet the object was worthy of an experiment, and that experiment could not be made with so much advantage in any way, as in that which has been fallen upon for the purpose.

Eighthly. That however justifiable it might be in the governor to oppose the appointment of a convention, if the measure were still under
deliberation; and if he sincerely believed it to be a pernicious one, yet
the general voice of America having decided in its favor, it is *unwarrantable* and *culpable in any man,* in so serious a posture of our national
affairs, to endeavour to prepossess the public mind against the hitherto
undetermined and unknown measures of a body to whose councils
America has, in a great measure, entrusted its future fate, and to whom
the people in general look up, under the blessing of heaven, for their
political salvation.

Ninthly. That such conduct in a man high in office, argues greater
attachment to his *own power* than to the *public good,* and furnishes strong
reason to suspect a dangerous predetermination to oppose whatever
may tend to diminish the *former,* however it may promote the *latter.*

If there be any man among us, who acts so unworthy a part, it becomes a free and enlightened people to observe him with a jealous eye,
and when he sounds the alarm of danger from another quarter, to
examine whether they have not more to apprehend from *himself.*

1. This item was written by Alexander Hamilton. It was reprinted in the *Hudson Weekly
Gazette,* 2 August; the first sentence only appeared in the *Northern Centinel,* 27 August,
which placed the words beginning with "reprobated" in large capital letters. The item
was also reprinted in whole or in part in sixteen out-of-state newspapers by 11 September:
Vt. (1), N.H. (2), Mass. (7), R.I. (1), Conn. (1), Pa. (2), Md. (1), S.C. (1). In reprinting
the article on 11 August, the *Massachusetts Centinel* signed it "A. B." Two other newspapers
also used the pseudonym.

2. The text within quotation marks was drawn by Hamilton from several sources: the
congressional resolution of 21 February 1787, the New York motion of 21 February in
Congress, and the report of the Annapolis Convention. (For these sources, see CDR,
181–87.)

3. Rhode Island did not appoint delegates to the Constitutional Convention.

4. A report by the Confederation Board of Treasury indicates that by 31 March 1788
the states had paid the following percentages of their shares of the specie and indents
levied by congressional requisitions from October 1781 to October 1787: New York (67),
Pennsylvania (57), South Carolina (55), Virginia (44), Massachusetts (39), Delaware (39),
Maryland (29), Rhode Island (24), Connecticut (20), New Jersey (19), New Hampshire
(12), and North Carolina (3). Georgia had paid nothing. (See PCC, Item 141, Estimates
and Statements of Receipts and Expenditures, 1780–88, Vol. I, 75, DNA.)

An Admirer of Anti-Federal Men
New York Daily Advertiser, 26 July 1787[1]

—Stand firm, and have a jealous Eye.

The conduct of several leading men, among us, has, of late, given
the friends to liberty much uneasiness. They tremble under an apprehension of becoming dupes to exalted ambition; and they see, with

deep concern, those men, who profess to be the fathers of their country, endeavouring by mean arts, to detach the affections of the people from every thing which bears the name of *federal.*

They see, with silent detestation, the low bias towards popularity, which evidently influences the conduct of those, from whom we have a right to expect examples of strict virtue and rigid impartiality:—And they see, with the most poignant sorrow, the evident ruin which the political doctrines of those creatures to wealth and influence, are likely to involve us in. But, while we deprecate such principles and conduct, let us not, my countrymen, sink down in a state of supinity. It is in our power to defeat the low cunning of the men we dread.—Let the recollection of past sufferings inspire our minds with a determined resolution to adhere to the general interests of the confederation; for, from this only, we must expect political welfare and happiness.

We embarked in the cause of freedom, and sacrificed *ease* and *affluence* to obtain it. The liberties of America were in danger, and, while our generous exertions contributed to rescue her from the chains of slavery, no partial interests induced us to sacrifice continental benefits to individual or even local advantages. Let us pursue the same wholesome system, and act like freemen:—should we deviate from this line of conduct, our country will be ruined. The time is fast approaching, when our virtue and patriotism will be proved. A gloomy cloud hangs over our heads; designing men will attempt to lead us astray with the most specious arguments:—but, *Stand Firm.*—In times of public danger, every citizen has a right, and should make it a duty, to come forward, and lend an aiding hand. The present period is pregnant with the most important consequences to this country. A confidence in those illustrious characters, which form the grand convention, now sitting, will have the most salutary effect.—The united wisdom of America is now forming a government adequate to the wants of our rising empire. Receive it, then, with gratitude: if it should seem deficient, proper alterations will be made, until it is rendered agreeably to the interests of the several states.—A WASHINGTON, surely, will never stoop to tarnish the lustre of his former actions, by having an agency in any thing capable of reflecting dishonor on himself or his countrymen:— and the philosophical FRANKLIN would not be guilty of embarking in any undertaking, which appeared futile and unnecessary. Rest assured, therefore, that those worthies, in conjunction with many others, have the good of America at heart.

July 25th, 1787.

1. Reprinted: *Pennsylvania Packet,* 23 August; Baltimore *Maryland Gazette,* 21 August; *Northern Centinel,* 10 September.

Pennsylvania Herald, 1 August 1787[1]

A gentleman from New-York informs us, that the anti-fœderal disposition of a great officer of that state, has seriously alarmed the citizens, as every appearance of opposition to the important measure upon which the people have reposed their hopes, creates a painful anticipation of anarchy and division. At this critical moment, men who have an influence upon society, should be cautious what opinions they entertain, and what sentiments they deliver,—yielding to the passions and exigencies of the country all dogmatic fondness for particular systems and arrangements.

1. Reprinted in the *Daily Advertiser*, 4 August, and *Northern Centinel*, 27 August (excerpt); and by 3 September in whole or in part in thirteen newspapers outside of New York: Vt. (1), N.H. (2), Mass. (4), R.I. (2), Conn. (1), Pa. (2), Md. (1).

Massachusetts Centinel, 18 August 1787[1]

IMPROMPTU

On reading in a late Centinel, of Gov. CLINTON'*s
insurgency and anti-federalism.*[2]

Since late events his *schemes* disclose,
That Clinton should *Dan. Shays* oppose,[3]
To save *one* State—what was the reason?
But this—he hop'd, though all unseen,
HIMSELF to wreck the *whole* THIRTEEN,
Without a *partner* in the *Treason.*

1. Reprinted: *Northern Centinel*, 3 September. For a response to "Impromptu," see "An Old Soldier," *Northern Centinel*, 10 September (below).

2. A reference to the *Massachusetts Centinel*, 11 August, reprinting of Alexander Hamilton's attack on Clinton that appeared in the *Daily Advertiser* on 21 July (above).

3. In March 1787, in response to an appeal from Massachusetts General Benjamin Lincoln, Governor Clinton personally took command of New York militia and cooperated with Lincoln in suppressing Shaysites who had crossed over into New York. See Kaminski, *Clinton,* 107–9.

A Republican
New York Journal, 6 September 1787[1]

"New ways he must attempt, his grov'ling name
To raise aloft, and wing his flight to fame."

DRYDEN.[2]

MR. GREENLEAF, In Mr. Child's Daily Advertiser, of the 21st of July, there appeared certain animadversions, on sentiments said to be expressed by his excellency the governour, respecting the Fœderal Convention.—On the first impressions made by that extraordinary publication, it was the wish of some of my fellow-citizens, that the governour would have made a reply to it; but, on a little reflection, it became the general opinion, that it would be highly improper, in the first magistrate of a respectable state, to enter the list in a newspaper with an anonymous scribler; and it cannot but afford pleasure to find, that it has accordingly been treated by him with silent and merited contempt.

It may not, however, be amiss for a private citizen, who feels himself deeply interested in the honour and welfare of the state, to make a few remarks on that production, and to unmask the motives from which it originated.

I think proper to premise, that I have but a slight personal acquaintance with the governour, and by no means such an intimacy, as would lead me to a knowledge of his opinion on public measures; whether he entertains the sentiments which that writer alledges, or, whether he ever delivered them in the manner asserted, I am not able to determine, and therefore shall neither attempt to justify or condemn them: I cannot, however, refrain from observing, that it is very extraordinary, that expressions, said to be used in a public company, *and currently reported and believed*, should never (as far as I have been able to learn) have reached the ear of a single citizen, before they appeared in the Daily Advertiser.

The ostensible design of that writer, is, to obviate any wrong impressions, which the conduct he ascribes to the governor, might make upon the public mind.—Let us then enquire, whether his actions correspond with his professions. It must be admitted, that, to justify the publication, the writer ought to have had the most conclusive evidence, that his excellency had (as is asserted) "in public company, and without reserve," expressed the sentiments ascribed to him, or, at least that it was "currently reported and generally believed" that he had; because, the only evil that could possibly result, must arise from the promulgation of those sentiments; for if they were not known, they could not influence. If the writer then proceeded on misinformation, he occasioned the very evil which he pretends, he was labouring to prevent. That the writer had no such testimony, will appear from his own words, for after stating the facts, he adds, "upon this conduct of his excellency, *if he is not misrepresented*, the following reflections will naturally occur to every considerate and impartial man."—Here he very strongly implies a doubt of the truth of the facts, on which he founds his production, while he admits, at the same time, that there could be no real use in his observations, since they would naturally, and without his suggesting them, have occurred to every "considerate and impartial man;" it must consequently appear, that this rude attack, which, by the author's own admission, could have no other object but to secure the opinion of the prejudiced and inconsiderate, was not the offspring of patriotism.

Lest I should be misunderstood, it is here necessary to observe, that I by no means assent to the reasoning of the writer, admitting it to be inferred from uncontrovertible facts; I deny that it is *unwarrantable and culpable*, in any citizen of a free state, [(]much less in a man, who is from office, one of the guardians of our liberties) freely and unreservedly to express his sentiments on public measures, however serious the posture of our national affairs may be; on the contrary, it is his essential duty; and the more critical our situation, the more loudly he is called upon to perform it, and to approve or disapprove, as he may think the public good directs. Should ever this inherent right be destroyed, it is easy to foresee, that a tyranny must, sooner or later, be the inevitable consequence.—Every attempt then to call it in question, I consider as high treason against the majesty of the people. In governments, conducted by intrigue and deception, and where ignorance is their chief support, candour will be arraigned as a vice, and reservedness construed into wisdom.—We ought to esteem it one of our greatest blessings, that the administration of our government does not depend upon such shallow and feeble artifices.

There is something extremely novel and singular in the manner, the performance under consideration is introduced, which cannot have escaped notice, and which must lead to a discovery of the spirit that dictated it.—It is founded on a report, of the truth of which, the writer himself expresses his doubts: is not this a refinement upon the system of slander? by adopting this new-invented mode of detraction, the reputation of any man, or family, may be wounded; nothing more is necessary than to have a malicious report circulated, which it will be easy to effect, by characters unworthy of notice, and then insert it in a newspaper, with an *if it is not a misrepresentation*, and deduce the most injurious traductions; and such is the depravity of human nature, that where party-spirit prevails, these productions will be read with pleasure, and command the applause of the malignant mind. It might have been wise in the author, to have reflected, that however elated with his *situation, connections* and *prospects*, they do not exempt *him* from the ungenerous attack.

An eminent author has predicted, that the opulent and ambitious, would never rest contented with the equality established by our democratic forms of government.

This was the case in the once free states of Athens and of Rome; the wealthy were continually harrassing and injuring the poor;—the eloquent were frequently luring them to destruction, by their pernicious orations. The ambitious were always at work to circumvent, and deprive them of their freedom. And they, unhappy people, were finally plunged into slavery. That this prediction, is already in some measure realized, must be obvious to every man of the least discernment; ⟨it cannot admit of a doubt, that a certain lordly faction exists in this state, composed of men, possessed of an insatiable thirst for dominion, and who, having forfeited the confidence of their fellow-citizens, and being defeated in their hopes of rising into power, have, for sometime past, employed themselves with unremitted industry, to embarrass every public measure; they reprobate our laws, censure our rulers, and decry our government, thereby to induce the necessity of a change, that they may establish a system more favorable to their aristocratic views, in which, honors and distinction shall not depend upon the opinion and suffrages of the people: every drone, every desparate debtor, and every other worthless character, though a despot in principle, even though he has drenched his hands in the blood of his fellow-citizens, that enlist under their banners, are received with applause, and dubbed patriots and fœderal men: no measure, which low cunning can devise, or wicked exertion effect, is omitted to ensure the attainment of their wishes; every virtuous man, who dares to stand in the way of their ambitious and arbitrary projects, becomes the victim of their keenest resentment, and is devoted to destruction—hence we find our newspapers daily disgraced with calumny, personal scurrility and falsehood⟩[3]— and hence we can trace the motives which influenced this writer.

I shall conclude with a few lines from the works of the celebrated Churchill, and leave the application to the reader.[4]

> "Smit with the love of honor, or the pence,
> O'er-run with wit, and destitute of sense,
> Legions of factious authors throng at once;
> Fool beckons fool, and dunce awakens dunce.
> To Hamilton's the ready lies repair;
> Ne'er was lie made which was not welcome there.
> Thence, on maturer judgment's anvil wrought,
> The polish'd falsehoods into public brought;

> Quick circulating slanders mirth afford,
> And reputation bleeds in ev'ry word."

1. Reprinted: *Hudson Weekly Gazette*, 13 September. For more reprints, see note 3 (below). For responses to "A Republican," see "Aristides" and Alexander Hamilton in the *Daily Advertiser*, 10 and 15 September (both below). The identity of "A Republican" has not been determined. New York Antifederalist Charles Tillinghast referred to Clinton as "the *Republican*." (See Tillinghast to Hugh Hughes, 27–28 January 1788, below.) In January 1787 a pamphlet signed by "A Republican" was published (Evans 20783). Melancton Smith appears to have been the author of the pamphlet.

2. *The Third Book of the Georgics*, lines 13–14. See John Dryden, *The Works of Virgil: Containing His Pastorals, Georgics, and Æneis. Translated into English Verse* (London, 1697).

3. The text in angle brackets was reprinted in the Philadelphia *Freeman's Journal*, 12 September, and Charleston *Columbian Herald*, 4 October.

4. The stanza is from Charles Churchill's *The Apology. Addressed to the Critical Reviewers* (London, 1761), in Douglas Grant, ed., *The Political Works of Charles Churchill* (Oxford, Eng., 1956), 35–48. Churchill referred to Archibald Hamilton (d. 1793), a London printer (*ibid.*, 476).

Aristides
New York Daily Advertiser, 10 September 1787[1]

To the EDITOR of the DAILY ADVERTISER.

SIR,

"When the administration of government is confided to improper hands, the strength and dignity of the state will be impaired, and a train of calamities must ensue."

In the New-York Journal of yesterday, a very sensible Citizen, under the signature of a Republican, has come forward with a justification of his Excellency the Governor's conduct, or rather his *silence*, against the pointed animadversions of a valuable citizen on the 21st of July; and by the selection of a poetic witticism, has dubbed one of our representatives in the Convention at Philadelphia, the author of them. Without stopping to dispute whether he is or not, I shall readily admit that the patriotism and manly spirit which have rendered this gentleman so eminently distinguished, appear sufficiently to justify the conjecture. I believe, indeed (and if I am right, why should it be concealed) that the author of the strictures alluded to, is Col. Alexander Hamilton— and what name in the State more worthy of credit? But before I proceed, let me recollect that the Republican has given me a lesson of caution and humility, and here I must profit by it. He has prefaced, that his acquaintance with Governor Clinton is too slight to enable him to judge of his sentiments on public measures, and acknowledges very frankly, that he is not *intimate enough* (I have no doubt but they will be better acquainted by and by) with his Excellency, to determine whether what has been asserted of him in the paper of July the 21st, be true or false.—In like manner with the gentleman, when speaking of the Governor, I have not the honor of much personal acquaintance with Col. Hamilton—scarcely any, but such as his public virtues have furnished me with; but it must be conceded, that an *unanswered attack* against a very influential officer, who sees clearly, and pursues industriously, his own interest, is strong evidence, that his Excellency *was not misrepresented* by that gentleman's publication; and whether his design was ostensibly, or *really* to obviate any wrong impressions which this conduct of the Governor might make on the public mind, must be judged of in a great measure, by the opinion which the public have formed of the *man*. That his Excellency has long been viewed as *secretly hostile* to such measures as were conceived absolutely necessary to the *support of a substantial Federal Government* cannot be denied—and if the animadversions alluded to are true, (and they remain uncontroverted) men will be disposed to consider him as *openly opposed* to any change which the wisdom of the present Convention may recommend—If this should prove to be the case, the Republican will please to observe, that I sport no opinions concerning the Governor's motives, and they are the less necessary since his friend appears so fertile of imagination, that this deficiency will be easily supplied.

The Republican's whole strength appears to be centered in his third paragraph, which I acknowledge he has handled in a very ingenious manner—He tells us, "In order to establish the charge against his Excellency, the most conclusive evidence ought to have been produced," &c.—Here, and elsewhere, pretty clearly, he admits culpability, but quibbles a good deal about the inexplicity of the testimony, and upon the whole, rather seems inclined to consider it as a personal and slanderous attack, than a *noble* and *patriotic alarm.*—Whether upon the whole, the Republican thinks the charge sufficiently established against the Governor; or, whether if it was proved beyond all controversy, *he* would admit it to be fraught with evil consequences, I cannot tell; but I may venture to assure him, that his Excellency knows, with more than tolerable certainty, the author, who publicly accused him of *expressing such sentiments* respecting the business and probable issue of the present Convention, as would, when disseminated throughout the State, have a powerful and direct tendency to pre-occupy the public mind, in a manner little calculated to give efficacy to the counsels of that great patriot band. If therefore he was innocently accused, why not apply an easy and certain remedy—the occasion to himself was interesting—the mode was easy—the antagonist every way his equal, *save one.* The fact, after all that has been said in his defence, remains undisproved; and its influence alarming; tho' I hope not undiminished.

I believe the Republican has a very exact knowledge of the rights and duties of Citizenship, and I presume from thence that he will admit, that a Chief Magistrate, from whose example each descending rank should learn obedience, is himself *most bound.* The reason is obvious:— the extent of his power renders the effects of his errors more diffused and dangerous, and, in the same measure that *they* are influential, I conceive *him* to be culpable. In my turn, I grant that his Excellency, both as Governor and as a free citizen, has an undeniable right to give an opinion on any public measure; and his authority, in cases of real danger and emergency, extends much farther: But at the same time I contend, that when such opinions are judged, by the enlightened part of the community, to be pregnant with pernicious consequences, they ought to be combated; and that citizen who, under such circumstances, feels himself impelled, from pure principles, to warn the people of impending danger, deserves well of the public. I concur most heartily in opinion with the Republican, when he says, "In governments conducted by *intrigue and deception,* and where ignorance is their chief support, *candor* will be arraigned as a vice; and reservedness, or *silence,* as the case may be, will be tortured, as is common enough, into wisdom and sagacity. While at the same time I admit, that the Republican has discovered himself to be a man of considerable penetration, I dispute the great postulata by which he endeavors to justify the Governor, and fix reprehension on Col. Hamilton, tho' they discover some *logical strength,* yet they, at the same time, shew much *political weakness.* Let us look at his own words. "The only evil (says he) that could possibly result, must arise from the *promulgation* of the Governor's sentiments on the present posture of public affairs; for, in this instance (mark his delusive inference) *if they were not known they could not influence."* Alas! the good gentleman appears little versed in the various modes, by which influence is communicable. The influence which even a great man's *silence* will communicate on *some occasions,* will speak loudly, and spread its contagion far and wide. Has the Republican ever cast his eyes over this state, and taken a view of the men in the different counties, who are in office? Does he know aught of the system of *connections and dependencies?* Has he considered the two distinct and strongly marked political classes, which obtain in it in common with the other States of the Union (for the sake of perspicuity I shall stile them Federal and Anti-Federal) and of whom, generally speaking, are they composed? The first I will venture to name:—they are the Clergy—the respectable body of Merchants—the intelligent, *independent* Country Gentlemen—and almost every citizen of discernment and public spirit. The second—but they are not of *my* acquaintance: I shall therefore leave the Republican to fill up the chasm; and, when he has completed his portraiture, and the motley group are honestly delineated, I shall crave permission to ask him one question:—Will the Republican think it necessary to play off much reasoning *with them?* His good understanding will tell him at once—that a few industrious coadjutors,—a *journey on horseback*,—and the whiff of a pipe, will save a world of trouble and anxiety, and answer the purpose equally as well. I should have followed the Republican a little farther, but he plunges himself into such a torrent of historical misapplication and invective, that I judge it improper to pursue him. I shall therefore conclude with observing, that the honorable citizen, against whom the Republican has levelled his poetry and wit, stands too highly in the estimation of his fellow-citizens, either to have his feelings or his fame injured, by the strongest efforts of jealousy, or the most envenomed shafts of malice. And I believe the generous part of the community will read, with abhorrence, a pointed attack against a gentleman, who is not only absent, but in the exercise of a most important duty, by which he is devoting, to a thankless people, a great portion of that time, which might be employed more profitably for himself and family; and joining the strength of his abilities with those other great characters, which the present awful conjuncture so evidently requires.

Friday, Sept. 7th.

1. Reprinted: *Hudson Weekly Gazette,* 20 September. On 8 September the printer of the *Advertiser* noted that "Aristides" was received but that on account of its length it would not be printed until 10 September. "Aristides" replies to "A Republican," *New York Journal,* 6 September, who answered Hamilton's attack on Clinton in the *Daily Advertiser* on 21 July (both above). For a response to "Aristides," see "Anti-Defamationis," *New York Journal,* 20 September (below).

An Old Soldier
Lansingburgh Northern Centinel, 10 September 1787[1]

Messrs. PRINTERS, That every person who has been any way active in opposing British tyranny, and establishing the freedom, independence, and liberty of the rising EMPIRE of AMERICA,—has secret enemies, I believe is not doubted:—⟨That there are scattered throughout the United States, private emissaries of Britain, in order to sow the seeds of division and discontent among the people, is generally acknowledged:—And Britain has not yet learnt to relinquish their favorite idea of subduing and reducing to abject slavery the free born sons of Columbia; they yet hope, by our folly and want of union among ourselves, to have an opportunity of subjugating us to their tyrannical sway.—A proof of this I observed in your Centinel, No. 16. in an "*Impromptu, on reading in a late Centinel of Gov. Clinton's insurgency and anti-federalism*," wherein the chief magistrate of this state is charged, by some incendiary, with an intention of treason against the United States; consequently to subvert a government he has uniformly, from the commencement of the late war, endeavoured, by every exertion in his power, to establish.—In the most gloomy hours of our warfare, who more readily drew his sword in our defence?—Who was more unwearied in his endeavours to defeat the vain attempts of our enemies to subdue us. Every one who knows his excellency's character, and is in any way acquainted with his conduct, must be convinced that he has rendered this country great and essential services, both in his civil and military capacities; and I think it the height of ingratitude to villify a character, which ought to be esteemed, and even revered, for his services.—If he is guilty of the charge exhibited in the Centinel, or any other against the people, let the author step forth, as a freeman, and boldly make them good;— if he is guilty by our laws, let him suffer;—if innocent, and still the faithful servant of the public we have ever found him—for God's sake let us not traduce a character so valuable to us, but by every means in our power, support him in all measures tending to the general good of our country, and let us ever detest those vile incendiaries, who (under British influence) secretly endeavour to sow the seeds of division, discontent and distrust among us.)

Confidence in our rulers will make us a great and happy people; a want of it will be our ruin. Our magistrates are not elected for life— we can change them when they act inconsistent with our welfare; but let us weigh and examine well their conduct before we dismiss them, least we repent our change, on proving those who are untried.

Lansingborough, Sept. 7, 1787.

1. The *New York Journal*, 20 September, reprinted the material in angle brackets. "An Old Soldier" responds to the author of a verse entitled "Impromptu" which was printed in the *Massachusetts Centinel* on 18 August (above) and reprinted in the *Northern Centinel* on 3 September.

Rusticus
New York Journal, 13 September 1787[1]

MR. GREENLEAF, I cannot but express my indignation at the many illiberal publications, which constantly crowd our newspapers, on the subject of politics.

It seems, by these publications, to be highly criminal, especially at this particular period, for any man to differ in opinion from a certain Aristocratic junto, who appear determined, by their writings, to silence, and traduce every person who will not subscribe to every part of their political creed.

In a free country, as this is, every man has an indubitable right to think for himself, and to express his approbation or disapprobation of public measures, when ever he supposes them consistent or inconsistent with the interest and happiness of the people. If this is not the case, then have we been fighting for a shadow, and lavishing our blood and treasure to very little purpose.

We are frequently informed by this junto, or their adherents, that the present Convention, in Philadelphia, is composed of the wisest and best characters in the United States, and that it is next to high treason to lisp a suspicion, that such a band of patriots can possibly recommend any system, or measure, inconsistent with the liberty, interest, and happiness, of those whom they represent. I am very sensible that there are many such characters in that honorable assembly as these writers have mentioned; but at the same time, it is well known, that there are too many of a very different character; perfect Bashaws! (saving a want of power) who would trample on the most sacred rights of the people, without the least reluctance or remorse; men who are possessed of the highest opinion of their own superlative, excellence, and importance; and who have worked themselves into a belief, that Heaven hath formed the bulk of mankind, to be mere slaves and vassals, to men of their superior genius, birth, and fortune.

The greatest part of the publications alluded to, are artfully calculated to prepare the minds of the people, implicitly to receive *any form* of government that may be offered them. If this is not the design, why anticipate? If the Convention recommend such measures as are not inconsistent with the union, but those that will promote the general interest of the confederation, and secure the essential rights of the people, every good and virtuous citizen will not only subscribe to them, but use all his influence; nay, strain every nerve to carry them into effect.

A paragraph has been introduced, as an article of intelligence, into the Daily Advertiser, and the papers published in this city, which was said to have been received from one of the counties in Pennsylvania, asserting, that the good people of that state are ready to receive, and implicitly acquiesce, in any kind of government that may be offered them by the Convention.[2]—This is paying but a poor compliment indeed, either to their understanding, or patriotism; and although it is asserted with so much confidence, I have too good an opinion of them, and the rest of my fellow-citizens, on the continent, to suppose, that such an enlightened people, who made so many strenuous exertions during the late war, to free themselves from the tyranny of Britain, can possibly be sunk into such a state of supineness, and so regardless of the essential interests of themselves, and their posterity, as to receive any form of government, that will not effectually secure their just rights and privileges, let it be recommended by any man, or, body of men, however wise, learned, or dignified.

Queens-County, *September* 10, 1787.

1. Reprinted: Boston *American Herald*, 24 September.

2. The reference is probably to an item reprinted in the *Daily Advertiser*, 29 August, that first appeared in the Philadelphia *Independent Gazetteer*, 22 August. This widely reprinted item states that "By letters and private accounts from most of the counties in Pennsylvania, we learn that the good people of this state, of all parties, are alike prepared and disposed to receive the new federal government. It is remarkable that Pennsylvania has in every great and necessary measure, set an example of a federal disposition to all the states" (CC:67). In New York City, this item was also reprinted in the *Independent Journal*, 29 August; *New York Journal*, 30 August; *New York Packet*, 31 August; and possibly also in the *New York Morning Post*, many issues of which are not extant. In the rest of New York state, the item was reprinted in the *Hudson Weekly Gazette*, 6 September, and *Northern Centinel*, 10 September. (For the remainder of the twenty-nine reprintings throughout America, see CC:67.)

New York Daily Advertiser, 15 September 1787[1]

Mr. Hamilton, in his absence from New-York, on public duty (with how much propriety and temper, his fellow citizens must decide) has been attacked by name, as the writer of a publication, printed in Mr. Childs's paper of the 21st of July last. In fixing that publication upon him, there is certainly no mistake; nor did he ever mean to be concealed. He left his name with the Printer, to be disclosed to any person who should apply for it, on the part of the Governor, with instructions to make that circumstance known, which was accordingly done. The fairness of this conduct speaks for itself. The Citizens of the state have too much good sense to be deceived into an opinion, that it could have been dictated by a wanton disposition to calumniate a meritorious character. They must and will consider it as an honorable and open attempt to unmask, what appeared to the writer, the pernicious intrigues of a man, high in office, to preserve power and emolument to himself, at the expence of the Union, the peace, and the happiness of America.

To say, that it would have been derogatory to the first Magistrate of the State, to enter the lists, in a news-paper, with an "anonymous scribbler" is a miserable subterfuge. Though Mr. Hamilton, to avoid the appearance of ostentation, did not put his name to the piece; yet, having left it with the Printer to be communicated to the party concerned, there is no pretence to consider it in the light of an anonymous publication. If the matter alledged had been false, the Governor had his choice of two modes of vindicating himself from the aspersion; one, by giving a simple and direct denial to it, in the public prints: the other, by having a personal explanation on the subject with the writer. Neither of these modes could have wounded his dignity. The first is practised in most governments where public opinion is respected. A short paragraph to the following effect, would have answered the purpose—"The Printer of this paper is authorised to assure the Public, that his Excellency the Governor never made use of the expressions attributed to him, in a publication contained in Mr. Childs's paper of the 21st July, nor of any other of similar import." This would have thrown it upon Mr. Hamilton, to bring forward to public view the sources of his information, and the proofs of his charge. And this he has too much regard for his reputation not to have been prepared to do. This he is still ready to do, whenever such a denial shall appear.

The Governor, if he had had any objections to this mode of proceeding, might have had recourse to the other—that of a personal explanation with the writer. Mr. Hamilton would have conceived himself bound by the principles of candor and honor, to declare on what grounds he had proceeded; and, if he could have been satisfied they were erroneous, to retract the imputations founded upon them. Would it have impaired the dignity of the first Magistrate of a Republic, to have had such an explanation with any *reputable* Citizen? Would it have impaired his dignity to have had such an explanation with a Citizen, who is at this moment acting in an important and delicate trust, by the appointment of the Legislature of the state?

Mr. Hamilton freely submits to the judgment of his fellow citizens, whether there was any thing in the manner of his animadversions that precluded such an explanation. They were strong and pointed; but he flatters himself they were free from indecorum. He states the charge as matter of report, and makes his observations hypothetically, even seeming to admit a possibility of misrepresentation. As he was not himself present at the conversation; but spoke from the information of those who were, he could not with propriety have expressed himself in more positive terms. As he was speaking of an officer of the first rank in the state, he was disposed to use as much moderation in the manner of exhibiting his misconduct, as was consistent with that explicitness and energy, which were necessary to place it in its proper light.

These remarks, while they explain Mr. Hamilton's motives, will serve to refute the cavil respecting his doubt of the truth of the fact alledged by him. He now declares, that from the nature of his information he had no doubt of the kind; and that since the publication he has understood from different partisans of the Governor, that he did not deny the expressions attributed to him to be in substance true, with some minute and unessential distinctions.

It is insinuated, that the circulation of the fact is calculated to produce the evil pretended to be guarded against, by diffusing through the community a knowledge of the Governor's sentiments. This remark admits of an obvious answer—If his Excellency was predetermined to oppose the measures of the Convention, as his conduct indicates, he would take care himself to propagate his sentiments, in the manner in which it could be done with most effect. This appears to have been his practice. It was therefore proper that the antidote should go along with the poison; and that the community should be apprised, that he was capable of forming such a predetermination, before, it can be presumed, he had any knowledge of the measures themselves, on which to found his judgment.

A cry is attempted to be raised against the publication of Mr. Hamilton, as if it were an invasion of the right of the first Magistrate of the state, to deliver his sentiments on a matter of public concern. The fallacy of this artifice will easily be detected. The Governor has an undoubted right to give his sentiments freely on every public measure. Under proper circumstances, it will be always his duty to do it. But every *right* may be abused by a *wrong exercise* of it. Even the constitutional powers vested in him may be so employed, as to subject him justly not only to censure, but to impeachment. The only question then is, whether he has in the present instance used his right properly, or improperly—whether it became him, by *anticipation*, to endeavor to prejudice the community against the "unknown and undetermined" measures of a body, to which the general voice of the union had delegated the important trust of concerting and proposing a plan for reforming the national constitution?—Let every man answer this question to himself.

The apologists for the Governor, in the intemperate ardor of their zeal for his character, seem to forget another *right*, very precious to the citizens of a free country, *that* of examining the conduct of their rulers. *These* have an undoubted right, within the limits of the constitution, to speak and to act their sentiments; but the citizen has an equal right to discuss the propriety of those sentiments, or of the manner of advancing or supporting them. To attempt to abridge this last right, by rendering the exercise of it odious, is to attempt to abridge a privilege, the most essential of any to the security of the people. The laws, which afford sufficient protection to the Magistrate, will punish the excess of this privilege: within the bounds ⟨they allow, it is the bulwark of public liberty.

But observations of either kind might mutually have been spared. There is no danger that the rights of a man, at the head of the Government (possessing all the influence to be derived from long continuance in office, the disposition of lucrative places, and *consummate talents* for popularity) can be injured by the voice of a private individual. There is as little danger, that the spirit of the people of this State will ever tolerate attempts to seduce, to awe, or to clamor them out of the privilege of bringing the conduct of men in power to the bar of public examination.

To all the declamation and invective, with which the Republican winds up his performance, and labors to mislead the public attention from its *true object,* a short answer will be given. It is the stale *trick* of the party to traduce every⟩[2] *independent man,* opposed to their views, the better to preserve to themselves that power and consequence, to which they have no other title than their arts of deceiving the people.

Mr. Hamilton can, however, defy all their malevolent ingenuity to produce a single instance of his conduct, public or private, inconsistent with the strictest rules of integrity and honor—a single instance, that may even denominate him selfish or interested—a single instance, in which he has either "*forfeited*" the confidence of the people, or failed in obtaining any proof of their favor, for which he has been a candidate. It would be ingratitude in him not to acknowledge, that the marks of their confidence have greatly exceeded his deserts.

1. This article, written by Alexander Hamilton, responds to "A Republican," *New York Journal,* 6 September, which answered Hamilton's attack on Clinton printed in the *Daily Advertiser,* 21 July (both above). The draft of this article is in the Hamilton Papers at the Library of Congress and is printed in Syrett, IV, 248–53. The manuscript and the newspaper printing differ slightly in punctuation, capitalization, and spelling. For an attack on this article, see "Inspector" I, *New York Journal,* 20 September (below).

2. The text in angle brackets is not in the manuscript version, apparently because a page is missing.

Anti-Defamationis
New York Journal, 20 September 1787[1]

MR. GREENLEAF, With great indignation I have observed several publications that have lately appeared, reflecting, in a most illiberal manner, on the Governor of this state, on account of some accidental expressions, concerning the Convention at Philadelphia; particularly one under the signature of *Aristides,* in the Daily Advertiser, No. 794.

For my part, I am not personally acquainted with the Governor, or with Col. Hamilton, and of course cannot be influenced by any undue partiality to either, but I cannot help thinking that the former (even admitting the assertions against him to be strictly true) has been very ill used.

I must beg leave to ask Aristides the following questions:

1st. Why should the Governor, or any other man, in a free state, be precluded from the privilege of speaking his sentiments in a matter of general concern?

2d. Why should the Governor, or any other man, be reprobated for differing in sentiment from a majority in Congress, or legislature of the state?

It is foreign to my purpose, at this time, to enter into a particular discussion, concerning the propriety of the appointment of the Convention at Philadelphia; but was I fully persuaded that their appointment was ill judged, and that much evil instead of good would result from their deliberations, I should conceive myself highly criminal in not communicating my ideas, although they might differ from the prevailing opinion.

The free citizens of this continent will never consent to have a constitution crammed down their throats. They have an undoubted right to examine before they accede, and to deny if they do not approve.

Although much is to be expected from the wisdom of the Convention in forming the constitution worthy of being received; it is still to be remembered, that the wisest men have often been guilty of very capital errors, and that, "notwithstanding the various forms of government hitherto recommended to the observance of men, very few are rendered better.["] If, therefore, our worthy Governor, or any other man, conceives, that by attempting a cure, the malady will be increased, it becomes his duty, as far as in him lies, to stem the tide of congressional, legislatorial, or popular prejudice.

But the design of Aristides and his colleague, in thus endeavouring, by unjust stigmas and innuendoes, to cast an odium on our Governor, is too obvious to be concealed. I must tell him plainly, that his trick wont take. The people are not so easily gulled. Let him forward his squibs to a certain northern county, where they may be useful to his friends at some future day; but here, and in other parts of the state, where the people have too much wisdom and spirit to be imposed upon, or browbeaten, they will only serve to bring the author, and his connections, into contempt.

1. Reprinted: *Hudson Weekly Gazette*, 27 September. On 13 September the printer of the *New York Journal* stated that "Anti-Defamationis" could not be inserted in that issue,

but that it would be printed on 20 September. "Anti-Defamationis" responds to "Aristides," *Daily Advertiser*, 10 September (above).

Inspector I
New York Journal, 20 September 1787

"Inspector" responds to Alexander Hamilton's article that appeared in the *Daily Advertiser* on 15 September (above). The first "Inspector" essay is not numbered, but two succeeding articles by "Inspector" are numbered II and III. The second number appeared in the *New York Journal* on 4 October, the third on 18 October (both in Mfm:N.Y.). "Aristides" and "Philopolitis" responded to the "Inspector" essays in the *Daily Advertiser* on 6 and 9 October, respectively, and on 11 October "A Customer" responded to "Aristides" and "Philopolitis" in the *New York Journal* (all in Mfm:N.Y.).

In this first number, "Inspector" refers to Hamilton as "Tom S**t"; to George Clinton as "steward George"; and to Philip Schuyler as "daddy" or "immaculate daddy." (In his other numbers, "Inspector" called Schuyler "Justice Midas.") When "Inspector" describes "Tom S**t" as "a mustee" in his first number, he is alluding to the alleged circumstances of Hamilton's birth. A "mustee" was a person of half-caste or the offspring of a white and a quadroon. Of illegitimate birth, Hamilton's enemies sometimes claimed that his mother was a West Indian slave. The name "Mungo," repeated three times in the two lines of quoted verse, was a typical name for a black slave.

MR. GREENLEAF, I have in general observed, that the most sensible men are usually modest and reserved, and that a man of consummate impudence, with but a moderate share of understanding, moves in the world with the greatest eclat; but although the world may some times over-rate a shallow capacity, it is often-times undeceived by a man's vanity leading him a step too far in his ridiculous sallies.

A man's knowledge is frequently over-rated in vulgar estimation in consequence of his having a memory good enough to retain a number of harmonious words which he can retail out at pleasure.—I know a negro who cannot read, and yet can deliver an extempore rhapsody, that will captivate weak minds, and give not offence, even to the ears of intelligent men.[1]

I have also known an upstart attorney, palm himself upon a great and good man, for a youth of extraordinary genius, and under the shadow of such a patronage, make himself at once known and respected; but being sifted and bolted to the brann, he was at length found to be a superficial, self-conceited coxcomb, and was of course turned off, and disregarded by his patron.[2]

I have known a blockhead publish pamphlets with borrowed phrases and arguments, by which he acquired a reputation he never was entitled to.[3]

I have also known a man publish pieces of his own composition, which, on examination, I have found to be mere froth, calculated only to bewilder the understanding.

I have a son, who is a lad of tolerable capacity, and great shrewdness. This boy, who is about 12 years old, reads the Newspapers to me, every morning; I have taught this young shaver to turn all the frothy publications he meets with, into plain English, and, as a specimen of his improvement, I shall give you his interpretation of a piece which appeared a few days ago in the Daily Advertiser, written in the Creolian taste, by Tom S**t, a mustee, viz.

> "*Mungo here, Mungo there, Mungo every where,*
> *What a terrible life am I led.*"
>
> PADLOCK.[4]

"My dear masters, I am indeed leading a very hard life in your service; you are driving me from post to pillar, without paying me for my trouble, and I could earn ten times as much by working at home. Consider the great sacrifices I have made for you; by birth a subject of his Danish Majesty;[5] I quitted my native soil in the Torrid Zone, and called myself a North American for your sakes.—I have since, not only ranted for you, and jockeyed for you, but even vouchsafed to give my august name to Phocion, a patriotic essay, manufactured by W. S. Esquire,[6] and sent from England just after the evacuation, under cover to Chrononhotontologos, the king's printer:[7] you have therefore scarcely done me justice, in simply giving me your suffrages, when I stood in need of them, to pave the way for my future agrandizement. I must however remember with gratitude, that when my ambition led me to become an honorary member of the whig Society,[8] I was not disappointed. My daddy, who was present to make interest for me, can evidence with how much chearfulness I was voted in.

"The important services I have rendered you, deserve much more than you will ever be able to pay me. I shall however be satisfied, with your compliance with one moderate request, which is, that you will be kind enough to discharge your old faithful steward George (who is grown so saucy, as to speak his mind without fearing any body) and put me, or my immaculate daddy, in his place.

"I am sorry you oblige me to speak so plainly, but I am constrained to do it, since your contempt and little notice taken of any late anonymous advertisement, convinces me, that you will not take a broad hint."   TOM S**T.

I have not leisure, at present, sir, to animadvert on the above curious performance, but shall conclude with a maxim of a great Philosopher which you will know how to apply.

Those actions which are denominated virtuous, have not any absolute and independant, but a relative beauty; and the source from which they derive their lustre, is the intention which guided them: if well intended, whether they produce good, or evil, they are equally virtuous: the producing good or evil are the accidents; the intention to produce good, is the essence of virtue.

1. Probably a reference to one or two lengthy speeches that Hamilton made earlier in the year. The first speech, delivered in the New York Assembly on 15 February, supported a bill to grant the Impost of 1783 to the Confederation Congress. (For the text of this speech, printed in the *Daily Advertiser*, 26 February, see Syrett, IV, 71–92.) The second speech, delivered in the Constitutional Convention on 18 June, criticized plans of government then under consideration and presented his own "sketch of a plan." In his second number, "Inspector" demonstrates that, despite the secrecy surrounding the Convention, he knew what Hamilton had said about the executive, especially his proposal that the executive serve during good behavior. (For the text of this speech, found in notes taken by Virginia delegate James Madison and by Hamilton's fellow New York delegates Robert Yates and John Lansing, Jr., see Farrand, I, 282–301; and Farrand, *Supplement*, 82–84.)

2. In 1777 Hamilton, a Continental Army captain, was invited by Commander in Chief George Washington to become his secretary and aide-de-camp with the rank of lieutenant colonel. Four years later, Washington and Hamilton had a falling out; Hamilton resigned and rejected Washington's request that he reconsider his resignation. Early in October 1787 Hamilton wrote Washington asking him "to put the matter [of "Inspector's" charge] in its true light," which Washington did in his reply to Hamilton. (See Hamilton to Washington, 8–10 October, and Washington to Hamilton, 18 October, both below.)

3. Hamilton published two pamphlets in 1774 and 1775 (Evans 13313, 14096), when not yet twenty years of age, supporting the Continental Congress against criticism levied by Loyalist Samuel Seabury, who wrote as "A. W. Farmer" (Evans 13602, 13603, 42697). In 1784 Hamilton, as "Phocion," published two pamphlets, calling for a more lenient legislative policy toward former Loyalists (Evans 18508, 18516).

4. These two lines (not successive in the original) are taken from Isaac Bickerstaff, *The Padlock: A Comic Opera* (London, 1768), Act I, scene VI. *The Padlock* was popular in both England and America, being performed in New York City as early as 1769.

5. As a child, Hamilton lived on the Danish West Indian island of St. Croix, but he had been born on the British Island of Nevis.

6. "W.S." was probably historian and former chief justice William Smith (1728–1793), one of New York's best-known Loyalists who moved to England in 1783 when the British evacuated New York City and to Canada in 1786. For Hamilton's "Phocion" pamphlets, see note 3 (above).

7. The king's printer was probably James Rivington, who was criticized and attacked by the Sons of Liberty. Rivington published the *Royal Gazette*, a Loyalist newspaper in British-occupied New York City from 1777 to 1783. Although Rivington was an American spy late in the war, unforgiving former Sons of Liberty prevented him from publishing his newspaper several weeks after the British evacuated the city. Nevertheless, Rivington remained in the city until his death in 1802.

8. The Whig Society was formed in New York City in January 1784 to make certain that remaining Loyalists would find adjusting to life difficult after the British evacuated on 25 November 1783. The creation of the society was just one example of the anti-Loyalist feeling that swept the city. The society pressured the city's aldermen and assem-

blymen to treat Loyalists harshly. It also assured the state legislature that the harsh anti-Loyalist laws already passed were not repugnant to the Treaty of Peace.

Edward Carrington to James Madison
New York, 23 September 1787 (excerpt)[1]

. . . The New York faction is rather active in spreading the seeds of opposition—this, however, has been expected, and will not make an impression so injurious as the same circumstance would in some other States. Colo. Hamilton has boldly taken his ground in the public papers and, having truth and propriety on his side, it is to be hoped he will stem the torrent of folly and iniquity. . . .

1. RC, Madison Papers, DLC. Printed: RCS:Va., 14–15. Carrington (1749–1810), a former Continental Army officer, sat in the Virginia House of Delegates, 1784–86, 1788–90 and Congress, 1786–88, and was U.S. marshal for Virginia, 1789–95. Madison (1751–1836) sat in the Virginia House of Delegates, 1776–77, 1784–87, 1799–1800; Congress, 1780–83, 1787–88; the Virginia Convention, 1788; and the U.S. House of Representatives, 1789–97. He was U.S. Secretary of State, 1801–9, and U.S. President, 1809–17. As one of three authors of *The Federalist*, Madison participated in the ratification debate in New York state. Having served as a Constitutional Convention delegate in Philadelphia, Madison was on his way to join Carrington in Congress.

Alexander Hamilton to George Washington
New York, 8–10 October 1787[1]

You probably saw some time since some animadversions on certain expressions of Governor Clinton respecting the Convention—You may have seen a piece signed a Republican, attempting to bring the fact into question and endeavouring to controvert the conclusions drawn from it, if true—My answer you will find in the inclosed.[2] I trouble you with it merely from that anxiety which is natural to every man to have his veracity at least stand in a fair light—The matter seems to be given up by the Governor and the fact with the inferences from it stand against him in full force, and operate as they ought to do.

It is however, of some importance to the party to diminish whatever credit or influence I may possess; and to effect this they stick at nothing. Among many contemptible artifices practiced by them, they have had recourse to an insinuation that I *palmed* myself upon you and that you *dismissed* me from your family—This I confess hurts my feelings, and if it obtains credit, will require a contradiction.[3]

You Sir will undoubtedly recollect the manner in which I came into your family and went out of it; and know how destitute of foundation such insinuations are. My confidence in your justice will not permit me to doubt your readiness to put the matter in its true light in your answer to this letter. It cannot be my wish to give any complexion to the affair which might excite the least scruple in you; but I confess it would mortify me to be under the imputation either of having obtruded myself into the family of a General or of having been turned out of it.

The New Constitution is as popular in this City as it is possible for any thing to be—and the prospect thus far is favourable to it throughout the state. But there is no saying what turn things may take when the full flood of official influence is let loose against it. This is to be expected, for, though the Governor has not publicly declared himself, his particular connections and confidential friends are loud against it. [P.S.] Mrs. Hamilton joins in respectful compliments to Mrs. Washington.

1. RC, Washington Papers, DLC. This undated letter was endorsed by Washington as received on 15 October. Since it took five to seven days for the post from New York City to reach Washington in Mount Vernon, this letter was probably written between 8 and 10 October. Washington (1732–1799) was Commander-in-Chief of the Continental Forces, 1775–83; President of the Constitutional Convention, 1787; and U.S. President, 1789–97.

2. Hamilton criticized Clinton in the *Daily Advertiser*, 21 July; "A Republican" responded in the *New York Journal*, 6 September; and Hamilton rejoindered in the *Daily Advertiser*, 15 September (all above).

3. See "Inspector" I, *New York Journal*, 20 September, at note 2 (above).

George Washington to Alexander Hamilton
Mount Vernon, 18 October 1787[1]

Your favor without date[2] came to my hand by the last Post.—It is with unfeigned concern I perceive that a political dispute has arisen between Governor Clinton and yourself.—For both of you I have the highest esteem and regard. But as you say it is insinuated by some of your political adversaries, and may obtain credit, "that you *palmed* yourself upon me, and was *dismissed* from my family;" and call upon me to do you justice by a recital of the facts.—I do therefore, explicitly declare, that both charges are entirely unfounded.—With respect to the first, I have no cause to believe that you took a single step to accomplish, or had the most distant ⟨ide⟩a of receiving, an appointment in my ⟨fam⟩ily 'till you were envited thereto.—And ⟨with⟩ respect to the second, that your quitting ⟨of it was⟩ altogether the effect of your own ⟨choic⟩e.—

When the situation of this Country ⟨calls⟩ loudly for unanimity & vigor, it is to be lamented that Gentlemen of talents and character should disagree in their sentiments for promoting the public weal. but unfortunately, this ever has been, and more than probable, ever will be the case, in the affairs of man.

Having scarcely been from home since my return from Philadelphia,[3]

I can give but little information with respect to the *general* reception of the New Constitution in *this* State.—In Alexandria however, and some of the adjacent Counties, it has been embraced with an enthusiastic warmth of which I had no conception.—I expect notwithstanding, violent opposition will be given to it by *some* characters of weight & influence, in the State.

Mrs. Washington unites with me in best wishes for Mrs. Hamilton and yourself

1. RC, Hamilton Papers, DLC. The words within angle brackets have been supplied from the letterbook copy because of a tear in the recipient's copy.
2. See immediately above.
3. Washington served as President of the Constitutional Convention.

Alexander Hamilton to George Washington
New York, 30 October 1787 (excerpt)[1]

I am much obliged to Your Excellency for the explicit manner in which you contradict the insinuations mentioned in my last letter— The only use I shall make of your answer will be to put it into the hands of a few friends.

The constitution proposed has in this state warm friends and warm enemies. The first impressions every where are in its favour; but the artillery of its opponents makes some impression. The event cannot yet be foreseen. The inclosed is the first number of a series of papers to be written in its defence.[2] . . .

1. RC, Washington Papers, DLC. Printed: Syrett, IV, 306–7.
2. See "Publius," *The Federalist* 1, *Independent Journal,* 27 October (below), which was written by Hamilton.

Rough Carver
New York Daily Advertiser, 3–4 September 1787[1]

Some Observations on the present Political situation of the United States.

When the question of the impost was agitated in our Legislature last winter, I took the liberty of addressing the citizens of the state of New-York, respecting it, and endeavored to treat the subject with freedom and candor. Pleased with the animating hope of seeing it meet a favorable termination, I repaired to the house of Assembly; but to my astonishment, a contemptuous silence succeeded the persuasive arguments offered by a very worthy character. The members appeared predetermined, having, as I was afterwards told, *made up their minds on the subject.* This conduct seemed to me so extremely inexplicable, that I resolved to pry into the probable causes of it, and soon found, that many of them were mere machines, to back the principles of others, and creatures to Jacobitish intrigue; controled in their sentiments by menial sycophants to British influence—by men, who in the time of our distress, exulting in the idea of British power, with an unremitting hand, confiscated the property of our unfortunate citizens. The British courts of Admiralty, held in this city at that time, teem with numberless instances. Perhaps it may be said in justification, that those who were instrumental in that business, should not be censured, because they were in the line of their duty. To this I answer, that if a great villain orders one, or more, smaller ones, to cut our throats, they are all guilty, as well those who execute, as he who directs. I will never believe any man's professions of friendship, who, from choice, could be capable of robbing me of my property, under the specious sanction of compulsion. Any allegations of being forced into the business, surely cannot be offered in mitigation, when nothing obligatory was imposed on the perpetrator. This same system in our governing Head, will, as long as the same characters remain in office, continue to thwart every improvement in the art of government, which may be conceived by the good and wise. These remarks being preparatory to my general plan, I will now proceed somewhat farther. We have all, no doubt, allowed ourselves to think more or less on the interesting question of a federal government. To state this in a proper point of view, is the object of my present endeavors; much hath already been written and said concerning it, but as it is of the highest magnitude to every man, who wishes to preserve his liberties inviolate, to be acquainted with the leading features in the politics of the present day, I shall not be ashamed of throwing out any thing, which, in its nature, is pregnant with, or may be made productive of either much good or evil to this country. The present critical situation of America is sufficient to engage our most anxious attention; unexampled in history, we see her tottering under every constitutional weakness, and fondly inviting the aid of all good men, to secure to her those blessings, for which she hath toiled and suffered. Shall the fair Genius of Columbia, in vain, wing her way from north to south, diffusing unanimity among her virtuous sons? In order to familiarize ourselves to the effects, which evils, yet at a distance, will certainly produce, let us suppose the confederation at present dissolved—and then enquire, what would be the natural consequences of such an event—to me, they stand thus. First *Those foreigners who have demands on us, would seize on the most valuable parts of our country, by way of security for their loans, and being once in possession, probably would not incline to restore them, but hold all, from a claim of right, founded on power; what the end of this would be, let every man judge for himself.*

Secondly. *Admitting that those evils would not follow a dissolution of the union; we must at least allow, that each state, would become a distinct independent sovereignty; each assuming to itself, a different interest, and rivalling each other in every political emolument.* Here, a contrariety of interests, operating on different local communities, must, of course, create a diversity of opposite pursuits, which in their turns, by an interference, will excite state cavils, producing wars, bloodshed, conquests, and doubtless slavery.—These things, from the circumstances naturally interwoven with such national commotions, generally happen. But to give the idea a full latitude, we will consider the United States at present unconnected, and independent of each other, by mutual consent. As sovereign states, a military force must be established in each, for its protection and defence, this cannot be, without an accumulation of taxes too great for the slender resources of an inconsiderable people, whose chief dependence must be on agriculture, and some commerce; not to say any thing of the dangers to which the liberties of the people would be exposed, from a standing army, which, in Republics, is at all times incompatible, unless an extensive dominion, exposed to the insults of a foreign foe, renders it necessary. The Executive in the Legislature, in this case, finds itself possessed of a balance in the scale of power, which depraved minds may use to answer the most iniquitous purposes. Thus situated, the complexion of the politics in the several States would be entirely European, if not altogether Germanic. Then, the high and mighty ones among us would bridle our tongues, and absolute dependence on the capricious favors of some ministerial brute, would be the highest reach of our warmest hopes; and seas of blood would flow throughout the land, to support the dignity of a thick-skulled and double-hearted Chief.[2]—To judge fairly of an object which attracts our attention, we should view it in its most natural colors: and to determine judiciously on any political question, we must strip it of every covering which may deceive the passive mind. The one now before us deserves all our attention; our own welfare, and the fate of millions yet unborn, are involved in it; another, so important, it is probable will never again rise in America. Without going into a tedious disquisition on any particular form of Federal Government, I must impress it on every friend to his country, to investigate, in order to understand, the nature and probable operation of an energetic, consolidated system of government, calculated on the broad basis of individual and state welfare.

Amid' the general bustle of popular enquiry, the most material objects are often neglected; namely, those local ingredients, which, in all good governments, are the pillars on which the liberties of the people

are erected; whose happiness being the end of all just laws, no exertion
of collective power should be made, but with an eye to promote it; and
into this common stream the worth, merit, and best deeds of individuals must flow, before a nation can be great and happy. These are
axioms, which none can contravert; yet we have men among us, who
will coolly oppose every thing, which does not bear the marks of *Self.*
Their intentions are as obvious, as the measures are despicable. The
great Anti-Impost Man,[3] after having disseminated the seeds of dissention, keeps aloof, gliding down the tide of popularity: it is, however, to
be hoped, that the same wisdom which dictated the necessity of revising
the Federal Government, will impress the citizens with just notions of
a governing Head; and, at the same time, a due regard for the rights
of individuals. The grand question, Whether we shall separate—or—
UNITE MORE FIRMLY IN FEDERAL TIES?—here opens to us: it is
an interesting one. The mutilated soldier—the ruined citizen—the distressed orphan—and the kindly stranger, are buried in anxious suspence for its fate. No man, in his proper senses, would prefer evil to
good; and no honest American can oppose that, which is intended and
calculated to render his situation eligible and happy; he detests every
idea of servile dependence on ambitious Rulers, who have nothing in
view but their own aggrandizement.

Sept. 1, 1787.

[4 September] We have men among us, who are assiduously striving
to form a party against Federal attachments: to cover their *contracted*
designs, many weak arguments are used.—They tell us, that the Confederation is sufficient, and that, by acceding to a well-balanced, energetic Government, we will delegate to the Supreme Head those powers, which we, as a State, should only possess. The alarming complexion
of the times requires truth and plainness. How vague is the reasoning
used by those gentlemen, in favor of their opinions!—I will ask, why
do we, as citizens, delegate to the Legislature the power of ruling us?
Is it not to secure to us those privileges which we enjoy? The propriety
of a ruling Head is so striking, that all mankind readily give into it:—
the most uncouth barbarian will tell you, that, in order to live in domestic security, he must come under some Government; that the whole
community, of which he is a member, are bound in the strictest ties of
reciprocal protection and preservation; and, as a member of the same
social compact, he is, in common with his fellow subjects, entitled to
the full protection of his life, liberty, and property. In this view the
United States must be considered: they each form a constituent part
of the grand body politic; by contributing to the same general stock, a

power may be created, and, being vested in the ruling Head, will prove sufficient for the protection and defence of each particular State; at the same time, by being well proportioned, no dangers need be apprehended from its operation.

Without this, none of them, in case of invasion, would have a right to solicit assistance from their neighbours. It would not be politic for either State to embroil itself in foreign or unnecessary disputes; having a different interest to pursue, a different system of politics must likewise be pursued. If the Legislature, in any one of the States, should oppress the People, they will have no other arbitrators to hear their grievances, but the very men from whom they flow. With regard to oppression from a Federal body, a combination of the Legislative powers, which the several States will possess, may at any time be opposed to the unwarrantable excursions in the field of power and dominion, which the depravity of human nature may incline it to make. With regard to external dangers—while closely united, we have none to dread; foes, who might, with impunity, destroy our habitations and lay waste our lands, if unconnected in political bonds, will, while the Union is preserved, hide their heads; and evils, which daily thicken under the generating clouds of discord, will shrink away, under the influential rays of unanimity. The mighty bugbears of despotic sway, from a well constituted body, will not weigh with thinking minds; men, in an enlightened age, are not satisfied without making proper enquiries themselves into the nature of the business before them. On a candid investigation, from the obvious tendency of the question under consideration, it must produce this rational conclusion—*That a collective energy, answering all the purposes of Government, should be lodged somewhere.* In no place, or body (provided the necessity of the Union is admitted) can this coercion be vested to advantage, but in that created by the general consent of the States. A dependent creature, of their own forming, they can always destroy; since, on their will and pleasure it must exist: and, while each State has a Legislature, such barriers can be raised, as will effectually frustrate every innovation, which an abandoned set of men might make. The method which was adopted to amend the Confederation, is a stern precedent:—a deficiency was sensibly felt by the States—their Government was weak and languid, and the people unanimously desired a more coercive one. Under such perswasions, we are easily induced to submit to impositions:—a better opportunity of rivetting chains on the Americans could not offer. Instead of this, the imbecility of the Federal Government was represented to the several States; and they, as the supreme arbitrators, nominated several of the first characters among them, to make such alterations as would be most productive of the common good. This right they will ever possess, while each State hath a distinct jurisdiction, blended with the general weal, in proportion to the cession of power which it was pleased to make. When we cease to be confederated States, we will also cease to enjoy that unbounded freedom which prevails throughout our land.

An annihilation of the Union would likewise tend to produce unhappy effects, from the ambitious views of the more powerful states; conscious of their own superior strength and importance, a thirst for dominion, would incite them to invade the rights of their weaker neighbours; and after driving the impetuous torrent of conquest and oppression, to the final subjugation of their depressed brethren, their own evident ruin would stare them in the face—the arms of their veteran bands, employed in the conquest of their best friends, would be turned against the advocates for freedom; and all their sighs, prayers, and supplications, would, with an unfeeling heart, be hurled down the common stream of unsatiated tyranny.—A revolution in the face of American politics, crowding into existence an Empire raised in blood and venality, would excite the compassion of the commiserating part of mankind, and cause the sensitive tear to flow, and the fair prospect of finding rest in a land of freedom, in being blasted would cast a gloom over the hopes of an enslaved world.—We will now reverse the picture, and indulge the anticipation of more agreeable events—instead of sinking under a hopeless despondency, we have some reason to promise ourselves, a saving turn to our national affairs—the characteristics of the present moment, should embolden us to place an assurance in the means used for that purpose. In a short time, we may reasonably expect, that from being the contempt of Europeans, America will rise triumphant, and spurn their low arts to injure her—that as mistress of her own seas, she will chastise all, who shall dare to insult her—and secure to her sons, independence, and the arts of peace. The universal tranquillity, which prevails, and the fixed confidence, dwelling in the countenance of every well-meaning individual, are strong indications of a happy issue.

New-York, Sept. 3, 1787.

1. On 1 September the *Daily Advertiser* announced that "Rough Carver" was received and it would appear on 3 September. "Rough Carver" was printed in two parts on 3 and 4 September, the first part being dated 1 September, the second 3 September. The term "Rough Carver" is a parody on Antifederalist Abraham Yates, Jr.'s, oft-employed pseudonym "Rough Hewer."

2. Governor George Clinton.

3. Governor George Clinton.

Editors' Note
The Publication of the Constitution in New York
21 September 1787–June 1788

The Constitutional Convention, meeting in Philadelphia, adjourned on 17 September 1787. John Dunlap and David C. Claypoole, printers to the Convention and publishers of the *Pennsylvania Packet*, quickly printed 500 official copies of a six-page broadside of the Convention's report that included in this order: (1) the Constitution, (2) two resolutions of 17 September, and (3) a letter dated 17 September from George Washington, the Convention's President, to the President of Congress. Each Convention delegate received several copies of this broadside, which were sent to state executives, families, and friends (Evans 20818. See CC:76 for this imprint.).

By the end of 1787 the Constitution was printed:
• in all nine New York state newspapers;
• in three pamphlet editions in New York City;
• in three broadside editions in New York City;
• in perhaps in a broadside edition in Poughkeepsie;
• in a Dutch-language broadside in Albany; and
• in two almanacs in New York City.

In the first six months of 1788 the Constitution was printed:
• in a Dutch-language and a German-language pamphlet in Albany;
• in the *Hudson Weekly Gazette* for the election campaign for the state Convention; and
• in an official pamphlet by a Poughkeepsie printer for the state Convention's delegates.

William Jackson, Secretary of the Constitutional Convention, left Philadelphia on 18 September and the next day he arrived in New York City, the meeting place of Congress. On 20 September the *Daily Advertiser* noted: "We are informed, from good authority, that the FEDERAL CONVENTION completed their business on Monday last; and that their proceedings will be immediately laid before Congress.—We purpose to give the whole of their proceedings in to-morrow's paper." On 19 September Jackson presented the engrossed Constitution (and probably some copies of Dunlap and Claypoole's broadside) to the Secretary of Congress, where the Constitution was read to the delegates on 20 September.

New York City newspapers were the first in the state to print the Constitution. On 21 September the Constitution and the accompanying documents were printed in the *Daily Advertiser* and the *New York Packet*. The *Daily Advertiser* printed these documents, without a heading, under a New York dateline of 21 September, although it changed their order, placing the letter of the Convention's President first. Most New York state newspapers arranged the documents in the same way as the *Advertiser*. Immediately below the documents, the *Advertiser* stated that "A few Copies of the preceding may be had of the Printer."

When printing the Constitution and accompanying documents, the *New York Packet* provided this heading: "*The* FŒDERAL CONVENTION *completed their Interesting Business on Monday last. The following is a Copy of the RESULT of the* Deliberations *of that IMPORTANT BODY.*" The printers, Samuel and John Loudon, encased the letter "W" in "We," the Preamble's first word, within an oval on top of which strode an eagle. They then put the illustration in a box. On 25 and 28 September the *New York Packet* noted that "A few Copies of the Result of the Deliberations of the Fœderal Convention, may be had at this Printing Office."

Before the *New York Packet's* type was broken up, the printers published (sometime before 20 October) the Constitution and accompanying documents, including the illustration along with other ornamentation, in an eight-page, double-column pamphlet whose title page reads *Result of the Deliberations of the Federal Convention of the United States of America, Convened at Philadelphia, in the Year 1787* (not in Evans). (On 20 October the French chargé d'affaires in New York City sent a copy of the pamphlet to the French foreign minister. See CC:180.) The Loudons also published a twelve-page pamphlet, using a similar title (Evans 20810). Unlike the eight-page pamphlet, the twelve-page pamphlet included neither a title page nor the Loudons' colophon. On 18 December the Loudons announced their publication and sale of Andrew Beers's *The Columbian Almanack . . .* for 1788 (Evans 20225), promising to annex the Constitution (probably this twelve-page pamphlet) to the almanac if so requested by purchasers.

On 22 September John M'Lean of the *Independent Journal* printed the Constitution and accompanying documents in a four-page supplement to the *Journal* of the same date under the heading "*Copy of the Result of the Deliberations of the FEDERAL CONVENTION*" (Evans 20812). Using the entire four pages, M'Lean placed the letter of the Convention's President first, following it with the Constitution and the Convention's resolutions. (M'Lean had informed his readers in his regular issue of 22 September that the Constitution would appear in the supplement.)

Using the type from the supplement, M'Lean followed quickly with three four-page broadside printings of the Constitution and accompanying documents. The first broadside, including his colophon, was headed "*Articles agreed upon by the Fœderal Convention of the United States of America, his Excellency George Washington, Esq. President."* The documents appeared in the same order that they had appeared in the *Independent Journal's* supplement of 22 September. To the second broadside, which had the same heading and M'Lean's colophon, he added (at the end) the 28 September resolution of Congress requesting that the states call conventions to consider the Constitution (Evans 20791). M'Lean also rearranged the documents, placing the Constitution first, followed by the resolutions and then the Convention President's letter.

In the third and last broadside, John M'Lean removed the heading and his colophon, kept the order of the documents as they appeared in the second broadside, and changed the setting of the 28 September resolution. This copy was attested by Secretary of Congress Charles Thomson and sent to the states on 28 September to be submitted to the state ratifying conventions (Evans 20817). It was probably this printing of the Constitution that most state conventions read, debated, and ratified. Although M'Lean printed this broadside, the actual publisher appears to have been John Dunlap of Philadelphia, the official printer for Congress (Leonard Rapport, "Printing the Constitution: The Convention and Newspaper Imprints, August–November 1787," *Prologue: The Journal of the National Archives,* 2 [1970], 84. Rapport also discusses in more detail all of the M'Lean printings.).

On 29 September, M'Lean began running the following advertisement in his *Independent Journal: "Just published, on a large Type and good Paper, (Price only* Six Pence) *and to be had at the Printing-Office, No.* 41, *Hanover-Square, the* ARTICLES *of the* CONFEDERATION.—*Those who wish to purchase by the hundred or thousand, will have them on very reasonable terms."* (This advertisement also ran on 3, 6, and 10 October.) M'Lean, of course, meant the Constitution, not the Articles of Confederation, which the Constitution was intended to replace. It should be remembered that M'Lean's first and second broadsides (above) described the Constitution as *"Articles agreed upon by the Fœderal Convention."* (He was probably selling one or both of these broadside printings.) M'Lean would again use this unique way of describing the Constitution when he first advertised for subscribers to the first volume of *The Federalist* in his *Independent Journal* on 2 January 1788. The advertisement revealed his intent to print the "ARTICLES of the CONVENTION" in the first volume (CC:406).

The *New York Morning Post* was probably the next New York City newspaper to print the Constitution and accompanying documents, although no extant issue of this newspaper contains those documents. On 26 September, however, the printer of the *Post* noted that he had

"A few Copies" of the Federal Convention's proceedings for sale. He ran this advertisement until at least 17 October.

On 27 September the *New York Journal* printed the Constitution and accompanying documents, under the same heading used in the *New York Packet* on 21 September (see above). In the same issue Thomas Greenleaf, the *Journal's* printer, stated that "*A number of* ADVERTISEMENTS, PIECES, *and* PARAGRAPHS, *are omitted, this week, to give place to the* FŒDERAL CONSTITUTION.— *It is presumed, that the* cause *of these omissions will operate as a sufficient apology to all interested therein.*" He also declared he had "*A few Copies*" of the Constitution for sale.

Greenleaf then struck off an eighteen-page pamphlet edition, entitled *The Fœderal Constitution, Being the Result of the Important Deliberations of the Fœderal Convention, Who Completed Their Business on the 17th September, 1787, at Philadelphia* (Evans 20805). On 11 October Greenleaf advertised that "*A few Copies of the* FŒDERAL CONSTITUTION, *in Pamphlets, with the Resolve of Congress annexed, to be had of the Printer hereof.*" He ran this advertisement until 28 November.

On 8 October New York City printer Hugh Gaine announced in the *New York Morning Post* that he had just published John Nathan Hutchins' almanac, *Hutchins Improved* . . . , for 1788 (Evans 20423). According to the advertisement, the almanac included the Constitution "as recommended by the Fœderal Convention, lately held at Philadelphia; the Design of which being to form a more perfect Union, insure Domestic Tranquility, provide for the common Defence, promote the general Welfare, and secure the Blessings of Liberty to the Subjects of these United States; it appears highly expedient that Copies thereof should be universally spread among them, therefore those who wish to possess themselves with one, have now an Opportunity, with the Advantage of an Almanack into the Bargain." The text of the Constitution and accompanying documents ran to twelve pages.

The Constitution was also published in the newspapers of the Hudson River towns of Poughkeepsie, Hudson, Lansingburgh, and Albany. On 26 September the Poughkeepsie *Country Journal* printed the Convention President's letter and the Constitution through section 7 of Article I preceded by this statement: "We have just received the proceedings of the Grand Convention, which being lengthy, and arriving late, we have only time to publish part, tho' the remainder will appear in our next." In this same issue, printer Nicholas Power told his readers that on 28 September he would publish the entire proceedings of the Convention in "a hand-bill" (not located). On 3 October the *Country Journal* printed the remainder of the Constitution and the Convention's resolutions. A week later, Power informed his readers that he still had "a few Copies" of the Constitution for sale.

On 27 September and 4 October, the *Hudson Weekly Gazette* printed the Constitution and accompanying documents prefaced by this statement: "On Monday, the 17th instant, the Federal Convention finished the business on which they met, adjourned, and the next day Major Jackson, their Secretary, set off to Congress with a copy of their proceedings." Printer Ashbel Stoddard noted on 11 October that "A few Copies of the FEDERAL CONSTITUTION, which every FREEMAN in the United States ought to be possessed of, to be sold at this office."

On 1 October the Constitution and accompanying documents were printed in the *Northern Centinel*, under the same heading used by the *New York Packet* on 21 September. Three days later the *Albany Gazette* printed these documents, and in the same issue Charles R. Webster, the *Gazette's* printer, noted that "A *few* COPIES *of the* FŒDERAL CONSTITUTION, *which every* FREEMAN *in the United States ought to be possessed of,* to be sold at this Office." (On 9 February and 8 March 1788, the recently established *Albany Journal,* which Webster operated with his brother George, ran this same advertisement.) Sometime in 1787 Albany printer John Babcock, at the behest of the Albany Federal Committee, printed a four-page Dutch-language broadside of the Constitution from John M'Lean's first broadside printing since the title and order of the documents are similar to those found in the M'Lean broadside (Evans 20792. With Thomas Claxton, Babcock published the *Northern Centinel.*).

In 1788 Charles R. Webster, also at the request of Albany's Federal Committee, published Dutch- and German-language pamphlets of the Constitution and accompanying documents, one of thirty-two pages and the other of twenty-four pages (Evans 21522, 45386). The thirty-two-page pamphlet lists on its title page the names of the first six states to ratify the Constitution. The shorter pamphlet makes no mention of the adoption of the Constitution by six states.

On 22 April 1788 the *Hudson Weekly Gazette* reprinted the Constitution and accompanying documents at the behest of "Amor Patriæ," who, with an eye on the coming election for state Convention delegates, made this statement: "Mr. STODDARD, Having collected the sentiments of a number of federalists concerning the republishment of the new constitution—I find it their unanimous wish that you should serve the cause of liberty and virtue by giving it a second insertion in your next gazette: And, as the decision of the United States is likely to close on the subject of its adoption, it is highly necessary that a copy of it should again be handed to the people—those who have not perused it carefully at first, will be more anxious now to preserve it from that unworthy fate, and lay it up unimpaired—on failure of memory they can have recourse to it. It must appear evidently necessary to the opposers as well as the advocates of federal government, that every man may judge for himself and his posterity, with a cautious and unprejudiced deliberation, that he may see who to place confidence in—who to trust to guard his property—and lastly, whether he will consent to delegate those patriots who freed their country in the field, to finish, in the cabinet of the United States, the permanent independence of America."

Lastly, on 18 June 1788 the New York Convention, meeting in Poughkeepsie, read the Constitution and accompanying documents and the congressional resolution of 28 September 1787 and ordered that Convention secretaries John McKesson and Abraham B. Bancker "procure a sufficient number of copies of the said report and resolutions, and letter, to be printed, to furnish a copy to each member of the Convention." As printer to the Convention, Nicholas Power of the Poughkeepsie *Country Journal* supplied the delegates with a twenty-page pamphlet, lacking a title page, that included the documents ordered printed by the Convention. Up to page 17, where the text of the Constitution ends, the text was printed on one side of the leaf so that the even-numbered pages are blank from page 2 through page 16 (Evans 21524).

John Pintard to Elisha Boudinot
New York, 22 September 1787[1]

My dear Elisha

Doctor Roorbach delivered me your letter of 19th. this morning his going out of town at 12. oclock as also my going in expectation of meeting Mrs. Pintard at Kingsbridge on her way home allows me but a few moments to say any thing respecting the New Constitution which was published yesterday[2] & has as you may well suppose occasioned great speculation among our citizens—The grand scale on which our Fœderal Government is to move (as I hope) far surpasses the general opinion—What that is I cannot attempt to describe for We have done nothing else but read it as yet—That opinion shd. vary in this State especially we need not be surprized at—I can more easily subscribe my assent to the plan held out—I have been for sometime perfectly settled in the persuasion that we must have an Energetic government for it must be evident to all by this time that our Utopian Ideas were to[o] fine spun for Execution—Were we all as upright as Yourself & a very few others Mankind might be ruled by opinion, but as that can never be the case in an extensive dominion the Laws ought to be sufficient

& the executive powerful enough to restrain the turbulent & support
the peaceable members of Society—As a merchant I am perfectly convinced that the Commerce of the U States must be governed by general
Laws to be productive of general benefit—As a Citizen I am also convinced that taxation ought to be equal & the funds arising whether
from Impost or otherwise to be equally applied—To carry these two
points into effect the plan proposed is perhaps the best that can be
imagined—I am not of that contracted Spirit as to fear the expence
attending the establishment of our Fœderal Government—decent salaries will produce respectable Characters to fill the posts & every duty
ought to be recompenced—Is the man who confines himself to the
functions of his post, to be thought compensated by gaining his daily
bread only—do we not all count it for worldly wisdom to be able to
lay up something for a rainey day & where must the public Officer
derive that something if not from his salary—There is a just mean
between prodigality & nigardliness in public as well as in private concerns—The Expence of the new Government begins to be resounded
& will I know be held forth as a strong objection—I hope to be able
to come over soon to digest this matter with you—This will depend
upon the health of my little boy who I fear is dangerously ill—Mrs. P.
will accompany me at least such is the plan—Let me hear from you
how Your time is to be applied that I may regulate my motions accordingly—I enclose you the supplement[3] containing the Constitution
which as our Liturgy says we ought to *waite, learn, & inwardly* digest
before we too hastily decide on it—I am obliged to you with regard to
the post you have given me under the new administration—Shd. I be
so fortunate as to obtain one I only wish that I may fill it with propriety
& honor—but I do not flatter myself as I dare say that every one is
aiming as Tristram Shandy wd. say to get a pr. of Breeches for himself
or a petticoat for his wife out of the peice of New Cloth that is yet in
the Loom & he will approve or disapprove of the Manufacture according to the Garment he may be able to obtain[4]—Independent of any
Sinister view I wish most ardently for the welfare of my country & the
peaceable adoption of the plan held forth—With love to Aunt Caty &
the little folks I am yours sincerely
[P.S.] Another Wicked & daring attempt was made last night to set the
city on Fire—near the Spot where the [– – –] was made within a few
yards of Mr Bleecker[5]—I cannot stay to relate particulars wh. Doctor
Roorbach may have heard & will tell you but the perserverance of these
rascals is truly alarming & there seems to be a steady plan in view to
effect their diabolical Scheme—

1. RC, Boudinot-Pintard Papers, NHi. Pintard (1759–1844), a 1776 graduate of the College of New Jersey (Princeton), was a deputy commissary of prisoners in New York City during the Revolution and a New York City insurance underwriter and a prosperous merchant involved in the East Indian trade. He lost his fortune during the Panic of 1792. Pintard moved to Newark, N.J., where he lived for eight years, serving some time in debtors' prison. In 1801 he returned to New York City and eventually recouped some of his fortune. Boudinot (1749–1819) was a Newark lawyer and former commissary of prisoners for New Jersey during the Revolution. He was an associate justice of the New Jersey Supreme Court from 1798 to 1804. His brother Elias was president of Congress, 1782–83.

2. The Constitution was printed in New York City on 21 September in the *Daily Advertiser* and *New York Packet.* See "The Publication of the Constitution in New York," 21 September 1787–June 1788 (immediately above).

3. The reference is to the separate four-page *Supplement to the Independent Journal* of 22 September.

4. The reference is to Laurence Sterne's well-known and popular novel, *The Life and Opinions of Tristram Shandy, Gentleman*, published in England in several parts between 1759 and 1767.

5. On 24 September the *Daily Advertiser* reported that "On Friday night, another daring attempt was made to consume, by fire, the stores in Gouverneur's alley, in order, as it is supposed, to communicate fire to a large part of the city. The combustibles were placed under a back building, and burnt some time before it was discovered. It seems that the constable of the ward, whose duty it was to summon and form the night's patrole, had neglected this necessary measure, and the consequences would have been alarming, if it had not been discovered and extinguished by the patrole of another ward, who were accidentally passing. It appears by this, that the incendiaries, upon the least relaxation of the patroles, will effect their villainous purpose."

At least three other attempts had recently been made to set fire to buildings, prompting the city's magistrates (Common Council) to recommend on 6 September that night watches be established by the inhabitants of the city's several wards (*New York Morning Post*, 7 September; and *Independent Journal*, 8 September). On 7 September the inhabitants met in their respective wards and established these watches. The East Ward, for example, stated that 24 inhabitants should patrol the street "every night, by rotation" (*Daily Advertiser*, 8 September). On 8 September Governor George Clinton issued a proclamation offering a reward of $1,000 for the apprehending and bringing to justice incendiaries who tried to set the city on fire (*New York Packet*, 11 September).

The *Daily Advertiser* noted on 7 September that it was of "some consolation" to the buildings' owners that their property could be insured at a low rate by the Mutual Assurance Company of New York. John Pintard was secretary of this newly formed company from May 1787 to February 1792.

Abraham Bancker to Evert Bancker
Staten Island, 23 September 1787 (excerpt)[1]

. . . I am much pleased with the proceedings of the fœderal Convention The Constitution, which they have proposed, and which, I hope, will be adopted by the United States, is very similar to the Constitution of Great Britain, and not very unlike the Constitution of this State; both of which, in my opinion, are admirably constructed for supporting the

Government, with becoming Dignity, and while it vests the Authority with Powers adequate to govern with Energy, it at the same time is calculated to secure and preserve inviolate the Rights of the Citizens. . . .

Your affectionate Nephew

1. RC, Bancker Family Correspondence, NHi. This letter was endorsed as received on 24 September and answered on the 25th. For the answer, see below. Abraham Bancker (1760–1832) attended the College of New Jersey (Princeton), 1774–76, and was an American spy on Staten Island during the Revolution. Bancker was Richmond County clerk, 1781–84; sheriff, 1784–88; and surrogate, 1792–1809. He represented Richmond in the Assembly, 1788–90, and in the state Convention, where he voted to ratify the Constitution in July 1788. Evert Bancker (1721–1803), the uncle of Abraham Bancker, was a merchant. He represented New York County in the Second, Third, and Fourth Provincial congresses, 1775–77, and in the Assembly, 1777–83, 1786–88 (speaker, 1779–83).

Marinus Willett to John Tayler
New York, 23 September 1787 (excerpt)[1]

. . . Well Sir what do you think of the ofspring of the Convention? They have laboured & brought fourth—Notwithstanding the General Idea that let this thing be what it might it must be received and that if it could not be chewed it must be swallowed It is now stared at as a Monster with open mouth and monsterous teeth ready to devour all before it—Peopel look at and numbers stand ready to strike—It is stared at with astonishment. many of Those who appeared determined to give it the most hospitable reception have taken up Clubs against it—Most undoubtedly it is an extrordinary conception—Fundamental principals have been totally departed from—our world is set afloat and unless this thing is laid we are like to become a wandering Commett. . . .

1. RC, Accession No. 3904, N. Willett (1740–1830), a 1776 graduate of King's College (Columbia) and a New York City merchant, was a Continental Army colonel during the Revolution and a member of the Assembly, 1784. Willett was sheriff of the County of New York, 1784–87, 1791–95, and mayor of the city, 1807–8. Tayler (1742–1829), a native of New York City and an Albany merchant, represented Albany County in the Third and Fourth Provincial congresses, 1776–77; the City and County of Albany in the state Assembly, 1777–79, 1780–81, 1786, and 1787; and the Eastern District in the state Senate, 1802, 1804–13 (president pro tempore, 1811). He was also lieutenant governor, 1813–22, and acting governor for several months in 1817.

New York Daily Advertiser, 24 September 1787[1]

The result of the deliberations of the National Convention is now laid before the public, and I congratulate each patriot heart on the important disclosure. The causes which have all pressed, as it were to a point, to render a thorough reform indispensably necessary, have been long the subject of general speculation. The Casuist has disputed—the Orator has harangued—and the Essayist has reasoned on them. Indeed, the necessity of the Convention has been generally admitted, and almost universally *felt*. We have now offered to us a Constitution, which, if happily received, will disappoint our enemies, render us safe and happy at home, and respected abroad. Heaven, in mercy to us, has furnished this auspicious event, in order to snatch us from impending ruin, and to re-establish this favored land on the substantial basis of liberty, honor and virtue. The means of wiping opprobrium from our country are now in our power; let us neither reject nor forego them. It will be the duty of all honest, well-disposed men, friends to peace and good government, as well in this State as throughout the Union, to cultivate and diffuse, as far as their walk may extend, a spirit of submission to the counsels of this great patriot band; who have sought to procure, and have been anxious in their endeavors to establish, our liberty, and aggrandize our fame. If the New Constitution is not as perfect in every part as it might have been, let it be considered, that it is much more so than the most friendly and sanguine expected; and, at the same time, let it be remembered, that "the *mutual deference and concession*," and that "*spirit of amity*,"[2] from which this Constitution has resulted, ought to have a strong operation on the minds of all generous Americans, and have due influence with every *State Convention*, when they come to deliberate upon its adoption.

Every good American, when he reflects, will exult with joy that his countrymen have calmly resorted to so temperate and wise a measure as the late Convention; not only on account of the advantages, which, by the blessing of Heaven, we are likely to derive from it; but also as it furnishes a valuable precedent, if it shall be found necessary hereafter. It will likewise teach foreign nations to reflect, that, tho' discord may rear its Hydra head, and state jealousies for a while prevail, yet the enlightened Americans will not consent that the fair fabric of Liberty, which they have established with their blood, shall be endangered by anarchy at home, or destroyed by violence from abroad. The conflict which America lately sustained in the cause of Freedom, will be historiated as an important lesson to distant nations and future ages. Let the present epoch be recorded as a lesson to future generations in these United States, as having given birth to *a revolution*, effected by good sense and deliberation: Let it be stiled the reign of reason, the triumph of discretion, virtue and public spirit!

Perhaps the greatest, if not the only difficulty, which will arise against the adoption of this New Federal System of Government, will be made by those ambitious citizens, in the different States, who either *now are in power*, or who will practise their political wiles on the ignorant and un-suspicious part of the people, in order to obtain their own *private purposes*. It is a lamentable consideration, that men of this stamp too frequently, by the folly and blindness of the people, are put in the exercise of such offices as give them a very dangerous degree of influence—Hence the social compact is often violated, and sometimes dissolved.

Let difficulties, if any unhappily arise, be no longer laid to *our charge*—and let us all, who are friends to order and good government, in the language of scriptural injunction, *"watch and pray."*[3]—*Watch, and, with open front*, manfully oppose every ambitious demagogue, however *high in office*, who may attempt to form combinations, with a wicked intent to destroy the labors of those distinguished worthies; and *pray the Governor of the world* to avert, and finally disappoint their nefarious purposes.—If the change, which genius and patriotism has presented to us, as the most advisable to be received, should be rejected, and if (which God avert) such evil-minded men should prevail, what is the alternative? Gorgon-headed anarchy, or a miserable aristocratic domination; all the wretchedness and wickedness of an aristocracy, without a single particle of its dignity.

Certain it is, we have no reason to fear (whatever pseudo-patriots may insinuate) a well digested system, which reconciles in a great measure, various interests, and embraces the happiness of the whole; which has been approved by the most dignified and patriotic citizens in the Union; and which at once gives a power that will be efficient and adequate to the support and happiness of the Confederation; and, at the same time, so guards and checks the administration of it, that there will be little danger of our running into a lawless Democracy, on the one hand, or of the Sovereign authority degenerating into Tyranny, on the other.—In short, a system, which it will be wise in us to accept with gratitude—the rejection of which might, perhaps, be dreadful.

Saturday.

1. Reprinted: *Albany Gazette*, 4 October; Litchfield, Conn., *Weekly Monitor*, 12 November.
2. Quoted from the 17 September letter of the President of the Constitutional Convention (George Washington) to the President of Congress, submitting the Constitution to Congress (Appendix III, below).
3. Matthew 26:41. "Watch and pray, that ye enter not into temptation: the spirit indeed is willing, but the flesh is weak."

Evert Bancker to Abraham Bancker
New York, 25 September 1787 (excerpt)[1]

. . . As for the Constitution proposed by the fœderal Convention I read it in great haste as Mr. Laurance[2] was to take it with him. It seemed to me to be a just & good one. At the same time [some?] do not like it. And [– – –] dislikes every thing that comes from others. I pray God in his Wisdom to Order, & direct all things for the Safety & prosperity of the American States. . . .

1. FC, Bancker Family Correspondence, NHi. Evert Bancker replies to Abraham Bancker's letter of 23 September (above).

2. Probably John Laurance, a New York City lawyer. See also "Newspaper Report of Senate Debates," 1 February 1788, note 2 (II below).

Elting & Varick to Peter Van Gaasbeek
New York, 25 September 1787 (excerpts)[1]

. . . The New Constitution is the Topick of the day and seems aproved of by many. Others wish some alterations, but it seems a Majority here will reather adopt it than remain without [turn]. . . .

N.B. from what I have said of the New Constitution you may be induced to think them my se[n]timents also on that Subject, My musing then was only to give you the most prevaling opinion of this City, which perhaps may Change in some shape on more Mature Consideration, (for my part I sincerely wish for a *Revisal of the Confœdiricy*) as I feel satisfied that the present is defeciant, But Cannot consent to give the President power to Call the Militia of any State in the field to any part of the United States and keep them their for any unlimited time without the Indulgence of Even furnishing a Substitute, (and that it may hereafter be granted by Congress, that the President shall have the sole appointment of all officers,) is such a barefaced attack upon our Liberties that I cannot reconcile to it, these two instances onely in my Opinion are sufficient to Inslave us in time to the worst of Tyranny— time will not permit me to add any more at present

1. RC, Van Gaasbeek Papers, Senate House State Historical Site, Library, Kingston, N.Y. This letter, probably in the handwriting of Peter Elting, was signed "Elting & Varick," while the postscript was signed "PE." Elting (1743–1805) was a native of Kingston and a brother-in-law of Richard Varick with whom he was in the iron business. Elting was a New York City alderman from the Dock Ward from 1787 to 1789. His first wife was a sister of Peter Van Gaasbeek; his second wife was Anne Varick, Richard Varick's sister. Varick (1753–1831) was a New York City lawyer, who between 1786 and 1789 worked with Samuel Jones on the codification of New York's laws. He was recorder of the city, 1784– 89; Assembly speaker, 1787–88; state attorney general, 1789; and mayor of the city, 1789– 1801.

Pennsylvania Herald, 25 September 1787[1]

We are informed that the constitution proposed by the late fœderal convention promises to be highly popular with the citizens in New-York; and that the distinguished person from whom an opposition was predicted, has expressed himself in terms favorably to the plan.[2] Perhaps there never was a subject indeed, upon which men were more unanimous, for even those who cavil at the system itself, are impressed with the necessity of adopting it.

1. Reprinted in the *New York Morning Post* and *Daily Advertiser*, 28 September, and by 16 October in twenty-five newspapers outside New York: N.H. (3), Mass. (9), R.I. (3), Conn. (1), Pa. (3), Md. (2), Va. (2), S.C. (1).
2. Probably Governor George Clinton.

Henry Chapman to Stephen Collins
New York, 26 September 1787 (excerpt)[1]

. . . I should like to hear Your sentiments on the new Fabric raised in Your City with so much care, Ability and deliberation, I am no Politician, but to the best of my Judgment it seems as little subject to exceptions as possible and I think the States in general will be wise if they adopt this second Child and disinherit its elder Brother[2]—

1. RC, The Papers of Stephen Collins & Son, DLC. Chapman was a New York City merchant. Collins (1733–1794) was a Philadelphia merchant.
2. On 1 October Chapman wrote Stephen Collins & Son again, stating that the Constitution was "I think unexceptionable as far as I can Judge" (Mfm:N.Y.).

A Citizen of New-York
New York Daily Advertiser, 26 September 1787[1]

Mr. CHILDS, Among other futile objections started against the New Federal Government, it is said we have no persons among us equal to the office of President. Without dwelling at present on the necessity of the Executive chalked out by this Constitution, or the salutary checks interposed to prevent abuses, I mean only to mention a few approved characters, who may safely be trusted with the powers delegated to this officer. Besides General Washington, whose election will doubtless be unanimous, unless he declines the trust, gentlemen are not wanting in each State, in whom these powers may be safely vested. In New-Hampshire, both Sullivan and Langdon have, during the war, discovered talents equal to the most arduous appointments. In Massachusetts, Hancock, John Adams, Cushing,[2] King, Gorham, and Knox, have a just title to be candidates. Doctor Johnson, Parsons, and Huntington reside in Connecticut. When Rhode-Island becomes Federal, we shall be at no loss to point out suitable characters in that state also. In New-York, Mr. Chancellor Livingston, General Schuyler, Governor Clinton, Mr. Duane, and Colonel Hamilton, have ability to discharge the duties of that important station. The present Governor of New-

Jersey[3] is deficient neither in abilities nor integrity. In Pennsylvania, Franklin, Robert Morris, and General Mifflin might be voted for. The name of John Dickenson will ever be respected in Delaware. In Virginia, the abilities of Richard Henry Lee, and the distinguished characters and integrity of Governor Jefferson and Maddison, could leave the electors at no loss, was that State not possessed of the illustrious Washington. North-Carolina, tho' she has lost her Nash, has, besides Governor Matthews,[4] other valuable citizens for competitors. In South-Carolina, General Pinckney and Governor Rutledge[5] will be worthy candidates. And, in Georgia, neither Walton nor Houstoun would disgrace that dignified station.

1. Reprinted: *Albany Gazette*, 4 October; *New Hampshire Spy*, 6 October; *Massachusetts Centinel*, 24 October; *Hampshire Chronicle*, 30 October; *Norwich Packet*, 8 November; and Litchfield, Conn., *Weekly Monitor*, 12 November. Fifteen of the twenty-nine men listed by "A Citizen of New-York" as being "equal to the office of President" had been delegates to the Constitutional Convention.

2. Probably a reference to Lieutenant Governor Thomas Cushing, but possibly to William Cushing, the chief justice of the Supreme Judicial Court.

3. William Livingston.

4. "A Citizen of New-York" probably meant either former Governor John Mathews of South Carolina or Governor George Mathews of Georgia.

5. John Rutledge. Edward Rutledge was not governor until 1798.

Philadelphia Independent Gazetteer, 26 September 1787 (excerpt)[1]

Extract of a letter from a Member of Congress,
dated New-York, September 23, 1787.

" . . . There will be some difficulty in getting it adopted in New-York—the *government* has already discovered strong marks of disapprobation, and its adherents are constantly employed in disseminating opinions unfavorable to its reception—but all their attempts will be unavailing, as the BODY OF THE PEOPLE will clearly view their own interests, as intimately connected with the establishment of this new government. . . ."

1. Printed: CC:99. The entire extract was reprinted in the *Daily Advertiser* and *New York Journal*, 4 October; *Country Journal*, 10 October; *Hudson Weekly Gazette*, 11 October; and by 20 October in twenty-two newspapers outside New York: Vt. (1), N.H. (1), Mass. (5), Conn. (5), Pa. (6), Md. (1), Va. (3).

Editors' Note
The Confederation Congress and the Constitution
26–28 September 1787

On 17 September the Constitution was signed and the Constitutional Convention resolved that it be laid before Congress and be submitted to state conventions chosen by the people, under the recommendations of the state legislatures. This final version, unlike earlier positions taken by the Convention, did not require congressional approval of the Constitution. Article VII of the proposed Constitution required that once the Constitution was ratified by nine state conventions it would go into effect among the ratifying states. (See Appendix III, below.) On 18 September Convention Secretary William Jackson carried the Constitution from Philadelphia to Congress in New York City, where he arrived the next day. On 20 September Congress read the Constitution.

From 26 to 28 September Congress considered the manner in which it should transmit the Constitution to the states. (As usual Congress was meeting in closed session.) Critics of the Constitution in Congress wanted to indicate to the state legislatures that the Constitutional Convention had violated Article XIII of the Articles of Confederation, the congressional resolution of 21 February 1787, and the instructions to the delegates from their state legislatures. Article XIII required the approval of Congress and the unanimous consent of the state legislatures to amend the Articles, while the congressional resolution called the Convention "for the sole and express purpose of revising the Articles," a proviso that some state legislatures, including New York, incorporated into their instructions to their Convention delegates. Supporters of the Constitution advocated that Congress should approve the Constitution before submitting it to the state legislatures. They also wanted to recommend that the legislatures call conventions to consider the Constitution. (For Article XIII of the Articles of Confederation and the congressional resolution of 21 February 1787, see CDR, 93, 187; and CC:1. For the appointment of Convention delegates, see CDR, 192–225.)

On 27 September Virginia delegate Richard Henry Lee, one of the leading critics of the Constitution in Congress, made a motion (seconded by New Yorker Melancton Smith), indicating that the Constitutional Convention violated Article XIII of the Articles of Confederation by creating a new confederacy of nine states. Since the Convention was constituted on the authority of twelve states, the resolution ordered that the Constitution be submitted to the state executives to be laid before the state legislatures. Abraham Clark of New Jersey countered with a motion, ordering that the Constitution be sent to the state executives to be laid before their state legislatures so that they could call state conventions.

After some debate, Congress voted ten states to one to postpone consideration of Lee's resolution so that it could consider Clark's resolution. Only New York voted against postponement; its three delegates, Melancton Smith, John Haring, and Abraham Yates, Jr., were joined only by Lee and fellow Virginian William Grayson. Clark's motion was then postponed so that Congress could consider the motion of Virginian Edward Carrington, stating that Congress agreed to the Constitution and that it also recommended that the state legislatures call conventions as speedily as possible so that the Constitution might be ratified and confirmed. During the debate over this motion, critics of the Constitution argued that it needed amendments. Near the end of this debate on 27 September, Lee proposed a series of amendments that included a bill of rights. According to Virginia delegate James Madison, Lee was supported by Melancton Smith (to George Washington, 30 September, CC:114). Congress refused to debate the substance of Lee's amendments and rejected his proposal.

On 28 September Congress reached a compromise. It agreed to transmit the Constitution and its accompanying documents to the state legislatures with a recommendation that they call conventions to consider the Constitution. Congress, however, did not endorse the Constitution, and all evidence of opposition to the Constitution was deleted from the journals. This compromise, then, followed the recommendation of the Constitutional Convention. (For the proceedings and debates in Congress, see CC:95; and CDR, 322–42. Melancton Smith took the notes of these debates.)

Newspapers throughout America printed the congressional resolution of 28 September (CC:95), but they were unaware of the heated debate that took place in Congress. It not was until 24 October, when the widely circulated "Centinel" II appeared in the Philadelphia *Freeman's Journal*, that the public learned that a debate had occurred, although "Centinel" said little about it (CC:190). The public became more fully aware of the extent of the controversy in Congress with the publication of Richard Henry Lee's proposed amendments and his 16 October letter to Virginia Governor Edmund Randolph in the Petersburg *Virginia Gazette* on 6 December (CC:325). For the circulation of "Centinel" II in New York state, see "New York Reprinting of the Centinel Essays," 17 October 1787–12 April 1788, and for the reprinting of Lee's 16 October letter and proposed amendments, see "New York Reprinting of Richard Henry Lee's Proposed Amendments to the Constitution," 22 December 1787–24 January 1788 (both below).

New York Journal, 27 September 1787[1]

The repeated breaches of public faith, says a correspondent, and the variety of laws, which have been passed in different states, countenancing the violation of private engagements, have had as ill an influence on our national morals, as on our national character. Honest men must rejoice to see a spirit of honesty running through the New Consti-tution.—Public spirited men must rejoice to see a prospect of our national reputation being rescued from approbrium and disgrace; and all good men, not blinded by party spirit, must rejoice to see an effort to erect barriers against the establishment of iniquity by law. The Con-vention have at least given a distinguished proof of their attachment to the principles of probity and rectitude.

1. Reprinted in the *New York Morning Post*, 11 October; *New York Packet*, 12 October; and by 6 November in eleven newspapers outside New York: Mass. (3), Conn. (5), N.J. (1), Pa. (1), Md. (1).

Cato I
New York Journal, 27 September 1787[1]

Seven essays signed "Cato," the first of which was unnumbered, appeared in the *New York Journal* between 27 September 1787 and 3 January 1788. The series was not widely reprinted. The first five numbers appeared in the *Albany Gazette*, the last five in the *Daily Advertiser*. No out-of-state newspaper reprinted more than two numbers.

Between October 1787 and January 1788 several newspaper writers sug-gested that Governor George Clinton was "Cato." Important among them are Federalist essayists "Curtius" II, *Daily Advertiser*, 18 October, and "Examiner" II, *New York Journal*, 14 December, both of whom refer to "Cato's" opposition to the Constitutional Convention, even before it adopted a new Constitution (both below). In a 21 July article in the *Daily Advertiser*, Alexander Hamilton had made such a charge against Clinton. (See "Alexander Hamilton Attacks Governor George Clinton," 21 July–30 October, above.) In the *Daily Advertiser*, 19 October, "a Man of no Party" stated that "Cato must undoubtedly be some little State Sovereign, as State Sovereignty seems to be the burden of the song" (Mfm:N.Y.). (For other newspaper items suggesting that Clinton was "Cato," see "Cato's Soliloquy," *Daily Advertiser*, 23 October [Mfm:N.Y.]; "The Syren's Songs," *Northern Centinel*, 11, 18 December [below]; and Extract of a Pough-keepsie Letter, *Northern Centinel*, 15 January, [II below].)

No private correspondence attributing authorship to Clinton has been found. However, in 1892 editor and bibliographer Paul Leicester Ford found a copy of a letter in the George Clinton manuscripts at the New York State Library that led him to assign authorship to Clinton. This letter to an unknown addressee, dated 18 October 1787 and signed "A. Hamilton," was in the hand-writing of Antifederalist leader John Lamb. No other historian has claimed to have seen this letter, which was probably destroyed in the great 1911 fire at the New York State Library. According to Ford, the letter states: "Since my last the chief of the state party has declared his opposition to the government proposed, both in private conversation and in print. That you may judge of the *reason* and *fairness* of his views, I send you the two essays, with a reply by Cæsar. On further consideration it was concluded to abandon this personal

form, and to take up the principles of the whole subject. These will be sent
you as published, and might with advantage be republished in your gazettes"
(Ford, *Essays*, 245). Ford identified Governor Clinton as "the chief of the state
party." (For an Antifederalist's reference to Clinton as "the chief," see Charles
Tillinghast to Hugh Hughes, 12 October, CC:155.)

Linda Grant De Pauw denies that Clinton was "Cato" and suggests that
Abraham Yates, Jr., who she maintains better fits the description "chief of the
state party," was more likely the author. De Pauw dismisses as inconclusive the
assertions made by some newspaper writers, claiming that these writers may
well have been referring to other Antifederalists. Furthermore, she questions
the authenticity of the letter found by Paul Leicester Ford. Most important,
De Pauw asserts that Clinton never submitted articles to newspapers and that
he lacked the intellect and learning to have written the essays. In turn, she
argues that Yates was a prolific newspaper essayist and that he wrote about the
Constitution under several other pseudonyms, among them "Rough Hewer"
and "Sidney." De Pauw admits, however, that she cannot positively identify
Yates as "Cato." Nevertheless, Yates, she says, is a more plausible choice than
Clinton (*The Eleventh Pillar: New York State and the Federal Constitution* [Ithaca, N.Y.,
1966], 283–92). John P. Kaminski, a Clinton biographer, and Herbert J. Storing
conclude that the evidence points to Clinton, but they admit that the question
remains open (*Clinton*, 309n–10n; and *Complete Anti-Federalist*, II, 101–4).

Nearly all of the responses to "Cato" were by New York writers. Most criticisms appeared in the *Daily Advertiser*: "Cæsar" I–II, 1, 17 October; "Curtius" II–III, 18 October, 3 November (supplement); and "Americanus" I–VI,
2, 23, 30 November, 5–6, 12 December, and 12 January 1788 (all below). Other
critics included: "Medium" and "Examiner" II–III, *New York Journal*, 21 November, 14, 19 December; and "The Syren's Songs," *Northern Centinel*, 11, 18
December (all below). No Antifederalist writer defended "Cato," although "A
Friend to Common Sense," *New York Journal*, 19 December, harshly criticized
"Examiner" for attacking "Cato" (below).

To the CITIZENS *of the* STATE *of* NEW-YORK.

The Convention, who sat at Philadelphia, have at last delivered to
Congress that system of general government, which they have declared
best calculated to promote your safety and happiness as citizens of the
United States. This system, though not handed to you formally by the
authority of government, has obtained an introduction through divers
channels; and the minds of you all, to whose observation it has come,
have no doubt been contemplating it; and alternate joy, hope, or fear
have preponderated, as it conformed to, or differed from, your various
ideas of just government.

Government, to an American, is the science of his political safety—
this then is a moment to you the most important—and that in various
points—to your reputation as members of a great nation—to your immediate safety, and to that of your posterity. In your private concerns
and affairs of life you deliberate with caution, and act with prudence;

your public concerns require a caution and prudence, in a ratio, suited to the difference and dignity of the subject. The disposal of your reputation, and of your lives and property, is more momentous than a contract for a farm, or the sale of a bale of goods; in the former, if you are negligent or inattentive, the ambitious and despotic will entrap you in their toils, and bind you with the cord of power from which you, and your posterity, may never be freed; and if the possibility should exist, it carries along with it consequences that will make your community totter to its center: in the latter, it is a mere loss of a little property, which more circumspection, or assiduity, may repair.

Without directly engaging as an advocate for this new form of national government, or as an opponent—let me conjure you to consider this a very important crisis of your safety and character—You have already, in common with the rest of your countrymen, the citizens of the other states, given to the world astonishing evidences of your greatness—you have fought under peculiar circumstances, and was successful against a powerful nation on a speculative question—you have established an original compact between you and your governors, a fact heretofore unknown in the formation of the governments of the world—your experience has informed you, that there are defects in the fœderal system, and, to the astonishment of mankind, your legislatures have concerted measures for an alteration, with as much ease as an individual would make a disposition of his ordinary domestic affairs: this alteration now lies before you, for your consideration; but beware how you determine—do not, because you admit that something must be done, adopt any thing—teach the members of that convention, that you are capable of a supervision of their conduct. The same medium that gave you this system, if it is erroneous, while the door is now open, can make amendments, or give you another, if it is required.—Your fate, and that of your posterity, depends on your present conduct—do not give the latter reason to curse you, nor yourselves cause of reprehension; as individuals you are ambitious of leaving behind you a good name, and it is the reflection, that you have done right in this life, that blunts the sharpness of death; the same principles would be a consolation to you, as patriots, in the hour of dissolution, that you would leave to your children a fair political inheritance, untouched by the vultures of power, which you had acquired by *an unshaken* perseverance in the cause of liberty—but how miserable the alternative—you would deprecate the ruin you had brought on yourselves—be the curse of posterity, and the scorn and scoff of nations.

Deliberate, therefore, on this new national government with coolness; analize it with criticism; and reflect on it with candour: if you find that the influence of a powerful few, or the exercise of a standing army, will always be directed and exerted for your welfare alone, and not to the agrandizement of themselves, and that it will secure to you and your posterity happiness at home, and national dignity and respect from abroad, adopt it—if it will not, reject it with indignation—better to be where you are, for the present, than insecure forever afterwards. Turn your eyes to the United Netherlands, at this moment, and view their situation; compare it with what yours may be, under a government substantially similar to theirs.[2]

Beware of those who wish to influence your passions, and to make you dupes to their resentments and little interests—personal invectives can never persuade, but they always fix prejudices which candor might have removed—those who deal in them have not your happiness at heart. Attach yourselves to measures, not to men.

This form of government is handed to you by the recommendations of a man who merits the confidence of the public;[3] but you ought to recollect, that the wisest and best of men may err, and their errors, if adopted, may be fatal to the community; therefore, in principles of *politics*, as well as in religious faith, every man ought to think for himself.

Hereafter, when it will be necessary, I shall make such observations, on this new constitution, as will tend to promote your welfare, and be justified by reason and truth.

Sept. 26, 1787.

1. Reprinted: Philadelphia *Freeman's Journal* and Philadelphia *Independent Gazetteer*, 3 October; *Albany Gazette*, 4 October; Boston *American Herald*, 8 October; *Pittsburgh Gazette*, 10 November. The Philadelphia *Freeman's Journal* inserted the heading "*To the People of America*" in place of "*To the* CITIZENS *of the* STATE *of* NEW-YORK," even though it indicated it was reprinting the article from the *New York Journal.*

2. For the political situation in The Netherlands, see RCS:Va., 1088n–89n. "A By-Stander," Philadelphia *Independent Gazetteer*, 9 October, criticized "Cato" for comparing the Constitution to the constitution of The Netherlands (Mfm:Pa. 116).

3. The reference is to George Washington, who as President of the Constitutional Convention, sent the Constitution to the President of Congress on 17 September (Appendix III, below). "Cæsar" I, *Daily Advertiser*, 1 October, attacked "Cato" for criticizing Washington (below).

Elias Boudinot to William Bradford, Jr.
Elizabethtown, N.J., 28 September 1787 (excerpt)[1]

. . . P.S. I forget to mention that from the best accounts I can get from New York, the Governor seems rather to be laying by and not decisive, waiting to see how the wind will blow—The People of Character & Property are universally for the Constitution of the Convention. . . .

1. RC, Wallace Papers, PHi. For a longer excerpt, see RCS:N.J., 134–35. Boudinot (1740–1821), an Essex County, N.J., lawyer, was a delegate to Congress, 1778, 1781–83 (president, 1782–83); a member of the U.S. House of Representatives, 1789–95; and the director of the U.S. Mint, 1795–1805. His son-in-law Bradford (1755–1795), a lawyer, was Pennsylvania attorney general, 1780–91; a justice of that state's Supreme Court, 1791–94; and U.S. Attorney General, 1794–95.

New York Morning Post, 28 September 1787[1]

Nothing (says a correspondent) is so essential to the happiness of a people, as the possession of a free government. Without this the most fertile country and the mildest climates, become scenes of misery and desolation; but with it, the most rugged regions of the earth are crowned with cheerfulness and plenty. This is one of those important truths of which all men seem to be sufficiently convinced; and yet very few nations have taken care to secure to themselves the inestimable blessing. In all ages, the bulk of mankind have been consigned to slavery and wretchedness. The reason of this is but too obvious. What concerns all men alike, is too often neglected by all; but the private interest of a few, selfish and ambitious individuals, is pursued with unremitted ardour. The wealthy and powerful combine together to make a property of their fellow citizens; and few governments have ever existed, in which a conspiracy has not been formed against the liberties of the people.

1. Reprinted: *Vermont Gazette,* 15 October.

Peter Tappen to George Clinton
Poughkeepsie, 29 September 1787 (excerpts)[1]

We arrived at poughkeepsie on Monday. . . . I find the New Constitution Sirculating here It has but few warm friends here Wm. Kent[2] Doctr. Thomas and Billings[3] but the Influence of the Last will not do it much good. I am happy Judge Platt opposes it warmly. I make no doubt but the common people here will generally oppose it. I should think that the Northern part of the County will be for adopting it. I judge from the leading men. I am fearfull that the many Publication in favour will Injure as none publish against. I shall use my Influence as far as I can and hope I have some here. . . .

1. Copy, Bancroft Transcripts, Clinton Papers, NN. Tappen (1748–1792), a former surgeon's mate in the Continental Army, was a Poughkeepsie merchant. Clinton was married to Tappen's sister Cornelia.
2. It is possible that the person who copied this letter for historian George Bancroft meant to write James Kent, not William Kent. For James Kent, see *Country Journal,* 3 October (below).

3. John Thomas, a native of Massachusetts, was a surgeon's mate and regimental surgeon in the Continental Army during the Revolution. After the war, Thomas moved to Poughkeepsie, where he practiced medicine. Andrew Billings, a silversmith, was a native of Connecticut. He moved to Poughkeepsie just before the Revolution and during the war he served as a captain in the Continental Army.

Curtius I
New York Daily Advertiser, 29 September 1787

On 29 September, 18 October, and 3 November, the *Daily Advertiser* published three essays signed "Curtius." The publication of the first of them was announced in the *Advertiser* on 28 September. This essay, which was unnumbered, was reprinted in toto in the *State Gazette of South Carolina*, 22, 25 October, and in the October issue of the Philadelphia *American Museum*. The first sentence and last three paragraphs of "Curtius" I were reprinted in the *Massachusetts Gazette* on 9 October. The *Gazette* printed this excerpt under a Boston, 9 October, dateline and omitted the pseudonym. The *Gazette's* excerpt was reprinted in the *New York Packet*, 16 October, and by 14 December in sixteen newspapers outside New York: N.H. (1), Mass. (5), R.I. (1), Conn. (3), Pa. (4), Md. (1), Va. (1). (See also note 4 below for another portion of "Curtius" reprinted by the *Massachusetts Gazette* on 9 October.) On 5 June 1788 the Boston *Independent Chronicle* reprinted the last three paragraphs of "Curtius." The *Chronicle's* version was reprinted in the *New York Packet*, 13 June, and by 7 August in seven newspapers outside New York: N.H. (1), Mass. (1), R.I. (1), Pa. (1), Md. (1), Va. (1), S.C. (1).

ADDRESS to all FEDERALISTS.

Friends and Countrymen, An individual, who never has been, nor has any ambition at present to be honored by marks of public distinction, presumes to address you. When Common Sense declared it to be the time to try men's souls,[1] he engaged in your service; nor left it, till the Court of Britain declared you independent. In common with yourselves, he felt a noble enthusiasm warm his breast in the cause of Freedom; and, he trusts, the generous flame is still unextinguished. Animated in the hope of your prosperity, he beheld, without a sigh, the fair expectations of affluence, to which he was born, blasted by the wanton cruelty of an enemy, and by injustice and fraud, sanctified by law: And now, should you embrace the heaven-sent opportunity to secure to yourselves the invaluable blessings of Liberty and Independence, he shall still glory in every sacrifice.

The Constitution of Government proposed to your acceptance, reflects the highest honor upon its compilers; and adds a lustre, even to the names of Washington and Franklin! Whether it meets your approbation, or not, it will excite the plaudit of the world; and your enlightened posterity will mark it as an exalted instance of American genius. Here we view the sources of *energy, wisdom* and *virtue,* delicately combined. Here the *Legislative, Executive,* and *Judicial* powers are completely separated, exactly defined, and accurately balanced. Here are instituted the wisest checks to ambition in the rulers, and to licentiousness in the ruled. Here we find the most admirable fetters to self-interest, and the most indestructible securities of civil liberty. Here we behold the greatest concessions made by the strongest; and, if any partiality is shewn, it is in favor of the weak.—Should it remind you of the Government of Poland, you will reflect, that the *mode* and *frequency* of electing our Executive Head, completely evade the confusion of an elective Monarchy. But, what is more probable, should it remind of a Government, once justly dear to us—then let us enquire, where, among foreign nations, are the people who may boast like Britons? In what country is justice more impartially administered, or the rights of the citizen more securely guarded? Had our situation been sufficiently contiguous; had we been justly represented in the Parliament of Great-Britain; to this day we should have gloried in the peculiar, the distinguished blessings of our political Constitution. But, even here, the Federal Government rises in the comparison. For in this we find the avenues of corruption and despotism completely closed. No Lords strut here with supercilious haughtiness, or swell with emptiness; but virtue, good sense and reputation alone ennoble the blood, and introduce the Plebeian to the highest offices of State. Our Executive Head is mediately dependent upon the People; he has no power to grant pensions, to purchase an undue influence, or to bribe in a fancied representation of the commons. All dignities flow from yourselves: those, indeed, of the Judicial kind, not so immediately, as your own experience must have convinced you is proper. That the people of a free Government mean right, when, frequently, they *think wrong,* is a truth which renders it indispensible, that certain of their servants should feel so independent, as to be unswayed by popular caprice and error. But, in forming this Constitution, your Delegates were not obliged to look abroad for assistance; many approved models were to be found at home, the excellencies and deficiencies of which experience had already discovered.

Perhaps, to point out such obvious advantages, some may deem affrontive to the good understanding of Americans, or unnecessary until attempts are made to deceive them. It is, moreover, beside the intention of this address; which was to exhort your most earnest attention to the present important crisis of public affairs. Never have you seen a period replete with more extensive consequences. Unbiassed and impartial, examine, then, for yourselves, how worthy that system of Government is, which the collected wisdom of the nation has recommended to your acceptance. Study and scrutinize its various parts; survey, with a jealous eye, the profound intelligence and policy it discloses. And, when once your minds are persuaded of its propriety, determine with unanimity, and with decided resolution to adopt, support, and perpetuate it.

Think not that such an eventful revolution, so great and so promising, should meet with no opposition. Nothing great or good, of the kind, ever commenced or ever existed without it. Opposition will arise from a variety of sources. A few will be actuated by a vain spirit of contention, or affectation of singularity. Some will prattle of chimerical dangers, to shew their superior discernment, or to obtrude themselves into notice. Even low wit and buffoonery shall raise their silly weapons. Perhaps you will be told, among Anti-Federalists, that, when the new Government is established, "money will grow upon the trees"—that "Washington has been duped"—that "Franklin has grown old"[2]—that "Pinckney and Hamilton are boys."[3]—Thus far opposition merits your contempt. But the fears of the jealous, of the undiscerning, and of the ignorant, among each of which classes there may be men of integrity and principle; the obstinacy of prepossession and party spirit; the secret intrigues of the ambitious; and clamours of avarice and self interest; these will be exerted to undermine your prospects of national felicity, and of these you should be aware. To hear from them any thing like solid argument, or calm discussion, is scarcely to be expected. From popular rumor, I have not as yet been able to collect an attempt of this kind, that merits your slightest regard. The ground of controversy is now changed. Every objection, from the purse and the sword being entrusted to one body of men, is now removed, by the different organization of the Federal Head: objections which had weight with many of your real friends, and have had their full force granted in the construction of the present system. These objections were formerly answered by an appeal to necessity. For, better was it that the efficient powers of Government should be lodged any where, than no where: better in one delegated Assembly, mutable in its members, and removable at your pleasure, than in no Assembly at all. For, certainly, rigid order, in society, is preferable to licentious disorder; and an absolute Monarchy, to an absolute Anarchy. ⟨The people of Virginia, some time since, in instructions to their Representatives, speaking of Congress, declare, "that the melioration of a Constitution, founded upon such false and incompatible principles, seems in every view almost impossible; but expedients proposed, which require the unanimous concurrence of thirteen separate Legislatures, differing in interests, distinct in habits, and opposite in prejudices, have so repeatedly failed, that they no longer furnish a ray of hope:—We pray, therefore, for the day, when we shall see a national Convention sit, composed of the best and

ablest men in the Union, a majority of whom shall be invested with the
power of altering it. It is now so bad, as to defy the malice of fortune
and ingenuity to make it worse.")[4]

If opposition is made in your public assemblies, which I have hope
will not be the case, from the means of information time will give all
classes of people, you will find ignorance and artifice endeavoring to
shroud themselves from public contempt, under an affected silence;
and perhaps not the shadow of an argument produced in support of a
dead vote. For shame, electors! let not the good sense of Americans be
thus represented; but if men do appear in your legislative bodies in
support of a bad cause, let them at least be able to gild its deformity.

But should you ratify the proceedings of your Convention, the happy
event will form an epocha, more peculiar in its nature, more felicitating
in its consequences, and more interesting to the philosophic mind,
than ever the political history of man has displayed. Where is the country in which the principles of civil liberty and jurisprudence are so well
understood as in this—and where has ever such an assembly of men
been deputed for such a purpose? To see an assemblage of characters,
most of them illustrious for their integrity, patriotism and abilities, representing many Sovereign States; framing a system of Government for
the whole, in the midst of a profound peace; unembarrassed by any
unfavorable circumstance abroad, uninfluenced by any selfish motive
at home; but making the most generous concessions to each other for
the common welfare, and directing their deliberations with the most
perfect unanimity—to see a Constitution of Government thus formed,
and fraught with wisdom, economy, and foresight, adapted to the political habits of their constituents, to the state of Society and civilization,
to the peculiar circumstances of their country, and to those enlightened sentiments of freedom and toleration, so dear to all good men—
and, finally, to see this Constitution ratified and adopted by several
millions of people, inhabiting an extensive country, not from any coer-
tion, but from mere principles of propriety, wisdom, and policy—these
are objects too great, and too glorious, to be viewed with common
admiration and delight—the idea alone is animating to every bosom,
susceptible of the emotions of patriotism or philanthropy—the attempt
alone reflects a dignity upon human nature, and the execution secures
freedom and public happiness to remote posterity.

This great event will disclose the meaning of those many astonishing
providences, which gave timely aid to American arms in the just struggle for independence. From this it will appear, that these were not
intended to usher in, upon this recent theatre of cultivated humanity,
the horrors of domestic jarring; but to establish, upon the firmest basis,

Union, freedom, and tranquillity. The prerogative of the great Guardian of Nations, to educe good from evil, will become illustrious. Our reproach abroad, and disarrangement at home, will but shew us, in contrast, the magnitude and propriety of our change. The light of prosperity will but shine the brighter, as just bursting from the dissipated clouds of injustice, avarice, and ambition.

Let us then be of one heart, and of one mind. Let us seize the golden opportunity to secure a stable Government, and to become a respectable nation. Let us be open, decided, and resolute, in a good cause. Let us render our situation worthy the ashes of our slaughtered brethren, and our own sufferings. Let us remember our emblem, the twisted serpent, and its emphatical motto, *Unite or Die.*[5] This was once written in blood; but it is as emphatical now as then. A house divided against itself cannot stand.[6] Our national existence depends as much as ever upon our Union; and its consolidation most assuredly involves our prosperity, felicity, and safety.

1. In "The American Crisis" No. I (December 1776), Thomas Paine stated that "These are the times that try men's souls." Paine also published the pamphlet *Common Sense* in January 1776.

2. "Curtius" anticipated similar charges made in "Centinel" I, Philadelphia *Independent Gazetteer*, 5 October, who stated "I would be very far from insinuating that the two illustrious personages alluded to, have not the welfare of their country at heart; but that the unsuspecting goodness and zeal of the one, has been imposed on, in a subject of which he must be necessarily inexperienced, from his other arduous engagements; and that the weakness and indecision attendant on old age, has been practised on in the other" (CC:133, p. 330).

3. Charles Pinckney of South Carolina was 29 years of age during the Constitutional Convention, while Alexander Hamilton was 30.

4. The text in angle brackets, without the pseudonym, was reprinted in the *Massachusetts Gazette*, 9 October; *New York Morning Post*, 16 October; *Pennsylvania Packet*, 19 October; *Albany Gazette*, 1 November; and *New Hampshire Spy*, 23 November.

5. At the time of the Albany Congress in 1754 Benjamin Franklin designed a cartoon with the legend "Join, or Die," that depicted a rattlesnake cut into parts representing the American colonies. Just before the Revolution a variation of this cartoon, with the legend "Unite or Die," was still in circulation. The rattlesnake symbol was very popular at the beginning of the Revolution.

6. Mark 3:25. "And if a house be divided against itself, that house cannot stand."

James Madison to George Washington
New York, 30 September 1787 (excerpt)[1]

. . . The general voice of this City seems to espouse the new Constitution. It is supposed nevertheless that the party in power is strongly opposed to it. The Country must finally decide, the sense of which is as yet wholly unknown. As far as Boston & Connecticut has been heard from, the first impression seems to be auspicious. I am waiting with anxiety for the eccho from Virginia but with very faint hopes of its corresponding with my wishes. . . .

1. RC, Washington Papers, DLC. Printed: CC:114.

John Stevens, Jr., to John Stevens, Sr.
New York, 1 October 1787 (excerpt)[1]

. . . Congress have resolved to recommend to the Legislatures of the several States to call conventions to ratify the new Constitution fraimed by the late general Convention at Philadelphia. From what I can collect there is like to be a considerable opposition made to the adoption of it in the State of New York. The Governor, Lamb, and Willet are openly opposed to it[2]—indeed it is natural to expect that men in office will set themselves against it—If however this Party should prevail in the State of New York and the new Constitution of course be rejected— They will throw the state into the utmost confusion and must finally submit in case the other States adopt it. . . .

1. RC, Stevens Family Papers, NjHi. John Stevens, Jr. (1749–1838), a 1768 graduate of King's College (Columbia) and owner of a large estate in present-day Hoboken, N.J., was trained in the law, but did not practice that profession. Stevens was New Jersey state treasurer, 1776–83. As "A Farmer, of New-Jersey," he published on 3 November 1787 in New York City *Observations on Government* . . ., a pamphlet supporting the Constitution (below). He was also the author of the seven essays of "Americanus," published in the *Daily Advertiser* between 2 November 1787 and 21 January 1788 (all below). His father, John Stevens, Sr. (1716–92), owner of a large estate in Lebanon Valley, N.J., and a former merchant and ship owner, served in the colonial Assembly and Council for many years. He was vice president of the Legislative Council, 1776–82, a delegate to Congress, 1784, and President of the New Jersey Convention, where he voted to ratify the Constitution in December 1787. At different times, both father and son lived in New York City.
2. On 3 October Virginia Antifederalist Arthur Lee, a member of the Confederation Board of Treasury, noted that "the Governor & all his friends are in opposition" (to John Adams, CC:127).

Cæsar I
New York Daily Advertiser, 1 October 1787

Two unnumbered essays signed "Cæsar" were published in the *Daily Advertiser* on 1 and 17 October. The first essay, which criticized "Cato" I, *New York Journal*, 27 September (above), was dated Friday (i.e., 28 September). On 29 September printer Francis Childs noted that the essay was received and would appear in his next issue, which was that of 1 October. "Cæsar" I was reprinted in the Philadelphia *Independent Gazetteer*, 6 October; *Albany Gazette*, 11 October; *Massachusetts Gazette*, 12 October; and *New York Journal*, 18 October (extraordinary). On 11 October the *New York Journal's* editor informed his readers that "*It was intended that* SYDNEY *should have had a place in this day's Journal, as likewise*

INSPECTOR *No. 3, and* CÆSAR, *from Mr. Child's paper of the* 1*st instant, in reply to* CATO, *No.* 1,—*but many* PIECES, *of the first importance, having intervened, the Editor was reluctantly obliged to postpone the publication of them until next week* [18 October], *together with several* ADVERTISEMENTS, *&c."* On 18 October the *Journal's* editor told his readers that "Cæsar" would appear in the *Journal's* extraordinary issue of that day.

In reprinting "Cæsar" I, the *Massachusetts Gazette* published this prefatory statement addressed to the printer: "In the [Boston] American Herald of Monday last, a writer, under the signature of Cato, has basely attempted to confuse the minds of the people, by insinuating, that the members of the Federal Convention were actuated, in their deliberations, by other motives than their country's good; when it is universally acknowledged that the legislatures of the different states could not have chosen a set of patriots whose characters for wisdom and virtue, firmness and integrity, stood more fair than theirs.—In answer to Cato, (who, by the way, is not to be compared with Cato, the patriotick, the wise Censor of Rome [see note 1, below]) you are requested to insert the following, extracted From the *(N. York)* DAILY ADVERTISER."

Editor-bibliographer Paul Leicester Ford attributed the "Cæsar" essays to Alexander Hamilton largely because of a copy of a letter said to have been written by Hamilton on 18 October (Ford, *Essays*, 245. For the text of this letter, see the headnote to "Cato" I, *New York Journal*, 27 September [above].). However, historian Jacob E. Cooke, former associate editor of *The Papers of Alexander Hamilton*, questioned the authenticity of the letter since it no longer exists and no one else besides Ford ever saw it. Cooke also argued that Hamilton could not have written "Cæsar" II, published on 17 October (below) as a reply to "Cato" II which was published on 11 October (below). Hamilton was in Albany attending the October term of the state Supreme Court, not in New York City, when "Cæsar" II was published; he could not have received "Cato" II, read and replied to it, and sent a reply to New York City in time for publication. Since Hamilton was not the author of "Cæsar" II, he could not have written "Cæsar" I since both essays were the work of the same person. Lastly, Hamilton had long since stopped writing in the style adopted by "Cæsar." (See Cooke, "Alexander Hamilton's Authorship of the 'Cæsar' Letters," *William and Mary Quarterly*, 3rd series, XVII [1960], 78–85.) Employing sophisticated statistical methods, Frederick Mosteller and David L. Wallace have also concluded that the "Cæsar" essays could not have been written by Hamilton (*Inference and Disputed Authorship: The Federalist* [Reading, Mass., 1964], 251–52.).

For articles praising "Cæsar," see "Curtius" II and "a Man of no Party," *Daily Advertiser*, 18, 19, and 20 October (below and Mfm:N.Y.). For criticisms, see "Cato" II, *New York Journal*, 11 October, and "A Countryman" IV (De Witt Clinton), *New York Journal*, 10 January 1788 (both below).

The Citizens of the State of New-York have received yesterday, from Cato (an ally of *Pompey*, no doubt)[1] an introductory discourse on the appearance of the New System for the Government of the United States: this, we are told, will be followed by such observations, on the constitution proposed to the Union, "as will promote our welfare and be justified by reason and truth." There is, in this preparatory lecture, little that is necessary to be dwelt on just now; and if Cato had not possessed his future investigations, in such terms as wore a *questionable shape*, they should have passed unheeded.

Cato tells us that he will not *directly engage as an advocate*, for this new form of Government—or as an *opponent*. Here Cato, without any dispute, acts prudently. It will be wise in him to rest a while; since he has given a *preface*, which, with small address, can easily be made to work on either side. When the sentiments of the Confederated States come to be generally known, it will be time enough to proceed—Cato will then *start fair*. A little caution, however, he thinks necessary to be given in the mean time. "Do not" says this prudent Censor, in addressing the Citizens, "because you admit that *something* must be done, adopt *any thing*." What, in the name of common sense, does this injunction import? I appeal to men of understanding, whether it is not obviously the language of distrust, calculated, as far as such a thing can influence, to prejudice the public opinion against the New Constitution; and, in effect, by a periphrastic mode of speech, recommending the rejection of it?— "*Teach* the Members of the Convention (Cato *very modestly* goes on) that you are capable of a supervision of their conduct; the same medium that gave you this system, if it is erroneous, while the door is now open, can make amendments, *or give you another.*" O excellent thought, and happily advised! Be clamorous, my friends—be discontented—assert your prerogative—for ever assert the power and *Majesty of the People! ! !*—I am not willing to suspect any man's intentions, when they aim at giving information; but when they come abroad, couched in such *magisterial* terms, I own I feel some indignation. If this demagogue had talents to throw light on the subject of Legislation, why did he not offer them when the Convention was in session? If they had been judged useful, no doubt they would have been attended to. But *is this now a time* for such insinuations? Has not the wisdom of America been drawn, as it were, into a focus, and the proffered Constitution sent forth with an unanimity, that is unequalled in ancient or modern story? And shall we now wrangle and find fault with that *excellent Whole*, because, perhaps, some of its parts *might have been* more perfect?— There is neither virtue nor patriotism in such conduct. Besides, how can Cato say, "That the door is *now open* to receive any amendments, or to give us *another Constitution*, if required.["] I believe he has advanced *this* without proper authority. I am inclined to believe that the *door of recommendation is shut, and cannot be opened by the same men*; that the Convention, in one word, is *dissolved*: if so, we must reject, IN TOTO, or, *vice versa*; just take it as it is; and be thankful. I deny the similarity betwixt the present Constitution and that of the United Netherlands.— Cato would here draw a very melancholy picture, but it wont apply. In my humble opinion, it has a much greater affinity with a Government, which, in all human probability, will remain when the History of the Seven Provinces shall be forgotten.—Cato tells us (what all America knows by this time) that the New Constitution comes sanctioned with the approbation of General Washington; and, though he appears to have some reverence for that great patriot chief, yet he very sagaciously observes, that the *best and wisest man may err*; and thence asserts, that every man in *politics*, as well as in religion, ought to judge for himself. This paragraph needs no comment, and, for that reason, I shall not touch it; but, with all deference to Cato's penetration, I would recommend to him, instead of entering into fruitless discussion of what has come from so many *clear heads, and good hearts*, to join his Fellow Citizens, and endeavour to reconcile this *excellent Constitution* to the *weak*, the *suspicious*, and the *interested*, who will be chiefly opposed to it; that we may enjoy the blessings of it as soon as possible. I would also advise him to give his vote (as he will probably be one of the *Electors*) to the American Fabius:[2] it will be more healthy for this country, and *this state*, that he should be induced to accept of the Presidency of the New Government, than that he should be solicited again to accept of the command of *an army*.

Cato, it appears, intends to adventure on perilous ground; it will therefore become him to be cautious on what terms he takes the field. "He advises us to attach ourselves to measures, and not to men." In this instance he advises well; and I heartily recommend to *himself*, not to forget the force of that important admonition: for Cato, in his future *marches*, will very probably be *followed* by CÆSAR.

Friday.

1. "Cæsar" refers to Marcus Porcius Cato Uticensis (95–46 B.C.), a bitter opponent of Julius Caesar and an ally of Pompey the Great. Cato committed suicide, when he learned of Caesar's great victory at Thapsus.

2. George Washington.

Poughkeepsie Country Journal, 3 October 1787

This item may have been written by James Kent (1763–1847), a graduate of Yale College (1781) and a Poughkeepsie lawyer who had read law with Egbert Benson, New York's Attorney General. Kent became the first law professor at Columbia College in 1793. Five years later, he was appointed a justice of the New York Supreme Court, becoming its chief justice in 1804. Kent became chancellor of the New York Court of Chancery in 1814, serving until 1823. He returned to Columbia College and delivered three courses of lectures (1824–26) that he revised and published in four volumes as *Commentaries on American Law* (1826–28, 1830).

On 6 October, three days after the article printed here appeared, Kent wrote a friend that "Nobody here agrees with me in politics or has as I conceive *just & liberal* Sentiments upon the Government of America. . . . As to Politics I was determined to speak my Mind & not to be silenced by mere authority or Party—I therefore wrote a short approbation of the new system which I inclose—It is declamatory but it answered my purpose—& if any person attacks the new Government here in print, I intend to attack *him*" (to Nathaniel Lawrence, Mfm:N.Y.). In his memoirs, Kent said that the discussions involving the Constitution "gave amazing impulse to my feelings and with an intensity of ardor I embarked in Federal politics and quite gained an ascendant in the local proceedings and discussions" (Mfm:N.Y. On the meager support for the Constitution in Poughkeepsie, see Peter Tappen to George Clinton, 29 September, above.).

This item was reprinted in the *Albany Gazette,* 11 October, the *Daily Advertiser,* 22 October, and in five newspapers outside New York by 6 November: N.H. (1), Mass. (1), Conn. (1), Pa. (2). See also note 1, below.

To the PRINTER of the Poughkeepsie Advertiser.

A Customer of your's would beg leave to remark, that every federal soul must feel at this moment, a persuasive impulse to congratulate his Countrymen on that fair and wise fabric of government which is now presented for the consideration of America. It discovers so much republican wisdom in the firm and equal balance of the powers of legislation—so much energy in the executive but so well guarded against excess—so much intelligence in the organization of the judicial department, and in removing every *local* impediment to the harmony of the *whole,* that he does not hesitate to yield it his ready and most unreserved admiration. It is armed to be sure with all the customary powers of sovereignty, but those powers are no more than necessary to the uniformity of the plan, and to give the system its proper balance and beautiful proportion. They exist in full latitude in all our state constitutions.—They are indeed co-existent with every effective government on earth, and therefore our true and only ground of security in this as well as in every other representative republic, consists in the election, the rotation, and the responsibility of those men to whom the administration of that government is committed.

Every discerning friend to his country has long wished for a firmer cement to the rational[1] union—for a correct and vigorous administration to recall the violated laws of justice—for respect abroad, and tranquility at home—for protection to our commerce and concert to our resources; in short, for some delegated power that might be able to defend our liberties from without, and to guard against the miseries of civil dissention. Those blessings are now presented to our hands. We ought to examine their nature and the foundations on which they are supported. But to examine with candour we presume is only to feel the instantaneous impressions of ardent gratitude and solid conviction. From the anxiety that lately vibrated through the breasts of every honest American, and from the warmth and congratulation that now attend the new system in its progress to every quarter, I will almost venture to say that *rubicun is passed*, and that the public reputation of America will be impressed for ages on the solid fabric.

Nor am I animated by intemperate zeal. My opinion is founded on a few plain political maxims. For if it be the interest of the American states to *be united*;—if the only effective and durable bond of union among states, as well as among individuals be *a coercive government*;—if the *republican form* of government be the safest, and the most compatible with the liberty, the honor and the happiness of mankind; and if the *perfection of that form* consists in the accurate distribution of the legislature, executive and judiciary powers, and in their harmonious union in one coercive point;—if these positions be true (and I think they carry their own evidence along with them) the expediency of adopting the new constitution comes as strongly enforced as any thing which can be offered to the human mind.

1. "Rational" in the original. Four of the seven newspapers that reprinted this item, including the two New York newspapers, changed "rational" to "national."

New York Journal, 4 October 1787

☞ The Editor of the New-York Journal, &c. having heard many ill-natured, and injudicious observations, on what the observers are pleased to stile *HIS PARTIALITY*, as a public printer, cannot refrain from remarking, that their suspicions are groundless—that their observations are puerile—and that *servile fetters* for the *FREE PRESSES* of this country would be the inevitable consequence, were printers easily terrified into a *rejection* of free and decent discussions upon public topics.—The Editor professes to print an *IMpartial* paper, and again declares, that, setting aside his private political sentiments, he will ever act *AS A PRINTER*, giving to every performance, that may be written with decency, free access to his Journal;—here is spacious ground for the rencounter of a *CATO* and a *CÆSAR*—for a *REPUBLICAN* and *ANONIMOUS*—for a *SIDNEY* and ——, &c. &c. &c.—either of whose communications will be received with pleasure, and, to give greater satisfaction, if desired, be inserted opposite to each other, in the same paper. For such interesting political investigations the Editor will conceive himself much obliged, as, by this means, he will be more effectually enabled to serve the national interest.[1]—CATO was received at too late an hour for this day's publication, but shall be inserted in our next.

1. The *Journal* reinforced its belief in the freedom of the press, when on 25 October it printed "Detector's" harsh criticism of Boston newspaper publishers who refused to publish Antifederalist articles unless their writers agreed to make their names public. "Detector" thought such action would lead to the replacement of justice and freedom with slavery. He concluded that "The printers of a free community are an important set of men—and, when *they* league to enslave it—it will be enslaved indeed." The article was preceded by a provision of the Massachusetts constitution, declaring that the freedom of the press was not to be restrained in Massachusetts (CC:131–H).

Editors' Note
New York Reprinting of the Essays of
An American Citizen, 6 October–29 November 1787

On 26, 28, and 29 September, the Philadelphia *Independent Gazetteer* published "An American Citizen" I–III, written by Federalist essayist Tench Coxe, a Philadelphia merchant (CC:100–A, 109, 112). These were the first of about thirty essays that Coxe published in support of the Constitution. Coxe's fourth essay signed "An American Citizen" appeared on or before 21 October in a Federalist broadside anthology issued by Hall and Sellers of the *Pennsylvania Gazette* (CC:183–A). This broadside also included, among other essays, James Wilson's 6 October speech before a Philadelphia public meeting (CC:134. See also "New York Reprinting of James Wilson's 6 October Speech Before a Philadelphia Public Meeting," 13–25 October, below.). The essays by "An American Citizen" circulated throughout America, although they elicited little response.

Tench Coxe quickly sent the first three numbers to James Madison, a Virginia congressmen in New York City, requesting that he consult with Alexander Hamilton about having the essays reprinted in New York and Virginia (to Madison, 27 and 28–29 September, CC:100–B; and RCS:Pa., 121). Madison praised the essays but informed Coxe that Hamilton was not then in the city. He would consult with Hamilton upon his return (to Coxe, 1 October, CC:100–C). Coxe also sent the broadside anthology to Madison, with a similar request (to Madison, 21 October, CC:183–B). Madison replied that he showed the anthology to Hamilton immediately, assuring Coxe that Hamilton "will make the best use of them" (to Coxe, 26 October, CC:183–C).

Numbers I–III of "An American Citizen" were reprinted in the *New York Packet*, 5, 9, and 16 October; and the *Hudson Weekly Gazette*, 18, 25

October, and 1 November. Number I was also reprinted in the *New York Morning Post* on 8 October, while numbers II and III were reprinted in the *Northern Centinel*, 15 and 29 October. On 15 November the *Hudson Weekly Gazette* informed its readers that the fourth essay would appear as soon as possible and on 22 and 29 November the *Gazette* printed the essay.

For a New York commentary on "An American Citizen," see "An Observer," *Northern Centinel*, 22 October (below).

Lansingburgh Northern Centinel, 8 October 1787[1]

From undoubted authority we can assure our readers, that a very large majority of the inhabitants of the southern part of this state, (particularly the city of New-York) are, after due consideration, fully convinced that the new constitution for the United States of America, is founded, by the greatest wisdom, on true principles of LIBERTY and JUSTICE: They are therefore determined to give it their warmest approbation, as its speedy adoption is the only means of preventing poverty, distrust and distress from prevailing universally in our country.

The generality of the inhabitants of the city of Albany, this town, and the country adjacent, highly approve the new constitution, and are fully determined to use their endeavours to have it take place as speedily as possible, as the only means left in our power to prevent our total ruin as individuals or a nation.

We can, from good authority, assure our readers, that a number of the friends of an officer of high rank, in the civil department in this state,[2] have lately waited on him and informed him, that although they highly esteemed him, both in his public and private capacities, yet, should he do any thing in opposition to the new federal constitution, they must and would immediately withdraw their friendship, and no longer consider him as a friend to the welfare and happiness of his country.

1. The second paragraph was reprinted in ten newspapers by 29 November: Vt. (1), N.H. (1), Mass. (2), R.I. (1), Conn. (1), N.J. (1), Pa. (3); while the third paragraph was reprinted in twelve newspapers by 22 November: Vt. (2), N.H. (1), Mass. (2), R.I. (1), Conn. (1), N.J. (2), Pa. (3). The *Vermont Gazette*, 15 October, which reprinted paragraphs two and three, was the only newspaper to reprint the first paragraph.

Two Rhode Island newspapers printed similar items. On 1 November the Providence *United States Chronicle* noted: "Recent Advices from New-York say, That the Federal Constitution will be received in that State by a large Majority—scarcely any Persons appearing against it, except a few in the City of New-York.—The County of Albany, almost to a Man, and nearly all the other back Counties, are in Favour of it." This item was reprinted three times in Pennsylvania and twice in Maryland by 5 December.

On 15 November the *Newport Herald* printed a brief item stating "And by letters from a gentleman of the utmost integrity at Albany, to his friend here,—he advises that in a tour on business thro' that State—he scarcely met with a man opposed to this constitution, and that there will be a very large majority for its immediate adoption." By 24 November this item was reprinted once each in New Hampshire and Massachusetts.

2. The reference is to Governor George Clinton. In reprinting this paragraph, the *Pennsylvania Journal*, 31 October, supplied a footnote identifying Clinton. Five other newspapers did the same.

Editors' Note
New York Reprinting of the Address of the
Seceding Members of the Pennsylvania Assembly
9–18 October 1787

On 18 September the Pennsylvania Assembly received the Constitution. In control of the Assembly, Federalists wanted to have a convention called to consider the Constitution before the Assembly adjourned on 29 September and before the early October elections for the next Assembly. Assemblymen knew that the Confederation Congress was considering the Constitution, which most members of Congress supported. On the morning of 28 September Federalists presented resolutions calling a convention to the Assembly which adopted one of them before adjourning at 4:00 P.M. When the Assembly reconvened, it lacked a quorum because nineteen delegates, most of the Antifederalists, had absented themselves. Therefore, the Assembly adjourned until 9:30 the next morning.

On 29 September, at about 7:00 A.M., a Federalist assemblyman received an unofficial copy of Congress' 28 September resolution transmitting the Constitution to the states. The Assembly reconvened at 9:30, still lacking a quorum. It read the congressional resolution and then ordered two of its officers to "require" the return of the absent members. Aided by a mob, the officers returned two members and a quorum was declared. The Assembly adopted the remaining resolutions and adjourned *sine die*.

Sixteen of the seceding assemblymen, all of them Antifederalists, signed an address dated 29 September, in which they complained about and described the forcible and highhanded methods employed on 28 and 29 September by the Assembly's Federalist members in obtaining the adoption of resolutions calling a state convention. The sixteen members also outlined their objections to the Constitution. On 2 October Philadelphia printer Eleazer Oswald, publisher of the *Independent Gazetteer*, printed a broadside entitled *An Address of the Subscribers Members of the late House of Representatives of the Commonwealth of Pennsylvania to their Constituents*. The next day Oswald reprinted the address in his newspaper. Six Federalist assemblymen responded to the seceding assemblymen in the *Pennsylvania Packet* on 8 October (RCS:Pa., 54–126; and CC:125).

On 9 October the *New York Morning Post* reprinted the address of the seceding assemblymen with this preface: "Fair Statement of a political and outrageous FRACAS, that lately took place in Philadelphia, in consequence of a virtuous minority of the Legislature refusing to vote against their Conscience;—an Event perhaps unparalelled in any Age or Country." The address was also reprinted in New York by the *New York Journal*, 11 October; *New York Packet*, 12 October; *Albany Gazette*, 18 October (including the *Post's* preface); and *Country Journal*, 24 October. The reply of the six Federalist assemblymen was reprinted in the *Albany Gazette*, 25 October. (For the circulation of both the address and the reply to it outside New York, see CC:125.)

Antifederalist Charles Tillinghast praised Oswald for upholding the principle of the freedom of the press by printing the address. In a 12 October letter, Tillinghast stated: "Oswald, was the only Printer who *dare* print the address of the seceding Members to their Constituents:—some of the *new Constitution* Gentry waited on him, and told him, that if he published *such pieces*, they would with draw their subscriptions; He replied, that they were very welcome, if they would first be pleased to discharge arrearages; for that whatever might be his *own sentiments*, yet his *Press* was *Free*, and he would *support its Freedom*—They knew him too well not to be convinced that he would not be frightened by any Threats which they might make use of, or it is highly probable, they would have held out to him some kind of Punishment" (to Hugh Hughes, CC:155).

Collin McGregor to Neil Jamieson
New York, 10 October 1787 (excerpt)[1]

. . . I am sorry to observe Mr. Miller does not act that part towards you which your indulgence to him merited; however there is no help for it.—I trust that he will not put off any longer; if he does I think he ought to have no further indulgence, if you can compell him, in consequence of any promise he may have made, or acceptance he may have come under.—The final settlement notes which gave rise to this transaction are still on hand.—The Indents drawn on them was only 'till Janry 1785, and as it would not do to sell them at prices going in Virga. which I find was 2/ @ 2/2.—I have ordered them all round here as I can readily get 2/6 for them;—These Certificates have rose ab[ou]t 2 @ 3d. ℔ 20/. within this little time in consequence of the Sale of some Lands which Congress have ordered to be sold on the Ohio.— these Sales are now going on but very slowly;[2] and as the Finances as well as the Government of this Continent must remain in a State of Uncertainty 'till the proceedings of the Convention are adopted, or rejected, it cannot be expected that the Public securities which are *Continental* will appreciate or depreciate much from their present situation.—All persons seem to agree that if the new Constitution (copy whereof goes herewith) is adopted, it will give a spring to securities.— A few months will determine this matter and the general belief is that the New Constitution will go down almost in every State.—Gov. Clinton & his associates in office are seriously opposed to it, as report goes; likewise a number of the Country members of this & the State of Pensylvania;—and Gov. Randolph & Mr Mason of Virga. are also against it; But it is to be hoped the great body of the people will overcome those Antifœderal characters, and fix the Government as the Convention have pointed out. . . .

1. FC, Collin McGregor Letterbook, 1787–88, NN. The name of the addressee does not appear. A notation at the top of the letter reveals that it was sent "⅌ Ship Betsey Watson." An advertisement that ran semiweekly in the *Independent Journal* from 19 September through 13 October states that the Ship *Betsey*, Thomas Watson, master, would sail for London on 12 October. The addressee was probably London merchant Neil Jamieson, for whom McGregor acted as a business agent. McGregor (d. 1801), a native of Scotland who came to America in 1781, was a New York City merchant and a speculator in land and securities. Jamieson, also a native of Scotland, came to America in 1760 as a member of a Scottish mercantile firm and settled in Norfolk, Va., where he prospered as a merchant. A Loyalist, he fled to New York City in 1776, and remained there until April 1785. While in New York City, Jamieson (like McGregor) was a member of the St. Andrew's Society.

2. On 27 October, following months of negotiations, the Ohio Company purchased 1,500,000 acres of land in the Northwest Territory. (For further details on these negotiations and purchases, see RCS:Va., 1174–75, notes 24–25.)

Philadelphia Freeman's Journal, 10 October 1787[1]

After all that has been spoken and written relative to the new code of government, (observes a N. York writer)[2] it is generally allowed, that with a very few alterations, that have been already hastily suggested by anonymous writers on the subject, it will gratify the most sanguine wishes of the public. Perfection, it has been often said, is not the lot of human nature, why then must this *Magna Charta* of American liberty be supposed to come at once into the world, like Minerva out of the head of Jupiter,[3] in every respect finished and perfect?—Be the matter as it may, no friend to the liberties of this country and the rights of the people can object to a liberal and decent discussion of a form of government which the public are yet to choose or reject, as their united wisdom shall hereafter determine, and not to saddle themselves with, merely because it may be agreeable to the men of great name and property amongst us.—I am convinced, also, that very few men of knowledge and reflection, unless interested, have already so fully made up their minds on the matter as to say that the plan proposed ought to be adopted as it stands, without any alteration or amendment. The subject is momentous, and involves the greatest consequences.

1. Reprinted: Philadelphia *Independent Gazetteer*, 12 October; New Jersey *Brunswick Gazette*, 16 October; Boston *American Herald*, 22 October; *State Gazette of South Carolina*, 29 October.

2. This item has not been located in any extant New York newspaper. It possibly appeared in the *New York Morning Post*, many issues of which are not extant. The *Morning Post* often printed Antifederalist items. Three of the newspapers that printed this item were Antifederalist.

3. Minerva, Roman goddess of wisdom and the arts, was produced, without a mother, out of the brain of Jupiter, the supreme Roman deity.

Cato II
New York Journal, 11 October 1787

This essay answers "Cæsar" I, *Daily Advertiser*, 1 October (above), who had attacked "Cato" I, *New York Journal*, 27 September (above). For replies to "Cato" II, see "Cæsar" II, *Daily Advertiser*, 17 October, and "Curtius" II, *Daily Advertiser*, 18 October (both below).

"Cato" II was reprinted in the Philadelphia *Freeman's Journal*, 17 October; Boston *American Herald*, 22 October; and *Albany Gazette*, 25 October.

To the Citizens *of the* State *of* New-York.

"Remember, O my friends! the laws, the rights,
The generous plan of power deliver'd down,
By your renown'd Forefathers;
So dearly bought, the price of so much blood!
O let it never perish in your hands!
But piously transmit it to your children." [1]

The object of my last address to you was to engage your dispassionate consideration of the new Fœderal government; to caution you against precipitancy in the adoption of it; to recommend a correction of its errors, if it contained any; to hint to you the danger of an easy perversion of some of its powers; to solicit you to separate yourselves from party, and to be independent of and uninfluenced by any in your principles of politics: and, that address was closed with a promise of future observations on the same subject which should be justified by reason and truth. Here I intended to have rested the introduction, but a writer under the signature of CÆSAR, in Mr. Childs's paper of the 1st instant, who treats you with passion, insult, and threat[,] has anticipated those observations which would otherwise have remained in silence until a future period. It would be criminal in me to hesitate a moment to appear as your advocate in so interesting a cause, and to resist the influence of such doctrines as this Cæsar holds.—I shall take no other cognizance of his remarks on the *questionable* shape of my future, or the *equivocal* appearance of my past reflections, than to declare, that in my past I did not mean to be misunderstood (for Cæsar himself declares, that it is obviously the language of distrust) and that in my future there will not be the semblance of doubt. But, what is the language of Cæsar—he redicules your prerogative, power, and majesty—he talks of this *proferred constitution* as the tender mercy of a benevolent sovereign to deluded subjects, or, as his tyrant name-sake, of his proferred grace to the virtuous Cato:—he shuts the door of free deliberation and discussion, and declares, that you must receive this government in manner and form as it is *proferred*—that you cannot revise nor amend it, and lastly, to close the scene, he insinuates, that it will be more healthy for you that the American Fabius[2] should be induced to accept of the presidency of this new government than that, in case you do not acquiesce, he should be solicited to command an army to impose it on you. Is not your indignation roused at this absolute, imperious stile?—For what did you open the veins of your citizens and expend their treasure?— For what did you throw off the yoke of Britain and call yourselves independent?—Was it from a disposition fond of change, or to procure new masters?—if those were your motives, you have your reward before you—go,—retire into silent obscurity, and kiss the rod that scourges you—bury the prospects you had in store, that you and your posterity would participate in the blessings of freedom, and the employments of your country—let the rich and insolent alone be your rulers—perhaps you are designed by providence as an emphatic evidence of the mutability of human affairs, to have the shew of happiness only, that your misery may seem the sharper, and if so, you must submit. But, if you had nobler views, and you are not designed by heaven as an example— are you now to be derided and insulted?—is the power of thinking, on the only subject important to you, to be taken away? and if per chance you should happen to dissent from Cæsar, are you to have Cæsar's principles crammed down your throats with an army?—God forbid!

In democratic republics the people collectively are considered as the sovereign—all legislative, judicial, and executive power, is inherent in and derived from them. As a people, your power and authority have sanctioned and established the present government—your executive, legislative, and judicial acknowledge it by their public acts—you are again solicited to sanction and establish the future one—yet this Cæsar mocks your dignity and laughs at the majesty of the people. Cæsar, with his usual dogmatism, enquires, if I had talents to throw light on the subject of legislation, why did I not offer them when the Convention was in session?—he is answered in a moment—I thought with him and you, that the wisdom of America, in that Convention, was drawn as it were to a Focus—I placed an unbounded confidence in some of the characters who were members of it, from the services they had rendered their country, without adverting to the ambitious and interested views of others. I was willingly led to expect a model of perfection and security that would have astonished the world. Therefore, to have offered observation, on the subject of legislation, under these impressions, would have discovered no less arrogance than Cæsar. The Convention too, when in session, shut their doors to the observations of the community, and their members were under an obligation of secrecy—Nothing transpired—to have suggested remarks on unknown and anticipated principles would have been like a man groping in the dark, and folly in the extreme. I confess, however, I have been disappointed, and Cæsar is candid enough to make the same declaration, for he thinks it *might* have been more perfect.

But to call in dispute, at this time, and in the manner Cæsar does, the right of free deliberation on this subject, is like a man's propounding a question to another, and telling him, at the same time, that if he does not answer agreeable to the opinion of the propounder, he will exert force to make him of the same sentiment:—to exemplify this, it will be necessary to give you a short history of the rise and progress of the Convention, and the conduct of congress thereon. The states in Congress suggested, that the articles of confederation had provided for making alterations in the confederation—that there were defects therein, and as a mean to remedy which, a Convention of delegates, appointed by the different states, was resolved expedient to be held for the sole and express purpose of revising it, and reporting to Congress and the different legislatures such alterations and provisions therein as should (when agreed to in Congress and confirmed by the several states) render the fœderal constitution adequate to the exigencies of government.[3] This resolution is sent to the different states, and the legislature of this state, with others, appoint, in conformity thereto, delegates for the purpose, and in the words mentioned in that resolve, as by the resolution of Congress, and the concurrent resolutions of the senate and assembly of this state, subjoined, will appear.[4]

For the sole and express purpose aforesaid a Convention of delegates is formed at Philadelphia:—what have they done? have they revised the confederation, and has Congress agreed to their report?—neither is the fact.—This Convention have exceeded the authority given to them, and have transmitted to Congress a new political fabric, essentially and fundamentally distinct and different from it, in which the different states do not retain separately their sovereignty and independency, united by a confederated league—but one entire sovereignty—a consolidation of them into one government—in which new provisions and powers are not made and vested in Congress, but in an assembly, senate, and president, who are not known in the articles of confederation.—Congress, without agreeing to, or approving of, this system *proferred* by the Convention, have sent it to the different legislatures, not for their confirmation, but to submit it to the people; not in conformity to their own resolution, but in conformity to the resolution of the Convention made and provided in that case. Was it then, from the face of the foregoing facts, the intention of Congress, and of this and the other states, that the essence of our present national government should be annihilated, or that it should be retained and only had an increase of substantial necessary power? Congress, sensible of this latter principle, and that the Convention had taken on themselves a power which neither they nor the other states had a right to delegate to them, and that they could not agree to, and approve of this consolidated system, nor the states confirm it—have been silent on its character; and though many have dwelt on their unanimity, it is no less than the unanimity of opinion that it originated in an assumption of power, which your voice alone can sanctify. This new government, therefore, founded in usurpation, is referred to your opinion as the origin of power not heretofore delegated, and, to this end, the exercise of the prerogative of free examination is essentially necessary; and yet you are unhesitatingly to acquiesce, and if you do not, the American Fabius, if we may believe Cæsar, is to command an army to impose it. It is not my view to rouse your passions, I only wish to excite you to, and assist you in, a cool and deliberate discussion of the subject, to urge you to behave like sensible freemen. Think, speak, act, and assert your opinions and rights—let the same good sense govern you with respect to the adoption of a future system for the administration of your public affairs that influenced you in the formation of the present.—Hereafter I do not intend to be diverted by either Cæsar, or any other—My object is to take up this new form of national government—compare it with the experience and the opinions of the most sensible and approved political authors— and to shew, that its principles, and the exercise of them, will be dangerous to your liberty and happiness.

1. Joseph Addison, *Cato. A Tragedy* (1713), Act III, scene 5. The lines were spoken by Cato himself. "Curtius" II, *Daily Advertiser*, 18 October (below) repeated a variation of these lines at the beginning of his essay.

2. George Washington.

3. For the 21 February 1787 resolution of the Confederation Congress calling the Constitutional Convention, see CDR, 185–88. This resolution was printed by the *New York Journal* immediately after "Cato" II.

4. For the 6 March 1787 resolution of the New York legislature appointing delegates to the Constitutional Convention, see Appendix II. This resolution was also printed by the *New York Journal* immediately after "Cato" II, and the congressional resolution of 21 February 1787 (see note 3).

New York Morning Post, 11 October 1787[1]

⟨On the 17th ult. the *Federal Convention*, which met in Philadelphia in May last, adjourned.

A correspondent, who has read the proceedings of the Convention at Philadelphia, begs leave to observe, that to him the seeds of Jealousy and Discord appear thickly sown through the whole of them; and indeed, that the very letter from the President of the Convention, introducing their proceedings to Congress, argues the difficulties, notwithstanding all their labours, that their Constitution must encounter, and doubts of its meeting with full approbation.⟩ The following extracts from it he ⟨quotes as⟩ proofs:

"It is obviously impracticable in the ⟨fede⟩ral government of the States, to secure all ⟨rights⟩ of independent sovereignty to each, and yet provide for the interest and safety of all. Individuals entering into society, must give up a share of liberty to preserve the rest. It is at all times difficult to draw with precision the line between those rights which must be surrendered, and those which may be reserved; and on the present occasion, this difficulty was increased by a difference among the several states as to their situation, extent, habits, and particular interests.

"That it will meet the full and entire approbation of every state is not perhaps to be expected, &c. &c."[2]

The above mentioned letter, our correspondent asserts, is sufficient of itself, to stifle this brat in the moment of its birth. Of all governments, the Americans detest a military one the most, and this is so nearly allied to it, and so likely in a short time to become an absolute one, that they will be very cautious indeed how they adopt it. And it cannot but strike the most cursory observer, in the plan proposed for electing a President, how the military have secured the election of their favourite Chief,[3] should such an election take place, which our correspondent supposes never will. Like *Friar Bacon*, he observes, they have toiled till they are weary, and have now left their servants to watch the

BRAZEN HEAD, while they sleep;[4] like his it will be laughed at, and, when that TIME, *that is,* (when *French Councils* are not altogether *absolute* among them) *is past,* it will tumble to pieces, and—*cætera desunt.*[5]

1. Almost all of the first two paragraphs of this item was torn from the top of the second page of the only extant copy of the *Morning Post.* The text in angle brackets is supplied from the *Boston Gazette,* 22 October, the only newspaper to reprint this item.

2. For the complete text of George Washington's 17 September letter as President of the Constitutional Convention to the President of Congress, see Appendix III (below).

3. George Washington.

4. According to legend, a brazen head was a head of brass that was omniscient and able to speak. In English legend, Roger Bacon (c. 1214–1292)—a Franciscan friar, philosopher, mathematician, alchemist, scientist, and inventor—constructed such a head. If Bacon heard it speak, he would be successful in his work; if not, he would fail. While a servant watched and listened, and while Bacon slept, the brazen head spoke three times: "Time is," a half hour later it said, "Time was," and after another half hour it said, "Time's past." Whereupon, the brazen head fell, breaking into atoms.

5. Latin: the rest is missing or these are all.

Editors' Note
New York Reprinting of James Wilson's 6 October Speech
Before a Philadelphia Public Meeting, 13–25 October 1787

On 6 October Federalist James Wilson, a Pennsylvania delegate to the Constitutional Convention, delivered a speech to "a very great concourse of people" at a public meeting at the Pennsylvania State House called to nominate candidates to represent the city of Philadelphia in the state assembly (CC:134). In this speech, first printed in the *Pennsylvania Herald,* 9 October (extra), Wilson advanced arguments defending and explaining the Constitution that would be often reiterated by Federalist writers. The *Herald* described the speech as "the first authoritative explanation of the principles" of the Constitution.

In New York, Wilson's speech was reprinted in the *Daily Advertiser,* 13 October, and the *Albany Gazette* and *Hudson Weekly Gazette,* 25 October. On 18 October the editor of the *New York Journal* (below) announced that he would reprint both Wilson's speech and "Centinel" I. The *Journal's* editor reprinted "Centinel" I in his extraordinary issue on 18 October, but he did not reprint Wilson's speech. The editor stated that he expected a reply to Wilson's speech, and he preferred to print them together. On 25 October the editor printed "A Republican" I, answering Wilson's speech (below), but he never reprinted the speech. Other major responses to Wilson printed in the *New York Journal* were "Cincinnatus" I–VI (Arthur Lee), 1, 8, 15, 22, 29 November, and 6 December; "Brutus" II, 1 November; "Timoleon," 1 November (extraordinary); and "Brutus, Junior, 8 November (all below).

For the national circulation of Wilson's speech and the national commentaries upon it, see CC:134.

James Madison to George Washington
New York, 14 and 18 October 1787 (excerpts)

[14 October][1] . . . The Newspapers here have contained sundry publications animadverting on the proposed Constitution & it is known that the Government party are hostile to it. There are on the other side so many able & weighty advocates, and the conduct of the Eastern States if favorable, will add so much force to their arguments, that there is at least as much ground for hope as for apprehension. . . .

[18 October][2] . . . The Newspapers here begin to teem with vehement & virulent calumniations of the proposed Govt. As they are chiefly borrowed from the Pensylvania papers, you see them of course. The reports however from different quarters continue to be rather flattering.

1. RC, Washington Papers, DLC. Printed: CC:159 (longer excerpt); and Rutland, *Madison*, X, 194–95).
2. RC, Washington Papers, DLC. Printed: CC:176. On the same day Don Diego de Gardoqui, the Spanish encargado de negocios to the U.S., wrote from New York City, stating "that the paper war in the Newspapers . . . is growing." This "war" indicated to him that ratification would be "delayed a long time, and that according to some respectable opinions it would not be surprising if they were to find it necessary to call another Convention next year" (to Conde de Floridablanca, 18 October, CC:174).

Marcus
New York Daily Advertiser, 15 October 1787[1]

The INTERESTS *of this* STATE.

It is the Interest of the Merchants to encourage the New Constitution, because Commerce may then be a national object, and nations will form treaties with us.

It is the Interest of the Mechanics to join the mercantile interest; because it is not their interest to quarrel with their *bread and butter.*

It is the Interest of the Farmer, because the prosperity of Commerce gives vent to his produce, raises the value of his lands, and commercial duties will alleviate the burthen of his taxes.

It is the Interest of the Landholder, because thousands in Europe, with moderate fortunes, will migrate to this country, if an efficient Government gives them a prospect of tranquillity.

It is the Interest of all Gentlemen and Men of Property, because they will see many low Demagogues reduced to their *tools*, whose upstart dominion insults their feelings, and whose passion for popularity will dictate laws[a], which ruin the minority of the Creditors, and please the majority of Debtors.

It is the Interest of all Public Creditors, because they will see the credit of the States[2] rise, and their Securities appreciate.

It is the Interest of the American Soldier, as the military profession will then be respectable, and the Floridas may be conquered in a campaign. The spoils of the West-Indies and South-America may enrich the next generation of Cincinnati.

It is the Interest of the Lawyers who have ability and genius, because the dignities in the Supreme Court will interest professional ambition, and create emulation which is not felt now. The dignities of the State Court, a Notary or the prosecutor of a bond will not aspire to, which has cheapened their value. Men also have enjoyed them without professional knowledge, and who are only versed in the abstract and learned science of the *plough*.

It is the Interest of the Clergy, as civil tumults excite every bad passion — the soul is neglected, and the Clergy starve.

It is the interest of all men, whose education has been liberal and extensive; because there will be a theatre for the display of talents, which have no influence in State Assemblies, where eloquence is treated with contempt, and reason overpowered by a *silent vote.*

It is *not* the Interest of those who enjoy State consequence, which would be lost in the Assemblies of the States. These insects and worms are only seen on their own dunghill. There are minds whose narrow vision can look over the concerns of a State or Town, but cannot extend their short vision to Continental concerns. Manners are essential in such a Government, and where the Union is represented, care should be taken to impress the other States with respectable opinions, and if this becomes a principle they must remain at home, and not presume to these national dignities.

(a) *Citation Laws.*[3]

New-York, Oct. 13.

1. The *Albany Gazette,* 6 December, reprinted "Marcus" from the *Salem Mercury,* 20 November, and changed the heading to read: "*The* INTERESTS *of this* STATE (*Massachusetts*) *and of every other* STATE *in the* UNION." (The *Gazette,* like every other reprint, deleted "Marcus's" footnote.) Outside New York, "Marcus" was reprinted in ten newspapers by 26 December: N.H. (1), Mass. (3), Conn. (2), N.J. (3), Pa. (1). On 19 October "a Man of no Party" in the *Daily Advertiser* wrote that "Marcus is so full of his *interest* that I suspect him to be an *usurer.* His pride seems hurt, and his disposition cynical. He would not have found fault, I imagine, with the old *batch,* if a loaf had come to his share" (Mfm:N.Y.).

2. Eight of the eleven reprints (not including the *Albany Gazette*) substituted "creditors of the states" for "credit of the states."

3. Perhaps a reference to the Roman law of citations (426 A.D.) which provided that the writings of only five named jurists should be cited as authorities and that a judge was bound by a majority of these five.

Cincinnatus
Lansingburgh Northern Centinel, 15 October 1787

To the People *of the State of* New-York.
FRIENDS and FELLOW CITIZENS.

Every true friend to America must feel the highest degree of real satisfaction on fully examining the new constitution for our federal government, lately submitted to the consideration of the citizens of America by our wise and patriotic convention—while every friend to this country, with heart-felt joy, observes how generally pleasing it is to the people, how few are averse to it, and how trifling the objections of those few are.

When we speak of our liberties, it is with pain every considerate man notices the mistaken idea some of our countrymen entertain of the word *liberty*:—There are those among us who conceive that it consists in every man's doing what he pleases: Let us for a moment suppose that was the case—what would be the consequence?—I will venture to say, confusion, distress, distrust, bloodshed, and every attendant evil.

From the first formation of society, it has been ever found absolutely necessary for the welfare, happiness and good of mankind, that they should give up a part of their liberties in trust for the preservation of the remainder.

As individuals, we have by our present excellent constitution, given those powers which were conceived necessary for our welfare to our fellow citizens and neighbours, chosen by ourselves; and of our own free will they have the preservation of our lives, liberties and properties, entrusted to their care.

If it is necessary that the several counties should delegate powers to certain men to form one body for the preservation and good of the state at large, in order to prevent that confusion and disorder which their several clashing interests would cause, and in order to strengthen and make more respectable the whole—how much more necessary will it appear to every reasoning man, to delegate sufficient powers from each individual state, to form one grand body to govern and bring to a point the united force of North-America?—And in doing this—in adopting the new constitution, as recommended to us, we do not, in my opinion, give up one particle of our liberties. The men to whom we delegate the necessary powers, our president, vice-president, senators and representatives, are still chosen by and from among ourselves.

Why then should we be more fearful or cautious in entrusting them with power than we now are in trusting the officers of our present government, who are also chosen by and from among ourselves?

The idea of being more fearful, or having a greater distrust of the one than the other appears to me truly ridiculous.

Long have the real friends of America lamented the want of a sufficient power;

To regulate our trade, and revive the present languishing state of our navigation and commerce;

To comply with the late treaty of peace with Great-Britain, and oblige them to give up the northern and western posts on our frontiers, and thereby throw an immense fur trade into our hands, which is now enjoyed by our inveterate enemies;

To make good our contracts with foreign nations, and thereby establish, at least, the character of an honest people, which would, to every feeling American, be highly preferable to our present character among the nations of Europe.

It is not known to ourselves only, but the world in general knows, that there is a want of force and energy in our federal government; the consequence of which is, no credit can or will be given to our engagements at home or abroad. Had we been so fortunate as to have had at this time a permanent and well established federal government, the present distracted and unhappy situation of the United Provinces of the Netherlands would, in all probability, have driven to this country thousands of worthy, opulent, industrious citizens, who would have brought with them the avails of many years' hard labour, industry and frugality, which would have considerably increased the number of our useful and industrious citizens, as well as added much to our wealth.

Our present feeble situation is well known to every person of the smallest information: From the close of the late war to the present day every one must have observed that a decline of trade and approaching poverty have rapidly gone on hand in hand; and should we continue, as we now are, without a power sufficient to govern and conduct the affairs of our nation, to what a miserable and impoverished state we shall in a few years be reduced, my pen has not power to describe—I can only faintly attempt it.

We are now greatly involved in immense debts, the farmer and mechanic to the country dealer, he to the importer, the importer to the foreign merchant, and the United States, as a nation, to France, Spain, Holland, &c. and our trade, by various nations, greatly cramped, and the balance thereof much against us. Will the foreign nations! will the foreign merchants wait much longer, when we do not even pay them the interest of what we justly ought to pay, not only the interest but principal also? I will venture to say no! they will not! their patience and long forbearance will be exhausted: What must be the dreadful consequence? the importer, the country dealer, the farmer and mechanic, not being able to pay their just debts, will be seized and thrown into loathsome prisons, their property (owing to the great poverty of the country) sold at public auction for one-fourth part of its real value, and they, their wives and tender offspring, turned out of doors, to encounter all the horrors of poverty, want and despair; and in all probability our vessels seized by the different nations for the payment of our honest debts. This, my countrymen, is not an exaggeration; every one who looks forward but a few years will see that it must certainly take place, unless we make a speedy alteration in our present continental government and politics—we have already too long neglected it.—Happy is it for us! happy for our posterity, that the wisdom of America, in the year 1787, saw the necessity of new modeling the federal constitution of their country; and still more happy ought we to esteem ourselves, that our choice of persons to revise our confederation fell on men of wisdom, who have recommended to us so excellent a constitution, that the most bitter of our internal enemies can scarcely find a fault in it. However, I am well aware that there are some few among us, who, from their late disappointment in their attempts to bring us to the feet of their late and still adored master, and others from sinister motives, who will yet endeavour to lead you astray. But I trust your good sense will not be imposed on, and that you will view and consider every article of the proposed federal constitution each one for himself, and I doubt not every real friend to America will heartily approve, and use every influence in his power to have it take place as speedily as possible.

Should we once be so happy as to have a sufficient and energetic government take place in America, how many thousands who are now in different parts of Europe, groaning under the chains of despotism, or languishing under the horrors of poverty and want, who would gladly fly to our then free and happy country, here to enjoy the blessings of liberty and the comforts of plenty. How greatly would our trade and navigation flourish, if under proper and general regulations for our whole empire; and how much would the increase of trade augment the demand for the produce of our country; and under a well regulated government, where every man is secure in his property, how much would the value of landed interest be enhanced. I believe I may venture to say that there is hardly a doubt but that every landholder may, as soon as the new constitution takes place, look upon his lands as of double the value they now are in our present confused, unsettled and feeble state.

In the present situation of our affairs, no real dependence can be put on contracts that look forward to any distance of time:—Who that values his interest would venture to make a contract for cash, to be received one, two or three years hence, when it is in the power of a party of men, destitute of honor or principle, to pay him in a depreciated currency at the rate of one for six, as is now the case in a sister state, where, under the sanction of a vile and unjust law, with the preface of a KNOW YE,[1] an honest industrious man is obliged to accept of one-sixth part for the full value of a just debt due on a solemn contract.

I think it unnecessary to particularize any more of the numerous evils and inconveniencies attending a want of a proper government for the United States; the good sense and judgment of the people will point out to them many others we now feel; and the many and still greater evils that are fast approaching with rapid strides, and must e're long fall upon us, unless speedily prevented. Then, my dear fellow citizens, let us haste to prevent that destruction and misery that now awaits us— Let none be swayed by persons or party; but let each of us examine and weigh well every article of the proposed constitution, and compare that with our present situation: I am fully confident, after mature deliberation, they must see the many advantages that must accrue to us as individuals and a nation, from adopting it,—as it appears to me to be founded on the most solid principles of liberty, and with much wisdom so modeled as to be adapted to the real good and happiness of every citizen of America, as nearly as their local situations would possibly admit.

The constitution of our state is generally admired by mankind, and particularly by our fellow citizens; it is looked upon as one of the best models for a free government that has yet appeared to the world. And it is visible, through the whole of the new proposed government, that the honorable and patriotic convention who framed it, had at all times our excellent constitution in view: It has so near a resemblance to our own internal government that I think our citizens will undoubtedly be among the foremost to adopt it. That some few men in high offices of honor and profit will oppose it, there is not a doubt, but their opposition cannot be supposed to proceed from patriotic principles, but from fear of lessening their power, their influence, or their emoluments: Their trifling and unsubstantial objections, and their interested views in making them, will readily be perceived by every observing citizen, and of course will have little weight.

After having thus long taken up the time of the public, I think it necessary to inform them, that the author is not swayed by party or interest: Through the whole course of the late war he served America as a soldier, and, since the peace, has retired to private business: He is not possessed of one shilling of public securities; he holds no kind of office under the present government, nor does he expect any from this or a future one; but is, and ever has been, anxious to see his country rival, in happiness, honor, glory, power and trade, all the nations of the earth.

Lansingburgh, Oct. 13.

1. "Know Ye" refers to the Rhode Island paper money act of May 1786. If creditors refused a tender in paper money, debtors could lodge the currency with a judge, who would advertise the lodgment in the state's newspapers introduced by the words "Know Ye." If the creditor remained adamant in his refusal to accept the depreciated paper money, the debt was cancelled and the lodgment, minus judge's and advertising fees, was forfeited to the state.

John Jay to John Adams
Office for Foreign Affairs, 16 October 1787 (excerpt)[1]

. . . The public Mind is much occupied by the Plan of fœderal Government recommended by the late Convention—many expect much Good from its Institution, and others will oppose its Adoption—The Majority seems at present to be in its Favor.[2] For my part I think it much better than the one we have, and therefore that we shall be Gainers by the Exchange; especially as there is Reason to hope that Experience and the good Sense of the People, will correct what may prove to be inexpedient in it. A Compact like this, which is the Result of Accommodation and Compromise, cannot be supposed to be perfectly consonant to the Wishes and Opinions of any of the Parties. It corresponds a good Deal with your favorite and I think just Principles of Government, whereas the present Confederation seems to have been formed without the least Attention to them. . . .

1. RC, Adams Family Papers, MHi. Printed: Johnston, *Jay,* III, 257–59. Adams (1735–1826) was U.S. minister to Great Britain in London, where he was engaged in writing and publishing his three-volume *A Defence of the Constitutions of Government of the United States of America* . . . (CC:16). A portion of Jay's letter (not printed here) reveals that Jay, the Confederation Secretary for Foreign Affairs, enclosed an act of Congress that complied with Adams's request to return to America and that expressed its thanks for his services.

2. On 24 October Jay wrote Thomas Jefferson that "What will be the fate of the new Constitution, as it is called, cannot easily be conjectured—at present the Majority seems to be in favor of it, but there will probably be a strong opposition in some of the States, particularly in this & Pensylvania" (Boyd, XII, 267).

Cæsar II
New York Daily Advertiser, 17 October 1787[1]

"The great source of all the evils which afflict Republics, is, that the People are too apt to make choice of Rulers, who

are either Politicians without being Patriots, or Patriots without being Politicians."

Mr. CHILDS, When I took notice of Cato's prefatory Address to the
Citizens of the State of New-York, in your paper of the first instant, I
had no serious intention of becoming a controversial defendant of the
New Constitution. Indeed, if the system required defence, I was neither
so weak, nor so vain, as to suppose myself competent to the task.—To
obviate difficulties which may arise, when such weighty affairs as the
principles of legislation are under discussion; I am sensible requires
talents far beyond my limited abilities. When I offered a few remarks
on Cato's introduction, I was strongly impressed with the idea, that even
the most substantial criticisms, promulgated by the most influential and
avowed Citizens, could have no good tendency at *this time*. I viewed the
public mind as wound up to a great pitch of dissatisfaction, by the
inadequacy of the powers of the present Congress, to the general good
and conservation of the Union—I believed then, as I do now, that the
people were determined and prepared for *a change:* I conceived, therefore, that the wish of every good man would be, that *this change might
be peaceably effected.* With this view, I opposed myself to Cato. I asserted,
in my last, *that the door of recommendation was shut, and cannot be opened
by the same men, that the Convention was dissolved.* If I am wrong, it will
be of great importance to Cato's future remarks, that he make it appear.
If he will declare, from sufficient authority, that the Members of the
late Convention have only adjourned, to give time to hear the sentiments of every political disputant, that, after the numerous presses of
America have groaned with the heavy productions of speculative politicians, they will *again meet*—weigh their respective merits, and accommodate accordingly:—I say, if Cato can do this, I make no hesitation
in acknowledging the utility of his plan. In the mean time, I positively
deny having any, the most distant desire of shutting the door of free
discussion, on any subject, which may benefit the people; but I maintain (until Cato's better information refutes me) that the door, as far
as relates *to this subject,* is already shut—not by me, but by the highest
possible authority which the case admits—even by those great Patriots
who were delegated by the people of the United States, to *open such a
door,* as might enable them to escape from impending calamities, and
political shipwreck. This distinction is clear, I conceive, and ought to
have some weight even with Cato, as well as those for whom he writes.—
I am not one of those who gain an influence by cajoling the unthinking
mass (tho' I pity their delusions) and ringing in their ears the gracious
sound of their *absolute Sovereignty.* I despise the trick of such dirty policy.

I know there are Citizens, who, to gain their own private ends, enflame the minds of the well meaning, tho' less intelligent parts of the community, by sating their vanity with that cordial and unfailing specific, that *all power is seated in the People.* For my part, I am not much attached to the *Majesty of the multitude,* and therefore wave all pretentions (founded on such conduct) to their countenance. I consider them in general as very ill qualified to *judge* for themselves what government will best suit their peculiar situations; nor is this to be wondered at:— The science of Government is not easily understood.—Cato will admit, I presume, that men of good education and deep reflection, only, are judges of the *form* of a Government; whether it is calculated to promote the happiness of society; whether it is constituted on such principles as will restrain arbitrary power, on the one hand, and equal to the exclusion of corruption, and the destruction of licentiousness, on the other. Whether the New Constitution, if adopted, will prove adequate to such desirable ends, time, the mother of events must shew. For my own part, I sincerely esteem it a system, which, without the finger *of God,*[2] never could have been suggested and agreed upon by such a diversity of interests. I will not presume to say, that a more perfect system might not have been fabricated;—but who expects perfection at once?—And it may be asked, *who are judges of it?* Few, I believe, who have leisure to study the nature of Government scientifically, but will frequently disagree about the quantum of power to be delegated to Rulers, and the different modifications of it. Ingenious men will give very plau[si]ble, and, it may be, pretty substantial reasons, for the adoption of two plans of Government, which shall be fundamentally different in their construction, and not less so in their operation:—yet both, if honestly administered, might operate with safety and advantage. When a new form of Government is fabricated, it lies with the people at large to receive or reject it:—this is their *inherent right.* Now, I would ask, (without intending to triumph over the weaknesses or follies of any men) how are the people to profit by this inherent right? By what conduct do they discover, that they are sensible of their own interest in this situation? Is it by the exercise of a well disciplined reason, and a correspondent education? I believe not. How then? As I humbly conceive, by a tractable and docile disposition, and by honest men endeavoring to keep their minds easy; while others, of the same disposition, with the advantages of genius and learning, are constructing the bark that may, by the blessing of Heaven, carry them to the port of rest and happiness; if they will embark without dissidence, and proceed without mutiny. I know this is blunt and ungracious reasoning: it is the best, however, which I am prepared to offer on this momentous business; and, since my own heart does not reproach me, I shall not be very solicitous about its reception. If truth, then, is permitted to speak, the mass of the people of America (any more than the mass of other countries) cannot judge with any degree of precision, concerning the fitness of this New Constitution to the peculiar situation of America:—they have, however, done wisely in delegating the power of framing a Government to those every way worthy and well qualified; and, if this Government is snatched, untasted, from them, it may not be amiss to enquire into the causes which will probably occasion their disappointment. Out of several, which present to my mind, I shall venture to select *One*, baneful enough, in my opinion, to work this dreadful evil. There are always men in society of some talents, but more ambition, in quest of *that* which it would be impossible for them to obtain in any other way than by working on the passions and prejudices of the less discerning classes of citizens and yeomanry.—It is the plan of men of this stamp to frighten the people with ideal bugbears, in order to mould them to their own purposes. The unceasing cry of these designing croakers is, my friends, your liberty is invaded! Have you thrown off the yoke of one tyrant, to invest yourselves with that of another! Have you fought, bled, and conquered, for *such a change!* If you have—go—retire into silent obscurity, and kiss the rod that scourges you.

To be serious: These state empirics leave no species of deceit untried to convince the unthinking people that they have power to do—what? Why truly to do much mischief, and to occasion anarchy and wild uproar. And for what reason do these political jugglers incite the peaceably disposed to such extravagant commotions? Because until the people really discover that they have *power*, by some outrageous act, they never can become of any importance. The misguided people never reflect during this frenzy, that the moment they become riotous, they renounce, from that moment, their independence, and commence vassals to their ambitious leaders, who instantly, and with a high hand, rob them of their consequence, and apply it to their own present, or future aggrandisement; nor will these tyrants over the people stick at sacrificing *their good*, if an advantageous compromise can be affected for *themselves.*

Before I conclude, I cannot refrain from observing, that Cato states very disingenuously the manner in which the Federal System came abroad. He tells us, Congress were sensible that the late Convention exercised a power which no authority could delegate to them. The Convention, says Cato, have taken upon them to make a perfectly new system, which, by its operation, will absorb the sovereignties of the individual States; this new government founded on *usurpation*, (Cato, this expression is very indecent—but I will rouse no passions against you) this consolidated system Congress did not approve, and *therefore* have been *silent* on its character. That Congress was silent on its character is true, but, could Cato find no other reason for their silence than that of disapprobation.—I believe Congress were by no means dissatisfied with the freedom the Convention took with the Articles of the Confederation; I believe further, that with very few exceptions, that honorable body approved of the New Constitution; and, that they did not accompany it to the States with a recommendatory capitation or circular letter, proceeded from a delicate attention to the Members of the late Convention, to a few of their own body, and to the people of America at large.[3] That the Convention went so earnestly into the business committed to their care, ought, instead of being matter of chagrin, to occasion the liveliest expressions of approbation and gratitude.—As matters stand just now, I think it may be fairly said, that no *generous plan of government* for the *United States* has ever been constructed, (the plan only excepted which is under consideration) so that it seems quite unnecessary in Cato to disturb the peace of society by a bombast appeal to their feelings, on the *generous plan of power delivered down by their renowned forefathers.* I venerate the memory of the slaughtered patriots of America, and rejoice as much as Cato, that they did not bleed in vain, but I would have America profit by their death in a different manner from him. I believe they fought to obtain liberty for no particular State, but for the whole Union, indissolubly connected under one controling and supreme head.

Cato complains of my anticipating parts of his subject which he intended for future periods. I shall break in no more upon his *arrangements*; all he can say against the New Constitution has been already disseminated in a neighbouring State, by the glorious defenders of *Shayism.* I shall therefore leave Cato to the wicked influences of his own heart, in the fullest persuasion that all good men, and good citizens, will combine their influence to establish the fair fabrick of American liberty, beyond the reach of suspicion, violence, anarchy, and tyranny. When this glorious work is accomplished, what may America not hope to arrive at! I will venture to prophecy that the day on which the Union under the new government shall be ratified by the American States, that *that day* will begin an era which will be recorded and observed by future ages, as a day which the Americans had marked by their wisdom in circumscribing the *power*, and ascertaining the *decline* of the ancient nations in Christendom.

Oct. 15.

1. Reprinted: *Albany Gazette*, 1 November. On 16 October the printer of the *Daily Advertiser* noted that "Cæsar" was "unavoidably postponed till to-morrow." "Cæsar" II

was part of an exchange between him and "Cato." See "Cato" I–II, *New York Journal,* 27 September and 11 October (both above), "Cato" III, *New York Journal,* 25 October (below); and "Cæsar" I, *Daily Advertiser,* 1 October (above).

2. Exodus, 31:18; Deuteronomy 9:10.

3. For the debate in Congress after it received the Constitution and for its transmittal of the Constitution to the states without taking a position on it, see "The Confederation Congress and the Constitution," 26–28 September (above).

Editors' Note
New York Reprinting of the Centinel Essays
17 October 1787–12 April 1788

On 5 October the Philadelphia *Independent Gazetteer* published "Centinel" I (Samuel Bryan), one of the earliest major attacks on the Constitution (CC:133). This was the first of eighteen "Centinel" essays published during the debate over the ratification of the Constitution, the last appearing on 9 April 1788. The first five numbers, filled with personal invective, presented many of the standard Antifederalist arguments against the Constitution.

"Centinel" circulated widely in New York. The *New York Journal* reprinted every essay except XVII between 18 October and 12 April 1788. The *New York Morning Post,* many issues of which are not extant, reprinted numbers I (17–18 October), II (25, 27 October), VI (1 January), VII (27 December), and VIII (5 January). "Centinel" I was also reprinted in the *Hudson Weekly Gazette,* 15 November, and *Albany Gazette,* 3 January. The *Albany Journal,* 3 March, reprinted essay XV.

The "Centinel" essays also circulated in New York as a broadside and as a pamphlet. Numbers I and II were reprinted in a two-page broadside (Evans 45045) by Thomas Greenleaf of the *New York Journal* in early November along with "Timoleon." (For "Timoleon," see *New York Journal,* 1 November [extraordinary], below.) In early April 1788 Greenleaf reprinted numbers I–IX in an Antifederalist anthology that New York Antifederalists distributed throughout the state (III below; and CC:666).

No original major responses to "Centinel" were printed in New York, although a number of writers commented upon "Centinel." See "Detector," *Daily Advertiser,* 24 November 1787, *Albany Gazette,* 20 December, "A Spectator," *Northern Centinel,* 1 January 1788 (all below); "A Countryman" VI (Hugh Hughes) and an unsigned essay, *New York Journal,* 14 February and 29 March 1788 (both III below); and "a Man of no Party," *Daily Advertiser,* 20 October 1787 (Mfm:N.Y.). For the national circulation of the "Centinel" essays and the national commentaries upon them, see the headnote to CC:133.

Curtius II
New York Daily Advertiser, 18 October 1787[1]

ADDRESS *to the* CITIZENS *of* NEW-YORK.

Remember, O my friends! the laws, the rights,
The generous plan of power delivered down
By your renowned *Convention*;
The price your *own*, not your forefathers' blood.
O let it never perish in your hands,
But piously transmit it to your children![2]

Can there be any, at this awful crisis, inattentive to their country's prosperity? Can there be any, so lost to every noble sentiment, as to disguise their principles, studious only, of what may eventually prove the current of popularity? The heart of the traitor will say yes! For, when contested questions, of such national consequence, engage our attention, we feel the justice of that Grecian decision, which ordained the man, who took no decided part in the civil commotions of his country, guilty of the worst species of treason.[3]

My first address was to excite you to a critical examination of the Constitution of Federal Government, framed, and proposed to your acceptance, by an uncorrupted delegation of our best and wisest citizens: but this is to awaken your attention to the insidious arts of your enemies. The period may soon arrive, when it may be of infinite importance to distinguish characters: now, then, is the time to mark well the conduct and political sentiments of individuals.

It has been observed to you, that so great and glorious a revolution, as now dawns in our political horizon, must in certain passions of society, find its enemies; and various sources of opposition have been pointed out. It might have been added, that the influence of office extends not only to dependants but to expectants. Employment from the man in power, or the grateful smile in the countenance of the great, is sufficient to lift the sycophant, to damn his conscience, and to sell his country. It is not, however, the fears or the desires of ambition and avarice in individuals alone, which would undermine your felicity; nor is your danger to be sought in the futile and wire-drawn arguments of the only champion who has as yet come boldly and honestly forward. The most you have to fear, is from your own supineness and inattention; and from a local and narrow policy, which has, on certain occasions, beguiled even your Legislature. From the first of these we find a diffusion and a reception given to the grossest lies, and to the most injurious misrepresentations. Thus it has been industriously spread,

and, by many, taken upon trust, that *the trial by jury* that inestimable
privilege of freemen, was forever sacrificed; that *a standing army* was *to
cram every thing down your throats*; and that *the Constitution itself might be
remolded*, either from caprice or craft, into any form best pleasing to
the holders of power and office. It is not my business to confute mere
reports, till such as these are more officially asserted. I shall, therefore,
consider them as mere lies, circulating upon the wings of ignorance,
jealousy and folly. The local and knavish policy of a Legislature is a far
more consequential object, and far more justly to be dreaded. The
genuine sentiments of this delusory guide are but seldom avowed. But,
altho' they veil themselves from the eye of public justice, under a silent
vote they can influence your most important concerns. Heaven knows
what may be your fate, should this demon of destruction insinuate her
poisons. "What! give up the impost! divide what providence has put
into our hands, what nature has allotted to us! What have we to do
with others? What, sacrifice our interest for fancied dangers! if these
are the terms at *present*, we need neither the protection nor the friendship of other States!" Here is the genuine language of this short-sighted
directress. Nor is it strange that ignorance, biassed by the influence
of power, should adopt what avarice dictates. Abbe Raynal, speaking
of that worst of all Governments, an Aristocracy, observes, that twenty
tyrants cannot blush;[4] but the same observation may be made concerning any Democratic Assembly, who are inveloped in blunders,
from being incapable of discovering the delicate intentions of a refined policy. But, should ever the important question before us unfold
the portals of civil war, and be written in American blood,—which
may God avert!—perhaps we may hear a language, similar to the
above, boldly, wisely, and openly retorted by some commercial cities,— "The impost *is ours*"— "Nature has allotted it to us"— "Providence has put it into our hands"— "But dangers are not fancied"—
"Let us seek the protection and friendship of the other states"— "Let
us give up *our* local advantages for lasting security to our inestimable
privileges"—["]Let us share all with those whose blood and treasure
assisted to procure them["]—["]With them we suffered and contended, not for the accidental emoluments of a seaport town, but for
Freedom, Independence and *Union*."

But who is Cato—whose elegant diction and long-spun argumentation would lead us to suspect him both the scholar and the sophist?—
Has he, as yet, however thrown out any thing calculated to enlighten
our minds, or to rectify our judgments, if in error? Did he, in his *first
number*,[5] affect a disgustful neutrality and was not the veil too thin to
hide his nefarious intentions? Did he bring arguments to the point in

question, or was his artful piece only a declamatory attempt to excite the prejudices of the ignorant, and the distrust of the jealous? These questions every candid and sensible reader must have determined. Of what materials, then, is his second production composed? Does he, in this, prove the Constitution of the Federal Government proposed, to be inferior to the ridiculous one under which we are, at present, said to live? Or, if he acknowledges it to be infinitely superior to this, or to any other of human invention, that has ever been enjoyed by any society of mankind; does he give any solid, substantial reasons, why we ought not immediately, by making the happy change, to immortalize ourselves, and bless our posterity? No, nothing like this appears. But his second number is made up, if of any thing, of six charges; three against his professed antagonist, and three against your Honorable Convention. The three first I shall leave with Cæsar,[6] contenting myself with barely mentioning them. 1st, then, Cæsar has ridiculed your power, prerogative, and majesty; by which, perhaps, is meant his own. 2dly, He hinders you to think; which can only mean, that Cæsar hinders him to deceive. 3dly. Cæsar would cram the whole fabric of Government down your throats with an army!—His charges against the Convention are more consequential. 1st, For an assumption of undelegated power—the very *sound* of the word *power* puts our patriot in the horrors. 2dly, For secrecy in their business—perhaps in *his* retirement Cato is but ill employed. 3dly, for shutting their doors. Dreadful impeachments!—But, had not those doors been shut, Cato would have been among the first, to have imputed every section of their system to the party influence of Philadelphia. He would have urged the present unanimity and federal spirit of that great city as incontestable evidences to the truth of his assertion.[7] One would think that this jealous republican, if he deserves so flattering an appellation, tortured by these instances of prudence in that illustrious body, had pictured in his frantic imagination the whole plan of conspiracy. He sees the Saviour, under God, of his country;[8] but instead of the immortal laurel, he wears the tiara of an unresisted despot. The venerable sage,[9] whose political wisdom and virtue have shone forth like the lightning of heaven, has become a state pensioner, and sinks into the grave with a salary of 40,000 eagles. Who is this dignified counsellor now metamorphosed into the Right Reverend High Lord Bishop of the United States?[10] See the Pennsylvania Farmer[11] has become a Duke. Phocion[12] is Prime Minister of State. The Pinckneys[13] are Lords of the Queen's Wardrobe—a long train of nobility succeeds—and alas! the virtuous Cato is forgotten! If such arrangements have really been made, we cannot too greatly lament the secession or neglect of our deputed servants. A Judge in the Supreme Court of this Sovereign and Independent State[14]—A Mayor of the ancient city of Albany[15]—these are, by the emoluments of office, above corruption—and from these we might have obtained the most authentic intelligence. "The Convention," says Cato, "have exceeded the authority given to them"—"they have transmitted *a new political fabric* to Congress, fundamentally different from the old"— "which consolidates the States into one Government"—"which vests *new* powers, not in Congress, but in an Assembly, Senate, and President, *not known in the Articles of Confederation.*" How truly ridiculous is this charge! Did Cato then suppose, that nothing *new* was to be expected from your Convention? Or had he *pre-determined* that they should *do no good?* Is he such a stickler for our present Constitution, that he wishes no change? Can his eye discern, with joy, the blemishes of the best, while his heart is wedded to the worst system of Government existing in Christendom? What an unhappy affair is it, to be *consolidated into one Government,* to secure our Union, perpetuate our peace, prosperity, and existence as a nation! But, observe Cato's wonderful criterion, "*not known in the Articles of Confederation.*" Our ingenious politician then supposes, that the Convention were deputed, not from a general persuasion of imbecility in the Federal Head; but, merely, to prune off the exuberances of its present power. For, to do any thing, they must either have added to, or have diminished, the present energetic powers of Congress. By Cato's criterion, the first could not have been done; for every *new power* proposed, would have been unknown to the Confederation: and any new power granted, would have made Congress a body politic, *not known in its Articles.* And yet, as Cato says, *he was led to expect,* they might have formed a perfect system, which would have astonished the world. Thus they might have ordained, and *have crammed the* ordination *down our throats* with Cato's visionary army, that Congress should no longer waste the public monies in the publication of their journals, bulls, and recommendations. A few such exertions would have made us perfectly free, mighty and Independent States. Perhaps in time the *Republican*[16] might hold the reins of government—Sidney[17] might become a Judge—the Inspector[18] might peep into some great man's kitchen—the Rough Hewer[19] might become our Chancellor— and even Cato himself enjoy some lucrative office. But let us suppose Cato's meaning to have been mistaken; and that he thinks new powers might have been granted. Where then would he have lodged them? What! with Congress as at present constructed? What! resign all the three powers, legislative, judicial and executive, in the hands of one body of men? Has not the Rough Hewer proved this to be fundamentally wrong? Our jealous Senator now launches from the extreme of distrust to the extreme of temerity. If this is his *own* sense, what ignorance he discovers! If it is the sense of his party, how contemptible is their inconsistency! Let us grant then it were true, that the Convention finding the present system to be *fundamentally* wrong, by exceeding the letter of their instructions, have merited our generous applause; what has this to do with the merit or demerit of the Constitution itself?

1. On 17 October the printer of the *Daily Advertiser* noted that "Curtius" was received and that it would appear "as soon as possible." "Curtius" replies to "Cato" II, *New York Journal*, 11 October (above).

2. "Curtius" varied the lines from Joseph Addison's *Cato. A Tragedy* that "Cato" II used as an epigraph (*New York Journal*, 11 October, above).

3. Plutarch states, in his life of Solon, the lawgiver, that "Amongst his [Solon's] other laws, one is very peculiar and surprising, which disfranchises all who stand neuter in a sedition; for it seems he would not have any one remain insensible and regardless of the public good, and securing his private affairs, glory that he has no feeling of the distempers of his country; but at once join with the good party and those that have the right upon their side, assist and venture with them, rather than keep out of harm's way and watch who would get the better" (*The Lives of the Noble Grecians and Romans* [New York: Modern Library Edition, 1932], 108–9). This edition of Plutarch was translated by John Dryden and revised by Arthur Hugh Clough.

4. This reference has not been identified, but the Abbé Guillaume Thomas François Raynal (1713–1796), French historian and philosopher, gave his ideas about aristocratic government in his most famous work—*A Philosophical and Political History of the Settlements and Trade of the Europeans in the East and West Indies* (6 vols., Edinburgh, 1782. This work was first printed in French in Amsterdam in 1770.). In Volume VI, Book XIX, Raynal stated that "The [British] government is formed between absolute monarchy, which is tyranny; democracy, which leads to anarchy; and aristocracy, which, fluctuating between one and the other, falls into the errors of both" (p. 140). He also stated that "The government of Venice would be the best of all governments, if an aristocracy were not, perhaps, the worst" (p. 149).

5. "Cato" I, *New York Journal*, 27 September (above).

6. "Cæsar" I–II, *Daily Advertiser*, 1, 17 October (both above).

7. For example, see the references to the petitions supporting the Constitution signed by more than 4,000 inhabitants of the city and county of Philadelphia in RCS:Pa., 62, 64, 64–65, 130, 134, 137–38. See also the reference to "a very great concourse of people" who attended the 6 October public meeting in Philadelphia at which Pennsylvania Constitutional Convention delegate James Wilson delivered an important speech praising and defending the Constitution (CC:134).

8. George Washington, a Virginia delegate to the Constitutional Convention, who signed the Constitution.

9. Benjamin Franklin, a Pennsylvania delegate to the Constitutional Convention, who signed the Constitution.

10. Possibly William Samuel Johnson, a lawyer and a Connecticut delegate to the Constitutional Convention, who signed the Constitution. A devout Anglican, Johnson had just become president of the Anglican-affiliated Columbia College in New York City.

11. In 1767 and 1768 John Dickinson, a Delaware delegate to the Constitutional Convention and a signer of the Constitution, published, under the signature "A Farmer," a series of twelve newspaper essays, attacking British imperial policy that also appeared as a pamphlet entitled *Letters from a Farmer in Pennsylvania to the Inhabitants of the British Colonies.*

12. Alexander Hamilton used the pseudonym "Phocion" while publishing two pamphlets in 1784. (See "Inspector" I, *New York Journal*, 20 September, note 3, above.)

13. Charles and Charles Cotesworth Pinckney, South Carolina delegates to the Constitutional Convention, who signed the Constitution.

14. Robert Yates, a New York delegate to the Constitutional Convention, who left the Convention on 10 July, never to return. He opposed the Constitution. Yates was a justice of the Supreme Court from 1777 to 1798, serving as chief justice beginning in 1790.

15. John Lansing, Jr., a New York delegate to the Constitutional Convention, who also left the Convention on 10 July, never to return. He also opposed the Constitution. Lansing was Albany's mayor from 1786 to 1790.

16. Governor George Clinton.

17. Abraham Yates, Jr., used this as a pseudonym.

18. See "Inspector" I, *New York Journal*, 20 September (above). "Inspector" has not been identified.

19. Abraham Yates, Jr., used this as a pseudonym.

New York Journal, 18 October 1787

☞ The Editor, having been obliged to omit a number of *PIECES*, &c. last week—and from a further consideration, of the expediency, in a *free* and *independent* country, of transmitting to the public cool and well written discussions on both sides of a subject that is closely connected with that freedom and independence—has judged it his duty, this week, to present his generous patrons, and the public, with a *JOURNAL EXTRAORDINARY.*—It was his intention to have subjoined to the *Centinel* the Address of Mr. *WILSON*, to his fellow citizens assembled at Philadelphia, which was intended as a refutation to the objections of the *Centinel* (and other writers) to the fœderal constitution—but, as a *REPLY* to Mr. *WILSON* is expected, it was thought best that they should both be inserted together in the same paper.—Accounts from the Indian country, which, however, are not of a very interesting nature, and "A SLAVE,"[1] from a correspondent, are unavoidably omitted.—Fortunately there is a dearth of news this week—for the few paragraphs prepared for this paper have also given place to more important political animadversions.

☞ *CENTINEL, CÆSAR, RESOLVE* of *CONGRESS*, of the 11th inst. *SIDNEY*,[2] &c. see Journal Extraordinary.

1. See "A Slave," *New York Journal*, 25 October (below).

2. See "Cæsar" I, *Daily Advertiser*, 1 October (above); and "Sidney," *New York Journal*, 18 October (extraordinary) (below). See also "New York Reprinting of the Centinel Essays," 17 October 1787–12 April 1788 (above). The congressional resolution of 11 October concerned the congressional requisition for 1787. For this resolution, see JCC, XXXIII, 649–58. This resolution was printed as a broadside (Evans 20763).

Brutus I
New York Journal, 18 October 1787[1]

Sixteen essays signed "Brutus" were published (in eighteen installments) in the *New York Journal* between 18 October 1787 and 10 April 1788. They were not reprinted in New York, but were reprinted in the newspapers of just six towns in four states (N.H., Mass., R.I., and Pa.). Responses to "Brutus" also appeared in towns where the essays were not reprinted. They were circulated and were read in a number of other towns. (For the circulation of "Brutus" outside New York, see CC:178, p. 411, and RCS:Mass. 172–73.)

The authorship of the "Brutus" essays is uncertain. Contemporaries of "Brutus" and scholars since then have suggested different authors. Hugh Hughes, an active New York Antifederalist polemicist, believed that Abraham Yates, Jr., wrote the essays (to Charles Tillinghast, 28 November, below). William Shippen, Jr., a Philadelphia Antifederalist, heard that "Brutus" was either Richard Henry Lee, a Virginia delegate to Congress, or John Jay (to Thomas Lee Shippen, 22 November, RCS:Pa., 288). An anonymous writer in the *Massachusetts Gazette*, 4 January 1788, declared that "Brutus" was "the anti-federal G——r of a sister state" (i.e., George Clinton) (RCS:Mass., 615).

Late in the nineteenth century, editor-bibliographer Paul Leicester Ford first concluded that Thomas Tredwell of Suffolk County, N.Y., was "Brutus" because Tredwell was known to have used that pseudonym in 1789. Ford, however, later changed his mind in favor of Robert Yates, although he offered no proof (*Pamphlets*, 117, 424). In 1981 Herbert J. Storing, in a comprehensive compilation of Antifederalist writings, declared that the considerable legal knowledge displayed in the "Brutus" essays "argues rather in favor of Yates' authorship" since he was a lawyer and a judge (*The Complete Anti-Federalist*, II, 363n). Most scholars have accepted Robert Yates as the author.

Morton Borden, however, has argued that Robert Yates was not "Brutus," but he has not named another author (*The Antifederalist Papers* [n.p., 1965], 42). William Jeffrey, Jr., published the sixteen "Brutus" essays and suggested that the author was possibly Melancton Smith, a merchant. Jeffrey recognized similarities between the "Brutus" essays and a pamphlet signed "A Plebeian" (17 April 1788, III below, and CC:689), which he believed to have been written by Smith and was published shortly after the last "Brutus" essay appeared. (See "The Letters of 'Brutus'—a Neglected Element in the Ratification Campaign of 1787–88," *University of Cincinnati Law Review*, XL [1971], 644–46.)

A letter that Smith wrote to Abraham Yates, Jr., on 23 January 1788, lends credence to the belief that Smith was "Brutus." In this letter, Smith requested that both Yates and Samuel Jones, another Antifederalist leader, provide him with their "observations" on the Constitution, "especially on the Judicial powers of it." Smith believed that the judicial powers "*clinch*" all the other powers of the Constitution (below. Yates had been chairman of the committee that drafted the state constitution in 1777; Jones, a lawyer, and Richard Varick were in the midst of codifying the laws of New York which they published in 1789.). "Brutus" XI–XV, published between 31 January and 20 March, expressed great concern about the creation of an uncontrollable federal judiciary.

The "Brutus" essays are among the finest Antifederalist writings on the Constitution. Throughout his essays, "Brutus" attacked the Constitution on several grounds: creating a dangerous consolidated government that would destroy the state governments (I, V, VI, XV); omitting a bill of rights that was needed to protect civil liberties (II, IX); providing inadequate representation in Congress (III–IV); giving Congress excessive powers, particularly over taxation and the military (V–X); creating an uncontrollable federal judiciary (XI–XV); and failing to separate the legislative, executive, and judicial branches of government (XVI).

Recognizing that "Brutus" was a formidable foe, supporters of the Constitution in New York responded quickly and sharply. Two days after "Brutus" I appeared, "a Man of No Party" noted that "*Brutus* may worry his antagonist, as he is *long-breathed*; but there is no immediate alarm from his '*weak efforts*' — to use his own happy and judicious expression" (*Daily Advertiser*, 20 October, Mfm:N.Y.). On 21 October James Madison declared that "a new Combatant, . . . with considerable address & plausibility, strikes at the foundation" of the new government (to Edmund Randolph, below, under a grouping of documents, dated 21–28 October). Although Alexander Hamilton ("Publius") did not name "Brutus" in *The Federalist* 1, *Independent Journal*, 27 October (below), he evidently had him in mind when he charged that certain Antifederalists advocated the idea of separate confederacies (see note 4, below). "Curtius" III maintained that "Brutus's" "mandates" would never "dissolve a union dictated by necessity and safety, supported by the dearest ties of national amity, and founded in principles, the propriety of which the experience of ages has demonstrated" (*Daily Advertiser*, 3 November [supplement], below). "Examiner" III (Charles McKnight) criticized "Brutus" "for giving sophistry the air of logical justness and argumentative precision" (*New York Journal*, 19 December, below). For other New York-based criticisms of "Brutus," see "Examiner" IV, *New York Journal*, 24 December; and "Curtiopolis," *Daily Advertiser*, 18 January 1788, both below.

A widely circulated response and criticism of "Brutus" was published in Philadelphia on 8 November by "A Citizen of Philadelphia" (Pelatiah Webster) in a twenty-three-page pamphlet entitled *The Weaknesses of Brutus Exposed . . .* (CC:244. This writer was responding to "Brutus" I which was reprinted in the Philadelphia *Pennsylvania Packet* on 26 October.). "A Citizen of Philadelphia" said that the "sentiments" of "Brutus" were "not only unsound, but wild and chimerical; the dreary fears and apprehensions, altogether groundless; and the whole tendency of the piece, in this important crisis of our politics, very hurtful." He then proceeded to answer "Brutus" in detail, giving numerous reasons why America needed a strong, energetic government. The first twenty pages of "A Citizen of Philadelphia" were reprinted in the *Daily Advertiser*, 20, 23, and 26 November, and 1 December. The *Advertiser* promised to continue publication but failed to do so. For additional criticisms and for defenses of "Brutus" outside New York state, see CC:178, p. 412.

In New York, "Brutus" was praised and defended by "Cato" V, *New York Journal*, 22 November, and an anonymous writer in the *Albany Gazette*, 20 December (both below). Rather than discussing the question of the small number of representatives in Congress, "Cato" referred his readers to "Brutus" who had discussed the issue "so ably and fully" in numbers III–IV. The writer in the *Albany Gazette* stated that "Publius," "Brutus," and "Cato" merited "the plaudits of all"; they were the "foremost" writers on the Constitution.

To the CITIZENS *of the* STATE *of* NEW-YORK.

When the public is called to investigate and decide upon a question in which not only the present members of the community are deeply interested, but upon which the happiness and misery of generations yet unborn is in great measure suspended, the benevolent mind cannot help feeling itself peculiarly interested in the result.

In this situation, I trust the feeble efforts of an individual, to lead the minds of the people to a wise and prudent determination, cannot fail of being acceptable to the candid and dispassionate part of the community. Encouraged by this consideration, I have been induced to offer my thoughts upon the present important crisis of our public affairs.

Perhaps this country never saw so critical a period in their political concerns. We have felt the feebleness of the ties by which these United-States are held together, and the want of sufficient energy in our present confederation, to manage, in some instances, our general concerns. Various expedients have been proposed to remedy these evils, but none have succeeded. At length a Convention of the states has been assembled, they have formed a constitution which will now, probably, be submitted to the people to ratify or reject, who are the fountain of all power, to whom alone it of right belongs to make or unmake constitutions, or forms of government, at their pleasure. The most important question that was ever proposed to your decision, or to the decision of any people under heaven, is before you, and you are to decide upon it by men of your own election, chosen specially for this purpose. If the constitution, offered to your acceptance, be a wise one, calculated to preserve the invaluable blessings of liberty, to secure the inestimable rights of mankind, and promote human happiness, then, if you accept it, you will lay a lasting foundation of happiness for millions yet unborn; generations to come will rise up and call you blessed.[2] You may rejoice in the prospects of this vast extended continent becoming filled with freemen, who will assert the dignity of human nature. You may solace yourselves with the idea, that society, in this favoured land, will fast advance to the highest point of perfection; the human mind will expand in knowledge and virtue, and the golden age be, in some measure, realised. But if, on the other hand, this form of government contains principles that will lead to the subversion of liberty—if it tends to establish a despotism, or, what is worse, a tyrannic aristocracy; then, if you adopt it, this only remaining assylum for liberty will be shut up, and posterity will execrate your memory.[3]

Momentous then is the question you have to determine, and you are called upon by every motive which should influence a noble and virtuous mind, to examine it well, and to make up a wise judgment. It is insisted, indeed, that this constitution must be received, be it ever so imperfect. If it has its defects, it is said, they can be best amended when they are experienced. But remember, when the people once part with power, they can seldom or never resume it again but by force. Many instances can be produced in which the people have voluntarily increased the powers of their rulers; but few, if any, in which rulers have willingly abridged their authority. This is a sufficient reason to induce you to be careful, in the first instance, how you deposit the powers of government.

With these few introductory remarks, I shall proceed to a consideration of this constitution.

The first question that presents itself on the subject is, whether a confederated government be the best for the United States or not? Or in other words, whether the thirteen United States should be reduced to one great republic, governed by one legislature, and under the direction of one executive and judicial; or whether they should continue thirteen confederated republics, under the direction and controul of a supreme federal head for certain defined national purposes only?[4]

This enquiry is important, because, although the government reported by the convention does not go to a perfect and entire consolidation, yet it approaches so near to it, that it must, if executed, certainly and infallibly terminate in it.

This government is to possess absolute and uncontroulable power, legislative, executive and judicial, with respect to every object to which it extends for by, the last clause of section 8th, article 1st, it is declared "that the Congress shall have power to make all laws which shall be necessary and proper for carrying into execution the foregoing powers, and all other powers vested by this constitution, in the government of the United States; or in any department or office thereof." And by the 6th article, it is declared "that this constitution, and the laws of the United States, which shall be made in pursuance thereof, and the treaties made, or which shall be made, under the authority of the United States, shall be the supreme law of the land; and the judges in every state shall be bound thereby, any thing in the constitution, or law of any state to the contrary notwithstanding." It appears from these articles that there is no need of any intervention of the state governments, between the Congress and the people, to execute any one power vested in the general government, and that the constitution and laws of every state are nullified and declared void, so far as they are or shall be inconsistent with this constitution, or the laws made in pursuance of it, or with treaties made under the authority of the United States.—The government then, so far as it extends, is a complete one, and not a confederation. It is as much one complete government as that of New-York or Massachusetts, has as absolute and perfect powers to make and execute all laws, to appoint officers, institute courts, declare offences, and annex penalties, with respect to every object to which it extends, as any other in the world. So far therefore as its powers reach, all ideas of confederation are given up and lost. It is true this government is limited to certain objects, or to speak more properly, some small degree of power is still left to the states, but a little attention to the powers vested in the general government, will convince every candid man, that if it is capable of being executed, all that is reserved for the individual states must very soon be annihilated, except so far as they are barely necessary to the organization of the general government. The powers of the general legislature extend to every case that is of the least importance—there is nothing valuable to human nature, nothing dear to freemen, but what is within its power. It has authority to make laws which will affect the lives, the liberty, and property of every man in the United States; nor can the constitution or laws of any state, in any way prevent or impede the full and complete execution of every power given. The legislative power is competent to lay taxes, duties, imposts, and excises;—there is no limitation to this power, unless it be said that the clause which directs the use to which those taxes, and duties shall be applied, may be said to be a limitation: but this is no restriction of the power at all, for by this clause they are to be applied to pay the debts and provide for the common defence and general welfare of the United States; but the legislature have authority to contract debts at their discretion; they are the sole judges of what is necessary to provide for the common defence, and they only are to determine what is for the general welfare: this power therefore is neither more nor less, than a power to lay and collect taxes, imposts, and excises, at their pleasure; not only the power to lay taxes unlimited, as to the amount they may require, but it is perfect and absolute to raise them in any mode they please. No state legislature, or any power in the state governments, have any more to do in carrying this into effect, than the authority of one state has to do with that of another. In the business therefore of laying and collecting taxes, the idea of confederation is totally lost, and that of one entire republic is embraced. It is proper here to remark, that the authority to lay and collect taxes is the most important of any power that can be granted; it connects with it almost all other powers, or at least will in process of time draw all other after it; it is the great mean of protection, security, and defence, in a good government, and the great engine of oppression and tyranny in a bad one. This cannot fail of being the case, if we consider the contracted limits which are set by this constitution, to the late governments, on this article of raising money. No state can emit paper money—lay any duties, or imposts, on imports, or exports, but by consent of the Congress; and then the net produce shall be for the benefit of the United States: the only mean therefore left, for any state to support its government and discharge its debts, is by direct taxation; and the United States have also power to lay and collect taxes, in any way they please. Every one who has thought on the subject, must be convinced that but small sums of money can be collected in any country, by direct taxes, when the fœderal government begins to exercise the right of taxation in all its parts, the legislatures of the several states will find it impossible to raise monies to support their governments. Without money they cannot be supported, and they must dwindle away, and, as before observed, their powers absorbed in that of the general government.

It might be here shewn, that the power in the federal legislative, to raise and support armies at pleasure, as well in peace as in war, and their controul over the militia, tend, not only to a consolidation of the government, but the destruction of liberty.—I shall not, however, dwell upon these, as a few observations upon the judicial power of this government, in addition to the preceding, will fully evince the truth of the position.

The judicial power of the United States is to be vested in a supreme court, and in such inferior courts as Congress may from time to time ordain and establish. The powers of these courts are very extensive; their jurisdiction comprehends all civil causes, except such as arise between citizens of the same state; and it extends to all cases in law and equity arising under the constitution. One inferior court must be established, I presume, in each state, at least, with the necessary executive officers appendant thereto. It is easy to see, that in the common course of things, these courts will eclipse the dignity, and take away from the respectability, of the state courts. These courts will be, in themselves, totally independent of the states, deriving their authority from the United States, and receiving from them fixed salaries; and in the course of human events it is to be expected, that they will swallow up all the powers of the courts in the respective states.

How far the clause in the 8th section of the 1st article may operate to do away all idea of confederated states, and to effect an entire consolidation of the whole into one general government, it is impossible to say. The powers given by this article are very general and comprehensive, and it may receive a construction to justify the passing almost any law. A power to make all laws, which shall be *necessary and proper*, for carrying into execution, all powers vested by the constitution in the government of the United States, or any department or officer thereof, is a power very comprehensive and definite, and may, for ought I know, be exercised in such manner as entirely to abolish the state legislatures. Suppose the legislature of a state should pass a law to raise money to support their government and pay the state debt, may the Congress repeal this law, because it may prevent the collection of a tax which they may think proper and necessary to lay, to provide for the general welfare of the United States? For all laws made, in pursuance of this constitution, are the supreme law of the land, and the judges in every state shall be bound thereby, any thing in the constitution or laws of the different states to the contrary notwithstanding.—By such a law, the government of a particular state might be overturned at one stroke, and thereby be deprived of every means of its support.

It is not meant, by stating this case, to insinuate that the constitution would warrant a law of this kind; or unnecessarily to alarm the fears of the people, by suggesting, that the federal legislature would be more likely to pass the limits assigned them by the constitution, than that of an individual state, further than they are less responsible to the people. But what is meant is, that the legislature of the United States are vested with the great and uncontroulable powers, of laying and collecting taxes, duties, imposts, and excises; of regulating trade, raising and supporting armies, organizing, arming, and disciplining the militia, instituting courts, and other general powers. And are by this clause invested with the power of making all laws, *proper and necessary*, for carrying all these into execution; and they may so exercise this power as entirely to annihilate all the state governments, and reduce this country to one single government. And if they may do it, it is pretty certain they will; for it will be found that the power retained by individual states, small as it is, will be a clog upon the wheels of the government of the United States; the latter therefore will be naturally inclined to remove it out of the way. Besides, it is a truth confirmed by the unerring experience of ages, that every man, and every body of men, invested with power, are ever disposed to increase it, and to acquire a superiority over every thing that stands in their way. This disposition, which is implanted in human nature, will operate in the federal legislature to lessen and ultimately to subvert the state authority, and having such advantages, will most certainly succeed, if the federal government succeeds at all. It must be very evident then, that what this constitution wants of being a complete consolidation of the several parts of the union into one complete government, possessed of perfect legislative, judicial, and executive powers, to all intents and purposes, it will necessarily acquire in its exercise and operation.

Let us now proceed to enquire, as I at first proposed, whether it be best the thirteen United States should be reduced to one great republic, or not? It is here taken for granted, that all agree in this, that whatever government we adopt, it ought to be a free one; that it should be so framed as to secure the liberty of the citizens of America, and such an one as to admit of a full, fair, and equal representation of the people. The question then will be, whether a government thus constituted, and founded on such principles, is practicable, and can be exercised over the whole United States, reduced into one state?

If respect is to be paid to the opinion of the greatest and wisest men who have ever thought or wrote on the science of government, we shall be constrained to conclude, that a free republic cannot succeed over a country of such immense extent, containing such a number of inhabitants, and these encreasing in such rapid progression as that of the whole United States. Among the many illustrious authorities which might be produced to this point, I shall content myself with quoting only two. The one is the baron de Montesquieu, spirit of laws, chap. xvi. vol. 1. "It is natural to a republic to have only a small territory, otherwise it cannot long subsist. In a large republic there are men of large fortunes, and consequently of less moderation; there are trusts too great to be placed in any single subject; he has interest of his own; he soon begins to think that he may be happy, great and glorious, by oppressing his fellow citizens; and that he may raise himself to grandeur on the ruins of his country. In a large republic, the public good is sacrificed to a thousand views; it is subordinate to exceptions, and depends on accidents. In a small one, the interest of the public is easier perceived, better understood, and more within the reach of every citizen; abuses are of less extent, and of course are less protected."[5] Of the same opinion is the marquis Beccarari.[6]

History furnishes no example of a free republic, any thing like the extent of the United States. The Grecian republics were of small extent; so also was that of the Romans. Both of these, it is true, in process of time, extended their conquests over large territories of country; and the consequence was, that their governments were changed from that of free governments to those of the most tyrannical that ever existed in the world.

Not only the opinion of the greatest men, and the experience of mankind, are against the idea of an extensive republic, but a variety of reasons may be drawn from the reason and nature of things, against it.

In every government, the will of the sovereign is the law. In despotic governments, the supreme authority being lodged in one, his will is law, and can be as easily expressed to a large extensive territory as to a small one. In a pure democracy the people are the sovereign, and their will is declared by themselves; for this purpose they must all come together to deliberate, and decide. This kind of government cannot be exercised, therefore, over a country of any considerable extent; it must be confined to a single city, or at least limited to such bounds as that the people can conveniently assemble, be able to debate, understand the subject submitted to them, and declare their opinion concerning it.

In a free republic, although all laws are derived from the consent of the people, yet the people do not declare their consent by themselves in person, but by representatives, chosen by them, who are supposed to know the minds of their constituents, and to be possessed of integrity to declare this mind.

In every free government, the people must give their assent to the laws by which they are governed. This is the true criterion between a free government and an arbitrary one. The former are ruled by the will of the whole, expressed in any manner they may agree upon; the latter by the will of one, or a few. If the people are to give their assent to the laws, by persons chosen and appointed by them, the manner of the choice and the number chosen, must be such, as to possess, be disposed, and consequently qualified to declare the sentiments of the people; for if they do not know, or are not disposed to speak the sentiments of the people, the people do not govern, but the sovereignty is in a few. Now, in a large extended country, it is impossible to have a representation, possessing the sentiments, and of integrity, to declare the minds of the people, without having it so numerous and unwieldly, as to be subject in great measure to the inconveniency of a democratic government.

The territory of the United States is of vast extent; it now contains near three millions of souls, and is capable of containing much more than ten times that number. Is it practicable for a country, so large and so numerous as they will soon become, to elect a representation, that will speak their sentiments, without their becoming so numerous as to be incapable of transacting public business? It certainly is not.

In a republic, the manners, sentiments, and interests of the people should be similar. If this be not the case, there will be a constant clashing of opinions; and the representatives of one part will be continually striving against those of the other. This will retard the operations of government, and prevent such conclusions as will promote the public good. If we apply this remark to the condition of the United States, we shall be convinced that it forbids that we should be one government. The United States includes a variety of climates. The productions of the different parts of the union are very variant, and their interests, of consequence, diverse. Their manners and habits differ as much as their climates and productions; and their sentiments are by no means coincident. The laws and customs of the several states are, in many respects, very diverse, and in some opposite; each would be in favor of its own interests and customs, and, of consequence, a legislature, formed of representatives from the respective parts, would not only be too numerous to act with any care or decision, but would be composed of such heterogenous and discordant principles, as would constantly be contending with each other.

The laws cannot be executed in a republic, of an extent equal to that of the United States, with promptitude.

The magistrates in every government must be supported in the execution of the laws, either by an armed force, maintained at the public expence for that purpose; or by the people turning out to aid the magistrate upon his command, in case of resistance.

In despotic governments, as well as in all the monarchies of Europe, standing armies are kept up to execute the commands of the prince or the magistrate, and are employed for this purpose when occasion requires: But they have always proved the destruction of liberty, and is abhorrent to the spirit of a free republic. In England, where they depend upon the parliament for their annual support, they have always been complained of as oppressive and unconstitutional, and are seldom employed in executing of the laws; never except on extraordinary occasions, and then under the direction of a civil magistrate.

A free republic will never keep a standing army to execute its laws. It must depend upon the support of its citizens. But when a government is to receive its support from the aid of the citizens, it must be so constructed as to have the confidence, respect, and affection of the people. Men who, upon the call of the magistrate, offer themselves to execute the laws, are influenced to do it either by affection to the government, or from fear; where a standing army is at hand to punish offenders, every man is actuated by the latter principle, and therefore, when the magistrate calls, will obey: but, where this is not the case, the government must rest for its support upon the confidence and respect which the people have for their government and laws. The body of the people being attached, the government will always be sufficient to support and execute its laws, and to operate upon the fears of any faction which may be opposed to it, not only to prevent an opposition to the execution of the laws themselves, but also to compel the most of them to aid the magistrate; but the people will not be likely to have such confidence in their rulers, in a republic so extensive as the United States, as necessary for these purposes. The confidence which the people have in their rulers, in a free republic, arises from their knowing them, from their being responsible to them for their conduct, and from the power they have of displacing them when they misbehave: but in a republic of the extent of this continent, the people in general would be acquainted with very few of their rulers: the people at large would know little of their proceedings, and it would be extremely difficult to change them. The people in Georgia and New-Hampshire would not know one another's mind, and therefore could not act in concert to enable them to effect a general change of representatives. The different parts of so extensive a country could not possibly be made acquainted with the conduct of their representatives, nor be informed of the reasons upon which measures were founded. The consequence will be, they will have no confidence in their legislature, suspect them of ambitious views, be jealous of every measure they adopt, and will not support the laws they pass. Hence the government will be nerveless and inefficient, and no way will be left to render it otherwise, but by establishing an armed force to execute the laws at the point of the bayonet— a government of all others the most to be dreaded.

In a republic of such vast extent as the United-States, the legislature cannot attend to the various concerns and wants of its different parts. It cannot be sufficiently numerous to be acquainted with the local condition and wants of the different districts, and if it could, it is impossible it should have sufficient time to attend to and provide for all the variety of cases of this nature, that would be continually arising.

In so extensive a republic, the great officers of government would soon become above the controul of the people, and abuse their power to the purpose of aggrandizing themselves, and oppressing them. The trust committed to the executive offices, in a country of the extent of the United-States, must be various and of magnitude. The command of all the troops and navy of the republic, the appointment of officers, the power of pardoning offences, the collecting of all the public revenues, and the power of expending them, with a number of other powers, must be lodged and exercised in every state, in the hands of a few. When these are attended with great honor and emolument, as they always will be in large states, so as greatly to interest men to pursue them, and to be proper objects for ambitious and designing men, such men will be ever restless in their pursuit after them. They will use the power, when they have acquired it, to the purposes of gratifying their own interest and ambition, and it is scarcely possible, in a very large republic, to call them to account for their misconduct, or to prevent their abuse of power.

These are some of the reasons by which it appears, that a free republic cannot long subsist over a country of the great extent of these states. If then this new constitution is calculated to consolidate the thirteen states into one, as it evidently is, it ought not to be adopted.

Though I am of opinion, that it is a sufficient objection to this government, to reject it, that it creates the whole union into one government, [un]der the form of a republic, yet if this objection was obviated, there are exceptions to it, which are so material and fundamental, that they ought to determine every man, who is a friend to the liberty and happiness of mankind, not to adopt it. ⟨I beg the candid and dispassionate attention of my countrymen while I state these objections—they are such as have obtruded themselves upon my mind upon a careful attention to the matter, and such as I sincerely believe are well founded. There are many objections, of small moment, of which I shall take no notice—perfection is not to be expected in any thing that is the production of man—and if I did not in my conscience believe that this scheme was defective in the fundamental principles—in the foundation upon which a free and equal government must rest—I would hold my peace.⟩[7]

1. Reprinted: *Pennsylvania Packet*, 26 October; Boston *Independent Chronicle*, 22 November; Northampton, Mass., *Hampshire Gazette*, 19, 26 December. See also notes 3 and 7 (below).

2. Luke 1:48. "For he hath regarded the low estate of his handmaiden: for, behold, from henceforth all generations shall call me blessed."

3. This paragraph was reprinted in the *Massachusetts Gazette*, 30 October, and *New Hampshire Recorder*, 18 December (RCS:Mass., 172–73).

4. It was probably this paragraph that made "Brutus" vulnerable to the charge levied by "Publius" in *The Federalist* 1, *Independent Journal*, 27 October, that "Brutus" favored separate confederacies. "Publius" referred to "the perverted ambition of another class of men, who will either hope to aggrandise themselves by the confusions of their country, or will flatter themselves with fairer prospects of elevation from the subdivision of the empire into several partial confederacies, than from its union under one government" (below. See also the last paragraph of *The Federalist* 1 and the internal note thereto.). Four days later the *Pennsylvania Gazette* printed this widely circulated paragraph: "What a variety of methods do the opposers of our new constitution pursue, to prevent the adoption of it. A New York writer, under the signature of BRUTUS, wishes to have three confederacies—that is, three times the officers, and three times the expence of the proposed plan. *If the union is preserved*, it can have nothing to fear from the British Colonies on the North, or the Spanish on the South; *but if it should be divided into three parts*, European politics would soon play off *one* against *another*." In New York, this paragraph was reprinted in the *Daily Advertiser*, 5 November; *Country Journal*, 14 November; and *Albany Gazette*, 15 November, and by 28 November it was reprinted six times outside New York: N.H. (1), Mass. (1), Conn. (1), Md. (1), Va. (1), S.C. (1).

5. Montesquieu, *Spirit of Laws*, I, Book VIII, chapter, XVI, 177.

6. Cesare Bonesana, Marchese di Beccaria, *An Essay on Crimes and Punishments* (3rd edition, London, 1770), chapter 26, "Of the Spirit of Family in States," pp. 92–97. This work was first published in Italian in Livorno (Leghorn) in 1764.

7. The *Pennsylvania Packet*, 26 October, omitted the text in angle brackets in this last paragraph; while Northampton, Mass., *Hampshire Gazette*, 19, 26 December, omitted all of the last paragraph except for the phrases following "the production of man."

Sidney
New York Journal, 18 October 1787 (extraordinary)[1]

"Sidney" published several Antifederalist essays between 18 October and 14 June 1788. In addition to the essay printed here, "Sidney" published four essays in the *Albany Gazette* between 24 January and 13 March 1788. The essay printed here was incorporated, with some changes, into the *Albany Gazette* article of 24 January. "Sidney" (now "Sydney") also published another essay (in two installments) in the *New York Journal* on 13 and 14 June.

The author of the "Sidney" essays was Abraham Yates, Jr. His papers at the New York Public Library contain his handwritten drafts of three of the four essays printed in early 1788. Moreover, one of his contemporaries quickly labeled him as the author of the earliest essay signed "Sidney." On 20 October 1787, "a Man of no Party," commenting upon the essay in the *Daily Advertiser*, noted that "It is a *rough-hewn* performance," clearly a reference to Yates, who, it was well known, had used the pseudonym "Rough Hewer" for several years (Mfm:N.Y. Drafts of some of Yates's early "Rough Hewer" essays are also in his papers at the New York Public Library.). On 8 April 1788, following the publication of the set of four essays, the *Daily Advertiser* reported that "By a gentleman from Albany we are informed, that a prosecution has been commenced by Abraham Yates, jun. against Messrs. Claxton and Babcock, printers of the Federal Herald, for the insertion of sundry pieces in their newspapers, reflecting on the conduct and principles of the author of the *Rough Hewer, Sydney,* &c.! ! !" Yates identified himself as the author of the 13–14 June 1788 essay, when on 15 June he wrote Abraham G. Lansing of Albany from New York City, informing him that the essay was published in "two papers" and that he was sending him ten sets of them. Yates also planned to transmit fifty sets to Poughkeepsie, where the New York Convention was scheduled to meet on 17 June. The sixty sets cost him thirty shillings. Yates also informed Lansing that mistakes in the essays "must be Rectified if they are Reprinted" (III below).

"To take the character of man, from history, he is a creature capable of any thing, the most infernally cruel and horrid when actuated by interest, or what is more powerful than interest, passion, and not in immediate fear of punishment from his fellow creatures; for, damnation out of sight, who would trust such a mischievous monkey with superfluous power?

"*Simia quam Similis turpissimi bestia nobis?*   Ovid.[2]

"The love of power is natural; it is insatiable; it is whetted, not cloyed, by possession. All men possessed of power may be expected to endeavour to prolong it beyond the due time, and to increase it beyond the due bounds; neither of which can be attempted without danger to liberty. Therefore government (by such frail and imperfect creatures as men) is impossible without continual danger to liberty. Yet we find that men in all ages, and nations have shewn an astonishing credulity, in their faithless fellow-creatures; they have hoped against hope; they have believed against the sight of their own eyes."   BURGH.[3]

The discussion, heretofore in favour of the requisitions of Congress of the third of February, 1781, and the 18th April, 1783,[a] for vesting that honorable body with an impost of 5 per cent. &c.[4] (and that called for in 1782)[b] "of one dollar for every hundred acres of land, and a pole tax of one dollar, on all freemen and slaves: and an excise of one eighth of a dollar upon all distilled spiritious liquors," have appeared under the favourable aspect, of a mere regulation, necessary and proper for the satisfaction of the public creditors, and the support of national faith; as if by investing Congress with a revenue, to be collected by officers in their own appointment, and laws of their own making; the public creditors would be the sooner paid, and the national faith the better preserved: but in its progression, it has received another form, we are now soon (perhaps too soon; for we have got into a way of doing business, either in secret or in haste) to be called upon, to change the very principles of our[c] government; contrary to the opinion of the best authors, and to adopt that reported by the Convention, lately assembled at Philadelphia; in which the thirteen states are to be consolidated, so as to become one republic, of upwards of four thousand[d] miles in circumference; Congress invested with legislative and judicial powers, and with it decide whether we shall establish a strong executive; as well as give up an *actual* for a *vertual* representation. The Dutch have tried both: by the one they have entirely lost the right of representation;[e] by the other, they have embarrassed themselves with a Stadtholder[f] (a strong executive) whose tyranny within the space of forty years, has become so intolerable, that the inhabitants to get rid of him, are at this day on the brink of ruin.

(a) See the journals of Congress.
(b) See the circular letters signed Robert Morris, dated the 27th February, and 29th September, 1782.[5]
(c) "Polibius having traced government up to its very origin, explains the principles by which different governments arose

to the summit of their power, and grandeur; and proves, that they sunk to ruin, by a more or less rapid progress, in proportion as they receded more or less from the first principles on which they were originally founded."   MONTAGUE.[6]

"When the efficacy of government, goes from where the constitution has placed it, into hands which have no right to it, that state is far gone to ruin."   BURGH.[7]

(d) "Political societies (says the Marquis De Baccaria) have their limits circumscribed, which they cannot exceed without disturbing their œconomy. An overgrown republic, can only be saved from despotism, by subdividing it into a number of confederated republics."[8]

"It is natural for a republic (says Montesquieu) to have only a small territory; otherwise it cannot long subsist. In a large republic, there are men of large fortunes, and consequently of less moderation: there are trusts too great to be placed in any single subject; he has interest of his own; he soon begins to think that he may be happy, great, and glorious, by oppressing his fellow citizens; and that he may raise himself to grandeur on the ruins of his country. In a large republic, the public good is sacrificed to a thousand views; it is subordinate to exceptions, and depends on accidents: in a small one, the interests of the public is easier perceived, better understood, and more within the reach of every citizen; abuses have a less extent, and of course are less protected."[9]

(e) "The magistrates of a certain city in Holland, so ordered the business, that the people in a general assembly gave up the right of election, since which time, the senators have filled up all in their own body; and this example has been followed by all the other towns in the provinces." See Bowen's system of geography, 547–549. 27 universal history 342–343.[10]

(f) "This affair [i.e., office] in a manner supercedes the constitution. The stadtholder is president of the states of every province, and such is his power, and influence, that he can change the deputies, magistrates, and officers, in every province or city: by this he has the moulding of the assembly of the states general, though he has no voice in it; in short, though he has not the title, he has more real power and authority than some kings."   Guthrie 481.[11]

1. Reprinted: *Massachusetts Gazette*, 13 November. On 11 October the editor of the *New York Journal* announced that he had intended to publish "Sidney" (and some other items) in this day's *Journal*, but that he had to postpone them to the following week because "*many* PIECES *of the first importance*" had intervened. On 18 October the editor again told his readers that the publication of "Sidney" was delayed but that it would appear in an extraordinary issue of the *Journal* for that day (above).

2. Latin: "How similar to us is the monkey, a very ugly beast." The phrase is attributed to Quintus Ennius by Cicero in *De Natura Deorum* (*On the Nature of the Gods*), Book I, section 97.

3. James Burgh, *Political Disquisitions* . . . (reprint ed., 1971; 3 vols., London, 1774–1775), I, Book III, chapter V, 106–7. When "Sidney" incorporated most of this article into the essay of 24 January 1788, he replaced this passage from Burgh with one from another source.

4. For the Imposts of 1781 and 1783, see CDR, 140–41, 146–48.

5. For Superintendent of Finance Robert Morris's circular letters of 9 February and 20 September 1782, see E. James Ferguson et al., eds., *The Papers of Robert Morris, 1781–1784* (9 vols., Pittsburgh, 1973–1999), IV, 191–97; VI, 408.

6. Edward Wortley Montagu, *Reflections on the Rise and Fall of the Ancient Republicks. Adapted to the Present State of Great Britain* (4th ed., London, 1778), 366. The first edition of this work appeared in 1759.

7. Burgh, *Political Disquisitions*, I, General Preface, xx–xxi. Burgh states: "In this volume, for instance, I have endeavoured to shew, that our parliaments are, at present, upon such a foot, as to the inadequate state of representation, the enormous length of their period, and ministerial influence prevailing in them, that their efficiency for the good of the people is nearly annihilated, and the subversion of the constitution, and ruin of the state is (without timely reformation of these abuses) the consequence unavoidably to be expected."

8. Cesare Bonesana, Marchese di Beccaria, *An Essay on Crimes and Punishments* (3rd ed., London, 1770), chapter 26, "Of the Spirit of Family in States," p. 96.

9. *Spirit of Laws*, I, Book VIII, chapter XVI, 177.

10. Emanuel Bowen, *A Complete System of Geography* (London, 1747), I, 547. *The Modern Part of an Universal History, from the Earliest Accounts to the Present Time. Compiled from Original Authors*, Vol. XXVII (London, 1782), 342–43. This edition, printed for C. Bathurst and others between 1779 and 1784, consists of 65 volumes, with volumes 22–65 being the *Modern Part*.

11. William Guthrie, *A New Geographical, Historical, and Commercial Grammar, and Present State of the Several Kingdoms of the World* (2 vols., London, 1776), II, 48. The first edition of this work appeared in 1770.

New York Journal, 18 October 1787 (extraordinary)[1]

How comes it, Mr. PRINTER, that the goddess *Liberty*, lately so much adored in the United States, should now be reprobated under the name of *Anarchy*? Suppose that we were to treat this fair lady Liberty as the Poet advises to treat another lady of much less consequence,

> "Be to her *faults* a little blind,
> Be to her *virtue* very kind."[2]

Perhaps this moderation of temper may arrest the *haste* with which some people would force the new constitution upon us, without suffering amendments to be made or offered, although amendments may be *necessary* to secure our liberties from weak or wicked rulers.

1. The *Journal* noted that this item was "Omitted last Week for want of Room."
2. Matthew Prior, *An English Padlock* (1705). "Be to her Virtues very kind:/Be to her Faults a little blind:/Let all her Ways be unconfin'd:/And clap your PADLOCK—on her Mind." Printed: H. Bunker Wright and Monroe K. Spears, eds., *The Literary Works of Matthew Prior* (2nd ed., 2 vols., Oxford, Eng., 1971), I, 229.

New York Daily Advertiser, 20 October 1787[1]

For fools admire, but men of sense approve.   *Pope.*[2]

Since *Constitution* is the word
    By men so often us'd,
And all it's meaning made absurd,
    By knaves and fools abus'd;

Pray, gentle reader, mark my scheme—
    Imprimis I must shew
What *Constitutions* an't my theme,
    Then item let you know:

'Tis not the *Constitution* nice,
    Which Metaphysics teach,
Of minds compos'd of Good and Vice,
    And strange effects of each:

'Tis not the Body's wondrous mold,
    Descried in every view;
Nor *Constitution* now call'd *old:*—
    I mean the *one* that's *new.*

A plan to govern Thirteen States
    Was erst imperfect found,
But Politicians made debates
    To *constitute* it sound;

These same debates, perus'd by most,
    Are hated or embrac'd,
Or damn'd (oh shocking!) or the boast
    Of all your *men of taste.*

The man whose *looks* bespeak him *wise*
    Protests they are not good,
Though not a sentence meets his eyes
    That well is understood:

[a]With shrug important, and a face
    Denoting thought profound,

He opes the snuff-box, then the case,
  While news-mongers surround.

"Pray, Sir, the Constitution—hah!—
  D'ye think 'twill stand the test?
Our new-form'd government, I say—
  Methinks 'tis not the best.

"The house of—Pshaw—'tis not thing,
  It's power will be too great,
The President will be a King;
  Besides, 'tis intricate."

"How, Sir, not good! beware, I pray,
  To hold the worst of Creeds,
Lest you be deem'd, as well you may,
  A foe to Fed'ral deeds;

"The scheme you must again review,
  Permit me to remark;
For, Sir, the Constitution's new,
  And therefore, Sir, is dark."

To little Critics dark it is:
  It's faults or excellence
Not seen by the sagacious phiz
  Of would-be men of sense.

In vulgar verse, permit a Bard
  His sentiment to tell,
(And Cato must not think it hard)
  He likes the system well;

And if some principle be there,
  That's opposite to mine,
How wise the plan! I still declare,
  What judgment in each line!

What, if my feeble thought can't soar
  It's highest good to find,
Is not a whole Convention's more
  Than one imperfect mind?

Yes, Patriots, by experience taught,
  (Their Country's guardian-guides)
Concert a plan, with wisdom fraught,
  And WASHINGTON presides!

Since he has led the virtuous band,
  They sure have counsel'd best;—

Oh! prosper, heaven, our parent land,
And make her people blest!
October 18*th*, 1787.

(a) With eager eyes and round unthinking face,
He first the Snuff-box open'd, then the Case.   *Pope.*[3]

1. Reprinted: *Pennsylvania Packet*, 29 October; Charleston *Columbian Herald*, 13 December. The editor of the *Daily Advertiser* probably had this item in mind when he announced on 19 October that "A POETICAL PIECE is received and shall have a place."
2. Alexander Pope, *An Essay on Criticism* (London, 1711), line 391.
3. Alexander Pope, *The Rape of the Lock. An Heroi-Comical Poem in Five Canto's* (London, 1714), Canto IV, lines 125–26.

Virginia Delegates to Congress Report on the Prospects of Ratification of the Constitution in New York, 21–28 October 1787

Between 21 and 30 October Virginia delegates to Congress James Madison and Edward Carrington wrote letters that included comments about the Constitution's prospects in New York. The letters were concerned about New York's previous stance on federal issues, the strength of the opposition to the Constitution, and Governor George Clinton's position on the Constitution.

James Madison to Edmund Randolph
New York, 21 October 1787 (excerpt)[1]

. . . The Newspapers in the middle & Northern States begin to teem with controversial publications. The attacks seem to be principally levelled agst. the organization of the Government, and the omission of the provisions contended for in favor of the Press, & Juries &c. A new Combatant[2] however with considerable address & plausibility, strikes at the foundation. He represents the situation of the U.S. to be such as to render any Govt. improper & impracticable which forms the States into one nation & is to operate directly on the people. Judging from the News papers one wd. suppose that the adversaries were the most numerous & the most in earnest. But there is no other evidence that it is the fact. . . .

Edward Carrington to Thomas Jefferson
New York, 23 October 1787 (excerpt)[3]

. . . Some symptoms of opposition have appeared in New York and Pensylvania; in the former, only in individual publications, which are attended with no circumstances evidencing the popular regard; the Governor[4] holds himself in perfect silence, wishing, it is suspected, for a miscarriage, but is not confident enough to commit himself in an open opposition. . . .

James Madison to Thomas Jefferson
New York, 24 October 1787 (excerpt)[5]

. . . There seems to be less agitation in this State than any where. The discussion of the subject seems confined to the newspapers. The principal characters are known to be friendly. The Governour's party which has hitherto been the popular & most numerous one, is supposed to be on the opposite side; but considerable reserve is practised, of which he sets the example. . . .

James Madison to William Short
New York, 24 October 1787 (excerpt)[6]

. . . It is difficult to say what is the prevailing sentiment in this State. The newspapers abound with anonimous publications on both sides, but there is a reserve in the general conversation which is scarcely seen elsewhere. The men of abilities are generally on the side of the Constitution. The Governour whose party is at least a very strong one is considered notwithstanding his reserve to be a decided adversary to it. . . .

Edward Carrington to William Short
New York, 25 October 1787 (excerpts)[7]

. . . in the Middle States appearances are generally for it, but not being in the habits of assembling for public objects, the people have given but few instances of collective declarations. Some Symptoms of opposition have appeared in New York & Pensylvania. . . . in the former some individual publications are exhibitted in the papers, but we have no evidence of their being regarded by the populace—the Men in Office in this State view, with great reluctance, the diminution of State emoluments and consequence—they hold their appointments under an influence which will not, in all probability, serve them upon a more extensive Scale of politics—the Governor is perfectly silent, but, it is suspected wishes the miscarriage of the measure, taking his usual guard against being committed in a fruitless opposition. . . .

James Madison to Edmund Pendleton
New York, 28 October 1787 (excerpt)[8]

. . . This State has long had the character of being antifederal. Whether she will purge herself of it on this occasion, or not, is yet to be ascertained. Most of the respectable characters are zealous on the right side. The party in power is suspected on good grounds to be on the wrong one.[9] . . .

1. RC, Madison Papers, DLC. Printed: CC:182 (longer excerpt); and Rutland, *Madison*, X, 199–200. Marked: "*Private*" by Madison. Randolph (1753–1813), a Williamsburg lawyer and governor of Virginia, had refused to sign the Constitution in the Constitutional Convention, but he voted to ratify it in the Virginia Convention in June 1788.

2. A reference to "Brutus" I, *New York Journal*, 18 October (above).

3. RC, Jefferson Papers, DLC. Printed: CC:185 (longer excerpt); and Boyd, XII, 252–57. Jefferson (1743–1826) was the American minister to France, 1785–89.

4. George Clinton.

5. RC, Jefferson Papers, DLC. Printed: CC:187 (longer excerpts); Boyd, XII, 270–86; and Rutland, *Madison*, 205–20.

6. RC, Short Papers, DLC. Printed: CC:188 (longer excerpt); and Rutland, *Madison*, X, 220–22. Short (1759–1849), a lawyer, was Thomas Jefferson's private secretary at the American legation in Paris, France.

7. RC, Short Papers, DLC. Printed: CC:191 (longer excerpt).

8. RC, Madison Papers, DLC. Printed: CC:205. Marked by Pendleton: "Answd. Jan. 29—88." Pendleton (1721–1803), a Virginia lawyer, was president of Virginia Supreme Court of Appeals and in June 1788 he was president of the Virginia Convention, where he voted to ratify the Constitution.

9. Two days later, Madison wrote Archibald Stuart that "The character of this State has long been antifederal, & is known that a very powerful party continue so" (CC:212).

An Observer
Lansingburgh Northern Centinel, 22 October 1787

Messrs. Printers, With pleasure I perused your Centinel of the 15th inst. No. 22, and was happy in seeing that the citizens of Philadelphia, of the opulent and ancient settlement of Germantown,[1] the inhabitants of the state of New-Hampshire,[2] &c. were so well satisfied with the new federal constitution:—Nor was I less pleased with a piece from the *Independent Gazetteer*, on the federal government, under the signature of *An American Citizen*:[3] There appears much judgment and good sense in this author's observations; and with great propriety he has pointed out the duties, powers, &c. of the intended president and vice-president, under the new recommended government. The comparison he so justly draws between the powers of the king of Britain and the proposed chief magistrate for the United states of America, will undoubtedly quiet the fears and apprehensions of those of our fellow citizens, who were fearful that the powers and dignities of a president-general, would approach too near royalty, and thereby give him too great an influence for an individual to possess under a free republican government. By the observations of the *American Citizen* (and on examination I find them strictly agreeable to the proposed constitution) it fully appears, that the powers to be vested in the intended president, by virtue of his office, are so greatly limited, and the duration thereof for so short a time, that should even a man void of honor, honesty or princple, be introduced to that dignified station (which, from the mode of our choosing him, is by no means probable) we should have very little to fear from him, his powers being so much confined that he is unable to do any thing of consequence, without the concurrrence of two-thirds of the senate, who are, in fact, elected by ourselves, and who, as well as the president, must have resided as citizens among us a time sufficient to, and have arrived at such an age, as will give every one an opportunity of judging whether their honesty and abilities qualify them to fill the important stations, to which they are call'd by the voice of a free and enlightened people. I most ardently wish my fellow citizens would examine critically the powers to be vested in the president, and I am fully satisfied they will then be convinced, that he will not be possessed of any authority, that is not so effectually guarded, as to prevent almost a possibility of his abuse of power; and that the adoption of the proposed federal constitution is our last resort and only hope, to avoid poverty, slavery, and all its concomitant horrors, which must speedily overtake us should we still neglect to put ourselves under a united government of force sufficient to answer the exigencies of our extended and growing empire. On the contrary, should we speedily adopt a government, founded with wisdom and justice on the principles of equal liberty, and of energy competent to the grand and good purposes of our union, he must be short sighted indeed, who cannot foresee the amazing advantages it will be to our country: among the many others, emigrations from the various nations of Europe to these states will, in all probability, be immense, as soon as it is known that we are under a proper established and well regulated government, which will add greatly to our strength as a nation, and put us in a situation to defend ourselves against any enemy who dare attempt to injure or insult us: and our trade must ere long, "under proper and general regulations," which equally affect our widely extended empire, be almost universal; for in our extensive country, possessing all the various climates of Europe, we shall have it in our power, after a few years, to rival the Europeans in almost every product of their several countries; and, in a short time, to equal them in manufactures of many kinds, and probably the period will come when we shall excel in most of them. The settlement of the vast extent of rich and fertile lands within our dominions, which now lies waste, and a proper cultivation of those already settled, will cause a great surplusage of produce in this country, which must of course throw the balance of trade in our favour, to our very great emolument: And should we continue a free and united nation, as it is now in our power to be, by the speedy adoption of a firm general government, in all probability, we shall continue such for many ages, and become the greatest, as well as the most happy and free people that has yet appeared on the face of the earth, and shall receive the blessings of unborn millions, for having amply provided for their happiness, honor and glory.

I cannot omit observing, that the sentiments of the author of a piece also published in your last Centinel, under the signature of *Cincinnatus*,[4] perfectly coincided with my own. The remarks he made appear to me just, and well founded; yet I am sorry he was not more full in giving the reasons why the real friends of America wish a revision of our confederation, as many other forcible and stubborn facts might have been observed, exclusive of those he has noticed, which makes an amendment in our union highly necessary to our welfare and political existence as a nation;—and his piece might have had a greater weight, had he more fully pointed out the numerous and various evils, in addition to those he has mentioned, that we must inevitably suffer as individuals and a people, should we continue, as now, destitute of a government of force sufficient to answer the purposes of our union. I could also wish he had more amply set forth the many and great advantages this country must, and most surely will, enjoy, by adopting a constitution so well calculated, in every point, to preserve equal liberty, and raise to power, opulence and glory, an empire of freedom, which will be an asylum to the oppressed of all nations, and the admiration of the world.

October 18, 1787.

1. On 21 September "a respectable number" of Germantown citizens resolved unanimously that they "do highly approve" the Constitution and supported the calling of a state convention to consider it (*Pennsylvania Packet* and Philadelphia *Independent Gazetteer*, 22 October, RCS:Pa., 134–35). In New York, this widely reprinted report was also printed in the *Daily Advertiser*, 27 September, and summarized in the *Hudson Weekly Gazette*, 4 October.

2. The *Northern Centinel* stated that "Our last papers from New-Hampshire inform, that the people in that state highly approve of the new federal government."

3. The reference is to "An American Citizen" I, Philadelphia *Independent Gazetteer*, 26 September (CC:100–A). See also "New York Reprinting of the Essays of An American Citizen," 6 October–29 November (above).

4. See "Cincinnatus," *Northern Centinel*, 15 October (above).

Cato III
New York Journal, 25 October 1787

For criticisms of "Cato" III, see "Americanus" I, III, and IV, *Daily Advertiser*, 2, 30 November, 5–6 December; and "Curtius" III, *ibid.*, 3 November (supplement) (all below).

"Cato" III was reprinted in the *Daily Advertiser*, 27 October, and *Albany Gazette*, 8 November. On 1 November the *Albany Gazette* had announced that "Cato" III would appear in its next issue.

To the CITIZENS *of the* STATE *of* NEW-YORK.

In the close of my last introductory address,[1] I told you, that my object in future would be to take up this new form of national government, to compare it with the experience and opinions of the most sensible and approved political authors, and to show you that its principles, and the exercise of them will be dangerous to your liberty and happiness.

Although I am conscious that this is an arduous undertaking, yet I will perform it to the best of my ability.

The freedom, equality, and independence which you enjoyed by nature, induced you to consent to a political power. The same principles led you to examine the errors and vices of a British superintendence, to divest yourselves of it, and to reassume a new political shape. It is acknowledged that there are defects in this, and another is tendered to you for acceptance; the great question then, that arises on this new political principle, is, whether it will answer the ends for which it is said to be offered to you, and for which all men engage in political society, to wit, the mutual preservation of their lives, liberties, and estates.[2]

The recital, or premises on which this new form of government is erected, declares a consolidation or union of all the thirteen parts, or states, into one great whole, under the firm of the United States, for all the various and important purposes therein set forth.—But whoever seriously considers the immense extent of territory comprehended within the limits of the United States, together with the variety of its climates, productions, and commerce, the difference of extent, and number of inhabitants in all; the dissimilitude of interest, morals, and policies, in almost every one, will receive it as an intuitive truth, that a consolidated republican form of government therein, can never *form a perfect union, establish justice, insure domestic tranquility, promote the general welfare, and secure the blessings of liberty to you and your posterity*, for to these objects it must be directed: this unkindred legislature therefore, composed of interests opposite and dissimilar in their nature, will in its exercise, emphatically be, like a house divided against itself.[3]

The governments of Europe have taken their limits and form from adventitious circumstances, and nothing can be argued on the motive of agreement from them; but these adventitious political principles, have nevertheless produced effects that have attracted the attention of philosophy, which has established axioms in the science of politics therefrom, as irrefragable as any in Euclid. It is natural, says Montesquieu, *to a republic to have only a small territory, otherwise it cannot long subsist: in a large one, there are men of large fortunes, and consequently of less moderation; there are too great deposits to intrust in the hands of a single subject, an ambitious person soon becomes sensible that he may be happy, great, and glorious by oppressing his fellow citizens, and that he might raise himself to grandeur, on the ruins of his country. In large republics, the public good is sacrificed to a thousand views; in a small one the interest of the public is easily perceived, better understood, and more within the reach of every citizen; abuses have a less extent, and of course are less protected*—he also shews you, that the duration of the republic of Sparta, was owing to its having continued with the same extent of territory after all its wars; and that the ambition of Athens and Lacedemon to command and direct the union, lost them their liberties, and gave them a monarchy.[4]

From this picture, what can you promise yourselves, on the score of consolidation of the United States, into one government—impracticability in the just exercise of it—your freedom insecure—even this form of government limited in its continuance—the employments of your country disposed of to the opulent, to whose contumely you will continually be an object—you must risque much, by indispensibly placing trusts of the greatest magnitude, into the hands of individuals, whose ambition for power, and agrandisement, will oppress and grind you—where, from the vast extent of your territory, and the complication of interests, the science of government will become intricate and perplexed, and too misterious for you to understand, and observe; and by which you are to be conducted into a monarchy, either limited or despotic; the latter, Mr. Locke remarks, *is a government derived from neither nature, nor compact.*[5]

Political liberty, the great Montesquieu again observes, *consists in security, or at least in the opinion we have of security;*[6] and this *security* therefore, or the *opinion*, is best obtained in moderate governments, where the mildness of the laws, and the equality of the manners, beget a confidence in the people, which produces this security, or the opinion. This moderation in governments, depends in a great measure on their limits, connected with their political distribution.

The extent of many of the states in the Union, is at this time, almost too great for the superintendence of a republican form of government, and must one day or other, revolve into more vigorous ones, or by separation be reduced into smaller, and more useful, as well as moderate ones. You have already observed the feeble efforts of Massachusetts against their insurgents;[7] with what difficulty did they quell that insurrection; and is not the province of main at this moment, on the eve of separation from her. The reason of these things is, that for the security of the *property* of the community, in which expressive term Mr. Lock makes life, liberty, and estate, to consist[8]—the wheels of a free republic are necessarily slow in their operation; hence in large free republics, the evil sometimes is not only begun, but almost completed, before they are in a situation to turn the current into a contrary progression: the extremes are also too remote from the usual seat of government, and the laws therefore too feeble to afford protection to all its parts, and insure *domestic tranquility* without the aid of another principle. If, therefore, this state, and that of N. Carolina, had an army under their controul, they never would have lost Vermont, and Frankland, nor the state of Massachusetts suffer an insurrection, or the dismemberment of her fairest district, but the exercise of a principle which would have prevented these things, if we may believe the experience of ages, would have ended in the destruction of their liberties.

Will this consolidated republic, if established, in its exercise beget such confidence and compliance, among the citizens of these states, as to do without the aid of a standing army—I deny that it will.—The mal-contents in each state, who will not be a few, nor the least important, will be exciting factions against it—the fear of a dismemberment of some of its parts, and the necessity to enforce the execution of revenue laws (a fruitful source of oppression) on the extremes and in the other districts of the government, will incidentally, and necessarily require a permanent force, to be kept on foot—will not political security, and even the opinion of it, be extinguished? can mildness and moderation exist in a government, where the primary incident in its exercise must be force? will not violence destroy confidence, and can equality subsist, where the extent, policy, and practice of it, will naturally lead to make odious distinctions among citizens?

The people, who may compose this national legislature from the southern states, in which, from the mildness of the climate, the fertility of the soil, and the value of its productions, wealth is rapidly acquired, and where the same causes naturally lead to luxury, dissipation, and a passion for aristocratic distinctions; where slavery is encouraged, and liberty of course, less respected, and protected; who know not what it is to acquire property by their own toil, nor to œconomise with the savings of industry—will these men therefore be as tenacious of the liberties and interests of the more northern states, where freedom, independence, industry, equality, and frugality, are natural to the climate and soil, as men who are your own citizens, legislating in your own state, under your inspection, and whose manners, and fortunes, bear a more equal resemblance to your own?

It may be suggested, in answer to this, that whoever is a citizen of one state, is a citizen of each, and that therefore he will be as interested in the happiness and interest of all, as the one he is delegated from;

but the argument is fallacious, and, whoever has attended to the history of mankind, and the principles which bind them together as parents, citizens, or men, will readily perceive it. These principles are, in their exercise, like a pebble cast on the calm surface of a river, the circles begin in the center, and are small, active, and forcible, but as they depart from that point, they lose their force, and vanish into calmness.

⟨The strongest principle of union resides within our domestic walls. The ties of the parent exceed that of any other; as we depart from home, the next general principle of union is amongst citizens of the same state, where acquaintance, habits, and fortunes, nourish affection, and attachment; enlarge the circle still further, &, as citizens of different states, though we acknowledge the same national denomination, we lose the ties of acquaintance, habits, and fortunes, and thus, by degrees, we lessen in our attachments, till, at length, we no more than acknowledge a sameness of species.⟩[9] Is it therefore, from certainty like this, reasonable to believe, that inhabitants of Georgia, or New-Hampshire, will have the same obligations towards you as your own, and preside over your lives, liberties, and property, with the same care and attachment? Intuitive reason, answers in the negative.

In the course of my examination of the principles of consolidation of the states into one general government, many other reasons against it have occurred, but I flatter myself, from those herein offered to your consideration, I have convinced you that it is both presumptious and impracticable consistent with your safety. To detain you with further remarks, would be useless—I shall however, continue in my following numbers, to anilise this new government, pursuant to my promise.

1. See "Cato" II, *New York Journal,* 11 October (above).

2. Locke, *Two Treatises,* Book II, chapter IX, section 123, p. 368. Locke stated "And 'tis not without reason, that he [Man] seeks out, and is willing to joyn in Society with others who are already united, or have a mind to unite for the mutual *Preservation* of their Lives, Liberties and Estates, which I call by the general Name, *Property.*"

3. Mark 3:25. "And if a house be divided against itself, that house cannot stand."

4. *Spirit of Laws,* I, Book VIII, chapter XVI, 177–78.

5. *Two Treatises,* Book II, chapter XV, section 172, p. 400. Locke stated that "*Despotical Power* is an Absolute, Arbitrary Power one Man has over another, to take away his Life, whenever he pleases. This is a Power, which neither Nature gives, for it has made no such distinction between one Man and another; nor Compact can convey, for Man not having such an Arbitrary Power over his own Life, cannot give another Man such a Power over it."

6. *Spirit of Laws,* I, Book XI, chapter VI, 222. Montesquieu states that "The political liberty of the subject is a tranquillity of mind arising from the opinion each person has of his safety. In order to have this liberty, it is requisite the government be so constituted as one man need not be afraid of another."

7. The reference is to Shays's Rebellion, 1786–87. See RCS:Mass., xxxviii–xxxix; and CC:18.

8. See note 2, above.

9. The text in angle brackets was quoted by "Americanus" VI, *Daily Advertiser*, 12 January 1788 (below), to illustrate the fact that it would be almost impossible for the central government under the Constitution to annihilate the state governments.

A Republican I: To James Wilson, Esquire
New York Journal, 25 October 1787

"A Republican" I answered the speech James Wilson delivered on 6 October to a Philadelphia public meeting (CC:134). In this essay "A Republican" quoted passages from Wilson's speech and from the Constitution, sometimes adding italics. Wilson's speech, printed in the *Pennsylvania Herald* in its extra issue of 9 October, was first reprinted in New York City in the *Daily Advertiser* on 13 October. (See "New York Reprinting of James Wilson's 6 October Speech Before a Philadelphia Public Meeting," 13–25 October, above.) "A Republican" was reprinted in the Philadelphia *Independent Gazetteer*, 30 October; *Massachusetts Centinel*, 3 November; *Hudson Weekly Gazette*, 8 November; and Providence *United States Chronicle*, 15 November. With the exception of the *Hudson Weekly Gazette*, each of these newspapers reprinted "A Republican" upon request. The person who made his request to the *Massachusetts Centinel* signed himself "Inimicus Tyrannis," while the person addressing the *United States Chronicle* signed himself "A Friend to the Confederation."

On 1 November the *New York Journal* announced that "Republican" II was received but that it would be postponed "for want of room." On 8 November the *Journal* announced that "The REPUBLICAN No. II. *is* again *unavoidably omitted for want of room.*" "A Republican" II was never printed, although an unnumbered essay signed "A Republican" appeared in the *Journal* on 27 December (below).

SIR, In Mr. Child's Daily Advertiser of the 13th inst. a publication appeared, which is said to be a speech delivered by you to the citizens of Philadelphia, and intended to explain and elucidate the principles and arrangements of the constitution formed by the Fœderal Convention for the United States, and submitted to public consideration.— When this performance was announced, as the first authoritative explanation of that system, it was read with avidity—by its advocates, because they were prejudiced in its favor, and possessed the fullest confidence (from your supposed abilities) that the objections raised against it would be refuted—by its opponents, because they were anxious to know what could be alledged in its favor—the former are disappointed and mortified—the latter ridicule the feeble attempt, as leading only to a discovery of the source from which the defects originated; for, from the text and comment it would appear, that you had a principal agency in the business.—Your address is confined to the citizens of a partial district, but the subject affects the happiness of America; it is therefore open to the examination of every citizen, and I shall make no apology for troubling you with the following animadversions.

You have prefaced your refutation (as you term it) of the charges alledged against this new system, by a discrimination between the state constitutions and the one under consideration. To prevent mistakes, I shall take the liberty to recite it in your own words—"When the people established the powers of legislation under their separate governments, they invested their representatives with every right and authority which they did not in explicit terms reserve; and therefore upon every question respecting the jurisdiction of the house of assembly, if the frame of government is silent, the jurisdiction is efficient and complete. But in delegating fœderal powers, another criterion was necessarily introduced, and the congressional authority is to be collected not from tacit implication, but from *the positive grant expressed in the instrument of union.* Hence, you add, it is evident, that in the former case every thing which is not reserved is given, but in the latter, the reverse of the proposition prevails, *and every thing which is not given is reserved.*"

As it is upon the truth of this distinction, which carries with it, at first blush, a degree of plausability, that you rest the defence of this constitution, in omitting a bill of rights, and particularly a stipulation for the security of the freedom of the press, it is proper that it should be carefully examined. Is there any thing in the nature of the two cases that will justify this discrimination? Do they not both depend on compact, and receive their sanction from the people, as the source and origin of all political power? Can the reasonable mind conceive of a compact granting what is not expressed in it, incident to, and necessary to the execution of the power given, or implied under the general terms in which they are expressed? certainly not; and the contrary would suppose, that the power was derived from the rulers, and not from the people—but in both cases the powers conferred will be considered as efficient, as far as the nature of the compact extends. It clearly follows then, that the criterion, you mention, was not *necessarily*, or naturally, *introduced*, and it only remains to examine, whether it depends upon stipulation.

In forming our present confederation, it was declared, "that each state shall retain its sovereignty, freedom, and independence, and every power, jurisdiction, and right, which is not by that confederation expressly delegated to the United States in Congress assembled."[1] This declaration would have been idle and useless, if the position, you state, was founded in fact—Is there any such *stipulation* to be found in this new constitution? there is not—But let us investigate this subject a little farther—let us compare it with the sense of the framers, as *expressed* in the instrument itself—this, perhaps, is the truest test. There are extensive powers of legislation granted to this new government—it would be needless, in me, to enumerate them; but there are also several exceptions made against the exercise of certain powers.—Now, according to your doctrine, unless these powers which are excepted were *expressly granted*; the exceptions would be *"superfluous and absurd."* For brevity sake, I shall instance one of those exceptions only. *"It is provided, that no title of nobility shall be granted by the United States."* Is this power *expressly* given to Congress by the new constitution? if it is not, then the exception must be to guard against an incidental or implied power.—And hence it clearly follows, that the framers of this new government, so far from adopting your construction, as to the origination of congressional power, adopted the very principle that you have laid down with respect to the individual states.

But in order the more fully to evince the fallacy of your observations, I must claim the liberty of quoting some other parts of your address.— You observe, "If indeed a power, similar to that which has been granted for the regulation of commerce, had been granted, *to regulate literary publications*, it would have been as necessary *to stipulate, that the liberty of the press should be preserved inviolate*, as that the impost should be general in its operation." But you assert as a fact, "That the proposed system *possesses no influence whatever upon the press*;" and thence infer, "That it would have been merely nugatory to have introduced a formal declaration upon the subject; nay, that very declaration might be construed to imply, that *some degree of power was given*, since it was undertaken to define its extent." Now it will be proper to enquire, whether the fact, from which you have drawn you inferences, is well founded. Does this constitution possess, as you assert, *no influence whatever upon the press?* Is there not a provision in it, "to secure for a limited time to authors and inventors the exclusive right to their respective *writings* and discoveries." I do not mean to call in question the propriety of this provision, but I would ask, whether under it the press may not be considered subject to the *influence* and controul of this government?—Will it be denied that this power includes in it (in some measure) *that of regulating literary publications?* certainly it cannot, unless we suppose what would be very absurd, "that authors, who are to be secured the exclusive right of their writings, are at the same time to be deprived of the use of the press." This then, being the case, it clearly follows, and you have admitted it, that *a stipulation for preserving inviolate the liberty of the press* was *necessary* and proper.—And hence too it evidently appears, that the *silence*, which is observed on this interesting subject, was not occasioned by the extremely delicate consideration to which you attribute it. To what cause then is the omission, and your attempts to deceive your fellow citizens, to be ascribed?—*The press is the scourge of tyrants and the grand paladium of liberty.*

I shall reserve the remarks I intend to make on the remainder of your speech for future letters, but before I close the present, permit me to ask, whether *the formal declaration, that no title of nobility shall be granted by the United States,* is to be construed to *imply, that some degree of power is given to introduce a nobility*? and whether America (as it would appear you are deep in her councils) among the other great blessings she may derive from the adoption of this new constitution, may expect (by the permission of Congress) to be favored with a foreign or self-created nobility.

New-York, October 19, 1787.

1. "A Republican" quotes Article II of the Articles of Confederation (CDR, 86).

A Slave and A Son of Liberty
New York Journal, 25 October, 8 November 1787

"A Slave" was apparently a response to a satirical Antifederalist piece printed in the Philadelphia *Independent Gazetteer* on 6 October (CC:136) that was reprinted in the *New York Morning Post* and *New York Packet* on 11 and 12 October, respectively. This Antifederalist piece listed thirteen "*blessings*" that could be expected from the Constitution, including the abolition of the liberty of the press and the establishment of a standing army. "A Slave" responded with an alternative list of thirteen "most salutary consequences" to expect from the Constitution.

"A Slave," "unavoidably omitted" from the *New York Journal* of 18 October, was reprinted in whole or in part nine times by 4 December. The entire piece appeared in the *Country Journal,* 31 October; *Massachusetts Gazette,* 2 November; and *New Hampshire Spy,* 6 November. The *Massachusetts Centinel,* 31 October, reprinted only the "salutary consequences." This shortened version was reprinted once each in New Hampshire, Connecticut, and South Carolina, and twice in Massachusetts. The *Centinel* reprinted the "salutary consequences" in combination with the Philadelphia *Independent Gazetteer's* thirteen "blessings."

"A Son of Liberty" responded to "A Slave" by enumerating thirteen "*curses*" that would result from the Constitution. It was reprinted in the Boston *American Herald,* 26 November; *Virginia Independent Chronicle,* 12 December; *New Hampshire Recorder,* 1 January 1788; and Philadelphia *Independent Gazetteer,* 16 June. Because the *New York Journal,* 1 November, announced that "A Son of Liberty" was "unavoidably postponed," the 4 November date is suspect.

A Slave
New York Journal, 25 October 1787

MR. GREENLEAF, I observe we have our doubting, fearful, and procrastinating brethren; those who, in the profundity of their penetration, not from interested motives, but a laudable zeal to serve the public, have discovered, and pronounced the new proposed Fœderal Government to be of the illegitimate and monstrous kind, like Pandora's box, pregnant with every evil, full of design, a fatal tendency, and diametrically repugnant to the true interests, happiness, and safety of the United States.

Whether these are chimeras of the brain or realities the public will determine: I must confess for myself I cannot perceive the danger of adopting it, and most sincerely wish it may speedily take place, fully persuaded that it will be attended with the most salutary consequences; I think I can foresee, under its benign influences,

1. Unity and peace at home.
2. Respect and honour from abroad.
3. The total abolition of paper money.
4. A sufficient specie medium.
5. A full treasury.
6. Public and domestic debts provided for.
7. Credit established.
8. The poor and industrious eased of their present burthensome taxes.
9. Agriculture, navigation, and population encouraged.
10. A well regulated commerce.
11. Navigation act, encouraging our own shipping, and seamen, now rotting, and starving in our harbours, in preference to foreigners.
12. Rebellion, and civil war, not so much as understood.
13. Policy, power, and spirit, to encourage virtue, punish vice, assert our rights, take possession of our territories, prevent encroachments, and repel invasions.

A Son of Liberty
New York Journal, 8 November 1787

Mr. Greenleaf, Having observed in your paper of the 25th ult. that a writer under the signature of *A Slave*, has pointed out a number of advantages or blessings, which, he says, will result from an adoption of the new government, proposed by the Convention:—I have taken the liberty to request, that you will give the following a place in your next paper, it being an enumeration of a *few* of the *curses* which will be entailed on the people of America, by this preposterous and newfangled system, if they are ever so infatuated as to receive it.

1st. A *standing army*, that bane to freedom, and support of tyrants, and their pampered minions; by which almost all the nations of Europe and Asia, have been enslaved.

2d. An arbitrary capitation or poll tax, by which the poor, in general, will pay more than the rich, as they have, commonly, more children, than their wealthy dissipated neighbours.

3d. A suppression of trial by a jury of your peers, in all civil cases, and even in criminal cases, the loss of the trial in the vicinage, where the fact and the credibility of your witnesses are known, and where you can command their attendance without insupportable expence, or inconveniences.

4th. Men of all ranks and conditions, subject to have their houses searched by officers, acting under the sanction of *general warrants*, their private papers seized, and themselves dragged to prison, under various pretences, whenever the fear of their lordly masters shall suggest, that they are plotting mischief against their arbitrary conduct.

5th. Excise laws established, by which our bed chambers will be subjected to be searched by brutal tools of power, under pretence, that they contain contraband or smuggled merchandize, and the most delicate part of our families, liable to every species of rude or indecent treatment, without the least prospect, or shadow of redress, from those by whom they are commissioned.

6th. The Liberty of the Press (that grand palladium of our liberties) totally suppressed, with a view to prevent a communication of sentiment throughout the states. This restraint is designedly intended to give our new masters an opportunity to rivet our fetters the more effectually.[a]

7th. A swarm of greedy officers appointed, such as are not known at present in the United States, who will riot and fatten on the spoils of the people, and eat up their substance.

8th. The militia of New-Hampshire, or Massachusetts, dragged to Georgia or South-Carolina, to assist in quelling an insurrection of Negroes in those states; and those of Georgia, to another distant quarter, to subdue their fellow citizens, who dare to rise against the despotism of government.

9th. The citizens of the state of New-Hampshire or Georgia, obliged to attend a trial (on an appeal) at the seat of government, which will, probably, be at the distance of at least five hundred miles from the residence of one of the parties, by which means, the expence of suits will become so enormous as to render justice unattainable but by the rich.

10th. The states perpetually involved in the wars of Europe, to gratify the *ambitious* views of their *ambitious* rulers, by which the country will be continually drained of its men and money.

11th. The citizens constantly subjected to the insults of *military* collectors, who will, by the magnetism of that most powerful of all attractives, the *bayonet*, extract from their pockets (without their consent) the exorbitant taxes imposed on them by their haughty lords and masters, for the purpose of keeping them under, and breaking their spirits, to prevent revolt.

12th. Monopolies in trade, granted to the favourites of government, by which the spirit of adventure will be destroyed, and the citizens subjected to the extortion of those companies who will have an exclusive right, to engross the different branches of commerce.

13th. An odious and detestable *Stamp act*, imposing duties on every instrument of writing, used in the courts of law and equity, by which the avenues to justice will, in a great measure, be barred, as it will enhance the expences on a suit, and deter men from pursuing the means requisite to obtain their right.—Stamp duties also, imposed on every *commercial* instrument of writing—on *literary productions*, and *particularly*, on *news papers*, which of course, will be a great discouragement to *trade*; an obstruction to *useful knowledge* in *arts, sciences agriculture*, and *manufactures*, and a prevention of *political information* throughout the states. Add to the above enumeration, the severest and most intolerable of all curses—that of being enslaved by men of our own creation (as to power) and for whose aggrandizement, many of us have fought and bled. Men who will, perhaps, construe our most innocent remarks and animadversions on their conduct, *treason*, misprision of treason, or high crimes and misdemeanours, which may be punished with unusual severity; we shall then be in a most forlorn and hopeless situation indeed.

> (a) *The Abbé Mably, one of the most sensible writers on government says, that the most despotic monarch in any nation whatever, if he had as many troops as the ability of the nation could support, would not long hold the reins of government, if the press was not shackled to prevent political disquisition.*

Orange-County, November 4, 1787.

New York Packet, 26 October 1787[1]

A correspondent observes, that the wisdom of the late Fœderal Convention is not doubted—but they *may* have erred. It is to be wished their report may have a *wise* and *temperate* discussion, and if it will not bear a *severe* trial, that it may not be adopted. A revolution every seven years must be very expensive and *dangerous*, and deprive us of the benefits we might derive from even an imperfect constitution.

1. Reprinted: *Hudson Weekly Gazette*, 1 November; *Pennsylvania Herald*, 3 November; *Northern Centinel* and Boston *American Herald*, 5 November; Winchester *Virginia Gazette*, 23 November.

Publius: The Federalist 1
New York Independent Journal, 27 October 1787[1]

PURPOSE AND AUTHORSHIP

The Federalist, a series of eighty-five essays signed by "Publius," was written by Alexander Hamilton, John Jay, and James Madison. Addressed to the "People of the State of New-York," these essays first appeared in New York City between 27 October 1787 and 28 May 1788. The purpose of the series, declared Hamilton in the first number, was to show the necessity of the "*UNION*," the weaknesses of the Articles of Confederation, and the nature and benefits of the Constitution. The essays were also intended to answer the objections raised to the Constitution.

Whether or not Hamilton or Jay originated the idea for the series is uncertain, but they asked others to be their collaborators. Gouverneur Morris of Pennsylvania, the most frequent speaker in the Constitutional Convention and the delegate most responsible for putting the Constitution into its final form, turned them down. Hamilton's close friend William Duer was asked and wrote four brief essays, signed "Philo-Publius," that did not become part of the series. (See "Philo-Publius" I, *Daily Advertiser*, 30 October, below.) James Madison was then asked and he agreed to participate, publishing his first essay (No. 10) on 22 November. Due to illness, Jay dropped out after publishing number 5 on 10 November, although he contributed one more essay (No. 64) in March 1788. Perhaps in response to the loss of Jay, Madison recommended Rufus King to Hamilton, but Hamilton did not think that King's talents were "as altogether of the sort required for the task in view." (For a fuller discussion of the choice of authors, see CC:Vol. 1, pp. 486–87.)

About three decades after the essays were printed, James Madison described the manner in which *The Federalist* essays were written and published, and to what extent the authors were responsible for each other's work. He stated that the essays "were written most of them in great haste, and without any ~~precise~~ special allotment of the different parts of the subject to the several writers, J. M. being at the time a member of the then Congress, and A. H. being also a member, and occupied moreover in his profession at the bar, it was understood that each was to write as their respective situations permitted, preserving as much as possible an order & connection in the papers successively published. This will account for ~~any~~ deficiencys in that respect, and also for an occasional repetition of the views taken of particular branches of the subject. The haste with which many of the papers were penned, in order to get thro' the subject whilst the Constitution was before the public, and to comply with the arrangement by which the printer was to keep his newspaper open for four numbers every week, was such that the performance must have borne a very different aspect, without the aid of historical and other notes which had been used in the Convention, and without the familiarity with the whole subject produced by the discussions there. It frequently happened that whilst the printer was putting into type parts of a number, the following parts were under the pen, & to be furnished in time for the press.

"In the beginning it was the practice, of the writers, of A. H. & J. M particularly to communicate each to the other, their respective papers before they were sent to the press. This was rendered so inconvenient, by the shortness of the time allowed, that it was dispensed with. Another reason was, that it was found most agreeable to each, not to give a positive sanction to all the doctrines and sentiments of the other; there being a known difference in the general complexion of their political theories" (Elizabeth Fleet, ed., "Madison's 'Detached Memoranda,'" *William and Mary Quarterly*, 3rd series, III [1946], 565). Madison also declared that occasionally the writers themselves "hardly" had time to read over their essays before they went to the printer (to Thomas Jefferson, 10 August 1788, CC:823).

In general, the authors did not refer by name to specific critics of the Constitution, although they were fully aware of and concerned with the influential Antifederalist literature appearing almost daily in newspapers, broadsides, and pamphlets. They did not engage in personal attacks, but they were not above deliberately misrepresenting Antifederalist positions. An example of such misrepresentation is their portrayal of Antifederalists as supporters of the idea of separate confederacies. (For example, see "Brutus" I, *New York Journal*, 18 October, note 4, above.)

In 1787 and 1788 the general public did not know the identity of "Publius." Four newspaper accounts, two of them originating in New York, implied that Hamilton was the author. While chiding the Antifederalist printer of the *New York Journal* for printing so many numbers of *The Federalist*, "Twenty-seven Subscribers" described "Publius" as a "*pert* adventurer, whose principles may be despotic, from habit in the wars and whose ideas of government cannot be satisfied with less than military execution: for a man whose sentiments have been viciated by one profession, will not easily recover virtuous dispositions by another" (*New York Journal*, 1 January 1788, below). In an essay commenting on the Antifederalist pamphlet by a "Federal Farmer," 8 November (below), Hugh Hughes, in "A Countryman" VI, referred to "Phocion" (i.e., Alexander Hamilton) who had "pretended to be as zealous an advocate for the constitution of the state, as Publius is now for the new [federal] constitution" (*New York Journal*, 14 February 1788, III below). In an earlier unpublished essay criticizing *The Federalist* 15, *Independent Journal*, 1 December 1787 (CC:312), Hughes suggested that Hamilton was "Publius," when he stated that "You really speak as tho' you had been a Member of the late Convention, and there experienced, in your own Person, *all the Improprieties and Excesses which a Spirit of Faction could* produce by mingling its Poison in your Deliberations, and which you so feelingly and emphatically now describe" ("Interrogator," post-1 December, below).

Outside New York, two newspaper contributors also hinted that Hamilton was "Publius." In the preface to a Boston reprinting of essay No. 13, "Philo Publius" referred to "A respectable and worthy member of the late Convention from New-York" who considered the question of separate republics in "one of a series of papers on the new Constitution" (*Massachusetts Centinel*, 8 December 1787, RCS:Mass., 404). A spurious letter said to be from Benjamin Rush to Alexander Hamilton, published in the highly partisan Antifederalist Philadelphia *Freeman's Journal*, identified the "60 numbers of Publius" as "your writings" (5 March 1788, Mfm:Pa. 487).

In private letters, New Yorkers—most of them Federalists—speculated about the authorship of *The Federalist*. James Kent, a young Poughkeepsie lawyer who met Hamilton for the first time at the October 1787 term of the state Supreme Court, declared that "The Author *must be* Hamilton who I think in Genius & political Research is not inferior to Gibbon, Hume or Montesquieu" (to Nathaniel Lawrence, 21 December, below). William Constable, a New York merchant and a partner of Gouverneur and Robert Morris, reported that "The New Constitution is the Sole Object of all our attention Hamilton has written in defence of it under the Signature of Publius" (to Marquis de Lafayette, 4 January 1788, Mfm:N.Y.). General Samuel Blachley Webb, a New York City merchant-factor and one of Hamilton's friends since the Revolution, identified Hamilton as "Publius" and praised him as "undoubtedly one of the most sensible men in America" (to Joseph Barrell, 13 January, below. See also Webb to Catherine Hogeboom, 24–25 June, VI below.). Walter Rutherfurd, another New York merchant, noted that "Madison has the principal hand in Publius and Hamilton assists" (to John Rutherfurd, post-22 January, Mfm:N.Y.). Although Brockholst Livingston drew no connection between Hamilton and *The Federalist*, he declared that in Antifederalist Ulster County, "they have burnt the Constitution accompanied with Coll. Hamilton in Effigy" (to William Livingston, 15 February, III below).

Confederation officeholders and foreign diplomats, stationed in New York City, also speculated about the authorship of *The Federalist*. Confederation Secretary at War Henry Knox, one of the best informed men in America, stated that "The publication signed *Publius* is attributed to the joint efforts of Mr Jay, Mr Maddison and Colo Hamilton It is highly probable that the general conjecture in this case is well founded" (to George Washington, 10 March, CC:610). Virginia congressman Edward Carrington also named all three men as the "supposed" authors of *The Federalist* (to Thomas Jefferson, 14 May, CC:743). On the other hand, Victor Marie DuPont, attaché to the French legation, gave full credit to Hamilton whose writings he described as "excellent." DuPont also asserted that "it is to him [Hamilton] that America owes its new constitution[;] it is he who by an adroit maneuver caused the plan to be adopted[;] and it is he who wrote every day during that time in order to prove the necessity of a government" (to Pierre Samuel DuPont de Nemours, 7, 18 April, below). The French chargé d'affaires Louis-Guillaume Otto, when describing the members of the Confederation Congress and the officers of the Confederation government, declared that Hamilton's "eloquence is often out of place in public debates, where precision and clarity are preferred to a brilliant imagination. It is believed that Mr. Hamilton is the author of the pamphlet entitled *The Federalist*. He has again missed his mark. This work is of no use to educated men and it is too learned and too long for the ignorant. It has, however, made him a great celebrity . . ." (post-July, Farrand, III, 234–35).

During the New York Convention in June 1788, some Antifederalist letter writers implied that Hamilton and "Publius" were one and the same. Convention observer Charles Tillinghast accused Hamilton of "*retailing*" the writings of "Publius" in the Convention (to John Lamb, 21 June, VI below). Apparently referring to Hamilton, Convention President George Clinton noted that most of the Federalist arguments were "only a second Edition of Publius, well delivered; One of the New York Delegates [i.e., Hamilton] has in Substance tho' not explicitly thrown off the Mask, his Arguments tending to Shew the Necessity of a Consolidated Continental, to the exclusion of any State Government" (to John Lamb, 21 June, VI below). Reporting on the Convention, delegate Melancton Smith stated that "Hamilton is the champion, he speaks frequently, very long and very vehemently—has, like publius, much to say not very applicable to the subject" (to Nathan Dane, 28 June, VI below. For a full discussion of the speculation about the authorship of *The Federalist* outside the state of New York, see CC:Vol. 1, pp. 488–89.).

Hamilton, Jay, and Madison themselves fueled the speculation about authorship since they identified themselves only to a few persons, such as Virginians George Washington, Edmund Randolph, and Thomas Jefferson, the latter being resident in Paris as American minister to France. Washington, in particular, eventually received either individual numbers or volumes of *The Federalist* from all three authors. (See CC:Vol. 1, p. 489.)

The authorship of sixty-nine of the eighty-five essays is certain. Hamilton wrote fifty essays—Nos. 1, 6–9, 11–13, 15–17, 21–36, 59–61, 65–85; Madison fourteen—Nos. 10, 14, 37–48; and Jay five, Nos. 2–5, 64. The disputed essays are Nos. 18–20, 49–58, and 62–63. The most definitive scholarship suggests that Madison probably wrote all of the disputed essays. (See Douglass Adair, "The Authorship of the Disputed Federalist Papers," *William and Mary Quarterly*, 3rd series, I [1944], 97–122, 235–64; Syrett, IV, 287–301; and Rutland, *Madison*, X, 259–63.) Robert Scigliano agrees that Madison wrote the disputed numbers, although he believes that Nos. 18–20 may have been jointly written by Madison and Hamilton (Scigliano, ed., *The Federalist* [Modern Library Edition, New York, 2000], xxiv–xli).

PUBLICATION AND CIRCULATION

Between 27 October 1787 and 2 April 1788, seventy-six numbers of *The Federalist* originated in four New York City newspapers—the *Independent Journal*, the *New York Packet*, the *Daily Advertiser*, and the *New York Journal*. John and Archibald M'Lean of the *Independent Journal* reprinted these essays in two volumes—the first volume appearing on 22 March 1788, the second on 28 May. The latter volume included eight new essays, making a total of eighty-four. The *Independent Journal* and the *Packet* printed or reprinted all eighty-four essays; the *Daily Advertiser*, Nos. 1–51; and the *New York Journal*, Nos. 23–39. (The latest reprinting of any essay of *The Federalist* by a newspaper occurred on 16 August.)

The numbering in the M'Lean volumes differs from that in the newspapers. Newspaper No. 35 is M'Lean No. 29; newspaper Nos. 29 and 30 are M'Lean Nos. 30 and 31. Newspaper No. 31 is divided into two becoming M'Lean Nos. 32 and 33. Consequently, newspaper Nos. 32 to 34 are Nos. 34 to 36 in M'Lean and newspaper Nos. 36 to 77 are one number higher in M'Lean. (The division of No. 31 into Nos. 32 and 33 increased the number of essays from eighty-four to eighty-five.)

In addition to the four originating newspapers, four other New York newspapers printed some of the "Publius" essays. The *Albany Gazette* reprinted at least fourteen numbers; the *Hudson Weekly Gazette* and *Northern Centinel* (later the *Federal Herald*), eleven each; and the *Country Journal* eight. No reprints have been found in the *New York Morning Post*, the *New-York Museum*, the *Im-*

partial Gazetteer, and the *Albany Journal*, all of which circulated at some time during the publication of *The Federalist*. Even though the *Albany Gazette* reprinted at least thirteen numbers by 7 February 1788, an Albany County resident complained that Antifederalist writings, which were published as broadsides and pamphlets, were "scattered all over the County, while the federalist remains at New York, & not a single piece (of which there are many more intelligible to the common people) is sent abroad" (William North to Henry Knox, 13 February, GLC 2437, The Henry Knox Papers, The Gilder Lehrman Collection, on deposit at the Pierpont Morgan Library, New York). For the out-of-state circulation of *The Federalist*, see CC:Vol. 1, pp. 490–91. See also the table of "Printings and Reprintings of *The Federalist*," Appendix IV, below.

The Federalist was so popular that by early December 1787 a New York City committee decided to strike a book edition of the essays. New York printers John and Archibald M'Lean were commissioned to produce 500 copies of the volume. (John M'Lean was the printer of the *Independent Journal*.) They were told that the volume would include twenty to twenty-five essays. On 2 January 1788 the M'Leans inserted an advertisement in the *Independent Journal*, stating that "The justness of the reasoning, the force of the arguments, and the beauty of the language, which distinguish this performance, have justly recommended it to general applause." The advertisement solicited advance subscribers to this projected volume of 200 to 250 pages. The M'Leans authorized printers and booksellers from all over America to accept subscriptions. With the publication and widespread reprinting of the advertisement, the newspaper reprinting of the essays began to subside. It had also become difficult for newspapers, most of them weeklies, to keep up with the avalanche of essays. (For the text and a full discussion of background and circulation of the *Journal's* advertisement, see "Advertisement for the Book Edition of *The Federalist*," *Independent Journal*, 2 January 1788, below.)

On 22 March the M'Leans advertised the publication and availability of the first volume of *The Federalist*, which included an unsigned preface by Alexander Hamilton and thirty-six essays, totalling 233 pages. The second volume, containing forty-nine essays and running to 390 pages, appeared on 28 May. The printers struck 500 copies of each of the two volumes. Hamilton, probably as a member of the committee that commissioned the volumes, paid for more than half the cost of printing them. These volumes circulated widely in New York and throughout America. Although their sale was good, "several hundred Copies" remained unsold in mid-October 1788. By May 1789, however, most of the volumes were sold. On 22 May the printer of the *New York Daily Gazette* noted that he had "a few copies" of *The Federalist* left for sale. "No publication respecting the New Constitution," stated the printer paraphrasing the *Independent Journal's* advertisement of 2 January 1788 (below), "has attracted so large a share of the public attention as the above work; the elegance of the language, the force of the reasoning, and the justness of the arguments which distinguished this performance, has deservedly entitled it to universal applause."

(For full discussions of the publication and circulation of these volumes in New York and throughout America, see "Publication and Sale of the Book Edition of *The Federalist*," 22 March 1788; and "Publication of Volume II of the Book Edition of *The Federalist*," 28 May, both III below.)

Public and Private Commentaries

In 1787 and 1788 *The Federalist* was praised in New York, both publicly and privately. Early in November 1787, "Curtius" III asserted that "the writings of Publius will reflect a pleasing lustre upon many of those beautiful intracacies, that are retired from superficial observation, and which require a master discernment to be brought into public notice" (*Daily Advertiser*, 3 November, supplement, below). "A Customer" of the *Northern Centinel* observed that *The Federalist* 1, whose reprinting he requested, suggested that future essays "will be written in the spirit of cool discussion, and will be directed to the judgment, and not the passions, of men." He hoped that the *Centinel's* printers would reprint future essays (*Northern Centinel,* 13 November, Mfm:N.Y.). Along these same lines, a writer in the *Northern Centinel* praised "the candid, cool demonstrations of Publius" (1 January 1788, below). James Kent recommended *The Federalist* "as the best thing I have seen hitherto in print on the federal side." Kent thought that "Publius" was "a most admirable writer & wields the sword of Party dispute with justice, energy, & inconceivable dexterity" (to Nathaniel Lawrence, 8 and 21 December 1787, both below). As "A Country Federalist," Kent also praised *The Federalist* in items printed in the *Country Journal* on 19 December (supplement) and 9 January 1788 (both below). "A Country Federalist" saw "the hand of a Master" in *The Federalist.* The essays, he continued, abounded in "new and brilliant thoughts" and they carried "along with them the most irresistable conviction." Kent also submitted several numbers of *The Federalist* to the *Country Journal* for reprinting (William Kent, *Memoirs and Letters of James Kent* . . . [Boston, 1898], 302 [Mfm:N.Y.]). He probably wrote the preface to the *Journal's* reprinting on 9 January 1788 of an excerpt from *The Federalist* 14 which declared that "Publius" had "treated on the necessity of the UNION of the United States with great energy of reasoning and with equal elegance of Language."

In four monthly issues from March through June 1788, the *American Magazine*—printed in New York City under the editorship of Noah Webster—summarized and reviewed both volumes of *The Federalist.* Commenting on the first volume in the March issue, the reviewer (probably Webster) remarked that "it would be difficult to find a treatise, which, in so small a compass, contains so much valuable political information, or in which the true principles of republican government are unfolded with such precision" (Mfm:N.Y.). At the end of his review in the June issue, the reviewer complimented the author of *The Federalist* for his "fair and candid" reasoning and "correct, smooth and elegant" language. He concluded that "these essays compose one of the most complete dissertations on government that ever has appeared in America, perhaps in Europe." The essays, he continued, would "remove objections to the new Constitution" and "would impress upon candid minds, just ideas of the nature of republican governments, of the principles of civil liberty, and of the genius and probable operation of the proposed Federal Constitution. They will be useful in diffusing political knowledge in the American republics, and will probably be re-published and read with pleasure and approbation, by the friends of liberty on the other side of the Atlantic" (Mfm:N.Y.). (For praise of *The Federalist* outside New York, see CC:Vol. 1, pp. 492–93.)

On the other hand, New York Antifederalists had harsh words for *The Federalist.* "An Observer" criticized "Publius" for "wilfully" trying to deceive "his fellow citizens" into thinking that Antifederalists supported the idea of separate confederacies. "An Observer" maintained that he had not read a single Antifederalist article advocating separate confederacies. Every friend to America, he stated, wanted to see "a confederated national government," but one that did not intrude into the internal affairs of the individual states. Such a government "would not encroach upon, or subvert our liberties at home" (*New York Journal,* 19 November, below). "Brutus" VI, VII, IX, and X castigated "Publius" for defending the new Congress' great financial and military powers and for his concept of federal-state relations. "Publius' " reasoning, "Brutus" continued, was "more specious than solid"; he lacked candor; and he "dressed" his arguments with "abundant verbages" (*New York Journal,* 27 December 1787, and 3, 17, and 24 January 1788, all below). "A Countryman" IV, written by DeWitt Clinton, Governor George Clinton's young nephew, remarked that all he had learned from "Publius" was "that it is better to be united than divided—that a great many people are stronger than a few" (*New York Journal,* 10 January 1788, below).

In a letter dated 14 January 1788, the "Federal Farmer" declared that, upon careful examination, the "voluminous productions" of "the lengthy writer in New-York . . . have but little relation to the great question, whether the constitution is fitted to the condition and character of this people or not" ("Federal Farmer," *An Additional Number of Letters to the Republican,* 2 May 1788 [III below and CC:723, p. 323]). This passage, along with some other remarks about "Publius," appeared in the *New York Journal,* 27 May, at the request of "A Customer," who referred to "the long-winded productions of Publius" [Mfm:N.Y.].). Similarly, "A Countryman" VI, written by Hugh Hughes, noted that "Publius" reminded him of "some of the gentlemen of the long robe, when hard pushed, in a bad cause, with a rich client. They frequently say a great deal, which does not apply; but yet, if it will not convince the judge nor jury, may, perhaps, help to make them forget some part of the evidence—embarrass their opponent, and make the audience stare, besides encreasing the practice" (*New York Journal,* 14 February, III below. For another published criticism of "Publius" by Hughes, see "Expositor" I, *New York Journal,* 7 February, below.). In an unpublished essay, Hugh Hughes described "Publius" as "*Solicitor General* for the New Constitution (perhaps with a View of being ATTORNEY GENERAL OR LD. CHIEF-JUSTICE under it)" ("Interrogator," post-1 December, below). (For criticism of *The Federalist* outside New York, see CC:Vol. 1, pp. 493–94.)

Only a small number of the eighty-five essays of *The Federalist* will appear in RCS:N.Y. Readers can find all eighty-five numbers in *Commentaries on the Constitution: Public and Private,* volumes XIII through XVIII of *The Documentary History of the Ratification of the Constitution.* The essays appear in *Commentaries on the Constitution* in chronological sequence with other major writings on the Constitution, both pro and con. The writings of "Publius" reveal that the authors were acutely aware of these writings. For single-volume editions of *The Federalist,* see the "Note on Sources" (above). See Appendix IV, for a table of "Printings and Reprintings of *The Federalist.*"

The FŒDERALIST. No. I.
To the People of the State of New-York.

After an unequivocal experience of the inefficacy of the subsisting
Fœderal Government, you are called upon to deliberate on a new Constitution for the United States of America. The subject speaks its own
importance; comprehending in its consequences, nothing less than the
existence of the UNION, the safety and welfare of the parts of which
it is composed, the fate of an empire, in many respects, the most interesting in the world. ⟨It has been frequently remarked, that it seems
to have been reserved to the people of this country, by their conduct
and example, to decide the important question, whether societies of
men are really capable or not, of establishing good government from
reflection and choice, or whether they are forever destined to depend,
for their political constitutions, on accident and force. If there be any
truth in the remark, the crisis, at which we are arrived, may with propriety be regarded as the æra in which that decision is to be made; and
a wrong election of the part we shall act, may, in this view, deserve to
be considered as the general misfortune of mankind.⟩[2]

This idea will add the inducements of philanthropy to those of patriotism to heighten the sollicitude, which all considerate and good
men must feel for the event. Happy will it be if our choice should be
decided by a judicious estimate of our true interests, unperplexed and
unbiassed by considerations not connected with the public good. But
this is a thing more ardently to be wished, than seriously to be expected. The plan offered to our deliberations, affects too many particular interests, innovates upon too many local institutions, not to involve
in its discussion a variety of objects foreign to its merits, and of views,
passions and prejudices little favourable to the discovery of truth.

Among the most formidable of the obstacles which the new Constitution will have to encounter, may readily be distinguished the obvious
interest of a certain class of men in every State to resist all changes
which may hazard a diminution of the power, emolument and consequence of the offices they hold under the State-establishments—and
the perverted ambition of another class of men, who will either hope
to aggrandise themselves by the confusions of their country, or will
flatter themselves with fairer prospects of elevation from the subdivision
of the empire into several partial confederacies, than from its union
under one government.[3]

It is not, however, my design to dwell upon observations of this nature. I am well aware that it would be disingenuous to resolve indis-
criminately the opposition of any set of men (merely because their
situations might subject them to suspicion) into interested or ambitious

views: Candour will oblige us to admit, that even such men may be actuated by upright intentions; and it cannot be doubted, that much of the opposition which has made its appearance, or may hereafter make its appearance, will spring from sources, blameless at least, if not respectable, the honest errors of minds led astray by preconceived jealousies and fears. So numerous indeed and so powerful are the causes, which serve to give a false bias to the judgment, that we upon many occasions, see wise and good men on the wrong as well as on the right side of questions, of the first magnitude to society. This circumstance, if duly attended to, would furnish a lesson of moderation to those, who are ever so much persuaded of their being in the right, in any controversy. And a further reason for caution, in this respect, might be drawn from the reflection, that we are not always sure, that those who advocate the truth are influenced by purer principles than their antagonists. Ambition, avarice, personal animosity, party opposition, and many other motives, not more laudable than these, are apt to operate as well upon those who support as upon those who oppose the right side of a question. Were there not even these inducements to moderation, nothing could be more illjudged than that intolerant spirit, which has, at all times, characterised political parties. For, in politics as in religion, it is equally absurd to aim at making proselytes by fire and sword. Heresies in either can rarely be cured by persecution.

And yet however just these sentiments will be allowed to be, we have already sufficient indications, that it will happen in this as in all former cases of great national discussion. A torrent of angry and malignant passions will be let loose. To judge from the conduct of the opposite parties, we shall be led to conclude, that they will mutually hope to evince the justness of their opinions, and to increase the number of their converts by the loudness of their declamations, and by the bitterness of their invectives. An enlightened zeal for the energy and efficiency of government will be stigmatised, as the off-spring of a temper fond of despotic power and hostile to the principles of liberty. An over-scrupulous jealousy of danger to the rights of the people, which is more commonly the fault of the head than of the heart, will be represented as mere pretence and artifice; the ____ bait[4] for popularity at the expence of public good. It will be forgotten, on the one hand, that jealousy is the usual concomitant of violent love, and that the noble enthusiasm of liberty is too apt to be infected with a spirit of narrow and illiberal distrust. On the other hand, it will be equally forgotten, that the vigour of government is essential to the security of liberty; that, in the contemplation of a sound and well informed judgment, their interest can never be separated; and that a dangerous ambition more often lurks behind the specious mask of zeal for the rights of the people, than under the forbidding appearance of zeal for the firmness and efficiency of government. History will teach us, that the former has been found a much more certain road to the introduction of despotism, than the latter, and that of those men who have overturned the liberties of republics the greatest number have begun their career, by paying an obsequious court to the people, commencing Demagogues and ending Tyrants.

In the course of the preceeding observations I have had an eye, my Fellow Citizens, to putting you upon your guard against all attempts, from whatever quarter, to influence your decision in a matter of the utmost moment to your welfare by any impressions other than those which may result from the evidence of truth. You will, no doubt, at the same time, have collected from the general scope of them that they proceed from a source not unfriendly to the new Constitution. Yes, my Countrymen, I own to you, that, after having given it an attentive consideration, I am clearly of opinion, it is your interest to adopt it. I am convinced, that this is the safest course for your liberty, your dignity, and your happiness. I affect not reserves, which I do not feel. I will not amuse you with an appearance of deliberation, when I have decided. I frankly acknowledge to you my convictions, and I will freely lay before you the reasons on which they are founded. The consciousness of good intentions disdains ambiguity. I shall not however multiply professions on this head. My motives must remain in the depositary of my own breast: My arguments will be open to all, and may be judged of by all. They shall at least be offered in a spirit, which will not disgrace the cause of truth.

I propose in a series of papers to discuss the following interesting particulars—*The utility of the UNION to your political prosperity—The insufficiency of the present Confederation to preserve that Union—The necessity of a government at least equally energetic with the one proposed to the attainment of this object—The conformity of the proposed constitution to the true principles of republican government—Its analogy to your own state constitution*—and lastly, *The additional security, which its adoption will afford to the preservation of that species of government, to liberty and to property.*

In the progress of this discussion I shall endeavour to give a satisfactory answer to all the objections which shall have made their appearance that may seem to have any claim to your attention.

It may perhaps be thought superfluous to offer arguments to prove the utility of the UNION, a point, no doubt, deeply engraved on the hearts of the great body of the people in every state, and one, which it may be imagined has no adversaries. But the fact is, that ⟨we already hear it whispered in the private circles of those who oppose the new constitution, that the Thirteen States are of too great extent for any general system, and that we must of necessity resort to seperate confederacies of distinct portions of the whole.⁽ᵃ⁾ This doctrine will, in all probability, be gradually propagated, till it has votaries enough to countenance an open avowal of it. For nothing can be more evident, to those who are able to take an enlarged view of the subject, than the alternative of an adoption of the new Constitution, or a dismemberment of the Union.)⁵ It will therefore be of use to begin by examining the advantages of that Union, the certain evils and the probable dangers, to which every State will be exposed from its dissolution. This shall accordingly constitute the subject of my next address.⁶

(a) *The same idea, tracing the arguments to their consequences, is held out in several of the late publications against the New Constitution.*

1. *The Federalist* 1—written by Alexander Hamilton—was reprinted in the *New York Packet* and *Daily Advertiser*, 30 October; *Northern Centinel*, 13 November; *Albany Gazette*, 15 November; *Hudson Weekly Gazette*, 22 November; the November issue of the nationally circulated Philadelphia *American Museum*; and in four newspapers outside New York: Mass. (1), R.I. (1), Pa. (1), Va. (1). See notes 2, 3, and 5 (below) for the publication of unattributed excerpts.

2. The text in angle brackets was reprinted in the Boston *Independent Chronicle* on 8 November under a Boston dateline, without identifying *The Federalist* 1 as the source. The *Chronicle's* text was reprinted in the *New Hampshire Mercury*, 9 November; *Hampshire Gazette*, 14 November; *Pennsylvania Packet*, 20 November; *Pennsylvania Gazette*, 21 November; and Charleston *Columbian Herald*, 6 December.

3. This paragraph was reprinted in the *Worcester Magazine*, 8 November, under a New York dateline of 27 October, without identifying *The Federalist* 1 as the source.

4. In the *Independent Journal*, a blank space appears before the word "bait." Some reprinting newspapers retained the blank space, others did not. In editions of *The Federalist* published in 1802 and 1818, the word "stale" preceded "bait."

5. The text in angle brackets was reprinted in the *Salem Mercury*, 6 November, under a New York dateline of 27 October, without identifying *The Federalist* 1 as the source.

6. *The Federalist* 2—printed in the *Independent Journal*, 31 October (CC:217)—was written by John Jay who noted in his concluding paragraph that the preservation and perpetuation of the Union was "the great object of the people" in calling the Constitutional Convention and that it was "the great object of the plan which the Convention has advised them to adopt." Jay could not understand why some men would suggest that three or four confederacies were better than one.

Lansingburgh Northern Centinel, 29 October 1787¹

The public prints from every quarter of the United States are filled with accounts of the unanimity with which the new federal constitution has been received, and the great happiness the people feel in the glorious prospect of being speedily relieved from their present feeble and declining state, and being put on a respectable footing among the nations, by the adoption of a united government, founded on so much wisdom, and so well calculated to preserve the rights of mankind, and raise to opulence and power the vast extended empire of America.

1. Reprinted: *New Hampshire Gazette*, 16 November; *Newport Herald*, 29 November; *Albany Gazette*, 6 December; *Pennsylvania Journal*, 19 December; *Maryland Journal*, 25 December.

Gouverneur Morris to George Washington
Philadelphia, 30 October 1787 (excerpt)[1]

. . . New York, hemmed in between the warm Friends of the Constitution could not easily (unless supported by powerful States) make any important Struggle, even tho her Citizens were unanimous, which is by no Means the Case. Parties there are nearly balanced. If the Assent or Dissent of the New York Legislature were to decide on the Fate of America there would still be a Chance, tho I believe the Force of Government would preponderate and effect a rejection. But the legislature cannot assign to the People any good Reason for not trusting them with a Decision on their own Affairs, and must therefore agree to a Convention—In the Choice of a Convention it is not improbable that the fœderal Party will prove strongest, for Persons of very distinct and opposite Interests have joined on this Subject. . . .

1. RC, Washington Papers, DLC. Printed: CC:213. Both the recipient's copy and Morris' draft of it (found in the Gouverneur Morris Collection in the Columbia University Libraries) are dated 30 October. The address page of the recipient's copy contains a postmark and an endorsement which cast doubt on that date. The postmark reads: "26 OC," and the endorsement reads "Alexandria 29th. Octr. 1787. The Northern Stage arrived at half past 7. OClock P M." Washington, however, docketed the letter "From Gouvr Morris Esqr 30th. Octr 1787."
Morris (1752–1816), a lawyer, represented New York in Congress, 1778–79, and signed the Articles of Confederation. He moved to Pennsylvania in 1779 and represented that state in the Constitutional Convention, where he signed the Constitution. A member of the Convention's Committee of Style, Morris was most responsible for putting the Constitution into its final form.

Philo-Publius I
New York Daily Advertiser, 30 October 1787

Alexander Hamilton and John Jay, the initial authors of *The Federalist* ("Publius"), solicited the aid of collaborators. Among those approached was William Duer, one of Hamilton's close friends. According to James Madison, who became the third author of *The Federalist*, Duer "wrote two or perhaps three more papers, which tho' intelligent & sprightly, were not continued; nor did they make a part of the printed Collection" (Elizabeth Fleet, ed., "Madison's 'Detatched Memoranda,'" *William and Mary Quarterly*, 3rd series, III [1946], 564). Apparently, it was no secret to others that Duer was "Philo-Publius." Two nephews of Governor George Clinton were aware of it. After reading some essays of "A Countryman," George Clinton told his brother DeWitt that "*Your Countrymans Letters* are very good and I think better adapted to the understanding of the Common People than any piece in the Newspapers. They seem to be wrote in imitation of Col. D—r" (22 December, Mfm:N.Y. See "A Countryman" I, *New York Journal*, 6 December, below.).

As "Philo-Publius," Duer published four essays, the first of which was not numbered, in the *Daily Advertiser*, 30 October, 1 December; the *New York Packet*, 16 November; and the *Independent Journal*, 28 November. Only the first essay was of an appreciable length. Numbers II and III were reprinted once each. On 2 January 1788 John and Archibald M'Lean announced that they would print the essays of "Publius" in a book edition. The M'Leans also promised subscribers that, to make this volume "more complete," they would include "Philo-Publius" and a copy of the Constitution (below). Although the M'Lean edition of *The Federalist* included the Constitution, it did not include any of the "Philo-Publius" essays.

Duer (1747–1799), a native of England and a wealthy New York City merchant and speculator in land and public securities, emigrated to America in 1769 and represented Washington County in the Fourth Provincial Congress, 1776–77, where he was a member of the committee that drafted the state constitution. He was a delegate to Congress, 1777–78; served as secretary of the Confederation Board of Treasury, 1785–89; represented New York County in the state Assembly, 1786; and served as Assistant to the Secretary of the U.S. Treasury, 1789–90. His insolvency, brought about by his financial and land speculations, helped to precipitate a financial crisis in New York in 1792. Duer was arrested for debt and spent most of the remainder of his life in prison.

In the first number of the Federalist, which appeared in the INDEPENDENT JOURNAL of Saturday, the interest of certain Officers, under the State establishments, to oppose an increase of Federal authority, is mentioned as a principal source of the opposition to be expected to the New Constitution. The same idea has appeared in other publications, but has not hitherto been sufficiently explained. To ascertain its justness and extent, would, no doubt, be satisfactory to the public; and might serve to obviate misapprehensions.

A very natural enquiry presents itself on the subject:—How happens it, that the interest of the Officers of a State should be different from that of its Citizens? I shall attempt an answer to this question.

The powers requisite to constitute Sovereignty, must be delegated by every people for their own protection and security. The people of each State have already delegated these powers; which are now lodged, partly in the PARTICULAR Government, and partly in the GENERAL Government. It is not necessary that they should grant greater or new ones. The only question with them is, in what manner the powers already granted shall be distributed; into what receptacles; and in what proportions. If they are represented in both, it will be immaterial to them, so far as concerns their individual authority, independence, or liberty, whether the principal share be deposited in the whole body, or in the distinct members. The re-partition, or division, is a mere question of expediency; for, by whatever scale it be made, their personal rights will remain the same. If it be their interest to be united, it will be their interest to bestow as large a portion upon the Union, as may be required to render it solid and effectual; and if experience has shewn, that the portion heretofore conferred is inadequate to the object, it will be their interest to take away a part of that which has been left in the State reservoirs, to add it to the common stock.

But such a transfer of power, from the individual members to the Union, however it may promote the advantage of the citizens at large, may subtract not a little from the importance, and, what is with most men less easily submitted to, from the emolument of those, who hold a certain description of offices under the State establishments. These have one interest as Citizens, and another as OFFICERS. In the latter capacity, they are interested in the POWER and PROFIT of their offices, and will naturally be unwilling to put either in jeopardy. That men love power is no new discovery; that they are commonly attached to good salaries does not need elaborate proof; that they should be afraid of what threatens them with a loss of either, is but a plain inference from plain facts. A diminution of State authority is, of course, a diminution of the POWER of those who are invested with the administration of that authority; and, in all probability, will in many instances produce an eventual decrease of salary. In some cases it may annihilate the offices themselves. But, while these persons may have to repine at the loss of official importance or pecuniary emolument, the private citizen may feel himself exalted to a more elevated rank. He may pride himself in the character of a citizen of America, as more dignified than that of a citizen of any single State. He may greet himself with the appellation of an American, as more honorable than that of a New-Yorker, a Pennsylvanian, or a Virginian.

From the preceding remarks, the distinction alluded to, between the private citizen and the citizen in office, will, I presume, be sufficiently apparent. But it will be proper to observe, that its influence does not reach near so far as might at first sight be imagined. The offices that would be affected by the proposed change, though of considerable importance, are not numerous. Most of the departments of the State Governments will remain, untouched, to flow in their accustomed channels. This observation was necessary, to prevent invidious suspicions from lighting where they would not be applicable.

Publius: The Federalist 2 (John Jay)
New York Independent Journal, 31 October 1787

Importance of Union versus separate confederacies. For text, see CC:217. For reprintings, see Appendix IV, below.

Albany Gazette, 1 November 1787[1]

A few OBSERVATIONS in favor of the NEW CONTINENTAL GOVERNMENT, now under the consideration of the Citizens of this State.

1. That it was formed by a Convention composed of the most sensible, virtuous, patriotic and independent characters that this, or perhaps any other country on the face of the globe, can produce.

2. That it is ushered to us under the respectable and illustrious signature of GEORGE WASHINGTON, whose disinterested and invaluable services to his country, has rendered him the admiration of the present age; and, to suppose that any act of his, could be intended, in the most distant degree, to injure a people whose freedom he has already established, at the risque of his life and fortune, would be a piece of base ingratitude, that no *honest* American can possibly be guilty of.

3. That it will unite under one head, and bring to one point, the resources, strength and commerce of this extensive country, and consequently serve to render us wealthy, respectable and powerful, as a mercantile as well as a warlike people.

4. That equal justice will be administered to each state, in the support of government, in proportion to its abilities and local situation, and no state be induced to furnish its full quota (which this state has frequently done)[2] when many others neglect furnishing a single shilling.

5. That in all probability the first good consequence, arising from a firm and a respectable government, will be the relinquishment of the WESTERN POSTS, by the British, according to the treaty of peace— which are now so unjustly detained from us, and for no other reason but a contempt of our government.

6. That the late disturbances, in Massachusetts, New-Hampshire, Pennsylvania, and even on the borders of this state,[3] shew a langor in our present government, that must alarm every thinking person; and which must, if not guarded against in future, end in anarchy and confusion. A

situation infinitely more to be dreaded, than all the evils that can be conceived from the tyranny of an absolute monarch.

7th and lastly. That it meets with opposition from few or none in this state, but persons who hold posts of profit and honor, and are fearful that a part of their state consequence must be swallowed up in the United States' government. A circumstance that should set every honest and well meaning citizen on his guard against all such opposers, however exalted their station may be, or respectable their private characters: For such is the weakness of frail nature, that none of us can act, or even think, with impartial justice, on any subject that interferes with our interest or ambition.

Albany, October 31, 1787.

1. Reprints by 18 December (6): N.H. (3), Mass. (1), Conn. (1), Pa. (1). Three reprints omitted the seventh observation.

2. A report of the Confederation Board of Treasury, dated 31 March 1788, revealed that New York ranked first among the states in paying congressional requisitions from 1781 to 1787. (See *Daily Advertiser*, 21 July, note 4, above.)

3. For the turmoil and unrest in these states, see CC:18.

An Enemy to Impostors
New York Daily Advertiser, 1 November 1787[1]

Mr. CHILDS, Please to insert the following Remarks upon *the incorruptible* PUBLIC PURSE HACKER, HEWER and SQUEEZER.

Should a person, who preferred living by his wits to living by labor, venture to disregard the good old maxim, which says, "The Shoemaker should not quit his Last;"[2] and, by that kind of address and decent assurance, which some might call cunning and effrontery, obtain a good [post?], the world might admire at his ingenuity.

Should he turn Politician, and undertake to cobble the State—should he string together, as party-colored and chequered as wampum, a number of common-place quotations from authors of note, on *Power*, and *the People*, and *Liberty*, and *Government*, and the PUBLIC MONEY, which, dealing out at random, he vainly imagined constituted him a Man of Science, and Statesman; the literary coxcomb, and pedantic ignoramus, might ride his hobbyhorse until he broke his neck with downright vainglory; and mistake the titter of contempt for the smiles of public applause.

Should such a genius (unluckily for him) be placed in a respectable public assembly, and there display his mule-headed ignorance and ill-timed obstinacy, by a fruitless and singular opposition to its general voice, on a matter of great public moment;[3] he would as naturally become the subject of merriment to its members, as of discredit to those he was sent to represent. But should this self-created *profound Politician*, and *immaculate Citizen*, after long and loud professions of his INCOR-RUPTIBLE PATRIOTISM, his great attachment to the liberties of THE PEOPLE, and the ECONOMY OF THEIR FINANCES,[4] fabricate an enormous account; and, on the most destructive principles of calcula-tion, attempt to extort from THE PEOPLE thirty-fold more than his stipulated allowance—should he, with an unparalleled effrontery, in-sult a whole empire, and, by his conduct, deny that there was either truth or justice in the general cry, of public grievances to be redressed and evils to be removed—should this pretended advocate for THE PEOPLE, with the spirit of an arbitrary Bashaw, and a despotic Tyrant, do his utmost to prevent THE PEOPLE even from deliberating upon a business of the last moment to them—upon *the result of the collected wisdom of their* SPECIAL *Delegates from all the States* (except the infamous ONE)[5]—upon the work of long and careful investigation, and agreed to with singular unanimity—I say, should such an arbitrary and avari-cious being oppose himself even to THE PEOPLE'S RIGHT OF DE-LIBERATION, on the present momentous occasion, because it did not suit HIS OWN private, narrow, selfish views—his name ought to be gibbeted with infamy throughout America, as an IMPOSTOR; who, with the spirit of a Tyrant, profanes with his blistered tongue the sacred word Liberty; and, with loud professions of *incorruptible integrity*, has exhibited himself to the world as notoriously enflamed with the rapa-cious spirit of an UNPRINCIPLED PUBLIC PECULATOR.

1. On 30 October the *Daily Advertiser* announced that "An Enemy to Impostors" would appear as soon as possible. "An Enemy to Impostors" attacks Abraham Yates, Jr., a former shoemaker and former Continental loan officer for New York, who was a prolific news-paper contributor, occasionally employing the pseudonyms "Rough Hewer" or "Rough Hewer, Jr." His detail-filled articles were often heavily footnoted; his learning was often ostentatiously displayed. Yates apparently made his living by holding public offices.

2. This maxim, often rendered "cobbler, stick to your last," is traced to Pliny the Elder (23–79 A.D.), *Natural History*, Book XXXV, section 85. Pliny credited the maxim to the Greek painter Apelles, who lived in the fourth century B.C.

3. As a state senator and as a delegate to Congress, Yates was known for casting the only negative vote on measures that would normally be adopted unanimously. For example, he cast the only nay vote against the Northwest Ordinance. On 16 July 1787 Nathan Dane, the Ordinance's principal author, wrote to Rufus King that Yates "appeared in this Case, as in most other not to understand the subject at all" (Smith, *Letters*, XXIV, 358).

4. Probably a reference to Yates's fierce opposition to the federal Impost of 1783, which he argued would result in the creation of numerous Continental officials who would harass the people in order to collect the tax.

5. Rhode Island was the only state that refused to send delegates to the Constitutional Convention.

Brutus II
New York Journal, 1 November 1787

"Brutus" II was one of three original Antifederalist items printed by the *New York Journal* on 1 November that were, in part, responses to Federalist James Wilson's influential 6 October speech before a Philadelphia public meeting (CC:134). (The other two items, "Cincinnatus" I and "Timoleon," are printed below.) On the same day, the *Journal* reprinted a fourth reply to Wilson, namely, "Centinel" II, Philadelphia *Freeman's Journal*, 24 October (CC:-190). "Brutus" II was reprinted in the Boston *Independent Chronicle*, 30 November.

To the CITIZENS *of the* STATE *of* NEW-YORK.

I flatter myself that my last address established this position, that to reduce the Thirteen States into one government, would prove the destruction of your liberties.

But lest this truth should be doubted by some, I will now proceed to consider its merits.

Though it should be admitted, that the argument against reducing all the states into one consolidated government, are not sufficient fully to establish this point; yet they will, at least, justify this conclusion, that in forming a constitution for such a country, great care should be taken to limit and define its powers, adjust its parts, and guard against an abuse of authority. How far attention has been paid to these objects, shall be the subject of future enquiry. When a building is to be erected which is intended to stand for ages, the foundation should be firmly laid. The constitution proposed to your acceptance, is designed not for yourselves alone, but for generations yet unborn. The principles, therefore, upon which the social compact is founded, ought to have been clearly and precisely stated, and the most express and full declaration of rights to have been made—But on this subject there is almost an entire silence.

If we may collect the sentiments of the people of America, from their own most solemn declarations, they hold this truth as self evident, that all men are by nature free. No one man, therefore, or any class of men, have a right, by the law of nature, or of God, to assume or exercise authority over their fellows. The origin of society then is to be sought, not in any natural right which one man has to exercise authority over another, but in the united consent of those who associate. The mutual wants of men, at first dictated the propriety of forming societies; and when they were established, protection and defence pointed out the necessity of instituting government. In a state of nature every individual pursues his own interest; in this pursuit it frequently happened, that the possessions or enjoyments of one were sacrificed to the views and designs of another; thus the weak were a prey to the strong, the simple and unwary were subject to impositions from those who were more crafty and designing. In this state of things, every individual was insecure; common interest therefore directed, that government should be established, in which the force of the whole community should be collected, and under such directions, as to protect and defend every one who composed it. The common good, therefore, is the end of civil government, and common consent, the foundation on which it is established. To effect this end, it was necessary that a certain portion of natural liberty should be surrendered, in order, that what remained should be preserved: how great a proportion of natural freedom is necessary to be yielded by individuals, when they submit to government, I shall not now enquire. So much, however, must be given up, as will be sufficient to enable those, to whom the administration of the government is committed, to establish laws for the promoting the happiness of the community, and to carry those laws into effect. But it is not necessary, for this purpose, that individuals should relinquish all their natural rights. Some are of such a nature that they cannot be surrendered. Of this kind are the rights of conscience, the right of enjoying and defending life, &c. Others are not necessary to be resigned, in order to attain the end for which government is instituted, these therefore ought not to be given up. To surrender them, would counteract the very end of government, to wit, the common good. From these observations it appears, that in forming a government on its true principles, the foundation should be laid in the manner I before stated, by expressly reserving to the people such of their essential natural rights, as are not necessary to be parted with. The same reasons which at first induced mankind to associate and institute government, will operate to influence them to observe this precaution. If they had been disposed to conform themselves to the rule of immutable righteousness, government would not have been requisite. It was because one part exercised fraud, oppression, and violence on the other, that men came together, and agreed that certain rules should be formed, to regulate the conduct of all, and the power of the whole community lodged in the hands of rulers to enforce an obedience to them. But rulers have the same propensities as other men; they are as likely to use the power with which they are vested for private purposes, and to the injury and oppression of those over whom they are placed, as individuals in a state of nature are to injure and oppress one another. It is therefore as proper that bounds should be set to their authority, as that government should have at first been instituted to restrain private injuries.

This principle, which seems so evidently founded in the reason and nature of things, is confirmed by universal experience. Those who have governed, have been found in all ages ever active to enlarge their powers and abridge the public liberty. This has induced the people in all countries, where any sense of freedom remained, to fix barriers against the encroachments of their rulers. The country from which we have derived our origin, is an eminent example of this. Their magna charta and bill of rights have long been the boast, as well as the security, of that nation. I need say no more, I presume, to an American, than, that this principle is a fundamental one, in all the constitutions of our own states; there is not one of them but what is either founded on a declaration or bill of rights, or has certain express reservation of rights interwoven in the body of them. From this it appears, that at a time when the pults of liberty beat high, and when an appeal was made to the people to form constitutions for the government of themselves, it was their universal sense, that such declarations should make a part of their frames of government. It is therefore the more astonishing, that this grand security, to the rights of the people, is not to be found in this constitution.

It has been said, in answer to this objection, that such declaration of rights, however requisite they might be in the constitutions of the states, are not necessary in the general constitution, because, "in the former case, every thing which is not reserved is given, but in the latter the reverse of the proposition prevails, and every thing which is not given is reserved."[1] It requires but little attention to discover, that this mode of reasoning is rather specious than solid. The powers, rights, and authority, granted to the general government by this constitution, are as complete, with respect to every object to which they extend, as that of any state government—It reaches to every thing which concerns human happiness—Life, liberty, and property, are under its controul. There is the same reason, therefore, that the exercise of power, in this case, should be restrained within proper limits, as in that of the state governments. To set this matter in a clear light, permit me to instance some of the articles of the bills of rights of the individual states, and apply them to the case in question.

For the security of life, in criminal prosecutions, the bills of rights of most of the states have declared, that no man shall be held to answer for a crime until he is made fully acquainted with the charge brought against him; he shall not be compelled to accuse, or furnish evidence against himself—The witnesses against him shall be brought face to face, and he shall be fully heard by himself or counsel. That it is essential to the security of life and liberty, that trial of facts be in the vicinity where they happen. Are not provisions of this kind as necessary in the general government, as in that of a particular state? The powers vested in the new Congress extend in many cases to life; they are authorised to provide for the punishment of a variety of capital crimes, and no restraint is laid upon them in its exercise, save only, that "the trial of all crimes, except in cases of impeachment, shall be by jury; and such trial shall be in the state where the said crimes shall have been committed." No man is secure of a trial in the county where he is charged to have committed a crime; he may be brought from Niagara to New-York, or carried from Kentucky to Richmond for trial for an offence, supposed to be committed. What security is there, that a man shall be furnished with a full and plain description of the charges against him? That he shall be allowed to produce all proof he can in his favor? That he shall see the witnesses against him face to face, or that he shall be fully heard in his own defence by himself or counsel?

For the security of liberty it has been declared, "that excessive bail should not be required, nor excessive fines imposed, nor cruel or unusual punishments inflicted—That all warrants, without oath or affirmation, to search suspected places, or seize any person, his papers or property, are grievous and oppressive."[2]

These provisions are as necessary under the general government as under that of the individual states; for the power of the former is as complete to the purpose of requiring bail, imposing fines, inflicting punishments, granting search warrants, and seizing persons, papers, or property, in certain cases, as the other.

For the purpose of securing the property of the citizens, it is declared by all the states, "that in all controversies at law, respecting property, the ancient mode of trial by jury is one of the best securities of the rights of the people, and ought to remain sacred and inviolable."[3]

Does not the same necessity exist of reserving this right, under this national compact, as in that of the states? Yet nothing is said respecting it. In the bills of rights of the states it is declared, that a well regulated militia is the proper and natural defence of a free government[4]—That as standing armies in time of peace are dangerous, they are not to be kept up,[5] and that the military should be kept under strict subordination to, and controuled by the civil power.[6]

The same security is as necessary in this constitution, and much more so; for the general government will have the sole power to raise and to pay armies, and are under no controul in the exercise of it; yet nothing of this is to be found in this new system.

I might proceed to instance a number of other rights, which were as necessary to be reserved, such as, that elections should be free, that

the liberty of the press should be held sacred; but the instances adduced, are sufficient to prove, that this argument is without foundation.—Besides, it is evident, that the reason here assigned was not the
true one, why the framers of this constitution omitted a bill of rights;
if it had been, they would not have made certain reservations, while
they totally omitted others of more importance. We find they have, in
the 9th section of the 1st article, declared, that the writ of habeas corpus shall not be suspended, unless in cases of rebellion—that no bill
of attainder, or expost facto law, shall be passed—that no title of nobility shall be granted by the United States, &c. If every thing which is
not given is reserved, what propriety is there in these exceptions? Does
this constitution any where grant the power of suspending the habeas
corpus, to make expost facto laws, pass bills of attainder, or grant titles
of nobility? It certainly does not in express terms. The only answer that
can be given is, that these are implied in the general powers granted.
With equal truth it may be said, that all the powers, which the bills of
rights, guard against the abuse of, are contained or implied in the
general ones granted by this constitution.

So far it is from being true, that a bill of rights is less necessary in
the general constitution than in those of the states, the contrary is
evidently the fact.—This system, if it is possible for the people of America to accede to it, will be an original compact; and being the last, will,
in the nature of things, vacate every former agreement inconsistent
with it. For it being a plan of government received and ratified by the
whole people, all other forms, which are in existence at the time of its
adoption, must yield to it. This is expressed in positive and unequivocal
terms, in the 6th article, "That this constitution and the laws of the
United States, which shall be made in pursuance thereof, and all treaties made, or which shall be made, under the authority of the United
States, shall be the supreme law of the land; and the judges in every
state shall be bound thereby, any thing in the *constitution*, or laws of
any state, *to the contrary* notwithstanding.[7]

"The senators and representatives before-mentioned, and the members of the several state legislatures, and all executive and judicial officers, both of the United States, and of the several states, shall be
bound, by oath or affirmation, to support this constitution."

It is therefore not only necessarily implied thereby, but positively
expressed, that the different state constitutions are repealed and entirely done away, so far as they are inconsistent with this, with the laws
which shall be made in pursuance thereof, or with treaties made, or
which shall be made, under the authority of the United States; of what

avail will the constitutions of the respective states be to preserve the rights of its citizens? should they be plead, the answer would be, the constitution of the United States, and the laws made in pursuance thereof, is the supreme law, and all legislatures and judicial officers, whether of the general or state governments, are bound by oath to support it. No priviledge, reserved by the bills of rights, or secured by the state governments, can limit the power granted by this, or restrain any laws made in pursuance of it. It stands therefore on its own bottom, and must receive a construction by itself without any reference to any other—And hence it was of the highest importance, that the most precise and express declarations and reservations of rights should have been made.

This will appear the more necessary, when it is considered, that not only the constitution and laws made in pursuance thereof, but all treaties made, or which shall be made, under the authority of the United States, are the supreme law of the land, and supersede the constitutions of all the states. The power to make treaties, is vested in the president, by and with the advice and consent of two thirds of the senate. I do not find any limitation, or restriction, to the exercise of this power. The most important article in any constitution may therefore be repealed, even without a legislative act. Ought not a government, vested with such extensive and indefinite authority, to have been restricted by a declaration of rights? It certainly ought.

So clear a point is this, that I cannot help suspecting, that persons who attempt to persuade people, that such reservations were less necessary under this constitution than under those of the states, are wilfully endeavouring to deceive, and to lead you into an absolute state of vassalage.

1. Quoted from James Wilson's 6 October speech (CC:134, p. 339). See also "New York Reprinting of James Wilson's 6 October Speech Before a Philadelphia Public Meeting," 13–25 October (above).

2. Quoted from the Maryland Declaration of Rights (1776), Articles XXII–XXIII (Thorpe, III, 1688). The declarations of Delaware, Massachusetts, New Hampshire, North Carolina, Pennsylvania, and Virginia also have provisions on some of the rights quoted by "Brutus" (Thorpe, III, 1891, 1892; IV, 2456, 2457; V, 2788, 3083, 3089; VII, 3813, 3814; and *American Historical Review* [*AHR*], III [1898], 646 [Delaware]).

3. Quoted from the North Carolina Declaration of Rights (1776), Article XIV (Thorpe, V, 2788). The declarations of Maryland, Massachusetts, New Hampshire, Pennsylvania, and Virginia also have provisions concerning jury trials (Thorpe, III, 1686–87, 1891–92; IV, 2456; V, 3083; and VII, 3814.

4. The declarations of rights of Delaware, Maryland, New Hampshire, and Virginia have this militia provision. New York and North Carolina also have provisions regarding the militia (Thorpe, III, 1688; IV, 2456; V, 2637, 2788; VII, 3814; and *AHR*, III [1898], 646 [Delaware]).

5. The declarations of rights of North Carolina, Pennsylvania, and Virginia stated that, since standing armies were "dangerous to liberty," they should be avoided (Thorpe, V, 2788, 3083; and VII, 3814). Those of Delaware, Maryland, Massachusetts, and New Hampshire prohibited the keeping of standing armies "without the consent of the legislature" (Thorpe, III, 1688, 1892; IV, 2456; and *AHR*, III [1898], 646 [Delaware]).

6. All seven of the state declarations of rights listed in note 5 (above) also provided for the subordination of the military to the civil power.

7. "Brutus" inserted the italics.

Cincinnatus I: To James Wilson, Esquire
New York Journal, 1 November 1787

Six essays signed "Cincinnatus"—addressed to "James Wilson, Esquire"— appeared in the *New York Journal* between 1 November and 6 December. They responded to Wilson's 6 October speech defending the Constitution before a Philadelphia public meeting (CC:134. See also "New York Reprinting of James Wilson's 6 October Speech Before a Philadelphia Public Meeting," 13–25 October, above.). None of the "Cincinnatus" essays was reprinted in New York, although each essay was reprinted in one or the other of Philadelphia's two Antifederalist newspapers, the *Independent Gazetteer* and the *Freeman's Journal*. Other reprints were scattered among five New England towns.

Contemporaries attributed the essays to Richard Henry Lee or to his brother Arthur. On 21 November the *Pennsylvania Gazette* printed an extract of a letter stating that "R——d H—y L.-e passed through this town [Wilmington, Del.] a few days ago, on his way to Virginia. He spent a whole evening in reading his Cincinnatusses, and in abusing Mr. Wilson and the new government. . . ." (CC:280. This extract was reprinted in the *Daily Advertiser*, 24 November. For another description of Lee's alleged activities in Wilmington, see Samuel Powel to George Washington, 13 November, CC:255.). On 22 November William Shippen, Jr., a Philadelphia physician and a brother-in-law to the Lees, wrote his son in London that "Brutus said to be by R. H. Lee or Jay, Cincinnatus by A Lee . . ." (to Thomas Lee Shippen, RCS:Pa., 288). In May 1788 William Short, secretary to American minister Thomas Jefferson in Paris, declared that he learned from John Paradise that Arthur Lee wrote the "Cincinnatus" essays (to Thomas Lee Shippen, 31 May 1788, RCS:Va., 896). Paradise, an English linguist who lived in London, was related to the Lees by marriage. He visited Virginia in 1787 with his wife Lucy Ludwell and sailed for France in late April or early May 1788, after having spent some time in New York City.

"Cincinnatus" attracted little response in New York, where he was criticized in general along with several other New York Antifederalist writers. For example, "Examiner" I (Charles McKnight), *New York Journal*, 11 December, referred to these writers as a "black train of sophists," while "A Lunarian," *Daily Advertiser*, 20 December, dismissed their writings as having "but little substance" (both below). "A Citizen of America," *Daily Advertiser*, 19 February 1788, charged that "Cincinnatus" belonged to a state party, some of whose members were "destitute of the principles of truth" (III below). The principal criticism of "Cincinnatus," however, was printed in the Northampton, Mass., *Hampshire Gazette*, 19 December, by "Anti-Cincinnatus," who rebutted "Cincinnatus" I point-by-point (RCS:Mass., 487–90. The *Gazette* had reprinted "Cincinnatus" I on 5 December.). "Anti-Cincinnatus," who, in particular, denied the need for a bill of rights and defended the Constitution's treaty-making powers, appeared on 29 December in the *New York Journal*, the only newspaper to reprint it. "Anti-Cincinnatus" also asserted that "Cincinnatus" I was "filled with little else but sarcastical taunts liberally bestowed both upon the Constitution, and Mr. Wilson, one of its framers and advocates."

In addition to appearing in the *Hampshire Gazette* on 5 December, "Cincinnatus" I—the most oft-reprinted number—appeared in the *Massachusetts Gazette*, 16 November; Philadelphia *Independent Gazetteer*, 16 November; *Vermont Gazette*, 26 November; and *Providence Gazette*, 8 December.

Arthur Lee (1740–1792), a Virginia lawyer and a former physician, received medical degrees from the University of Edinburgh and the University of Leyden, and studied law at Middle Temple and Lincoln's Inn. A prolific pamphleteer who supported American independence, Lee was treaty commissioner to France, 1776–79, and a signer of the Treaties of Alliance and Commerce with France, 1778. He represented Prince William County in the Virginia House of Delegates, 1781–84; was a delegate to Congress, 1782–84; and was a member of the three-member Confederation Board of Treasury, 1785–89.

MR. GREENLEAF, A speech made to the citizens of Philadelphia, and said to be by MR. WILSON, appears to me to abound with sophistry, so dangerous, as to require refutation. If we adopt the new Constitution, let us at least understand it. Whether it deserves adoption or not, we can only determine by a full examination of it, so as clearly to discern what it is that we are so loudly, I had almost said, indecently called upon to receive. Such an examination is the object of the papers which I am to entreat you to lay before the public, in answer to Mr. Wilson, and under the signature of— Cincinnatus.

SIR, You have had the graciousness, Sir, to come forward as the defender and panegyrist of the plan of a new Constitution, of which you was one of the framers. If the defence you have thought proper to set up, and the explanations you have been pleased to give, should be found, upon a full and fair examination, to be fallacious or inadequate; I am not without hope, that candor, of which no gentleman talks more, will render you a convert to the opinion, that some material parts of the proposed Constitution are so constructed—that a *monstrous aristocracy springing from it, must necessarily swallow up the democratic rights of the union, and sacrifice the liberties of the people to the power and domination of a few.*

If your defence of this new plan of power, has, as you say, been matured by four months constant meditation upon it, and is yet so very weak, as I trust will appear, men will begin to think, that—the thing itself is indefensible. Upon a subject so momentous, the public has a right to the sentiments of every individual that will reason: I therefore do not think any apology necessary for appearing in print; and I hope to avoid, at least, the indiscriminate censure which you have, with so much candor and liberality, thrown on those who will not worship *your idol*—"that they are industriously endeavouring to prevent and destroy it, by insidious and clandestine attempts." Give me leave just to suggest, that perhaps these clandestine attempts might have been owing to the terror of *your mob*, which so nobly endeavoured to prevent all freedom of action and of speech.[1] The *reptile Doctor*, who was employed to blow the trumpet of persecution, would have answered the public reasoning of an opponent, by hounding on him the rage of a deluded populace.[2]

It was to such men, and under such impressions, that you made the speech which I am now to examine; no wonder then that it was received with loud and unanimous testamonies of their approbation. They were vociferating through you the panegyric of their own intemperate opinions.

Your first attempt is to apologize for so very obvious a defect as— the omission of a declaration of rights. This apology consists in a very ingenious discovery; that in the state constitutions, whatever is not re- served is given; but in the congressional constitution, whatever is not given, is reserved. This has more the quaintness of a conundrum, than the dignity of an argument. The conventions that made the state and the general constitutions, sprang from the same source, were delegated for the same purpose—that is, for framing rules by which we should be governed, and ascertaining those powers which it was necessary to vest in our rulers. Where then is this distinction to be found, but in your assumption? Is it in the powers given to the members of conven- tion? no—Is it in the constitution? not a word of it:—And yet on this play of words, this dictum of yours, this distinction without a difference, you would persuade us to rest our most essential rights. I trust, however, that the good sense of this free people cannot be so easily imposed on by professional figments. The confederation, in its very outset, de- clares—that what is not expressly given, is reserved.[3] This constitution makes no such reservation. The presumption therefore is, that the framers of the proposed constitution, did not mean to subject it to the same exception.

You instance, Sir, the liberty of the press; which you would persuade us, is in *no* danger, though not secured, because there is no express power granted to regulate literary publications. But you surely know, Sir, that where general powers are expressly granted, the particular ones comprehended within them, must also be granted. For instance, the proposed Congress are empowered—to define and punish offences against the law of nations—mark well, Sir, if you please—to *define* and punish. Will you, will any one say, can any one even think that does not comprehend a power to define and declare all publications from the press against the conduct of government, in making treaties, or in any other foreign transactions, an offence against the law of nations? If there should ever be an influential president, or arbitrary senate, who do not choose that their transactions with foreign powers should be discussed or examined in the public prints, they will easily find pretexts to prevail upon the other branch to concur with them, in restraining what it may please them to call—the licentiousness of the press. And this may be, even without the concurrence of the representatives of the people; because the president and senate are empowered to make treaties, and these treaties are declared the supreme law of the land.

What use they will make of this power, is not now the question. Certain it is, that such power is given, and that power is not restrained by any declaration—that the liberty of the press, which even you term, the sacred palladium of national freedom, shall be forever free and inviolable. I have proved that the power of restraining the press, is necessarily involved in the unlimited power of defining offences, or of making treaties, which are to be the supreme law of the land. You acknowledge, that it is not expressly excepted, and consequently it is at the mercy of the powers to be created by this constitution.

Let us suppose then, that what has happened, may happen again: That a patriotic printer, like Peter Zenger, should incur the resentment of our new rulers, by publishing to the world, transactions which they wish to conceal. If he should be prosecuted, if his judges should be as desirous of punishing him, *at all events,* as the judges were to punish Peter Zenger, what would his innocence or his virtue avail him? This constitution is so admirably framed for tyranny, that, by clear construction, the judges might put the verdict of a jury out of the question. Among the cases in which the court is to have appellate jurisdiction, are—controversies, to which the United States are a party:—In this appellate jurisdiction, the judges are to determine, *both law and fact.* That is, the court is both judge and jury. The attorney general then would have only to move a question of law in the court below, to ground an appeal to the supreme judicature, and the printer would be delivered up to the mercy of his judges. Peter Zenger's case will teach us, what mercy he might expect. Thus, if the president, vice-president, or any officer, or favorite of state, should be censured in print, he might effectually deprive the printer, or author, of his trial by jury, and subject him to something, that will probably very much resemble the—Star Chamber of former times.[4] The freedom of the press, the sacred palladium of public liberty, would be pulled down;—all useful knowledge on the conduct of government would be withheld from the people— the press would become subservient to the purposes of bad and arbitrary rulers, and imposition, not information, would be its object.

The printers would do well, to publish the proceedings of the judges, in Peter Zenger's case—they would do well to publish lord Mansfield's conduct in, the King against Woodfall;—that the public mind may be properly warned of the consequences of agreeing to a constitution, which provides no security for the freedom of the press, and leaves it controversial at least—whether in matter of libels against any of our intended rulers; the printer would even have the security of trial by jury. Yet it was the jury only, that saved Zenger, it was a jury only, that saved Woodfall, it can only be a jury that will save any future printer from the fangs of power.[5]

Had you, Mr. Wilson, who are so unmerciful against what you are pleased to call, the disingenuous conduct of those who dislike the constitution; had you been ingenuous enough to have stated this fairly to our fellow citizens; had you said to them—gentlemen, it is true, that the freedom of the press is not provided for; it is true, that it may be restrained at pleasure, by our proposed rulers; it is true, that a printer sued for a libel, would not be tried by a jury; all this is true, nay, worse than this is also true; but then it is all necessary to what I think, *the best form of government that has ever been offered the world.*

To have stated these truths, would at least have been acting like an honest man; and if it did not procure you such unanimous testimonies of approbation, what you would have received, would have been *merited.*

But you choose to shew our fellow citizens, nothing but what would flatter and mislead them. You exhibited, that by a rush-light only, which, to dissipate its darkness, required the full force of the meridian sun. When the people are fully apprized of the chains you have prepared for them, if they choose to put them on, you have nothing to answer for. If they choose to be tenants at will of their liberties, by the new constitution; instead of having their freehold in them, secured by a declaration of rights; I can only lament it. There was a time, when our fellow citizens were told, in the words of Sir Edward Coke—For a man to be tenant at will of his liberty, I can never agree to it—*Etiam si* Dominus *non sit molestus, tamen miserremum est,* posse, *se vebit*—Though a despot may not act tyrannically; yet it is dreadful to think, that if he *will*, he *may*. Perhaps you may also remember, Sir, that our fellow citizens were then warned against those—"smooth words, with which the most dreadful designs may be glossed over." You have given us a lively comment on your own text. You have varnished over the iron trap that is prepared, and *bated with some illustrious names, to catch the liberties of the people.*

1. On 29 September 1787 a mob forced two Antifederalist assemblymen to attend the Pennsylvania Assembly so that the Assembly would attain the quorum needed to adopt resolutions calling a state convention to consider the Constitution. (See "New York Reprinting of the Address of the Seceding Members of the Pennsylvania Assembly," 9–18 October, above.)

2. Benjamin Rush, a prominent Philadelphia physician who would become a Federalist polemicist.

3. Article II of the Articles of Confederation states: "Each state retains its sovereignty, freedom and independence, and every Power, Jurisdiction and right, which is not by this confederation expressly delegated to the United States, in Congress assembled" (CDR, 86).

4. The Court of Star Chamber evolved in 15th-century England from the judicial sittings of the King's Council at Westminster. It began as a juryless court of equity and prerogative, but extended its jurisdiction, particularly under the Tudors, to criminal matters and libels. Under the Stuart kings James I and Charles I, the Star Chamber became tyrannical and arbitrary. The Court of Star Chamber was abolished by the Long Parliament in 1641.

5. Both New York City newspaper printer John Peter Zenger and London newspaper printer Henry Sampson Woodfall were tried for committing seditious libel against royal authority. In November 1734 Zenger was imprisoned at the order of the William Cosby, New York's royal governor, because Zenger attacked the governor and his administration for corruption and abuse of power. In August 1735 Zenger, who had been in jail since being arrested, went on trial for publishing seditious libel against the governor. The jury was instructed to bring in a special verdict, determining only if Zenger was guilty of publishing the material and whether the material was aimed at the governor and his administration. Under English common law, judges alone could determine whether or not the attacks were libelous. The jury, however, brought in a general verdict of not guilty. Zenger spent only one more night in jail, being released the next morning.

Henry Sampson Woodfall published one of the letters of "Junius" that attacked the King. In the case of *Rex* v. *Woodfall* (1770), the Chief Justice of King's Bench, Lord Mansfield (William Murray, 1705–1793), instructed the jury that it was to consider two points: whether Woodfall had published the letter and whether the innuendoes and blank spaces in the letter referred to the King and his ministers. The issue of whether or not the letter was a libel published with malicious or criminal intent, Lord Mansfield reserved to the court. The jury found Woodfall guilty of printing and publishing *only*, implying that Woodfall was not guilty of libel. Since the jury's meaning was unclear and the court term was nearing an end, the justices of King's Bench took the verdict under advisement. The next term, Lord Mansfield, speaking for the court, set the verdict aside and ordered a new trial. Only when two other printers were acquitted outright for the same offense did the Crown decide against further prosecution. Mansfield, however, consistently maintained this position before the American Revolution and continued to do so after the Revolution, particularly in the famous case (1784) of the Rev. W. D. Shipley, the Dean of St. Asaph, who was indicted for seditious libel for printing a pamphlet favoring parliamentary reform.

Timoleon
New York Journal, 1 November 1787 (extraordinary)

On 25 October editor Thomas Greenleaf of the *New York Journal* announced that he had received "Timoleon" but for "Want of room" he was postponing publication of Timoleon and other "interesting pieces upon public topics" until the following week. "Timoleon" appeared on 1 November in a two-page extra issue that also included only "Centinel" II (Philadelphia *Freeman's Journal*, 24 October, CC:190). In Greenleaf's regular issue of 1 November, he informed his readers that they could find the two essays in this extraordinary issue.

Not long after the extraordinary issue appeared, Greenleaf reprinted "Centinel" I, Philadelphia *Independent Gazetteer*, 5 October (CC:133), "Centinel" II, and "Timoleon," in that order, in a two-page broadside that did not display his colophon (Evans 45045). The two-page broadside circulated in the Hudson River Valley, as far north as Albany and Lansingburgh. New York Antifederalists also sent hundreds of broadsides into Connecticut, an action condemned by Connecticut Federalists (*New Haven Gazette*, 22 November and 13 December, CC:283–A and C; and RCS:Conn, 330, 458, 470–71, 495–96, 507, 514. For more on the reprinting of "Centinel," see "New York Reprinting of the Centinel Essays," 17 October 1787–12 April 1788, above.). "A Countryman" II (Roger Sherman), *New Haven Gazette*, 22 November, listed several prominent New York and Pennsylvania Antifederalists, "Timoleon" included, whose "declamations" he denounced. According to "A Countryman," "Timoleon" was "more contemptible" than any of these writers (CC:284. "A Countryman" II was reprinted in the *New York Journal* on 3 December.).

MR. GREENLEAF, I was lately invited to pass the evening with a club of grave and sensible men, who are in the practice of assembling weekly to converse on public affairs; and having been previously made acquainted, by my introducing friend, with the characters, situations, and circumstances of the persons who composed this club, I found that they were not officers of the present government, and that there was little probability of any among them becoming suitors (or seekers, as now called) for place, or employment under the *new Constitution*, if it should succeed. I judged from their contented and independent characters, that they had no view to place of *finance*, of *judge*, or *attorney-general*, or *tax collectors*, or any other office of emolument, which so often drives men to prostitute their abilities for the support of bad measures, from expectation of *great profit*.

I accepted, with pleasure, an opportunity of hearing the sentiments of such respectable characters, on so interesting a subject as public affairs, especially at this crisis, when the minds of men are *on one side violently agitated and active;* on the other, and the greater part, *a sleepy indolence and inattention* seems to prevail. As I expected, so it happened, that the conversation turned upon the new Constitution offered by the late Convention.

After some judicious reflections on this subject, which tended to shew the necessity of the most plain and unequivocal language in the all important business of constituting government, which necessarily conveying great powers, is always liable (from the natural tendency of power to corrupt the human heart and deprave the head) to great abuse; by perverse and subtle arguments calculated to extend dominion over all things and all men. One of the club supposed the following case:—A gentleman *in the line of his profession* is appointed a *judge* of the supreme court under the new Constitution, and the *rulers,* finding that the rights of conscience and the freedom of the press were exercised in such a manner, by *preaching* and *printing* as to be troublesome to the new government—which event would probably happen, if the rulers finding themselves possessed of great power, should so use it as to oppress and injure the community.—In this state of things the *judge* is called upon, *in the line of his profession,* to give his opinion—whether the *new Constitution* admitted of a legislative act to *suppress the rights of conscience,* and *violate the liberty of the press?* The answer of the learned *judge* is conceived in didactic mode, and expressed in learned phrase; thus,—In the 8th section of the first article of the *new Constitution,* the Congress have power given *to lay and collect taxes for the general welfare of the United States.* By this power, the right of taxing is co-extensive with the *general welfare,* and the *general welfare* is as unlimitted as actions and things are that may disturb or benefit that general welfare. A right being given to *tax* for the general welfare, necessarily includes the right of judging what is for the general welfare, and a right of judging what is for the general welfare, as *necessarily* includes a power of protecting, defending, and promoting it by all such laws and means as are fitted to that end; for, qui dat finem dat media ad finem necessaria, who gives the end gives the means necessary to obtain the end. The Constitution must be so construed as not to involve an absurdity, which would clearly follow from allowing the end and denying the means. A right of *taxing* for the general welfare being the highest and most important mode of providing for it, cannot be supposed to exclude inferior modes of effecting the same purpose, because the rule of law is, that, omne majus continet in se minus.[1]

From hence it clearly results, that, if *preachers* and *printers* are troublesome to the new government; and that in the opinion of its rulers, it shall be for the general welfare to restrain or suppress both the one and the other, it may be done consistently with the new Constitution. And that this was the opinion of the community when they consented

to it, is evident from this consideration; that although the all comprehending power of the new legislature is fixed, by its acts being made
the *supreme law* of the land, any thing in the *Constitutions* or laws of any
state to the contrary notwithstanding: Yet no *express* declaration in favor
of the *rights of conscience* or *liberty* of the *press* is to be found in the new
Constitution, as we see was carefully done in the *Constitutions* of the
states composing this union—Shewing clearly, that what was *then* thought
necessary to be specially reserved from the pleasure of power, is *now*
designed to be yielded to its will.

A grave old gentleman of the club, who had sat with his head re-
clined on his hand, listening in pensive mood to the argument of the
judge, said, "I verily believe, that neither the logic or the law of that
opinion will be hereafter doubted by the professors of power, who,
through the history of human nature, have been for enlarging the
sphere of their authority. And thus the dearest rights of men and the
best security of civil liberty may be sacrificed by the sophism of a lawyer,
who, Carneades like, can to day shew that to be necessary, before the
people, which to-morrow he can likewise shew to be unnecessary and
useless—For which reason the sagacious Cato advised, that such a man
should immediately be sent from the city, as a person dangerous to the
morals of the people and to society."[2] The old gentleman continued,
"I now plainly see the necessity of express declarations and reservations
in favor of the great, unalienable rights of mankind, to prevent the
oppressive and wicked extention of power to the ruin of human liberty.
For the opinion above stated, absolutely refutes the sophistry of 'that
being retained which is not given,' where the words conveying power
admit of the most extensive construction that language can reach to,
or the mind conceive, as is the case in this new Constitution. By which
we have already seen how logically it may be proved, that both *religion*
and the *press* can be made to bend before the views of power. With as
little ceremony, and similar constructive doctrine, the inestimable trial
by jury can likewise be depraved and destroyed—because the Constitution in the 2d section of the 3d article, by expressly assuming the
trial by jury in *criminal cases*, and being silent about it in *civil causes*,
evidently declares it to be unnecessary in the latter. And more strongly
so, by giving the supreme court jurisdiction in appeals, '*both as to law
and fact.*' If to this be added, that the trial by jury in criminal cases is
only stipulated to be '*in the state*,' not in the county where the crime is
supposed to have been committed; one excellent part of the jury trial,
from the vicinage, or at least from the county, is even in criminal cases
rendered precarious, and at the mercy of rulers under the new Constitution.—Yet the danger to liberty, peace, and property, from restrain-

ing and injuring this excellent mode of trial, will clearly appear from the following observations of the learned Dr. Blackstone, in his commentaries on the laws of England, Art. Jury Trial Book 3. chap. 33.— 'The establishment of jury trial was always so highly esteemed and valued by the people, that no conquest, *no change of government*, could ever prevail to abolish it. In magna charta it is more than once insisted upon *as the principal bulwark of our liberties*—And this is a species of knowledge most absolutely necessary for every gentleman; as well, because he may be frequently called upon to determine in this capacity the rights of others, his fellow subjects; as, *because his own property, his liberty, and his life, depend upon maintaining in its legal force the trial by jury*—In settling and adjusting a question of *fact*, when intrusted to any single magistrate, partiality and injustice have an ample field to range in; either by boldly asserting that to be proved which is not so, or by more artfully suppressing some circumstances, stretching and warping others, and distinguishing away the remainder. Here therefore a competent number of sensible and upright jurymen, *chosen from among those of the middle rank, will be found the best investigators of truth, and the surest guardians of public justice.* For the most powerful individual in the state will be cautious of committing any flagrant invasion of anothers right, when he knows that the *fact* of his oppression must be examined and decided by twelve indifferent men, not appointed until the hour of trial; and that when once the *fact* is ascertained, *the law must*, of course, redress it. *This, therefore, preserves in the hands of the people that share, which they ought to have* in the administration of public justice, *and prevents the encroachments of the more powerful and wealthy citizens. Every new tribunal, erected for the decision of facts, without the intervention of a jury* (whether composed of justices of the peace, commissioners of the revenue, judges of a court of conscience, or any other standing magistrates) *is a step towards establishing aristocracy, the most oppressive of absolute governments.* And in every country as the trial by jury has been *gradually disused*, so the great have increased in power, until the state has been torn to pieces by rival factions, and oligarchy in effect has been established, though under the shadow of regal government; unless where the miserable people have taken shelter under absolute monarchy, as the lighter evil of the two. And, particularly, it is worthy of observation, that in Sweden the trial by jury, that bulwark of liberty, continued long in its full force, but is now fallen into disuse; and that there, though the regal power is in no country so closely limitted, yet the liberties of the commons are extinguished, and the government is degenerated into a mere aristocracy. *It is therefore upon the whole, a duty which every man owes to his country, his friends, his posterity, and himself, to maintain, to the utmost of his power, this valuable trial by jury in all its rights.'* ["]³ Thus far the learned Dr. Blackstone.—"Could the Doctor, if he were here, at this moment, continued the old gentleman, have condemned those parts of the new Constitution in stronger terms, which give the supreme court jurisdiction both as to law and *fact;* and which have weakened the jury trial in criminal cases, and which have discountenanced it in all civil causes? At first I wondered at the complaint that some people made of this new Constitution, because it led to the government of a few; but it is fairly to be concluded, from this injury to the trial by jury, that *some* who framed this new system, saw with Dr. Blackstone, how operative jury trial was in preventing the tyranny of the great ones, and therefore frowned upon it, as this new Constitution does. But we may hope that our fellow citizens will not approve of this new plan of government, before they have well considered it, and that they will insist on such amendments to it, as will secure from violation the just rights and liberty of the people." The club listened, with great attention, to the worthy old gentleman, and joined him in hearty wishes, that the people may be upon their guard, and not suffer themselves to be deprived of liberty, under the notion of strong federal government—because the design of all government should be the happiness of the people, and it is not necessary for the purpose of securing happiness, that power should be given rulers to destroy happiness. I was an attentive hearer, Mr. Greenleaf, of what passed in this honest club, and I have given it to you as nearly as my memory (which is not a bad one) enables me to do. I confess to you, that I felt my mind much informed upon this all important business, the new Constitution, which, when first I saw it, and hastily read it, I found my imagination quickly taken with the good parts of it, and so passed over those great and fundamental errors, which, if agreed to, must inevitably convert the people of this free country into hewers of wood and drawers of water⁴ for the few great ones, into whose hands all power will be thereby unwarily delivered.

New-York, October 24, 1787.

1. Latin: "Every greater contains in itself the less" or "The greater always contains the less."

2. Carneades of Cyrene (214–129 B.C.), a philosopher noted for his dialetical and rhetorical abilities, was famous for his method of arguing for and against any given point of view. The Athenians sent him and several others on an embassy to Rome, where Carneades so captivated the youth of Rome with his method that Cato the Censor (234–149 B.C.) demanded that Carneades and the others leave Rome immediately for fear that Carneades would corrupt Roman youth.

3. Blackstone, *Commentaries,* Book III, chapter XXIII, 350–51, 380–81.

4. Joshua 9:21, 23, 27.

Americanus I
New York Daily Advertiser, 2 November 1787[1]

Seven essays signed "Americanus" that answered critics of the Constitution appeared in the *Daily Advertiser* between 2 November 1787 and 21 January 1788. In numbers I–VI "Americanus" criticizes the New York writer "Cato" (see "Cato" I, *New York Journal*, 27 September, above). In number VI "Americanus" also attacks "The Dissent of the Minority of the Pennsylvania Convention," *Pennsylvania Packet*, 18 December (CC:353). Number VII responds to Virginia Governor Edmund Randolph's letter to the speaker of the Virginia House of Delegates, first printed as a pamphlet around 27 December (CC:385). (See also "New York Reprinting of the Dissent of the Minority of the Pennsylvania Convention," 27 December 1787–April 1788, and "New York Reprinting of Virginia Governor Edmund Randolph's 10 October 1787 Letter to the Speaker of the Virginia House of Delegates," 8 January–April 1788 [both below].) None of the seven "Americanus" essays was reprinted; nor did any of them evoke any significant commentary.

"Americanus" was John Stevens, Jr., of Hoboken, N.J., who identified himself as the author when he wrote to his father on 14 December that "If you get the New York Daily advertiser you will see some pieces signed Americanus written by a friend of yours" (Stevens Family Papers, NjHi).

Cato has at length opened his batteries on the Constitution, submitted to us by the late Convention.[2] He begins with an endeavor to impress us with this idea, that "the axioms of Montesquieu, Locke, &c. in the science of politics, are as irrefragable as any in Euclid." And can we possibly believe Cato to be really in earnest? Wretched indeed would be our political institution[s], had we been governed by the "axioms" of European writers on politics, in the formation of them. As we are placed in a situation totally new, instead of absurdly hunting for precedents in the old world, we must think, we must reason, for ourselves. Every American breast, retaining the least degree of spirit, must spurn, with indignation, at this insidious attempt to shackle our understandings.

Montesquieu, it seems, tells us, that a *Republic must have only a small territory*. But how, I would ask, would he, or Locke, or any other political writer in Europe, be warranted in insisting on this assertion as *an irrefragable axiom?* Had they formed any conceptions of a republican Government instituted upon the plan of the Constitution now under consideration? Because the wretched attempts that have been made in the old world, to constitute Republican Governments, have necessarily failed of attaining the desired purpose, are we to be told the thing is "impracticable," when attempted upon principles as different, as light is from darkness? Montesquieu's maxim may be just, for aught I know, when applied to such republican Governments as Sparta. This commonwealth affords us a striking instance of the absurdities mankind are capable of when they blindly submit themselves to the guidance of *passion* and *prejudice*. Had we not the undoubted evidence of history, it could never be believed, at this time of day, that such a monstrous political prodigy could really have existed. This institution was founded upon Montesquieu's principle of Republican Government, viz. virtue: by virtue, here, is not meant morality; but an enthusiastic attachment to the political system of the country we inhabit. By the force of this mistaken principle, however, the Government, which Lycurgus established in Sparta, was supported for ages. It is unnecessary for me to attempt a delineation of this wonderful institution, against which the feelings of humanity, every generous sentiment of the human heart, revolt with horror. And what is the tendency of Cato's reasoning, but to form Governments, like that of Sparta, in every State in the Union? Should we be able to support separate independent sovereignties (which, with submission to Cato, I think would be "impracticable") we should soon become mere nests of hornets. The austere hostile spirit of Lacedemon, must be substituted in the place of that benign temper of universal philanthropy which the Constitution offered to us is so eminently calculated to diffuse; and which is so congenial to the habits and sentiments of Americans. Away with this Spartan virtue and black broth; we'll have none of them: and Cato must not think to cram them down our throats, by telling us it is the prescription of a great political doctor. The "axioms" of Montesquieu, or any other great man, tho' Cato shall deem them "as irrefragable as any in Euclid," shall never persuade me to quarrel with my bread and butter.

"A Republic must have only a small territory, otherwise it cannot long subsist." But I utterly deny the truth of this "axiom" of the celebrated civilian. This ought not to be deemed arrogant in me, or in any man, at this time of day, and on this side the Atlantic. The learned Frenchman formed his principles of Government in conformity to the lights he possessed. Had he been an American, and now living, I would stake my life on it, he would have formed different principles. A collection of smaller States, united under one federal head, by a Constitution of Government similar to the one at present under consideration, is capable of a greater degree of real permanent liberty, than any combination of power I can form an idea of. The grand evil which all popular governments have hitherto labored under, is an inveterate tendency to faction. We are naturally inclined, without the aid of reason and experience, to suppose that in a free government every man should have a right to a personal vote on every measure. This is the rock on which all Democratic Governments have split. And, indeed, were we to admit this principle in the formation of a Republic, Mr. Montesquieu's maxim would be perfectly just; for it would be utterly "impracticable" for a people to exercise this right, who were not confined to a "small territory." But reason and experience have at length convinced us of the impropriety of the people themselves interfering, in any shape, in the administration of Government. The powers of Government must, of necessity, be delegated. It was the English who first discovered the secret, of which the ancients were totally ignorant, of Legislation by Representation. This is the hinge on which all Republican Governments must move. But we must proceed a step farther. It has also been discovered, that faction cannot be expelled even from a *Representative* body, while possessed *singly* of the whole of the Legislative power. Hence two distinct Legislative bodies have been contrived, farther to check this turbulent spirit. But even this, too, has been found insufficient. To give, therefore, the last finish to this beautiful model of Republican Government, it has been found necessary to place one more check, by giving the Executive and Judicial a revisory power. But, so prone is the spirit of man to party and faction, that even this admirable system will not prevent their mischivous effects, in a state possessing a "small territory." The next expedient, then, is to unite a number of these lesser communities under one Federal Head. The chain of dependence, thus lengthened, will give a permanency, consistency, and uniformity to a *Federal* Government, of which that of a *single* State is, in its nature, incapable. The gusts of passion, which faction is ever flowing up in "*a small territory*," lose their force before they reach the seat of *Federal* Government. Republics, limited to *a small territory*, ever have been, and, from the nature of man, ever will be, liable to be torn to pieces by faction. When the citizens are confined within a narrow compass, as was the café of Sparta, Rome, &c. it is within the power of a factious demagogue to scatter sedition and discontent, instantaneously, thro' every part of the State. An artful declaimer, such as Cato, for instance, by infusing jealousy and rage into the minds of the people, may do irreparable mischief to a small State. The people, thrown suddenly into passion, whilst this paroxysm, whilst this fit of insanity continues, commit a thousand enormities; and it is well if the Government itself escapes from total subversion. Had the commotion, which Shays excited in Massachusetts, happened in a state of *small territory*, what would have been the probable consequences? Before the people had recovered from their madness, perhaps all would have been lost.

"The employments of your country, disposed of to the opulent, to whose contumely you will continually be an object."—"You must risque much, by indispensibly placing trusts of the greatest magnitude in the hands of individuals, whose ambition for power and aggrandizement will oppress and grind you." This is *argumentum ad populum.*[3] Cato knows better: he knows that the powers vested, by this Constitution, in the Federal Government, are incapable of abuse.

The different powers are so modified and distributed, as to form mutual checks upon each other. The State Legislatures form a check on the Senate and House of Representatives, infinitely more effectual than that of the people themselves on their State Legislatures. The people, so far from entertaining a jealousy of, in fact place the highest confidence in, *their* Representatives; who, by giving false colorings to bad measures, are too often enabled to abuse the trust reposed in them. But widely different is the situation in which the Federal Representatives stand, in respect to the State Legislatures. Here the mutual apprehensions of encroachments, must for ever keep awake a jealous, watchful spirit, which will not suffer the smallest abuse to pass unnoticed. The Senate and House of Representatives form mutual checks on each other, and the President on both. Cato's apprehensions of Monarchy are chimerical, in the highest degree; and calculated in the same manner as what he says of the rich oppressing and grinding the poor—to catch the attention of the unwary multitude.

1. On 30 October the *Daily Advertiser* announced that "Americanus" was received and that it "will appear as soon as possible."

2. See "Cato" III, *New York Journal,* 25 October (above).

3. Latin: An appeal to the people (i.e., to their lower nature rather than to their intellect).

Curtius III
New York Daily Advertiser, 3 November 1787 (supplement)[1]

An ADDRESS to FEDERALISTS.

One who has no other motive than the public good to influence his political sentiments, congratulates you upon the Federal spirit now so universally pervading the Union; incontestible evidences of which are daily received.

A late respectable Convention of Clergymen, in this city,[2] have done honor to their society, by intimating to us the general sense of the serious and sedate. The proposed Constitution appeared to them so evidently calculated to promote the happiness of mankind, and to secure the liberties of their country, as to draw forth their public and warmest commendations. By those, in every State, who have long been most eminent for wisdom and integrity, it is regarded as the mean to expand the wings of commerce, science and religion; to convert our deserts into populous and cultivated villages; to reward the toils of smiling industry; to banish frowning discord from our peaceful borders; to exalt the scale of justice, to restore the crown of righteousness to the brow of America, and to perpetuate the blessings for which she has bled.

The numbers of that enlightened order in society, the *mercantile*, are too sensible of the importance of national respectability, of public credit abroad, and of just commercial regulations at home, to hesitate long as to its adoption. They perceive that, under it, the most excellent provisions will be instituted, with respect to such objects; while they know, that, notwithstanding every real or pretended defect, it surpasses any system of Government, that has ever as yet regulated an extensive empire. Hence it is that the cities of Boston, New-York, Philadelphia, Annapolis, and our other trading towns, are so undivided in sentiment. Boston warmly espouses the opinion of her worthy Governor;[3] but it is to be hoped she has not burnt in effigy a seceding member of the Convention;[4] or that, from Alexandria, another has been formally banished by its Mayor and Corporation.[5] An honest indignation of patriotism is often commendable: but when it flames to a devouring enthusiasm; when respectable characters become its victims, philanthropy must sigh at the frailties of humanity.

But it is not our cities alone that are attentive to the instructions of sound policy. The intelligent farmer, and the industrious mechanic, perceive the oppressions of ignorance, the injustice of ex post facto laws, the want of encouragement to labor, the instability of Government, and the insecurity of property. Hence it is, we find the interior counties of many of the States, particularly of Virginia,[6] so warmly expressing their attachment to the new Constitution. Hence it is, that several of the State Conventions are already appointed. Hence the odium that rests upon the seceding members throughout Pennsylvania.[7] The town of Carlisle, so far from resenting the conduct of Philadelphia towards her representatives, as Anti-Federalists supposed, unanimously declared them unworthy, in future, to hold any office of place or trust.[8] The Federal dagger is half unsheathed in the State of Jersey; and her counties, composed principally of farmers, pledge their lives and fortunes in support of the glorious revolution.[9]

The last mentioned circumstance might convince any candid mind, how cowardly is the fear, how idle is the pretence of despotism. If the Constitution was, in reality, thus dangerously constructed, by the encroachments of power, the great would at length overwhelm the small, and the State of Jersey would be among the first to fall a sacrifice to her powerful and ambitious neighbours. Jealousy, in different degrees, is the blessing and the bane of liberty. In free countries it is constantly verging to an excess of distrust. But the State which would be most in danger, had these cowardly pretences any foundation, is not only ardently favorable to Federal measures, but wisely conceiving her safety and her interest connected thereto, willingly concedes one half of her present consequence in the Federal councils.[10] It is not, my countrymen, the fear of any encroachments from despotism, so much as an attachment to local advantages, that any where excites opposition. While the latter is secretly operating upon the minds of the avaricious, the pretence of the former is an artful invention of ambition, to rouse the distrust of the jealous.

But, as history has shewn the danger of great national revolutions, and as reason pronounces that the frequency of change must beget an habit of inconstancy in the minds of the people, let us for once enquire, why an alteration in the government of these states is considered as necessary—why it is so fervently wished for, and so confidently expected? This enquiry is easily resolved. For, besides the reasons furnished by the foregoing reflections, the federal government in its present situation is utterly incapable of combining or of supporting the various interests of the union. Nor ought, what should have been expected, to create the least degree of surprise; since the confederation was formed, when the principles of legislation were comparatively but ill understood; when the common cause of liberty and the sense of common danger united us in the most indissoluble bonds; and when the great object of all our patriotic reflections was, not to form a political system, but to repel a powerful enemy. The present construction of our union being, therefore, as it were by accident, radically repugnant to every wise principle in jurisprudence, any trifling alteration rendering it efficient to temporary purposes, would as certainly cause its final operation to be both absurd and oppressive. While its laws, or rather its *recommendations* are the subjects of ridicule, while its exertions excite opposition and abhorrence, can we conceive of a government more open to anarchy, or more destructive in its issue? Our foreign politics and our domestic economy are equally deranged. Our friends are disgusted, and our enemies treat us with contempt. The states are disobedient to the most constitutional requisitions, and an energy is wanting necessary to the support of any government. The state of New-York and the state of Delaware bear an equal weight in the federal councils, and the inconveniencies of so disproportionate a representation must sooner or later be felt. In fine, an incapacity to regulate the common concerns of the union is daily experienced, or to discharge its most indispensible obligations, either at home or abroad. It may be added, that among the states themselves, we trace the symptoms of growing disaffection, mutual jealousy, separate interest, and local prejudice. Injustice, faction and confusion, call into birth the deadliest animosities.—Such is the real, but awful situation of our public affairs!

Whether should opposition most excite, our pity, our indignation, or our contempt? Is it possible, that, as the moderate Publius supposes, there may, from human fallability, be men so blind to the interest of their country, as to oppose from principle the most obvious dictates of wisdom?[11] Can there be any, who from an honest motive, would suffer such an important period to pass unimproved? If once the golden opportunity wings its departure, it may never return, unless conducted back by the sanguinary horrors of civil discord. ⟨When the illustrious Father of his country was called on by the Convention to ratify the Constitution as its President—holding the pen, after a short pause, he pronounced these words, too remarkable to be forgotten or unknown—"*Should the states reject this excellent Constitution, the probability is, an opportunity will never again offer to cancel another in peace—the next will be drawn in blood!*"—Great Heaven, avert the direful catastrophe! But may the rising glories of his country gild his declining horizon, and her smiling prosperity chear his heart as sinking into the embrace of death!⟩[12]

But what are we to feel when the dark arcana of opposition are disclosed? What, when the judgment of common sense is affronted by a denial of the most interesting truths? Anti-federal writers scruple not to declare that our interest consists in *dis-union*. Go then, my countrymen, forget your weakness and your danger when divided. Forget the experience of ancient Greece. Forget your mutual sufferings, and the blood you mingled for a dear-bought Independence. Forget the endearing ties by which you are related, that you are friends and brethren. Go then, destroy your emblems of your union, and bury your standards in the dust.

Cato seems to dread the too energetic powers of the proposed Constitution, and bids us "beware of despotism as the greatest of all evils:" but anon, it is metamorphosed by his versatile imagination into a pure republican construction, "incapable of combining or of preserving the peace of these states."[13] Brutus is equally consistent. "We have felt (he acknowledges) the feebleness of our ties and the want of sufficient energy;" and yet he is dismally apprehensive, that what he declares, will amount to "a perfect and entire consolidation," will render our disunion the more probable.[14] Under our present impotent and despised government, while the states are guilty of unjust practices and malicious retaliations towards each other, neither of these writers appear to have any apprehensions; but the instant the union is to be strengthened, and such practices over-ruled, they give an alarm: to their bewildered fancies or pretended fears, our "climates, productions and customs grow varient," and our interests begin to draw with an irresistible force into opposite direction. And "this forbids (says Brutus) that we should be connected under one government." But why did not Brutus forbid that the counties of New-York should be consolidated into one government? Behold through what a variety of climates she extends her variegated territory; from the commercial ocean, through the frigid regions of the North, and along the uncultivated borders of the Great Ontario! But be assured that neither the mandates of Brutus, nor the threatened *factions* of Cato, with his "powerful mal-contents," shall ever dissolve a union dictated by necessity and safety, supported by the dearest ties of national amity, and founded in principles, the propriety of which the experience of ages has demonstrated.

Both these writers appeal to the authority of the celebrated Montesquieu, to shew the impropriety of an extensive republic, and the impossibility under such a government to take cognizance of, or to do justice to the local necessities of its subjects. But Brutus and Cato pervert his sense by their confounding the *simple democracy* of which he treats, with the complex plan of the federal constitution. Thus they disguise those peculiar circumstances which ought to characterise our political situation from all others. To furnish a solution to objections drawn from this favorite source, we have only to attend to the two following distinctions: First, the president of the United States is to possess certain executive powers, which will give the federal government the guarded efficience of an elective monarchy. For the abuse of these powers he *alone* is answerable, and by the representatives of the people he may at any time be impeached. But as his accuser and his judge ought not to be the same, his trial is before a senate, in which each state bears an equal sway; so that although he be a *favorite* of *the strong* he may be made to tremble before the *justice* of the *weak*. Secondly, the existence and office of the state legislatures. How vain, how invidious is the pretence that these must perish under the operation of the supreme jurisdiction; when, from the very mode of appointing the different branches of the federal government, it must, at the same time, thus work its own annihilation. Brutus artfully throws a veil over the existence of the state legislatures, by endeavouring to confound them with the supreme. For this purpose, he observes, that "it will be impossible for the supreme legislature to attend to the various internal concerns of so extensive an empire." But the duties to be attended to by this supreme legislative head, are to be drawn from the letter of the constitution. They are principally of the great national kind, while the local concerns of states, or the necessities of particular districts fall not within the sphere of its jurisdiction, but are left under the direction of the states individually. From this beautiful arrangement, subjects so different in their nature, instead of being confounded, will for ever claim the unembarrassed attention of men best competent to their discussion.

The existence, office, and mutual dependence of these *inferior* and *superior powers*, might have in part originated in a delicate unwillingness in your Convention to break in upon the already formed habits of their constituents. From the same free people, both are immediately derived; which can therefore never be interested in each other's destruction. But should our ambitious designs be cherished by the former, the latter stand the centinels of freedom to sound an alarm. And should ever the improbable event take place, (but which however may take place under *any* government); should ever the liberties of the people be violated by the execution of such designs; from this constitution they must experience a peculiar advantage. For while under other governments in such circumstances, the people are obliged, in order to obtain redress, to resolve themselves into a state of anarchy and tumult, in which they often fall a sacrifice to the demagogues of their own party: here they may do themselves justice, and resist every encroachment of despotism, with the advantages of combination, system, and arrangement under their state legislatures. On the other hand, should the latter, which is quite as probable, usurp an undue or oppressive authority over them, the union is bound to guard the rights of the injured, and to guarantee to each state a republican form of government.

Having thus considered a part of the admirable construction of the proposed Constitution, it appears that the objections of its enemies serve but to display and to elucidate its excellencies. I view this fair, this stately edifice of liberty, as rising under the forming hand of Heaven to render America the blissful seat of human glory and perfection. Its structure, fitness and proportion, attract our admiration, and become more illustriously conspicuous upon every review; while it rests upon thirteen pillars of adamant,[15] and new states must but add stability to its immovable basis. From the specimens we have received, it may be justly expected, that the writings of Publius will reflect a pleasing lustre upon many of those beautiful intricacies, that are retired from superficial observation, and which require a master discernment to be brought into public notice.

1. On 2 November the *Daily Advertiser* informed its readers that "Curtius" was received.

2. From 2 to 5 October the Philadelphia Baptist Association, composed of churches in the Middle States, met in New York City, and, among other things, it adopted a circular letter supporting the Constitution that was printed for distribution to the churches. A report of this meeting was published in the *New York Packet*, 12 October, and reprinted in the *Daily Advertiser*, 22 October; *Hudson Weekly Gazette* and *Albany Gazette*, 25 October; and *Country Journal*, 31 October. For the report and its circulation outside New York, see CC:156–A.

3. In the months of September and October, reports came into New York City that Boston strongly supported the Constitution. For example, see the letters written from New York City by Virginia congressman James Madison (RCS:Mass., 1078, 1079, 1080). With respect to Governor John Hancock, his 18 October speech to the Massachusetts legislature presenting the Constitution to that body, first printed in the *Massachusetts Gazette* on 19 October, was reprinted in the *New York Morning Post* on 1 November. (The portion on the Constitution appeared in the *Northern Centinel* on 13 November.) Although Hancock did not discuss the merits of the Constitution, his remarks were construed as being favorable to it. For the speech and its circulation throughout America, see CC:177.

4. The reference is to Elbridge Gerry, a Massachusetts delegate to the Constitutional Convention, who refused to sign the Constitution. On 17 October the *Pennsylvania Journal* reported that letters from Boston revealed that Gerry "is not only censured by the public in general, but by his best friends, for not signing the Constitution." This item was reprinted in five New York newspapers: *Daily Advertiser*, 22 October; *New York Packet*, 23 October; *Independent Journal*, 24 October; and *Hudson Weekly Gazette* and *Albany Gazette*, 1 November. For this report and its circulation throughout America, see CC:171–A.

5. On 17 October the *Pennsylvania Journal* reported that when George Mason arrived in Alexandria the mayor and the corporation expressed "their abhorrence" for his refusal to sign the Constitution in the Constitutional Convention. They advised him to leave Alexandria "within an hour, for they could not answer for his personal safety, from an enraged populace, should he exceed that time." The New York newspapers that reprinted the report about Gerry (see note 4) also reprinted this report. For the report on Mason and its circulation throughout America, see CC:171–A.

"A Lover of Truth," *New York Packet*, 30 October, quoted this report and denied that the incident ever took place. "The laws of the country," he wrote, "the decency of the people of Alexandria, and the very great *respectability* of Mr. Mason forbidding such a *foolish outrage* to have been committed" (Mfm:N.Y.).

6. Probably a reference to the 28 September meeting held in Berkeley County, where the inhabitants voted unanimously to support the Constitution. The meeting's proceedings, printed in the Winchester *Virginia Gazette*, 12 October, were reprinted in the *Daily Advertiser*, 31 October; *Country Journal*, 7 November; and *Northern Centinel*, 13 November. For these proceedings and for their circulation throughout America, see RCS:Va., 22.

7. See "New York Reprinting of the Address of the Seceding Members of the Pennsylvania Assembly," 9–18 October (above).

8. On 15 October, the *Pennsylvania Packet* reported that on 3 October a meeting of the inhabitants of Carlisle in Cumberland County, Pa., called to nominate persons for the Supreme Executive Council and Assembly, adopted a resolution "most warmly" approving the Constitution and praising the Assembly majority for calling a state convention to consider the Constitution. The inhabitants censured the seceding members of the Assembly who tried to prevent the calling of the convention, declaring that they were "unworthy of the confidence of the people, and unfit to represent them." (Three Cumberland County assemblymen were among the sixteen seceding members.) The proceed-

ings of this meeting were reprinted in the *Daily Advertiser*, 18 October. For the proceedings and their circulation throughout America, see RCS:Pa., 173–74.

9. In October at least six of New Jersey's thirteen counties either sent petitions to the state legislature requesting that it call a convention to ratify the Constitution or instructing their representatives to support the calling of a convention. (See RCS:N.J., 135–37, 139–40.) The petition and proceedings of the Burlington County meeting—published in the Philadelphia *Independent Gazetteer*, 16 October—were reprinted in the *Daily Advertiser* and *New York Packet*, 19 October; and *Country Journal*, 24 October. The proceedings of the Somerset County meeting—published in the New Jersey *Brunswick Gazette*, 16 October—were reprinted in the *New York Packet*, 19 October; *Country Journal*, 24 October; *Daily Advertiser*, 26 October; *Northern Centinel*, 29 October; and *Independent Journal*, 31 October. The proceedings of the Essex County meeting—published in the *New Jersey Journal*, 24 October—were reprinted in the *Daily Advertiser*, 26 October.

10. Under the Constitution, New Jersey was allotted only four representatives in the House of Representatives, while its neighbors New York and Pennsylvania were allotted six and eight, respectively. In the Senate, however, the three states were each allotted two senators.

11. See "Publius," *The Federalist* 1, *Independent Journal*, 27 October (above).

12. The text in angle brackets appeared in the *New Jersey Journal* on 7 November (CC:233–A). The *Journal* changed "the illustrious Father of his country" to "the illustrious Washington." By 29 December this text was reprinted thirty-eight times, including the *New York Packet*, 20 November; *Hudson Weekly Gazette*, 29 November; *Northern Centinel*, 4 December; and *Country Journal*, 5 December. Both the *New York Packet* and the *Country Journal* indicated that this text was reprinted from the *New Jersey Journal*. All four New York reprintings omitted the last sentence of the text.

13. See "Cato" III, *New York Journal*, 25 October (above). The other reference to "Cato" in this essay is also from "Cato" III. "Curtius" took considerable liberties with the text that he quoted.

14. See "Brutus" I, *New York Journal*, 18 October (above). Other references to "Brutus" in this essay are also from "Brutus" I. "Curtius" took considerable liberties with the text that he quoted.

15. An adamant is a legendary stone of extreme hardness, sometimes the diamond.

Publius: The Federalist 3 (John Jay)
New York Independent Journal, 3 November 1787

Importance of Union in foreign relations. For text, see CC:228. For reprintings, see Appendix IV, below.

A Farmer, of New-Jersey: Observations on Government
New York, 3 November 1787 (excerpt)

On 3 November New York City printer William Ross announced in the *Daily Advertiser* the publication and sale of a fifty-six page pamphlet by "A Farmer, of New-Jersey" entitled *Observations on Government, including some Animadversions on Mr. Adams's Defence of the Constitutions of Government of the United States of America: and on Mr. De Lolme's Constitution of England* (Evans 20465). The excerpts below, which recommend amendments to the Constitution, appear on pages 53–56 of the pamphlet. They were reprinted in the *Daily Advertiser* on 17 November. (For Adams's *Defence*, see CC:16.)

Although often attributed to New Jersey Governor William Livingston, a former delegate to the Constitutional Convention, the pamphlet was written by John Stevens, Jr., of Hoboken, the author of the "Americanus" essays, the first essay of which appeared on 2 November in the *Daily Advertiser* (above). A manuscript draft of the first part of the pamphlet, in Stevens' handwriting, is in the Stevens Family Papers at the New Jersey Historical Society. Moreover, Stevens identified himself as the author. On 30 December, he wrote his father that "I have Sent Mama a political Pamphlet which was written by a very good friend of hers the sentiments of which I hope will not displease her" (to John Stevens, Sr., Mfm:N.Y. On 9 December Stevens had written his father that he had sent a copy of the pamphlet to John Cox, requesting that his father read the pamphlet and give him his opinion of it [Mfm:N.Y.].). Lastly, Stevens paid the printing costs for 500 copies, and he sent copies to several individuals.

The pamphlet appears to have circulated only in New York, New Jersey, and Pennsylvania. After the initial advertisement, the *Daily Advertiser* advertised the sale of the pamphlet on 25 December, and 3 and 25 January 1788. Advertisements for the pamphlet also appeared in the *New York Morning Post*, 17 November; and the *Pennsylvania Herald*, 5, 7, and 14 February 1788. On 16 May 1788 William Ross wrote Stevens that 100 copies had been sent to a Philadelphia bookseller, twenty-four had been forwarded to Stevens himself, and twenty had been sold in New York City. Ross retained 364 copies. Ross also provided Stevens with a receipt for the balance of the money sent to him for printing the pamphlet (Mfm:N.Y.). Like the "Americanus" essays, this pamphlet did not provoke any significant commentary.

In his pamphlet, Stevens criticized both John Adams and Jean Louis De Lolme for favoring a powerful executive and he proposed amendments to curtail the power of the executive branch under the Constitution. The amendments, however, also curtailed the power of the legislative branch. Stevens also rejected Adams's notion of a balance of power among the executive, legislative, and judicial branches. In a democracy, stated Stevens, the legislature was supreme because it most directly represented the people. For this reason, he praised the state constitutions since they made the legislatures responsive to the people. For Stevens, the state governments approached the ideal of representative democracy. Even though Stevens recommended amendments, he fully supported the ratification of the Constitution without amendments. He wrote his father on 9 December that "The Constitution must either be wholly received or wholly rejected. It is in vain to expect that any kind of federal government can ever take place, if the State Conventions are to make amendments" (Mfm:N.Y.).

. . . But after all, every thing that has hitherto been done will signify nothing without an effectual Foederal Government. The plan that has been submitted to our consideration by the late Convention, surpasses my most sanguine expectation. When we consider the multiplicity of jarring interests, which mutual concession alone could reconcile, it really becomes matter of astonishment that a system of legislation could have been effected in which so few imperfections are to be found. The man who can deliberately go about to oppose the adoption of this plan, must evidently be actuated by sinister motives; for admitting it to be much more faulty than it really is, can we form any reasonable hope of obtaining a better?

What a glorious spectacle would the adoption of this constitution exhibit! an event so totally contradictory to the habits and sentiments which prevail every where but in America, would scarcely be credited. Elevated infinitely beyond even the conceptions of the wisest men of the East, our situation would excite the envy and admiration of all the world; and we should probably have the honor of teaching mankind this important, this interesting lesson, THAT MAN IS ACTUALLY CAPABLE OF GOVERNING HIMSELF, and not (thro' the imbecility of his nature) "*unavoidably*" necessitated to resign himself to the guidance of one or more masters.

It might be deemed arrogant in me should I presume to suggest amendments to a constitution, in the formation of which the ablest political artists of the nation have been employed. To vindicate myself from this charge, I think it will be sufficient for me to say that the constitution, tho' excellent, is acknowledged on all hands to have its defects: how indeed could it be otherwise? The wonder is, that so few are to be found. The following are the amendments I would propose:

That the *executive* be divided into THREE GRAND DEPARTMENTS.

I. The PRESIDENT vested with all the powers given him by the constitution, except such as are hereafter proposed to be lodged in other hands. To make appointments *without* the advice and consent of the Senate.

II. The CHIEF JUSTICE to have the appointment of the Judges, and every other officer necessary to the administration of justice;—to hold his office during good behaviour.

III. The SUPERINTENDENT OF FINANCE to have the management of all matters relative to the collection and expenditure of the foederal revenues; to have the appointment of all officers of the revenue; the treasurer or receiver general, treasurers and receivers in each State, customhouse officers, excise officers, &c.—to hold his office during good behaviour.

These three great executive officers, to constitute a council to revise all bills which have passed the house of representatives and the senate, in the same manner as by the constitution it is directed to be done by the President. A majority to determine the sense of the council on all questions that may come before them.

An Auditor General to be chosen by a majority of the House of Representatives;—to continue in office during *their pleasure*. He must have the appointment of as many deputies as he may deem necessary.

I must beg leave to make a few observations on the above distribution.

I. The powers that must *necessarily* be intrusted in the hands of the President, are amply sufficient to preserve his respectability and independence; were they greater, he might become dangerous: for which reason the revision of the laws is not left *solely* to him; and the appointments under the Chief Justice and Superintendent of Finance, are given to each respectively. But there is another reason in favour of this last arrangement;—as each in his department must know, better than any other person can, whether those who may offer themselves as candidates for office are properly qualified, we may presume that they will of course be more competent to this business, and at the same time more responsible.

[II.] By giving the revision *altogether* to a President, the judicial is left *unprotected*; and for want of a technical legal knowledge, the laws may be destitute of uniformity and consistency. Again, as a thorough knowledge of the fittest modes of raising and collecting a revenue is not easily acquired, we may reasonably apprehend that Congress, who cannot be supposed scientifically acquainted with this business, might, without the assistance, and in some measure controul of a Superintendent of Finance, proceed upon mistaken principles, and run themselves into most fatal mistakes.

III. It is manifest there would be danger in intrusting the powers of a President in the same hands for more than three or four years without a new election. This *necessary* dependence of the President on the voice of the people for his continuance in office, renders him, so far forth an unfit person to place in opposition to a bad measure, if it should happen to be popular.

IV. From the nature of the offices of Chief Justice and Superintendent of Finance, a greater degree of permanency may be given to them, without danger to liberty; it is therefore proposed that these offices should be held during good behaviour, and be in the appointment of the President. These circumstances will render the possessors so totally independent of all popular influence, that they may be safely relied on, should an opposition to Congress be at any time necessary.

V. The President should have the chusing of his own advisers, as he will of consequence be the more responsible.—But at any rate, the *Senate* are very improper for this office, as they are to sit as judges in case of an impeachment of the President.

VI. To guard against any danger there may be, of collusion between the Superintendent or any of his officers, and the Auditor or his deputies, it is necessary the Auditor be wholly under the power of Congress, and removeable at any time.

New York Daily Advertiser, 5 November 1787[1]

From a Correspondent.
PALPABLE TRUTHS.
Fools! not to know that half exceeds the whole.[2]

It is a palpable truth, that, as Messrs. Randolph, Mason, and Gerry, did not sign the Convention [i.e., Constitution]—the majority were all in the wrong.

It is also a truth, that, as Rhode-Island and, perhaps, New-York, are Anti-Federal—the Federal States will be all in the wrong.

It is also a truth, that, as State Officers do not chuse to risk the loss of office—their opponents are all in the wrong.

It is also a truth, that, as some of the European Powers wish to keep us a disunited people, and, for that purpose, will, *perhaps*, employ the grey-goose quill of every venal scribbler to disseminate fears and jealousies—that every honest advocate of the Federal Government must be in the wrong.

In short, my dear Countrymen, if we suffer ourselves to be guided by the majority—we shall assuredly be all in the wrong.

1. Reprinted: *Albany Gazette*, 15 November; *Pennsylvania Packet*, 17 November; *Vermont Gazette*, 26 November; *Massachusetts Centinel*, 1 December; *Boston Gazette*, 3 December; *New Hampshire Mercury*, 4 December. On 3 November the *Daily Advertiser* announced that "Palpable Truths" would "appear as soon as possible."
2. Hesiod (c. 700 B.C.), *The Works and Days*, lines 40–41.

Publius: The Federalist 4 (John Jay)
New York Independent Journal, 7 November 1787

Importance of Union in protecting America from foreign invasion. For text, see CC:234. For reprintings, see Appendix IV, below.

Philadelphia Freeman's Journal, 7 November 1787[1]

Extract of a letter from N. York, *Nov.* 4.

"It is astonishing with what a high hand matters are carried in Massachusetts, relative to the adoption of the New Constitution. Freedom of enquiry, particularly among the Bostonians, seems to be put entirely out of countenance.[2] *John Adam's Chickens* (commonly called the *Well Born*) are already, in imagination, completely mounted upon the shoulders of the populace.[3]—Some nations have been cheated out of their freedom by a long concatenation of subtilty and deceit; there are, in this country, too many that would carry the *same point* by downright impudence and effrontery:

'Who first the generous steed opprest
Not kneeling did salute the beast;
But with high courage, life, and force
Approaching, tam'd the unruly horse.'

"The clergy, I find, are, generally, very busy in proving by their present (as well as by some past) conduct, that *politics* and *theology* are by no means incompatible. I had hitherto imagined, this order of men were paid and maintained by the people to keep them in mind of their duty to GOD and their neighbours. But, it seems, they have a sufficiency of leisure upon their hands to fix, at least, *one eye* pretty steadily upon the political affairs of the world we are in."[4]

1. Reprinted: *Maryland Journal*, 13 November; *Virginia Independent Chronicle*, 21 November; Boston *American Herald*, 26 November; *State Gazette of South Carolina*, 10 January 1788.

2. At issue in Boston was the principle of open access to and the impartiality of the town's newspapers. Antifederalists complained that in order to get their articles printed they had to leave their names with the publishers of some newspapers. For other New York Antifederalist commentaries on the dispute in Boston, see "Detector," *New York Journal*, 25 October (CC:131–H); "Brutus, Junior," *New York Journal*, 8 November (below); "Federal Farmer," 8 November (below); and *New York Journal*, 27 December (RCS:Mass., 539–40). For the dispute in Boston, see RCS:Mass., 41–50, and for the issue of the press on the national level, see CC: 131.

3. One of the principal criticisms made against the first volume of John Adams's *Defence of the Constitutions*, which was available in England in January 1787 and in America by mid-April, was that Adams diminished the role of the people and gave too much prominence to the rich and well born. (See CC:16, pp. 84, 85, 89–90.)

4. Possibly a reference to the October meeting in New York City of the Baptist clergy of the Middle States that expressed support for the Constitution. (See "Curtius" III, *Daily Advertiser*, 3 November, supplement, note 2, above.) Under Article XXXIX of the New York constitution of 1777, clergymen were not permitted to hold any civil or military office or place (Appendix I, below).

P. Valerius Agricola
Albany Gazette, 8 November 1787[1]

AN ESSAY,
On the CONSTITUTION recommended by the FEDERAL CONVENTION to the UNITED STATES.   By P. VALERIUS AGRICOLA.
My BANE *and* ANTIDOTE *are both before me!*
Addison's Cato.[2]

The hour of anxious expectation and vague conjecture has at length elapsed—The GRAND FEDERAL CONVENTION is dissolved—before us lies the result of their deliberations—and demands from every citizen a strict and impartial examination.

It is again "The time to try men's souls"[3]—The fate of America is once more at stake! Stand firm, my countrymen, and act like men on whose decision depends the happiness or misery of millions!

On a subject of such high importance to ourselves and to posterity, it becomes us to deliberate with temperance and caution—to speak with decent freedom, and to act with manly fortitude.

"Let us be neither rash nor diffident."[4]

It is told of an illustrious personage, that when any new project was introduced, he always asked, CUI BO NO? *(whom will it profit?)*[5] When the proposed *Constitution* is mentioned, we all naturally make this enquiry:—A Citizen of America, concealed in the shades of obscurity, unconnected with party, and uninfluenced by power, respectfully offers, in the following pages, to his countrymen, a series of reflections, that, perhaps, may conduce to a solution of the Important Question.

In order to form an adequate opinion of a remedy, it is requisite that the disease should be thoroughly explored—A skilful physician must have frequent recourse to the principles of his art, and critically mark such indications as are peculiar to the disorder—cautious of trusting to theory, however specious, he consults the history of similar cases, handed down in the writings of the learned and experienced of the faculty; with equal pains he investigates the nature and properties of the medicine, and upon mature consideration only, will he venture to pronounce it proper.

Let such be our conduct.

I cannot flatter them, who may deem this essay deserving their perusal, with a promise of a speedy dismission—a prospect of the business before me, makes it necessary to solicit their candor and patient attention.

The investigation of truth, always laborious, will, in the present instance, be attended with peculiar embarrassments—we must have frequent recourse to political principles—we must pay unremitted attention to perspicuity of stile and accuracy of distinction, and be content to sacrifice to these objects, a degree of ease, the desire of novelty and the embellishment of language.

Three grand questions seem naturally to rise from the subject.

I. What is the design of civil government?

II. Does the present political system of the United States answer this design, and what are its deficiencies?

III. Is the constitution now recommended by the Convention to the states, well calculated to supply those deficiencies, and what are the advantages and disadvantages that may probably attend its adoption?

CHAP. I.

THE FIRST QUESTION DISCUSSED.

"Emollit mores, nec sinit esse feros."[6]

WHATEVER were the distinguishing privileges and advantages of the parent of mankind, it is a melancholy truth, that his apostate posterity are exposed to numberless wants which they cannot supply, to dangers which they can neither shun nor resist—surrounded by errors that darken the understanding, and laden with infirmities that degrade the dignity of our nature.

To meliorate, as far as possible, circumstances so unhappy, at a period of time too remote for the cognizance of history, the sons of men first associated themselves for the purposes of mutual convenience and defence.

It was then, that the individual, impelled by fear and attentive to the suggestions of reason, intrusted a portion of his natural liberty to the care of community, which became thus enabled to afford him protection against the dangers incident to a state of nature: the urgency of which dangers, could alone have induced a being, with whom the love of freedom is congenial, to forego the minutest privilege and submit to the shackels of power.

"Society being thus formed, government results of course, as necessary to keep that society in order."

From a review of the foregoing observations, we may then infer, that the design of civil government is, the security and happiness of community, and by no means the aggrandisement of an individual or a few—or, as the preamble to the proposed constitution has in more words expressed it, "To form a more perfect union—establish justice—ensure domestic tranquility—provide for the common defence—promote the general welfare, and secure the blessings of liberty to ourselves and our posterity."

Having already observed, that these inestimable privileges can only be purchased by a partial surrender of natural liberty, it concerns us next to consider the magnitude of the cession.

It is obvious, from the slightest reflection, that there are certain *rights*, of so extensive and transendant a nature, that were they left in the exercise of individuals, would produce infinite mischiefs to society—subvert its utility, and eventually occasion its dissolution.

These are called by the civilians the JURA SUMMI IMPERII, or, *the rights of sovereignty*, "which constitutes[(a)] that supreme, absolute, uncontrolled authority, which is and must be in every government, of what form or description soever."

These we may reckon,

First, LEGISLATION, and the consequent EXECUTIVE and JUDICIAL rights.

Second, The rights of making war and peace, consequently of raising troops, establishing navies, arsinals, &c. of concluding treaties and alliances, and whatsoever is directly or indirectly conducive to the public security;—as the means of effecting which, we induce.

Third, The right of raising money by coinage, by loan, or assessment on the subject—of making commercial regulations, and promoting, by all suitable measures, the wealth and happiness of community.

The propositions adduced in this chapter, we trust will readily be received as political axioms, which we have only mentioned, that the subject [in] question might be fairly stated, and a standard established to which we might occasionally have recourse, in the subsequent discussion. *Ab ovo deducimus verum.*[7]

CHAP. II.

THE SECOND *general* QUESTION DISCUSSED.

⟨*"There is something rotten in the state of Venice."*⟩[8]

"FACTS are stubborn things"[9]—One argument founded on facts, outweighs a thousand utopeian speculations.—The projector may construct wings and by mathematical reasoning, evince the possibility of soaring to the moon—the alchymist may talk plausibly of his universal menstruum and elixer of life: But, when experience shews us the former dashed like *Icarus* on the ground, and the latter ending a life of futile researches, in poverty and disgrace, we must conclude either, that they proceeded upon false principles, or made sophistical inductions.

From every quarter of the continent, our ears have long been stunned with complaints of state injustice, of state debility, and of state embarrasment—mean while the sovereignty of America, like the expiring lion in the fable, has alternately been spurned and insulted by the ass and the lamb:[10]—even the voice of public authority has, at length pronounced the disastrous CRAVEN! and thus given sanction to the clamors of the continent.⟩[11]

(a)I Black. § 2. 49.[12]

(To be continued.)

1. On 15 November the *Albany Gazette* announced that the continuation of this essay was "unavoidably postponed" until its issue of 22 November. Instead, the continuation did not appear until 6 December (below).

2. Joseph Addison, *Cato. A Tragedy* (1713), Act V, scene 1. The words are spoken by Cato himself.

3. Thomas Paine, "The American Crisis," No. I (December 1776).

4. Joseph Addison, *Cato. A Tragedy* (1713), Act II, scene 1. Cato states: "Let us appear nor rash nor diffident:/Immoderate valor swells into a fault,/And fear, admitted into public councils,/Betrays like treason."

5. Marcus Tullius Cicero (106–43 B.C.), *Pro T. Annio Milone (Speech on Behalf of Titus Annius Milo)*, Chapter XII, section 32.

6. Ovid (43 B.C.–17 A.D.), *Epistulae ex Ponto (Letters from Pontus)*, Book II, chapter 9. The complete sentence which contains this phrase reads "*ingenuas didicisse fideliter artes/ emollit mores, nec sinit esse feros.*" Translation: "A faithful study of the liberal arts humanizes character and permits it not to be cruel." This sentence (in Latin) appears in David Hume, "Of the Delicacy of Taste and Passion," *Essays, Moral, Political, and Literary*, ed. Eugene F. Miller (rev. ed., Indianapolis, 1987), 6. This essay first appeared in 1741 in a volume entitled *Essays, Moral and Political.*

7. Latin: From the egg, we deduce the truth.

8. William Shakespeare, *Hamlet*, Act I, scene 4. "Something is rotten in the state of Denmark."

9. Alain René Le Sage, *The Adventures of Gil Blas of Santillane* (2 vols., London and New York, [1910]), II, Book X, chapter I, 199. This picaresque novel first appeared as *Histoire de Gil Blas de Santillane* (4 vols., Paris, 1715–1735).

10. A reference to an Æsop's fable, "The Old Lion" or "The Sick Lion."

11. The text in angle brackets, along with an excerpt from the 6 December continuation of this essay, was reprinted, without the pseudonym, in the *Massachusetts Centinel*, 22 December (Mfm:Mass).

12. Blackstone, *Commentaries*, Book I, "Introduction," section 2, p. 49.

Albany Gazette, 8 November 1787[1]

The happiness of a state, says a correspondent, consists not in its number or wealth, but in the good disposition, wise regulation and good conduct of its inhabitants. Hence,

That state is happy, whose laws and rulers are good, and its inhabitants industrious, frugal and in a just subordination. And,

That state is wretched and miserable, where pride, idleness and dissipation prevail, men and not laws govern, and the rulers are ignorant, or wicked.

A government without a directing and controuling power, is like a ship without master, pilot or rudder.

A government without faith, is a government without credit; and a government without credit, is a government without energy; and a government without energy, is no government at all. And,

A government too popular borders upon tyranny.

1. Reprinted in the *Country Journal*, 14 November; *New York Packet*, 16 November; and by 4 February 1788 in six newspapers outside New York: Vt. (1), N.H. (2), Mass. (1), Conn. (1), Md. (1).

Brutus, Junior
New York Journal, 8 November 1787

The authorship of "Brutus, Junior" is uncertain. On 28 November Hugh Hughes asked fellow Antifederalist Charles Tillinghast "Are you not wrong as to the Author of Brutus—I supposed him to have been Brutus Junior & Mr. A Y. [Abraham Yates, Jr.] to have been the Author of Brutus" (below). Almost identical passages and references to the same events appear in "Brutus, Junior" and Letters I and V of the "Federal Farmer," 8 November (below). Both "Brutus, Junior" and the pamphlet by "Federal Farmer" were available to the public on the same day.

"Brutus, Junior" was reprinted in the Philadelphia *Independent Gazetteer* on 14 November, at the request of a number of subscribers who believed that "it seems to be better calculated for the meridian of Pennsylvania, than the one it was written for." For commentary on "Brutus, Junior" in Connecticut, Pennsylvania, and Maryland, see the headnote to CC:239, and "A Countryman" II, *New Haven Gazette*, 22 November (CC:284).

MR. GREENLEAF, I have read with a degree of attention several publications which have lately appeared in favour of the new Constitution; and as far as I am able to discern—the arguments (if they can be so termed) of most weight, which are urged in its favour may be reduced to the two following:

1st. That the men who formed it, were wise and experienced; that they were an illustrious band of patriots, and had the happiness of their country at heart; that they were four months deliberating on the subject, and therefore, it must be a perfect system.

2d. That if the system be not received, this country will be without any government, and of consequence, will be reduced to a state of anarchy and confusion, and involved in bloodshed and carnage; and in the end, a government will be imposed upon us, not the result of reason and reflection, but of force and usurpation.

As I do not find that either Cato or the Centinel, Brutus, or the Old Whig,[1] or any other writer against this constitution, have undertaken a particular refutation of this new species of reasoning, I take the liberty of offering to the public, through the channel of your paper, the few following animadversions on the subject; and the rather, because I have discovered, that some of my fellow citizens have been imposed upon by it.

With respect to the first, it will be readily perceived, that it precludes all investigation of the merits of the proposed constitution, and leads to an adoption of the plan, without enquiring whether it be good or bad. For if we are to infer the perfection of this system from the characters and abilities of the men who formed it, we may as well determine to accept it without any enquiry as with.—A number of persons in this as well as the other states, have, upon this principle, determined to submit to it without even reading or knowing its contents.

But supposing the premises from which this conclusion is drawn, to be just, it then becomes essential, in order to give validity to the argument, to enquire into the characters of those who composed this body, that we may determine whether we can be justified in placing such unbounded confidence in them.

It is an invidious task, to call in question the characters of individuals, especially of such as are placed in illustrious stations. But when we are required implicitly to submit our opinions to those of others, from a consideration that they are so wise and good as not to be liable to err, and that too in an affair which involves in it the happiness of ourselves and our posterity; every honest man will justify a decent investigation of characters in plain language.

It is readily admitted, that many individuals who composed this body, were men of the first talents and integrity in the union. It is at the same time, well known to every man, who is but moderately acquainted with the characters of the members, that many of them are possessed of high aristocratic ideas, and the most sovereign contempt of the common people; that not a few were strongly disposed in favour of monarchy; that there were some of no small talents and of great influence, of consummate cunning, and masters of intrigue, whom the war found poor, or in embarrassed circumstances, and left with princely fortunes, acquired in public employment, who are at this day to account for many thousands of public money; that there were others who were young, ardent, and ambitious, who wished for a government corresponding with their feelings, while they were destitute of that experience which is the surest guide in political researches; that there were not a few who were gaping for posts of honour and emolument; these we find exulting in the idea of a change, which will divert places of honour, influence and emolument, into a different channel, where the confidence of the people, will not be necessary to their acquirement. It is not to be wondered at, that an assembly thus composed should produce a system liable to well founded objections, and which will require very essential alterations. We are told by one of themselves (Mr. Wilson of Philadelphia) the plan was matter of accommodation; and it is not unreasonable to suppose, that in this accommodation, principles might be introduced which would render the liberties of the people very insecure.[2]

I confess I think it of no importance, what are the characters of the framers of this government, and therefore should not have called them in question, if they had not been so often urged in print, and in conversation, in its favour. It ought to rest on its own intrinsic merit. If it is good, it is capable of being vindicated; if it is bad, it ought not to be supported. It is degrading to a freeman, and humiliating to a rational one, to pin his faith on the sleeve of any man, or body of men, in an affair of such momentous importance.

In answer to the second argument, I deny that we are in immediate danger of anarchy and commotions. Nothing but the passions of wicked and ambitious men, will put us in the least danger on this head: those who are anxious to precipitate a measure, will always tell us that the present is the critical moment; now is the time, the crisis is arrived, and the present minute must be seized. Tyrants have always made use of this plea; but nothing in our circumstances can justify it.

The country is in profound peace, and we are not threatened by invasion from any quarter: the governments of the respective states are in the full exercise of their powers; and the lives, the liberty, and property of individuals are protected: all present exigencies are answered by them. It is true, the regulation of trade and a competent provision for the payment of the interest of the public debt is wanting; but no immediate commotion will arise from these; time may be taken for calm discussion and deliberate conclusions. Individuals are just recovering from the losses and embarrassments sustained by the late war: industry and frugality are taking their station, and banishing from the community, idleness and prodigality. Individuals are lessening their private debts, and several millions of the public debt is discharged by the sale of the western territory.[3] There is no reason, therefore, why we should precipitately and rashly adopt a system, which is imperfect or insecure; we may securely deliberate and propose amendments and alterations. I know it is said we cannot change for the worse; but if we act the part of wise men, we shall take care that we change for the better: It will be labour lost, if after all our pains we are in no better circumstances than we were before.

If any tumults arise, they will be justly chargeable on those artful and ambitious men, who are determined to cram this government down the throats of the people, before they have time deliberately to examine it. All the measures of the leaders of this faction have tended to this point. In Congress they attempted to obtain a resolution to approve the constitution, without going into an examination of it.[4] In Pennsylvania, the chiefs of the party, who themselves were of the convention, that framed this system, within a few days after it dissolved, and before Congress had considered it, indecently brought forward a motion in their general assembly for recommending a convention; when a number of respectable men of that legislature, withdrew from the house, refusing to sanction with their presence, a measure so flagrantly improper, they procured a mob to carry a sufficient number of them by force to the house, to enable them to proceed on the business.[5]

In Boston, the printers have refused to print against this plan, and have been countenanced in it.[6] In Connecticut, papers have been handed about for the people to sign, to support it, and the names of those who decline signing it, have been taken down in what was called, a black list, to intimidate them into a compliance, and this before the people had time to read and understand the meaning of the constitution.[7] Many of the members of the convention, who were charged with other public business, have abandoned their duty, and hastened to their states to precipitate an adoption of the measure. The most unwearied pains has been taken, to persuade the legislatures to recommend conventions to be elected to meet at early periods, before an opportunity could be had to examine the constitution proposed; every art has been used to exasperate the people against those, who made objections to the plan. They have been told that the opposition is chiefly made by state officers, who expect to lose their places by the change,[8] though the propagators of this falsehood, know, that very few of the state offices will be vacated by the new constitution, and are well apprized, that should it take place, it will give birth to a vast number of more lucrative and permanent appointments, which its principal advocates in every state are warmly in the pursuit of. Is it not extraordinary, that those men who are predicting, that a rejection of this constitution will lead to every evil, which anarchy and confusion can produce, should at the same moment embrace and pursue with unabating industry, every measure in their power, to rouse the passions, and thereby preclude calm and dispassionate enquiry. It would be wise in them, however, to reflect in season that should public commotion take place, they will not only be answerable for the consequences, and the blood that may be shed, but that on such an event, it is more than probable the people will discern the advocates for their liberties, from those who are aiming to enslave them, and that each will receive their just deserts.

1. Like the essays of "Centinel," those of "An Old Whig" were published in the Antifederalist Philadelphia *Independent Gazetteer*. The eight numbers of "An Old Whig" appeared in the *Gazetteer* between 12 October 1787 and 6 February 1788. Numbers I to VII were reprinted in the *New York Journal* between 27 November and 15 December; while numbers IV and V appeared in the *New York Morning Post* on 3 and 10 November. For more on "An Old Whig," see CC:157. For "Centinel," see "New York Reprinting of the Centinel Essays," 17 October 1787–12 April 1788 (above).

2. See "New York Reprinting of James Wilson's 6 October Speech Before a Philadelphia Public Meeting," 13–25 October (above).

3. For the sale of western lands in October, see RCS:Va., 1174n–75n.

4. See "The Confederation Congress and the Constitution," 26–28 September (above).

5. See "New York Reprinting of the Address of the Seceding Members of the Pennsylvania Assembly," 9–18 October (above).

6. For the Boston press, see Philadelphia *Freeman's Journal*, 7 November, note 2 (above).

7. On 8 October Connecticut Lieutenant Governor Oliver Wolcott, Sr., wrote that he "heard that it has been proposed to send out Subscription Papers to be signed by those

who may be for and against the Constitution." He hoped that such a measure would not be carried out (to Oliver Wolcott, Jr., CC:141). On 21 January 1788 the Philadelphia *Independent Gazetteer* reported that before the people of Connecticut "could possibly have time scarcely to read the new constitution, they were compelled to sign to their perfect approbation of it, or be posted in a black list" (CC: Vol. 3, p. 570). This item was reprinted in the *New York Journal*, 10 March, and seven times outside New York by 28 February: Mass. (1), Conn. (4), Md. (2).

8. See especially "Alexander Hamilton Attacks Governor George Clinton," 21 July–30 October (above).

Cato IV
New York Journal, 8 November 1787

This essay, along with several others and some advertisements, were ready for publication on 1 November, but they were "unavoidably postponed, for want of room" (*New York Journal*, 1 November. For the *Journal's* change from a weekly to a daily because it lacked the space to print all that it received, see "Note on Sources," above.). "Cato" IV's objections to the executive branch as outlined in the Constitution were criticized in detail by "Americanus" II, *Daily Advertiser*, 23 November (below). See also "Americanus" IV, *Daily Advertiser*, 5–6 December (below). "Cato" IV was reprinted in the *Daily Advertiser*, 9 November, and in a two-page supplement to the *Albany Gazette* of 17 November.

To the CITIZENS of the STATE of NEW-YORK.

Admitting, however, that the vast extent of America, together with the various other reasons which I offered you in my last number,[1] against the practicability of the just exercise of the new government are insufficient to convince you; still it is an undeniable truth, that its several parts are either possessed of principles, which you have heretofore considered as ruinous, and that others are omitted which you have established as fundamental to your political security, and must in their operation, I will venture to assert—fetter your tongues and minds, enchain your bodies, and ultimately extinguish all that is great and noble in man.

In pursuance of my plan, I shall begin with observations on the executive branch of this new system; and though it is not the first in order, as arranged therein, yet being the *chief*, is perhaps entitled by the rules of rank to the first consideration. The executive power as described in the 2d article, consists of a president and vice-president, who are to hold their offices *during* the term of four years; the same article has marked the manner and time of their election, and established the qualifications of the president; it also provides against the removal, death, or inability of the president and vice-president—regulates the salary of the president, delineates his duties and powers; and lastly, declares the causes for which the president and vice-president shall be removed from office.

Notwithstanding the great learning and abilities of the gentlemen who composed the convention, it may be here remarked with deference, that the construction of the first paragraph of the first section of the second article, is vague and inexplicit, and leaves the mind in doubt, as to the election of a president and vice-president, after the expiration of the election for the first term of four years—in every other case, the election of these great officers is expressly provided for; but there is no explicit provision for their election in case of the expiration of their offices, subsequent to the election which is to set this political machine in motion—no certain and express terms as in your state constitution, that *statedly* once in every four years, and as often as these offices shall become vacant, by expiration or otherwise, as is therein expressed, an election shall be held as follows, &c.—this inexplicitness perhaps may lead to an establishment for life.

It is remarked by Montesquieu, in treating of republics, that *in all magistracies, the greatness of the power must be compensated by the brevity of the duration; and that a longer time than a year, would be dangerous.*[2] It is therefore obvious to the least intelligent mind, to account why, great power in the hands of a magistrate, and that power connected, with a considerable duration, may be dangerous to the liberties of a republic— the deposit of vast trusts in the hands of a single magistrate, enables him in their exercise, to create a numerous train of dependants—this tempts his *ambition,* which in a republican magistrate is also remarked, *to be pernicious* and the duration of his office for any considerable time favours his views, gives him the means and time to perfect and execute his designs—*he therefore fancies that he may be great and glorious by oppressing his fellow citizens, and raising himself to permanent grandeur on the ruins of his country.*[3]—And here it may be necessary to compare the vast and important powers of the president, together with his continuance in office with the foregoing doctrine—his eminent magisterial situation will attach many adherents to him, and he will be surrounded by expectants and courtiers—his power of nomination and influence on all appointments—the strong posts in each state comprised within his superintendance, and garrisoned by troops under his direction—his controul over the army, militia, and navy—the unrestrained power of granting pardons for treason, which may be used to screen from punishment, those whom he had secretly instigated to commit the crime, and thereby prevent a discovery of his own guilt—his duration in office for four years: these, and various other principles evidently prove the truth of the position— that if the president is possessed of ambition, he has power and time sufficient to ruin his country.

Though the president, during the sitting of the legislature, is assisted by the senate, yet he is without a constitutional council in their recess—he will therefore be unsupported by proper information and advice, and will generally be directed by minions and favorites, or a council of state will grow out of the principal officers of the great departments, the most dangerous council in a free country.

The ten miles square, which is to become the seat of government, will of course be the place of residence for the president and the great officers of state—the same observations of a great man will apply to the court of a president possessing the powers of a monarch, that is observed of that of a monarch—*ambition with idleness—baseness with pride—the thirst of riches without labour—aversion to truth—flattery—treason—perfidy—violation of engagements—contempt of civil duties—hope from the magistrates weakness; but above all, the perpetual ridicule of virtue*[4]—these, he remarks, are the characteristics by which the courts in all ages have been distinguished.

The language and the manners of this court will be what distinguishes them from the rest of the community, not what assimilates them to it, and in being remarked for a behaviour that shews they are not *meanly born*, and in adulation to people of fortune and power.

The establishment of a vice president is as unnecessary as it is dangerous. This officer, for want of other employment, is made president of the senate, thereby blending the executive and legislative powers, besides always giving to some one state, from which he is to come, an unjust pre-eminence.

It is a maxim in republics, that the representative of the people should be of their immediate choice; but by the manner in which the president is chosen he arrives to this office at the fourth or fifth hand, nor does the highest votes, in the way he is elected, determine the choice—for it is only necessary that he should be taken from the highest of five, who may have a plurality of votes.

Compare your past opinions and sentiments with the present proposed establishment, and you will find, that if you adopt it, that it will lead you into a system which you heretofore reprobated as odious. Every American whig, not long since, bore his emphatic testimony against a monarchical government, though limited, because of the dangerous inequality that it created among citizens as relative to their rights and property; and wherein does this president, invested with his powers and prerogatives, essentially differ from the king of Great-Britain (save as to name, the creation of nobility and some immaterial incidents, the offspring of absurdity and locality) the direct prerogatives of the presi-

dent, as springing from his political character, are among the following:—It is necessary, in order to distinguish him from the rest of the
community, and enable him to keep, and maintain his court, that the
compensation for his services; or in other words, his revenue should
be such as to enable him to appear with the splendor of a prince; he
has the power of receiving ambassadors from, and a great influence on
their appointments to foreign courts; as also to make treaties, leagues,
and alliances with foreign states, assisted by the senate, which when
made, become the supreme law of the land: he is a constituent part of
the legislative power; for every bill which shall pass the house of representatives and senate, is to be presented to him for approbation; if
he approves of it, he is to sign it, if he disapproves, he is to return it
with objections, which in many cases will amount to a compleat negative; and in this view he will have a great share in the power of making
peace, coining money, &c. and all the various objects of legislation,
expressed or implied in this Constitution: for though it may be asserted
that the king of Great-Britain has the express power of making peace
or war, yet he never thinks it prudent so to do without the advice of
his parliament from whom he is to derive his support, and therefore
these powers, in both president and king, are substantially the same:
he is the generalissimo of the nation, and of course, has the command
& controul of the army, navy and militia; he is the general conservator
of the peace of the union—he may pardon all offences, except in cases
of impeachment, and the principal fountain of all offices & employments. Will not the exercise of these powers therefore tend either to
the establishment of a vile and arbitrary aristocracy, or monarchy? The
safety of the people in a republic depends on the share or proportion
they have in the government; but experience ought to teach you, that
when a man is at the head of an elective government invested with
great powers, and interested in his re-election, in what circle appointments will be made; by which means *an imperfect aristocracy* bordering
on monarchy may be established.

   You must, however, my countrymen, beware, that the advocates of
this new system do not deceive you, by a fallacious resemblance between it and your own state government, which you so much prize; and
if you examine, you will perceive that the chief magistrate of this state,
is your immediate choice, controuled and checked by a just and full
representation of the people, divested of the prerogative of influencing
war and peace, making treaties, receiving and sending embassies, and
commanding standing armies and navies, which belong to the power
of the confederation, and will be convinced that this government is no

more like a true picture of your own, than an Angel of darkness resembles an Angel of light.

1. See "Cato" III, *New York Journal*, 25 October (above).
2. *Spirit of Laws*, I, Book II, chapter III, 20.
3. *Ibid.*, Book VIII, chapter XVI, 177.
4. *Ibid.*, Book III, chapter V, 34.

Cincinnatus II: To James Wilson, Esquire
New York Journal, 8 November 1787

> This essay, a response to James Wilson's 6 October speech (CC:134), was ready for publication on 1 November, but it was "unavoidably postponed, for want of room" (*New York Journal*, 1 November). It was reprinted in the Philadelphia *Independent Gazetteer*, 16 November, and *Providence Gazette*, 8 December. The *Vermont Gazette*, 3 December, reprinted the first two paragraphs without identifying "Cincinnatus" as the author. (For more on Wilson's speech in New York, see "New York Reprinting of James Wilson's 6 October Speech Before a Philadelphia Public Meeting," 13–25 October [above].)

SIR, I have proved, sir, that not only some power is given in the constitution to restrain, and even to subject the press, but that it is a power totally unlimited; and may certainly annihilate the freedom of the press, and convert it from being the palladium of liberty to become an engine of imposition and tyranny. It is an easy step from restraining the press to making it place the worst actions of government in so favorable a light, that we may groan under tyranny and oppression without knowing from whence it comes.

But you comfort us by saying,—"there is no reason to suspect so popular a privilege will be neglected." The wolf, in the fable, said as much to the sheep, when he was persuading them to trust him as their protector, and to dismiss their guardian dogs.[1] Do you indeed suppose, Mr. Wilson, that if the people give up their privileges to these new rulers they will render them back again to the people? Indeed, sir, you should not trifle upon a question so serious—You would not have us to suspect any ill. If we throw away suspicion—to be sure, the thing will go smoothly enough, and we shall deserve to continue a free, respectable, and happy people. Suspicion shackles rulers and prevents good government. All great and honest politicians, *like yourself*, have reprobated it. Lord Mansfield is a great authority against it, and has often treated it as the worst of libels.[2] But such men as Milton, Sidney, Locke, Montesquieu, and Trenchard, have thought it essential to the preservation of liberty against the artful and persevering encroachments of those with whom power is trusted. You will pardon me, sir, if

I pay some respect to these opinions, and wish that the freedom of the press may be *previously* secured as a *constitutional* and *unalienable right*, and not left to the precarious care of popular privileges which may or may not influence our new rulers. You are fond of, and happy at, quaint expressions of this kind in your observation—that a formal declaration would have done harm, by implying, that some degree of power was given when we undertook to define its extent. This thought has really a brilliancy in it of the first water. But permit me, sir, to ask, why any saving clause was admitted into this constitution, when you tell us, every thing is reserved that is not expressly given? Why is it said in sec. 9th, "The migration or importation of such persons as any of the states now existing shall think proper to admit, shall not be prohibited by Congress, prior to the year, 1808." There is no power expressly given to the Congress to prohibit migrations and importations. By your doctrine then they could have none, and it was, according to your own position, nugatory to declare they should not do it. Which are we to believe, sir,—you or the constitution? The text, or the comment. If the former, we must be persuaded, that in the contemplation of the framers of the constitution implied powers were given, otherwise the exception would have been an absurdity. If we listen to you we must affirm it to be a distinctive characteristic of the constitution, that—"what is not expressly given is reserved." Such are the inconsistenc[i]es into which men over ingenuous, like yourself, are betrayed in advocating a bad cause. Perhaps four months more consideration of the subject, would have rendered you more guarded.[3]

I come now to the consideration of the trial by jury in civil cases. And here you have, indeed, made use of your professional knowledge—But you did not tell the people that your profession was always to advocate one side of a question—to place it in the most favorable, though false, light—to rail where you could not reason—to pervert where you could not refute—and to practice every fallacy on your hearers—to mislead the understanding and pervert judgment. In light of this professional practice, you make a refutable objection of your own, and then triumphantly refute it. The objection you impute to your opponents is—the trial by jury is abolished in civil cases. This you call a disingenuous form—and truly it is very much so on your part and of your own fabrication. The objection in its true form is, that—trial by jury is not secured in civil cases. To this objection, you could not possibly give an answer; you therefore ingenuously coined one to which you could make a plausible reply. We expected, and we had a right to expect, that such an inestimable privilege as this would have been secured—that it would not have been left dependent on the arbitrary exposition of future judges, who, when it may suit the arbitrary views of the ruling powers will explain it away at pleasure. We may expect Tressellians, Jeffrees's, and Mansfield's here,[4] and if they should not be native with us, they may possibly be imported.

But, if taken even on your own ground it is not so clearly tenable. In point of legal construction, the trial by jury does seem to be taken away in civil cases. It is a law maxim, that the expression of one part is an exclusion of the other. In legal construction therefore, the reservation of trial by jury in criminal, is an exclusion of it in civil cases. Why else should it be mentioned at all? Either it followed of course in both cases, or it depended on being stipulated. If the first, then the stipulation was nugatory—if the latter, then it was in part given up. Therefore, either we must suppose the Convention did a nugatory thing; or that by the express mention of jury in criminal, they meant to exclude it in civil cases. And that they did intend to exclude it, seems the more probable, as in the appeal they have taken special care to render the trial by jury of no effect by expressly making the court judges both of law and fact. And though this is subjected to the future regulation of Congress, yet it would be absurd to suppose, that the regulation meant its annihilation. We must therefore conclude, that in appeals the trial by jury is expressly taken away, and in original process it is by legal implication taken away in all civil cases.

Here then I must repeat—that you ought to have stated fairly to the people, that the trial by jury was not secured; that they might know what, it was they were to consent to; and if knowing it, they consented, the blame could not fall on you. Before they decide, however, I will take leave to lay before them the opinion of that great and revered Judge Lord Camden,[5] whose authority is, I hope, at least equal to that of Mr. Wilson.—"There is, says he, scarce any matter of challenge allowed to the judge, but several to the jurors, and many of them may be removed without any reason alledged. This seems to promise as much impartiality as human nature will admit, and absolute perfection is not attainable, I am afraid, either in judge or jury or any thing else. The trial by our country, is in my opinion, the great bulwark of freedom, and for certain, the admiration of all foreign writers and nations. The last writer of any distinguished note, upon the principles of government, the celebrated Montesquieu, is in raptures with this peculiar perfection in the English policy. From juries running riot, if I may say so, and acting wildly at particular seasons, I cannot conclude, like some Scottish Doctors of our law and constitutions, that their power should be lessened. This would, to use the words of the wise, learned, and intrepid Lord Chief Justice Vaughan, be—a strange newfangled conclusion, after a trial so celebrated for so many hundreds of years."[6]

Such are the opinions of Lord Camden and Vaughan, and multitudes of the first names, both English and other foreigners might be cited, who bestow unbounded approbation on this best of all human modes for protecting, life, liberty, and property.

I own then, it alarms me, when I see these Doctors of our constitutions cutting in twain this sacred shield of public liberty and justice. Surely my countrymen will think a little before they resign this strong hold of freedom. Our state constitutions have held it sacred in all its parts. They have anxiously secured it. But that these may not shield it from the intended destruction in the new constitution, it is therein as anxiously provided, that "this constitution, and the laws of the United States, which shall be made in pursuance thereof; or which shall be made under the authority of the United States, shall be the supreme laws of the land; and the judges in every state, shall be bound thereby; any thing in the constitution and laws of any state, to the contrary notwithstanding."

Thus this new system, with one sweeping clause, bears down every constitution in the union, and establishes its arbitrary doctrines, supreme and paramount to all the bills and declarations of rights, in which we vainly put our trust, and on which we rested the security of our often declared, unalienable liberties. But I trust the whole people of this country, will unite, in crying out, as did our sturdy ancestors of old—*Nolumus leges anglicæ mutari.*[7]—We will not part with our birthright.

1. Aesop's fable "The Wolves and the Sheep."

2. For Lord Mansfield's views in cases involving the freedom of the press, see "Cincinnatus" I, *New York Journal,* 1 November, note 5 (above).

3. The Constitutional Convention, of which James Wilson was a member, had met for four months.

4. Robert Tresilian (d. 1388), George Jeffreys (1648–1689), and Mansfield (see note 2 above) were all prominent English judges, notorious for conducting illegal proceedings and for rendering harsh and unjust decisions.

5. Charles Pratt (1714–1794), the first Earl of Camden and Chief Justice of the Court of Common Pleas, was perhaps best known for his decision in *Entick* v. *Carrington* (1765) in which he denied the Secretary of State the power to imprison persons except on the charge of treason. Pratt also denied the legality of general warrants issued by the Secretary. Two years earlier, Pratt had declared general warrants illegal in the case *Wilkes* v. *Wood* (1763). Both decisions were praised by American colonists, who also hailed his constitutional positions on the taxing of the American colonies, the Stamp Act (1765), and the Declaratory Act (1766). In his "Letters from a Farmer in Pennsylvania," John Dickinson referred to Lord Camden as "that great and excellent man."

6. A quote from the decision of Chief Justice John Vaughan (1603–1674) in *Bushell's Case* (1670). Edward Bushell, a member of a jury who was fined and imprisoned for giving a false verdict, sought a writ of *habeas corpus* to challenge the legality of his imprisonment. Vaughan found for Bushell, stating that judges could not punish a juror for his verdict contrary to the judge's instruction. Vaughan had used the phrase "new-found conclusion."

7. During the reign of Henry III (1216–1272), the Magna Carta (1215), the principal body of statute law, was added to twice. The first addition was the Statute of Merton (1236), the most famous clause of which—*nolumus leges Angliae mutare*—included the declaration that the barons would not change the laws of England.

Federal Farmer
Letters to the Republican, 8 November 1787

The best Antifederalist writing on the Constitution was a forty-page pamphlet entitled *Observations Leading to a Fair Examination of the System of Government Proposed by the Late Convention; and to Several Essential and Necessary Alterations in It. In a Number of Letters from the Federal Farmer to the Republican.* This pamphlet consists of five numbered letters, dated 8, 9, 10, 12, and 13 October. "Four editions, (and several thousands)" of the *Letters* were "in a few months printed and sold in the several states" ("Advertisement," *An Additional Number of Letters from the Federal Farmer to the Republican . . .* , 2 May 1788, CC:723, p. 266). A newspaper advertisement for *An Additional Number of Letters* stated that the first set of the *Letters* had "undergone several impressions in the different states, and several thousands of them have been sold" (*New York Journal* and *New York Packet*, 2 May, CC:723, pp. 265–66).

Copies of three editions of the *Letters*, and possibly four, have been located. Since the place of publication and the name of the printer do not appear on the title pages of any of these extant copies, it is a matter of conjecture as to when, where, and by whom each edition was printed. Bibliographers have generally attributed the publication of these editions to Thomas Greenleaf of the *New York Journal.* However, an analysis of the texts of the extant copies, of the advertisements offering them for sale, and of other evidence suggests that two editions were published by one printer and that the third was published by someone else.

On 8 November the weekly *New York Journal* advertised that the *Letters* was "Just received, and to be SOLD, at *T. Greenleaf's Printing-Office.* And by Mr. Hodge, and T. Allen, Book-sellers, in Queen-street, and at Mr. Loudon's, Printing-Office, Water-street." The next day the semiweekly *New York Packet*, printed by Samuel and John Loudon, advertised the *Letters* as "Just Published, and to be Sold by the Printers hereof, And by most of the Printers and Booksellers in this city." The printing of the pamphlet had probably been completed a few days before the appearance of the advertisements because, by 9 November, James Kent, a young lawyer, read the *Letters* in Poughkeepsie, about eighty-five miles north of New York City (below).

The first edition of the *Letters*, which was misdated 1777 (instead of 1787) on the title page, was filled with errors (Evans 20454). Consequently, a corrected edition was struck, apparently from the same forms (Evans 20455). This corrected edition was evidently printed before 14 November because, on that day, the Poughkeepsie *Country Journal* began reprinting the *Letters* with the corrections. A third edition—"RE-PRINTED BY ORDER OF A SOCIETY OF GEN-TLEMEN"—was published incorporating the corrections made in the second edition, as well as some additional changes (Evans 20456). There are also typographical differences to indicate that the third edition was struck by another printer. The only advertisement that referred to this edition appeared in Eleazer Oswald's Philadelphia *Independent Gazetteer* on 23 November. A fourth edition of the *Letters* was probably printed by Edward E. Powars of the Boston *American Herald* in January 1788, although no copies of it are extant (RCS: Mass., 544, 545, 547–48).

The authorship of the *Letters* had long been attributed to the well-known Revolutionary patriot Richard Henry Lee of Virginia, who was serving in the Confederation Congress in New York City at the time the letters were dated. This attribution was first made in a Federalist newspaper essay signed "New England" and published in the Hartford *Connecticut Courant* on 24 December (CC:372. See also "The New York Reprinting of New England's Response to the Federal Farmer's Letters to the Republican," 4 January 1788, below.). "New England" accused Lee of writing the *Letters*, although he offered no evidence for such a statement. Well known for his opposition to the Constitution, Lee was a good target because of his alleged personal hostility to George Washington, the former President of the Constitutional Convention and a strong supporter of the Constitution. "New England" maintained that this hostility arose "from a low envy of the brilliant virtues and unbounded popularity, of that illustrious character." In writing the "Federal Farmer," Lee was assisted, according to "New England," by "several persons of reputed good sense in New-York." "New England" was referring to Antifederalist leaders, especially John Lamb, of whose motives and methods for opposing the Constitution he was harshly critical. Four Massachusetts newspaper items derived from "New England" also identified Lee as the "Federal Farmer" (*Massachusetts Gazette,* 1 January 1788, *Massachusetts Centinel,* 2 January, and Boston *American Herald,* 7 January, [CC:390 E–H]).

Private letters offer few clues as to the authorship of the *Letters.* On 28 November 1787 Hugh Hughes wrote fellow Antifederalist Charles Tillinghast that "The federal Farmer, I think I am sure of, as one of the Letters contains some Part of a Conversation I once had, when I spent an Evening with him—Perhaps this may bring him to your Memory—If not, please to observe the first Part of the 2nd Paragraph in the 7th Page, and you will recollect, I expect, as I told you that he was perfectly in Sentiment with me on that Subject—I think he has great Merit, but not as much as he is capable of meriting—But, perhaps, he reserves himself for another Publication; if so, it may be all very right" (below).

Writing as "A Countryman" VI, Hughes repeated that "Federal Farmer" had "great merit" and added that he "well deserves the thanks of his country" (*New York Journal,* 14 February 1788, III below). However, "A Countryman" had several criticisms of the "Federal Farmer," and he declared that he did not know the identity of the "Federal Farmer." (See notes 2, 13, 15, and 33, below, for these criticisms.) In his fourth "Countryman" essay, Hughes attacked "Federal Farmer" for not being sufficiently critical of the supremacy clause of the Constitution (*New York Journal*, 15 December, below). Several weeks after the *Additional Letters* appeared in early May 1788, Virginia congressman Edward Carrington noted that the *Letters* and the *Additional Letters* "are reputed the best of any thing that has been written" against the Constitution (to Thomas Jefferson, 9 June, RCS:Va., 1591).

Since the 1950s, scholars have effectively challenged Lee's authorship of the *Letters*, but only three of them, Robert H. Webking, Joseph Kent McGaughy, and John P. Kaminski, have suggested a substitute. For the debate over the authorship of the *Letters*, in which some scholars still accept Lee's authorship of the *Letters*, see William Winslow Crosskey, *Politics and the Constitution in the History of the United States* (2 vols., Chicago, 1953), II, 1300; Gordon S. Wood, "The Authorship of the *Letters from the Federal Farmer*," *William and Mary Quarterly*, 3rd series, XXXI (1974), 299–308; Steven R. Boyd, "The Impact of the Constitution on State Politics: New York as a Test Case," in James Kirby Martin, ed., *The Human Dimensions of Nation Making, Essays on Colonial and Revolutionary America* (Madison, Wis., 1976), 276n; Walter Hartwell Bennett, ed., *Letters from the Federal Farmer to the Republican* (University, Ala., 1978), xiv–xx; Herbert J. Storing, ed., *The Complete Anti-Federalist* (7 vols., Chicago, 1981), II, 215–16; Robert H. Webking, "Melancton Smith and the *Letters from the Federal Farmer*," *William and Mary Quarterly*, 3rd series, XLIV (1987), 510–28; Joseph Kent McGaughy, "The Authorship of *The Letters from the Federal Farmer*, Revisited," *New York History*, LXX (1989), 153–70; and John P. Kaminski, "The Role of Newspapers in New York's Debate Over the Federal Constitution," in Stephen L. Schechter and Richard B. Bernstein, eds., *New York and the Union: Contributions to the American Constitutional Experience* (Albany, 1990), 286–87. Webking and McGaughy argue that Melancton Smith was the "Federal Farmer," while Kaminski recommends Elbridge Gerry of Massachusetts as a more likely choice.

Most historians have been so preoccupied with the question of Lee's authorship that they have ignored "The Republican"—the person to whom the *Letters* were addressed. In New York politics, Governor George Clinton was known by this sobriquet. (See Charles Tillinghast to Hugh Hughes, 27–28 January 1788, below.)

The *Letters* circulated throughout New York for months. On 8 November almost identical passages and references to similar events in the "Federal Farmer's" Letters I and V appeared in "Brutus, Junior," in the *New York Journal* (above). The *New York Packet* ran its 9 November advertisement for the *Letters* weekly until 30 November. Beginning on 15 November, the *New York Journal*, which became a daily on 19 November, published seven advertisements, each slightly different from the others, more than fifty times by mid-February 1788. (For these seven advertisements, see "The New York Journal Advertises the Sale of the Letters from the Federal Farmer to the Republican," 15 November 1787–18 February 1788, Mfm:N.Y.) On 22 December the *New York Journal* announced that the *Letters* had been "Just PUBLISHED, and to be SOLD. . . ." This advertisement possibly indicates that a new printing had just become available (*ibid.*). (A variant copy of the *Letters* found in the Rare Book Room of the

New York Public Library, with the letter "s" dropped from the word "Observations" on the title page, was possibly part of a new printing of the *Letters.* Except for this change on the title page, this printing is identical to the second edition of the *Letters* mentioned above.) In March 1789 Greenleaf still had copies of the *Letters* for sale, along with several other Antifederalist pamphlets (*New York Journal,* 12 March 1789, Mfm:N.Y. A week later, on 19 March, Edward E. Powars of the Worcester *American Herald* also advertised that he had copies for sale.).

At the request of "A CUSTOMER" the *Country Journal* reprinted the entire pamphlet in weekly installments from 14 November 1787 to 2 January 1788. Addressing the *Journal's* printer "A CUSTOMER" stated: "It is my opinion that every well-written piece in favor or against the new Constitution, ought to be laid before the public. You have published several pieces on both sides, and being sensible of your impartiality, the republication of the following letters cannot but afford general satisfaction." (For excerpts of the *Letters* reprinted by the *Massachusetts Gazette* and the *Newport Mercury,* see notes 3 and 38 below.) On 11 January 1788 Federalist Abraham Van Vechten of Johnstown, N.Y., wrote Antifederalists Henry Oothoudt and Jeremiah Van Rensselaer of Albany thanking them for a copy of the *Letters* that they had sent him on 2 January. He declared that he would deliver it to some "Friends here for their perusal" (James T. Mitchell Autograph Collection, PHi). A month later Federalist William North wrote from Albany that the *Letters,* "Centinel," and other Antifederalist publications "are scattered all over the County" (to Henry Knox, 13 February, III below). (For the circulation of the *Letters* outside New York, especially in Pennsylvania, Connecticut, and Massachusetts, see CC:Vol. 2, pp. 17–18. New York Antifederalists were involved in the circulation of the pamphlet in Connecticut and perhaps in the other two states.)

The response of New York Federalists to the *Letters* was mixed; nor did they respond in any significant detail to its arguments. James Kent wrote that the Constitution had "considerable Defects" and that the "Federal Farmer" had "illustrated those Defects in a candid & rational manner" (to Nathaniel Lawrence, 9 November, below). "Pat. O'Balaghan" in the *Country Journal* dismissed "Federal Farmer" as one of "those polity-errant writers who create monsters on purpose to destroy them" (19 December, Mfm:N.Y.). Also writing for the *Country Journal,* "Cato" warned his readers to beware of the sophistry of the "Federal Farmer" who agreed that the Confederation needed to be reformed but who thought reform was impractical (19 December, supplement, below). *The Federalist* 29 (Alexander Hamilton), *Independent Journal,* 9 January 1788 (CC:429), attacked "Federal Farmer" for criticizing the provision of the Constitution permitting the calling out of the militia to enforce the laws of the United States. "Curtiopolis," adopting a satirical stance, makes the writings of the "Federal Farmer" and other Antifederalists appear to be ridiculous (*Daily Advertiser,* 18 January, below). In *The Federalist* 68, "Publius" admitted that the "Federal Farmer" was the "most plausible" of the Antifederalists (*Independent Journal,* 12 March, CC:615, p. 376). A reviewer, probably Noah Webster, of the *Letters* and the *Additional Letters,* stated that the "Federal Farmer" wrote "with more candor and good sense" than most Antifederalists even though his "arguments want method, and the reader is consequently fatigued with numberless repetitions." He also responded to several of the arguments (*American*

Magazine, May 1788 issue, III below. Webster was the editor of the *American Magazine* and a contributor to it.).

A Pennsylvania Federalist, however, did write a point-by-point refutation of the *Letters,* but it was not published. On 24 December, a month after Charles Tillinghast had sent him a copy of the *Letters* and had requested his opinion of the Constitution, Timothy Pickering of Luzerne County, Pennsylvania, began writing an eighteen-page letter refuting the "Federal Farmer." On 27 January 1788 Tillinghast sent a copy of Pickering's letter to Hugh Hughes, stating that he believed that Pickering wanted the letter printed. However, Tillinghast, who acted as a go-between for inserting Antifederalist pieces in the *New York Journal,* did not have the letter printed. (For Pickering's letter of 24 December, see CC:288–C; and for Tillinghast's letter of 24 November, in which Tillinghast agreed with the "Federal Farmer" that the Constitution was "very dangerous to the liberties of the People," see below. Pickering had received Tillinghast's request while a delegate to the Pennsylvania Convention and he did not begin writing his refutation of the *Letters* until twelve days after that Convention had ratified the Constitution.).

LETTER I.

OCTOBER 8th, 1787.

DEAR SIR, My letters to you last winter, on the subject of a well-balanced national government for the United States, were the result of free enquiry; when I passed from that subject to enquiries relative to our commerce, revenues, past administration, &c. I anticipated the anxieties I feel, on carefully examining the plan of government proposed by the convention. It appears to be a plan retaining some federal features; but to be the first important step, and to aim strongly to one consolidated government of the United States. It leaves the powers of government, and the representation of the people, so unnaturally divided between the general and state governments, that the operations of our system must be very uncertain. My uniform federal attachments, and the interest I have in the protection of property, and a steady execution of the laws, will convince you, that, if I am under any biass at it,[1] it is in favor of any general system which shall promise those advantages. The instability of our laws increase my wishes for firm and steady government; but then, I can consent to no government, which, in my opinion, is not calculated equally to preserve the rights of all orders of men in the community. My object has been to join with those who have endeavoured to supply the defects in the forms of our governments by a steady and proper administration of them. Though I have long apprehended that fraudulent debtors, and embarrassed men, on the one hand, and men, on the other, unfriendly to republican equality, would produce an uneasiness among the people, and prepare the way, not for cool and deliberate reforms in the governments, but for changes calculated to promote the interests of particular orders of men. Acquit me, sir, of any agency in the formation of the new system; I shall be satisfied with seeing, if it should be adopted, a prudent administration. Indeed I am so much convinced of the truth of Pope's maxim, that—"That which is best administered is best,"[2] that I am much inclined to subscribe to it from experience. I am not disposed to unreasonably contend about forms. I know our situation is critical, and it behoves us to make the best of it. A federal government of some sort is necessary. We have suffered the present to languish; and whether the confederation was capable or not originally of answering any valuable purposes, it is now but of little importance. I will pass by the men, and states, who have been particularly instrumental in preparing the way for a change, and, perhaps, for governments not very favourable to the people at large. A constitution is now presented, which we may reject, or which we may accept, with or without amendments; and to which point we ought to direct our exertions, is the question. To determine this question, with propriety, we must attentively examine the system itself, and the probable consequences of either step. This I shall endeavour to do, so far as I am able, with candour and fairness; and leave you to decide upon the propriety of my opinions, the weight of my reasons, and how far my conclusions are well drawn. Whatever may be the conduct of others, on the present occasion, I do not mean, hastily and positively to decide on the merits of the constitution proposed. I shall be open to conviction, and always disposed to adopt that which, all things considered, shall appear to me to be most for the happiness of the community. It must be granted, that if men hastily and blindly adopt a system of government, they will as hastily and as blindly be led to alter or abolish it; and changes must ensue, one after another, till the peaceable and better part of the community will grow weary with changes, tumults and disorders, and be disposed to accept any government, however despotic, that shall promise stability and firmness.

The first principal question that occurs, is, Whether, considering our situation, we ought to precipitate the adoption of the proposed constitution? If we remain cool and temperate, we are in no immediate danger of any commotions; we are in a state of perfect peace, and in no danger of invasions; the state governments are in the full exercise of their powers; and our governments answer all present exigencies, except the regulation of trade, securing credit, in some cases, and providing for the interest, in some instances, of the public debts; and whether we adopt a change, three or nine months hence, can make but little odds with the private circumstances of individuals; their happiness and prosperity, after all, depend principally upon their own exertions. We are hardly recovered from a long and distressing war: The farmers, fishmen, &c. have not yet fully repaired the waste made by it. Industry and frugality are again assuming their proper station. Private debts are lessened, and public debts incurred by the war, have been, by various ways, diminished; and the public lands have now become a productive source for diminishing them much more. I know uneasy men, who wish very much to precipitate, do not admit all these facts; but they are facts well known to all men who are thoroughly informed in the affairs of this country. It must, however, be admitted, that our federal system is defective, and that some of the state governments are not well administered; but, then, we impute to the defects in our governments, many evils and embarrassments which are most clearly the result of the late war. We must allow men to conduct on the present occasion, as on all similar one's. They will urge a thousand pretences to answer their purposes on both sides. When we want a man to change his condition, we describe it as miserable, wretched, and despised; and draw a pleasing picture of that which we would have him assume. And when we wish the contrary, we reverse our descriptions. Whenever a clamor is raised, and idle men get to work, it is highly necessary to examine facts carefully, and without unreasonably suspecting men of falshood, to examine, and enquire attentively, under what impressions they act. It is too often the case in political concerns, that men state facts not as they are, but as they wish them to be; and almost every man, by calling to mind past scenes, will find this to be true.

Nothing but the passions of ambitious, impatient, or disorderly men, I conceive, will plunge us into commotions, if ⟨time should be taken fully to examine and consider the system proposed. Men who feel easy in their circumstances, and such as are not sanguine in their expectations relative to the consequences of the proposed change, will remain quiet under the existing governments. Many commercial and monied men, who are uneasy, not without just cause, ought to be respected; and, by no means, unreasonably disappointed in their expectations and hopes; but as to those who expect employments under the new constitution; as to those weak and ardent men who always expect to be gainers by revolutions, and whose lot it generally is to get out of one difficulty into another, they are very little to be regarded: and as to those who designedly avail themselves of this weakness and ardor, they are to be despised. It is natural for men, who wish to hasten the adoption of a measure, to tell us, now is the crisis—now is the critical moment which must be seized, or all will be lost: and to shut the door against free enquiry, whenever conscious the thing presented has defects in it, which time and investigation will probably discover. This has been the custom of tyrants and their dependants in all ages. If it is true, what has been so often said, that the people of this country cannot change their condition for the worse, I presume it still behoves them to endeavour deliberately to change it for the better. The fickle and ardent, in any community, are the proper tools for establishing despotic government. But it is deliberate and thinking men, who must establish and secure governments on free principles. Before they decide on the plan proposed, they will enquire whether it will probably be a blessing or a curse to this people.)³

The present moment discovers a new face in our affairs. Our object has been all along, to reform our federal system, and to strengthen our governments—to establish peace, order and justice in the community—but a new object now presents. The plan of government now proposed, is evidently calculated totally to change, in time, our condition as a people. Instead of being thirteen republics, under a federal head, it is clearly designed to make us one consolidated government. Of this, I think, I shall fully convince you, in my following letters on this subject. This consolidation of the states has been the object of several men in this country for some time past. Whether such a change can ever be effected in any manner; whether it can be effected without convulsions and civil wars; whether such a change will not totally destroy the liberties of this country—time only can determine.

To have a just idea of the government before us, and to shew that a consolidated one is the object in view, it is necessary not only to examine the plan, but also its history, and the politics of its particular friends.

The confederation was formed when great confidence was placed in the voluntary exertions of individuals, and of the respective states; and the framers of it, to guard against usurpation, so limited and checked the powers, that, in many respects, they are inadequate to the exigencies of the union. We find, therefore, members of congress urging alterations in the federal system almost as soon as it was adopted. It was early proposed to vest congress with powers to levy an impost, to regulate trade, &c.⁴ but such was known to be the caution of the states in parting with power, that the vestment, even of these, was proposed to be under several checks and limitations. During the war, the general confusion, and the introduction of paper money, infused in the minds of people vague ideas respecting government and credit. We expected too much from the return of peace, and of course we have been disappointed. Our governments have been new and unsettled; and several legislatures, by making tender, suspension, and paper money laws, have given just cause of uneasiness to creditors. By these and other causes, several orders of men in the community have been prepared, by degrees, for a change of government; and this very abuse of power in the legislatures, which, in some cases, has been charged upon the democratic part of the community, has furnished aristocratical men with those very weapons, and those very means, with which, in great measure, they are rapidly effecting their favourite object. And should an oppressive government be the consequence of the proposed change, posterity may reproach not only a few overbearing, unprincipled men, but those parties in the states which have misused their powers.

The conduct of several legislatures, touching paper money, and tender laws, has prepared many honest men for changes in government, which otherwise they would not have thought of—when by the evils, on the one hand, and by the secret instigations of artful men, on the other, the minds of men were become sufficiently uneasy, a bold step was taken, which is usually followed by a revolution, or a civil war. A general convention for mere commercial purposes was moved for— the authors of this measure saw that the people's attention was turned solely to the amendment of the federal system; and that, had the idea of a total change been started, probably no state would have appointed members to the convention. The idea of destroying, ultimately, the state government, and forming one consolidated system, could not have been admitted—a convention, therefore, merely for vesting in congress power to regulate trade, was proposed. This was pleasing to the commercial towns; and the landed people had little or no concern about it. September, 1786, a few men from the middle states met at Annapolis, and hastily proposed a convention to be held in May, 1787, for the purpose, generally, of amending the confederation—this was done before the delegates of Massachusetts, and of the other states arrived[5]— still not a word was said about destroying the old constitution, and making a new one—The states still unsuspecting, and not aware that they were passing the Rubicon, appointed members to the new convention, for the sole and express purpose of revising and amending the confederation[6]—and, probably, not one man in ten thousand in the United States, till within these ten or twelve days, had an idea that the old ship was to be destroyed, and he put to the alternative of embarking in the new ship presented, or of being left in danger of sinking—The States, I believe, universally supposed the convention would report alterations in the confederation, which would pass an examination in congress, and after being agreed to there, would be confirmed by all the legislatures, or be rejected. Virginia made a very respectable appointment, and placed at the head of it the first man in America:[7]—In this appointment there was a mixture of political characters; but Pennsylvania appointed principally those men who are esteemed aristocratical.[8] Here the favourite moment for changing the government was evidently discerned by a few men, who seized it with address. Ten other states appointed, and tho' they chose men principally connected with commerce and the judicial department, yet they appointed many good republican characters—had they all attended we should now see, I am persuaded, a better system presented. The non-attendance of eight or nine men, who were appointed members of the convention, I shall ever consider as a very unfortunate event to the United States.[9]—Had they attended, I am pretty clear that the result of the convention would not have had that strong tendency to aristocracy now discernable in every part of the plan. There would not have been so great an accummulation of powers, especially as to the internal police of the country, in a few hands, as the constitution reported proposes to vest in them—the young visionary men, and the consolidating aristocracy, would have been more restrained than they have been. Eleven states[10] met in the convention, and after four months close attention, presented the new constitution, to be adopted or rejected by the people. The uneasy and fickle part of the community may be prepared to receive any form of government; but, I presume, the enlightened and substantial part will give any constitution, presented for their adoption, a candid and thorough examination: and silence those designing or empty men, who weakly and rashly attempt to precipitate the adoption of a system of so much importance—We shall view the convention with proper respect—and, at the same time, that we reflect · there were men of abilities and integrity in it, we must recollect how disproportionably the democratic and aristocratic parts of the community were represented.—Perhaps the judicious friends and opposers of the new constitution will agree, that it is best to let it rest solely on its own merits, or be condemned for its own defects.[11]

In the first place, I shall premise, that the plan proposed, is a plan of accommodation—and that it is in this way only, and by giving up a part of our opinions, that we can ever expect to obtain a government founded in freedom and compact. This circumstance candid men will always keep in view, in the discussion of this subject.

The plan proposed appears to be partly federal, but principally however, calculated ultimately to make the states one consolidated government.

The first interesting question, therefore, suggested, is, how far the states can be consolidated into one entire government on free principles. In considering this question extensive objects are to be taken into view, and important changes in the forms of government to be carefully attended to in all their consequences. The happiness of the people at large must be the great object with every honest statesman, and he will direct every movement to this point. If we are so situated as a people, as not to be able to enjoy equal happiness and advantages under one government, the consolidation of the states cannot be admitted.

There are three different forms of free government under which the United States may exist as one nation; and now is, perhaps, the time to determine to which we will direct our views. 1. Distinct republics connected under a fœderal head. In this case the respective state governments must be the principal guardians of the peoples rights, and exclusively regulate their internal police; in them must rest the balance of government. The congress of the states, or federal head, must consist of delegates amenable to, and removeable by the respective states: This congress must have general directing powers; powers to require men and monies of the states; to make treaties; peace and war; to direct the operations of armies, &c. Under this federal modification of government, the powers of congress would be rather advisory or recommendatory than coercive. 2. We may do away the several state governments, and form or consolidate all the states into one entire government, with one executive, one judiciary, and one legislature, consisting of senators and representatives collected from all parts of the union: In this case there would be a compleat consolidation of the states. 3. We may consolidate the states as to certain national objects, and leave them severally distinct independent republics, as to internal police generally. Let the general government consist of an executive, a judiciary and balanced legislature, and its powers extend exclusively to all foreign concerns, causes arising on the seas, to commerce, imports, armies, navies, Indian affairs, peace and war, and to a few internal concerns of the community; to the coin, post-offices, weights and measures, a general plan for the militia, to naturalization, *and, perhaps to bankruptcies,* leaving the internal police of the community, in other respects, exclusively to the state governments; as the administration of justice in all causes arising internally, the laying and collecting of internal taxes, and the forming of the militia according to a general plan prescribed. In this case there would be a compleat consolidation, *quoad* certain objects only.

Touching the first, or federal plan, I do not think much can be said in its favor: The sovereignty of the nation, without coercive and efficient powers to collect the strength of it, cannot always be depended on to answer the purposes of government; and in a congress of representatives of foreign states, there must necessarily be an unreasonable mixture of powers in the same hands.

As to the second, or compleat consolidating plan, it deserves to be carefully considered at this time by every American: If it be impracticable, it is a fatal error to model our governments, directing our views ultimately to it.

The third plan, or partial consolidation, is, in my opinion, the only one that can secure the freedom and happiness of this people. I once had some general ideas that the second plan was practicable, but from long attention, and the proceedings of the convention, I am fully satisfied, that this third plan is the only one we can with safety and propriety proceed upon. Making this the standard to point out, with candour and fairness, the parts of the new constitution which appear to be improper, is my object. The convention appears to have proposed the partial consolidation evidently with a view to collect all powers ultimately, in the United States into one entire government; and from its views in this respect, and from the tenacity, of the small states to have an equal vote in the senate, probably originated the greatest defects in the proposed plan.

Independant of the opinions of many great authors, that a free elective government cannot be extended over large territories, a few reflections must evince, that one government and general legislation alone never can extend equal benefits to all parts of the United States: Different laws, customs, and opinions exist in the different states, which by a uniform system of laws would be unreasonably invaded. The United States contain about a million of square miles, and in half a century will, probably, contain ten millions of people; and from the center to the extremes is about 800 miles.

Before we do away the state governments, or adopt measures that will tend to abolish them, and to consolidate the states into one entire government several principles should be considered and facts ascertained:—These, and my examination into the essential parts of the proposed plan, I shall pursue in my next.

LETTER II.

October 9, 1787.

Dear Sir, The essential parts of a free and good government are a full and equal representation of the people in the legislature, and the jury trial of the vicinage in the administration of justice—a full and equal representation, is that which possesses the same interests, feelings, opinions, and views the people themselves would were they all assembled—a fair representation, therefore, should be so regulated, that every order of men in the community, according to the common course of elections, can have a share in it—in order to allow professional men, merchants, traders, farmers, mechanics, &c. to bring a just proportion of their best informed men respectively into the legislature, the representation must be considerably numerous—We have about 200 state senators in the United States, and a less number than that of federal representatives cannot, clearly, be a full representation of this people, in the affairs of internal taxation and police, were there but one legislature for the whole union. The representation cannot be equal, or the situation of the people proper for one government only— if the extreme parts of the society cannot be represented as fully as the central—It is apparently impracticable that this should be the case in this extensive country—it would be impossible to collect a representation of the parts of the country five, six, and seven hundred miles from the seat of government.

Under one general government alone, there could be but one judiciary, one supreme and a proper number of inferior courts. I think it would be totally impracticable in this case, to preserve a due administration of justice, and the real benefits of the jury trial of the vicinage—there are now supreme courts in each state in the union; and a great number of county and other courts subordinate to each supreme court—most of these supreme and inferior courts are itinerant, and hold their sessions in different parts every year of their respective states, counties and districts—with all these moving courts, our citizens, from the vast extent of the country must travel very considerable distances from home to find the place where justice is administered. I am not for bringing justice so near to individuals as to afford them any temptation to engage in law suits; though I think it one of the greatest benefits in a good government, that each citizen should find a court of justice within a reasonable distance, perhaps, within a day's travel of his home; so that, without great inconveniences and enormous expences, he may have the advantages of his witnesses and jury—it would be impracticable to derive these advantages from one judiciary—the one supreme court at most could only set in the centre of the union, and move once a year into the centre of the eastern and southern extremes of it—and, in this case, each citizen, on an average, would travel 150 or 200 miles to find this court—that, however, inferior courts might be properly placed in the different counties, and districts of the union, the appellate jurisdiction would be intolerable and expensive.

If it were possible to consolidate the states, and preserve the features of a free government, still it is evident that the middle states, the parts of the union, about the seat of government, would enjoy great advantages, while the remote states would experience the many inconveniences of remote provinces. Wealth, officers, and the benefits of government would collect in the centre: and the extreme states; and their principal towns become much less important.

There are other considerations which tend to prove that the idea of one consolidated whole, on free principles, is ill-founded—the laws of a free government rest on the confidence of the people, and operate gently—and never can extend their influence very far—if they are executed on free principles, about the centre, where the benefits of the government induce the people to support it voluntarily; yet they must be executed on the principles of fear and force in the extremes—This has been the case with every extensive republic of which we have any accurate account.

There are certain unalienable and fundamental rights, which in forming the social compact, ought to be explicitly ascertained and fixed—a free and enlightened people, in forming this compact, will not resign all their rights to those who govern, and they will fix limits to their legislators and rulers, which will soon be plainly seen by those who are governed, as well as by those who govern: and the latter will know they cannot be passed unperceived by the former, and without giving a general alarm—These rights should be made the basis of every constitution; and if a people be so situated, or have such different opinions that they cannot agree in ascertaining and fixing them, it is a very strong argument against their attempting to form one entire society, to live under one system of laws only.—I confess, I never thought the people of these states differed essentially in these respects; they having derived all these rights, from one common source, the British systems; and having in the formation of their state constitutions, discovered that their ideas relative to these rights are very similar. However, it is now said that the states differ so essentially in these respects, and even in the important article of the trial by jury, that when assembled in convention, they can agree to no words by which to establish that trial, or by which to ascertain and establish many other of these rights, as fundamental articles in the social compact. If so, we proceed to consolidate the states on no solid basis whatever.

But I do not pay much regard to the reasons given for not bottoming the new constitution on a better bill of rights. I still believe a complete federal bill of rights to be very practicable. Nevertheless I acknowledge the proceedings of the convention furnish my mind with many new and strong reasons, against a complete consolidation of the states. They tend to convince me, that it cannot be carried with propriety very far—that the convention have gone much farther in one respect than they found it practicable to go in another; that is, they propose to lodge in the general government very extensive powers—*powers* nearly, if not altogether, complete and unlimited, over the purse and the sword. But, in its organization, they furnish the strongest proof that the proper limbs, or parts of a government, to support and execute those powers on proper principles (or in which they can be safely lodged) cannot be formed. These powers must be lodged somewhere in every society; but then they should be lodged where the strength and guardians of the people are collected. They can be wielded, or safely used, in a free country only by an able executive and judiciary, a respectable senate, and a secure, full, and equal representation of the people. I think the principles I have premised or brought into view, are well founded—I think they will not be denied by any fair reasoner. It is in connection with these, and other solid principles, we are to examine the constitution. It is not a few democratic phrases, or a few well formed features, that will prove its merits; or a few small omissions that will produce its rejection among men of sense; they will enquire what are the essential powers in a community, and what are nominal ones, where and how the essential powers shall be lodged to secure government, and to secure true liberty.

In examining the proposed constitution carefully, we must clearly perceive an unnatural separation of these powers from the substantial representation of the people. The state governments will exist, with all their governors, senators, representatives, officers and expences; in these will be nineteen twentieths of the representatives of the people; they will have a near connection, and their members an immediate intercourse with the people; and the probability is, that the state governments will possess the confidence of the people, and be considered generally as their immediate guardians.

The general government will consist of a new species of executive, a small senate, and a very small house of representatives. As many citizens will be more than three hundred miles from the seat of this government as will be nearer to it, its judges and officers cannot be very numerous, without making our government very expensive. Thus will stand the state and the general governments, should the constitution be adopted without any alterations in their organization: but as to powers, the general government will possess all essential ones, at least on paper, and those of the states a mere shadow of power. And therefore, unless the people shall make some great exertions to restore to the state governments their powers in matters of internal police; as the powers to lay and collect, exclusively, internal taxes, to govern the militia, and to hold the decisions of their own judicial courts upon their own laws final, the balance cannot possibly continue long; but the state governments must be annihilated, or continue to exist for no purpose.

It is however to be observed, that many of the essential powers given the national government are not exclusively given; and the general government may have prudence enough to forbear the exercise of those which may still be exercised by the respective states. But this cannot justify the impropriety of giving powers, the exercise of which prudent men will not attempt, and imprudent men will, or probably can, exercise only in a manner destructive of free government. The general government, organized as it is, may be adequate to many valuable objects, and be able to carry its laws into execution on proper principles in several cases; but I think its warmest friends will not contend, that it can carry all the powers proposed to be lodged in it into effect, without calling to its aid a military force, which must very soon destroy all elective governments in the country, produce anarchy, or establish despotism. Though we cannot have now a complete idea of what will be the operations of the proposed system, we may, allowing things to have their common course, have a very tolerable one. The powers lodged in the general government, if exercised by it, must ultimately[12] effect the internal police of the states, as well as external concerns; and there is no reason to expect the numerous state governments, and their connections, will be very friendly to the execution of federal laws in those internal affairs, which hitherto have been under their own immediate management. There is more reason to believe, that the general government, far removed from the people, and none of its members elected oftener than once in two years, will be forgot or neglected, and its laws in many cases disregarded, unless a multitude of officers and military force be continually kept in view, and employed to enforce the execution of the laws, and to make the government feared and respected. No position can be truer than this,—That in this country either neglected laws, or a military execution of them, must lead to a revolution, and to the destruction of freedom. Neglected laws must first lead to anarchy and confusion; and a military execution of laws is only a shorter way to the same point—despotic government.

LETTER III.

OCTOBER 10th, 1787.

DEAR SIR, The great object of a free people must be so to form their government and laws and so to administer them as to create a confidence in, and respect for the laws; and thereby induce the sensible and virtuous part of the community to declare in favor of the laws, and to support them without an expensive military force. I wish, though I confess I have not much hope, that this may be the case with the laws of Congress under the new Constitution. I am fully convinced that we must organize the national government on different principles, and make the parts of it more efficient, and secure in it more effectually the different interests in the community; or else leave in the state governments some powers proposed to be lodged in it—at least till such an organization shall be found to be practicable. Not sanguine in my expectations of a good federal administration, and satisfied, as I am, of the impracticability of consolidating the states, and at the same time of preserving the rights of the people at large, I believe we ought still to leave some of those powers in the state governments, in which the people, in fact, will still be represented—to define some other powers proposed to be vested in the general government, more carefully, and to establish a few principles to secure a proper exercise of the powers given it. It is not my object to multiply objections, or to contend about inconsiderable powers or amendments. ⟨I wish the system adopted with a few alterations; but those, in my mind, are essential ones; if adopted without, every good citizen will acquiesce,⟩[13] though I shall consider the duration of our governments, and the liberties of this people, very much dependant on the administration of the general government. A wise and honest administration, may make the people happy under any government; but necessity only can justify even our leaving open avenues to the abuse of power, by wicked, unthinking, or ambitious men. I will examine, first, the organization of the proposed government in order to judge; 2d. with propriety, what powers are improperly, at least prematurely lodged in it. I shall examine, 3d, the undefined powers; and 4th, those powers, the exercise of which is not secured on safe and proper ground.

First. As to the organization—the house of representatives, the democrative branch, as it is called, is to consist of 65 members; that is, about one representative for fifty thousand inhabitants, to be chosen biennially—the federal legislature may increase this number to one for every thirty thousand inhabitants, abating fractional numbers in each state.—Thirty-three representatives will make a quorum for doing business, and a majority of those present determine the sense of the house.—I have no idea that the interests, feelings, and opinions of three or four millions of people, especially touching internal taxation, can be collected in such a house.—In the nature of things, nine times in ten, men of elevated classes in the community only can be chosen—

Connecticut, for instance, will have five representatives—not one man in a hundred of those who form the democrative branch in the state legislature,[14] will on a fair computation, be one of the five—The people of this country, in one sense, may all be democratic; but if we make the proper distinction between the few men of wealth and abilities, and consider them, as we ought, as the natural aristocracy of the country, and the great body of the people, the middle and lower classes, as the democracy, this federal representative branch will have but very little democracy in it, even this small representation is not secured on proper principles.—The branches of the legislature are essential parts of the fundamental compact, and ought to be so fixed by the people, that the legislature cannot alter itself by modifying the elections of its own members. This, by a part of Art. 1. Sect. 4. the general legislature may do, it may evidently so regulate elections as to secure the choice of any particular description of men.—It may make the whole state one district—make the capital, or any place in the state, the place or places of election—it may declare that the five men (or whatever the number may be the state may chuse) who shall have the most votes shall be considered as chosen—In this case it is easy to perceive how the people who live scattered in the inland towns will bestow their votes on different men—and how few men in a city, in any order or profession, may unite and place any five men they please highest among those that may be voted for—and all this may be done constitutionally, and by those silent operations, which are not immediately perceived by the people in general.—I know it is urged, that the general legislature will be disposed to regulate elections on fair and just principles:—This may be true—good men will generally govern well with almost any constitution: But why in laying the foundation of the social system, need we unnecessarily have a door open to improper regulations?—This is a very general and unguarded clause, and many evils may flow from that part which authorises the congress to regulate elections—Were it omitted, the regulations of elections would be solely in the respective states, where the people are substantially represented; and where the elections ought to be regulated, otherwise to secure a representation from all parts of the community, in making the constitution, we ought to provide for dividing each state into a proper number of districts, and for confining the electors in each district to the choice of some men, who shall have a permanent interest and residence in it; and also for this essential object, that the representative elected shall have a majority of the votes of those electors who shall attend and give their votes.

In considering the practicability of having a full and equal representation of the people from all parts of the union, not only distances and different opinions, customs, and views, common in extensive tracts of country, are to be taken into view, but many differences peculiar to Eastern, Middle, and Southern States. These differences are not so perceivable among the members of congress, and men of general information in the state, as among the men who would properly form the democratic branch. The Eastern states are very democratic, and composed chiefly of moderate freeholders: they have but few rich men and no slaves; the Southern states are composed chiefly of rich planters and slaves; they have but few moderate freeholders, and the prevailing influence, in them, is generally a dissipated aristocracy: The Middle states partake partly of the Eastern, and partly of the Southern character.

Perhaps, nothing could be more disjointed, unweildly and incompetent to doing business with harmony and dispatch, than a federal house of representatives properly numerous for the great objects of taxation, &c. collected from the several states; whether such men would ever act in concert; whether they would not worry along a few years, and then be the means of separating the parts of the union, is very problematical?—View this system in whatever form we can, propriety brings us still to this point, a federal government possessed of general and complete powers, as to those national objects which cannot well come under the cognizance of the internal laws of the respective states, and this federal government, accordingly, consisting of branches not very numerous.

The house of representatives is on the plan of consolidation, but ⟨the senate is entirely on the federal plan;⟩[15] and Delaware will have as much constitutional influence in the senate, as the largest state in the union; and in this senate are lodged legislative, executive and judicial powers: Ten states in this union urge that they are small states, nine of which were present in the convention.[16]—They were interested in collecting large powers into the hands of the senate, in which each state still will have its equal share of power. I suppose it was impracticable for the three large states, as they were called, to get the senate formed on any other principles:—But this only proves, that we cannot form one general government on equal and just principles—and proves, that we ought not to lodge in it such extensive powers before we are convinced of the practicability of organizing it on just and equal principles. The senate will consist of two members from each state, chosen by the state legislature, every sixth year. The clause referred to, respecting the elections of representatives, empowers the general legislature to regulate the elections of senators also, "except as to the places of chusing senators."—There is, therefore, but little more security in the elections than in those of representatives:—Fourteen senators make a quorum for business, and a majority of the senators present give the vote of the senate, except in giving judgment upon an impeachment, or in making treaties, or in expelling a member, when two thirds of the senators present must agree.—The members of the legislature are not excluded from being elected to any military offices, or any civil offices, except those created, or the emoluments of which shall be increased by themselves: two-thirds of the members present, of either house, may expel a member at pleasure.—The senate is an independent branch of the legislature, a court for trying impeachments, and also a part of the executive, having a negative in the making of all treaties, and in appointing almost all officers.

The vice-president is not a very important, if not an unnecessary part of the system—he may be a part of the senate at one period, and act as the supreme executive magistrate at another—The election of this officer, as well as of the president of the United States seems to be properly secured;[17] but when we examine the powers of the president, and the forms of the executive, shall perceive that the general government, in this part, will have a strong tendency to aristocracy, or the government of the few. The executive is, in fact, the president and senate in all transactions of any importance; the president is connected with, or tied to the senate; he may always act with the senate, never can effectually counteract its views: The president can appoint no officer, civil or military, who shall not be agreeable to the senate; and the presumption is, that the will of so important a body will not be very easily controuled, and that it will exercise its powers with great address.

In the judicial department, powers ever kept distinct in well balanced governments, are no less improperly blended in the hands of the same men—in the judges of the supreme court is lodged, the law, the equity and the fact. It is not necessary to pursue the minute organical parts of the general government proposed.—There were various interests in the convention, to be reconciled, especially of large and small states; of carrying and non-carrying states: and of states more and states less democratic—vast laboured attention[18] were by the convention bestowed on the organization of the parts of the constitution offered; still it is acknowledged, there are many things radically wrong in the essential parts of this constitution—but it is said, that these are the result of our situation:—On a full examination of the subject, I believe it; but what do the laborious inquiries and determinations of the convention prove? If they prove any thing, they prove that we cannot consolidate the states on proper principles: The organization of the government presented proves, that we cannot form a general government in which all power can be safely lodged; and a little attention to the parts of the one proposed will make it appear very evident, that all the powers proposed to be lodged in it, will not be then well deposited, either for the purposes of government, or the preservation of liberty. I will suppose no abuse of powers in those cases, in which the abuse of it is not well guarded against—I will suppose the words authorising the general government to regulate the elections of its own members struck out of the plan, or free district elections, in each state, amply secured.—That the small representation provided for shall be as fair and equal as it is capable of being made—I will suppose the judicial department regulated on pure principles, by future laws, as far as it can be by the constitution, and consist with the situation of the country—still there will be an unreasonable accumulation of powers in the general government, if all be granted, enumerated in the plan proposed. The plan does not present a well balanced government: The senatorial branch of the legislative and the executive are substantially united, and the president, or the first executive magistrate, may aid the senatorial interest when weakest, but never can effectually support the democratic, however it may be oppressed;—the excellency, in my mind, of a well balanced government is that it consists of distinct branches, each sufficiently strong and independant to keep its own station, and to aid either of the other branches which may occasionally want aid.

The convention found that any but a small house of representatives would be expensive, and that it would be impracticable to assemble a large number of representatives. Not only the determination of the convention in this case, but the situation of the states, proves the impracticability of collecting, in any one point, a proper representation.

The formation of the senate, and the smallness of the house, being, therefore, the result of our situation, and the actual state of things, the evils which may attend the exercise of many powers in this national government may be considered as without a remedy.

All officers are impeachable before the senate only—before the men by whom they are appointed, or who are consenting to the appointment of these officers. No judgment of conviction, on an impeachment, can be given unless two thirds of the senators agree. Under these circumstances the right of impeachment, in the house, can be of but little importance: the house cannot expect often to convict the offender; and, therefore, probably, will but seldom or never exercise the right. In addition to the insecurity and inconveniences attending this organization beforementioned, it may be observed, that it is extremely difficult to secure the people against the fatal effects of corruption and influence. The power of making any law will be in the president, eight senators, and seventeen representatives, relative to the important objects enumerated in the constitution. Where there is a small representation a sufficient number to carry any measure, may, with ease, be influenced by bribes, offices and civilities; they may easily form private juntoes, and out-door meetings, agree on measures, and carry them by silent votes.

Impressed, as I am, with a sense of the difficulties there are in the way of forming the parts of a federal government on proper principles, and seeing a government so unsubstantially organized, after so arduous an attempt has been made, I am led to believe, that powers ought to be given to it with great care and caution.

In the second place it is necessary, therefore, to examine the extent, and the probable operations of some of those extensive powers proposed to be vested in this government. These powers, legislative, executive, and judicial, respect internal as well as external objects. Those respecting external objects, as all foreign concerns, commerce, impost, all causes arising on the seas, peace and war, and Indian affairs, can be lodged no where else, with any propriety, but in this government. Many powers that respect internal objects ought clearly to be lodged in it; as those to regulate trade between the states, weights and measures, the coin or current monies, post-offices, naturalization, &c. These powers may be exercised without essentially effecting the internal police of the respective states: But powers to lay and collect internal taxes, to form the militia, to make bankrupt laws, and to decide on appeals, questions arising on the internal laws of the respective states, are of a very serious nature, and carry with them almost all other powers. These taken in connection with the others, and powers to raise armies and build navies, proposed to be lodged in this government, appear to me to comprehend all the essential powers in the community, and those which will be left to the states will be of no great importance.

A power to lay and collect taxes at discretion, is, in itself, of very great importance. By means of taxes, the government may command the whole or any part of the subject's property. Taxes may be of various kinds; but there is a strong distinction between external and internal taxes. External taxes are impost duties, which are laid on imported goods; they may usually be collected in a few seaport towns, and of a few individuals, though ultimately paid by the consumer; a few officers can collect them, and they can be carried no higher than trade will bear, or smuggling permit—that in the very nature of commerce bounds are set to them. But internal taxes, as poll and land taxes, excise, duties on all written instruments, &c. may fix themselves on every person and species of property in the community; they may be carried to any lengths, and in proportion as they are extended, numerous officers must be employed to assess them, and to enforce the collection of them. In the United Netherlands the general government has compleat powers, as to external taxation; but as to internal taxes, it makes requisitions on the provinces. Internal taxation in this country is more important, as the country is so very extensive. As many assessors and collectors of federal taxes will be above three hundred miles from the seat of the federal government as will be less. Besides, to lay and collect internal taxes, in this extensive country, must require a great number of congressional ordinances, immediately operating upon the body of the people; these must continually interfere with the state laws, and thereby produce disorder and general dissatisfaction, till the one system of laws or the other, operating upon the same subjects, shall be abolished. These ordinances alone, to say nothing of those respecting the militia, coin, commerce, federal judiciary, &c. &c. will probably soon defeat the operations of the state laws and governments.

Should the general government think it politic, as some administrations (if not all) probably will, to look for a support in a system of influence, the government will take every occasion to multiply laws, and officers to execute them, considering these as so many necessary props for its own support. Should this system of policy be adopted, taxes more productive than the impost duties will, probably, be wanted to support the government, and to discharge foreign demands, without leaving any thing for the domestic creditors. The internal sources of taxation then must be called into operation, and internal tax laws and federal assessors and collectors spread over this immense country. All these circumstances considered, is it wise, prudent, or safe, to vest the powers of laying and collecting internal taxes in the general government, while imperfectly organized and inadequate; and to trust to amending it hereafter, and making it adequate to this purpose? It is not only unsafe but absurd to lodge power in a government before it is fitted to receive it? It is confessed that this power and representation ought to go together. Why give the power first? Why give the power to the few, who, when possessed of it, may have address enough to prevent the increase of representation? Why not keep the power, and, when necessary, amend the constitution, and add to its other parts this power, and a proper increase of representation at the same time? Then men who may want the power will be under strong inducements to let in the people, by their representatives, into the government, to hold their due proportion of this power. If a proper representation be impracticable, then we shall see this power resting in the states, where it at present ought to be, and not inconsiderately given up.

When I recollect how lately congress, convention, legislatures, and people, contended in the cause of liberty, and carefully weighed the importance of taxation, I can scarcely believe we are serious in proposing to vest the powers of laying and collecting internal taxes in a government so imperfectly organized for such purposes. Should the United States be taxed by a house of representatives of two hundred members, which would be about fifteen members for Connecticut, twenty-five for Massachusetts, &c. still the middle and lower classes of people could have no great share, in fact, in taxation. I am aware it is said, that the representation proposed by the new constitution is sufficiently numerous; it may be for many purposes; but to suppose that this branch is sufficiently numerous to guard the rights of the people in the administration of the government, in which the purse and sword is placed, seems to argue that we have forgot what the true meaning of representation is. I am sensible also, that it is said that congress will not attempt to lay and collect internal taxes; that it is necessary for them to have the power, though it cannot probably be exercised.—I admit that it is not probable that any prudent congress will attempt to lay and collect internal taxes, especially direct taxes: but this only proves, that the power would be improperly lodged in congress, and that it might be abused by imprudent and designing men.

I have heard several gentlemen, to get rid of objections to this part of the constitution, attempt to construe the powers relative to direct taxes, as those who object to it would have them; as to these, it is said, that congress will only have power to make requisitions, leaving it to the states to lay and collect them. I see but very little colour for this construction, and the attempt only proves that this part of the plan cannot be defended. By this plan there can be no doubt, but that the powers of congress will be complete as to all kind of taxes whatever— Further, as to internal taxes, the state governments will have concurrent powers with the general government, and both may tax the same objects in the same year; and the objection that the general government may suspend a state tax, as a necessary measure for the promoting the collection of a federal tax, is not without foundation.—As the states owe large debts, and have large demands upon them individually, there clearly would be a propriety in leaving in their possession exclusively, some of the internal sources of taxation, at least until the federal representation shall be properly encreased: The power in the general government to lay and collect internal taxes, will render its powers respecting armies, navies and the militia, the more exceptionable. By the constitution it is proposed that congress shall have power "to raise and support armies, but no appropriation of money to that use shall be for a longer term than two years; to provide and maintain a navy; to provide for calling forth the militia to execute the laws of the union; suppress insurrections, and repel invasions: to provide for organizing, arming, and disciplining the militia: reserving to the states the right to appoint the officers, and to train the militia according to the discipline prescribed by congress;" congress will have unlimited power to raise armies, and to engage officers and men for any number of years; but a legislative act applying money for their support can have operation for no longer term than two years, and if a subsequent congress do not within the two years renew the appropriation, or further appropriate monies for the use of the army, the army, will be left to take care of itself. When an army shall once be raised for a number of years, it is not probable that it will find much difficulty in getting congress to pass laws for applying monies to its support. I see so many men in America fond of a standing army, and especially among those who probably will have a large share in administering the federal system; it is very evident to me, that we shall have a large standing army as soon as the monies to support them can be possibly found. An army is a very agreeable place of employment for the young gentlemen of many families. A power to raise armies must be lodged some where; still this will not justify the lodging this power in a bare majority of so few men without any checks; or in the government in which the great body of the people, in the nature of things, will be only nominally represented. In the state governments the great body of the people, the yeomanry, &c. of the country, are represented: It is true they will chuse the members of congress, and may now and then chuse a man of their own way of thinking; but it is impossible for forty, or thirty thousand people in this country, one time in ten to find a man who can possess similar feeling, views, and interests with themselves: powers to lay and collect taxes and to raise armies are of the greatest moment; for carrying them into effect, laws need not be frequently made, and the yeomanry, &c. of the country ought substantially to have a check upon the passing of these laws; this check ought to be placed in the legislatures, or at least, in the few men the common people of the country, will, probably, have in congress, in the true sense of the word, "from among themselves." It is true, the yeomanry of the country possess the lands, the weight of property, possess arms, and are too strong a body of men to be openly offended—and, therefore, it is urged, they will take care of themselves, that men who shall govern will not dare pay any disrespect to their opinions. It is easily perceived, that if they have not their proper negative upon passing laws in congress, or on the passage of laws relative to taxes and armies, they may in twenty or thirty years be by means imperceptible to them, totally deprived of that boasted weight and strength: This may be done in a great measure by congress, if disposed to do it, by modelling the militia. Should one fifth, or one eighth part of the men capable of bearing arms, be made a select militia, as has been proposed, and those the young and ardent part of the community, possessed of but little or no property, and all the others put upon a plan that will render them of no importance, the former will answer all the purposes of an army, while the latter will be defenceless. The state must train the militia in such form and according to such systems and rules as Congress shall prescribe: and the only actual influence the respective states will have respecting the militia will be in appointing the officers. I see no provision made for calling out the *posse commitatus* for executing the laws of the union, but provision is made for Congress to call forth the militia for the execution of them—and the militia in general, or any select part of it, may be called out under military officers, instead of the sheriff to enforce an execution of federal laws, in the first instance and thereby introduce an entire military execution of the laws.[19] I know that powers to raise taxes, to regulate the military strength of the community on some uniform plan, to provide for its defence and internal order, and for duly executing the laws, must be lodged somewhere; but still we ought not to lodge them, as evidently to give one another of them in the community, undue advantages over others; or commit the many to the mercy, prudence, and moderation of the few. And so far as it may be necessary to lodge any of the peculiar powers in the general government, a more safe exercise of them ought to be secured, by requiring the consent of two-thirds or three-fourths of Congress thereto—until the federal representation can be increased, so that the democratic members in Congress may stand some tolerable chance of a reasonable negative, in behalf of the numerous, important, and democratic part of the community.

I am not sufficiently acquainted with the laws and internal police of all the states to discern fully, how general bankrupt laws, made by the union, would effect them, or promote the public good. I believe the property of debtors, in the several states, is held responsible for their debts in modes and forms very different. If uniform bankrupt laws can be made without producing real and substantial inconveniences, I wish them to be made by Congress.

There are some powers proposed to be lodged in the general government in the judicial department, I think very unnecessarily, I mean powers respecting questions arising upon the internal laws of the respective states. It is proper the federal judiciary should have powers co-extensive with the federal legislature—that is, the power of deciding finally on the laws of the union. By Art. 3. Sect. 2. the powers of the federal judiciary are extended (among other things) to all cases between a state and citizens of another state—between citizens of different states—between a state or the citizens thereof, and foreign states, citizens or subjects. Actions in all these cases, except against a state government, are now brought and finally determined in the law courts of the states respectively; and as there are no words to exclude these courts of their jurisdiction in these cases, they will have concurrent jurisdiction with the inferior federal courts in them; and, therefore, if the new constitution be adopted without any amendment in this respect, all those numerous actions, now brought in the state courts between our citizens and foreigners, between citizens of different states, by state governments against foreigners, and by state governments against citizens of other states, may also be brought in the federal courts; and an appeal will lay in them from the state courts, or federal inferior courts, to the supreme judicial court of the union. In almost all these cases, either party may have the trial by jury in the state courts; excepting paper money and tender laws, which are wisely guarded against in the proposed constitution; justice may be obtained in these courts on reasonable terms; they must be more competent to proper decisions on the laws of their respective states, than the federal courts can possibly be. I do not, in any point of view, see the need of opening a new jurisdiction to these causes—of opening a new scene of expensive law suits—of suffering foreigners, and citizens of different states, to drag each other many hundred miles into the federal courts. It is true, those courts may be so organized by a wise and prudent legislature, as to make the obtaining of justice in them tolerably easy; they may in general be organized on the common law principles of the country: But this benefit is by no means secured by the constitution. The trial by jury is secured only in those few criminal cases, to which the federal laws will extend—as crimes committed on the seas against the laws of nations, treason and counterfeiting the federal securities and coin: But even in these cases, the jury trial of the vicinage is not secured, particularly in the large states, a citizen may be tried for a crime committed in the state, and yet tried in some states 500 miles from the place where it was committed; but the jury trial is not secured at all in civil causes. Though the convention have not established this trial, it is to be hoped that congress, in putting the new system into execution, will do it by a legislative act, in all cases in which it can be done with propriety. Whether the jury trial is not excluded [in] the supreme judicial court, is an important question. By Art. 3. Sect. 2. all cases affecting ambassadors, other public ministers, and consuls, and in those cases in which a state shall be party, the supreme court shall have jurisdiction. In all the other cases before mentioned, the supreme court shall have appellate jurisdiction, both as to LAW and FACT, with such exception, and under such regulations, as the congress shall make. By court is understood a court consisting of judges; and the idea of a jury is excluded. This court, or the judges, are to have jurisdiction on appeals, in all the cases enumerated, as to law and fact; the judges are to decide the law and try the fact, and the trial of the fact being assigned to the judges by the constitution, a jury for trying the fact is excluded; however, under the exceptions and powers to make regulations, Congress may, perhaps, introduce the jury, to try the fact in most necessary cases.

There can be but one supreme court in which the final jurisdiction will centre in all federal causes—except in cases where appeals by law shall not be allowed: The judicial powers of the federal courts extends in law and equity to certain cases: and, therefore, the powers to determine on the law, in equity, and as to the fact, all will concentre in the supreme court:—These powers, which by this constitution are blended in the same hands, the same judges, are in Great-Britain deposited in different hands—to wit, the decision of the law in the law judges, the decision in equity in the chancellor, and the trial of the fact in the jury. It is a very dangerous thing to vest in the same judge power to decide on the law, and also general powers in equity; for if the law restrain him, he is only to step into his shoes of equity, and give what judgment his reason or opinion may dictate; we have no precedents in this country, as yet, to regulate the divisions as in equity in Great-Britain; equity, therefore, in the supreme court for many years, will be mere discretion. I confess in the constitution of the supreme court, as left by the constitution, I do not see a spark of freedom or a shadow of our own or the British common law.

This court is to have appellate jurisdiction in all the other cases before mentioned: Many sensible men suppose that cases before-mentioned respect, as well the criminal cases as the civil ones, mentioned antecedently in the constitution, if so an appeal is allowed in criminal cases—contrary to the usual sense of law. How far it may be proper to admit a foreigner or the citizen of another state to bring actions against state governments, which have failed in performing so many promises made during the war, is doubtful: How far it may be proper so to humble a state, as to bring[20] it to answer to an individual in a court of law, is worthy of consideration; the states are now subject to no such actions; and this new jurisdiction will subject the states, and many defendants to actions, and processes, which were not in the contemplation of the parties, when the contract was made; all engagements existing between citizens of different states, citizens and foreigners, states and foreigners; and states and citizens of other states were made the parties contemplating the remedies then existing on the laws of the states—and the new remedy proposed to be given in the federal courts, can be founded on no principle whatever.

LETTER IV.

OCTOBER 12th, 1787.

DEAR SIR, It will not be possible to establish in the federal courts the jury trial of the vicinage so well as in the state courts.

Third. There appears to me to be not only a premature deposit of some important powers in the general government—but many of those deposited there are undefined, and may be used to good or bad purposes as honest or designing men shall prevail. By Art. 1, Sect. 2, representatives and direct taxes shall be apportioned among the several states, &c.—same art. sect. 8, the Congress shall have powers to lay and collect taxes, duties, &c. for the common defence and general welfare, but all duties, imposts and excises, shall be uniform throughout the United States: By the first recited clause, direct taxes shall be apportioned on the states. This seems to favour the idea suggested by some sensible men and writers, that Congress, as to direct taxes, will only have power to make requisitions; but the latter clause, power to[21] tax immediately individuals, without the intervention of the state legislatures[;] in fact the first clause appears to me only to provide that each state shall pay a certain portion of the tax, and the latter to provide that Congress shall have power to lay and collect taxes, that is to assess upon, and to collect of the individuals in the state, the states quota; but these still I consider as undefined powers, because judicious men understand them differently.

It is doubtful whether the vice president is to have any qualifications; none are mentioned; but he may serve as president, and it may be inferred, he ought to be qualified therefore as the president; but the qualifications of the president are required only of the person to be elected president. By art. the 2, sect. 2. "But the Congress may by law vest the appointment of such inferior officers as they think proper in the president alone, in the courts of law, or in the heads of the departments:" Who are inferior officers? May not a Congress disposed to vest the appointment of all officers in the president, under this clause, vest the appointment of almost every officer in the president alone, and destroy the check mentioned in the first part of the clause, and lodged in the senate. It is true, this check is badly lodged, but then some check upon the first magistrate in appointing officers, ought, it appears by the opinion of the convention, and by the general opinion, to be established in the constitution. By art. 3, sect. 2, the supreme court shall have appellate jurisdiction as to law and facts with such exceptions, &c. to what extent it is intended the exceptions shall be carried—Congress may carry them so far as to annihilate substantially the appellate jurisdiction, and the clause be rendered of very little importance.

4th. There are certain rights which we have always held sacred in the United States, and recognized in all our constitutions, and which, by the adoption of the new constitution, its present form will be left unsecured. By article 6, the proposed constitution, and the laws of the United States, which shall be made in pursuance thereof; and all treaties made, or which shall be made under the authority of the United States, shall be the supreme law of the land; and the judges in every state shall be bound thereby; any thing in the constitution or laws of any state to the contrary notwithstanding.

It is to be observed that when the people shall adopt the proposed constitution it will be their last and supreme act; it will be adopted not by the people of New-Hampshire, Massachusetts, &c. but by the people of the United States; and whenever this constitution, or any part of it, shall be incompatible with the antient customs, rights, the laws or the constitutions heretofore established in the United States, it will entirely abolish them and do them away: And not only this, but the laws of the United States which shall be made in pursuance of the federal constitution will be also supreme laws, and whenever they shall be incompatible with those customs, rights, laws or constitutions heretofore established, they will also entirely abolish them and do them away.

By the article before recited, treaties also made under the authority of the United States, shall be the supreme law: It is not said that these treaties shall be made in pursuance of the constitution—nor are there any constitutional bounds set to those who shall make them: The president and two thirds of the senate will be empowered to make treaties indefinitely, and when these treaties shall be made, they will also abolish all laws and state constitutions incompatible with them. This power in the president and senate is absolute, and the judges will be bound to allow full force to whatever rule, article or thing the president and senate shall establish by treaty, whether it be practicable to set any bounds to those who make treaties, I am not able to say: If not, it proves that this power ought to be more safely lodged.

The federal constitution, the laws of congress made in pursuance of the constitution, and all treaties must have full force and effect in all parts of the United States; and all other laws, rights and constitutions which stand in their way must yield: It is proper the national laws should be supreme, and superior to state or district laws; but then the national laws ought to yield to alienable[22] or fundamental rights—and national laws, made by a few men, should extend only to a few national objects. This will not be the case with the laws of congress: To have any proper idea of their extent, we must carefully examine the legislative, executive and judicial powers proposed to be lodged in the general government, and consider them in connection with a general clause in art. 1. sect. 8. in these words (after enumerating a number of powers) "To make all laws which shall be necessary and proper for carrying into execution the foregoing powers, and all other powers vested by this constitution in the government of the United States, or in any department or officer thereof."—The powers of this government as has been observed, extend to internal as well as external objects, and to those objects to which all others are subordinate; it is almost impossible to have a just conception of these powers, or of the extent and number of the laws which may be deemed necessary and proper to carry them into effect, till we shall come to exercise those powers and make the laws. In making laws to carry those powers into effect, it will be expected, that a wise and prudent congress will pay respect to the opinions of a free people, and bottom their laws on those principles which have been considered as essential and fundamental in the British, and in our government: But a congress of a different character will not be bound by the constitution to pay respect to those principles.

It is said, that when the people make a constitution, and delegate powers, that all powers not delegated by them to those who govern, is reserved in the people; and that the people, in the present case, have reserved in themselves, and in there state governments, every right and power not expressly given by the federal constitution to those who shall administer the national government. It is said, on the other hand, that the people, when they make a constitution, yield all power not expressly reserved to themselves. The truth is, in either case, it is mere matter of opinion, and men usually take either side of the argument, as will best answer their purposes: But the general presumption being, that men who govern, will, in doubtful cases, construe laws and constitutions most favourably for encreasing their own powers; all wise and prudent people, in forming constitutions, have drawn the line, and carefully described the powers parted with and the powers reserved. By the state constitutions, certain rights have been reserved in the people; or rather, they have been recognized and established in such a manner, that state legislatures are bound to respect them, and to make no laws infringing upon them. The state legislatures are obliged to take notice of the bills of rights of their respective states. The bills of rights, and the state constitutions, are fundamental compacts only between those who govern, and the people of the same state.

In the year 1788 the people of the United States make a federal constitution, which is a fundamental compact between them and their federal rulers; these rulers, in the nature of things, cannot be bound to take notice of any other compact. It would be absurd for them, in making laws, to look over thirteen, fifteen, or twenty state constitutions, to see what rights are established as fundamental, and must not be infringed upon, in making laws in the society. It is true, they would be bound to do it if the people, in their federal compact, should refer to the state constitutions, recognize all parts not inconsistent with the federal constitution, and direct their federal rulers to take notice of them accordingly; but this is not the case, as the plan stands proposed at present; and it is absurd, to suppose so unnatural an idea is intended or implied, I think my opinion is not only founded in reason, but I think it is supported by the report of the convention itself. If there are a number of rights established by the state constitutions, and which will remain sacred, and the general government is bound to take notice of them—it must take notice of one as well as another; and if unnecessary to recognize or establish one by the federal constitution, it would be unnecessary to recognize or establish another by it. If the federal constitution is to be construed so far in connection with the state constitutions, as to leave the trial by jury in civil causes, for instance, secured; on the same principles it would have left the trial by jury in criminal causes, the benefits of the writ of habeas corpus, &c. secured; they all stand on the same footing; they are the common rights of Americans, and have been recognized by the state constitutions: But the convention found it necessary to recognize or re-establish the benefits of that writ, and the jury trial in criminal cases. As to EXPOST FACTO laws, the convention has done the same in one case, and gone further in another. It is a part of the compact between the people of each state and the rulers, that no EXPOST FACTO laws shall be made. But the convention, by Art. 1. Sect. 10. have put a sanction upon this part even of the state compacts. In fact, the 9th and 10th Sections in Art. 1. in the proposed constitution, are no more nor less, than a partial bill of rights;

they establish certain principles as part of the compact upon which the federal legislators and officers can never infringe. It is here wisely stipulated, that the federal legislature shall never pass a bill of attainder, or EXPOST FACTO law; that no tax shall be laid on articles exported, &c. The establishing of one right implies the necessity of establishing another and similar one.

On the whole, the position appears to me to be undeniable, that this bill of rights ought to be carried farther, and some other principles established, as a part of this fundamental compact between the people of the United States and their federal rulers.

It is true, we are not disposed to differ much, at present, about religion; but when we are making a constitution, it is to be hoped, for ages and millions yet unborn, why not establish the free exercise of religion, as a part of the national compact. There are other essential rights, which we have justly understood to be the rights of freemen; as freedom from hasty and unreasonable search warrants, warrants not founded on oath, and not issued with due caution, for searching and seizing men's papers, property, and persons. The trials by jury in civil causes, it is said, varies so much in the several states, that no words could be found for the uniform establishment of it. If so the federal legislation will not be able to establish it by any general laws. I confess I am of opinion it may be established, but not in that beneficial manner in which we may enjoy it, for the reasons beforementioned. When I speak of the jury trial of the vicinage, or the trial of the fact in the neighbourhood,—I do not lay so much stress upon the circumstance of our being tried by our neighbours: in this enlightened country men may be probably impartially tried by those who do not live very near them: but the trial of facts in the neighbourhood is of great importance in other respects. Nothing can be more essential than the cross examining witnesses, and generally before the triers of the facts in question. The common people can establish facts with much more ease with oral than written evidence; when trials of facts are removed to a distance from the homes of the parties and witnesses, oral evidence becomes intolerably expensive, and the parties must depend on written evidence, which to the common people is expensive and almost useless; it must be frequently taken ex-parte, and but very seldom leads to the proper discovery of truth.

The trial by jury is very important in another point of view. It is essential in every free country, that common people should have a part and share of influence, in the judicial as well as in the legislative department. To hold open to them the offices of senators, judges, and officers to fill which an expensive education is required, cannot answer any valuable purposes for them; they are not in a situation to be brought forward and to fill those offices; these, and most other offices of any considerable importance, will be occupied by the few. The few, the well born, &c. as Mr. Adams calls them,[23] in judicial decisions as well as in legislation, are generally disposed, and very naturally too, to favour those of their own description.

The trial by jury in the judicial department, and the collection of the people by their representatives in the legislature, are those fortunate inventions which have procured for them in this country, their true proportion of influence, and the wisest and most fit means of protecting themselves in the community. Their situation, as jurors and representatives, enables them to acquire information and knowledge in the affairs and government of the society; and to come forward, in turn, as the centinels and guardians of each other. I am very sorry that even a few of our countrymen should consider jurors and representatives in a different point of view, as ignorant, troublesome bodies, which ought not to have any share in the concerns of government.

I confess I do not see in what cases the Congress can, with any pretence of right, make a law to suppress the freedom of the press; though I am not clear, that Congress is restrained from laying any duties whatever on printing and from laying duties particularly heavy on certain pieces printed, and perhaps Congress may require large bonds for the payment of these duties. Should the printer say, the freedom of the press was secured by the constitution of the state in which he lived, Congress might, and perhaps, with great propriety, answer, that the federal constitution is the only compact existing between them and the people; in this compact the people have named no others, and therefore Congress, in exercising the powers assigned them, and in making laws to carry them into execution, are restrained by nothing beside the federal constitution, any more than a state legislature is restrained by a compact between the magistrates and people of a county, city, or town of which the people, in forming the state constitution, have taken no notice.

It is not my object to enumerate rights of inconsiderable importance; but there are others, no doubt, which ought to be established as a fundamental part of the national system.

It is worthy of observation, that all treaties are made by foreign nations with a confederacy of thirteen states—that the western country is attached to thirteen states—thirteen states have jointly and severally engaged to pay the public debts.—Should a new government be formed of nine, ten, eleven, or twelve states, those treaties could not be considered as binding on the foreign nations who made them. However, I believe the probability to be, that if nine states adopt the constitution, the others will.

It may also be worthy our examination, how far the provision for amending this plan, when it shall be adopted, is of any importance. No measures can be taken towards amendments, unless two-thirds of the Congress, or two-thirds of the legislatures of the several states shall agree.—While power is in the hands of the people, or democratic part of the community, more especially as at present, it is easy, according to the general course of human affairs, for the few influential men in the community, to obtain conventions, alterations in government, and to persuade the common people they may change for the better, and to get from them a part of the power: But when power is once transferred from the many to the few, all changes become extremely difficult; the government, in this case, being beneficial to the few, they will be exceedingly artful and adroit in preventing any measures which may lead to a change; and nothing will produce it, but great exertions and severe struggles on the part of the common people. Every man of reflection must see, that the change now proposed, is a transfer of power from the many to the few, and the probability is, the artful and ever active aristocracy, will prevent all peaceable measures for changes, unless when they shall discover some favorable moment to increase their own influence. I am sensible, thousands of men in the United States, are disposed to adopt the proposed constitution, though they perceive it to be essentially defective, under an idea that amendment of it, may be obtained when necessary. This is a pernicious idea, it argues a servility of character totally unfit for the support of free government; it is very repugnant to that perpetual jealousy respecting liberty, so absolutely necessary in all free states, spoken of by Mr. Dickinson.[24]—However, if our countrymen are so soon changed, and the language of 1774, is become odious to them, it will be in vain to use the language of freedom, or to attempt to rouse them to free enquiries: But I shall never believe this is the case with them, whatever present appearances may be, till I shall have very strong evidence indeed of it.

LETTER V.

OCTOBER 13th, 1787.

DEAR SIR, Thus I have examined the federal constitution as far as a few days leisure would permit. It opens to my mind a new scene; instead of seeing powers cautiously lodged in the hands of numerous legislators, and many magistrates, we see all important powers collecting in one centre, where a few men will possess them almost at discretion.

And instead of checks in the formation of the government, to secure the rights of the people against the usurpation of those they appoint to govern, we are to understand the equal division of lands among our people, and the strong arm furnished them by nature and situation, are to secure them against those usurpations. If there are advantages in the equal division of our lands, and the strong and manly habits of our people, we ought to establish governments calculated to give duration to them, and not governments which never can work naturally, till that equality of property, and those free and manly habits shall be destroyed; these evidently are not the natural basis of the proposed constitution.—No man of reflection, and skilled in the science of government, can suppose these will move on harmoniously together for ages, or even for fifty years. As to the little circumstances commented upon, by some writers, with applause—as the age of a representative, of the president, &c.—they have, in my mind, no weight in the general tendency of the system.

There are, however, in my opinion, many good things in the proposed system. It is founded on elective principles, and the deposits of powers in several hands, is essentially right.—The guards against those evils we have experienced in some states in legislation are valuable indeed: but the value of every feature in this system is vastly lessened for the want of that one important feature in a free government, a representation of the people. Because we have sometimes abused democracy, I am not among those men who think a democratic branch a nuisance; which branch shall be sufficiently numerous, to admit some of the best informed men of each order in the community into the administration of government.

While the radical defects in the proposed system are not so soon discovered, some temptations to each state, and to many classes of men to adopt it, are very visible. It uses the democratic language of several of the state constitutions, particularly that of Massachusetts; the eastern states will receive advantages so far as the regulation of trade, by a bare majority, is committed to it: Connecticut and New-Jersey will receive their share of a general impost:[25]—The middle states will receive the advantages surrounding the seat of government:—The southern states will receive protection, and have their negroes represented in the legislature, and large back countries will soon have a majority in it.—This system promises a large field of employment to military gentlemen, and gentlemen of the law; and in case the government shall be executed without convulsions, it will afford security to creditors, to the clergy, salary-men and others depending on money payments. So far as the system promises justice and reasonable advantages, in these respects, it ought to be supported by all honest men; but whenever it promises unequal and improper advantages to any particular states, or orders of men, it ought to be opposed.

I have, in the course of these letters observed, that there are many good things in the proposed constitution, and I have endeavoured to point out many important defects in it. I have admitted that we want a federal system—that we have a system presented, which, with several alterations, may be made a tolerable good one—I have admitted there is a well founded uneasiness among creditors and mercantile men. In this situation of things, you ask me what I think ought to be done? My opinion in this case is only the opinion of an individual, and so far only as it correspondents[26] with the opinions of the honest and substantial part of the community, is it entitled to consideration. Though I am fully satisfied that the state conventions ought most seriously to direct their exertions to altering and amending the system proposed before they shall adopt it—yet I have not sufficiently examined the subject, or formed an opinion, how far it will be practicable for those conventions to carry their amendments. As to the idea, that it will be in vain for those conventions to attempt amendments, it cannot be admitted; it is impossible to say whether they can or not until the attempt shall be made: and when it shall be determined, by experience, that the conventions cannot agree in amendments, it will then be an important question before the people of the United States, whether they will adopt or not the system proposed in its present form. This subject of consolidating the states is new; and because forty or fifty men have agreed in a system, to suppose the good sense of this country, an enlightened nation, must adopt it without examination, and though in a state of profound peace, without endeavouring to amend those parts they perceive are defective, dangerous to freedom, and destructive of the valuable principles of republican government—is truly humiliating. It is true there may be danger in delay; but there is danger in adopting the system in its present form; and I see the danger in either case will arise principally from the conduct and views of two very unprincipled parties in the United States—two fires, between which the honest and substantial people have long found themselves situated. One party is composed of little insurgents, men in debt, who want no law, and who want a share of the property of others; these are called levellers, Shayites, &c. The other party is composed of a few, but more dangerous men, with their servile dependents; these avariciously grasp at[27] power and property; you may discover in all the actions of these men, an evident dislike to free and equal governments, and they will go systematically to work to change, essentially, the forms of government in this

country; these are called aristocrates, morrisites,[28] &c. &c. Between
these two parties is the weight of the community; the men of middling
property, men not in debt on the one hand, and men, on the other,
content with republican governments, and not aiming at immense fortunes, offices, and power. In 1786, the little insurgents, the levellers,
came forth, invaded the rights of others, and attempted to establish
governments according to their wills.[29] Their movements evidently gave
encouragement to the other party, which, in 1787, has taken the political field, and with its fashionable dependents, and the tongue and
the pen, is endeavouring to establish in great haste, a politer kind of
government. These two parties, which will probably be opposed or
united as it may suit their interests and views, are really insignificant,
compared with the solid, free, and independent part of the community.
It is not my intention to suggest, that either of these parties, and the
real friends of the proposed constitution, are the same men. The fact
is, these aristocrats support and hasten the adoption of the proposed
constitution, merely because they think it is a stepping stone to their
favourite object. I think I am well founded in this idea; I think the
general politics of these men support it, as well as the common observation among them, That the proffered plan is the best that can be got
at present, it will do for a few years, and lead to something better. The
sensible and judicious part of the community will carefully weigh all
these circumstances; they will view the late convention as a respectable
assembly of men—America probably never will see an assembly of men
of a like number, more respectable. But the members of the convention
met without knowing the sentiments of one man in ten thousand in
these states respecting the new ground taken. Their doings are but the
first attempts in the most important scene ever opened. Though each
individual in the state conventions will not, probably, be so respectable
as each individual in the federal convention, yet as the state conventions will probably consist of fifteen hundred or two thousand men of
abilities,[30] and versed in the science of government, collected from all
parts of ⟨the community and from all orders of men, it must be acknowledged that the weight of respectability will be in them—In them
will be collected the solid sense and the real political character of the
country. Being revisers of the subject, they will possess peculiar advantages. To say that these conventions ought not to attempt, coolly and
deliberately, the revision of the system, or that they cannot amend it,
is very foolish or very assuming. If these conventions, after examining
the system, adopt it, I shall be perfectly satisfied, and wish to see men
make the administration of the government an equal blessings[31] to all
orders of men. I believe the great body of our people to be virtuous

and friendly to good government, to the protection of liberty and property; and it is the duty of all good men, especially of those who are
placed as centinels to guard their rights—it is their duty to examine
into the prevailing politics of parties, and to disclose them—while they
avoid exciting undue suspicions, to lay facts before the people, which
will enable them to form a proper judgment. Men, who wish the people
of this country to determine for themselves, and deliberately to fit the
government to their situation, must feel some degree of indignation at
those attempts to hurry the adoption of a system, and to shut the door
against examination. The very attempts create suspicions, that those
who make them have secret views, or see some defects in the system,
which, in the hurry of affairs, they expect will escape the eye of a free
people.

What can be the views of those gentlemen in Pennsylvania, who precipitated decisions on this subject?[32] What can be the views of those
gentlemen in Boston, who countenanced the Printers in shutting up
the press against a fair and free investigation of this important system
in the usual way.[33] The members of the convention have done their
duty—why should some of them fly to their states—almost forget a
propriety of behaviour, and precipitate measures for the adoption of a
system of their own making? I confess candidly, when I consider these
circumstances in connection with the unguarded parts of the system I
have mentioned, I feel disposed to proceed with very great caution,
and to pay more attention than usual to the conduct of particular characters. If the constitution presented be a good one, it will stand the
test with a well informed people: all are agreed there shall be state
conventions to examine it; and we must believe it will be adopted, unless we suppose it is a bad one, or that those conventions will make
false divisions respecting it. I admit improper measures are taken
against the adoption of the system as well as for it—all who object to
the plan proposed ought to point out the defects)[34] objected to, and
to propose those amendments with which they can accept it, or to
propose some other system of government, that the public mind may
be known, and that we may be brought to agree in some system of
government, to strengthen and execute the present, or to provide a
substitute. I consider the field of enquiry just opened, and that we are
to look to the state conventions for ultimate decisions on the subject
before us; it is not to be presumed, that they will differ about small
amendments, and lose a system when they shall have made it substantially good; but touching the essential amendments, it is to be presumed the several conventions will pursue the most rational measures
to agree in and obtain them; and such defects as they shall discover

and not remove, they will probably notice, keep them in view as the ground work of future amendments, and in the firm and manly language which every free people ought to use, will suggest to those who may hereafter administer the government, that it is their expectation, that the system will be so organized by legislative acts, and the government so administered, as to render those defects as little injurious as possible.—Our countrymen are entitled to an honest and faithful government; to a government of laws and not of men; and also to one of their chusing—as a citizen of the country, I wish to see these objects secured, and licentious, assuming, and overbearing men restrained; if the constitution or social compact be vague and unguarded, then we depend wholly upon the prudence, wisdom and moderation of those who manage the affairs of government; or on what, probably, is equally uncertain and precarious, the success of the people oppressed by the abuse of government, in receiving it from the hands of those who abuse it, and placing it in the hands of those who will use it well.

In every point of view, therefore, in which I have been able, as yet, to contemplate this subject, I can discern but one rational mode of proceeding relative to it; and that is to examine it with freedom and candour, to have state conventions some months hence, which shall examine coolly every article, clause, and word in the system proposed, and to adopt it with such amendments as they shall think fit. How far the state conventions ought to pursue the mode prescribed by the federal convention of adopting or rejecting the plan in toto, I leave it to them to determine. Our examination of the subject hitherto has been rather of a general nature. The republican characters in the several states, who wish to make this plan more adequate to security of liberty and property, and to the duration of the principles of a free government, will, no doubt, collect their opinions to certain points, and accurately define those alterations and amendments they wish; if it shall be found they essentially disagree in them, the conventions will then be able to determine whether to adopt the plan as it is, or what will be proper to be done.

Under these impressions, and keeping in view the improper and unadvisable lodgment of powers in the general government, organized as it at present is, touching internal taxes, armies and militia, the elections of its own members, causes between citizens of different states, &c. and the want of a more perfect bill of rights, &c.—I drop the subject for the present, and when I shall have leisure to revise and correct my ideas respecting it, and to collect into points the opinions of those who wish to make the system more secure and safe, perhaps I may proceed to point out particularly for your consideration, the amendment[35] which ought to be ingrafted into this system, and[36] only in conformity to my own, but the deliberate opinions of others—you will with me perceive, that the objections to the plan proposed may, by a more leisure examination be set in a stronger point of view, especially the important one, that there is no substantial representation in the people provided for in a government, in which the most essential powers, even as to the internal police of the country, is proposed to be lodged.

⟨I think the honest and substantial part of the community, will wish to see this system altered, permanency and consistency given to the constitution we shall adopt; and therefore they will be anxious to apportion the powers to the features and organization of the government, and to see abuse in the exercise of power more effectually guarded against. It is suggested, that state officers, from interested motives will oppose the constitution itself[37]—I see no reason for this, their places in general will not be effected, but new openings to offices and places of profit must evidently be made by the adoption of the constitution in its present form.⟩[38]

1. In the second printing of the *Letters* "it" was changed to "all."

2. Pope's maxim is usually quoted as a couplet: "For forms of government let fools contest,/Whate'er is best administred, is best." Alexander Pope, *An Essay on Man* (London, 1758), Epistle III, lines 301–2. The third epistle was first published in 1733. (See RCS:Mass., 507n–8n.) "A Countryman" VI (Hugh Hughes) criticized the "Federal Farmer" for laying "rather too much stress on Mr. Pope's maxim." "With the greatest deference for the Fœderal Farmer's good sense," declared "A Countryman," "I beg leave to ask, whether this jingling maxim will not militate as much for the worst form of government, as for the best?" (*New York Journal*, 14 February 1788, III below).

3. The text in angle brackets was incorporated into an item that was printed in the *Massachusetts Gazette* on 1 February 1788. The person who submitted the item declared that he no longer supported the Constitution after listening to the debates of the Massachusetts Convention and reading the *Letters* and other writings on the Constitution. The *Newport Mercury* reprinted the item on 18 February. See at note 38 for another excerpt quoted in the *Massachusetts Gazette* on 1 February and reprinted in the *Newport Mercury* on 18 February. It is possible that the *Massachusetts Gazette* reprinted these excerpts from the edition of the *Letters* that probably was printed in Boston in January 1788 since there are minor differences in spelling and punctuation in the *Massachusetts Gazette's* text when compared with the first New York edition. (For the excerpts as printed in the *Massachusetts Gazette*, see RCS:Mass., 840–41.)

4. For various attempts to strengthen the Articles of Confederation, see CDR, 140–74; CC:Vol. 1, pp. 11–34; and the "Introduction" (above).

5. For the proceedings of the Annapolis Convention, held in September 1786 and attended by only five states (including New York), see CDR, 181–85.

6. For the congressional resolution of 21 February 1787 calling the Constitutional Convention, see CC:1. For New York's appointment of delegates to the Constitutional Convention, see Appendix II (below).

7. For the appointment of the Virginia delegation to the Constitutional Convention, headed by George Washington, see RCS:Va., xxxv–xxxvi, 540–42.

8. For the appointment of the Pennsylvania delegation to the Constitutional Convention, see CDR, 199–200. For the debate in Pennsylvania over the nature of its delegation, see CC:150, note 5; and RCS:Pa., 112, 117–19, 185, 502, 504, 619–20.

9. Among those delegates who did not attend the Constitutional Convention were Abraham Clark of New Jersey, Willie Jones of North Carolina, and Patrick Henry and Richard Henry Lee of Virginia. For a complete list of the delegates who did not attend, see CC:Vol. 1, xlvii.

10. Rhode Island never sent delegates to the Constitutional Convention. After Robert Yates and John Lansing, Jr., left the Convention on 10 July, New York's vote was not counted, although the remaining delegate, Alexander Hamilton, signed the Constitution. See the "Introduction" (above).

11. In speculating on the authorship of the *Letters*, Hugh Hughes claimed that he discussed the first part of this paragraph with the person he believed wrote the *Letters*, although he did not reveal the name of the person (to Tillinghast, 28 November, below).

12. In the second printing of the *Letters* "ultimately" was changed to "intimately."

13. "A Countryman" VI quoted the text in angle brackets and stated that he wished that the "Federal Farmer" "had either been more explicit, or silent; as, in the first case, his meaning would have appeared to more advantage, and, in the other, there would have been no necessity for any observation" (*New York Journal*, 14 February 1788, III below).

14. About 170 delegates were elected to the Connecticut House of Representatives that met in October 1787 (RCS:Conn., 341–44).

15. After quoting the text in angle brackets, "A Countryman" VI stated "which to me appears somewhat singular, when each senator is to have one vote. Either I do not comprehend his meaning, or there is a mistake, which ought to be corrected, for, by the present confederation, which is a union of the states, not a consolidation, *all the delegates*, from a state, have but one vote, and in the state senate, which is on the plan of consolidation, *each* senator has a vote" (*New York Journal*, 14 February 1788, III below).

16. Rhode Island, a small state, was not present. Massachusetts, Pennsylvania, and Virginia were the three large states.

17. *The Federalist* 68 is referring to "Federal Farmer," when he states that "The most plausible of these [opponents of the Constitution], who has appeared in print, has even deigned to admit, that the election of the president is pretty well guarded" (*Independent Journal*, 12 March 1788, CC:615).

18. The second printing of the *Letters* reads: "vast labour and attention."

19. Although *The Federalist* 29 (Alexander Hamilton), *Independent Journal*, 9 January (CC:429), does not refer to "Federal Farmer" by name, the essay is a reply to "Federal Farmer's" discussion of the militia. The proposed "select militia" that "Federal Farmer" mentions is probably a reference to a proposal made by Baron von Steuben in a pamphlet entitled *A Letter on the Subject of an Established Militia, and Military Arrangements, Addressed to the Inhabitants of the United States* (New York, 1784) (Evans 18796). For another reference to this pamphlet, see "A Countryman" V (Hugh Hughes), *New York Journal*, 22 January (below).

20. In the second printing of the *Letters* "bring" was changed to "oblige."

21. At this point in the second printing of the *Letters* the following was inserted: "lay and collect taxes, &c. seems clearly to favour the contrary opinion, and, in my mind, the true one, that congress shall have power to."

22. In the second printing of the *Letters* "alienable" was changed to "unalienable."

23. For John Adams's use of the term, "the well born," see the Philadelphia *Freeman's Journal*, 7 November, note 3 (above).

24. In Letter XI of *Letters from a Farmer in Pennsylvania,* John Dickinson stated: "A perpetual *jealousy,* respecting liberty, is absolutely requisite in all free-states." See Paul Leicester Ford, ed., *The Writings of John Dickinson* (*Memoirs* of the Historical Society of Pennsylvania, XIV [Philadelphia, 1895]), 386. Letter XI was first published in the *Pennsylvania Chronicle* on 8 February 1768.

25. Both of these states, which imported foreign goods and merchandise from New York, complained that they paid more for such imports because of the New York state impost, the proceeds of which did not benefit either of them. See "Introduction" (above).

26. In the second printing of the *Letters* "correspondents" was changed to "corresponds."

27. In the second printing of the *Letters* the word "all" was inserted here.

28. In the second printing of the *Letters* "morrisites" was rendered "m——ites." The reference is to the followers of former Confederation Superintendent of Finance Robert Morris, the leader of Pennsylvania's Federalists.

29. For Shays's Rebellion in Massachusetts in 1786 and 1787 and for examples of agrarian discontent in other states, see CC:18; and RCS:Mass., xxxviii–xl.

30. Approximately 1,650 delegates were elected to the state ratifying conventions.

31. In the second printing of the *Letters* "blessings" was changed to "blessing."

32. For the actions taken by Federalists on 28 and 29 September, inside and outside the Pennsylvania Assembly, to call a state ratifying convention, see "New York Reprinting of the Address of the Seceding Members of the Pennsylvania Assembly," 9–18 October (above).

33. For the refusal of some Boston printers to publish Antifederalist material unless the authors were willing to have their names divulged to the public, see CC:131; and "The Boston Press and the Constitution," 4 October–22 December (RCS:Mass., 41–50).

34. The text in angle brackets is on page 38 of the *Letters.* "A Countryman" VI stated that "In page 38, there is an expression, which does not seem to be altogether consistent with the general tenor of the whole, but, perhaps not worth your notice at this time" (*New York Journal,* 14 February 1788, III below).

35. In the second printing of the *Letters* "amendment" was changed to "amendments."

36. In the second printing of the *Letters* "and" was changed to "not."

37. In the second printing of the *Letters* "itself" was changed to "presented."

38. See note 3 above.

James Kent to Nathaniel Lawrence
Poughkeepsie, 9 November 1787[1]

I have not had leisure till now, owing to one intervening circumstance & another, to answer your favor of some time since on the politics of the Day—You expressed your Sentiments quite unfavorably of the new Constitution, & tho you acknowledged that our only alternative if we rejected it, was to expect our next form of Government from the Sword, yet you seemed to be in doubt whether it would not be our least evil to take our chance of a new one & reject it.—I do not wish my Friend, to make our friendly Correspondence the Subject of altercation & therefore I shall not dwell on the Subject—I however certainly know in my Conscience that my Heart, as far as it engages itself in public Concerns, is ardently attached to the true Spirit & the true Principles of Liberty; & If I did believe with you, that the Government would necessarily introduce an aristocracy, I would run any Hazard rather than submit to so odious a dominion. The new System like all other human Institutions has considerable Defects. I have read the Pamphlet from the federal farmer to the Republican[2] & most of the other publications on the Subject & I think the first particularly has illustrated those Defects in a candid & rational manner—But still I do not think, it tends to an aristocracy in my Idea of the word, but that it has all the essential features of a well ballanced representative republic—The Pamphlet above alluded to calls men of talents & Property the natural Aristocracy of the Country—In that Case I trust & hope I shall always be governed by an aristocracy—But to consider an aristocracy, as I have always considered it, as defining a Government of a few permanent Nobles independent of & not chosen by nor amenable to the great body of the People, In that Case I think the assertion that the constitution would necessarily introduce an aristocracy, to be unsupported by a single argument drawn from the Principles or tendency of the System—This is modestly *my Opinion*, but as I said before, I do not mean to make my correspondence the vehicle of Dispute & therefore I will now adhere more steadily to my first word of dismissing the Subject.

How much more soothing to the mind & awakening to the tender & elegant Sentiments of the Heart are the Studies of Poetry, History & Philosophy? I speak this not from affectation, but from recent experience—I find all the political Disputes I have had here only tend to sour the mind & leave the combatants more irritated at Opposition & more confirmed in their Opinions than before—In Politics as in Religion, it is only the Progress of time, & calm temperate Discussions that can make converts—Persecution indeed, whenever that is made use of, always multiplies the Party that is persecuted—but that is a most outrageous violation of the rights of Humanity & I hope it never may be begun in the utmost violence of Party—You see I mean to be cool & a man of moderation. Every Person is entitled to his Opinion & I would no sooner quarrel with my Friend for differing with me on a speculative point of Politics, than on one of Religion—I hope your professional affairs are promising & that you have no reason to adopt the maxim which is sometimes propagated, that men of talents are neglected—In some cases, it certainly is the case & Dunces are elevated to a most profitable flow of Business. But this cannot continue long in general when things are in their natural settled order—I wish I could know what your general Employment is, & whether you are silently preparing to undermine the reputation of Coke by setting him below the top of his Profession. I have just been reading Smith *on the Wealth of Nations* & he has taught me to look with an unfavorable eye on monopolies— But a monopoly of the mental kind I take to be laudable & an exception to the Rule—

I hope Mrs. Lawrence is better than when you wrote last—

1. RC, Dreer Collection, American Lawyers, PHi.
2. This pamphlet is printed immediately above.

William Grayson to William Short
New York, 10 November 1787 (excerpts)[1]

I have recieved your favor, for which I am much obliged; the Convention at Philada. about which I wrote you, have at length produced (contrary to expectation) an entire new constitution; This has put us all in an uproar:—Our public papers are full of attacks and justifications of the new system: And if you go into private companies, you hear scarcely any thing else. . . . In this State, I believe there is a great majority against it: the reason assigned by it's favorers is that she they derives great advantages by imposing duties on the imports of Jersey & Connecticut,—In Jersey, nothing is more popular

There was something singular in the affair which is that the one was determined to adopt & the other to reject the new constitution before it had made its appearance. . . .

NB . . . Inclosed are the papers of the day. You are not [to] suppose I mean to reflect on the members of the Convention: I highly respect the chief of them: but they could not act otherwise so circum[stanced?].

1. RC, Short Papers, DLC. Printed: CC:248 (longer excerpts).

Publius: The Federalist 5 (John Jay)
New York Independent Journal, 10 November 1787

Importance of Union in preventing sectional rivalries and conflicts. For text, see CC:252. For reprintings, see Appendix IV, below.

Middletown, Conn., Middlesex Gazette, 12 November 1787[1]

Extract of a letter from a gentleman, to his friend in this town.

"I have of late made an excursion into the state of New-York, through Albany, Schenectady, and up the Mowhawk-River, as far as Johnstown.

It is very mortifying to observe the depreciated idea that the inhabitants on that river possess, of the honesty of these New-England states. I am ready from this conduct to believe, that but few, except our horse-jockies, and most notorious villains, have visited those parts. It is impossible for a gentleman from this state to negotiate any business, or conclude any bargain on credit with any of their merchants or other inhabitants, without a previous personal acquaintance, let his recommendations be what they may. It is an universal complaint, that scarce a debt contracted by people from these states is punctually discharged; but every artifice is employed, to procrastinate and finally evade the payment of their contracts.

"How unhappy is the consideration, that the justice of these complaints is notoriously evident among ourselves. Knavery is a science, in which if not the bulk, yet great numbers of our people are astonishing proficients, and assiduous students; and has become so fashionable, that with many an honest man, who cancels a debt which might have been evaded, becomes an object of ridicule. This, tho' it had no evil influence on our future existence, is pregnant with a train of mischievous effects and consequences, that are severely felt at present, and of necessity must ever attend it. It involves mechanicks in ruin, merchants in difficulties, and brings perplexity and discouragement upon the honest farmer. By this we render ourselves unable and unworthy to be credited at home or abroad, but upon extravagant advance. By dishonesty we ruin the market of the commodities which we export, and load ourselves with a long rearage of forgotten debts. Knavery is the pest of society, and the bane of good neighbourhood; by so large a proportion of this class of people among us, there is a constant necessity of suspicious vigilance among all; and the ill, and apparently lucrative example, makes a deplorable impression on the rising generation. By these destructive villains the honest, as well as the deserving, become the prey of attornies who are in this respect a people *(sui generis)* by themselves, that always find their accounts in the dishonesty of themselves and all the world about them. Should dishonesty become general, and be the true characteristic of a republican people, it must of course produce a knavish legislature, and the same spirit would at once corrupt the executive department of government, destroy distributive justice and public liberty, and reduce the people to anarchy, which never fails of producing monarchy. A lively instance of which R—de I—d has already begun to exhibit, as a warning to our view. ⟨For since all officers in a republican government are elected by the people, it must be expected that they will partake of the prevailing temper of their constituents; nor ought a people to be surprised if themselves are fraudulent, should they see corruption, bribery and the most avowed injustice in every branch of government, since it is their duty fairly to represent their constituents, and conform to their minds. And notwithstanding the excellency of the characters that for the most part fill up the offices of our government, yet we have so many dishonest inhabitants that they are sufficient to destroy public credit, enlarge the charges of government, and add a mischievous increase to taxes. For my part I wish the civil laws would in all cases take cognizance of every act of dishonesty, and punish it with the utmost severity, equal to the penalties of theft. The happy consequences which would attend this mode of discipline, are too obvious to need a mention.")

1. Reprinted: Philadelphia *Independent Gazetteer*, 19 November; Baltimore *Maryland Gazette*, 27 November; *Northern Centinel*, 11 December (excerpt). The text in angle brackets was omitted in the *Northern Centinel*.

Publius: The Federalist 6 (Alexander Hamilton)
New York Independent Journal, 14 November 1787

Danger of domestic turmoil and insurrections. For text, see CC:257. For reprintings, see Appendix IV, below.

The News-Mongers' Song for the Winter of 1788
Albany Gazette, 15 November 1787[1]

Good news, brother dealers in metre & prose!
The world has turn'd *buffer* and coming to blows;
Write *good sense* or *non sense*, my boys, it's all one,
All persons may fire when the battle's begun.
                              Down, down, down derry down.
Our tutors and sages would oftentimes say,
"*Sit omnibus hora*,"[2] each dog has his day:
Queen Ann's was the æra of genius 'tis known,
Arguendo[3] this day is for scribblers alone.
                              Down, down &c.
Now *Claxton* & *Babcock* and *Webster* and *Stoddard*,
Hall, Sellers, Childs, Loudon, Oswald, Morton and *Goddard*
Russell, Haswell, Green, Thomas, Meigs, Powers and *Draper*.[4]
May thank the kind stars for such luck to their paper.
                              Down, down, &c.
Come on brother scribblers, 'tis idle to lag.
The CONVENTION has let the cat out of the bag,
Write something at randum, you need not be nice,
Public spirit, Montesquieu, and *great Dr. Price*,
                              Down, down, &c.

Talk of *Holland* & *Greece*, and of *purses* & *swords*,
Democratical mobs and congressional Lords:
Tell what is surrendered and what is enjoy'd,
All things weigh alike, boys, we know, in a void.
                                        Down, down, &c.
Much joy, brother printers! the day is our own,
A time like the present sure never was known:
Predictions are making—predictions fulfil,
All nature seems proud to bring grist to our mill.
                                        Down, down, &c.
Huge Comets once more thro' the system will stroll,
The Moon, they inform us is burnt to a coal;
Old Saturn is tumbling—the Sun has a spot,
The world and its glory are going to pot.
                                        Down, down, &c.
All *Europe*, we hear, is in horrible pother,
They jockey, they bully and kill one another:
In *Holland*, where freedom is lustily bawling,
All's fighting and swearing, and pulling & ha[u]ling.
                                        Down, down, &c.
The *Empress* and *Poland* fresh mischief are carving,
The *Porte* is in motion, and *Ireland* is starving,
While the *Dey of Algiers*, sirs, so haughty is grown,
That he swears by the prophet, the WORLD's all his own.
                                        Down, down, &c.
In *England*, blest island![5] what wonders we view,
NORTH blind as a bat,[6] Lord GEORGE GORDON a *Jew*,[7]
Or halters or peerage on HASTINGS[8] await,
And faction *pro more*, dismembers the state.
                                        Down down, &c.
PRINCE GEORGE[9] has relinquish'd the *stews* for the *church*,
And struts like a true-blue in Solomon's porch:[10]
Corruption pervades thro' both country and town,
And the tune of the nation is *Down derry down*
                                        Down, down &c.
We bid Europe farewell, the Atlantic is past,
O free born COLUMBIA you're welcome at last!
Hail *Congress, Conventions, Mobs, Shayites* & *Kings*,
With *Bankrupts* & *Know ye's*,[11] & all pretty things!
                                        Down, down, &c.
The state's had a fall and received a contusion,
And all things are tumbled in jumbled confusion:

State quacks and state midwives are huddling all round,
But in spite of their drugs we go *Down derry down.*
                                          Down; down, &c.
Write then, brother scribblers, your talents display,
This world is a *stage* and man's life is a play;[12]
When the curtain is drawn and the ranting is o'er,
Kings, heroes and waiters are equal once more.
                                          Down, down, &c.
Old Time, with his brass-eating teeth shall consume,
The works of a *Homer*, a *Newton*, a *Hume*;
And who, when all things are consumed by Old Time,
Can tell but we scribblers were writers sublime?
                                    Down, down, down derry down.

1. Reprinted in the *Daily Advertiser* and *New York Morning Post*, 23 November; the December issue of the nationally circulated Philadelphia *American Museum*; and by 2 January 1788 in twelve newspapers outside New York: Vt. (1), N.H. (2), Mass. (4), R.I. (1), Conn. (2), Pa. (1), Md. (1). For a parody of this item, see "Parody of the News-Mongers' Song," *Northern Centinel*, 27 November (below).
2. Latin: All in good time.
3. Latin: for the sake of argument. (Used in the law.)
4. Those named here were newspaper printers from Vermont to Maryland.
5. William Shakespeare, *Richard II*, Act II, scene 1, line 50. "This blessed plot, this earth, this realm, this England."
6. A reference to Lord North (1732–1792), who began losing his sight in early 1787 and who soon became totally blind.
7. In June 1780 Lord George Gordon (1751–1793) was the leader of the Protestant riots in London that erupted in opposition to toleration for Roman Catholics. He had recently converted to Judaism.
8. Warren Hastings (1732–1818) had been governor general of India. He returned to England in 1785 and was impeached by the House of Commons two years later for corruption and cruelty in office. He was acquitted by the House of Lords in 1795.
9. George Augustus Frederick, Prince of Wales (1762–1830), who became George IV in 1820.
10. Solomon's porch was attached to the original temple built by Solomon. It was the porch of judgment, where Solomon rendered judgments and exercised justice. See 1 Kings 6:3; 1 Kings 7:6–7. See also John 10:23–39. Jesus was questioned after he entered Solomon's porch as to whether or not he was the Christ.
11. For the meaning of "Know Ye," see "Cincinnatus," *Northern Centinel*, 15 October, note 1 (above).
12. William Shakespeare, *As You Like It*, Act II, scene 7, lines 139–40. "All the world's a stage,/And all the men and women merely players."

New York Journal, 15 November 1787[1]

Southern Mail yesterday brought no papers!—It is greatly to be wished, that some reform might take place with respect to the public mails, as by the great negligence, within a few weeks, the means of intelligence, from every quarter, is almost entirely cut off.

1. Reprinted: *Country Journal,* 21 November. On 17 December the *New York Journal* again complained about the southern mails (below), but these complaints did not become common until after the beginning of the new year, when Philadelphia Antifederalist "Centinel" began to complain about the post office and its policy toward the carrying of newspapers through the mails. (See "New York Journal and the Post Office," 10 January–25 March 1788, below; and CC:Vol. IV, Appendix II, "The Controversy over the Post Office and the Circulation of Newspapers.")

Brutus III
New York Journal, 15 November 1787[1]

To the Citizens of the State of New-York.

In the investigation of the constitution, under your consideration, great care should be taken, that you do not form your opinions respecting it, from unimportant provisions, or fallacious appearances.

On a careful examination, you will find, that many of its parts, of little moment, are well formed; in these it has a specious resemblance of a free government—but this is not sufficient to justify the adoption of it—the gilded pill, is often found to contain the most deadly poison.

You are not however to expect, a perfect form of government, any more than to meet with perfection in man; your views therefore, ought to be directed to the main pillars upon which a free government is to rest; if these are well placed, on a foundation that will support the superstructure, you should be satisfied, although the building may want a number of ornaments, which, if your particular tastes were gratified, you would have added to it: on the other hand, if the foundation is insecurely laid, and the main supports are wanting, or not properly fixed, however the fabric may be decorated and adorned, you ought to reject it.

Under these impressions, it has been my object to turn your attention to the principal defects in this system.

I have attempted to shew, that a consolidation of this extensive continent, under one government, for internal, as well as external purposes, which is evidently the tendency of this constitution, cannot succeed, without a sacrifice of your liberties; and therefore that the attempt is not only preposterous, but extremely dangerous; and I have shewn, independent of this, that the plan is radically defective in a fundamental principle, which ought to be found in every free government; to wit, a declaration of rights.

I shall now proceed to take a nearer view of this system, to examine its parts more minutely, and shew that the powers are not properly deposited, for the security of public liberty.

The first important object that presents itself in the organization of this government, is the legislature. This is to be composed of two branches; the first to be called the general assembly, and is to be chosen by the people of the respective states, in proportion to the number of their inhabitants, and is to consist of sixty five members, with powers in the legislature to encrease the number, not to exceed one for every thirty thousand inhabitants. The second branch is to be called the senate, and is to consist of twenty-six members, two of which are to be chosen by the legislatures of each of the states.

In the former of these there is an appearance of justice, in the appointment of its members—but if the clause, which provides for this branch, be stripped of its ambiguity, it will be found that there is really no equality of representation, even in this house.

The words are "representatives and direct taxes, shall be apportioned among the several states, which may be included in this union, according to their respective numbers, which shall be determined by adding to the whole number of free persons, including those bound to service for a term of years, and excluding Indians not taxed, three fifths of all other persons."—What a strange and unnecessary accumulation of words are here used to conceal from the public eye, what might have been expressed in the following concise manner. Representatives are to be proportioned among the states respectively, according to the number of freemen and slaves inhabiting them, counting five slaves for three free men.

"In a free state," says the celebrated Montesquieu, "every man, who is supposed to be a free agent, ought to be concerned in his own government, therefore the legislature should reside in the whole body of the people, or their representatives."[2] But it has never been alledged that those who are not free agents, can, upon any rational principle, have any thing to do in government, either by themselves or others. If they have no share in government, why is the number of members in the assembly, to be increased on their account? Is it because in some of the states, a considerable part of the property of the inhabitants consists in a number of their fellow men, who are held in bondage, in defiance of every idea of benevolence, justice, and religion, and contrary to all the principles of liberty, which have been publickly avowed in the late glorious revolution? If this be a just ground for representation, the horses in some of the states, and the oxen in others, ought to be represented—for a great share of property in some of them, consists in these animals; and they have as much controul over their own actions, as these poor unhappy creatures, who are intended to be described in the above recited clause, by the words, "all other persons."

By this mode of apportionment, the representatives of the different parts of the union, will be extremely unequal; in some of the southern states, the slaves are nearly equal in number to the free men; and for all these slaves, they will be entitled to a proportionate share in the legislature—this will give them an unreasonable weight in the government, which can derive no additional strength, protection, nor defence from the slaves, but the contrary. Why then should they be represented? What adds to the evil is, that these states are to be permitted to continue the inhuman traffic of importing slaves, until the year 1808—and for every cargo of these unhappy people, which unfeeling, unprincipled, barbarous, and avaricious wretches, may tear from their country, friends and tender connections, and bring into those states, they are to be rewarded by having an increase of members in the general assembly. There appears at the first view a manifest inconsistency, in the apportionment of representatives in the senate, upon the plan of a consolidated government. On every principle of equity, and propriety, representation in a government should be in exact proportion to the numbers, or the aids afforded by the persons represented. How unreasonable, and unjust then is it, that Delaware should have a representation in the senate, equal to Massachusetts, or Virginia? The latter of which contains ten times her numbers, and is to contribute to the aid of the general government in that proportion? This article of the constitution will appear the more objectionable, if it is considered, that the powers vested in this branch of the legislature are very extensive, and greatly surpass those lodged in the assembly, not only for general purposes, but, in many instances, for the internal police of the states. The other branch of the legislature, in which, if in either, a faint spark of democracy is to be found, should have been properly organized and established—but upon examination you will find, that this branch does not possess the qualities of a just representation, and that there is no kind of security, imperfect as it is, for its remaining in the hands of the people.

It has been observed, that the happiness of society is the end of government—that every free government is founded in compact; and that, because it is impracticable for the whole community to assemble, or when assembled, to deliberate with wisdom, and decide with dispatch, the mode of legislating by representation was devised.

The very term, representative, implies, that the person or body chosen for this purpose, should resemble those who appoint them—a representation of the people of America, if it be a true one, must be like the people. It ought to be so constituted, that a person, who is a stranger to the country, might be able to form a just idea of their character, by knowing that of their representatives. They are the sign—the people are the thing signified. It is absurd to speak of one thing being the representative of another, upon any other principle. The ground and reason of representation, in a free government, implies the same thing. Society instituted government to promote the happiness of the whole, and this is the great end always in view in the delegation of powers. It must then have been intended, that those who are placed instead of the people, should possess their sentiments and feelings, and be governed by their interests, or, in other words, should bear the strongest resemblance of those in whose room they are substituted. It is obvious, that for an assembly to be a true likeness of the people of any country, they must be considerably numerous.—One man, or a few men, cannot possibly represent the feelings, opinions, and characters of a great multitude. In this respect, the new constitution is radically defective.—The house of assembly, which is intended as a representation of the people of America, will not, nor cannot, in the nature of things, be a proper one—sixty-five men cannot be found in the United States, who hold the sentiments, possess the feelings, or are acquainted with the wants and interests of this vast country. This extensive continent is made up of a number of different classes of people; and to have a proper representation of them, each class ought to have an opportunity of choosing their best informed men for the purpose; but this cannot possibly be the case in so small a number. The state of New-York, on the present apportionment, will send six members to the assembly: I will venture to affirm, that number cannot be found in the state, who will bear a just resemblance to the several classes of people who compose it. In this assembly, the farmer, merchant, mec[h]anick, and other various orders of people, ought to be represented according to their respective weight and numbers; and the representatives ought to be intimately acquainted with the wants, understand the interests of the several orders in the society, and feel a proper sense and becoming zeal to promote their prosperity. I cannot conceive that any six men in this state can be found properly qualified in these respects to discharge such important duties: but supposing it possible to find them, is there the least degree of probability that the choice of the people will fall upon such men? According to the common course of human affairs, the natural aristocracy of the country will be elected. Wealth always creates influence, and this is generally much increased by large family connections: this class in society will for ever have a great number of dependents; besides, they will always favour each other—it is their interest to combine—they will therefore constantly unite their efforts to procure men of their own rank to be elected—they will concenter all their force in every part of the state into one point, and by acting together, will most generally carry their election. It is probable, that but few of the merchants, and those the most opulent and ambitious, will have a representation from their body—few of them are characters sufficiently conspicuous to attract the notice of the electors of the state in so limited a representation. The great body of the yeomen of the country cannot expect any of their order in this assembly—the station will be too elevated for them to aspire to—the distance between the people and their representatives, will be so very great, that there is no probability that a farmer, however respectable, will be chosen—the mechanicks of every branch, must expect to be excluded from a seat in this Body—It will and must be esteemed a station too high and exalted to be filled by any but the first men in the state, in point of fortune; so that in reality there will be no part of the people represented, but the rich, even in that branch of the legislature, which is called the democratic.—The well born, and highest orders in life, as they term themselves, will be ignorant of the sentiments of the middling class of citizens, strangers to their ability, wants, and difficulties, and void of sympathy, and fellow feeling. This branch of the legislature will not only be an imperfect representation, but there will be no security in so small a body, against bribery, and corruption—It will consist at first, of sixty-five, and can never exceed one for every thirty thousand inhabitants; a majority of these, that is, thirty-three, are a quorum, and a majority of which, or seventeen, may pass any law—a majority of the senate, or fourteen, are a quorum, and eight of them pass any law—so that twenty-five men, will have the power to give away all the property of the citizens of these states—what security therefore can there be for the people, where their liberties and property are at the disposal of so few men? It will literally be a government in the hands of the few to oppress and plunder the many. You may conclude with a great degree of certainty, that it, like all others of a similar nature, will be managed by influence and corruption, and that the period is not far distant, when this will be the case, if it should be adopted; for even now there are some among us, whose characters stand high in the public estimation, and who have had a principal agency in framing this constitution, who do not scruple to say, that this is the only practicable mode of governing a people, who think with that degree of freedom which the Americans do—this government will have in their gift a vast number of offices of great honor and emolument. The members of the legislature are not excluded from appointments; and twenty-five of them, as the case may be, being secured, any measure may be carried.

The rulers of this country must be composed of very different materials from those of any other, of which history gives us any account, if the majority of the legislature are not, before many years, entirely at the devotion of the executive—and these states will soon be under the absolute domination of one, or a few, with the fallacious appearance of being governed by men of their own election.

The more I reflect on this subject, the more firmly am I persuaded, that the representation is merely nominal—a mere burlesque; and that no security is provided against corruption and undue influence. No free people on earth, who have elected persons to legislate for them, ever reposed that confidence in so small a number. The British house of commons consists of five hundred and fifty-eight members; the number of inhabitants in Great-Britain, is computed at eight millions—this gives one member for a little more than fourteen thousand, which exceeds double the proportion this country can ever have: and yet we require a larger representation in proportion to our numbers, than Great-Britain, because this country is much more extensive, and differs more in its productions, interests, manners, and habits. The democratic branch of the legislatures of the several states in the union consists, I believe at present, of near two thousand; and this number was not thought too large for the security of liberty by the framers of our state constitutions: some of the states may have erred in this respect, but the difference between two thousand, and sixty-five, is so very great, that it will bear no comparison.

Other objections offer themselves against this part of the constitution—I shall reserve them for a future paper,[3] when I shall shew, defective as this representation is, no security is provided, that even this shadow of the right, will remain with the people.

1. Reprinted: Philadelphia *Freeman's Journal*, 21 November (upon request); Philadelphia *Independent Gazetteer*, 23 November (upon request); Boston *Independent Chronicle*, 13 December. For an out-of-state response to "Brutus" III, see "Mark Antony," Boston *Independent Chronicle*, 10 January 1788 (RCS:Mass., 672–77).

2. *Spirit of Laws*, I, Book XI, chapter VI, 226.

3. See "Brutus" IV, *New York Journal*, 29 November (below).

Cincinnatus III: To James Wilson, Esquire
New York Journal, 15 November 1787[1]

SIR, Your speech has varnished an iron trap, ba[i]ted with some illustrious names, to catch the liberties of the people. And this you are pleased to call a constitution—"the best form of government that was ever offered to the world." May Heaven then have mercy on the world and on us. And in this prayer, I am persuaded, you will join me when you come to consider temperately, the unbounded powers given to this best of all possible governments; and then recollect, from your reading, what horrible abuses have grown from too unlimited a confidence of the people in their rulers. It is always both easier and safer, to add to powers, which are found to be insufficient, than to recall those which are injuriously large. This is a maxim, which no people, who mean to be free, should ever forget. While the people have something to give, they will be respected by their rulers. When with Cappadocian baseness,[2] they resign all at once, they will be deemed fit only to be hewers of wood and drawers of water.[3]

In my former papers, I have shewn, that the freedom of the press is left at the mercy of the proposed government—that the sacred trial by jury, in civil cases, is at best doubtful; and in all cases of appeal expressly taken away. In equal insecurity, or rather equally at mercy, are we left as to—liberty of conscience. We find nothing that regards it, except the following;—"but no religious test shall every be required as a qualification to any office or public trust under the United States." This exception implies, and necessarily implies, that in all other cases whatever liberty of conscience may be regulated. For, though no such power is expressly given, yet it is plainly meant to be included in the general powers, or else this exception would have been totally unnecessary— For why should it be said, that no religious test should be required as a qualification for office, if no power was given or intended to be given to impose a religious test of any kind? Upon the omission of the trial by jury in civil cases, you observe—"when this subject was in discussion, we were involved in difficulties which pressed on all sides, and no precedent could be discovered to direct our course. The cases open to trial by jury differed in the different states, it was therefore impracticable on that ground to have made a general rule."—So, because the extent of the trial by jury varied in the different states, therefore it was proper to abolish it in all. For what else can your words—"it was impracticable to have made a general rule" mean?—If ever the rule is made, it must be general. And if this is impracticable—it surely follows, that in the fœderal court we must go without it in civil cases. What sense is there in supposing, that what, for the reasons you alledge, was impracticable with the Convention, will be practicable with the Congress? What faculty can the one body have more than the other, of reconciling contradictions? But the sophistry of this excuse consists in the word *made*—*make* you might not, but surely nothing hindered your *proposing* the general rule, which, if approved by the several state Conventions, would *make* the rule. You have made nothing. You have only proposed. It rests with the several conventions, to make your propositions, rules. It is not possible to say, that the Convention could not have proposed, that there should be one similar general mode of trial by jury in the Fœderal court in all cases whatever. If the states would not have acceded to the proposition, we should only be where we are. And that this trial by jury is best, even in courts where the civil law process now prevails, I think no unbigoted man can doubt. Judge Blackstone is so explicit on this head, that I need only quote him to enforce conviction on every unprejudiced mind.—"This open examination of witnesses viva voce, in the presence of all mankind, is much more conducive to the clearing up of truth, than the private and secret examination taken down in writing before an officer, or his clerk, in the ecclesiastical courts, and all others that have borrowed their practice from the civil law; where a witness may frequently depose that in private which he will be ashamed to testify in a public and solemn tribunal. Where an artful or careless scribe may make a witness speak what he never meant, by dressing up his depositions in his own forms and language; but he is here at liberty to correct and explain his meaning, if misunderstood, which he can never do after a written deposition is once taken. Besides the occasional questions of the judge, the jury, and the counsel, propounded to the witnesses on a sudden, will sift out the truth much better than a formal set of interrogatories previously penned and settled; and the confronting of adverse witnesses is also another opportunity of obtaining a clear discovery, which can never be had on any other method of trial. Nor is the presence of the judge, during the examination, a matter of small importance; for besides the respect, &c. with which his presence will naturally inspire the witness, he is able by use and experience to keep the evidence from wandering from the point in issue. In short, by this method of examination, and this only, the persons who are to decide upon the evidence, have an opportunity of observing the quality, age, education, understanding, behaviour, and inclinations of the witness; in which points all persons must appear alike, when their depositions are reduced to writing and read to the judge, in the absence of those who made them; and yet as much may be frequently collected from the manner in which the evidence is delivered as from the matter of it. These are a few of the advantages attending this way of giving testimony oretenus; which was also, indeed, familiar among the ancient Romans."[4]

They who applaud the practice of civil law courts, must either have seen very little of such practice not to know that it is liable to infinite fraud, corruption, and oppression. As far as it prevails in the English system of jurisprudence, from which we derive ours, it is a remnant of ecclesiastical tyranny. The free and pure part of the system, that is the common law courts, have ever cautiously guarded against its encroachments, and restrained its operation. All great judges have reprobated it, except Lord Mansfield. He indeed, has been as desirous of extending it in England, as he was of extending parliamentary power into America; and with the same view—to establish tyranny. This noble Lord's principles, if we may judge from the proposed constitution, has too many admirers in America.

But I shall be told, that almost all the nations in Europe have adopted the civil law. This is true; and it is equally true, that almost all European nations have adopted arbitrary power with the civil law. This ought to be a warning to us how we admit it, even as England has done. It would never have been admitted there, but from the ecclesiastical influence in the days of superstition. This, thank Heaven, is now no more; and I sincerely wish its offspring was also extinct.

I have been thus particular on the subject of civil law, to shew how little propriety there was in leaving it upon as respectable a foot, as the common law, in civil cases. In fact, the constitution leaves them both to shift for themselves, in original process, and in appeal seems to favor the former by placing both law and fact, in the arbitrament of the judges.

Upon standing armies, sir, your professional dexterity has not abandoned you. The Constitution proposes to give the power of raising and supporting armies—and this without any limitation as to number; and to appropriate money to that object for two years at a time. This you justify by saying, that you "do not know a nation in the world which has not found it necessary and useful to maintain the appearance of strength, in a season of profound tranquility:" your knowledge then, sir, has not extended to free nations. Your phraseology, it is true, is somewhat equivocal; but unless by the term, appearance of strength, we understand, a standing army, we must suppose you to have meant a disingenuous evasion. Your reading might have informed you, sir,— that the Grecian republics, while free, never kept up any standing army—that the Roman republic, while free, never kept up a standing army, but that with them, a standing army and tyranny were co-eval, and concomitant—that in the free Swiss Cantons, no standing army, was ever, or is now permitted; no, sir, in all these great and glorious republics, though surrounded with enemies, their military array was occasional, or at the utmost, annual; nor was there formerly, nor is there now, in the Swiss Cantons, any more appearance of strength kept up in time of peace, than their militia gives: and yet they are free and formidable.

You say a standing army has always been, "a topic of popular declamation." Is it indeed nothing more, sir? Is that which all free nations
have studiously avoided, as the rock on which their liberties would suffer shipwreck; that which in fact, is the source and security of tyranny;
that which all great political writers concur in condemning; that which
has animated the ardor, and inflamed the eloquence of the first orators
in the two houses of parliament, in Great-Britain—that which all the
art and influence of the crown could never obtain from the people for
more than a year[5]—is all that, sir, nothing more but a topic of popular
declamation? Is it surprising, that such knowledge, and such sentiments, as this declaration holds out, should have given us such a constitution? But the weightiest reason is, that without a standing army,
"the government must declare war, before they are prepared to carry
it on." This is without question a most warlike paragraph: whether we
are to invade Great-Britain, France, Spain, Portugal, or all together,
under the new constitution, and with the standing army it has given,
you have not been pleased to inform us. To do this, a navy too will be
necessary, and I see no provision for that: however, I suppose that, as
well as every thing else, is included in the power "to make all laws
which shall be necessary and proper for carrying into execution the
foregoing, and all other powers vested by this constitution, in the government of the United States, or in any department or officer thereof."
Let then the people rightly understand, that one blessing of the constitution will be, the taxing them to support fleets and armies to con-
quer other nations, against whom the ambition of their new rulers may
declare war.

1. This item, an answer to James Wilson's 6 October speech before a Philadelphia
public meeting (CC:134), was reprinted in the Philadelphia *Independent Gazetteer*, 21 November. For Wilson's speech, see also "New York Reprinting of James Wilson's 6 October
Speech Before a Philadelphia Public Meeting," 13–25 October (above).

2. The ancients considered the Cappadocians or Syrians a mean, perfidious, dull, and
submissive people who were addicted to every vice. When offered their freedom by the
Romans, the Syrians refused it and begged for a king. Many of the slaves employed by
the Romans were Syrians; the word "syrus" is often applied to slaves. The ancients used
this epigram to describe the Cappodocians: "*Vipera Cappodocem nocitura momordit; at ailla
Gustato periit sanguine Cappadocis.*" (I.e., The snake about to do harm has bitten a Cappadocian, but that snake has perished once the blood of the Cappadocian has been
tasted.)

3. Joshua 9:21, 23, 27.

4. Blackstone, *Commentaries*, Book III, chapter XXIII, 373–74.

5. In 1689 the English Parliament passed the Mutiny Act, providing for military discipline of officers and soldiers of the regular army by courts-martial. From that time
forward, the mutiny act—which was essentially a military budget—was reenacted annually. Its annual passage gave Parliament leverage against the Crown. For example, in
1784 the House of Commons delayed passage of the mutiny act in order to assert its

independence and forestall a threatened dissolution by the King. Not only were annual
acts passed respecting the regular army, but annual acts also provided for the payment
of the militia.

Philopœmen
New York Daily Advertiser, 16 November 1787[1]

> "Those who cannot write, and those who can,
> All rhyme, and scrawl, and scribble to a man."[2]

Though from the justness at all times of these lines of a poet, and
their peculiar aptitude to the present times, no one can doubt their
application; it may not be amiss among the present professional and
undistinguished rage for authorities (which when grave, are always absurd, if too strained and remote to be believed, or too obvious and trite
to be doubted) to add a second liable to neither objection.

> Gladly they coil beneath the Statesman's pains,
> Give them but credit for a Statesman's brains,
> All would be deemed, e'en from the cradle fit
> To rule in politics as well as wit.
> The grave, the gay, the cobler and the dunce,
> Start up (God bless us!) Statesmen all at once.

Were it not for our present critical and important situation, admitted
to be so by honest men on all sides, and which to deny, would be an
insult on truth, common sense, and mankind; for it must appear so to
all in some point of view or other; I should have declined the above
invidious sarcasms and a comment upon them, which, whether just or
not, will be displeasing to many of both parties; but which I deem
absolutely necessary to the interest of truth and our common country:
because, while the present mistakes, misrepresentations and scurrility
prevail, and are exulted in, a true estimate and decision cannot be
attained, because truth and right are not only eclipsed, but absolutely
hidden and lost amidst this inundation of error. In such a state not an
argument, but of passion and party finds access; for, from such a scene,
men of delicacy, judgment and philosophy, which are generally found
together, will fly with horror: but should love of their country induce
them to adventure, they would pass unheeded by and disregarded—
Here then would be a worse political mob, than Athens e'er was cursed
with. For these men, capable of directing the mob, were compellable
under the heaviest penalties, to take part in every cabal in the state,
and the utility of the measure sufficiently justifies its establishment in
their situation: but our's is a different and superior lot, exhibiting other

prospects, other dangers, and consequently requiring other remedies. We aspire, and with reason, to be a nation of statesmen. Unhappily we anticipate the course of nature, and suppose ourselves what it will require ages to make us, or even a majority of us, consummate politicians as well as freemen. Remote as is the prospect, and ideal as it is deemed by most of the old world, I still trust to see them reconciled, and already in idea behold them both carried to the utmost human perfection in this country. Am I asked how? I answer by means of the Press and this new Constitution; for so far from being inimical, I see them the best of friends—and did I not, I should be the first to condemn the latter.— The weakness and intemperance with which the contrary opinion is maintained, convince me of the safety of the former:—But of this by the by— for the present let me advert to a source of greater danger and inconvenience to the press and community, as well as to the cause they intend to advocate—and that is this very cloud of illiberal, indiscriminate and total reprobation of this new form of Government. Well grounded objections (if any) will thus be discouraged or overlooked, if made; while the friends to the Constitution will too probably, with equal silence and perhaps justice, pass over the one as the other. And truly I cannot account for the silence of so many moderate men and worthy patriots; but from this prostitution of party talents, and prostration of all justice and candor—and surely this affords but too good an apology.

From this grievance it is my object, in some measure, to relieve the public; persuaded that, with my small abilities, I cannot, at this juncture, render them a more essential service; and hoping that, as a mere private citizen, who has equal prospects and advantages under all the Constitutions, because he has none under any, he will be the more readily forgiven, as he certainly deserves to be. His task he will attempt, not so much with ridicule, generally unsavory and often hurtful to best cause (indeed more likely to such than any other) as by a candid statement and stricture on such parts of the many compositions that have appeared, as appear to merit it, and can be recollected: for, tho' I have read every thing which has appeared on this important subject in this city (and which I believe includes almost every thing) with the utmost impartiality, that the above described situation admits, I have not the Herculean resolution of revising such a disgusting chaos as most of them present; and from this, as well as a desire of avoiding the intrusion of partiality, have declined giving any of them above one attentive reading. Nothing, however, shall be remarked on, but what has made a distinct impression; and will, in the manner it is introduced, have a clear recollection in minds of all the attentive and impartial, who have had, and embraced, the like opportunities of satisfying a mind, anxious after truth alone.

To begin with what has been the real or pretended ground of most of the observations against the Constitution, Mr. Wilson's address, candor (as far as recollection serves, and I speak from nothing else) must confess that it is worthy of neither the object, the occasion, nor the speaker; unless we suppose it, as it in fact appears to have been, an extemporaneous harangue, to a few particular friends, intended more as a sample of oratory than of logic; and which their partiality for the man led them to imagine worthy of an use for which it was never designed—a logical, written defence and recommendation of the new Constitution. But has it produced better logic in answer? I fear not; but rather that his radical errors, like the nightly meteor, have, according to the nature of things, added to, and been surpassed by, *their* fruitless wanderings. But let us, for the present, confine ourselves to the detection and true estimate of this deluding star, and then pursue our course, with double certainty and double vigilance.

For error on error, whether the latter be on the same or opposite side to the former, is not otherwise to be rectified.

The introductory observation of Mr. Wilson is the only one that comes within the above description, and it, with the animadversions upon it, justly do; tho' one part of his antithesis (and, what candor must be loth to suspect, this the material one) is certainly true: so that we have the consolation of having been amused with endless refutations and remarks on what, tho' false, is perfectly immaterial to the merits or demerits of the Constitution before us; unless indeed, if what Mr. Wilson here tells us, about the nature of our State Governments, be true; and what his antagonists, rather than lose the shadow of an argument, tho' a real one is lost by it, have admitted, nay affirmed, to be true; unless, I say, it is in contemplation soon to alter and accommodate to circumstances, our State Governments also, as most if not all the States have just reason to alter them if they have been thus used: for it is impossible that Constitutions framed at the time, and under the circumstances they were, should not need an alteration.

To what lengths and absurdities will not the fervor of altercation carry unhappy mortals? It has been observed that men; predeterminately setting out on the most contrary principles, have insensibly or unavoidably fallen into the same conclusions at last. If this has happened, with respect to the ultimate destination of the doctrines of party zealots, much more frequent, and more at the expence of truth, will be their herding together in hotels by the way, for mutual convenience, and from mutual confidence and security, as to the great object of their pursuit; and without having recourse to some of the foregoing principles, it must be difficult, if not impossible, to account how both or either party should assent to so strange a position, as that of Mr. Wilson, concerning our State Governments, "that whatever is not reserved is given" to the rulers. This is at once telling us, either that "all power *is not* derived from the people," or that notwithstanding our boasted privileges and extravagant love of independence, we have been already *usurped upon* and divested of our just and natural rights *by force*; for this includes every mode of attaining power, but by *general consent*, the only legal one, and that no otherwise than as recognised by the Constitution. Whatever is not surrendered by this, is retained, and we cannot be deprived of it, but by a violence, which would well deserve to be taught, that *vox populi vox dei est;*[3] and that neither is to be imposed upon with impunity.

If any thing could be clearer than this principle, I would endeavor to illustrate it, and perhaps the following might then have some effect; that as the stream is derived from and dependent on its fountain, the latter can never be destroyed or greatly depressed without violence of some kind or other, and without drawing after its injury or ruin that of its offspring. But it is as impossible to add light to that which has attained the summit of brightness or evidence, as it is to increase the blackness of that which has received the utmost tinge of darkness. I will, therefore, desist from so wild an undertaking, by accounting for its having been denied.

The candid and discerning will not need to be told, that all the mistakes on this subject have arisen from too partial a view of the subject. The objectors to Mr. Wilson, instead of taking up this important rule of construction upon its own genuine principles, have diverted our attention to particular clauses in Mr. Wilson's harangue, in the old and new Federal Government, and other more remote and trifling objects; contenting themselves with general assertions of what, from its importance, as well as singularity to the eye of unbiassed reason, well required the most unequivocal demonstration.

A desire of security and certainty, induces men in all their transactions, to stipulate many things which are by no means absolutely necessary. This is more frequently practised in affairs of moment, length and intricacy, where, from the nature of language, there will be many general clauses which require modifications, that otherwise never would have been thought of. These two obvious reflections sufficiently answer every argument of the nature above-mentioned, which are the only ones of the objectors to the new Government to that point. Thus do we find the explicitness, caution and prudence of the Convention, relied upon as fatal to a system, which was never exceeded in any of those respects, as must appear from their being made the chief proofs of the want of them.

What cannot prejudice convert to its own purposes? Take for another example, and as a recurrence to what I promised near the beginning about the safety of the press, the two following and only attempts (except general declamation of which all are capable) to call it in question; the former of which appeared a considerable time since, and is grounded on that clause of the eighth section, which gives Congress the power "to promote the progress of science and useful arts, by securing for limited times to authors and inventors, the exclusive right to their respective writings and discoveries."

The latter is of a birth so late as the first appearance of Cincinnatus,[4] and has its weighty foundation in the second clause from the other. This enables Congress "to define and punish piracies and felonies committed on the high seas, and offences against the law of nations."

Had I not already twice mentioned the objections which are raised to these paragraphs, and perhaps as it is, I might venture any wager, that not one out of fifty of any common understanding, can persuade himself that such an inference has ever been drawn by a rational man, much less by a public writer against the Convention; that he would sooner suspect any other, or any thing than the fact; that it must have been quoted by the opposite party for a directly contrary purpose. But unluckily, neither this nor almost any other part of the Constitution, has been produced in its defence, and what may seem strange to the illiterate, and to them only, its advocates seem less zealous and assuming, with the most express and unanimous approbation of near half a hundred patriots, and the concurrence of all America on their side, than its opponents with arguments like those which have been noticed.

It may be asked, if such the prospects and inequality, why this anxiety in you? I answer, that for our honor and interest, as well as that of the world (unhappily beyond the views of individuals too little regarded) the subject may have as cool, disinterested and discreet an examination, and as peaceable and unanimous a determination as the subject admits, and our situation requires.

1. On 15 November the *Daily Advertiser* announced that "Philopœmen" would appear the next day. This essay is a commentary on James Wilson's 6 October speech before a Philadelphia public meeting (CC:134). For Wilson's speech, see also "New York Reprinting of James Wilson's 6 October Speech Before a Philadelphia Public Meeting," 13–25 October (above).

2. Alexander Pope, *The First Epistle of the Second Book of Horace, Imitated* (1737).

3. Latin: the voice of the people is the voice of God.
4. "Cincinnatus" I, *New York Journal*, 1 November (above).

Philo-Publius II
New York Packet, 16 November 1787[1]

The government of Athens was a democracy. The people, as is usual in all democratical governments, were constantly alarmed at the spectre of ARISTOCRACY; and it was common in that republic as it is in the republics of America to pay court to them by encouraging their jealousies, and gratifying their prejudices. Pericles to ingratiate himself with the citizens of Athens, whose favor was necessary to his ambition, was a principal agent in mutilating the privileges and the power of the court of AREOPAGUS; an institution acknowleged by all historians to have been a main pillar of the State.[2] The pretence was that it promoted the POWER of the ARISTOCRACY.

The same man undermined the constitution of his country TO ACQUIRE popularity—squandered the treasures of his country to PURCHASE popularity—and to avoid being accountable to his country precipitated it into a war which ended in its destruction. Pericles was, nevertheless, a man endowed with many amiable and shining qualities, and, except in a few instances, was always the favorite of the people.

1. Reprinted: Boston *American Herald*, 10 December; *Hudson Weekly Gazette*, 20 December.

2. The ancient aristocratic Athenian Council or Court of Areopagus held the guardianship of the law and could declare as null any laws in violation of the Athenian constitution. In 462/1 B.C. Pericles joined with popular leader Ephialtes to deprive the Court of Areopagus of its guardianship of the law as well as some of its other jurisdiction, whereby the Court lost much of its political influence. The Court remained, however, the court for deliberate homicide, wounding, and arson. After Ephialtes was murdered, he was succeeded as popular leader by Pericles.

Ebenezer Hazard to Jeremy Belknap
New York, 17 November 1787 (excerpt)[1]

. . . The Foederal Constitution is but little talked of here, but the Presses attack & defend it with Spirit: whether it will be adopted or not must rest with the Conventions: I wish to see some Government, for I declare I am sick of Anarchy. . . .

1. RC, Belknap Papers, MHi. Printed: "The Belknap Papers," *Collections* of the Massachusetts Historical Society, 5th series, Vols. II–III (Boston, 1877), II, 495–96. Hazard (1744–1817), a 1762 graduate of the College of New Jersey (Princeton), was Confederation postmaster general, 1782–89. Belknap (1744–1798), a Harvard College graduate (1762), was pastor of the Congregational Church in Long Lane, Boston, 1787–98.

Publius: The Federalist 7 (Alexander Hamilton)
New York Independent Journal, 17 November 1787

Danger of interstate conflict. For text, see CC:269. For reprintings, see Appendix IV, below.

An Observer
New York Journal, 19 November 1787[1]

MR. GREENLEAF, A writer, under the signature of PUBLIUS, or the FEDERALIST, No. V. in the Daily Advertiser, and in the New-York Packet, with a view of proving the advantages which, he says, will be derived by the states if the new Constitution is adopted—has given extracts of a letter from Queen Anne to the Scotch parliament, on the subject of a union, between Scotland and England, and which I shall also here insert.

"An entire and perfect union will be the solid foundation of lasting peace: It will secure your religion, liberty and property, remove the animosities among yourselves, and the jealousies and differences betwixt our two kingdoms. It must increase your strength, riches and trade; and by this union the whole island, being joined in affection and free from all apprehensions of different interest, will be ⟨enable[d] to resist all its enemies⟩." "We most earnestly recommend to you calmness and unanimity in this great and weighty affair, that the union may be brought to a happy conclusion, being the only ⟨effectual⟩ way to secure our present and future happiness; and disappoint the designs of our and your enemies, who will doubtless, on this occasion, ⟨use their utmost endeavours to prevent or delay this union⟩."[2]

I would beg leave to remark, that Publius has been very unfortunate in selecting these extracts as a case in point, to convince the people of America of the benefits they would derive from a union under such a government, as would be effected by the new system—It is a certainty, that when the union was the subject of debate in the Scottish legislature, some of their most sensible and disinterested nobles, as well as commoners (who were not corrupted by English gold) violently opposed the union, and predicted, that the people of Scotland, would, in fact, derive no advantages from a consolidation of government with England, but, on the contrary, bear a great proportion of her debt, and furnish large bodies of men to assist in her wars with France, with whom, before the union, Scotland was at all times on terms of the most cordial amity. It was also predicted, that the representation in the parliament of Great-Britain, particularly in the house of commons, was too small;—forty-five members being very far from the proportion of Scotland, when its extent and numbers were duly considered; and that even they, being so few, might (or at least a majority of them might) at all times be immediately under the influence of the English ministry; and, of course, very little of their attention would be given to the true interests of their constituents, especially if they came in competition with the projects or views of the ministry. How far these predictions have been verified, I believe it will not require much trouble to prove; as it must be obvious to every one, the least acquainted with the English history, since the union of the two nations, that the great body of the people in Scotland, are in a much worse situation now, than they would be, were they a separate nation. This will be fully illustrated, by attending to the great emigrations which are made to America; for if the people could have but a common support at home, it is unreasonable to suppose, that such large numbers would quit their country, break from the tender ties of kindred and friendship, and trust themselves on a dangerous voyage across a vast ocean, to a country of which they can know but little, except by common report. I will only further remark, that it is not above two or three years since a member of the British parliament (I believe Mr. Dempster) gave a most pathetic description of the sufferings of the commonality of Scotland, particularly on the sea coast, and endeavoured to call the attention of parliament to their distresses, and afford them some relief, by encouraging their fisheries.[3] It deserves also to be remembered, that the people of Scotland, in the late war, between France and Great-Britain, petitioned to have arms and ammunition supplied them by their general government, for their defence, alledging that they were incapable of defending themselves, and their property, from an invasion, unless they were assisted by government. It is a truth that their petitions were disregarded, and reasons were assigned, that it would be dangerous to intrust them with the means of defence, as they would then have it in their power to break the union. From this representation of the situation of Scotland, surely no one can draw any conclusion, that this country would derive happiness or security from a government which would, in reality, give the people but the mere name of being free; for if the representation, stipulated by the constitution, framed by the late Convention, be attentively and dispassionately considered, it must be obvious to every disinterested observer (besides many other weighty objections which will present themselves to his view) that the number is not, by any means, adequate to the present inhabitants of this extensive continent, much less to those it will contain at a future period.

I observe that the writer above-mentioned, takes great pains to shew the disadvantages which would result from three or four distinct confederacies of these states.[4] I must confess that I have not seen, in any of the pieces published against the proposed constitution, any thing which gives the most distant idea that their writers are in favor of such governments; but it is clear these objections arise from a consolidation not affording security for the liberties of their country; and from hence it must evidently appear, that the design of Publius, in artfully holding up to public view such confederacies, can be with no other intention than wilfully to deceive his fellow citizens.

I am confident it must be, and that it is, the sincere wish of every true friend to the United States, that there should be a confederated national government, but that it should be one which would have a controul over national and external matters only, and not interfere with the internal regulations and police of the different states in the union. Such a government, while it would give us respectability abroad, would not encroach upon, or subvert our liberties at home.

November 13, 1787.

1. Reprinted: *Daily Advertiser*, 20 November; Boston *American Herald*, 3 December (minus the excerpts from Queen Anne's letter). On 15 November the printer of the *New York Journal* announced that "An Observer" had been prepared for printing, but that it was "unavoidably omitted." "An Observer" attacks "Publius," *The Federalist* 5, *Independent Journal*, 10 November. For the text of *The Federalist* 5, see CC:252. For reprintings, see Appendix IV, below. For a defense of *The Federalist* 5 against the criticism of "An Observer," see "Detector," *Daily Advertiser*, 24 November (below).

2. Queen Anne's letter is in Daniel Defoe, *The History of the Union of Great Britain* (Edinburgh, 1709), "Of the Carrying on of the Treaty in Scotland," 6–7. The text in angle brackets in this paragraph was italicized in *The Federalist* 5.

3. See the 23 June 1784 speech of George Dempster in the British House of Commons, [T. C. Hansard], *The Parliamentary History of England from the Earliest Period to the Year 1803* . . . (36 vols., London, 1806–1820), XXIV, 1015–16.

4. *The Federalist* 5 gives considerable space to criticizing the alleged advocates of separate confederacies. *The Federalist* 1, *Independent Journal*, 27 October (above), first made the charge that some Antifederalists favored separate confederacies.

Publius: The Federalist 8 (Alexander Hamilton)
New York Independent Journal, 20 November 1787

Wars between nations can lead to militarism and a military state. For text, see CC:274. For reprintings, see Appendix IV, below.

Alexander Hamilton to Benjamin Rush
New York, 21 November 1787[1]

I send you herewith a series of political papers under the denomination of the Federalist published in favor of the new Constitution.

They do good here and it is imagined some of the last numbers might have a good effect upon some of your Quaker members of Convention. They are going on and appear evidently to be written by different hands and to aim at a full examination of the subject.[2] Perhaps even if they are not wanted with you, it might be well to give them a passage through your papers to your more Southern neighbors.[3]

Upon the whole I think we have a good majority thus far in this State in favor of the Constitution.

1. Copy, Bancroft Collection, Letters to Benjamin Rush, NN. Rush (1745–1813), a Philadelphia physician, was a prolific writer on medical subjects, social reforms, and national and Pennsylvania state politics, who had supported the establishment of a strong central government since 1776. In December 1787 he voted to ratify the Constitution in the Pennsylvania Convention, and early in 1788 he was a Federalist polemicist.

2. Between 14 and 21 November, Hamilton himself contributed numbers 6–9 of *The Federalist*, in which he discussed the importance of a strong union in the prevention of and in dealing with internal dissensions and convulsions, interstate conflicts, internal wars, and domestic insurrections. Such a union, Hamilton argued, would avoid the need for a standing army, which Quakers feared. (See "Publius," *The Federalist* 6–9, *Independent Journal*, 14, 17, 21 November, and *New York Packet*, 20 November, CC:257, 269, 274, 277.)

3. In Philadelphia, the semiweekly *Pennsylvania Journal* had already begun to print *The Federalist*, numbers 1 to 3 appearing between 7 and 17 November. The widely circulated *Pennsylvania Gazette*, a weekly and Philadelphia's leading Federalist newspaper, printed numbers 2 through 19 (almost every week) between 14 November 1787 and 19 March 1788. (See the table of "Printings and Reprintings of *The Federalist*," Appendix IV, below.)

Publius: The Federalist 9 (Alexander Hamilton)
New York Independent Journal, 21 November 1787

Union as check on factions and domestic insurrections. For text, see CC:277. For reprintings, see Appendix IV, below.

A Countryman I (Hugh Hughes)
New York Journal, 21 November 1787

Between 21 November 1787 and 14 February 1788, the *New York Journal* published six letters signed "A Countryman" that were written by "a gentleman in Dutchess county" to his friend in New York City. "A Countryman" was Hugh Hughes, a New York Son of Liberty before the Revolution and a Continental deputy quartermaster general during the Revolution. Among Hughes's Papers in the Library of Congress are his drafts of "Countryman" letters IV, V, and VI. Hughes also identified himself as "A Countryman" in private letters that he wrote to Charles Tillinghast, one of Hughes's assistants during the Revolution, a son-in-law of Antifederalist leader John Lamb, and secretary of the Antifederalist New York Federal Republican Committee. On 28 November Hughes wrote to Tillinghast requesting that Hughes's son (James Miles Hughes) and Tillinghast read letter III before it went to press (below). Tillinghast informed Hughes on 27 January 1788 that letter V had appeared in the

New York Journal. Hughes also wrote under the pseudonym, "Expositor." (See
"Expositor" I, *New York Journal,* 24 January, below.)

In New York, only an excerpt from letter IV was reprinted and that excerpt
was reprinted not from the *New York Journal* but from an out-of-state newspaper
(see below). Outside New York, at least one letter—in whole or in part—was
reprinted at one time or another in Rhode Island, Pennsylvania, Maryland,
and South Carolina. All six letters were reprinted in the daily Antifederalist
Philadelphia *Independent Gazetteer* from 26 April through 3 May 1788. The *Gazetteer* dropped Dutchess County from the heading and identified "A Countryman" only as being from New York state. Even before the *Gazetteer* began to
reprint the series, it had reprinted an excerpt from letter IV on 28 February
that was reprinted in the *New York Morning Post,* 5 March, and Baltimore *Maryland Gazette,* 11 March. (For the reprinting of letter I, see note 1, below.)

During this same time, the *New York Journal* printed two other series of essays
signed "A Countryman," one of which also originated in New York while the
other first appeared in Connecticut. The second New York series, written by
Antifederalist DeWitt Clinton, began publication on 6 December and ended
with number V on 17 January 1788 (all below). Four of five numbers of the
Connecticut series, written by Federalist Roger Sherman, were reprinted in the
New York Journal between 30 November and 17 December. (Sherman's essays
appeared in the *New Haven Gazette* between 15 November and 20 December,
CC:261, 284, 305, 322, 361.)

MR. GREENLEAF, Enclosed you have a copy of a letter[1] I lately received
from a gentleman in Dutchess county, and as it contains some very
proper and important remarks on the Constitution proposed by the
late Convention, I must request the favor of your publishing it in your
useful paper. The writer has promised, occasionally, to continue his
remarks; and as they come to hand, I shall, without farther introduction, send them to you for publication.   A CUSTOMER.
New-York, Nov. 20, 1787.

DEAR SIR, As you have several Times intimated a Wish to know my
Sentiments, relative to the conduct of the late Convention, as well as
of the Constitution, which they have offered to the Consideration of
the People, I shall freely, as often as convenient, communicate whatever
occurs to me on the Subject, as most worthy of Observation, if not
already publicly discussed. When the Latter is the Case, perhaps I may
drop a Sentiment concerning the Propriety, or Impropriety, of the Discussion, &c. But all this, my Friend, will, in a great Measure, depend
on your reciprocating; for I am too phlegmatic to write, unless answered.

In the first Place then, most unfeignedly do I wish, and that for the
Sake of Humanity, that the Convention never had existed; and, for the
Sake of our old illustrious Commander in chief,[2] I wish, as they have

departed from their Institution, that they had offered a Constitution more worthy of so great a Character. But, as he has acted entirely in a Ministerial Capacity, so I wish to consider him, whenever I am obliged to mention his venerable Name, or allude to it. Not that I think any Name, however great, can justify Injustice, or make Slavery more eligible than Freedom, and beg to be so understood.

Yet, ⟨when I consider the original Confederation, and Constitutions of the States which compose the Union, as well as the Resolutions of several of the States, for calling a Convention to *amend* the Confederation, which it admits, but not *a new one*, I am greatly at a Loss to account for the surprizing Conduct of so many wise Men, as must have composed that honorable Body. In fact, I do not know, at present, whether it can be accounted for; unless it be by supposing a Predetermination of a Majority of the Members to reject their Instructions, and all authority under which they acted.

If this be the Case, the Transition to prostrating every Thing that stood in their Way, though ever so serviceable or sacred to others, was natural and easy.—However, I do not even wish to think so unfavorably of the Majority; but rather, that several of them, were, by different Means, insidiously drawn into the Measures of the more artful and designing Members, who have long envied the great Body of the People, in the United States, the Liberties which they enjoy.—And, as a Proof of their being Enemies to the Rights of Mankind, permit me to refer you to the first Clause, of the 9th Section, of the first Article of the new Constitution, which is framed to deprive Millions of the human Species of their natural Rights, and, perhaps, as many more of their Lives in procuring others! That Clause, you will immediately perceive, has been purposely so contrived for reviving that wicked and inhuman Trade to Africa.—That Trade in Blood, and every Vice, of which the Avarice, Pride, Insolence and Cruelty, of Man is capable! A Trade, which, if ever permitted, will entail eternal Infamy on the United States, and all that they have ever said or done in Defence of Freedom.⟩—Will it not be said, that the greatest Sticklers for Liberty, are its worst Enemies?—For these Gentlemen, no doubt, mean to treat the United States, if they adopt the new Constitution, as they have some of their Colleagues; that is, make Cloaks of them, to cover their Wickedness.

At the Moment it is adopted by the States, in its present Form, that Moment the *external* Turpitude of it is transferred to the Adoptors; and the Framers of it will immediately say, it was called for by the People, of whom they were but the Servants, and, that the Adoption is a Proof of the Assertion.

Perhaps you may next enquire what can be done?—If you should, I will tell you, on Condition that you pardon the Anticipation, the Legislature may, and with the greatest Propriety, as its Delegate[3] has exceeded his Powers, or rejected them, consider all that he has done as a Nullity.—Would not this be a useful Lesson for Usurpers?

Indeed, I cannot see the Consistency or Propriety of Congress's sending it, or even permitting it to be sent, to the Legislatures that compose the present Union, when it entirely annihilates the Confederation under which they act, and which admits not of any thing more than an Emendation, as is evident by the 13th article.

But, as I have often told you, such is the unfortunate Lot of Humanity, that there are a Thousand brilliant Characters, to one that is always consistent, and, of this, Dr. Franklin, and Mr. John Dickinson, are two recent Examples among the Many. The Doctor is at the Head of a humane Institution for promoting the Emancipation of Slaves, or abolishing Slavery;[4] yet lends his Assistance to frame a Constitution which evidently has a Tendency not only to enslave all those whom it ought to protect; but avowedly encourages the enslaving of those over whom it can have no Manner of Right, to exercise the least shadow of Authority.

Mr. Dickinson, a few Years before the Revolution, publicly impeached the Doctor's Conduct for offering to attempt a Change in the chartered Privileges of Pennsylvania,[5] and now joins him in destroying a far superior Constitution, yes, thirteen far superior Constitutions, and opening a Trade which is a Disgrace to Humanity! Will not such Conduct leave these Gentlemen Monuments of much departed Fame? As I have several of their Publications by me, which, I imagine you never saw, I purpose in my Next, to let them speak for themselves, if you have no Objection.

I am, Dear Sir, very respectfully, yours, A COUNTRYMAN.
November 10, 1787.

1. This letter was reprinted in toto in the Providence *United States Chronicle*, 13 December; and the Philadelphia *Independent Gazetteer*, 26 April 1788. The text in angle brackets was reprinted in the Philadelphia *Freeman's Journal*, 28 November; Baltimore *Maryland Gazette*, 7 December; and *State Gazette of South Carolina*, 27 December.

2. George Washington.

3. Alexander Hamilton.

4. Benjamin Franklin was president of The Pennsylvania Society for Promoting the Abolition of Slavery, for the Relief of Free Negroes Unlawfully Held in Bondage, and for Improving the Condition of the African Race.

5. See "A Protest against the Appointment of Benjamin Franklin as Agent for the Colony of Pennsylvania," 26 October 1764, in Paul Leicester Ford, ed., *The Writings of John Dickinson* (*Memoirs* of the Historical Society of Pennsylvania, XIV [Philadelphia, 1895]), 147. The protest was printed in the *Pennsylvania Journal* on 1 November 1764.

Medium
New York Journal, 21 November 1787[1]

⟨MR. GREENLEAF, I have read with attention most of the publications respecting the new constitution, without bias or prejudice in favor of either fœderal or antifœderal party—my researches have been solely directed to one grand object, which was to discover which of them had the greatest share of reason on its side.⟩

In all controversial matters, and especially those of a political nature, men are apt to run into extremes, to what party soever they belong, and for the sake of supporting an argument, which is friendly to a favorite system, will wade through thick and thin, and often put reason and conscience to the torture. How far such a method of speaking and acting is repugnant to the dictates of moral honesty and genuine pa triotism, is too obvious not to be easily discerned.

⟨My candid opinion is, that most of the anonymous publications which have lately come forth on both sides of the question, are well intended, and whether right or wrong, the public is certainly indebted to the authors for the pains they have taken to investigate a subject, on which the welfare of millions, yet unborn, so evidently depends.⟩

I find that all are clearly agreed in the truth of this position; that an energetic Fœderal Government is essential to our happiness and existence as a nation.

Now, sir, I presume no one has yet called in question the sufficiency of the new constitution in point of energy. The only thing, therefore, remaining to be decided is, whether under this constitution our essential freedom can be maintained.

An hot brained Fœderalist will tell you, that it must be adopted, hastily adopted, without limitation or reserve; and I have known some go so far, as to call in the assistance of *tar* and *feathers*[2] against such as were of different sentiment.

The Anti-Fœderalists, in general, are more moderate, but equally obstinate. Some of them would reject the whole, purely, because some few parts of it do not meet with their approbation.

Persons of the above description are swayed by passion, not by reason, and should not be regarded by the honest and sensible part of the community. ⟨For my own part, I look with contempt upon the sophistry of the self conceited Cato, who promised a great deal and has performed nothing; and smile at the bombast of Curtius, whose "universal knowledge" seems to be but a medley of hard words.⟩

I really think, sir, that if a bill of rights had accompanied our new constitution, little or no opposition would have been made to it. It may be true, that it is defective, but none have yet been able to maintain that it is materially so. We have, however, much reason to expect amendments, if necessary, from our representatives who act under it in the first instance. In short, we cannot hazard much, provided we are previously secured by a bill of rights. This with the Anti-Fœderalists seems to be the thread on which hangs suspended all their hopes and wishes.

Let those, therefore, who call themselves Fœderalists, lay aside a little of their arrogance, and instead of abusing, endeavour to convince their fellow citizens of the necessity of embracing the constitution as it stands, the impracticability of securing a better one; and that anarchy will be the consequence of its rejection. Let them unite with their brethren in recommending a bill of rights, which is, in fact, the best security we can have against the encroachments of despotism, and I dare flatter myself, that our state will not be the last that shall accede to it.

1. Reprinted: Boston *American Herald,* 3 December; *Worcester Magazine,* 13 December; Philadelphia *Independent Gazetteer,* 24 December; Springfield, Mass., *Hampshire Chronicle,* 25 December. The last three newspapers omitted the text in angle brackets. For a response to "Medium," see "A Citizen," *New York Journal,* 24 November (below).

2. Probably a reference to a Federalist article signed "Tar and Feathers" that appeared in the Philadelphia *Independent Gazetteer* on 28 September (RCS:Pa., 148–49). "Tar and Feathers" was reprinted in the *New York Morning Post* on 4 October. This writer threatened an Antifederalist author with "a coat of TAR and FEATHERS." "Tar and Feathers" appeared again in the *Gazetteer* on 2 October (RCS:Pa., 152–53).

Publius: The Federalist 10 (James Madison)
New York Independent Journal, 22 November 1787

Union as check on inevitable factions. For text, see CC:285. For reprintings, see Appendix IV, below.

Cato V
New York Journal, 22 November 1787

On 19 November the printer of the *New York Journal* announced that "Cato" V and "Cincinnatus" IV were "reserved for next Thursday's [22 November] Paper." The *New York Journal* had become a daily newspaper on 19 November and the printer wanted to continue to publish the "Cato" and "Cincinnatus" essays on Thursdays because that day's newspaper had "*a more general Circulation in the Country*" (see "Note on Sources," above). "Cato" V was reprinted in the *Daily Advertiser,* 24 and 26 November, and *Albany Gazette,* 6 December. For a response to "Cato" V, see "Americanus" V, *Daily Advertiser,* 12 December (below).

To the CITIZENS *of the State of* NEW-YORK.

In my last number[1] I endeavored to prove that the language of the article relative to the establishment of the executive of this new government was vague and inexplicit, that the great powers of the President, connected with his duration in office would lead to oppression and ruin. That he would be governed by favorites and flatterers, or that a dangerous council would be collected from the great officers of state;—that the ten miles square, if the remarks of one of the wisest men,[2] drawn from the experience of mankind, may be credited, would be the asylum of the base, idle, avaricious and ambitious, and that the court would possess a language and manners different from yours; that a vice-president is as unnecessary, as he is dangerous in his influence— that the president cannot represent you, because he is not of your own immediate choice, that if you adopt this government, you will incline to an arbitrary and odious aristocracy or monarchy—that the president possessed of the power, given him by this frame of government differs but very immaterially from the establishment of monarchy in Great-Britain, and I warned you to beware of the fallacious resemblance that is held out to you by the advocates of this new system between it and your own state governments.

And here I cannot help remarking, that inexplicitness seems to pervade this whole political fabric: certainty in political compacts, which Mr. Coke *calls the mother and nurse of repose and quietness*,[3] the want of which induced men to engage in political society, has ever been held by a wise and free people as essential to their security; as on the one hand it fixes barriers which the ambitious and tyrannically disposed magistrate dare not overleap, and on the other, becomes a wall of safety to the community—otherwise stipulations between the governors and governed are nugatory; and you might as well deposit the important powers of legislation and execution in one or a few and permit them to govern according to their disposition and will; but the world is too full of examples, which prove that *to live by one man's will became the cause of all men's misery*.[4] Before the existence of express political compacts it was reasonably implied that the magistrate should govern with wisdom and justice, but mere implication was too feeble to restrain the unbridled ambition of a bad man, or afford security against negligence, cruelty, or any other defect of mind. It is alledged that the opinions and manners of the people of America, are capable to resist and prevent an extension of prerogative or oppression; but you must recollect that opinion and manners are mutable, and may not always be a permanent obstruction against the encroachments of government; that the progress of a commercial society begets luxury, the parent of inequality, the foe to virtue, and the enemy to restraint; and that ambition and voluptuousness aided by flattery, will teach magistrates, where limits are not explicitly fixed to have separate and distinct interests from the people, besides it will not be denied that government assimilates the manners and opinions of the community to it. Therefore, a general presumption that rulers will govern well is not a sufficient security.—You are then under a sacred obligation to provide for the safety of your posterity, and would you now basely desert their interests, when by a small share of prudence you may transmit to them a beautiful political patrimony, which will prevent the necessity of their travelling through seas of blood to obtain that, which your wisdom might have secured:— It is a duty you owe likewise to your own reputation, for you have a great name to lose; you are characterised as cautious, prudent and jealous in politics; whence is it therefore, that you are about to precipitate yourselves into a sea of uncertainty, and adopt a system so vague, and which has discarded so many of your valuable rights:—Is it because you do not believe that an American can be a tyrant? If this be the case you rest on a weak basis, Americans are like other men in similar situations, when the manners and opinions of the community are changed by the causes I mentioned before, and your political compact inexplicit, your posterity will find that great power connected with ambition, luxury, and flattery, will as readily produce a Caesar, Caligula, Nero, and Domitian in America, as the same causes did in the Roman empire.

But the next thing to be considered in conformity to my plan, is the first article of this new government, which comprises the erection of the house of representatives and senate, and prescribes their various powers and objects of legislation. The most general objections to the first article, are that bi-ennial elections for representatives are a departure from the safe democratical principles of annual ones—that the number of representatives are too few; that the apportionment and principles of increase are unjust; that no attention has been paid to either the numbers or property in each state in forming the senate; that the mode in which they are appointed and their duration, will lead to the establishment of an aristocracy; that the senate and president are improperly connected, both as to appointments, and the making of treaties, which are to become the supreme law of the land; that the judicial in some measure, to wit, as to the trial of impeachments is placed in the senate a branch of the legislative, and some times a branch of the executive: that Congress have the improper power of making or altering the regulations prescribed by the different legislatures, respecting the time, place, and manner of holding elections for representatives; and the time and manner of choosing senators; that standing armies may be established, and appropriation of money made for their support, for two years; that the militia of the most remote state may be marched into those states situated at the opposite extreme of this continent; that the slave trade, is to all intents and purposes permanently established; and a slavish capitation, or poll-tax, may at any time be levied—these are some of the many evils that will attend the adoption of this government.

But with respect to the first objection, it may be remarked that a well digested democracy has this advantage over all others, to wit, that it affords to many the opportunity to be advanced to the supreme command, and the honors they thereby enjoy fills them with a desire of rendering themselves worthy of them; hence this desire becomes part of their education, is matured in manhood, and produces an ardent affection for their country, and it is the opinion of the great Sidney, and Montesquieu that this in a great measure produced by annual election of magistrates.[5]

If annual elections were to exist in this government, and learning and information to become more prevalent, you never will want men to execute whatever you could design—Sidney observes *that a well governed state is as fruitful to all good purposes as the seven headed serpent is said to have been in evil; when one head is cut off, many rise up in the place of it.* He remarks further, that *it was also thought, that free cities by frequent elections of magistrates became nurseries of great and able men, every man endeavoring to excel others, that he might be advanced to the honor he had no other title to, than what might arise from his merit, or reputation,*[6] but the framers of this *perfect government,* as it is called, have departed from this democratical principle, and established bi-ennial elections, for the house of representatives, who are to be chosen by the people, and sextennial for the senate, who are to be chosen by the legislatures of the different states, and have given to the executive the unprecedented power of making temporary senators, in case of vacancies, by resignation or otherwise,[7] and so far forth establishing a precedent for virtual representation (though in fact, their original appointment is virtual) thereby influencing the choice of the legislatures, or if they should not be so complaisant as to conform to his appointment—offence will be given to the executive and the temporary members, will appear ridiculous by rejection; this temporary member, during his time of appointment, will of course act by a power derived from the executive, and for, and under his immediate influence.

It is a very important objection to this government, that the representation consists of so few; too few to resist the influence of corruption, and the temptation to treachery, against which all governments ought to take precautions—how guarded you have been on this head, in your own state constitution, and yet the number of senators and representatives proposed for this vast continent, does not equal those of your own state;[8] how great the disparity, if you compare them with the aggregate numbers in the United States. The history of representation in England, from which we have taken our model of legislation, is briefly this, before the institution of legislating by deputies, the whole free part of the community usually met for that purpose; when this became impossible, by the increase of numbers, the community was divided into districts, from each of which was sent such a number of deputies as was a complete representation of the various numbers and orders of citizens within them; but can it be asserted with truth, that six men can be a complete and full representation of the numbers and various orders of the people in this state?[9] Another thing may be suggested against the small number of representatives is, that but few of you will have the chance of sharing even in this branch of the legislature; and that the choice will be confined to a very few; the more complete it is, the better will your interests be preserved, and the greater the opportunity you will have to participate in government, one of the principal securities of a free people; but this subject has been so ably and fully treated by a writer under the signature of Brutus,[10] that I shall content myself with referring you to him thereon, reserving further observations on the other objections I have mentioned, for my future numbers.

1. See "Cato" IV, *New York Journal*, 8 November (above).

2. Montesquieu, *Spirit of Laws*, I, Book III, chapter V, 34–35.

3. Edward Coke, *The Second Part of the Institutes of the Laws of England* . . . (2 vols., London, 1797), I, *A Proeme*. The second part of the *Institutes* was first published in 1642, eight years after Coke's death.

4. Richard Hooker, *Of the Lawes of Ecclesiasticall Politie, Books I–V, [1594]* (Menston, Eng., 1969), Book I, chapter 10, p. 72. Book I was published around 1594.

5. Algernon Sidney, *Discourses Concerning Government*, ed. Thomas G. West (Indianapolis, 1990), Chapter 2, section 21, pp. 200–1; and Montesquieu, *Spirit of Laws*, I, Book II, chapter III, 20. Sidney's *Discourses* were first published in 1698, fifteen years after his death. On 21 June 1788 Antifederalist John Williams repeated this argument, almost in the same words, in the New York Convention (V below).

6. Sidney, *Discourses*, Chapter 2, section 23, pp. 211–12; section 28, pp. 270–71.

7. In *The Federalist* 67, "Publius" charged that "Cato" had incorrectly assumed that the President would fill all vacancies in the U.S. Senate (*New York Packet*, 11 March 1788, CC:612).

8. Under the Constitution, if all thirteen states ratified, Congress was to consist of 26 Senators and 65 Representatives, making a total of 91. Under the New York constitution of 1777, the legislature was to consist of at least 24 senators and at least 70 assemblymen, making a total of at least 94 (Thorpe, V, 2629, 2631).

9. Under the Constitution, New York had only six representatives in the U.S. House of Representatives. On 21 June 1788 Antifederalist John Williams repeated this argument, almost in the same words, in the New York Convention (V below).

10. See "Brutus" III, *New York Journal*, 15 November (above).

Cincinnatus IV: To James Wilson, Esquire
New York Journal, 22 November 1787

The printer of the *New York Journal* received "Cincinnatus" IV on 15 November, stating that it "will be attended to." Four days later, he announced that the essay was "reserved for next Thursday's [22 November] Paper." (For the significance of wanting to print on Thursday, see the headnote to "Cato" V, *New York Journal*, 22 November, immediately above.) On 11 December the *Salem Mercury* reprinted paragraphs two through four of "Cincinnatus" IV which answered James Wilson's 6 October speech before a Philadelphia public meeting (CC:134. See also "New York Reprinting of James Wilson's 6 October Speech Before a Philadelphia Public Meeting," 13–25 October, above.). The *Mercury* preceded these paragraphs from "Cincinnatus" with a preface stating that the essay was "Supposed to have been written" by Virginia congressman Richard Henry Lee. This attribution undoubtedly came from an extract of a Wilmington, Del., letter asserting that Lee was "Cincinnatus" (*Pennsylvania Gazette*, 21 November, CC:280). The *Mercury* reprinted this extract immediately after the paragraphs taken from "Cincinnatus."

On 30 January 1788 the Antifederalist Philadelphia *Freeman's Journal* reprinted "Cincinnatus" IV with this prefatory statement by "L. M.": "Mr. BAILEY, Inclosed is the Fourth Number of Cincinnatus which you did not receive, owing to some mishap; it is no matter of surprise to me, that it was stopped." "L. M." refers to "Centinel's" charge that major Antifederalist articles from the *New York Journal*, such as "Brutus," "Cato," and "Cincinnatus," were not reprinted in Philadelphia during the meeting of the Pennsylvania Convention (20 November–15 December) because they had "miscarried in their conveyance." Federalist newspapers, however, did not miscarry ("Centinel" IX and XI, Philadelphia *Independent Gazetteer*, 8, 16 January, CC:427, 453. See also CC:Vol. 4, Appendix II, "The Controversy over the Post Office and the Circulation of Newspapers," especially pp. 540–47; and "New York Journal and the Post Office," 10 January–25 March, below.).

SIR, The public appear to me, sir, to be much indebted to you, for informing them; for what purpose a power was given by the proposed Constitution, of raising and supporting armies.—Some, indeed, might have suspected, that such a power, uncontrouled by any declaration, that the military should always be subject to the civil power, might be intended for the purposes of ambition. Your declaration has removed all doubt. Every principle of policy, you say, would be subverted unless we kept up armies—for what—for our defence?—no,—to support declarations of war—to strike home, with dispatch and secrecy, before the enemy can be apprized of your intention. Upon the same principle a small army would be ridiculous. Nothing less than the Prussian number, about 200,000 men would embrace this salutary object. And as you now say—"no man that regards the dignity and safety of his country can deny the necessity of a military force."—You will next affirm, that no one, for the same reason, can deny the necessity of a large army. The safety of the country, we have already experienced to depend, upon the militia. Switzerland has often experienced the same. Why then, sir, should you be so very positive, that for this purpose a military force is necessary?—But for the dignity of the country, that is for the ambition of its rulers, armies I confess are necessary; and not less in number than other ambitious rulers maintain, by grinding the face of the people. For every thousand in these armies a million of dollars must be levied upon the public, and such armies—raised and supported, would at once maintain the dignity of government, and ensure the submission of the people. We shall be as dignified as the Turks, and equally free.— The sole power of voting men, and money, is retained by the representative of the people in England. This is their shield and their defence against arbitrary power. Never has the King been able to obtain the extension of this vote beyond a year. But we are called upon, with all the solemnity of a constitutional act, to give it up for two years. And yet, sir, you talk of the controul and the restrictions which the new Constitution provides. There is, I confess, some dexterity in the negative terms in which this power is conceived—not more than two years. But what the Constitution permits, and what it grants are essentially the same. And since it seemed necessary to this almost all confiding Convention, to limit our confidence in this particular, the only rule that observation suggests is, that of England; where this confidence has never exceeded one year.

I come now, sir, to the most exceptionable part of the Constitution— the senate. In this, as in every other part, you are in the line of your profession, and on that ground assure your fellow citizens, that—"perhaps there never was a charge made with less reason, than that which predicts the institution of a baneful aristocracy in the Fœderal Senate." And yet your conscience smote you, sir, at the beginning, and compelled you to prefix a—perhaps to this strange assertion. The senate, you say, branches into two characters—the one legislative and the other executive. This phraseology is quaint, and the position does not state the whole truth. I am very sorry, sir, to be so often obliged to reprehend the suppression of information at the moment that you stood forth to instruct your fellow citizens, in what they were supposed not to understand. In this character, you should have abandoned your professional line, and told them, not only the truth, but the whole truth. The whole truth then is, that the same body, called the senate, is vested with— legislative—executive—and judicial powers. The two first you acknowlege; the last is conveyed in these words, sec. 3d. The senate shall have the sole power to try all impeachments. On this point then we are to come to issue—whether a senate so constituted is likely to produce a baneful aristocracy, which will swallow up the democratic rights and liberties of the nation.

To judge on this question, it is proper to examine minutely into the constitution and powers of the senate; and we shall then see with what anxious and subtle cunning it is calculated for the proposed purpose. 1st. It is removed from the people, being chosen by the legislatures— and exactly in the ratio of their removal from the people, do aristocratic principles constantly infect the minds of man. 2d. They endure, two thirds for four, and one third for six years, and in proportion to the duration of power, the aristocratic exercise of it, and attempts to extend it, are invariably observed to increase. 3d. From the union of the executive with the legislative functions, they must necessarily be longer together, or rather constantly assembled; and in proportion to their continuance together, will they be able to form effectual schemes for extending their own power, and reducing that of the democratic branch. If any one would wish to see this more fully illustrated, let him turn to the history of the Decemviri in Rome.[1] 4th. Their advice and consent being necessary to the appointment of all the great officers of state, both at home and abroad, will enable them to win over any opponents to their measures in the house of representatives, and give them the influence which, we see, accompanies this power in England; and which, from the nature of man, must follow it every where. 5th. The sole power of impeachment being vested in them, they have it in their power to controul the representative in this high democratic right; to screen from punishment, or rather from conviction, all high offenders, being their creatures, and to keep in awe all opponents to their power in high office. 6th. The union established between them and the vice president, who is made one of the corps, and will therefore be highly animated with the aristocratic spirit of it, furnishes them a powerful shield against popular suspicion and enquiry, he being the second man in the United States who stands highest in the confidence and estimation of the people. And lastly, the right of altering or amending money-bills, is a high additional power given them as a branch of the legislature, which their analogous branch, in the English parliament, could never obtain, because it has been guarded by the representatives of the people there, with the most strenuous solicitude as one of the vital principles of democratic liberty.

Is a body so vested with means to soften & seduce—so armed with power to screen or to condemn—so fortified against suspicion and enquiry—so largely trusted with legislative powers—so independent of and removed from the people—so tempted to abuse and extend these powers—is this a body which freemen ought ever to create, or which freemen can ever endure? Or is it not a monster in the political creation, which we ought to regard with horror? Shall we thus forge our own fetters? Shall we set up the idol, before which we shall soon be obliged, however, reluctantly to bow? Shall we consent to see a proud aristocracy erect his domineering crest in triumph over our prostrate liberties?

But we shall yet see more clearly, how highly favored this senate has been, by taking a similar view of the representative body. This body is the true representative of the democratic part of the system; the shield and defence of the people. This body should have weight from its members, and the high controul which it should alone possess. We can form no idea of the necessary number in this untried system, to give due weight to the democratic part, but from the example of England. Had it not been intended to humble this branch, it would have been fixed, at least, at their standard. We are to have one representative for every thirty thousand—they have nearly one for ten thousand souls. Their number is about six millions; their representatives five hundred and fifteen. When we are six millions, we shall have only two hundred representatives. In point of number therefore and the weight derived from it, the representative proposed by the constitution is remarkably feeble. It is farther weakened by the senate being allowed not only to reject, but to alter and amend money-bills. Its transcendent and incommunicable power of impeachment—that high source of its dignity and controul—in which alone the majesty of the people feels his sceptre, and bears aloft his fasces—is rendered ineffectual, by its being triable before its rival branch, the senate, the patron and prompter of the measures against which it is to sit in judgment. It is therefore most manifest, that from the very nature of the constitution the right of impeachment apparently given, is really rendered ineffectual. And this is contrived with so much art, that to discover it you must bring together various and distant parts of the constitution, or it will not strike the examiner, that the same body that advises the executive measures of government which are usually the subject of impeachment, are the sole judges on such impeachments. They must therefore be both party and judge, and must condemn those who have executed what they advised. Could such a monstrous absurdity have escaped men who were not determined, at all events, to vest all power in this aristocratic body? Is it not plain, that the senate is to be exalted by the humiliation of the democracy. A democracy which, thus bereft of its powers, and shorn of its strength; will stand a melancholy monument of popular impotence.

Hitherto I have examined your senate by its intrinsic and its comparative powers. Let us next examine, how far the principles of its constitution are compatible with what our own constitutions lay down, and what the best writers on the subject have determined to be essential to free and good government.

In every state constitution, with a very trifling exception in that of Massachusetts, the legislative and executive powers are vested in different and independent bodies.—Will any one believe, that it is because we are become wiser, that in twelve years we are to overthrow every system which reason and experience taught us was right. Or is it, that a few men, forming a plan at Philadelphia subversive of all former principles, then posting to Congress, and passing it there, and next dispersing themselves in the several states to propagate their errors, and, if they can, get chosen into the state conventions; are actuated by motives of interest and bad ambition? I should be very unwilling to believe the latter, and yet it is utterly incomprehensible, how such a systematic violation of all that has been deemed wise and right, from which no other result can be expected, but the establishment of a baneful aristocracy, could have been recommended to a free and enlightened people.

"Lorsque dans la meme personne, says Montesquieu, ou dans le meme corps de magistrature, la puissance legislative est re-unie a la puissance executive; il n'y a point de liberte; parce qu'on peut craindre que le meme monarque, ou le memc Scnat ne fasse des loix tyranniques, pour les executer tyranniquement." "When the legislative and executive powers are united in the same person, or in the same corps, there can be no liberty. Because, it may be feared, that the same monarch or senate will make tyrannical laws, that they may execute them tyrannically."[2] I am aware that this great man is speaking of a senate being the whole legislative; whereas the one before us is but a branch of the proposed legislature. But still the reason applies, inasmuch as the legislative power of the senate will enable it to negative all bills that are meant to controul the executive, and from being secure of preventing any abridgment, they can watch every pliant hour of the representative body to promote an enlargement of the executive powers. One thing at least is certain, that by making this branch of the legislature participant in the executive, you not only prevent the legislature from being a check upon the executive, but you inevitably prevent its being checked or controuled by the other branch.

To the authority of Montesquieu, I shall add that of Mr. de Lolme; whose disquisition on government, is allowed to be deep, solid, and ingenious. ["]Il ne suffisoit pas, says he, d'oter aux legislateurs l'execution des loix, par consequent, l'exemption qui en est la suite immediate; il falloit encore, leur oter ce qui eut produit les memes effects—l'espoir de jamais se l'attribuer["]—["]It is not only necessary to take from the legislature the executive power which would exempt them from the laws; but they should not have even a hope of being ever able to arrogate to themselves that power."[3] To remove this hope from their expectation, it would have been proper, not only to have previously laid down, in a declaration of rights, that these powers should be forever separate and incommunicable; but the frame of the proposed constitution, should have had that separation religiously in view, through all its parts. It is manifest this was not the object of its framers, but, that on the contrary there is a studied mixture of them in the senate as necessary to erect it into that potent aristocracy which it must infallibly produce. In pursuit of this darling object, than which no greater calamity can be brought upon the people, another egregious error in constitutional principles is committed. I mean that of dividing the executive powers, between the senate and the president. Unless more harmony and less ambition should exist between these two executives than ever yet existed between men in power, or than can exist while human nature is as it is: this absurd division must be productive of constant contentions for the lead, must clog the execution of government to a mischievous, and sometimes to a disgraceful degree, and if they should unhappily harmonize in the same objects of ambition, their number and their combined power, would preclude all fear of that responsibility, which is one of the great securities of good, and restraints on bad governments. Upon these principles M. de Lolme has foreseen that "the effect of a division of the executive power is the establishment of absolute power in one of continual contention"; he therefore lays it down, as a general rule "pour q'un etat soit tranquille il faut que le pouvoir executif y soit rèunie"—for the tranquillity of the state it is necessary that the executive power should be in one.[4] I will add, that this singlehood of the executive, is indispensably necessary to effective execution, as well as to the responsibility and rectitude of him to whom it is entrusted.

By this time I hope it is evident from reason and authority, that in the constitution of the senate there is much cunning and little wisdom; that we have much to fear from it, and little to hope, and then it must necessarily produce a baneful aristocracy, by which the democratic rights of the people will be overwhelmed.

It was probably upon this principle that a member of the convention, of high and unexceeded reputation for wisdom and integrity, is said to have emphatically declared, that *he would sooner lose his right hand, than put his name to such a constitution.*[5]

1. In 451 B.C. a Commission of Ten was created in the Roman Republic in response to pressure brought by plebeians who wanted laws published so that patricians could not interpret custom as they saw fit. These *decemvirs*, all patricians, issued a code of laws consisting of ten tables. These laws were sanctioned by the *Comitia Centuriata*, or legislative assembly, that was composed of both patricians and plebeians. The next year another commission, which included some plebeians, added two more tables, which Cicero later labeled as unjust. The commission began to rule dictatorially, bringing on a reign of terror. Eventually, the plebeians seceded from the commission, the *decemvirs* abdicated, and constitutional government was restored in 449. The code of the Twelve Tables, however, remained in effect.

2. *Spirit of Laws*, I, Book XI, chapter VI, 222.

3. Jean Louis De Lolme, *The Constitution of England* . . . (London, 1816), Book II, chapter X, 281. This book was first published in 1771.

4. *Ibid.*, Book II, chapter III, 221–22.

5. The reference is to George Mason, a Virginia delegate to the Constitutional Convention, who declared in the Convention on 31 August "that he would sooner chop off his right hand than put it to the Constitution as it now stands" (Farrand, II, 479). On 25 October, in a debate in the Virginia House of Delegates, Mason said that "I would have lost this hand, before it should have marked my name to the new government" (RCS:Va., 114. Reports of this debate were reprinted in the *Daily Advertiser* and *New York Morning Post* on 17 November.). See also Philadelphia *Independent Gazetteer*, 27 October, for a similar statement (RCS:Va., 125. The *Gazetteer's* item was reprinted in the *New York Morning Post* on 1 November.).

Americanus II
New York Daily Advertiser, 23 November 1787

Experience has produced ample conviction in the minds of all of us, that a Federal Government, which admits of an Independent Sovereignty in the States individually, can never be so construed as to command the resources, and bring into action the collective force of the nation. Indeed, had our situation been similar to that of the Swiss Cantons, the inconveniencies of such a confederation would probably not have been greatly felt. Inhabiting a country rough and mountainous throughout; so inaccessible that there can exist no motive to provoke hostilities either with their neighbours or amongst themselves—from poverty and remoteness from navigation rendered incapable of ever becoming commercial: Amongst a people thus circumstanced, there can happen but few occasions for national exertion. How widely does the country we possess differ from this—extending a length of two thousand miles along a sea coast, indented by innumerable harbours, and comprehending infinite variety with respect to soil, climate and product. From the natural consequences of such a situation, we feel at every turn the most pressing necessity for the vigorous and unremitted exertions of a National Government. The Convention have certainly acted wisely in throwing the Confederation totally aside, and erecting in its place an entire new fabric. This was a decisive boldness I had not looked for. I was therefore the more strongly impressed in its favor, when, for the first time, I saw this Constitution. The writings of those gentlemen in opposition to it, whatever effects they may have produced on others, have hitherto tended only to fix more firmly the sentiments I had imbibed in the first instance. For my own part, I must say, it has pleased me much, that some of these champions have shown themselves *openly* in the field of controversy—had they remained altogether *under cover*, and kept up only a sort of Indian fight, we must have remained in a great measure ignorant of their total strength. I have, however, a strong suspicion that Cato has nearly exhausted his quiver, and will be put to some difficulty to proceed without renewing the attack in the same quarter, or in other words, repeating the same story over again.

In his last number,[1] he has urged his objections against "the Executive branch of this new System." The first paragraph of the 1st sect. of the 2d article, is thus expressed. ["]The Executive power shall be vested in a President of the United States of America. He shall hold his office during the term of four years, and, together with the Vice-President, chosen for the same term, be elected as follows." "This inexplicitness," he tells us, "perhaps may lead to an establishment for life." Cato must certainly be hard pushed for argument, when he can advance so paltry a cavil as this. Without a total change of sentiment in the majority of the people of these States, such "an establishment for life" could never be effected, though the words of the above quoted paragraph were much more inexplicit, than Cato pretends they are at present.

The comparison which he has thought to his purpose to institute between a BRITISH MONARCH and a PRESIDENT under the Constitution is surely unworthy of attention. It must excite ridicule and contempt in every man when he considers on one side, the dreadful catalogue of unnecessary, but dangerous, prerogatives, which, in the British Government, is vested in the Crown; and, on the other side, takes a view of the powers with which this Constitution has cloathed the President. Imperial dignity, and hereditary succession—constituting an independent branch of the Legislature—the creation of Peers and distribution of titles and dignities—the supremacy of a national church—the appointment of Arch-bishops and Bishops—the power of convening, proroguing, and dissolving the Parliament—the fundamental maxim that the King can do no wrong—to be above the reach of all Courts of law—to be accountable to no power whatever in the nation—his person to be sacred and inviolable—all these unnecessary, but dangerous prerogatives, independent of many others, such as the sole power of making war and peace—making treaties, leagues and alliances—the collection, management and expenditure of an immense revenue, deposited annually in the Royal Exchequer—with the appointment of an almost innumerable tribe of officers, dependent thereon—all these prerogatives, besides a great many more, which it is unnecessary to detail here, (none of all which are vested in the President) put together, form an accumulation of power of immense magnitude; but which, it seems, are only "immaterial incidents."

Let the arrangement and distribution of the executive branch, be what it may, whether it be split and divided into a variety of distinct parts—or put into commission and executed by a body of ten or twenty members, this however I will aver, and challenge Cato to gainsay it if he can, that every power which by this Constitution is vested in a President, is *indispensably necessary* to good Government, and must of consequence be entrusted somewhere. If Cato therefore, in the place of forming the above idle and ridiculous comparison, had pointed out to us in what manner the powers of the executive branch could have been modified, and distributed to more advantage, and with greater security to liberty, he had certainly done more to the purpose.

But you do not, Cato, deal fairly either with us or your friend Montesquieu. You institute a comparison between a King of England, and a President, and because you find that some of the powers necessarily vested in this President, and some of the prerogatives of that King are alike, you place them on a footing, and talk "of a President possessing the powers of a Monarch." But admitting that a President, and a King of England, were as like as two peas; this, however, will by no means serve your turn. Montesquieu is here speaking expressly of the Court of an absolute Monarch. What similitude Cato's ingenuity may discover between a President, and a King of Spain, or a Grand Monarch, I can form no conjecture.

But he quarrels too with the revisory power vested in the President. Of what strange heterogeneous materials are we poor mortals compounded! What Cato here reprobates, I must confess I esteem as one of the most excellent things in the Constitution.

But as Cato is so fond of Montesquieu as to quote him at every turn, and has attempted to establish his positions as "irrefragable axioms,"[2] it is surprising to me that he has never met, in the course of his reading in this favorite author, an authority exactly in point. With a view therefore, of easing his apprehensions respecting the dangerous powers of a President, I shall here transcribe it. "The Executive power ought to be in the hands of a Monarch, because this branch of Government

having need of dispatch, is better administered by one than by many."³
He is here speaking of the Constitution of England, which he afterwards tells us is "the best that could possibly be imagined by men."⁴

"The safety of the people in a Republic depends on the share or
proportion they have in the Government."⁵ The justness of this proportion appears at first view so obvious, that the mind gives it its assent
without a thought of examination. But notwithstanding this plausible
appearance, it happens a little unfortunately for this pretty theory, that
experience has afforded us the most ample proofs that the people
themselves are totally unfit for the exercise of *any* of the powers of
Government. They are obliged from necessity, to confide in others for
the execution of these important trusts. Indeed good Government depends altogether on the proper delegation of the several powers
thereof. I might here, after the example of our worthy Minister at the
Court of Great-Britain, cause all the Republican Governments that have
ever existed in the world, whether ancient or modern, to pass in review
before my gentle readers.⁶ But in pity to them I shall refrain. I will
resist the temptation though great, and forego this glorious opportunity
(which may perhaps never offer again during the course of a long life)
of displaying an immensity of erudition. Suffice it to say, that on such
an investigation it would be found invariably, that exactly in proportion
to "the share the people have in the Government," has anarchy, violence, and the most shocking outrages and enormities of every kind
prevailed. All power however in a free Government, must be derived
originally from the people. *But of themselves they are absolutely incapable
of the exercise of any.* This is an "axiom," I will venture to assert, much
more "irrefragable" than any Cato has yet thought fit to give us from
Montesquieu's spirit of laws, but which, by the by, if it had suited his
purpose, he might have found there.

What Montesquieu has said of Harrington may in some measure be
applied to Cato and his coadjutors. "Harrington," says he, "in his
Oceana, has also enquired into the utmost degree of liberty to which
the *Constitution* of a State may be carried. But of him indeed it may be
said, that for want of *knowing* the nature of *real* liberty, he busied himself in the pursuit of an *imaginary* one; and that he built a Chalcedon,
tho' he had a Byzantium before his eyes.["]⁷

1. See "Cato" IV, *New York Journal,* 8 November (above).
2. In his third number, "Cato" states that "The governments of Europe have taken
their limits and form from adventitious circumstances, and nothing can be argued on
the motive of agreement from them; but these adventitious political principles, have
nevertheless produced effects that have attracted the attention of philosophy, which has
established axioms in the science of politics therefrom, as irrefragable as any in Euclid"
(*New York Journal,* 25 October, above).

3. *Spirit of Laws*, I, Book XI, chapter VI, 229.

4. *Spirit of Laws*, I, Book XI, chapter, VIII, 240.

5. See "Cato" IV, *New York Journal*, 8 November (above).

6. A reference to John Adams's *Defence of the Constitutions*, which, in part, is a detailed study of ancient and modern confederacies (CC:16).

7. *Spirit of Laws*, I, Book XI, chapter VI, 237. *Oceana* was published in 1656 by English political theorist James Harrington.

A Countryman II (Hugh Hughes) New York Journal, 23 November 1787[1]

Letters from a Gentleman in Dutchess County, to his Friend in New-York.

In the Conclusion of my First, of the 19th [i.e., 10th] current,[2] I promised that Mr. Dickenson, or the famous Author of the Farmer's Letters, and Doctor Franklin should speak for themselves; I now offer you as a Specimen of the Farmer's Rhetoric, the second Paragraph of his first Letter, which appears thus—"From my Infancy I was taught to love Humanity and Liberty. Enquiry and Experience have since confirmed my Reverence for the Lessons then given me, by convincing me more fully of their Truth and Excellence. Benevolence towards Mankind excites Wishes for their Welfare, and such Wishes endear the Means of fulfilling them. Those can be found in Liberty alone, and therefore her sacred Cause ought to be espoused by every Man, on every occasion, to the utmost of his Power. As a Charitable, but poor, Person does not withhold his Mite, because he can not relieve all the Distresses of the Miserable; so let not any honest Man suppress his Sentiments concerning Freedom, however small their Influence is likely to be. Perhaps he may touch some Wheel that will have a greater Effect than he expects."[3] What gracious Sentiments, and how sweetly expressed!—But what are Sentiments, or the tenderest Expressions, when not accompanied by corresponding Actions? They certainly render the Author a greater Object of our Pity, if not of Contempt.—How is it possible to reconcile the first Clause of the 9th Section, in the first Article of the new Constitution,[4] with such universal Benevolence to all Mankind?

Will this Gentleman say, that the Africans do not come within the Description of "Mankind?" If he should, will he be believed?—Besides, he seems to have run counter to a generally received Maxim in educating the rational as well as the irrational Creation; as he acknowledges, that he was early instituted in Virtue, which, now, in advanced Life, he seems either to have forgotten or stiffled?

Had Cornwallis, Rawdon, Arnold, or any of the British, Marauding,

Butchers, signed such a Clause, there would have been a Consistency; but, for the benevolent Author of the Farmer's Letters, which every where seem to breathe the pure Spirit of Liberty and Humanity, to lend his once venerated Name, for promoting that which the Framers of the Clause were either ashamed or afraid, openly, to avow, exceeds Credulity itself, were it not for occular Demonstration.

Is this the Way by which we are to demonstrate our Gratitude to Providence, for his divine Interposition in our Favor, when oppressed by Great Britain?—Who could have even imagined, that Men lately professing the highest Sense of Justice and the Liberties of Mankind, could so soon and easily be brought to give a Sanction to the greatest Injustice and Violation of those very Liberties? Strange Inconsistency and painful Reflection!—And the more so, when it is considered, that not only Individuals in Europe, as well as in each of these states; but that several of the Nations in Europe have, for some years before the Revolution, been endeavouring to put a Stop to a Trade, which was a Disgrace to the very Name of Christianity itself.—Nay, that Numbers among those whom we so lately considered as Enemies to Liberty, are now using every Means in their Power to abolish Slavery! Will not a contrary Conduct of the States tarnish the Lustre of the American Revolution, by violating the Law of Nations, and entailing endless Servitude on Millions of the human Race, and their unborn Posterity? Can any Person, who is not deeply interested in enslaving this Country, believe, that the Contrivers of such a diabolical Scheme had any Regard for the most sacred Rights of human Nature?

It really seems to have been, as Mr. Wilson acknowledged, a mere Matter of Accomodation between the Northern and Southern States; that is, if you will permit us to import Africans as Slaves, we will consent that you may export Americans, as Soldiers;[5] for this the new Constitution clearly admits, by the 2d Clause of the 6th Article, which says, "that this Constitution and the Laws of the United States which shall be made in pursuance thereof, and all Treaties made, or which shall be made under the Authority of the United States, shall be the supreme Law of the Land, &c. any Thing in the Constitution or Laws of any State to the Contrary notwithstanding."

May not Treaties be immediately entered into with some of the Nations of Europe for assisting them with Troops, which, if they do not enlist voluntarily, may, by this Clause, be detached and transported to the West or East-Indies, &c.?

I ask the Doctor's Pardon, I promised in my first, that he should be permitted to speak for himself in this; but Time will not now admit of it—He shall have the Preference of opening my next.

I am, with every Sentiment of Esteem, Dear Sir, Your most Obedient,
A COUNTRYMAN.
November 17, 1787.

1. Reprinted: Philadelphia *Independent Gazetteer*, 28 April 1788.

2. See "A Countryman" I, *New York Journal*, 21 November (above).

3. John Dickinson, *Letters from a Farmer in Pennsylvania*. See Paul Leicester Ford, ed., *The Writings of John Dickinson* (*Memoirs* of the Historical Society of Pennsylvania, XIV [Philadelphia, 1895]), Letter I, 307–8. Dickinson placed the phrase "may touch some wheel" within quotation marks and indicated that it was taken from Alexander Pope. (See Pope, *An Essay on Man* [1733], Epistle I, line 59.) "Letters of a Farmer in Pennsylvania" were printed in twelve installments in the Philadelphia *Pennsylvania Chronicle* between 2 December 1767 and 15 February 1768, and in March 1768 they appeared as a pamphlet.

4. This clause prohibited Congress from closing the African slave trade before 1808.

5. In James Wilson's widely circulated 6 October speech to a Philadelphia public meeting (CC:134), no mention is made of a compromise or bargain between the Northern and Southern states that involved the slave trade.

New York Journal, 23 November 1787

MR. GREENLEAF, *Please to insert the following Extract of a Letter from a Gentleman in Massachusetts to his Friend—and you will oblige*
A CUSTOMER.

My dear Brother, I have perused the constitution with as much attention as I am capable of. I have read the pieces that have been written for, and against it.—The first appear to be founded in general observations and declamations; many of the last take up the constitution fairly, and the observations and arguments have not been answered— nor have there been any attempts to answer some of the most important of them. I did not at first comprehend all that is contained in the plan proposed. It is extremely well calculated not to make unfavorable impressions at the first reading. Many have acknowledged to me, that on the first perusal it pleased them—but that the more they consider upon it, the less they liked it.

The three important powers to be conveyed by the people to the legislature, by this constitution, are,

First. To make laws affecting the life, liberty, and property of the citizens of the United States, in every possible case.

Secondly. To abolish the trial by jury in all cases.

Thirdly. To alter the constitution itself, so far as amendments will ever be necessary.

The two first have been amply discussed in the public papers. It has been established, incontrovertibly, that the plan contains these two powers.

The first, is founded as follows, Art. 1. sec. 8. paragraph 18. "To make all laws which shall be necessary and proper for carrying into execution the foregoing powers, and all other powers vested by this constitution in the government of the United States, or in any department or office thereof." The primary objects of the constitution are expressed, "to form a more perfect union, establish justice, insure domestic tranquility, provide for the common defence, promote the general welfare, and secure the blessings of liberty to ourselves and our posterity." The legislature will alone be the judges of what laws will be necessary and proper, relative to these indefinite objects. The next is the second paragraph of the sixth article. "This constitution, and the laws of the United States, which shall be made in pursuance thereof, and all treaties made, or which shall be made under the authority of the United States, shall be the supreme law of the land; and the judges, in every state, shall be bound thereby, any thing in the constitutions, or laws of any state, to the contrary notwithstanding."

The legislatures of the states have annexed very different penalties to the crime of forgery. But when Congress, or the proposed legislature, annex a penalty to this crime, without limiting the extent of the operation of the act to citizens of different states, or to forging the public securities, or other papers of the United States, as they may do, it will then be the supreme law of the land. I do not see, but Congress must make laws for all the variety of cases that can possibly happen; and then will the municipal laws of the different states be wholly annihilated, by the supreme law of the land.

With respect to the second article—It is founded upon the 3d article, 2d sec. and 1st paragraph. "The judicial power shall extend to all cases, in law and equity arising under this constitution, the laws of the United States, &c." And second paragraph—"In all cases affecting ambassadors, other public ministers, and consuls, and those in which a state shall be a party, the supreme court shall have original jurisdiction. In all the other cases before mentioned, the supreme court shall have appellate jurisdiction, both as to law and fact, with such exceptions, and under such regulations as the Congress shall make." As the supreme court are expressly vested with jurisdiction, both as to law and fact, in cases of appeal, and are only vested with original jurisdiction, in cases affecting ambassadors, other public ministers and consuls, and states; it seems, that in these last cases, the supreme court are not judges of the fact. A power expressly given in certain cases, strongly implies that it is not given, and is not to be exercised in any other case. This distinction was not attended to until writing down the last paragraph. I am willing to give it all the weight it is entitled to.

I do not recollect that the idea contained in the third proposition has yet made its appearance in public:—It however appears, to me, to

be an important one, and worthy of critical examination. My reasons
for this opinion, are contained in the primary objects, for which the
constitution is to be made—which are, to insure domestic tranquility,
promote the general welfare, and secure the blessings of liberty to ourselves and our posterity.—In the 1st art. sec. 8, paragraph 18, already
quoted, and in the 5th art.—"The Congress, whenever two thirds of
both houses shall deem it necessary, shall propose amendments to this
constitution, or, on the application of the legislatures of two thirds of
the several states, shall call a Convention for proposing amendments,
which, in either case, shall be valid to all intents and purposes, as part
of this constitution, when ratified by the legislatures of three fourths
of the several states, or by conventions in three fourths thereof, as the
one, or the other mode of ratification may be proposed by the Congress. Provided, that no amendments, which may be made prior to the
year 1808, shall in any manner affect the first and fourth clause in the
9th sec. of the 1st art. And that no state, without its consent, shall be
deprived of its equal suffrage in the senate."

There is no stipulation in this article, that no amendments shall be
made to the constitution, but by the legislatures of three fourths of the
states, or of conventions, as the case may be. It is not stipulated that
Congress shall, on the application of the legislatures of two thirds of
the states, call a convention for proposing amendments.

The plain language of this article is this, if two thirds of both houses
deem the proposing amendments necessary; not if they deem amendments necessary, they shall propose them. The word "propose" holds
a very important station in this article, and if it is intended that the
states alone shall amend the constitution, it ought to be removed to
the other side of the word "amendments."

If, therefore, Congress shall think amendments necessary to be
made, they will make them, and they will not think it necessary to
propose them to any body of men whatever.

It appears, to me, that the people, if they adopt this constitution, will
convey all the power they possess to the government of the United
States.—They will therefore want no amendment in this respect; for if
there should be any on this ground, to a diminution of power. It must,
therefore, be evident now, that no alterations can be made, or proposed, but such as will relate to the president, senate, and house of
representatives. It is not provided expressly, that there shall be a president and vice president chosen every four years; that the senate shall
be chosen every six years, and that the members of the house of representatives shall be chosen every two years. If therefore Congress
should deem it necessary to insure domestic tranquility, and to promote

the general welfare to make the president and senate hereditary in their offices, and to make the time and service of the members of the house seven years instead of two; it appears, to me, the constitution gives them a legal power to pass the necessary acts.

It is pretty evident, that the small states in the convention had an idea, that this power was lodged in Congress; and upon this principle only can we account for the last part of the article—"That no state, without its consent, shall be deprived of its equal suffrage in the senate."

To make a provision, at this time, that it shall not be in the power of the legislatures of three fourths of the states to alter the principles of representation in the senate, seems to be a useless and unnecessary precaution. The late convention have fully demonstrated what regard is to be paid to such provision—for notwithstanding, the present confederation provides, that no alteration shall be made in it, without the consent of all the legislatures,[1] yet, we find a plan proposed which may entirely exclude four states from the union. The provision, therefore, in this view has no weight in it. But in the other view, it is wise and cautious in the small states. Yet, there may hereafter be found an ambiguity in the words "equal suffrage." And the large states may insist upon having the number of their senators encreased, so as to give them an equal suffrage with the small states. This constitution will undoubtedly be the most unexceptionable—Therefore I do not see that the small states have secured any thing more, than a representation in the senate upon the principles of equity. It is expressly stipulated, that there shall be two senators from each state, and that each senator shall have one vote—yet, I do not find that it is stipulated that there shall be only two and no more.

I have several more observations to make, which I must postpone to another opportunity, and conclude with repeating, that the people are by the constitution to convey all the power they possess, or can convey, to the legislature.

That it is left with the legislature to alter the arrangement and deposit of the powers, in such manner as they may deem necessary.

On these principles alone can I account for Mr. Wilson's high encomium on the constitution,[2] for otherwise, it seems to contain the seeds of its own dissolution.

1. Article XIII of the Articles of Confederation states that "the Articles of this confederation shall be inviolably observed by every state, and the union shall be perpetual; nor shall any alteration at any time hereafter be made in any of them; unless such alteration be agreed to in a congress of the united states, and be afterwards confirmed by the legislatures of every state" (CDR, 93).

2. A reference to James Wilson's 6 October speech to a Philadelphia public meeting (CC:134). See also "New York Reprinting of James Wilson's 6 October Speech Before a Philadelphia Public Meeting," 13–25 October (above).

Charles Tillinghast to Timothy Pickering
New York, 24 November 1787[1]

On 24 November Charles Tillinghast wrote to Timothy Pickering, requesting his opinion on the Constitution. Enclosed with his letter, Tillinghast included a copy of the Antifederalist pamphlet *Letters from the Federal Farmer* that had gone on sale on 8 November (above). On 6 December Pickering, then serving as a Federalist delegate in the Pennsylvania Convention, replied that he would give his opinion as soon as he had time to write a long letter. He also stated that the Constitution should be adopted and that the "federal farmer is not a fair reasoner" (CC:288–B). On 24 December, nine days after the adjournment of the Pennsylvania Convention which ratified the Constitution, Pickering began a detailed and harsh criticism of "Federal Farmer" that he eventually sent to Tillinghast, hoping to alleviate his fears about the Constitution. According to Pickering who had voted to ratify the Constitution, it was the "best" that Americans "at present have any right to expect"; it should be "readily" adopted; and if experience dictated, it could eventually be amended (CC:288–C).

On 27 January 1788 Tillinghast sent a copy of Pickering's 24 December letter to fellow Antifederalist Hugh Hughes, to whom he had already sent Pickering's 6 December letter. Tillinghast told Hughes that he believed Pickering wanted the letter criticizing "Federal Farmer" published. Tillinghast, however, refused to do so because Pickering's reasons did not convince him. Pickering, declared Tillinghast, showed "more *Temper* in this last letter, than he ordinarily does" (below).

During the Revolution, Tillinghast served under Pickering as assistant Continental quartermaster general. Pickering (1745–1829) was adjutant general of the Continental Army, 1777–78, and Continental quartermaster general, 1780–85. After the Revolution, he moved from Massachusetts to Pennsylvania. Pickering was U.S. postmaster general, 1791–94; U.S. Secretary of War, 1795; U.S. Secretary of State, 1795–1800; U.S. Senator (Mass.), 1803–11; and U.S. Representative (Mass.), 1813–17.

Presuming on the many Proofs of Friendship and Confidence, with which you have been pleased to Honour me, I have taken the Liberty to enclose a Pamphlet lately published here, on the Constitution proposed by the late Convention from an attentive reading of which, and a serious Examination of the Constitution itself, I cannot but consider it as very dangerous to the liberties of the People of this Continent— I do not consider myself competent to a perfect Knowledge of the more intricate parts of Government, but as I conceive the one in Question to be deficient in the grand Essentials requisite for the Security of those Rights for which we have so ably and successfully contended with Great-Britain, I have concluded, and I hope not impertinently, to ask your sentiments on this momentous Business.

If I am wrong in making this request, permit me to plead the indulgence you have always, generously, given me, in permitting me freely to write and speak my sentiments on every Subject, and as I have the utmost confidence in your disinterestedness in matters of a public as well as of a private nature, and that you never had, nor do I believe you ever will have, any views inconsistent with what you consider to be the true interest of the States, your Opinion, if you are so obliging as [to] give it, I shall receive with the greatest Pleasure, and as I have the greatest confidence in your judgment, it will enable me to view the Government proposed in its true light.

1. RC, Pickering Papers, MHi.

Detector
New York Daily Advertiser, 24 November 1787[1]

A Petulant OBSERVER in the DAILY ADVERTISER of Monday, is of opinion, that Publius[2] has been unfortunate in his reference to the case of the Union between England and Scotland—the latter Kingdom, it seems, for want of an adequate representation, has been a sufferer by the Union; and the proofs of this are the pathetic harangues of a member of Parliament, and the emigration of Scotchmen to America.

That the first is not a very satisfactory piece of evidence will be manifest to all those, who know how easy a thing it is for members of a popular Assembly to declaim when they have a favorite point to carry. The efforts of Mr. Dempster to obtain a parliamentary patronage of the Scotch fisheries, is a curious proof, that the nation itself is in a worse condition, by its incorporation with England under one Government. As to the circumstance of emigrations to this country, it is matter of surprise, that they have been so limited. Considering the real temptations, which America holds out to the industrious poor of all nations, and the enthusiasm inspired in her favor, by the first impressions of the late Revolution, most men have been disappointed in the small number of emigrants, that have arrived from Scotland; a country, the physical or natural advantages of which are so greatly inferior to those of the United States. There is a love of novelty in the human heart, that is often an over-match for the attachment to native soil. How else does it appear, that such swarms of people abandon the most fertile and flourishing parts of our Atlantic settlements, to make establishments beyond the Ohio? Many circumstances conspire to place, in a seducing light, the advantages of expatriating to America; and if we should see people from any part of Europe flocking hither, it would be a fallacious argument, either of the badness of the Government, or of the distress of the country from which they came.

It is true, as the Observer intimated, that there was a strong party in Scotland, violent in their opposition to the incorporation of the two Kingdoms. These men, like the Anti-federalists of America, pronounced that measure to be unnatural and impracticable, and predicted an endless train of mischiefs from its adoption. There was also a considerable party in England whose prognostics were not more favorable; but the friends to the Union in both countries triumphed; and experience has confirmed the justness of their views, in the reciprocal prosperity of the two nations. At the present day, there is not an enlightened man in either Kingdom, that doubts the utility of that great event to both.

The no less judicious than elegant Robertson, a Scotch historian, gives the following account of the effects of the Union. "The political POWER[a] of the NOBLES (says he) already broken by the Union of the two Crowns, was almost annihilated by the UNION of THE TWO KINGDOMS." "As the Nobles were deprived of power, THE PEOPLE ACQUIRED LIBERTY. Exempted from burthens to which they were formerly subject, screened from oppression, to which they had been long exposed, and adopted into a Constitution, whose genius and laws were more liberal than their own, THEY HAVE EXTENDED THEIR COMMERCE, REFINED THEIR MANNERS, MADE IMPROVEMENTS IN THE ELEGANCIES OF LIFE, AND CULTIVATED THE ARTS AND SCIENCES."—"Since the Union the COMMONS, anciently neglected by their Kings, and despised by their Nobles, have emerged into dignity, and being admitted to a participation of all the privileges, which the English had purchased, at the expence of so much blood, must now be esteemed a body not less considerable in one Kingdom than they long have been in the other."

The impartial and enlightend Goldsmith, an English historian, delivers himself upon the same subject, in these terms. "The Scotch[b] were fired with indignation at the thoughts of losing their ancient and independent Government. The Nobility found themselves degraded in point of dignity and influence, by being excluded from their seats in Parliament. The trading part of the nation beheld their commerce loaded with heavy duties, and considered their new privilege of trading to the English plantations, in the West-Indies, as a very uncertain advantage. In the English houses also, it was observed, that the Union of a rich with a poor nation, would be always beneficial to the latter, and that the former could only hope for a participation of their necessities. It was said, that the Scotch reluctantly yielded to this coalition, and that it might be likened to a marriage with a woman against her consent. It was supposed to be an Union, made up of so many *unmatched pieces*, and such *incongruous ingredients*, that it could never take effect. It was complained, that the proportion of the land tax paid by the Scotch was small, and unequal to their share in the Legislature. To these arguments in both nations, besides the shew of a particular answer to each, one great argument was used, which preponderated against all the lesser ones. *It was observed that all inconveniences were to be overlooked in the attainment of one great and solid advantage; that of acting with uniformity of counsels for the benefit of a community naturally united.* The party, therefore, for the Union prevailed; AND THIS MEASURE WAS CARRIED IN BOTH NATIONS THROUGH ALL THE OBSTACLES OF PRETENDING PATRIOTISM AND PRIVATE INTEREST, from which we may learn, that many great difficulties are surmounted because they are not seen by those who direct the operation; and that SCHEMES, which THEORY deems IMPRACTICABLE will OFTEN SUCCEED in EXPERIMENT."

Thus we find the historians of both countries bearing testimony to the advantages derived from the adoption of a measure, which the candid and well informed OBSERVER treats as having been ruinous to one of them. As it cannot well be supposed, that the two historians were in a conspiracy with PUBLIUS to deceive the people of America, there will be no resource left for the Observer, but to hint in his next publication, that they were bribed with British gold to be the panegyrists of the Union. Who can be wise, or honest, that lisps a sentiment or retails a fact, in contradiction to the representations of the wise and virtuous militants against the proposed Constitution.

The Observer states, as one of the arguments used in Scotland against the consolidation of the two Governments, that it would oblige her to take part in the wars of England against France, with which nation, Scotland, before the Union, had at all times been upon terms of the most cordial amity. The true amount of this argument is precisely this:—Scotland, by her Union with England, will be compelled to engage in the wars of the latter kingdom against France, a DISTANT POWER, and able, from that circumstance, to do her LITTLE INJURY; and, if not united with England, she will commonly be enlisted on the side of France against England, and must sacrifice considerations of immediate safety to her connection with a power incapable, from *its distance*, of securing her effectually against the attacks of a *near formidable neighbor*. But this argument could not have been used against the consolidation of the two kingdoms, because the Union of the Crowns, which had preceded that event, included the evil, if it was an evil, against which the force of that argument was directed. The Observer knows enough of the history of the two kingdoms, to be convinced, that lessons still more instructive to this country might be drawn from the operation of the alliances, in which Scotland was engaged prior to the Union.

As to the cavil against those remarks of PUBLIUS, which are designed to shew the dangerous consequences of disunion, whether it terminates in a total separation of the States, or in several smaller Confederacies, it will be sufficient to establish facts to detect its futility.[3] PUBLIUS no where alledges, that the doctrine of two or three separate Confederacies has been advanced by any of the writers against the New Constitution. He only asserts that it has been held up in private circles, a fact which the Observer cannot be ignorant of; and that the tendency of the arguments, which have been urged in some publications that have appeared on the other side of the question, is towards the same point. To make out this conclusion, he undertakes to shew, that no Government less comprehensive, or energetic, than the one proposed, can be adequate to the preservation of the Union; and that therefore the tenets of the authors of those publications, which aim at narrowing the boundaries of the Federal authority, must lead to the alternative of entire disunion, or partial confederacies. This is the evident scope of Publius's observations. In this view of the subject, which is the true one, is there any thing disingenuous, or improper, in displaying the disadvantages that would attend such a situation? Is there any thing unnatural in the order he has chosen of preceding the arguments, which are to explain the principles of a Government, adapted to the preservation of the UNION, by an examination of the utility of the *thing itself*, and the mischiefs of its *opposite*, under whatever shape?

Let the people judge whether Publius or the Observer aims most at deception, from the attempts he has made to disparage the benefit of the Union to Scotland. There is indeed a degree of enterprize in that attempt, which was hardly to be looked for, even from the adventurous spirit, that so highly distinguishes the adversaries of the New Constitution. The means of detection were so near at hand, that we cannot be indifferent to that undaunted disregard of the ordinary rules of prudence, which marks so singular an experiment. There are few causes so bad as entirely to destroy the merit of noble daring; and in the present instance, the temerity of the undertaking is forgotten, in the admiration we feel for the spirit, that dictated it. Indeed on the score of spirit, it is impossible to do complete justice to that meritorious class of citizens who stand forth in print the champions of the public liberty, against the meditated invasions of a Washington and a Franklin; who compliment the heroism of the first at the expence of his understanding, and expatiate on the past merits of the latter, as an apology for the errors of his present dotage;[4] who brand, as men of arbitrary principles and dishonest views, all those who in the Convention, or out of it, have ventured to depart from their infallible notions of Government; and who represent, as conspirators against the liberties of the people, the best and brightest characters of the community—men whose patriotism can stand the test of unequivocal facts, and who through every vicissitude of fortune, were the firmest and most useful supporters of the American Revolution.

(a) History of Scotland, vol. 2, page 29[8], 299.[5]
(b) History of England, vol. 4, page 131, 132.[6]

1. On 23 November the *Daily Advertiser* announced that "Detector" would appear "tomorrow." On 26 November "Detector"—a reply to "An Observer," *New York Journal*, 19 November (above)—was reprinted in the *New York Journal* preceded by this statement from "A Reader": "By inserting the DETECTOR, in reply to AN OBSERVER, which originated in your DAILY PATRIOTIC REGISTER of Monday last, you will oblige many, and greatly evince your Impartiality."

2. See "Publius," *The Federalist* 5, *Independent Journal*, 10 November (CC:252).

3. The first five numbers of *The Federalist* all emphasized the importance of Union.

4. See, for example, "Centinel" I, Philadelphia *Independent Gazetteer*, 5 October, at note 3 (CC:133, p. 330). For the "Centinel" essays, see also "New York Reprinting of the Centinel Essays," 17 October 1787–12 April 1788 (above).

5. William Robertson (1721–1793), *The History of Scotland* . . . [1542–1603] in *The Works of William Robertson, D.D.* . . . (12 vols., Edinburgh, 1818), III, Book VIII, 193, 194, 195. "Detector" added the capital letters. Robertson's two-volume history first appeared in 1759 in London.

6. Oliver Goldsmith (1728–1774), *The History of England, from the Earliest Times to the Death of George II* (4 vols., London, 1771), IV, 131–32. "Detector" added the italics and the capital letters.

Publius: The Federalist 11 (Alexander Hamilton)
New York Independent Journal, 24 November 1787

Union will promote commerce and lead to establishment of a navy. For text, see CC:291. For reprintings, see Appendix IV, below.

A Querist
New York Journal, 24 November 1787

MR. GREENLEAF, A gentleman rented a house for one hundred years, and agreed to pay down 50l. and to pay 50l. for it every second year. That if it was not demanded when due, it should not be paid; also, if any dispute arose respecting the contract, the tenant was to appoint his own judge to settle it finally.

The third year the second 50l. was demanded—being due that year by contract. The tenant refuses to pay it, and beginning with 1787, asks how many second years there are in one hundred years—The proprietor answers, every other year, or one year intervening between 1787 and 1789, and so on, will solve the question. But, answers the tenant, in a series of numbers, say from one to one hundred—can you find, making one the datum, more than one second number, which immediately follows number one.

Query. Does the above supposed contract contain any certain principle whereby it can be fairly and consistently explained?

My reason for asking the above question in this plain way, arises from a clause in the proposed constitution which I have read, and that I understood clearly; yet my mind has frequently reverted to it seemingly, not perfectly, satisfied—a few days since it impressed me so strongly, that I sat down to calculate upon it.

"The house of representatives shall consist of members chosen every second year by the people of the several states."

If the words had been "the house of representatives shall consist of members chosen (or to be chosen) for two years and no longer," the meaning would have been plain; and I ask, if this is not the idea that every person, almost in reading the clause, affixes to the words?—and if it is, are they not deceived?—The time that the members shall be chosen for, is not mentioned—but it seems to be implied, that, if the people chose members every second year, the new members must supercede the old members. What is every second year?—for example— the new members are first chosen in 1788—is not 1789 the second year?—Are the members then to be chosen every year?—If the time of every choice made, is the datum to begin to count from, to find out when another choice is to be made—then 1790 is the second year from 1789.

Is not this clause so worded, that the new Congress will find themselves obliged, on account of the general welfare, to give it a meaning; and if so, is it possible for us now to know what that meaning may be?

A candid answer to these enquiries will be very candidly acknowledged.

A Citizen
New York Journal, 24 November 1787

MR. GREENLEAF, On reading your Daily Patriotic Register of the 21st inst., a political piece, under the signature of MEDIUM,[1] engaged my attention—From the name which the author has taken, I flattered myself, that his writings would have been influenced by candor and impartiality; his declarations in the first paragraph, of his having perused the publications for and against the new constitution, "without bias or prejudice," and that his researches had been solely directed to discover on which side the greatest reason prevailed—and, his indiscriminate censures of writers (without my stopping to enquire into the justice of them) confirmed my opinion in favor of his performance: you may judge then of my disappointment when I came to the two last paragraphs; these plainly discover that little dependence can be placed on appearances, and that the people ought to guard against the cunning and insidious arts, employed by designing men to mislead and betray them; for, it is evidently discernible, that the name which the writer assumes, and the candor that he effects, were purposely designed the better to carry on the business of deception, and to effect the great end which a certain lordly party have in view—the adoption of the new constitution with all its defects; and, of course, risking the dearest rights of mankind to the precarious chance of being secured by future amendments.

In the first place, Medium asserts, that "It may be true, that the constitution is defective, but none have yet been able to prove that it is materially so;" he, however, admits, that it is not accompanied with a bill of rights, which he allows "to be the best security we can have against the encroachments of despotism"—Here it is granted, that the omission of a bill of rights is (whether proved so by other writers or not) "a material defect;"—With what degree of consistency then can he urge "the embracing the constitution as it now stands;" certainly, he cannot be ignorant, that if it is agreed to without "that best security against the encroachments of despotism," that our liberties must, hereafter, entirely depend upon acts of an imperfect and unequal congressional legislature, which may be repealed at their pleasure, and, whenever it suits their arbitrary designs.

The stale and hackneyed reasons, that have been alledged for the adoption of the proposed system, in all its parts, are the only ones made use of by this writer, viz. The impracticability of getting a better, and the anarchy which will ensue its rejection. In order to shew the futility and absurdity of these positions, it may be proper to give the following concise account of the commencement and progress of this business.

A convention was appointed by the respective legislatures, at the recommendation of Congress, for the sole purpose of *revising* and *amending* the articles of confederation; Congress had no power to concur in any measures for alteration, but such as should be assented to by all the states; nor had the legislatures the least authority to confer powers for the purposes of violating or abridging the state constitutions; the commission of the delegates to the late Fœderal Convention, consequently, could not, by any possible construction, invest them with powers which Congress and the legislatures themselves did not possess: the business of the *conventioneers* was then evidently not to form a new constitution for the United States, but to revise and amend the old one, as far as was necessary and consistent with their delegation. It was well understood, that the account of provisions, for the general regulation of commerce, and for ensuring a compliance with requisitions made under the fœderal compact, were principal causes which induced the appointment of the convention. These being the main objects, the representations, from all the states, were small, principally taken from commercial cities, and composed chiefly of merchants, practitioners of the law, and judicial officers; of the two latter professions, nearly one half of the convention consisted. This imperfect representation of the people, both as to numbers and descriptions, when assembled, shut their doors against their fellow citizens, and laid themselves under obligations of secrecy, and, by keeping from the world a knowledge of the important business which they had assumed upon themselves, they were precluded from all opportunities of receiving light or information, upon so interesting a subject, from the animadversions which their constituents would probably have made upon the different points under their deliberation. Under these unfavorable circumstances, this new constitution was formed, and it must therefore be considered as an unauthorized essay, which can only receive sanction from the assent of the people; it has already become the subject of general discussion, and, besides the omission of a bill of rights (which even Medium admits to be essential) many other radical defects have been pointed out; but, instead of attempting to amend them, it is insisted that it must, for the groundless and puerile reasons above-mentioned, be accepted in toto. What is there in the nature of our situation that imposes this disagreeable necessity upon us? Is it probable, that we shall ever be in a situation, in which we can with more temper and greater safety, deliberate upon this momentous concern than at present? From abroad, we have nothing to fear—the interesting affairs of the European powers will engage their attention beyond the atlantic—at home, we are in a state of perfect tranquility—for, although there are defects in the existing articles of confederation, yet the governments of the different states have energy sufficient to command obedience to their laws, and preserve domestic peace; America has not been subjected to as many tumults and disasters since the conclusion of the war, as countries, of an earlier foundation, have suffered in the same space of time. Some of the states have, already, with great calmness and temper, directed conventions of the people to assemble and take the proposed constitution into consideration—they ought, and it is unquestionably their duty to give every article a free and fair discussion; it would be inconsistent with, and derogatory to, every idea of the rights of freemen, to presume that they must approve of such parts as, in their opinions, are improper and dangerous, or, on the other hand, that they would reject what merited their approbation—it should also be their duty, to point out such amendments and alterations, as to them appear necessary and salutary—and they, or the legislatures, should appoint delegates to compose a new general convention; the members of which, being furnished with the remarks of the respective state conventions, will be enabled to form a system much less exceptionable, more perfect, and coincident with the wishes of the people; by this means the present animosities and divisions, which now prevail will, in all probability, be healed, and a government introduced that will engage the attachment, promote the felicity, and receive the support, of all ranks of people.

If the advocates, for the unqualified adoption of the new constitution, could be induced to divest themselves of prejudice, and reflect seriously and candidly, perhaps they would discover greater danger of anarchy and civil discord through their unjustifiable endeavors to establish a government (universally allowed to be defective) than by a concurrence in this practicable and rational mode of proceedure. They ought deliberately to consider, whether the proposed constitution will ensure to the people all those great advantages they are led to expect from the encomiums which its advocates so lavishly bestow upon it, in order to obtain its establishment; for, if the contrary (which is predicted by many) should happen, and the people, instead of having their happiness and interest promoted, find themselves deprived of their invaluable liberties, and their burdens increased by an expensive government, the inevitable consequences will be anarchy and discord, which may prove, when beyond the power of remedy, dangerous to the community, and *dreadfully fatal* to the authors of their deception.

New-York, Nov. 22, 1787.

1. See "Medium," *New York Journal*, 21 November (above).

John Jay and the Constitution
24 November–7 December 1787

The first known reaction to the Constitution by John Jay, the Confederation Secretary for Foreign Affairs, was favorable. On 16 October Jay wrote John Adams, the American minister in London, that the Constitution was "much better" than the Articles of Confederation (above). In late October Jay joined Alexander Hamilton in anonymously writing *The Federalist*, a series of essays (signed "Publius") that supported the Constitution. (For Jay's authorship, see the headnote to *The Federalist* 1, *Independent Journal*, 27 October, above.) Between 31 October and 10 November, New York City newspapers published essays two through five written by Jay (CC:217, 228, 234, 252). Shortly after publishing *The Federalist* 5, illness prevented Jay from continuing his writing.

As Confederation Secretary for Foreign Affairs, Jay probably thought that he should not take a public stance on the Constitution (see note 5, below). As a result of this public silence, some observers, especially those outside New York, thought that Jay actually opposed the Constitution. For instance, on 22 November Philadelphia Antifederalist William Shippen, Jr., declared that the "Brutus" essays were "said to be by R. H. Lee or Jay" (RCS:Pa., 288). On 24 November a correspondent in the Philadelphia *Independent Gazetteer* reported that Jay was no longer "carried away" with the Constitution and that he was "now very decidedly against it" (below). This report was reprinted in the *Daily Advertiser*, 29 November, the *New York Journal*, 30 November, and in eleven newspapers outside New York by 24 December: Mass. (5), R.I. (1), Conn. (3), Md. (1), N.C. (1). The *Massachusetts Centinel*, 8 December, reprinted the report under the heading "RANK ANTIFEDERALISM."

On the same day that the *Independent Gazetteer's* report appeared, Philadelphia merchant John Vaughan wrote Jay a letter, enclosing a copy of the report. On 26 November another Philadelphia merchant Tench Coxe wrote New York merchant David S. Franks that the report "has astonished many here." Coxe enclosed a copy of the report and asked Franks to show it to Jay (Tench Coxe Papers, Series II, Correspondence and General Papers, PHi).

Jay authorized Vaughan on 1 December to deny the *Gazetteer's* report, to indicate that he supported the Constitution, and to publish his letter, if Vaughan so desired. Vaughan received the letter on 5 December and two days later an extract of it was printed in the *Gazetteer* and *Pennsylvania Packet*, with Jay being identified as the writer and Vaughan as the recipient. Jay's excerpted letter was reprinted in the *Daily Advertiser* and *New York Morning Post*, 13 December; the *New York Journal* and *New York Packet*, 14 December; the *Independent Journal*, 15 December; the *Albany Gazette*, 20 December; the *Country Journal*, 26 December; and by 19 January 1788 in twenty-three newspapers outside New York: N.H. (2), Mass. (10), R.I. (2), Conn. (5), Pa. (2), Md. (1), Va. (1).

Immediately below Jay's excerpted letter, the *Albany Gazette*, 20 December, printed the following paragraph preceded by a hand device: "A correspondent presents his compliments to the Antifederalists, begs that in their future publications they would pay a *little* regard to TRUTH. Their compliance in this particular, will give much satisfaction to the honest part of the community." (The *Gazette* had not printed the false report, claiming that Jay opposed the Constitution.)

Twelve of the thirteen newspapers, including the *Daily Advertiser* and the *New York Journal*, that printed the Philadelphia *Independent Gazetteer's* report of 24 November also printed the excerpt from Jay's 1 December letter. Three of the twelve included both items in the same issue. The *New Haven Gazette*, 20 December, and the Hartford *American Mercury*, 24 December, printed both items under the heading "Antifœderal Dishonesty detected," while the Middletown, Conn., *Middlesex Gazette*, 24 December, printed both together without comment.

Writing in the *Daily Advertiser* on 12 December, "D——" accused the "Antifederal party" of "base purposes." He was certain that Jay supported the Constitution (below). George Washington questioned James Madison about Jay's alleged change of heart on 7 December, and two weeks later Madison replied that the *Gazetteer's* report was "an arrant forgery" (CC:328, 359). For other comments outside New York, see "One of the People," *Maryland Journal*, 25 December (CC:377); and "A Traveller," *Pennsylvania Chronicle*, 6 February 1788 (Mfm:Pa. 407).

Philadelphia Independent Gazetteer, 24 November 1787

A correspondent says, "his Excellency John Jay, (a gentleman of the first rate abilities, joined to a good heart) who at first was carried away with the new plan of government, is now very decidedly against it, and says it is as deep and wicked a conspiracy as has been ever invented in the darkest ages against the liberties of a free people. In New-York it goes by the name of the *gilded trap*, and very properly, for when we find men of the first abilities and best intentions at first taken with it, how very artfully must it be drawn up and glossed over, and who will then wonder that General Washington or any body else, should have signed it in Convention. The Governor of New-York[1] is very active against it, and will not call the Assembly, who in that case will not meet this some months,[2] in the mean time the people there will have time to think for themselves on this important subject."

Philadelphia Independent Gazetteer, 7 December 1787[3]

Mr. OSWALD, I send you an extract of a letter I have received from Mr. Jay, which I beg you will insert in your paper.

JOHN VAUGHAN.

Philadelphia, 7th Dec. 1787.

"New-York, 1st Dec. 1787.

"Dear Sir, I thank you for your obliging letter of the 24th ult. enclosing a paragraph respecting me in Mr. Oswald's paper of the same date. You have my authority to deny the change of sentiments it imputes to me, and to declare, that in my opinion, *it is adviseable*[4] *for the people of America to adopt the constitution proposed by the late Convention.* If you should think it expedient to publish this letter, I have no objections to its being done.

JOHN JAY."[5]

1. George Clinton.

2. The Assembly convened on 1 January 1788, but it did not attain a quorum until 11 January. (See II, below.)

3. This item was also published on 7 December in the *Pennsylvania Packet*, where it was addressed to Messrs. Dunlap and Claypoole, the printers of the *Packet*. The manuscript letter, which has no italics, is in the Madeira-Vaughan Collection at the American Philosophical Society in Philadelphia. The manuscript letter was endorsed as received on 5 December and as answered. This manuscript also includes these remarks by Jay: "Your Letter found me much indisposed—I am so still—but the Doctr. tells me the violence of my Complaint is broken, and as my Feelings accord with his opinion, I hope by Degrees to regain the Blessings of Health."

4. In reprinting this letter, the *New York Morning Post*, 13 December, substituted "admissible" for "adviseable." The next day, however, the *Morning Post* informed its readers of its error.

5. On 4 January 1788 Jay wrote to his brother-in-law in Baltimore that "It would give me Pleasure to make you a visit, and compare notes on the new Constitution & other interesting Topics, but my official Situation forbids it—as to the Constitution the Convention appear to me to have acted & written candidly respecting it, and the various Reasons for adopting it induce me to think it adviseable" (to Matthew Ridley, Jay Papers, Columbia University Libraries, Rare Book and Manuscript Library).

Louis Guillaume Otto to Comte de Montmorin
New York, 26 November 1787 (excerpt)[1]

. . . The debates, My Lord, for and against the new Constitution continue to absorb public attention and while the individual States are preparing to call conventions in order to adopt or reject this new plan, the two parties abuse each other in the public papers with a rancor which sometimes does not even spare insults and personal invectives. As in these sorts of political commotions, the men and the issues usually disguise themselves so as to become unrecognizable, the partisans of the innovation are called *Federalists* and the others more commonly *Whigs*, although neither of these names has a direct relation to the object in question. This spirit of argument is even pushed to intolerance in regard to foreigners and they absolutely want us to take a side for or against the new Constitution. Some politicians trying to be shrewder than others have even suggested that this Constitution was bad since it was approved by foreign Ministers. According to one side Despotism will be the necessary consequence of the proposed Constitution; according to the others the united States will reach the summit of glory and power with this same Constitution. Indifferent Spectators agree that the new form of Government, well executed will be able to produce good results; but they also think that if the states really had the desire to be united the present Confederation would be adequate for all their needs. Meanwhile they are unable to conceal that after having excited this general ferment there is no longer a means to stop it, that the old edifice is almost destroyed, and that any fabric whatsoever must be substituted for it. In effect it was impossible to carry out a more violent coup to the authority of Congress, than in saying to all America, to the entire Universe, that this body is inadequate to the needs of the Confederation and that the united States have become the laughingstock of all the powers. This principle repeated over and over by all the Innovators seems as false as their spirits are excited; the united States held the place among nations which their youth and means assigned them; they are neither rich enough, populated enough, nor well established enough to appear with more luster and perhaps one ought to reproach them only for the impatience of anticipating their future grandeur. . . .

1. RC (Tr), Correspondance Politique, États-Unis, Vol. 32, ff. 401–4, Archives du Ministère des Affaires Étrangères, Paris, France. Printed: CC:294. Otto (1754–1817) had served as France's chargé d'affaires since 1785 and continued to be its principal diplomatic representative in America until the arrival of the Comte de Moustier early in 1788. The Comte de Montmorin (1745–1792) was France's Minister of Foreign Affairs.

Publius: The Federalist 12 (Alexander Hamilton)
New York Packet, 27 November 1787

Union will ensure creation of a national revenue. For text, see CC:297. For reprintings, see Appendix IV, below.

Lansingburgh Northern Centinel, 27 November 1787

To say (remarks a correspondent) that *all antifederalists are tories,* would be a very severe reflection on some persons high in office in this state;—but this we all know, that it may be asserted, without the least deviation from veracity, that *all tories are antifederalists.*

Lansingburgh Northern Centinel, 27 November 1787[1]

Messrs. Printers, *By inserting the following in the Northern Centinel, you will oblige a* large Number *of your Readers.*

A PARODY *of the* NEWS-MONGERS' SONG.
Odd news brother dealers in prose and in rhymes,
Some *law-quack* lampooners are blacking the times;
They're patroniz'd daily by black & nut brown,
And the tune of each ruffian is down derry down.
                                    Fal lal, &c.

Some fancy they're sages, and say with a jeer,
Sit omnibus annus[2] each skunk has his year.
Queen Ann's was an æra of geniuses past,
Arguendo[3] a day's come for parchment at last.

Now Draper, Meigs, Powers, Green, Thomas, Hall, Haswell,
Childs, Stoddard, Green, Goddard, Loudon, Oswald, and Russell.
Morton, Greenleaf and Webster, and Babcock and Claxton,[4]
May thank for their luck the sly readers of Blackstone.

Come on brother scribblers, 'tis high time ye learn.
The calf must be catch'd that's got out of the barn;
A feast boys is cooking, the whiskey is good,
We've fire & molasses, we've Honey & wood.

Of Holland the orange, of Can'an the goards,
Of Greece the law-sophists, of Britain the lords.
American Shayites, antifedrals and laws,
All fine twisting matters adopted to flaws.

Much joy to ye, printers, ye'll now get your part,
The *law* and *land jobbers* are losing the start:
The *new constitution* has still to undo her,
In front, the *sly CATO*—in rear the *ROUGH HEWER.*

Huge commets are strolling and rambling this way,
The moon at the full is as bright as a bay;
Old Saturn is rolling, the sun's all on fire,
And *Satan himself* has a *fee* like a *'Squire.*

All Europe we hear is most horrible mad,
They sue, jockey, bully and all that is bad;
In Holland where freedom is cowardly squeeling,
All's cussing and robbing and cheating & stealing.

The empress of Russia is sitting her work,
While Ireland is starving, she sports with the Turk;
The Algerine Dey struts about in his robe
And swears by Mahomet he owns all the globe.

In blaithe bon[n]y Scotslaundt a bannok's the cheer,
In Derry they've cherry, good ale and strong beer;
America and Holland in England's the theme,
And faction *pro more*[5] dismembers each scheme.

Will. Henry's[6] relinquish'd the whores for the waves,
And rides like a Don o'er dead heroes and knaves;
Yet none but the long robe, the fops nigh the crown,
And fools of the nation sing down derry down.

Adieu growling Europe, atlantic's between us,
Blest free-born Columbia can better convene us;
Hail *governors, assemblies, mobs, Shayites* and *kings,*
Quacks, bankrupts and *know ye's*[7] and all *needless things.*

Our timber is fallen air castles to build,
And tho' *roughly hew'd* many coffers has fill'd;
To share in the booty each knave huddles round,
While sweeps on the chimneys cry down derry down.

Write then brother scribblers, your talents prolong,
This ball is a concert and life is a song:
When the music is o'er, at the end of each strain,
Kings, heroes and waiters are equal again.

Old raw-boned Time, with his lamper jaws ope,
Will soon eat an Ossian,[8] a Dryden or Pope;
And who, when all things are eat up by old Time,
Can tell but *Song Scribblers* were writers sublime.
  Albany Nov. 17.   *Fal lal,* &c.

1. Reprinted: *Daily Advertiser,* 11 December; *Massachusetts Gazette,* 14 December; *New Hampshire Spy,* 21 December. This item is a parody of "The News-Mongers' Song for the Winter of 1788" that was printed in the *Albany Gazette,* 15 November (above). For a response to this parody, see *Northern Centinel,* 18 December (Mfm:N.Y.).
 2. Latin: Let the year be for all.
 3. Latin: For the sake of argument. (Used in the law.)
 4. Those named here were newspaper printers from Vermont to Maryland.

5. Latin: For the sake of habit.

6. The reference is to William Henry (1765–1837), the third son of George III, who in 1830 became William IV. In 1786–87 William Henry went to the West Indies and Quebec as captain of the frigate *Pegasus*.

7. For the meaning of "Know Ye," see "Cincinnatus," *Northern Centinel*, 15 October, note 1.

8. Ossian was a legendary blind Gaelic poet of the third century, who sang the exploits of *Finn mac Cumhail* and his Fenian cohorts. James Macpherson (1736–1796), a Scottish poet, claimed to have discovered a hitherto unknown epic poem of Ossian, and he published this find in 1762. Some individuals, including David Hume, Horace Walpole, and especially Samuel Johnson, questioned the authenticity of the epic, but nevertheless it became very popular. It went through several editions and was translated into many languages. The debate over the epic's authenticity continued for decades and it was not definitively demonstrated to be a forgery until the end of the nineteenth century.

Hugh Hughes to Charles Tillinghast
28 November 1787 (excerpts)[1]

My dear Friend,

. . . Are you not wrong as to the Author of Brutus[2]—I supposed him to have been Brutus Junior[3] & Mr. A Y.[4] to have been the Author of Brutus—The federal Farmer, I think I am sure of, as one of the Letters contains some Part of a Conversation I once had, when I spent an Evening with him—Perhaps this may bring him to your Memory—If not, please to observe the first Part of the 2nd Paragraph in the 7th Page,[5] and you will recollect, I expect, as I told you that he was perfectly in Sentiment with me on that Subject—I think he has great Merit, but not as much as he is capable of meriting—But, perhaps, he reserves himself for another Publication; if so, it may be all very right—I wish you and Miles[6] to run the C——n over, before it goes to Press.[7] . . .

NB. If you have any thing to send, that is, Letters or Papers, the Bearer will take Charge of them, which will save a Trip to the Landing.

1. RC, Misc. MSS, Hugh Hughes Folder, NHi. Printed: CC:298 (longer excerpt). The place of writing does not appear on the letter. At this time Hughes was tutoring John Lamb's children at Lamb's farm in Yonkers, Westchester County.

2. See "Brutus" I, *New York Journal*, 18 October (above).

3. See "Brutus, Junior," *New York Journal*, 8 November (above).

4. Abraham Yates, Jr.

5. See "Federal Farmer," *Letters to the Republican*, 8 November, at note 11 (above).

6. A reference to Hughes's son, James Miles Hughes, a New York City lawyer.

7. Probably a reference to Hugh Hughes's "A Countryman" III, which appeared in the *New York Journal* on 3 December (below).

Publius: The Federalist 13 (Alexander Hamilton)
New York Independent Journal, 28 November 1787

Union will produce a less expensive government. For text, see CC:300. For reprintings, see Appendix IV, below.

Philo-Publius III
New York Independent Journal, 28 November 1787[1]

Publius has shewn us in a clear light the utility, it might be said, the necessity of Union to the formation and support of a navy. There is one point of view however on which he has left the subject untouched—the tendency of this circumstance to the preservation of liberty. Will force be necessary to repell foreign attacks, or to guard the national rights against the ambition of particular members? A navy will be a much safer as well as a more effectual engine for either purpose. If we have a respectable fleet there will be the less call on any account for an army. This idca is too plain to need enlargement.—Thus the salutary guardianship of the Union appears on all sides to be the palladium of American liberty.

1. Reprinted: *Daily Advertiser*, 29 November.

Brutus IV
New York Journal, 29 November 1787[1]

To the PEOPLE *of the State of* NEW-YORK.

There can be no free government where the people are not possessed of the power of making the laws by which they are governed, either in their own persons, or by others substituted in their stead.

Experience has taught mankind, that legislation by representatives is the most eligible, and the only practicable mode in which the people of any country can exercise this right, either prudently or beneficially. But then, it is a matter of the highest importance, in forming this representation, that it be so constituted as to be capable of understanding the true interests of the society for which it acts, and so disposed as to pursue the good and happiness of the people as its ultimate end. The object of every free government is the public good, and all lesser interests yield to it. That of every tyrannical government, is the happiness and aggrandisement of one, or a few, and to this the public felicity, and every other interest must submit.—The reason of this difference in these governments is obvious. The first is so constituted as to collect the views and wishes of the whole people in that of their rulers, while the latter is so framed as to separate the interests of the governors from that of the governed. The principle of self love, therefore, that will influence the one to promote the good of the whole, will prompt the other to follow its own private advantage. The great art, therefore, in forming a good constitution, appears to be this, so to frame it, as that those to whom the power is committed shall be subject to the same feelings, and aim at the same objects as the people do, who transfer to them their authority. There is no possible way to effect this but by an equal, full and fair representation; this, therefore, is the great desideratum in politics. However fair an appearance any government may make, though it may possess a thousand plausible articles and be decorated with ever so many ornaments, yet if it is deficient in this essential principle of a full and just representation of the people, it will be only like a painted sepulcher—For, without this it cannot be a free government; let the administration of it be good or ill, it still will be a government, not according to the will of the people, but according to the will of a few.

To test this new constitution then, by this principle, is of the last importance—It is to bring it to the touch-stone of national liberty, and I hope I shall be excused, if, in this paper, I pursue the subject commenced in my last number,[2] to wit, the necessity of an equal and full representation in the legislature.—In that, I showed that it was not equal, because the smallest states are to send the same number of members to the senate as the largest, and, because the slaves, who afford neither aid or defence to the government, are to encrease the proportion of members. To prove that it was not a just or adequate representation, it was urged, that so small a number could not resemble the people, or possess their sentiments and dispositions. That the choice of members would commonly fall upon the rich and great, while the middling class of the community would be excluded. That in so small a representation there was no security against bribery and corruption.

The small number which is to compose this legislature, will not only expose it to the danger of that kind of corruption, and undue influence, which will arise from the gift of places of honor and emolument, or the more direct one of bribery, but it will also subject it to another kind of influence no less fatal to the liberties of the people, though it be not so flagrantly repugnant to the principles of rectitude. It is not to be expected that a legislature will be found in any country that will not have some of its members, who will pursue their private ends, and for which they will sacrifice the public good. Men of this character are, generally, artful and designing, and frequently possess brilliant talents and abilities; they commonly act in concert, and agree to share the spoils of their country among them; they will keep their object ever in view, and follow it with constancy. To effect their purpose, they will assume any shape, and, Proteus like,[3] mould themselves into any form—where they find members proof against direct bribery or gifts of offices, they will endeavor to mislead their minds by specious and false reasoning, to impose upon their unsuspecting honesty by an affectation of zeal for the public good; they will form juntos, and hold

out-door meetings; they will operate upon the good nature of their
opponents, by a thousand little attentions, and seize them into compliance by the earnestness of solicitation. Those who are acquainted
with the manner of conducting business in public assemblies, know how
prevalent art and address are in carrying a measure, even over men of
the best intentions, and of good understanding. The firmest security
against this kind of improper and dangerous influence, as well as all
other, is a strong and numerous representation: in such a house of
assembly, so great a number must be gained over, before the private
views of individuals could be gratified that there could be scarce a hope
of success. But in the fœderal assembly, seventeen men are all that is
necessary to pass a law. It is probable, it will seldom happen that more
than twenty-five will be requisite to form a majority, when it is considered what a number of places of honor and emolument will be in the
gift of the executive, the powerful influence that great and designing
men have over the honest and unsuspecting, by their art and address,
their soothing manners and civilities, and their cringing flattery, joined
with their affected patriotism; when these different species of influence
are combined, it is scarcely to be hoped that a legislature, composed
of so small a number, as the one proposed by the new constitution, will
long resist their force. A farther objection against the feebleness of the
representation is, that it will not possess the confidence of the people.
The execution of the laws in a free government must rest on this confidence, and this must be founded on the good opinion they entertain
of the framers of the laws. Every government must be supported, either
by the people having such an attachment to it, as to be ready, when
called upon, to support it, or by a force at the command of the government, to compel obedience. The latter mode destroys every idea of
a free government; for the same force that may be employed to compel
obedience to good laws, might, and probably would be used to wrest
from the people their constitutional liberties.—Whether it is practicable to have a representation for the whole union sufficiently numerous
to obtain that confidence which is necessary for the purpose of internal
taxation, and other powers to which this proposed government extends, is an important question. I am clearly of opinion, it is not, and
therefore I have stated this in my first number,[4] as one of the reasons
against going into so an entire consolidation of the states—one of the
most capital errors in the system, is that of extending the powers of
the fœderal government to objects to which it is not adequate, which
it cannot exercise without endangering public liberty, and which it is
not necessary they should possess, in order to preserve the union and
manage our national concerns; of this, however, I shall treat more fully

in some future paper—But, however this may be, certain it is, that the representation in the legislature is not so formed as to give reasonable ground for public trust.

In order for the people safely to repose themselves on their rulers, they should not only be of their own choice. But it is requisite they should be acquainted with their abilities to manage the public concerns with wisdom. They should be satisfied that those who represent them are men of integrity, who will pursue the good of the community with fidelity; and will not be turned aside from their duty by private interest, or corrupted by undue influence; and that they will have such a zeal for the good of those whom they represent, as to excite them to be deligent in their service; but it is impossible the people of the United States should have sufficient knowledge of their representatives, when the numbers are so few, to acquire any rational satisfaction on either of these points. The people of this state will have very little acquaintance with those who may be chosen to represent them; a great part of them will, probably, not know the characters of their own members, much less that of a majority of those who will compose the fœderal assembly; they will consist of men, whose names they have never heard, and of whose talents and regard for the public good, they are total strangers to; and they will have no persons so immediately of their choice so near them, of their neighbours and of their own rank in life, that they can feel themselves secure in trusting their interests in their hands. The representatives of the people cannot, as they now do, after they have passed laws, mix with the people, and explain to them the motives which induced the adoption of any measure, point out its utility, and remove objections or silence unreasonable clamours against it.—The number will be so small that but a very few of the most sensible and respectable yeomanry of the country can ever have any knowledge of them: being so far removed from the people, their station will be elevated and important, and they will be considered as ambitious and designing. They will not be viewed by the people as part of themselves, but as a body distinct from them, and having separate interests to pursue; the consequence will be, that a perpetual jealousy will exist in the minds of the people against them; their conduct will be narrowly watched; their measures scrutinized; and their laws opposed, evaded, or reluctantly obeyed. This is natural, and exactly corresponds with the conduct of individuals towards those in whose hands they intrust important concerns. If the person confided in, be a neighbour with whom his employer is intimately acquainted, whose talents, he knows, are sufficient to manage the business with which he is charged, his honesty and fidelity unsuspected, and his friendship and zeal for the service of his principal unquestionable, he will commit his affairs into his hands

with unreserved confidence, and feel himself secure; all the transactions
of the agent will meet with the most favorable construction, and the
measures he takes will give satisfaction. But, if the person employed be
a stranger, whom he has never seen, and whose character for ability or
fidelity he cannot fully learn—If he is constrained to choose him, because it was not in his power to procure one more agreeable to his
wishes, he will trust him with caution, and be suspicious of all his conduct.

If then this government should not derive support from the good
will of the people, it must be executed by force, or not executed at all;
either case would lead to the total destruction of liberty.—The convention seemed aware of this, and have therefore provided for calling out
the militia to execute the laws of the union. If this system was so framed
as to command that respect from the people, which every good free
government will obtain, this provision was unnecessary—the people
would support the civil magistrate. This power is a novel one, in free
governments—these have depended for the execution of the laws on
the Posse Comitatus, and never raised an idea, that the people would
refuse to aid the civil magistrate in executing those laws they themselves
had made. I shall now dismiss the subject of the incompetency of the
representation, and proceed, as I promised, to shew, that, impotent as
it is, the people have no security that they will enjoy the exercise of the
right of electing this assembly, which, at best, can be considered but as
the shadow of representation.

⟨By section 4, article 1, the Congress are authorized, at any time, by
law, to make, or alter, regulations respecting the time, place, and manner of holding elections for senators and representatives, except as to
the places of choosing senators. By this clause the right of election
itself, is, in a great measure, transferred from the people to their rulers.—One would think, that if any thing was necessary to be made a
fundamental article of the original compact, it would be, that of fixing
the branches of the legislature, so as to put it out of its power to alter
itself by modifying the election of its own members at will and pleasure.
When a people once resign the privilege of a fair election, they clearly
have none left worth contending for.⟩

It is clear that, under this article, the fœderal legislature may institute
such rules respecting elections as to lead to the choice of one description of men. The weakness of the representation, tends but too certainly to confer on the rich and *well-born*, all honours; but the power
granted in this article, may be so exercised, as to secure it almost beyond a possibility of controul. The proposed Congress may make the
whole state one district, and direct, that the capital (the city of New-
York, for instance) shall be the place for holding the election; the con-

sequence would be, that none but men of the most elevated rank in society would attend, and they would as certainly choose men of their own class; as it is true what the *Apostle Paul* saith, that "no man ever yet hated his own flesh, but nourisheth and cherisheth it."[5]—They may declare that those members who have the greatest number of votes, shall be considered as duly elected; the consequence would be that the people, who are dispersed in the interior parts of the state, would give their votes for a variety of candidates, while any order, or profession, residing in populous places, by uniting their interests, might procure whom they pleased to be chosen—and by this means the representatives of the state may be elected by one tenth part of the people who actually vote. This may be effected constitutionally, and by one of those silent operations which frequently takes place without being noticed, but which often produces such changes as entirely to alter a government, subvert a free constitution, and rivet the chains on a free people before they perceive they are forged. Had the power of regulating elections been left under the direction of the state legislatures, where the people are not only nominally but substantially represented, it would have been secure; but if it was taken out of their hands, it surely ought to have been fixed on such a basis as to have put it out of the power of the fœderal legislature to deprive the people of it by law. Provision should have been made for marking out the states into districts, and for choosing, by a majority of votes, a person out of each of them of permanent property and residence in the district which he was to represent.

⟨If the people of America will submit to a constitution that will vest in the hands of any body of men a right to deprive them by law of the privilege of a fair election, they will submit to almost any thing. Reasoning with them will be in vain, they must be left until they are brought to reflection by feeling oppression—they will then have to wrest from their oppressors, by a strong hand; that which they now possess, and which they may retain if they will exercise but a moderate share of prudence and firmness.

I know it is said that the dangers apprehended from this clause are merely imaginary, that the proposed general legislature will be disposed to regulate elections upon proper principles, and to use their power with discretion, and to promote the public good. On this, I would observe, that constitutions are not so necessary to regulate the conduct of good rulers as to restrain that of bad ones.—Wise and good men will exercise power so as to promote the public happiness under any form of government. If we are to take it for granted, that those who administer the government under this system, will always pay proper attention to the rights and interests of the people, nothing more was necessary than to say who should be invested with the powers of government, and leave them to exercise it at will and pleasure. Men are apt to be deceived both with respect to their own dispositions and those of others.⟩ Though this truth is proved by almost every page of the history of nations, to wit, that power, lodged in the hands of rulers to be used at discretion, is almost always exercised to the oppression of the people, and the aggrandizement of themselves; yet most men think if it was lodged in their hands they would not employ it in this manner.—Thus when the prophet *Elisha* told *Hazael*, "I know the evil that thou wilt do unto the children of Israel; their strong holds wilt thou set on fire, and their young men, wilt thou slay with the sword, and wilt dash their children, and rip up their women with child." Hazael had no idea that he ever should be guilty of such horrid cruelty, and said to the prophet, "Is thy servant a dog that he should do this great thing." Elisha, answered, "The Lord hath shewed me that thou shalt be king of Syria."[6] The event proved, that Hazael only wanted an opportunity to perpetrate these enormities without restraint, and he had a disposition to do them, though he himself knew it not.

1. Reprinted: Philadelphia *Independent Gazetteer*, 8 December; Boston *Independent Chronicle*, 20 December. The text in angle brackets appeared in the Philadelphia *Freeman's Journal*, 12 December, with this prefatory statement: "A sensible writer on the proposed constitution, in the New-York Journal, under the signature of BRUTUS, makes the following judicious remarks on the powers therein granted to Congress respecting elections." On 1 January 1788 the *Maryland Journal* reprinted the *Freeman's Journal* preface and the text in angle brackets.

2. See "Brutus" III, *New York Journal*, 15 November (above).

3. In Greek mythology, Proteus was a minor sea god who had the power to change shapes.

4. See "Brutus" I, *New York Journal*, 18 October (above).

5. Ephesians 5:29.

6. 2 Kings 8:12–13.

Cincinnatus V: To James Wilson, Esquire
New York Journal, 29 November 1787

On 27 November the *New York Journal* reported that "Cincinnatus" V and VI were received and that they "shall be attended to as soon as possible." Both essays were continuations of "Cincinnatus' " response to James Wilson's speech of 6 October before a Philadelphia public meeting (see "New York Reprinting of James Wilson's 6 October Speech Before a Philadelphia Public Meeting," 13–25 October, above). "Cincinnatus" V was reprinted in the Philadelphia *Independent Gazetteer* on 15 December, three days after the Pennsylvania Convention ratified the Constitution.

"Centinel" XIV charged that "Cincinnatus" V was not reprinted in Philadelphia until "two or three days after the convention rose" because it "contained very material information about the finances of the union, which strikes at some of the principal arguments in favor of the new constitution" (Philadelphia *Independent Gazetteer*, 5 February 1788, CC:501, p. 38. For a similar charge made earlier by "Centinel," see the headnote to "Cincinnatus" IV, *New York Journal*, 22 November, above.).

Sir, In my former observations on your speech, to your fellow-citizens,[1] explanatory and defensive of the new constitution; it has appeared, by arguments to my judgment unanswerable, that by ratifying the constitution, as the convention proposed it, the people will leave the liberty of the press, and the trial by jury, in civil cases, to the mercy of their rulers—that the project is to burthen them with enormous taxes, in order to raise and maintain armies, for the purposes of ambition and arbitrary power—that this power is to be vested in an aristocratic senate, who will either be themselves the tyrants, or the support of tyranny, in a president, who will know how to manage them, so as to make that body at once the instrument and the shield of his absolute authority.—Even the Roman Emperors found it necessary to have a senate for this purpose. To compass this object, we have seen powers, in every branch of government, in violation of all principle, and all safety condensed in this aristocratic senate: we have seen the representative, or democratic branch, weakened exactly in proportion to the strength[en]ing the aristocratic, or, what means the same thing, and will be more pleasing to your ear, Mr. Wilson, the republican branch. We have seen with what cunning the power of impeachment is apparently given to the representative of the people, but really to the senate; since, as they advise these measures of government, which experience has shewn, are the general matters of impunity the executive officers will be sure of impeachment when they act in conformity to their will. Impeachment will therefore have no terrors, but for those who displease or oppose the senate.

Let us suppose that the privy councils who advise the executive government in England, were vested with the sole power of trying impeachments; would any man say that this would not render that body absolute; and impeachment to all popular purposes, negatory? I shall appeal to those very citizens, Mr. Wilson, whom you was misleading, for the propriety of what I am going to observe. They know that their constitution was democratic—that it secured the powers of government in the body of the people. They have seen an aristocratical party rise up against this constitution, and without the aid of such a senate, but from the mere influence of wealth, however unduly obtained, they have seen this aristocracy, under the originatical title of republicans, procure such a preference in the legislature, as to appoint a majority of the state members in the late convention, out of their body.[2] Had such a senate, as they have now proposed, been part of your constitution, would the popular part of it, have been in effect more than a name. Can your fellow citizens then doubt that these men planned this senate, to effect the very purpose which has been the constant object of their endeavors, that is to overthrow the present constitution. And can you, O citizens of Philadelphia, so soon forget the constitution which you formed, for which you fought, which you have solemnly engaged to defend—can you so soon forget all this, as to be the willing ministers of that ambition, which aims only at making you its footstool—the confirmers of that constitution, which gives your aristocratic enemies their wish, and must trample your state constitution in the dust. Reflect a moment—who wish to erect an aristocracy among you—Mr. Wilson and his party; who were your delegates in framing the constitution now proposed to you—Mr. Wilson, and his party; who harangues you to smooth its passage to your approbation—Mr. Wilson; who have you chosen to approve of it in your state convention—Mr. Wilson.—O sense where is your guard! shame where is your blush![3] the intention of a state convention is, that a work of so great moment to your welfare, should undergo an examination by another set of men, uninfluenced by partiality or prejudice in its favor. And for this purpose you are weak enough to send a man, who was in the former convention, and who has not only signed his approbation of it, but stands forward as an agitator for it: is this man unprejudiced? would any man who did not suffer party to overcome all sense of rectitude, solicit or accept so improper a trust? He knows, in the line of his profession, that the having given an opinion upon the same question is a constant ground of challenge to a juryman. And does he think that this question is of less importance and ought less to be guarded against partiality and prejudice, than a common jury cause? He knows that a conscientious man will not sit as a juryman twice on the same cause: and is he in this most momentous cause, less conscientious than a common juryman? What are we to expect from the work of such hands? But you must permit me to lay before you, from your own transactions, farther proofs of Mr. Wilson's consistency, and of his sacred attention to your rights, when he counsels you to adopt the new constitution.

You know that he was one of the convention that formed, and recommended to you, your state constitution. Read what is there laid down as a fundamental principle of liberty—"As standing armies, in the time of peace, *are dangerous to liberty*, they ought not to be kept up."[4] Read now what this identical Mr. Wilson says to you in his speech—"This constitution, it has been farther urged, is of a pernicious tendency, because it tolerates a standing army in time of peace. This has always been a topic of popular declamation, and yet I do not know a nation in the world, which has not found it necessary and useful to maintain the appearance of strength, in a season of the most profound peace." What a change of tone is here.—Formerly the mischief of standing armies was of sufficient moment, to find a place in a most solemn recognition of the fundamental rights of the people; standing armies were dangerous to liberty; but *now* they are only a topic of popular declamation, and are both useful and necessary in a season of the most profound tranquility:—O citizens of Philadelphia! do your hear, do you read, do you reflect? can you believe that the man means either wisely or honestly, who thus palpably contradicts himself, who treats with such levity, what your constitution declares to be one of your most sacred rights; and who betrays so little knowledge of ancient and modern history, as not to know, that some of the freest republics in the world, never kept up a standing army in time of peace! Can you, O deluded men, not see that the object of all this, is to fix upon you, with your own consent, a strong government that will enable a few proud, intriguing, aristocratical men, to make you the instruments of their avarice and ambition, and trample upon your privileges at pleasure. Your privileges, did I say, I beg your pardon; after a surrender of every thing on your part, into the hands of a few, their pleasure will be your only privileges.

I beg you will pardon me, Mr. Wilson, for this digression: it is not a pleasant one, and I wish the cause of it had never existed. We will return, if you please, to your speech. "When we reflect, you say, how various are the laws, commerce, habits, population, and extent, of the confederated states, this evidence of mutual concession and accommodation ought rather to command a generous applause, than to excite a jealousy and reproach. For my part, my admiration can only be equalled by my astonishment in beholding so perfect a system formed from such heterogeneous materials." What a rhapsody is here; it certainly must have excited equal admiration and astonishment in your audience, and called forth those loud and unanimous testimonies of applause which Doctor Panegyric tells us, accompanied your speech.[5] Nil admirari,[6] Mr. Wilson, is a wise lesson, and when you recover from your admiration and astonishment which are always incompatible with truth and reason; I shall ask you what union in the world is so similar in their laws, commerce, habits, population and extent? Is there such difference between Rhode-Island and Virginia, as between Holland and Overyssel; between Massachusetts and Georgia, as between Berne and Switzs? Do not the several states harmonize in trial by jury of the vicinage; taxation by representation; habeas corpus; religious toleration; freedom of the press; separation of the legislative, executive and judicial functions. Are not these the great principles on which every constitution is founded? In these the laws and habits of the several states are uniform. But I suppose, because the citizens of New-York are not in the habit of being so ostentatious as those of Philadelphia, nor its merchants, of being such speculators in commerce as to fill the papers with bankruptcies; because in Carolina they are in the habit of eating rice, and in Maryland of eating homony; therefore the materials are heterogeneous, out of which this perfect, system; his subject of amazement, was formed.

What was this wonder working concession and accommodation? If they consisted in giving up, or hazarding any of the above fundamental principles of liberty, which I confess seems probable, because some furious spirits in the convention, and such there were, insisted upon it, such conduct may command your generous applause; but trust me, sir, when the people come to feel that their rights have been so basely betrayed by those they trusted, it will command a general execration: And here I cannot avoid remarking on what I have heard and for the truth of which I appeal to you. It is that a member of the late convention said, not very honorably distinguished for his moral or political virtue, admonished his associates that, unless they carried the constitution through before there was time for considering it, there would be no probability of its being adopted.[7] When I couple this profligate declaration, with the equally profligate measures taken by some persons to force it down in Philadelphia, and with the indecent speed with which others posted to Congress, and then to their several states, to hurry it forward[8]—I confess I cannot help apprehending that such advice has not only [been] given, but followed.

You would next induce us, Mr. Wilson, to believe, that the state sovereignties will not be annihilated, if the general one be established as the convention recommends. Your reason for this is as curious as it is conclusive. Because the state legislatures must nominate the electors of the President once in four years, and chuse a third of the Senate once in two years; therefore they will continue to be sovereign. Sovereignty then consists in electing the members of a sovereignty; to make laws—preside over the administration of justice—command the militia, or force of the state—these I suppose, do not constitute its sovereignty, for these are totally taken away, and yet you are clear the sovereignty remains. Did you think, Sir, that you was speaking to men or to children, when you hazarded such futile observations. Nor are they compensated by the very profound erudition you display in defining the meaning of the word corporation. In common *parlance* we should call this egregious pedantry. Such is the anxiety manifested by the framers of the proposed constitution, for the utter extinction of the state sovereignties, that they were not content with taking from them every

attribute of sovereignty, but would not leave them even the name.—
Therefore, in the very commencement they prescribe this remarkable
declaration—*We the People of the United States.* When the whole people
of America shall be thus recognized by their own solemn act, as the
people of the United States, I beseech you Sir, to tell us over whom the
sovereignty, you say you leave to the several states, is to operate. Did
the generous confidence of your fellow citizens, deserve this mockery
of their understandings; or inebriated with so unusual a thing as popularity, did you think that every rhapsody you uttered, would be received as reason? That you may not expose yourself again on this subject, give me leave to recommend to you to read Mr. Locke, in whom
you will find that sovereignty consists in three things—the legislative,
executive, and negociating powers, all which your constitution takes
absolutely away from the several states. In Barbeyrac's Puffendorf, you
will find these words, "La souvèraintee entant quelle prescrit des regles
generales pour la conduite de la vie civile, s'appelle pouvoir legislatif—
entant qu'elle prononce sur les demeles des citoiens, conformement a
ces regles, pouvoir judiciaire—entant q'uelle arme les citoiens contre
un ennemie etranger, ou qu'elle leur ordonne de mettre fin aux acts
d'hostilitès; pouvoir de faire la guerre et la paix; entant qu'elle se
choisit des Ministres pour lui aider a prendre soin des affaires pub-
liques; pouvoir d'etablir des magistrats. The sovereignty, inasmuch as
it prescribes general rules for the conduct of civil life, is called the
legislative power—in deciding controversies among its citizens, con-
formably to those laws it is called the judiciary power—in arming its
citizens against a foreign enemy, or ordering them to cease hostilities;
it has the power of war and peace—the appointment of officers to aid
it in the case of the public, is the power of establishing magistrates."[9]
Now, Sir, all these attributes of sovereignty, being vested exclusively in
your new government, is it not a mockery of common sense to tell us,
the state sovereignties are not annihilated? and yet you undertake to
prove, that upon their existence depends the existence of the fœderal
plan—and when this mighty undertaking is explained, it is because
they must meet once in two years to elect part of the federal sovereignty. O fie! O fie![10] Mr. Wilson! you had yet some character to lose,
why would you hazard it in this manner?

On the subject of taxation, in which powers are to be given so largely
by the new constitution, you lull our fears of abuse by venturing to
predict "that the great revenue of the United States must and always
will be raised by impost"—and you elevate our hopes by holding out,
"the reviving and supporting the national credit." If you have any other
plan for this, than by raising money upon the people to pay the interest

of the national debt, your ingenuity will deserve our thanks. Supposing however, that raising money is necessary to payment of the interest, and such payment requisite to support the credit of the union; let us see how much will be necessary for that end, and how far the impost will supply what we want.

	Dollars.
The arrearages of French and Spanish interest amount now to	1,500,000
Interest and instalments of do. for 1788,	850,227
Support of government, and its departments, for 1788,	500,000
Arrears and anticipations of 1787,	300,000
Interest of domestic debt,	500,000
	4,650,227

The new Congress then, supposing it to get into operation towards October, 1788, will have to provide for this sum, and for the additional sum of 3,000,000 at least for the ensuing year; which together will make the sum of 7,650,227.[11]

Now let us see how the impost will answer this: Congress have furnished us with their estimate of the produce of the whole imports of America at five per cent. And that is 800,000 dollars:[12] there will remain to provide for, by other taxes, 6,850,227.

We know too, that our imports diminish yearly, and from the nature of things must continue to diminish; and consequently that the above estimate of the produce of the impost, will in all probability, fall much short of the supposed sum. But even without this, it must appear, that you was either intentionally misleading your hearers, or very little acquainted with the subject when you ventured to predict, that the great revenue of the United States would always flow from the impost. The estimate above is from the publications of Congress, and I presume is right. But the sum stated, is necessary to be raised by the new government, in order to answer the expectations they have raised, is not all. The state debts, independent of what each owes to the United States, amount to about 30,000,000 dollars;[13] the annual interest of this is 1,800,000.

It will be expected, that the new government will provide for this also; and such expectation is founded, not only on the promise you hold forth, of its reviving and supporting public credit among us, but also on this unavoidable principle of justice, that is the new government takes away the impost, and other substantial taxes, from the produce of which the several states paid the interest of their debt, or funded the paper with which they paid it. The new government must find ways and means of supplying that deficiency, or in other words of paying the interest in hard money, for in paper as now, it cannot, without a violation of the principles it boasts, attempt to pay. The sum then which it must annually raise in specie, after the first year, cannot be less than 4,800,000:[14] at present, there is not one half of this sum in specie raised in all the states; and yet the complaints of intolerable taxes has produced one rebellion, and will be mainly operative in the adoption of your constitution.—How you will get this sum is inconceivable, and yet get it you must, or lose all credit. With magnificent promises you have bought golden opinions of all sorts of people, and with gold you must answer them.

1. See "Cincinnatus" I–IV, *New York Journal*, 1, 8, 15, 22 November (all above).

2. Four of the eight Pennsylvania delegates to the Constitutional Convention were also members of the Pennsylvania Assembly. A fifth delegate, Benjamin Franklin, was President of the state's Supreme Executive Council. (For the election of Pennsylvania's delegates to the Constitutional Convention, see CDR, 199–200.) For the principal complaint against the election of Pennsylvania's delegates to the Constitutional Convention, see "The Address of the Seceding Assemblymen," and for the major Pennsylvania response to this complaint, see "The Reply of Six Assemblymen" (RCS:Pa., 112–20). See also "New York Reprinting of the Address of the Seceding Members of the Pennsylvania Assembly," 9–18 October (above).

3. William Shakespeare, *Hamlet*, Act III, scene 4, line 81.

4. Article XIII of the Pennsylvania Declaration of Rights (Thorpe, V, 3083).

5. "Doctor Panegyric" was Benjamin Rush. The *Pennsylvania Herald's* report of Wilson's speech indicated that Wilson "was frequently interrupted with loud and unanimous testimonies of approbation" (RCS:Pa., 172).

6. Latin: To be undisturbed in spirit, or to be astonished at nothing. See Horace (65–8 B.C.), *Epistles*, Book I, epistle VI, line 1.

7. Probably a reference to Gouverneur Morris of Pennsylvania who, along with Charles Pinckney of South Carolina, proposed in the Constitutional Convention on 31 August that state legislatures should call ratifying conventions "as speedily as circumstances will permit." Morris explained that "his object was to impress in stronger terms the necessity of calling Conventions in order to prevent enemies to the plan, from giving it the go by. When it first appears, with the sanction of this Convention, the people will be favorable to it. By degrees the State officers, & those interested in the State Govts will intrigue & turn the popular current against it." Luther Martin of Maryland responded that "the people would be agst. it [the Constitution]. but for a different reason from that alledged. . . . they would not ratify it unless hurried into it by surprize" (Farrand, II, 478. See also Luther Martin's reply to the Maryland "Landholder," *Maryland Journal*, 21 March 1788, CC:636.).

8. For the precipitate action taken in Pennsylvania, see "New York Reprinting of the Address of the Seceding Members of the Pennsylvania Assembly," 9–18 October (above). For Congress' transmittal of the Constitution to the states, see "The Confederation Congress and the Constitution," 26–28 September (above).

9. Jean Barbeyrac, trans., *Le Droit de la Nature et des Gens. . . . Traduit du Latin de feu Mr. Le Baron de Pufendorf* (2 vols., Basel, Swit., 1732), II, Book VII, chapter IV, section I, 258. The Baron Samuel von Pufendorf's work was first published in 1672, and Barbeyrac's translation was first printed in 1706.

10. William Shakespeare, *Troilus and Cressida*, Act IV, scene 5, lines 54–57. "Fie, fie upon her!/There's language in her eye, her cheek, her lip,/Nay, her foot speaks; her wanton spirits look out/At every joint and motive of her body."

11. These figures (and those immediately above) appear to be based upon a report on the 1787 congressional requisition made to Congress by the three-member Confederation Board of Treasury, of which Arthur Lee, the author of the "Cincinnatus" essays, was a member. Congress read the report on 29 September 1787, and made the report the order for the day on 5, 8, and 11 October. It ordered 100 copies of the report to be printed (JCC, XXXIII, 569–85, 616, 632–36, 650–58. For the fourteen-page printed report, see Evans 20756.).

12. When it proposed the Impost of 1783, Congress estimated that the tariff would yield annually about $915,000 (JCC, XXIV, 277–83, 285–87. For the text of the Impost of 1783, see CDR, 146–48.).

13. In 1790 Alexander Hamilton, the Secretary of the Treasury in the new government under the Constitution, estimated the state debts to be $25,000,000.

14. For a response to some of the financial statements made by "Cincinnatus," see "A Lunarian," *Daily Advertiser*, 20 December (below).

Americanus III
New York Daily Advertiser, 30 November 1787[1]

"It is natural for a Republic to have only a small territory."[2] It may be thought by some an unpardonable piece of temerity in me to deny the truth of this maxim of the celebrated Civilian, in so decisive a tone as I have ventured to do in a former paper. To satisfy those therefore, whose delicacy may be hurt on this occasion, I hope I shall be able before I finish this paper to bring about a perfect reconciliation between the Baron and myself; and thus deprive Cato of the assistance of this powerful auxiliary, on this occasion at least. It is manifest from a variety of passages, that Montesquieu's idea of a Republic, was a Government in which the collective body of the people, as in Democracy, or of the nobles, as in Aristocracy, possessed a share in the management of public affairs: Thus he tells us "the people in whom the supreme power resides ought to have the management of every thing within their reach."[3] "It is likewise a fundamental law in Democracies, that the people should have the sole power to enact laws."[4] It is obvious that to collect the suffrages of a numerous people, scattered over a wide extent of country on every law, on every public measure, would be utterly impracticable. According therefore to his idea of a Republican Government, this maxim of his, that a Republic should be confined to a small territory, is certainly a very just one. Should I be able to prove that the Governments of these States are founded on principles totally different from those which Montesquieu here had in view, it will then be manifest that Cato has lugged him into a controversy in which he is no ways concerned.

The Republics of antiquity were chiefly Democratic, those of modern date are chiefly Aristocratic. As to Aristocracies we have nothing to do with them. But let us enquire a little into the nature and genius of the antient Republics of Greece and Rome. Cato's maxim, "that the safety of the people in a Republic depends on the share or proportion they have in the Government,"[5] seem[s] to have been deemed by them indispensibly necessary; indeed, as they had no idea of appointing representatives to legislate for them, they had no other alternative; either the people collectively must retain to themselves a voice in the management of public affairs, or all pretensions to liberty must be resigned. To obviate the natural tendency of this radical defect in the frame of their Governments, they were under an absolute necessity of recurring to violent methods. To support these wretched institutions, the laws of nature herself were subverted. The life of a citizen was one continued effort of self-denial and restraint. Every social passion—all the finer feelings of the heart—the tender ties of parent and child—every enjoyment, whether of sentiment or of sense—every thing in short which renders life desirable, was relinquished. The Romans did not carry this system of self-denial to that extreme as was done by some of the Grecian States. They found however that a rigid attention to manners was indispensibly necessary. Magistrates were appointed for the express purpose of inspecting into the lives and conduct of every citizen—the public good superceded every consideration of a private nature—fathers condemned their own sons to the axe. Let it not be thought however that this exalted degree of patriotism—this rigid system of mortification and self-denial was the effect of choice; no! far from it! it was necessity that imposed it on them.—This magnanimous people saw plainly that their safety depended upon keeping up this austerity of manners. As from the very nature of this sort of Government there can be no regular checks established for preventing the abuse of power, the people are in a great measure constrained to rely on the patriotism and personal virtue of those citizens who compose the Government.

The Grecians and Romans have however infinite merit in subjecting themselves to so severe a discipline, in foregoing so many of the blessings and enjoyments of this life, for the sake of liberty.

The history of these States affords us very striking instances of the astonishing force of this passion of the human heart, when man is placed in a situation proper for displaying it.

Without a due attention to these distinctive properties of the Republics of antiquity, we cannot form an adequate idea of the immense advantages of a representative legislature. The people of Rome, of

Sparta, &c. were obliged to keep a constant eye on the conduct of their rulers for this reason, and that they might be enabled to exercise their right of a personal vote on public affairs, it was absolutely necessary that the citizens be confined within a small compass.

But if matters can be so ordered, that by appointing Representatives, the people can have the business of the State transacted in a better manner than they can possibly do it themselves, there is then no determining what may be the extent of the state. Thus it will be found that the Government of the most extensive State of the Union, though greater perhaps than all the States of Greece put together, may be administered with infinitely more care and safety than was any one of them, though comprehended within the limits of a few square miles.

The major part of mankind are slaves to sound—the writings of a great man, who has distinguished himself in any of the walks of science, in a short time become "irrefragable axioms."[6] Thus, thro' the indolence and inattention of some, and the knavery of others, error becomes at length so firmly established as to baffle, for a long time, the assaults of philosophy and truth.

And thus it is, that with those who suffer themselves to be carried away by a name, and attend not to things, the application Cato makes of Montesquieu's maxim to the Government of these States, would pass currently and without opposition. But this would be to sacrifice sense to sound with a vengeance.

The political institutions we have contrived and adopted in this new world differ as widely from the republics of the old, whether antient or modern, as does a well constructed edifice, where elegance and utility unite and harmonize, differ from a huge mishapen pile reared by Gothic ignorance and barbarity.

I have already remarked, that a Republic confined to a small territory, must, from its own nature, be incident to great inconvenience. Faction, instability, and frequent revolutions, are inherent properties. Besides, that its weakness exposes it to continual danger from the enterprizes of ambitious neighbours. What a capital improvement then is representation to a Republican Government. By this simple expedient can the sense of the people of an extensive Empire be collected with ease and certainty. By this admirable contrivance, the care and attention of Government is extended equally to every part—the wants and wishes of the most remote corners are known and attended to. But what is of infinite importance, a Government on this plan can be so constructed, as that the different parts of it shall form mutual checks on each other. This is not all, a number of lesser communities may be

united under one head; and thus form an extensive Empire. But this
new combination will give still greater security to liberty, because more
checks will be added. The Government of the Union, and those of the
States individually, will be watchful centinels on the conduct of each
other. By this means the usurpations of power are guarded against, and
liberty secured without the interference of the collective body of the
people. Until this important discovery in the art of Government was
made, the people themselves formed almost the only check on the
Government. For, from the necessity of the case, the right of proposing
new laws to the consideration of the people, necessarily devolved upon
those who were entrusted with the execution of those laws. Now it may
easily be conceived, that to counteract the sinister views of their rulers,
it required the utmost circumspection in the people—indeed it was
impossible, by the most active and vigilant attention to public officers,
for the people to avoid being dupes to the artifices of designing men.
This indeed is a business the people are by no means calculated for.
Conscious of this inability, the Romans procured the establishment of
tribunes, who were to be the guardians of the people's rights, and to
defend their privileges against the power of the Senate and the Consuls.
How well this expedient answered the end, history will inform us. All
that train of unavoidable mischiefs, which necessarily attends the interference of the people in the management of public affairs, instantly
vanish when we have recourse to a representative Legislature. Nothing
more is then necessary to place liberty on the firmest basis, than the
frequent recurrence of elections—that representation be adequate and
proportionate—and that the Representatives be tied down from interfering in any shape, in the Executive parts of Government, but confined absolutely to the business of their mission, which should be Legislation solely. If these things are attended to, the people need be under
no apprehensions about the management of affairs. From the very nature of things, these Representatives cannot fail of proving the faithful
and effectual guardians of the people. Here then we have that grand
desideratum, that has hitherto been wanting in all the popular Governments we are acquainted with, that the people may repose confidence in Government, without danger of its being abused. As these
Representatives are chosen only for a short period, at the expiration of
which, they are again reduced to the level of their fellow-citizens; and
as, during their continuance in this service, they are absolutely prohibited from interfering in any of the Executive branches of the Government; thus it becoming impossible for them to form an interest separate from that of the community at large, they can have no motive
whatever for betraying that of their Constituents. A Government

formed on this plan, requires in the execution of it, none of those heroic virtues which we admire in the antients, and to us are known only by story. The sacrifice of our dearest interests, self-denial, and austerity of manners, are by no means necessary. Such a Government requires nothing more of its subjects than that they should study and pursue merely their own true interest and happiness. As it is adapted to the ordinary circumstances of mankind, requiring no extraordinary exertions to support it, it must of course be the more firm, secure and lasting. A Government thus founded on the broad basis of human nature, like a tree which is suffered to retain its native shape, will flourish for ages with little care or attention. But like this same tree, if distorted into a form unnatural and monstrous, will require the constant use of the pruning knife, and all the art and contrivance of a skilful operator, to counteract the efforts of nature against the violence which has been offered her.

I would not however, wish it to be thought, that it is in any degree my design to depreciate that amor patriæ, which is a sentiment so natural to the human breast, and which, when well directed, is capable of such glorious effects—but unfortunately for mankind, the majority possess it in a very gross degree. It is with them generally nothing more than a blind attachment to a party, or to the local interests of a narrow district.

1. On 28 November the *Daily Advertiser* announced that "Americanus" III would appear on 30 November and that "Americanus" IV had been received. "Americanus" III responds to "Cato" III–IV, *New York Journal*, 25 October, 8 November (both above. See also notes 2, 5, and 6 below.).

2. *Spirit of Laws*, I, Book VIII, chapter XVI, 177. "Cato" III, *New York Journal*, 25 October, cited this passage (above).

3. *Spirit of Laws*, I, Book II, chapter II, 12.

4. *Ibid.*, I, Book II, chapter II, 17.

5. Quoted from "Cato" IV, *New York Journal*, 8 November (above).

6. "Cato" III stated that "The governments of Europe have taken their limits and form from adventitious circumstances, and nothing can be argued on the motive of agreement from them; but these adventitious political principles, have nevertheless produced effects that have attracted the attention of philosophy, which has established axioms in the science of politics therefrom, as irrefragable as any in Euclid" (*New York Journal*, 25 October, above).

A Baptist
New York Journal, 30 November 1787

"A Baptist" criticizes an action taken by the Philadelphia Baptist Association at its meeting in New York City from 2 to 5 October. On the last day, the Association (comprising the churches of the Middle States) adopted a circular letter, the bulk of which was concerned with "the important subject of Sanc-

tification." Most of the first paragraph of the letter, however, was an endorsement of the Constitution. ("A Baptist" quoted this endorsement in his article
printed below. See at notes 8 and 10.) The part of the circular letter endorsing
the Constitution appeared in the *New York Packet* on 12 October. The *Packet's*
report was then reprinted throughout America (CC:156–A. In New York, the
Packet's report appeared in the *Daily Advertiser*, 22 October; the *Hudson Weekly
Gazette* and *Albany Gazette*, 25 October; and the *Country Journal*, 31 October.).
The complete circular letter, preceded by the Association's minutes, was published in an eight-page pamphlet by New York City printer John Patterson
(Evans 20218).

For a New York newspaper item praising the Association's action on the
Constitution, see "Curtius" III, *Daily Advertiser*, 3 November, supplement
(above), and for out-of-state commentaries on its action, see the headnote to
CC:156.

TO THE *BAPTIST CHURCHES* BELONGING
TO THE PHILADELPHIA ASSOCIATION.

It is a fundamental principle upon which our churches are founded
that the "kingdom of Christ is not of this world."[1] By this is meant not
only that the great objects of a christian's faith and hope, are good
things reserved for them in a future state, but also, that christian
churches, which are the visible representation of the kingdom of Christ
in the world, are not governed by worldly maxims, influenced by
worldly hopes or fears, ambitious of worldly power or honours, and
that they do not concern themselves, as churches, with worldly policy,
or meddle with the government of states, or the politics of them.—
The great design of visible churches, is to hold forth the word of life,
not only by a public profession of the truth, as it is in Jesus, and by
contending earnestly for the faith once delivered to the saints, but by
rendering obedience to all the laws of Christ, who is alone King and
head of his church.[2] They are intended by their Lord and Master to be
the light of the world, as a city set on an hill which cannot be hid.[3] It
becomes them, therefore, to let their light so shine before men, that
others seeing their good works, may glorify their father which is [in]
heaven.[4] It is their duty to exercise benevolence to all men, brotherly
love to each other, and to observe the laws of Christ in all things,[5] and
thus to manifest, that they are blameless and harmless, the sons of God,
without rebuke in the midst of a crooked and perverse generation,
among whom they ought to shine as lights in the world.[6] But they have
nothing to do as christian societies, with the policy of the kingdoms of
this world. The only command given them on this head, is, "To submit
themselves to every ordinance of man for the Lord's sake."[7] As men,
connected with civil society, it is lawful for them to exercise the rights
of that society; but as christians, united in the fellowship of the gospel,

according to the laws of Christ's house, they are bound to concern themselves only with those things which appertain to the kingdom of heaven.

I was led to these reflections by reading the circular letter of the messengers of the several baptist churches, belonging to the Philadelphia association, met in the city of New-York, in October last.

After congratulating us on the tidings they had receiv'd from different parts, of the advancement of the Redeemer's kingdom, they proceed and say, "As also, on the kind interposition of divine providence, visible in that happy union which obtaincd among the members of the late federal convention, to agree upon and report to the states in this union, a form of a federal government, which promises, on its adoption, to rescue our dear country from that national dishonour, injustice, anarchy, confusion and bloodshed, which have already resulted from the weakness and inefficiency of the present form; and which we have the greatest reason to fear is but the beginning of sorrow, unless the people lay hold on this favourable opportunity offered, to establish an efficient government, which, we hope, may, under God, secure our invaluable rights, both civil and religious; which it will be in the power of the great body of the people, if hereafter found necessary, to controul and amend.["] [8]

I cannot conceive what the association had to do with the new constitution—they were a body composed of messengers from the several churches, to communicate to each other the state of the several congregations, who sent them. To advise on cases and questions which were difficult or doubtful; "to provoke one another, to love and good works," [9] and to concert measures to promote and diffuse the knowledge of the great things which concern that kingdom, which cannot be moved. Why then did they undertake to congratulate us on the unanimity which prevailed in an assembly that had been employed in devising a form of civil government for a nation of this world? One would imagine, from the dreadful picture that is drawn of the country in this paragraph, that the churches were just delivered from a severe persecution, similar to the one, which the church at Jerusalem endured at the first establishment of christianity; or resembling that, which the churches suffered in the primitive times, under those bloody tyrants, Nero and Dioclesian:—And that this new constitution was so framed as to secure them against a like calamity in future.

For what circumstance short of this, could induce the messengers, from a number of churches, who had assembled for the express purpose of advising on religious matters; after "congratulating the church on ⟨the glorious tidings brought from different parts of the advancement of our Redeemer's cause, as portentious of the speedy accomplishment of the promises made by the Father to Christ the King of Zion:⟩[10]—To add, as also on the kind interposition of Providence, &c.—which promises on its adoption to rescue our dear country from—anarchy, confusion and bloodshed, which have already resulted from the weakness and inefficiency of the present form, and which we have the greatest reason to fear, is but the beginning of sorrows, unless the people lay hold on this favourable opportunity to establish an efficient government."

Had the churches, to which these messengers belonged, been suffering for conscience sake, a language of this kind would have been perfectly proper; but we know of no country in the world, at any period since the first establishment of Christianity, where there has been such perfect liberty of conscience, and such entire freedom in the exercise of religion, as in these States, and under the present existing government. This liberty in religion is secured to the people of every one of the states by their several constitutions, and it is out of the power of their legislatures, should they be weak or wicked enough to attempt it, ever to deprive them of it—For this inestimable privilege, which so many christians in former days prayed for, but did not enjoy. I do sincerely congratulate all the churches of Christ—For this Christians are bound with fervent hearts, to offer up their thanks to the God of all Grace who hath in this respect, distinguished them from many of their pious forefathers, who were called to suffer for the faith of the Gospel in their estates, and in their persons even unto death.

It is remarkable, that this constitution, which the association recommends, has no clause in it that secures to us this invaluable blessing.—if it should supplant the constitutions of the individual states, as it certainly will, the only security we shall have for the enjoyment of this privilege, will be the grace and favour of the federal legislature.

The Baptists ought seriously to reflect, how feeble a security this will be—if they recollect the sufferings they have endured, both in the eastern and southern parts of the continent, within a few years past, for their adherence to what they believed to be the doctrines of Christ; however improbable it may seem that these sufferings may be revived, yet they ought most ardently to wish, and by all lawful means to endeavor to have the rights of conscience expressly reserved in any government that may be established over this country.

I think it extraordinary, that the association should have recommended this new constitution, not only because it was a subject which they had nothing to do with—but also because, I am well informed, it was never read in the association, and many of the members had never heard or understood the contents. I believe I may venture to affirm with truth, that few, if any of the members had considered the subject with that attention which is necessary, to understand the powers which this government will convey, or the operation they will have in exercise. Indeed when the association sat, sufficient time, and opportunity, had not been given after the publication of the new system, to acquire that knowledge of the subject which is requisite to form a rational judgment on the matter: It requires a good deal of time, study, and attention, to become master of a subject, so complicated in its nature, extending to so many objects, and consisting of so many parts, as this constitution does: Is it not wonderful, that in this situation, they should take it upon them to recommend it? It justifies an observation which has often been made, that when ministers of religion undertake to meddle with politics, they generally conduct weakly or wickedly. The history of mankind confirms the truth of this remark: I had hoped that our Baptist ministers had better understood the nature of their duty, than so improperly, I may say so indecently, to have interfered in a political question, concerning which I am sure very few of them had used the necessary means to obtain proper information. They are generally men of little wor[l]dly knowledge, and in this respect more resemble the primitive ministers of the new testament, than perhaps the ministers of any other denomination of christians. But alas! we find even among them a portion of the same leaven of pride which has worked in the hearts of some of the teachers of christianity ever since the days of the Apostles; some among them are ambitious to figure in the world. It was this class, as I am well informed, that originated this clause at the moment the association were about adjourning: It was agreed to without much debate, contrary to the sentiments of a number of the most serious and prudent members.

As christian churches, as I before observed, I am persuaded you have nothing to do with political questions? your duty in that capacity is, to study the policy of the kingdom of our Lord Jesus Christ—I exhort you therefore brethren, that you keep the ordinances as they have been delivered to you by our Lord and his apostles[11]—hold fast the form of sound words, which ye have heard from the oracles of truth, in faith and love, which is in Christ Jesus;[12] take heed that your minds be not corrupted, from the simplicity that is in Christ,[13] that you be not carried about, with every wind of doctrine, by the sleight of men, and cunning craftiness, whereby they lie in wait to deceive.[14] Search the laws of Christ's house, mark well the orders of it, the coming in and going out thereof, and all the laws and ordinances thereof, to do them; study to do all things whatsoever Christ commands; so shall you be his disciples indeed—walk in love, even as Christ also loved you.[15] Finally, brethren, whatsoever things are true, whatsoever things are honest, whatsoever things are just, whatsoever things are pure, whatsoever things are of good report, if there be any virtue, and if there be any praise, think on these things.[16]

As members of civil society you have a right to examine for yourselves, any political question submitted to you, and it is your duty to take pains to understand it and give your sentiments like honest men and lovers of your country—in this view, this new system of government should be examined; but you ought to be careful not to be deluded into an opinion, that it must be adopted, be it ever so imperfect, under an idea, that it can easily be amended by the people, if it should prove, on experiment defective.—This sentiment is suggested by the association; it is an evidence they had not investigated the plan, for it is not founded in truth: before any amendment can be proposed, two thirds of both houses of the federal legislature, or two thirds of those of the several states, must agree to it; and after any amendment is agreed to by a convention of the states, three fourths of the legislatures of the respective states must ratify them before they become valid: if this government is calculated to transfer power from the *many* to the *few*, it is easy to foresee, that those in power will be able to influence one fourth of the legislatures in such manner as to prevent any change in favor of the people.

It is not my design to enter upon a discussion of this system of government, but as a freeman, and a citizen of America, I beg leave to intreat you well to examine and thoroughly to understand it before you give it your assent. And in your investigation enquire,

1st. Whether there is any security provided in it, for liberty of conscience in matters of religion—for the liberty of the press—the tryal by jury in matters of property, or a fair and impartial trial by a jury of the vicinage, in matters of a criminal nature.

2d. Whether the representation in the legislature is not so small, as to afford no reasonable ground for the confidence of the people, or security to liberty? and whether there is any security that the people shall retain in their hands, the right of a fair and impartial choice of its members?

3d. Whether the general legislature can exercise the power to lay and collect internal taxes and excises, to organize and govern the militia, and call them out *to execute the laws of the union,* and suppress insurrections, without grievously oppressing the people, and greatly endangering public liberty?

4th. Whether the federal judiciary, will not supplant the courts of the several states—render the obtaining justice extremely burdensome and oppressive, and sacrifice the poor to the avarice and oppression of the rich?

5th. Whether the government will not be intolerably expensive, by increasing the number of officers to be supported by the people—and whether it will not lead to the establishment of a court in America, similar to the venal courts of Europe, where will exist *ambition with idleness—baseness with pride—the thirst of riches without labour—aversion to truth—flattery—treason—perfidy—violation of engagements—contempt of civil duties—hope from the magistrates weakness; but above all, the perpetual ridicule of virtue, and the sacred doctrines and precepts of religion.*

Finally, Whether in all its parts it has not a manifest tendency to confer the heighth of power and happiness, on the *few*, and to reduce the *many* to weakness and misery?

To enable you to give just answers to these queries, and a number of others that might be suggested—examine cooly and dispassionately the system itself—keep your minds open to conviction—read the several publications for and against it, and judge for yourselves.

Truth will stand the test of free enquiry; but error shuns fair investigation. That you may be directed, by the father of light, to act in this important matter, as becomes free and virtuous men, is the prayer of A BAPTIST.

New-York, November 26, 1787.

1. John 18:36. Jesus said: "My kingdom is not of this world."
2. Ephesians 5:23. "For the husband is the head of the wife, even as Christ is the head of the church: and he is the saviour of the body."
3. Matthew 5:14.
4. Matthew 5:16.
5. Romans 12:10–11. "Be kindly affectioned one to another with brotherly love; in honour preferring one another; Not slothful in business; fervent in spirit; serving the Lord."
6. Philippians 2:15.
7. 1 Peter 2:13.
8. Quoted from the Association's circular letter.
9. Hebrews 10:24.
10. The text in angle brackets appeared in the Association's circular letter before the part quoted above at note 8.
11. 1 Corinthians 11:2.
12. 2 Timothy 1:13.
13. 2 Corinthians 11:3.

14. Ephesians 4:14.
15. Ephesians 5:2.
16. Philippians 4:8.

Publius: The Federalist 14 (James Madison)
New York Packet, 30 November 1787

Large representative republic superior to a small direct democracy. For text, see CC:310. For reprintings, see Appendix IV, below.

Editors' Note
New York Reprinting of George Mason's Objections
to the Constitution, 30 November–13 December 1787

As a delegate to the Constitutional Convention, Virginian George Mason favored a strong central government, but he demanded protection for the rights and liberties of the people. When the Convention, on 15 September, refused to appoint a committee to draft a bill of rights that both he and Elbridge Gerry of Massachusetts had insisted upon, both men refused to sign the Constitution two days later. Before Mason left the Convention, he drew up a list of his objections that circulated in manuscript form in New York, New Hampshire, Pennsylvania, and Virginia before the objections were published. (For the circulation of the objections in manuscript in Pennsylvania and Virginia, see "George Mason: Objections to the Constitution," CC:138, 276.)

In New York, the objections were possibly put into circulation by Virginia congressman Richard Henry Lee, who may have received a copy from Mason in a letter dated 18 September, and by Elbridge Gerry, who had been allowed by Mason to copy them before Gerry left Philadelphia. Both Lee and Gerry were in New York City during the month of October. Either Gerry's or Lee's copy of the objections was possibly the one that Antifederalist leader John Lamb read at Governor George Clinton's house in mid-October. Lamb declared that the objections demonstrated that Mason was "a Man of the first rate Understanding." (See Charles Tillinghast to Hugh Hughes, 12 October, CC:155.)

The widespread circulation of Mason's objections in manuscript prompted Federalists to publish them so that Federalist essayists could reply to them. (It was deemed inappropriate to respond in print to items that had not been previously printed.) On 21 November the *Massachusetts Centinel*— claiming that it had obtained the objections from a New York correspondent who "frequently" furnished it with "authentick information from that quarter"—printed the objections, although it omitted a paragraph criticizing the Constitution for allowing a simple majority of Congress to enact navigation laws (CC:276–A). On 19 December the *Centinel* printed the omitted paragraph as part of an extract of a 7 December letter from the New York correspondent. The correspondent stated that he had obtained the objections from "a certain antifederal character" in New York City who omitted Mason's "principal" objection "which he well knew, would, if published in the northern States, be an inducement to them to accept of the Constitution." "I shall only remark," continued the correspondent, "on this his Machiavelian conduct—that the enemies to the Federal plan, ought no longer to complain of deception" (CC:276–D).

The *Massachusetts Centinel's* incomplete version of the objections was reprinted in the *Daily Advertiser* and *New York Packet*, 30 November, and in twenty other newspapers outside New York by 7 January 1788: N.H. (2), Mass. (6), R.I. (1), Conn. (4), N.J. (1), Pa. (3), Md. (1), S.C. (2). The omitted paragraph was reprinted in only four of these twenty-two newspapers by 3 January: N.H. (1), Mass. (1), R.I. (1), Pa. (1). On 27 December the *New Haven Gazette*, which had not printed the incomplete version of the objections, printed the missing paragraph.

On 22 November the Alexandria *Virginia Journal*, at the behest of "Brutus" (Tobias Lear), printed a complete version of Mason's objections. (Lear was private secretary to George Washington, who had received a copy of the objections from Mason in early October. Lear probably got his copy from Washington.) In a lengthy preface, "Brutus" criticized the previous "clandestine manner" in which the objections had circulated; he wanted to see the objections submitted "to the test of a public investigation." "Brutus" scored the influential Mason for not openly and candidly submitting his objections to the public. Immediately following the objections, "Brutus" concluded that "Many of the foregoing objections and the reasonings upon them, appear to be calculated more to alarm the fears of the people, than to answer any good or valuable purpose.—Some of them are raised upon so slender a foundation as would render it doubtful whether they were the production of Col. *Mason's* abilities, if an incontestible evidence of their being so could not be adduced" (CC:276–B). The *Journal's* version was reprinted in the *Virginia Independent Chronicle*, 5 December; the *Albany Gazette*, 13 December; the *Worcester Magazine*, 13 December; the December issue of the Philadelphia *American Museum*; and in two Richmond pamphlet anthologies (CC:350). It was also printed as a folio broadside by the publisher of the Richmond *Virginia Gazette and Weekly Advertiser*. Only the *Albany Gazette* reprinted "Brutus's" preface and concluding statement. A last version of the objections appeared on 23 November in the Winchester *Virginia Gazette*, but this version was never reprinted.

The public commentary on the objections was widespread and hostile, but no original article attacking Mason's objections appeared in any New York newspaper. Only an occasional reference to Mason's objections appeared. For instance, "A Citizen" declared that the Constitution "has been misconstrued by its enemies, by Messrs. M. and R. H. L. in particular" (*Hudson Weekly Gazette*, 24 January, below). Nor did Antifederalists write in defense of Mason. (For the criticism and defense of Mason outside New York, see the headnote to CC:276.) Lastly, it should be noted that New York Antifederalists did not include Mason's objections in the important Antifederalist pamphlet anthology that they printed and distributed throughout the state early in April 1788 (III below).

Edmund Prior to Moses Brown
New York, 1 December 1787 (excerpt)[1]

Thy favour of the 18th Ulto.[2] I duly recd., and should have answered it Long since, but a Member of the Late Convention, who I had some acquaintance with, being Absent, I was unable to obtain that information I wished for, and altho he is yet away I shall nevertheless endeavour to reply to thine,[3] The Great oversight of the Convention in respect to securing universal Liberty & Impartial Justice is generally attributed to the influence of the Southern Members, who had they duly ad[v]erted to the Publick declarations made in the days of their fear and distress, a very different determination in respect to Slavery would have taken place; With us it is however agreed that the State Legislatures will not be restrained from enacting such Laws for the prevention of the Odious traffick, as they may Judge expedient, for themselves, and I wish it may be the Case, hoping the advocates for the poor afflicted & oppress'd Africans will not be discouraged from pursuing their Laudable purpose—Its nevertheless allowed that should the Constitution be adopted the State of Massachusetts will no Longer be an Assylum to the Negroes,[4] unless they Should, except that Article, in their adoption Nothwithstandg our Testimony is so opposite to the sentiments of that body yet cannot see, how we shall move in the business, farther than a Pat[i]ent gradual Perseverance, for the Work is evidently on its way, and I have no doubt will in time be effected, hope our Pat[i]ence may keep Pace with the Success & we Steadily press forward—at times I have been possessed with a fear Least from the Cause being so good and the unrighteousness & Cruelty of Slavery, we should be induced to attempt to drive, & thereby be in danger of Shifting our ground,— ~~This fear has~~ which would then become an uncertain foundation,

Thine of the 19th with its inclosures was very acceptable, I had no expectation of any State going so far yet, its an excellent example for the others and I hope they will, adopt or enact Similar Laws—It has been published here[5] & in Jersey & have no Doubt but in Philada. also. . . .

1. RC, Moses Brown Papers, Rhode Island Historical Society. The letter was addressed to "Moses Brown/near Providence/Care of John Hadwin/New Port." Prior (1755–1841), was a New York City merchant, who was clerk of the (Quaker) New York Yearly Meeting from 1784 to 1786. Brown (1738–1836), a former Providence merchant and slave trader, became a Quaker in 1773, freed his slaves, and became an influential and active advocate for emancipation.

2. This letter has not been located, but for one that Brown wrote to a Philadelphia Quaker merchant about the slave trade on 17 October, see Brown to James Pemberton, 17 October (CC:Vol. 2, pp. 506–10).

3. Perhaps a reference to Rufus King, who had not yet returned to New York City from Newburyport, Mass., in order to be with his pregnant wife and her family in the city. On 18 March 1787 Prior had written to James Pemberton that "Rufus King suggested to James Parsons in some conversation he lately had with him, that as the Convention proposed to be held in your city [Philadelphia] for Fœderal purposes, was also to take into consideration the Commerce of the States in which the Slave Trade would be a material Subject, whether some hints thrown before that body on that business might not be useful" (Pemberton Papers, PHi). Like Prior, James Parsons was a Quaker and a merchant in New York City.

4. The Massachusetts constitution (1780) declares that "All men are born free and equal" (RCS:Mass., 440). During the 1780s the Massachusetts Supreme Court in the cases of Walker-Jennison and others interpreted this provision as abolishing slavery. Consequently, slaves sued for their freedom, while others left their masters. In 1790 the federal census reported no slaves in Massachusetts. The U.S. Constitution's fugitive slave clause would eliminate Massachusetts as an asylum for runaway slaves.

5. Led by Brown, Rhode Island Quakers petitioned the state legislature to prohibit the slave trade. They were successful on 31 October 1787 when the legislature adopted an act prohibiting Rhode Islanders, under the threat of heavy fines, from taking part in the slave trade. This act was reprinted in the *Daily Advertiser*, 23 November, and the *New York Journal*, 26 November. Both newspapers also printed the Quaker petition of June 1787, sponsored by Brown, that prompted the act. In February 1788 the New York legislature passed an act that tightened an act of 1785 on the slave trade.

Publius: The Federalist 15 (Alexander Hamilton)
New York Independent Journal, 1 December 1787

Inadequacy of Confederation Congress as a legislature. For text, see CC:312. For reprintings, see Appendix IV, below.

Philo-Publius IV
New York Daily Advertiser, 1 December 1787

Upon what basis does our Independence rest, so far as respects the recognition of Foreign Powers? Upon the basis of the UNION.—In what capacity did France first acknowledge our Independence? In the capacity of UNITED STATES. In what capacity did Britain accede to it, and relinquish her pretensions? In the capacity of UNITED STATES.— In what character have we formed Treaties with other Nations? In the character of UNITED STATES.—Are we, in short, known in any other Independent character to any Nation on the face of the Globe?

I admit, that in theory, our Independence may survive the Union; but can the Anti-federalists guarantee the efficacy of this theory upon the Councils of Europe? Can they ensure us against a fate, similar to that which lately befel the distracted and devoted Kingdom of Poland?

Interrogator: To Publius or the Pseudo-Federalist Post-1 December 1787

> This undated, unpublished manuscript written by Hugh Hughes responded to Alexander Hamilton's *The Federalist* 15 (CC:312) which first appeared in the *Independent Journal* on 1 December and was reprinted in the *New York Packet* on 4 December, and the *Daily Advertiser* on 4 and 5 December. Hughes's draft essay, which was addressed to "Publius or the Pseudo-Federalist" asked "a few plain questions," was laced with invectives against "Publius" and the Constitutional Convention, and insinuated that Hamilton was "Publius" (at note 6, below). Hughes probably submitted his essay for publication under the pseudonym "Interrogator," but it was never published. Charles Tillinghast told Hughes that "I put the *Interrogator* into the hands of *Cato*, who gave it to *Brutus* to read, and between them, I have not been able to get it published" (27–28 January 1788, below).
>
> The manuscript essay is in the Hughes Papers in the Library of Congress.

Sir, As you appear to me, from your much laboured & multitudinous Publications, to be *Solicitor General* for the New Constitution (perhaps with a View of being ATTORNEY GENERAL OR LD. CHIEF-JUSTICE under it) and have addressed all your Publications, in it's Favour, "To the People of the State of New York"—in particular; I beg your Permission, *as one of those very Persons*, to request the Solution of a few plain Questions, which (I imagine) are easily solved by a Gentleman of your *Knowledge* and *Identity*.—

This Favour, I think, you can not, reasonably, deny me, especially when you reflect, that you, yourself, have been the Means of inducing it; for, had you not addressed your Publications *to me*, I should not, now, interrogate you.

Will you please to reconcile the 1st. Clause of the 9th. Section, of the first Article[1] of the New Constitution (or your political Creed) with an Assertion of yours, at the latter End of the 3rd [10th][2] Paragraph, in the Conclusion of your 15th Number, where, you say—"We must extend the Authority of the Union to the Persons of the Citizens—*the only proper Objects of Government.*"[3]—Taking you at your Word, what Right, or even a Pretension to Right, could the late Convention have had, for extendg the Authority of Government, had they really been properly authorised to frame a Constitution, to Importing, enslaving and murdering the Africans, who, certainly, are not Citizens of the United States? Could not they complete the Measure of their Iniquity deceiving and enslaving their Fellow Citizens, without having Recourse to the Revival of that which all Christendom are ashamed of, and wish to suppress

In the latter Part of the next Paragraph you assert, that—"In an Association where the general Authority is confined to collective Bodies of the Communities that compose it, every Branch of the Laws must involve a State of War, and military Execution must become the only Instrument of civil Obedience. Such a State of Things can certainly not deserve the Name of Government, nor would any prudent Man chuse to commit his Happiness to it."—And does not the Clause referred to, *involve a State of War and military Execution* to the Persons who are the objects of it?—Nay, does it not do much worse? Does it not involve *a Dissolution of all the tenderest Ties of Nature by an endless Servitude,* the severest Labour, and all its horrid Consequences? that the Wantonness of a lazy, Lordly southern Tobacco—Rice or Indigo, Planter can suggest, or his savage Overseer execute, and that without any Regard to Age, Sex or Condition?

You say—"Such a State of Things can certainly not deserve the Name of Government"—And I ask, by what Name ought the Government, which you are advocating, to be called, when founded in Fraud, Violence Murder and Slavery?—You say—"Nor would any prudent Man chuse to commit his Happiness to it."—And I ask, would any Man whose Pride, Avarice or Lust of Power had not gotten the Better of his Humanity and Love of Justice, advocate the Cause of such an Institution as the late Convention have exhibited—I care not who were the Suggesters, Promoters or Framers of that Clause, nor who has lent his Name to the Adoption of it. I pronounce it to be fraught with every Species of Wickedness, Cruelty and Injustice, of which the Mind of Man is susceptible.—Nor do I believe that the Contrivers of it had, at that Time, either the Love of God, or Man, in their Hearts.

When, in the Middle of the 5th. [12th] Paragraph you ask—"Why has Government been instituted at all?" And answer—"Because the Passions of Men will not conform to the Dictates of *Reason and Justice,*

without Constraint."[4]—Your Conduct seems to me, very much like that
of a Prostitute recommending Chastity to her Sex, lest they should divide the Profits of the Business with her, as one that thought herself
intitled to an exclusive Right to ruin her Adherents.—What else can
you there mean by prostituting the *sacred Names of Reason and Justice?*

Have the Framers of that disgraceful & wicked Clause, or their Adherents, any Pretensions to speak of Reason and Justice, unless it be to
deceive?—But, when you ask the following Question—"Has it been
found that Bodies of Men act with more Rectitude or greater Disinterestedness than Individuals?"—And answer—"The Contrary of this has
been inferred by all accurate Observers of the Conduct of Mankind;
and the Inference is founded upon obvious Reasons. Regard to Reputation has a less active Influence, when the *Infamy* of a bad Action is
to be divided among a Number, than when it is to fall singly upon one.
A *Spirit of Faction* which is apt to mingle its *Poison* in the Deliberations
of all Bodies of Men, will often hurry the Persons of whom they are
composed into Improprieties and Excesses, for which they would blush,
in a private Capacity."[5]—You really speak as tho' you had been a Member of the late Convention,[6] and there experienced, in your own Person, *all the Improprieties and Excesses which a Spirit of Faction could* produce
by mingling its Poison in your Deliberations, and which you so feelingly
and emphatically now describe. I shall be happy to know whether you
had an eye generally, to the Conduct of the Convention, [and?] to the
particular Conduct of one of its Members or Both,—when you assert,
in the 5th. Period, of the 6th [13th] Paragraph that—"Power controled
or abused is almost always the Rival and Enemy of that Power by which
it is controlled or abridged."—For, if one may be permitted to use
some of your own Words, there seems to have been a very considerable
*excentric Tendency in the inferiour Orbs of Both to fly off from the common
Centre.* But this you have very justly & laconicly accounted by saying—
"It has its origin in the love of Power."[7]—This was as [– – –] and you
see that I am willing to allow you all the Credit which it merits. I hope
your Patience is not quite exhausted, because the Joes[8] have not [ap-
peared?], as I yet wish to learn of so able an Informant, by what Authority the Delegate from this State to the late Convention acceded to
their Proceedings? Have you ever seen, heard, or understood that the
Legislature, or either Branch of it, impowered or encouraged him, directly or indirectly, to the accession?

Or, have you ever seen, or heard of, Petitions from a Majority of the
Freeholders and Inhabitants of this State, requesting a new Constitution for the U. States? Or, have you any official or authentic Documents

to prove that any of the States in the Union requested an entire new Constitution by a Consolidation of the Whole?—

If you can Answer all or any of these Questions in the Affirmative, I beg you will be so condescending; as I really wish for Information, and have Reason to think, that many others are in the like Situation.—

If you do not, comply with such reasonable Requisitions, you will please to remember that you subject yourself and Cause to some very unfavourable Inferences.—

Finally, as you appear to be much bloated by a vain Opinion of a little Learning and Knowledge, and not infrequently to have written like a Person, who considered himself as the sole Proprietor of all common Sense, permit me to remind you of the Fable of the Ox and the Frog,[9] who, ambitious to make as great an Appearance as the Former, kept straining its lankey Sides till it burst, which, must be the Fate of every Individual whatever, that attempts to put his scanty Knowledge or Acquirements in Competition with the Aggregate Knowledge of a Nation.—Only reflect on how little you know of your own mental and corporeal Composition, as well as of what daily and momently contributes to your Support and Existence or, that many of the most simple Plebians, or Mechanicks, can teach you some of the first Principles of Philosophy. Or how very little you know of any Thing, when compared with what is unknow[n] to you and Thousands who are much wiser, & you will not find much Cause to value yourself on your Omniscience.

You can not convince "The People of the State of N.Y." nor a Majority of them, that they had better make a Surrender of all their most invaluable Rights, and Property, into the Hands [of] Power, and then to receive as much back as their Lords & Masters may think fit to spare. It is not impossible but your Judgement may have become the Dupe of your Vanity; but you may rely, that you can not Nor can you, by the utmost Effort of all the Rhetoric & Logic you are Master of, persuade the World that either you are, or the Convention, were actuated by the true Principles of Patriotism, or Philanthropy—Posterity will speak of it as it deserves, when you and they are reduced to Dust and Silence[10]—

P.S. How would you relish making a Trip to Algiers in Company with the Authors, Promoters and Abbettors of the Section already mentioned, and there spend the Remainder of your Days at the Chain and Oar or to be driven like Cattle into the interior Parts of the Country and there distributed as might best suit the Captors or Purchasers &c.? Yet Monsters in Wickedness as you and they are! Believe me, I do not wish you nor them a worse Fate, than to experience it long enough to produce a *permanent Contrition.*

1. Article I, section 9, clause 1, of the Constitution reads: "The Migration or Importation of such Persons as any of the States now existing shall think proper to admit, shall not be prohibited by the Congress prior to the Year one thousand eight hundred and eight, but a Tax or duty may be imposed on such Importation, not exceeding ten dollars for each Person."

2. The paragraph number in brackets in this and two other instances in Hughes's draft identify the actual paragraphs in *The Federalist* 15. The differences in the numbers can be explained by the fact that Hughes used the *Daily Advertiser* reprinting in which *The Federalist* 15 appeared in two parts in the issues of 4 and 5 December. As a result, the tenth paragraph in *The Federalist* 15 appears as the third paragraph in the *Advertiser's* issue of 5 December.

3. The italics in the quoted text were supplied by Hughes.

4. The italics in the quoted text were supplied by Hughes.

5. The italics in the quoted text were supplied by Hughes. In the right margin opposite this quoted text, Hughes wrote the word "Lexiphanisms," meaning bombastic phrases.

6. At this point, Hughes is insinuating that Hamilton, one of New York's delegates to the Constitutional Convention, was "Publius."

7. When quoting and paraphrasing a portion of the 13th paragraph of *The Federalist* 15, Hughes took some liberties. That portion of the paragraph reads: "From this spirit it happens, that in every political association which is formed upon the principle of uniting in a common interest a number of lesser sovereignties, there will be found a kind of excentric tendency in the subordinate or inferior orbs, by the operation of which there will be a perpetual effort in each to fly off from the common center. This tendency is not difficult to be accounted for. It has its origin in the love of power. Power uncontrouled or abused is almost always the rival and enemy of that power by which it is controuled or abriged."

8. A "half Joe" or "half Johannes" was a Portuguese gold coin. In English money it was worth eighteen shillings.

9. See Æsop's fable "The Frog and the Ox," the moral of which is "self-conceit may lead to self-destruction."

10. Probably taken from Psalm 6, "Temptations in Sickness Overcome" (long meter), written by English clergyman Isaac Watts (1674–1748) and printed in his *The Psalms of David, Imitated in the Language of the New Testament.* . . . First printed in 1719, these psalms went through many editions and were reprinted numerous times in America, beginning in 1729. The fifth stanza of Psalm 6 reads:

"I feel my flesh so near the grave,
My thoughts are tempted to despair;
But graves can never praise the Lord,
For all is dust and silence there."

James Madison to Edmund Randolph
New York, 2 December 1787 (excerpt)[1]

. . . The inclosed paper contains two numbers of the Federalist.[2] This paper was begun about three weeks ago, and proposes to go through that subject. I have not been able to collect all the numbers, since my return from Philada. or I would have sent them to you. I have been the less anxious as I understand the printer means to make a pamphlet of them, when I can give them to you in a more convenient form. You will probably discover marks of different *pens*. I *am not at liberty* to *give you any* other *key* than that I *am in myself for a few numbers* & that *one besides myself* was a *member* of *the Convention*.[3]

1. RC, Madison Papers, DLC. Printed: CC:314 (longer excerpt); Rutland, *Madison*, X, 289–90. Madison marked the letter "*private*." He encoded the italicized words employing a number code that Randolph had sent to him in 1782. Years later Madison translated the numbers, writing the words above them.

2. The enclosed newspaper was probably either the *New York Packet* of 30 November which printed *The Federalist* 13–14 (CC:300, 310), or the *Independent Journal* of 1 December which printed *The Federalist*, 14–15 (CC:310, 312). Madison wrote number 14, while Alexander Hamilton authored numbers 13 and 15.

3. For the publication of *The Federalist* essays in book form, see *The Federalist* 1, *Independent Journal*, 27 October (above); and "Advertisement for the Book Edition of *The Federalist*," *Independent Journal*, 2 January 1788 (below).

A Countryman III (Hugh Hughes)
New York Journal, 3 December 1787[1]

Letters from a Gentleman in Dutchess County,
to his Friend in New-York.

DEAR SIR, My second Letter[2] was concluded by a Promise that Dr. Franklin should have the Preference in this. However, I do not know, whether, upon the Whole, I ought not to make the Doctor some Acknowledgement, as he does not appear, all Circumstances considered, quite so inconsistent as Mr. Dickenson, or the Author of the Farmer's Letters, who, before this violent Attack on the present Confederation, has not, to my Knowledge, ever been concerned in subverting the Rights or Liberties of the People.

For the sake of America and Humanity, I wish the same could, with Truth, be said of his Colleague, the Doctor, who, as you will presently perceive by his own Words, as well as by Mr. Dickenson's, has long been endeavouring to reconcile this Country to a standing Army, and, I think, an episcopal Hierarchy also; but, the Latter you will be better able to judge of, when you hear him speak for himself, and I do not wish to misrepresent a single Syllable to the Prejudice of him, or any other Person. Perhaps it may not be amiss to acquaint you, that the Doctor's Speech, of which I am going to transcribe a Part, was not an extemporaneous one; but written in Philadelphia, April the 12th, 1764, as appears by the Date, by Way of Letter, to a Friend in the Country, and afterwards published under the Title of "Cool Thoughts on the present Situation of our public Affairs."[3]

He thus begins—"Sir, your Apology was unnecessary. It will be no ⟨Trouble,⟩ but a ⟨pleasure⟩, if I can give you the Satisfaction you desire.

I shall therefore immediately communicate to you my Motives for approving the Proposal of endeavouring to obtain a ⟨Royal Government⟩ in Exchange for this of the Proprietaries; with such Answers to the Objections you mention, as, in my Opinion, fully obviate them."[4]— Then follows, to the 15th Page, a Number of Observations, &c. on the Conduct of the Proprietaries and their Government, &c. with neither of which, at this Time, have we any Concern.

But the 2d. Paragraph in the Page mentioned above, exhibits a Case more in Point, if I may be allowed the Phrase, and begins thus,—⟨"It is farther objected, you tell me, that if we have a Royal Government, we must have with it a Bishop, and a Spiritual Court, and must pay Tythes to support an Episcopal Clergy.⟩ A Bishop for America has been long talked of in England, and probably from the apparent Necessity of the Thing, will sooner or later be appointed; because a Voyage to England for Ordination, is extreamly inconvenient and expensive to the young Clergy educated in America; and the Episcopal Churches and Clergy in these Colonies cannot so conveniently be governed and regulated by a Bishop residing in England, as by one resided among those committed to his Care. But this Event will happen neither sooner nor later for our being, or not being, under a Royal Government. And the spiritual Court, if the Bishop should hold one, can have no Authority only with his own People, &c."[5]—The 2d Paragraph, in the 16th Page, I believe you will readily allow to be more to the Purpose, it being less equivocal; as the Doctor, in his usual Manner, avows his Sentiments, in the following Words—"That ⟨we shall have a standing Army to maintain,⟩ is another Bugbear raised to terrify us from endeavouring to obtain a King's Government. It is very possible that the Crown may think it necessary to keep Troops in America henceforward, to maintain its Conquests, and defend the Colonies; and that the Parliament may establish some Revenue arising out of the American Trade to be applied towards supporting those Troops. It is possible too, that we may, after a few Years Experience, be generally very well satisfied with the Measure, from the steady Protection it will afford us against foreign Enemies, and the Security of internal Peace among ourselves without the Expence or Trouble of a Militia. But assure yourself, my Friend, that whether we like it or not, our continuing under a Proprietary Government will not prevent it, nor our coming under a Royal Government promote and forward it, any more than they would prevent or procure Rain or Sunshine, &c. &c."[6]—To the last Paragraph in the 20th Page, which, as a Part of it, is so exceedingly applicable to the Doctor's, and his Colleague's late Conduct, as well as our Feelings. I presume you will

have no Objection to hearing him conclude, as follows—"On the
Whole, I cannot but think, the more the Proposal is considered, of ⟨an
humble Petition to the⟩ King, ⟨to take this Province under his immediate Protection and Government,⟩ the more unanimously we shall go
into it. We are chiefly People of ⟨three Countries:⟩ British Spirits can
no longer bear the Treatment they have received, nor will they put on
Chains prepared for them by a fellow Subject. And the Irish and Ger-
mans have felt too severely the Oppressions of ⟨hard-hearted Land-
lords⟩ and ⟨arbitrary Princes,⟩ to wish to see, in the proprietaries of
Pennsylvania, both united, &c."[7]—Had he said,—"Nor will they put
on Chains prepared for them by fellow Citizens," it might, perhaps,
have been considered as prophetic of the present Era.—Of this intended Change of Government, in Pennsylvania, Mr. Dickenson, in a
Publication, speaks as follows,—"Benjamin Franklin, Esq. was accordingly chosen Speaker, and in the Afternoon of the same Day, signed
the Petition, as one of his first Acts; an Act which —— but Posterity
will best be able to give it a Name!"[8]—If Mr. Dickenson's Opinion, of
the Doctor's Conduct, was then just, which I believe all honest, unprejudiced Men thought it was, must not the Language we now speak,
become much more copious and expressive than it is, to enable Posterity to give a proper Name to their late joint Act, the new Constitution, as it is called?

I have been the more particular on these Gentlemen's Conduct, as
I perceive that much Stress is laid, by some Writers, on their Patriotism
&c. especially the Doctor's; and many at this time in your City, either
from a State of Minority, or their former Residence, cannot be acquainted with all the Facts and Circumstances which I have produced.
That Dr. Franklin countenanced and encouraged the Stamp Act, I have
had sufficient Proof from several of his most intimate Friends; from his
Conduct in favoring unasked, as they said, several of those Friends Appointments for carrying that Act into Execution,[9] and, lastly, from several Letters to some of those very Persons who were appointed: I saw
a Letter *of the Doctor's own Writing*, in the Hands of his Attorney, in your
City, wherein he was directed to acquaint the Printer of the New-York
Journal, the late Mr. John Holt, *of most respected memory*, that, if he persisted in printing against the Ministry, he must not expect that his Papers would be permitted to circulate by the Post-riders; and this whilst
the Doctor was in England, and the Execution of the Stamp Act was in
Suspence. But Mr. Holt was neither to be cajoled nor intimidated; he
wrote the Doctor, and told his Agent, that, if his Papers were refused
the same Conveyance as the other Printers, he would appeal to the

Public, and hire a Rider, who should carry his Papers, as well as Letters, to his Customers. This, and the Opposition to the Stamp Act, had the desired Effect, an absolute Refusal was not made; but, Mr. Holt's Papers were continually delayed, and not infrequently destroyed by the Doctor's Deputies.[10]

But granting that the Doctor is really as great a Patriot as he has been represented, or, as ever existed, and that his Confederates were all as patriotic and wise as he, nay, supposing that they were all, *in their private Capacities of Divine Descent,* to what does it amount? As Members of the Convention, they were but Deputies of Deputies, not Representatives of the People. Whence then could they derive any Authority for offering a new and unheard of Constitution to the Inhabitants of the United States; when the Legislatures themselves, from whom the Convention derived its very existence, have not Power even to alter a single Sentence of the present Confederation; but only to confirm such Alterations as may be agreed to in a Congress of the United States? To save you the Trouble of looking for the Confederation, as it is now before me, I will transcribe the last Period of the 13th Article, which reads thus—"And the Articles of this Confederation shall be inviolably observed by every State, and the Union shall be perpetual: nor shall any Alteration at any Time hereafter be made in any of them; unless such Alterations be agreed to in a Congress of the United States, and be afterwards confirmed by the Legislatures of every State."—Can any thing be more plain and comprehensive?—With what Consistency or Propriety can the Legislature of this, or any other State, consent to calling a Convention to consider of such a manifest insult offered by their Deputies to the Sovereignties of the States, as well as a most atrocious Attempt to dissolve the Union, when they were deputed solely for the Purpose of improving it, or rather perhaps for devising Means to improve it? If a Convention should be called, of which I confess, I cannot see either the Necessity, or even a Propriety, ought it not to be for impeaching the insidious Contrivers of such deep laid Designs, as appear from the Conduct of some of the late Convention, and the proffered Constitution? As a Grand-Juror, had the Convention sat in this State, I should have been for preferring a Bill against them, as Violators of the present Confederation, and Disturbers of the Public Tranquility. And, as it is, they appear to me, to be proper Objects of Impeachment in the respective States to which they belong; and that as well for a most unparalleled Breach of Trust and Usurpation, as for attempting to destroy the present Confederacy.—Should there, in Consequence of these Men's Conduct, be any Secession or Separation of the States, though I cannot believe that even a Majority will adopt it, as it is; must not they, the Contrivers, be considered as the Authors of all the Evil which may flow from a Dissolution of the Union? And yet, dreadful as the bare Apprehension of a Disunion may be, I do not really know, but it might be more eligible than the Adoption of what is offered us. For, though several very ingenious, sensible and patriotic Writers have undertaken to shew of what the different Parts of the new Constitution deprives us, not one, that I have seen, has attempted to shew in what it has fully and indefeasibly secured us, unless it be in building a Federal Town, with as many Seraglios as may be wanted, and supporting a standing army, to defend them against foreign Invasions, &c. Nor do I believe it in the Power of the Projectors and all their Adherents, to prove that we are sufficiently Secure in any one essential Right, either Civil or Religious, when such unlimited Powers are vested in a haughty Senate, and a hungry Monarchy, both of which may be continued as long as exorbitant Grants of Land, Contracts, Places, Pensions, and every Species of Bribery and Corruption, have an Influence. But more of this some other Time; I have not leisure, at present, to enlarge. I am, Dear Sir, Very respectfully, your's, &c. A COUNTRYMAN.

1. Reprinted: Philadelphia *Independent Gazetteer*, 30 April 1788.

2. See "A Countryman" II, *New York Journal*, 23 November (above).

3. See Leonard W. Labaree et al., eds., *The Papers of Benjamin Franklin* (36 vols. to date, New Haven and London, 1959–), XI, 153–73. Franklin's essay, signed "A.B.," first appeared in the supplement to the *Pennsylvania Journal*, 26 April 1764. In the same year, two Philadelphia printers printed the essay as separate pamphlet editions entitled *Cool Thoughts on the Present Situation of Our Public Affairs. In a Letter to a Friend in the Country* (Evans 9663–64). The text in angle brackets in the paragraphs that follow were italicized in the Franklin pamphlet but not in the *New York Journal.*

4. Labaree, *Franklin Papers*, XI, 157.

5. *Ibid.*, 168.

6. *Ibid.*, 169–70.

7. *Ibid.*, 172–73.

8. The quotation is from the preface to Dickinson's "Speech on a Petition for a Change of Government of the Colony of Pennsylvania," 24 May 1764. The preface was written, not by Dickinson, but by the Reverend William Smith, the provost of the College of Philadelphia (University of Pennsylvania) (Paul Leicester Ford, ed., *The Writings of John Dickinson*, in *Memoirs* of the Historical Society of Pennsylvania, XIV [Philadelphia, 1895], 14). In 1764 two pamphlet editions of this lengthy speech were printed in Philadelphia by William Bradford (Evans 9641–42).

9. In early 1765, when the Stamp Act was being considered, Benjamin Franklin was in London as a special agent to persuade the British government to take Pennsylvania away from its proprietors, the Penn family, and convert it into a royal colony, thereby benefiting the Quaker Party of which he was a leader. Franklin's mission was opposed by the Proprietary Party. Along with agents from other colonies, Franklin opposed the Stamp Act before its adoption, but after the act became law on 22 March 1765 he obtained the appointment of political ally John Hughes as stamp agent for Pennsylvania and of William Cox for New Jersey. Franklin also wrote members of the Quaker Party, advising them that

it would be wise to submit to the act. (John Hughes was the brother of Hugh Hughes, the author of "A Countryman" and a Son of Liberty who vigorously opposed the Stamp Act.)

10. The Franklin and Holt letters described by "A Countryman" have not been located. Holt was one of the most vociferous critics of the Stamp Act, thereby winning favor with the Sons of Liberty. However, when Holt wanted to suspend publication of his *New York Gazette* after the Stamp Act went into effect on 1 November 1765, the Sons of Liberty wrote him a letter, stating that it would be best if he continued to publish without stamped paper. If Holt refused to publish, he could "depend upon it, your House, Person and Effects, will be in imminent Danger." Holt agreed to continue publishing his newspaper and he printed the letter of the Sons of Liberty in it on 7 November 1765.

The Circulation of New York Antifederalist Material in Connecticut
New York Daily Advertiser, 4 December 1787[1]

Because Connecticut's nine newspapers printed or reprinted very little Antifederalist material, New York Antifederalists began, sometime in early to mid-November, to disseminate Antifederalist literature in neighboring Connecticut. Soon, the *New York Journal*, the *Letters from the Federal Farmer*, and the broadside or handbill versions of Antifederalist essays (originating in Philadelphia and New York City) were circulating widely in Connecticut, to the chagrin of both Connecticut and New York Federalists.

On 22 November the *New Haven Gazette* decried the industrious circulation of "Centinel" I (CC:133), which had originated in Philadelphia in early October and which, among other things, declared that George Washington and Benjamin Franklin, both signers of the Constitution, had been duped. Without naming Antifederalist leader John Lamb, the *New Haven Gazette* referred to Lamb as a longtime "furious and violent" opponent of "all federal measures" who was responsible for the circulation of Antifederalist material in Connecticut (CC:283–A). On 1 December the *New Haven Gazette's* piece was reprinted, without comment, in the *New York Morning Post*. On 4 December a correspondent of the *Daily Advertiser* attacked New York's Antifederalists for circulating Antifederalist literature in Connecticut in order "to delude the people and excite jealousies." The next day the *Advertiser* reprinted the *New Haven Gazette's* piece of 22 November with a prefatory statement by "An Old Customer," indicating that the *Gazette's* piece well illustrated "the paragraph" printed by the *Advertiser* on the 4th. (The *New Haven Gazette's* item was also reprinted in the *Albany Gazette* on 6 December. For reprints of the *Daily Advertiser* item of 4 December, see note 1, below.)

On 13 December the *New Haven Gazette* printed a satirical "ADVERTISE-MENT" warning the public that "a large overgrown Creature marked *and branded* CENTINEL" had broken into Connecticut. It had been driven out of Pennsylvania by "the lash of Mr. [James] Wilson." The "ADVERTISEMENT" left little doubt as to who was responsible for the circulation of "Centinel" in Connecticut, as it revealed that the creature "was lately in the keeping of J——— L———of New-York" (CC:283–C). Four days later the Hartford *American Mercury* conjectured that handbills received in Hartford were sent by "a LAMB, or rather a Wolf in Sheep's cloathing." The *New Haven Gazette's* "ADVERTISE-

MENT" was reprinted in the *Daily Advertiser*, 19 December; *Country Journal*, 26 December; *Northern Centinel*, 1 January 1788; and *New York Journal*, 7 January; while the *American Mercury's* piece was reprinted in the *Albany Gazette*, 3 January. The "ADVERTISEMENT" was reprinted in the *Country Journal* at the request of "A Customer" who noted that "It is an entertaining burlesque on a most detestable performance, and which has been circulated in this State no less than in Connecticut; and for the same gracious purpose of poisoning and inflaming the passions of the people."

When the *New York Journal* reprinted the "ADVERTISEMENT," it placed (in brackets) below the "ADVERTISEMENT" a commentary defending John Lamb and attacking Federalists that had first appeared in the Philadelphia *Independent Gazetteer*, 27 December, also in tandem with the "ADVERTISE-MENT." This commentary reads: "The advocates of the new system of government must be very much exhausted in point of argument indeed, when they have recourse to such wretched abuse as is contained in the above *advertisement*. Unfortunately for this horrid scribbler, the gentleman, at whom he has levelled his scurrility and low ribaldry, is held in the highest estimation by his fellow-citizens for his honor, integrity, and unshaken attachment to the cause of liberty—And the name of the patriotic LAMB of New-York, 'will be sweet in the mouths' of a grateful and applauding country—when those of his infamous political adversaries,—the *upstarts and mushrooms* of an hour,—the *totos* and *major tiffanies*—the *time-serving* tools, the *Phocions and Publiuses* of our day,— 'will stink in the very nostrils of posterity.' " (The phrase "*Phocions and Publiuses* of our day" was probably an allusion to Alexander Hamilton who used both pseudonyms.)

For more on the circulation and impact of New York and Philadelphia Antifederalist material in Connecticut, see CC:283. See also "New York Reprinting of the Centinel Essays," 17 October 1787–12 April 1788 (above).

Nothing, says a correspondent, can equal the meanness of the Anti-Federal junto in America, but the low arts of our enemies during the war. Like them the Anti-Federal men are circulating hand-bills, fraught with sophistry, declamation and falshoods, to delude the people and excite jealousies. A few days ago a packet was sent from New-York to Connecticut, enclosed and addressed to a very respectable gentleman, with an anonymous letter, requesting him to circulate the hand-bills among the people. The hand-bills contained Anti-federal essays. The gentleman determined at first to commit them to the flames, as they deserved; but reflecting that the people are above the influence of such despicable arts, he sent them into the country. What a poor cause is that which its advocates are ashamed to avow and support, but by the dirty arts that would have disgraced the enemies of liberty, during the struggle for Independence! But such stratagems are useless in Connecticut. Every man has taken his side, and almost every man of information, on the side of the Constitution. On the other side are ranged a few weak people and the friends of Shays.

1. Reprinted: *Northern Centinel*, 18 December; *Albany Gazette*, 20 December; *Massachusetts Gazette*, 4 January 1788; *New Hampshire Mercury*, 9 January; Exeter, N.H., *Freeman's Oracle*, 18 January.

Publius: The Federalist 16 (Alexander Hamilton)
New York Independent Journal, 4 December 1787

Confederation Congress lacks powers of enforcement. For text, see CC:317. For reprintings, see Appendix IV, below.

Publius: The Federalist 17 (Alexander Hamilton)
New York Independent Journal, 5 December 1787

Balance of powers between states and central government. For text, see CC:321. For reprintings, see Appendix IV, below.

Americanus IV
New York Daily Advertiser, 5–6 December 1787[1]

The investigation of the principles and probable tendency of the new plan of Government, is evidently the most important discussion that ever employed the pen or engaged the attention of man: The immense magnitude of the subject fills the mind with the most awful impressions. To suffer ourselves to be governed in a business of so interesting a nature by the maxims and principles of systematic writers, however celebrated, would be an unpardonable indiscretion. Let us avail ourselves of every light they can afford; but would it not be downright madness to shackle ourselves with maxims and principles which are clearly inapplicable to the nature of our political institutions? The path we are pursuing is new, and has never before been trodden by man. Our principal dependance, then, in this arduous business, must be derived from the resources of our own minds: As we can find no rule or precedent to which we can appeal, our determinations must result from the dispassionate but vigorous exertions of our own good sense and judgment. From this view of the subject I feel the incumbent weight on my shoulders. I am sensible how hard a task it is to root out and abolish errors sanctified and established by time and the reputation of celebrated writers.

In every science this rule must invariably hold good, that new combinations require new principles. Montesquieu tells us, "it is a fundamental law in Democracies, that the people should have the sole power to enact laws."[2] From this fundamental law, all his reasonings, all his inferences on the nature of this species of Government are drawn. That a Republic should be confined to a small territory—heroic virtues—self-denial—and the sacrifice of our dearest interests are essentially necessary, and are consequences flowing immediately from the nature of this fundamental law. For, was the Government extensive, the people would find the exercise of their sovereignty impracticable, and was it not for the patriotism and self-denial of individuals, the public interest would be neglected or betrayed.

But has this law been established as a fundamental in the Constitution of any of our Governments? I believe Cato himself will not venture to answer this question in the affirmative. It is a fact notorious to all the world, to the unlearned as well as learned, that the people of these States have in no instance retained the exercise of sovereignty in their own hands; but have universally appointed representatives to legislate for them. Here then there obviously appears a most material and essential difference between the fundamental law of Democracy laid down by Montesquieu, and the fundamental law established in the several Constitutions of these States. From this difference of the fundamental law, there of course flow principles and consequences as different. And as we manifestly can have no recourse to precedent, our political institutions being founded upon a fundamental law altogether new in Republican government, the principles and consequences resulting therefrom must be sought after and discovered from our own experience, and from deductions drawn from the peculiar nature of these institutions.

Having, as I presume, cleared the question (as the mathematician does his equation from co-efficients) of these non-essentials, which can serve no other purpose but to perplex and embarrass our enquiries, I shall now proceed to the further consideration of Cato's objections; and glean up every sentence which carries the least shadow of an argument, and which has not yet been fully answered.

"This consolidated Republic cannot do without the aid of a standing army." It is readily admitted that a moderate military establishment will be necessary. But, "will not political security, and even the opinion of it, be extinguished?" By no means. There are various circumstances which will render it impossible for a standing army to become dangerous; provided these States continue United. The causes which require large military establishments in Europe, do not exist on this side the Atlantic. But why is the trifling force which it may be necessary for us to keep up, made so great a bug-bear of? Does not Great-Britain support a standing army vastly greater than we can ever have occasion for? Yet, if we go out of our own country, where shall we find more "political security;" less "force," less "violence," in the exercise of the powers of Government? But, "the malecontents in each State," who, as Cato informs us, "will *not be a few*, nor *the least important*, will be exciting factions against it."[3] What will be the numbers of these malecontents, I know not. It will be sufficient if the majority in favor of the Constitution be clear and decided, which I sincerely hope, and firmly believe it will be. Indeed, should an Angel come down from Heaven, and present us with a Constitution of Government altogether spotless and free from blemish; should we not still have malecontents amongst us? Would there not be Cato's and Brutus's ready to disseminate groundless jealousies and vain fears? If a plan of Government must be rejected because some are opposed to it, is it not evident that none can ever be adopted? One remark, however, I must beg leave to address more immediately to Cato and his party: If there is any one "axiom in the science of politics," which may be deemed "irrefragable," it must certainly be this;—that in a free Government the majority must necessarily govern; and that, therefore, it becomes the indispensable duty of good citizens to acquiesce; to attempt an opposition by means of force and violence, would be to commit a crime of the blackest dye.

[6 December] Cato insinuates that a large Republic is less capable of suppressing domestic insurrections than a small one. From what causes do insurrections generally arise? Some turbulent individual infuses jealousy and discontent into the minds of the people. But the personal influence of an individual cannot extend far. The contagion therefore must spread progressively, if it spreads at all; indeed, it can never happen but from some gross error in Government, that the great body of the people, spread over a large extent of country, can all be infected with this spirit of discontent at one and the same time. The time that must necessarily be consumed in communicating the flame of sedition from one quarter of an extensive territory to another, will also give time to Government to collect her strength. The passion of the insurgents will cool—wild uproar will give place to calm reflection—negociation will ensue—matters will be accommodated, and peace restored. But should Government be drove to the disagreeable necessity of recurring to the use of arms; it will then be a matter of no small moment that, from the extent of her territories, she is able to collect her forces from parts remote from the scene of action. From hence, this capital advantage, among many others, will be derived; that, on the restoration of peace, harmony and cordial reconciliation will probably ensue, as personal resentment and rancor will not be engendered between parties who will of course be strangers to each other.

Cato tells us that the Government of small States will be more mild and also more vigorous than that of larger ones. But if it is true that small States ever have been, and from the nature of man ever must be the nurseries of parties, factions, discord, discontent, wild uproar, and seditious tumults; this observation of his must manifestly be erroneous. The characteristics of a *mild* Government are Liberty without Licentiousness, and Government without Tyranny; of a *vigorous* one, unanimity, consistency, and uniformity in its councils.

We are told that extent of territory, variety of climates, productions and commerce, difference of extent, and number of inhabitants, dissimilitude of interests, morals and politics, will render this consolidated Republican form of Government impracticable. But what is the drift and tendency of this mode of argumentation? It evidently militates with equal force against every species of general Government—call it by what name you will, whether Consolidation or Confederation, it matters not, all must be equally impracticable. Nay! this mode of argumentation leads immediately to consequences which I cannot suppose Cato could have had in contemplation. If diversity of interest arising from various contingencies, such as climate, productions, commerce, morals, politics, &c. &c. form invariable bars against the due exercise of the powers of Government; then, I say there is an end of every thing.

For, if the infinite number and variety of distinct and jarring interests, which necessarily prevail among the individuals of a society in a state of civilization cannot be controled and reconciled by the energetic exertions of the powers of Government, we must then relinquish all our ideas of the efficiency of Government as mere chimeras. The very end, purpose and design of all Government is to prevent the destructive effects of these clashing interests on the peace, security and happiness of society. Strange mode of argumentation! that the very circumstances which require and call aloud for all the energy of such an efficient Government as this constitution has delineated, should, by an unaccountable perversity of all the rules of just reasoning, be urged as an argument against the Constitution itself.

We are told that the strongest principle of Union exists between the members of the same family. The next general principle of Union is amongst citizens of the same state; but when we still enlarge the circle so as to comprehend the citizens of other States, affection and attachment are lost.—"Is it therefore, from certainty like this, reasonable to believe the inhabitants of Georgia or New-Hampshire will have the same obligations towards you as your own, and preside over your lives, liberties and property with the same care and attachment?" It is by no means necessary. The principles I have endeavored to establish as resulting from the nature of our Governments, form a sufficient answer to this question. This attachment to the particular interest of our own State, if too strong, becomes a very pernicious principle; and I view it as a capital advantage that the nature of our Governments renders it in a great measure unnecessary. It is sufficient that we have the most ample and clearest assurances which the nature of the thing will admit of, that the interests of the States individually can never be wantonly sacrificed. That the general interests of the Union should be first attended to and provided for, is but just and proper.

I come next to the consideration of Cato's fifth number,[4] a great part of which is taken up with a long and labored harangue against trusting discretionary power in the hands of any man. Propriety of language, elegance of diction, and justness of remark, it must be allowed are by no means wanting here: but how these remarks apply to a Constitution in which the powers of Government are ascertained and defined with accuracy and precision, I am at a loss to conceive. From want of explicitness in this Constitution, he again urges the probability of a Monarchial establishment.

That the fecund womb of time may hereafter produce causes and events tending to such an establishment, is to be sure not impossible, but, in my opinion, very improbable. This inexplicitness which Cato complains of, can operate only as a drop to the bucket. A free people are not to be deprived of their liberty by logical refinements and mere verbal criticisms. To effect this purpose more efficacious means must be recurred to.

After revolving this subject in my own mind, in every light I can place it, I can see none of those dangerous consequences, apprehended by Cato, from investing the Executive power in the hands of a single person. The most effectual way, perhaps, of effacing these gloomy fears from our minds, is to compare the distribution of power made by this Constitution, with the distribution of power which has taken place in the Government of Great-Britain. It is a fact, universally admitted, that no people have ever enjoyed real liberty, in so eminent a degree, as do the people of England. But what an immense disparity is there between this celebrated Government, and the Constitution offered for our acceptance, with respect to the limitations and restrictions in favor of liberty! We find there an hereditary Monarch, invested with such an host of dangerous prerogatives as appears incompatible with any degree of liberty. He has the sole prerogative of making war and peace; of making treaties, leagues and alliances, on whatever condition he thinks proper; sends and receives Ambassadors; he forms a distinct branch of the Legislature; he has the sole command of the fleets and armies, with the appointment of all the offices and places dependent thereon, both military and civil; he alone can levy troops, equip fleets and build fortresses. He is the source of all the Judicial power in the State; he is the chief of all the tribunals, and the Judges are only his substitutes; every thing is transacted in his name; the judgments must be with his seal, and are executed by his officers. By a fiction in the law, he is looked upon as the universal proprietor of the kingdom. He can pardon offences. He is the fountain of honor, office and privilege; creates Peers of the realm, and distributes titles and dignities. He is the head and supreme governor of the national Church. In this capacity he appoints the Bishops, and the two Archbishops; he alone convenes, prorogues or dissolves the Convocation of the Clergy; his assent likewise is necessary to the validity of their acts. He is the Superintendent of Commerce; he has the prerogative of regulating weights and measures; he alone can coin money, and can give currency to foreign coin. He possesses the power of convening, proroguing and dissolving the Parliament; the collection, management and expenditure of an immense revenue, deposited annually in the Royal Exchequer, with the appointment of an almost innumerable tribe of officers dependent thereon. In fine, what seems to carry so many powers to the height, is its being a fundamental maxim, that THE KING CAN DO NO WRONG; he is above the reach of all Courts of law; he is accountable to no power whatever in the nation; and his person is sacred and inviolable.

In the next place, we find an hereditary Nobility, and an order of gownsmen totally dependent on the Crown, who form another distinct branch of the Legislature, and a Court of Judicature in cases of appeal. This body of Nobility are created and encreased at the will of the Crown. Here are then, two branches out of three of the Legislature, wholly independent of the people. The House of Commons are, to be sure, an elective body, and the only part of the Government in any degree dependent on the people. They form, however, a very imperfect representation of the collective body of the people. Out of 513, the number of Members sent by England to Parliament, the Boroughs and Cinque Ports send no less than 382. Some of these Boroughs contain but one voter; many of them not more than ten; and the major part of them less than one hundred. But if representation is so imperfect and unequal, there still remains a most capital defect, as to the frequency of elections, and the vague, uncertain footing this privilege of the people, so indispensibly necessary to liberty, stands upon. No fixed rule has been established for the duration of Parliament. But it is left to the discretion of Parliament itself to lengthen or shorten its own duration, as they in their wisdom shall judge expedient; and accordingly we find Parliaments to have been annual, triennial, septennial, duodennial, and octodennial. At present they are septennial.[5]

When we consider maturely all these circumstances in the Government of Great-Britain, so unfriendly to liberty, instead of supposing them the freest people on earth (ourselves excepted) it must really appear wonderful, that any degree of liberty whatever can be supported. But it must add greatly to our surprise on this occasion, when we consider further, that this people, so celebrated for liberty, have emerged, by slow and almost imperceptible degrees; from a state of the vilest vassalage, to their present pre-eminent station among nations. Indeed the history of the rise and progress of liberty amongst this people, in circumstances so extremely unfavorable and adverse, has convinced me fully, that it is impossible to subjugate a numerous and free people, spread over a wide extent of country, without the intervention and concurrence of adventitious and extrinsic causes. The ordinary powers of a well constructed Government are inadequate to this purpose. Let not, therefore, my fellow-countrymen, the gloomy apprehensions of Cato fright your imaginations. Nothing surely can be more chimerical than this idea of the powers of a President finally degenerating into an establishment for life.

1. On 28 November the *Daily Advertiser* announced that "Americanus" IV was received. This essay responds to "Cato" III–V, *New York Journal*, 25 October, and 8 and 22 November (all above). See also note 4, below.

2. *Spirit of Laws*, I, Book II, chapter II, 17.

3. "Americanus" added the italics in this quotation from "Cato" III (above).

4. "Cato" discussed the executive in his fourth and fifth essays, but primarily in the former.

5. The Septennial Act (1716) provided that Parliament not continue longer than seven years.

Don Diego de Gardoqui to Conde de Floridablanca
New York, 6 December 1787 (excerpt)[1]

. . . It seems likely that the plan of government proposed by the [Constitutional] Convention will be ratified by the required nine States, perhaps during next year, in spite of the opposition that is expected from the two most considerable [states] of Virginia and New York.

The first [state] is divided into two parties composed of its leading subjects, and they have postponed the Meeting of their special Convention to consider the matter until May.

Although no one knows what will happen in this [state], it is asserted that the Governor[2] and his party, which is the strongest, are violently opposed to the plan. It is likely that their Assembly will meet at the beginning of the year and that they will reveal themselves.

Meanwhile, a great deal is written for and against [the Constitution], but it appears that the majority inclines toward acceptance, rather, in my opinion, because of the depleted state of their Treasury and Commerce, than because of the knowledge of the sacrifices that the people are making for the Government.

They expect great benefits from it [the Constitution], but I confess that I do not find it as they do, because having compared their Commerce in general to that of other nations, I see no reason why these [other nations] should change their system of exclusion which they have imposed upon them [the Americans], so that even after this experiment they will not be much better off. . . .

1. RC (Tr), Estado, Legajo 3893, Apartado 3, Reservado 18, pp. 433–44, Archivo Histórico Nacional, Madrid. Printed in D. C. Corbitt and Roberta Corbitt, trans. and eds., "Papers from the Spanish Archives Relating to Tennessee and the Old Southwest, 1783–1800," East Tennessee Historical Society *Publications*, XVI ([Knoxville], 1944), 90–95. Longer excerpts appear in RCS:Va., 204–7. Gardoqui (1735–1798), Spain's encargado de negocios, arrived in America in 1785 to negotiate a commercial treaty with the United States, with instructions not to surrender Spain's claim to the exclusive navigation of the Mississippi River. Gardoqui was also instructed to negotiate certain boundary disputes between the United States and Spain. He remained in America until 1789. Floridablanca (1728–1808) was Spain's Secretary of State.

2. George Clinton.

P. Valerius Agricola
Albany Gazette, 6 December 1787[1]

AN ESSAY, On the CONSTITUTION recommended by the FEDERAL CONVENTION to the UNITED STATES.   By P. VALERIUS AGRICOLA.

⟨So frequently has the catalogue of public calamities been recited, so long have its gloomy contents engrossed our attention, that I would gladly wa[i]ve coming to particulars, were it less essential to the present enquiry.

These are stubborn facts,[2] too apparent we presume to be contested.

—That the UNION of the American States, if not merely nominal is at best imperfect, inefficient and precarious.

—That our national character has become contemptible in the sight of mankind.

—That our finances are deranged, our resources exhausted, and we [are] consequently unable to satisfy the demands of the national creditors, now clamorous for justice.

—That no uniform continental system of justice has been yet established, but that to the disgrace of the American name, there are at this day existing, in several of the states, laws incompatible with the principles of morality, destructive of that good faith, by which our domestic and foreign interests can alone be maintained.

—That a spirit of discord and rebellion which too visibly pervades the continent on the one hand, and the recent hostilities of the savages, on the other, evince the necessity of a spirited, energetic government, to ward off the calamities of war and insure our domestic tranquility.

—That while thus endangered we are destitute, of the means of defence, without an army to secure us from domestic violence, without a navy to guard our sea coasts, from piratical depredations, without money to raise and maintain an armament, and without that credit which might enable us to make use of foreign resources.

That our deranged and enfeebled situation being known to the world, we are become the prey of European policy, ever ready to take advantages of our embarrassments, and deprive us of the many benefits incident to our local situation, and which a wise system of policy might undoubtedly secure.

That our commerce is dwindled to a sound—the trifling trade we carry on, being fettered with restrictions equally injurious and degrading.

And finally that in our present situation, we have no reasonable prospect of securing the blessings of liberty to ourselves and our posterity.)[3](a)

A question now naturally occurs, how came we in this embarrassed situation? so complicated a series of difficulties, could scarcely proceed from circumstances merely adventitious, but rather argue that something is radically defective in the constitution.(b)

The history of mankind has afforded us these two cases in politics; each of which is replete with mischief to [the] community.

I. When the constitution of a state, is so vague and imperfect, that it becomes dubious to what part of the community; many of the *powers of government* are instrusted.

II. When the constitution has so injudiciously disposed the *powers of government* in the community, that they cannot co-operate nor act to advantage.

In the first case, we find the source of these calamities, which ordinarily attend nations, just emerging from a state of nature and as yet unacquainted with many principles of civil policy. Such are the erratic tribes of Asia and America, barbarous and unpolished as they are, we can yet discern among them the faint traces of sovereignty, some few and simple regulations formed on the spur of the occasion, and adapted to their immediate exigences.

Yet as no actual compact has been ever made, as their ideas and their wants are comparitively few, their constitutions are very defective, and in numerous instances it becomes impossible to determine what rights belong to the community, and what to the individual; involved in this obscurity they are put into confusion by every new occurrence in their politics, and fall an easy prey to the first more civilized invader.

In justice to ourselves we must own that we are yet some degrees removed, from absolute barbarity—Perhaps all the members of sovereignty may be found scattered here and there in our unwieldy system of state and federal policy, and at one period or other of our national existence, we have exercised or attempted to exercise all the rights of a state.—We have exercised legislation, proclaimed and carried on war—concluded peace—made treaties—sent and received ambassadors—established loans—opened loans—laid assessments and levies—emitted bills of credit—established commercial regulations, &c. We must therefore apply to the second case mentioned, viz. An injudicious disposition of the *rights of sovereignty*:—For as it is well known, that a piece of machinery, for instance, a clock or a watch may contain all the necessary springs, wheels and pivots, but these being improperly disposed may produce an effect quite contrary to the design of the artist;—so from an unskilful disposition of the *jura summi imperij*,[4] the politician has often seen his fine spun theories, his darling systems, fall into confusion,

> "And like the baseless fabric of a vision,
> Leave not a trace behind."[5]

And here we beg leave to advance certain political axioms: That the *rights of sovereignty* combined, form our grand and national law, to which UNIVERSALITY, PERMANENCY and UNIFORMITY are essential—consequently any system will be defective in proportion as either or all of these requisites are wanting. That as in mechanics when equal forces oppose, they mutually destroy each other as in domestics; when several members of a family pretend to an equal share in the government, discontent and confusion will ensue—so in politics, when the *parts* pretend to an exercise of those transcendent and sovereign rights, which the safety of government requires should be vested in the confederacy, the community will naturally be reduced to debility, and distraction, for this reason, civilians have ever exploded the *imperium in imperio*[6] as an absurdity in government.

A person superficially acquainted with the system of American policy might, perhaps, conclude, that the sovereignty of the states is lodged in *Congress*, as several of the grand rights of sovereignty are actually, and others ostensibly, vested in that body by the confederation, but, upon enquiry, he would find that certain of the *jura summi imperij* are not expressly deposited in the federal government—that others are participated by Congress with the particular States, and that the most pernicious consequences have, in every instance, attended this participation.

Suffer us here to particularize.

One of the *rights of sovereignty* is, the assessing of money for the public service, and this right is lodged in Congress—Congress may ascertain the *quantum* of supplies, and assign the quota of the several states.

But it belongs, likewise, to sovereignty to levy the supplies when assessed; for [(c)] *qui dat finem dat media ad illum necessaria.* In this instance, however, the power of Congress is merely recommendatory; Congress may request, but cannot compel.—The right of levying money, the extreme caution of our political fathers, has lodged in the individual states: here the sovereignty is participated between the *whole* and the *parts*, and an absolute *imperium in imperio* at once created.

It is essential to a law that it be *compulsory*; for law acts upon the unwilling; but where is the power lodged of compelling the individual states to comply with the will of the *whole* signified in the requisition of Congress? The state, it will be said, has contracted that it *will* comply; but contracts act only on the willing, and require the intervention of a compulsory power to carry them into effect—This power is not in *Congress*—they can only recommend; it is not in the delinquent state, for a power of forcing one's selves, is an absurdity in terms—it is not lodged in any other state in the confederacy, for the states are equals and [(d)] *inter pares nulla est potestas.*—Thus, in this instance, both the cases afore mentioned are exemplified.

Here it has been answered, that although a state cannot *quasi* be said to compel itself, yet, a state may compel its delinquent members, which will eventually be the same thing; and that we may safely rely on the wisdom and patriotism of the states in a matter so essential to their own happiness and security.

Reasoning of this sort may argue the honest, unsuspicious man, but can give us no high opinion of his acquaintance with human nature.

The history of mankind will inform us that public bodies, like individuals, are capable of acting foolishly, and directly contrary to their interests; and that *patriotism*, when the spur of danger ceases to impel, dwindles to a sound and becomes the mere watch word of party.

In the moment of imminent danger, of the *Hannibal ad portas*,[7] *public spirit*, like the gods of Homer, may descend from heaven and support the combatants; but when that critical moment is past, she mixes again with the divinities and leaves man to himself. The experience of every age has confirmed this truth—and the founders of our policy might have remembered that Americans were but men.

A few years ago, and these sentiments had been censured as visionary and malevolent, and the author stigmatized as unfriendly to the liberties of this country; but he is unhappy to observe, that innumerable facts have but too well realised the facts he apprehended in theory.— We have seen in Rhode-Island, a striking example of political madness and perve[r]seness—we have seen the plains of Springfield red with gore, and an armed banditti hovering o'er the heights of Pelham![8]

Quos Deus perdat prius dementat.[(e)]

Come hither, ye opposers of a reform, and inform us what is the state of the public finances? what progress has been made (we will not ask) in discharging the principal, but the interest of the national debt? What are our resources, in case invasion from abroad or rebellion at home should render it necessary to appeal to arms? Inform us how far the states have complied with congressional requisitions—whether any of the states, excepting *New York*, have paid any considerable part of their quotas into the public treasury?[9] What is the probability of their speedy compliance, and whether many of the public embarrassments must not be charged to these deficiencies; and finally, whether they imagine that the sounds of *public spirit* and DEMOCRACY will prove as effectual a charm in blunting the tomahawk and dagger, as they have been in lulling the senses and fears of the multitude? Let truth reply, and on the answer we will venture to rest the question.

> (a) We presume that the reader will excuse us for presenting him in this place with the following lines; written by the ingenuous author of the *Anarchiad*,[10] lately published in Connecticut.
>
> And lo! th' expected scene advances near,
> The promis'd age; the fiends' *millenial* year!
> At that fam'd æra, rais'd by angry fates,
> What countless imps shall throng the new born states!
> See from the shades on tiny pinions swell,
> And rise the young *democracy* of hell!
> Before their face the powers of Congress fade
> And *public credit* sinks an empty shade;
> Wide severance rages, wars intestine spread,
> Their boasted *union* hides its dying head,
> The forms of government in ruin hurl'd,

Reluctant empire quits the western world!
Oh glorious throng, beyond expression wise,
Expert to act, excentric to devise!
In retrogressive march, what schemes advance,
What vast resources and what strange finance!
Chimeras sage with plans commercial fraught,
Sublime abortions of projecting thought!
To paper coin how copper mints succeed!
How Indian wars in brains prolific breed!
What strength, what firmness guide the public helm,
How troops disbanded guard the threat'ned realm!
How treaties thrive, and midst the sons of Ham,
The LYBIAN LION[11] shrinks before the LAMB![12]
New modes of taxing spring from WOGLOG's[13] hands.
And peerless WIMBLE[14] sells the western lands.

(b) The author of this essay takes it for granted, that the present political system of the states, as expressed in the articles of confederation, is materially defective—as even the warmest opposers of the constitution, proposed by the convention have not scrupled, of late to acknowledge it, however, they differ in their ideas of reform. Indeed the resolutions of Congress, which recommended the convention at Philadelphia; the concurring acts of the state legislatures, have authoritatively fixed this a maxim, in American politics—that the confederation is inadequate to the exigencies, of the community and requires a revision.

(c) *He who gives the end also gives the means conducive thereto.*

(d) *Equals have not the right of coercion.*

(e) *God first infatuates those he gives up to destruction.*[15]

(To be continued)

1. For the first part of this essay, see "P. Valerius Agricola," *Albany Gazette*, 8 November (above). On 15 November the *Albany Gazette* had announced that this essay was "unavoidably postponed" until 22 November. Instead, it did not appear until 6 December.

2. See "P. Valerius Agricola," *Albany Gazette*, 8 November, at note 9 and note 9 (above).

3. The text in angle brackets, along with the end of the first part of this essay, was reprinted without the pseudonym, in the *Massachusetts Centinel*, 22 December (Mfm:Mass.).

4. William Blackstone defines this phrase as "the rights of sovereignty" (*Commentaries*, Book I, section 2, p. 49).

5. William Shakespeare, *The Tempest*, Act IV, scene 1, lines 151, 156.

6. Latin: A sovereignty within a sovereignty, or an absolute authority within the jurisdiction of another.

7. Latin: Hannibal is at the gates, or the enemy is close at hand.

8. In early 1787 Shaysites were routed by Massachusetts militia at Springfield. Another body of militia pursued the Shaysites through several towns, including Pelham (the home of Daniel Shays) and finally defeated them at Petersham, ending the rebellion.

9. See *Daily Advertiser*, 21 July, note 4 (above).

10. *The Anarchiad*—written by Connecticut poets Joel Barlow, Lemuel Hopkins, David Humphreys, and John Trumbull—was published in twelve installments under the title "American Antiquities" in the *New Haven Gazette* between 26 October 1786 and 13 September 1787. The eleventh installment, an extract of which is printed here, appeared first in the *Connecticut Courant* on 6 August; it was the only installment that was not first printed in the *New Haven Gazette*, the *Gazette* reprinted it on 16 August. *The Anarchiad*, a work that supported strengthening the central government and vilified the opponents of such a government, was widely reprinted. In New York, the eleventh installment was reprinted in the *Daily Advertiser*, 11 August, and the *Hudson Weekly Gazette*, 23 August.

11. The phrase "LYBIAN LION" was apparently borrowed from English poet John Dryden's translation of Virgil's *Aeneid*, Book XII. Dryden's famous translation was first printed in London in 1697. The authors of *The Anarchiad* mention Virgil in their prose introductions to their eleventh and twelfth installments.

12. Possibly a reference to John Lamb.

13. Probably a reference to Connecticut Antifederalist leader Erastus Wolcott, a member of the Council, who earlier in 1787 published newspaper articles recommending that farmers pay lower taxes and that the burden of taxes be shifted to merchants and professional men. The term "woglog" was probably borrowed from John Newbery, the English author of books for children. In 1758 he published *Fables in Verse, for the Improvement of Young and Old, by Abraham Aesop, Esq.; to which are added Fables in Verse and Prose, with the Conversations of Birds and Beasts at their several Meetings, Routs, and Assemblies, by Woglog the (great) Giant . . .*; and in 1759 he published *A Pretty Book of Pictures for little Masters and Misses; or, Tommy Trip's History of Birds and Beasts. . . . To which is added, the History of little Tom Trip himself, of his Dog Jowler, and of Woglog the great Giant.*

14. A reference to Connecticut Antifederalist William Williams, a member of the state Council, who suspected that members of the Society of the Cincinnati and land speculators were seeking control of the Western Reserve (Ohio) which the Confederation Congress had guaranteed to Connecticut in exchange for the cession of its other claims to western lands. He was nicknamed "William Wimble" after his suspicions were published. The sobriquet "William Wimble" was probably based upon a character appearing in number 108 of *The Spectator* which was written by Joseph Addison and published on 4 July 1711. Written largely by Addison and Richard Steele, 635 numbers of *The Spectator* appeared between 1 March 1711 and 20 December 1714. "Will Wimble embodies in himself all the traits of the idle younger son in an ancient family, 'bred to no Business and born to no Estate.' " The Latin motto of essay number 108 in translation reads: "Puffing hard, and making much ado about nothing." See Donald F. Bond, ed., *The Spectator* (5 vols., Oxford, Eng., 1965), I, 446–49.

15. Or, more commonly, "Those whom God wishes to destroy, he first makes mad" (an anonymous Latin saying based on a fragment from Euripides).

Cincinnatus VI: To James Wilson, Esquire
New York Journal, 6 December 1787[1]

Sir, When I stated the monied difficulties, which the new government will have to encounter, my chief object was to prove to our fellow citizens, the delusion into which you have led them in your speech, when you ventured "to predict that the great revenue of the United States, must, and always will be, raised by impost." This is not the land, Sir, of *second sight*; and I have shewn that your prediction, is not founded on any knowledge of the subject. It is one of those numerous deceptions, that are practised upon the people to delude them into the toils that are spread for them by the proposed constitution.

To satisfy them more fully on the subject of the revenue, that is to be raised upon them, in order to give enormous fortunes to the jobbers in public securities, I shall lay before them a proposition to Congress, from Mr. Robert Morris, when superintendant of finance. It is dated, I think,[a] the 29th of June, 1782, and is in these words:—"The requisition of a five per cent. impost, made on the 3d of February, 1781,[2] has not yet been complied with by the state of Rhode-Island, but as there is reason to believe, that their compliance is not far off, this revenue may be considered as already granted.—It will, however, be very inadequate to the purposes intended. If goods be imported, and prizes introduced to the amount of twelve millions annually, the five per cent. would be six hundred thousand, from which at least one sixth must be deducted, as well for the cost of collection as for the various defalcations which will necessarily happen, and which it is unnecessary to enumerate. It is not safe therefore, to estimate this revenue at more than, half a million of dollars; for though it may produce more, yet probably it will not produce so much. It was in consequence of this, that on the 27th day of February last, I took the liberty to submit the propriety of asking the states for a land tax of one dollar for every hundred acres of land—a poll-tax of one dollar on all freemen, and all male slaves, between sixteen and sixty, excepting such as are in the federal army, or by wounds or otherwise rendered unfit for service; and an excise of one eighth of a dollar [per gallon], on all distilled spiritous liquors. Each of these may be estimated at half a million; and should the product be equal to the estimation, the sum total of revenues for funding the public debts, would be equal to two millions."[3]

You will readily perceive, Mr. Wilson, that there is a vast difference between your prediction and your friends proposition. Give me leave to say, Sir, that it was not discreet, in you, to speak upon finance without instructions from this great financier. Since, independent of its delusive effect upon your audience, it may excite his jealousy, lest you should have a secret design of rivalling him in the expected office of superintendant under the new constitution. It is true, there is no real foundation for it; but then you know jealousy makes the food it feeds on. A quarrel between two such able and honest friends to the United States, would, I am persuaded, be felt as a public calamity. I beseech you then to be very tender upon this point in your next harrangue. And if four months study will not furnish you with sufficient descretion, we will indulge you with six.

It may be said, that let the government be what it may, the sums I have stated must be raised, and the same difficulties exist. This is not altogether true. For first, we are now in the way of paying the interest of the domestic debt, with paper, which under the new system is utterly reprobated. This makes a difference between the specie to be raised of 1,800,000 dollars per annum. If the new government raises this sum in specie on the people, it will certainly support public credit, but it will overwhelm the people. It will give immense fortunes to the speculators; but it will grind the poor to dust. Besides the present government is now redeeming the principal of the domestic debt by the sale of western lands. But let the full interest be paid in specie, and who will part with the principal for those lands. A principal, which having been generally purchased for two shillings and six pence on the pound, will yield to the holders two hundred and forty per cent. This paper system therefore, though in general an evil, is in this instance attended with the great benefit of enabling the public to cancel a debt upon easy terms, which has been swelled to its enormous size, by as enormous impositions. And the new government, by promising too much, will involve itself in a disreputable breech of faith, or in a difficulty of complying with it, insuperable.

The present government promises nothing.—The intended government, every thing.—From the present government little is expected:—From the intended one, much. Because it is conceived that to the latter much is given—to the former, little. And yet the inability of the people to pay what is required in specie, remaining the same, the funds of the one will not much exceed those of the other. The public creditors are easy with the present government from a conviction of its inability—they will be urgent with the new one from an opinion, that as it promises, so it can and will perform every thing. Whether the change will be for our prosperity and honour, is yet to be tried. Perhaps it will be found, that the supposed want of power in Congress to levy taxes, is at present a veil happily thrown over the inability of the people; and that the large powers given to the new government, will to every eye, expose the nakedness of our land. Certain it is, that if the expectations which are grafted on the gift of these plenary powers, are not answered, our credit will be irretrievably ruined.

Once more, Mr. Wilson, be pleased to pardon me for digressing. We come now to your last argument, or rather observation, which is in these terms—That as establishing the new government will—"turn the stream of influence and emolument into a new channel, therefore every person who enjoys or expects to enjoy a place of profit under the present establishment, will object to the proposed innovation, not in truth, because it is injurious to the liberties of his country, but because it affects his schemes of wealth and consequence."

This reflection, sir, is as ingenious as it is liberal. It reaches every man who will not worship the new idol. It is the shibboleth of your party. Every man who differs in opinion with you, upon the new constitution, if he is not actually a placeman under the present establishment, may be an expectant; and then, according to your liberal and gentlemanly conclusion, his opinion must be imputed to his pursuit of wealth and consequence.

But how could it escape you, that this was a two-edged argument, and might cut its inventor. Perhaps these very violent gentlemen for the new establishment, may be actuated by the same undue motives. Perhaps some of its framers, might have had its honours and emoluments in view. When you have let loose suspicion, Mr. Wilson, there is no knowing where it will end. Perhaps some may be audacious enough to suspect even—you. They may think, that the emoluments of an attorney generalship, or of a chief justice largely provided for, under a government gifted with almost chemic powers to extract gold from the people, might happily repair your shattered fortunes. Let us, Sir, suppose a man fallen from opulence into the most gloomy depths of monied distress, by an unsatiable love of wealth and as unwise a pursuit of it:[4] would not such a man be a fit instrument in the hands of others to agitate the introduction of the new constitution. Such a man would have no objection to the golden speculations which such a constitution holds forth. Such a man, albeit unused to speak without a fee, and a large one too, would deign to harangue gratis for such an object. His crest would be brightened, his eloquence animated by an anticipation of that happy hour, when he might sail down this new pactolean channel, accompanied by his pathetic Doctor,[5] to sing a requiem to our expired liberties, and chant hallelujahs to his approach—to wealth and consequence. Such a man, Sir, in such a mood, would, as you do, regard the new constitution, in every point of view, with a candid and disinterested mind, and be bold to assert, "that it is the best form of government which has ever been offered to the world."

Such a man as I have painted, you know, Mr. Wilson, is not a fiction. What I have said was not to insult his distresses, but to admonish his discretion. He ought not to have touched ground, on which he, and his swelled superior,[6] who dances him forth to the people, is so very vulnerable. Upon my honor, Sir, I do not know two men in the United

States more tender in this point. Permit me then to admonish them, through you, never again to insult the patience of the public with insinuations about the judgment of men on the proposed constitution, being affected by schemes of wealth and consequence.

There is one very material power given to the proposed Congress, on which you have thought proper to be silent, and which as not coming within the scope of your speech I have reserved to this place. In the 4th section, it is said—"The times, places, and manner of holding elections for senators and representatives shall be prescribed in each state by the legislature thereof; but the Congress may at any time, by law, make or alter such regulations, except as to the places of chusing senators."

In all our constitutions, the regulation of elections is fixed; not left to the legislature, because it is a fundamental right, in which the essence of liberty resides.

It is in fact the root of all rights. Nothing can be plainer than that Congress, under the pretence of regulating, might in various ways annihilate the freedom of elections. If ever the aristocracy should meet with a pliant representative, it will be easy so to regulate the times, places, and manner of holding elections—as to secure the complaisance of future representatives.

This power over elections is another proof of a prediction for the senate, and a determination to have a complete controul over the people. It participates precisely of the spirit, which dictated the rendering the power of impeachment nugatory, by the manner in which it is to be executed.

Thus too, the right of election, under controul from time to time, in point of manner, times, and places, is but a shadow in the people; while the substance will necessarily reside with those to whom the regulation of it is resigned. But the senate was too sacred to be subjected to this unhallowed touch. The aristocracy is elevated on high, while the democracy is trampled in the dust. If the people can indeed be deluded into such a surrender of their most sacred rights; it must arise from the precipitation with which they are called upon to decide. Still, however, I trust, that they will have discernment to discover the parts which are incompatible with their rights and liberties, and spirit to insist upon those parts being amended.

(a) *I say, I think, because, by accident, the month is erased in the note I have, and I have not access to public papers which would enable me to supply the defect.*

1. Reprinted: Philadelphia *Freeman's Journal,* 12 December.

2. For the Impost of 1781 that Rhode Island never ratified, see CDR, 140–41.

3. This is an excerpt from Morris' report of 29 July 1782, which had been submitted to a congressional committee composed of Samuel Osgood, Abraham Clark, and Arthur Lee (the author of these "Cincinnatus" essays). On 5 August 1782 the committee reported that Morris' proposal was "in general too exceptionable to meet with the approbation of Congress; as it would operate very unequally, as well with respect to the different States, as to the inhabitants of each State" (JCC, XXII, 429–47).

4. The reference is to James Wilson himself who had far-flung interests in land, manufacturing, and commerce and whose projects sometimes lost money, putting him into debt.

5. The reference is to Benjamin Rush, whom "Cincinnatus" had criticized earlier. (See "Cincinnatus" I, *New York Journal,* 1 November, at note 2, above.)

6. The reference is to Robert Morris, for whom Wilson was often a spokesman on political and financial matters. Consequently, Wilson's enemies sometimes accused him of being a tool or agent of Morris.

A Countryman I (De Witt Clinton)
New York Journal, 6 December 1787

Between 6 December 1787 and 17 January 1788, the *New York Journal* published five Antifederalist essays signed "A Countryman," the second New York Antifederalist series employing this pseudonym. The other series, written by Hugh Hughes, began publication on 21 November 1787 (above). This second series was written by the youthful De Witt Clinton, a nephew of Governor George Clinton. On 22 December De Witt Clinton's brother George wrote to him and told him that "*Your Countrymans Letters* are very good and I think better adapted to the understanding of the Common People than any piece in the Newspapers. They seem to be wrote in imitation of Col. D——r" (Mfm:N.Y.). "Col. D——r" was probably William Duer who published four brief essays signed "Philo-Publius." (See "Philo-Publius," *Daily Advertiser* 30 October, above.) Duer had been recruited to contribute to *The Federalist,* written by "Publius," but his essays never became part of the series. (See *The Federalist* 1, *Independent Journal,* 27 October, above.) None of De Witt Clinton's "Countryman" essays was reprinted. The *New York Journal* on 5 December announced that the first number would appear the next day.

De Witt Clinton (1769–1828), a native of Little Britain, Orange County, and a graduate of Columbia College (1786), was studying law in New York City with Antifederalist leader Samuel Jones of Queens County. Not long after New York ratified the Constitution, Clinton became private secretary to his uncle Governor George Clinton. De Witt Clinton served in the state Assembly, 1798; state Senate, 1798–1802, 1806–11; and U.S. Senate, 1802–3. He was also mayor of New York City almost continuously between 1803 and 1815 and was governor of New York from 1817 to 1822 and from 1825 until his death.

WORTHY AND ESTEEMED SIR, I received your letter of the 21st of last month with the new constitution and several pieces for and against it, which you were kind enough to send me, and for which I return you my hearty thanks. You condescend to ask my opinion of it, which, I fear, will scarcely be worth the trouble it will give you in reading. All I know about politics, I learnt during the late troubles, and that chiefly by reading the votes of our assembly and the journal of Congress, which you were good enough, now and then, to lend me. In the fore part of the war, I had a very good opinion of our Congress and principal men, that were employed in public business—they appeared to me very honest and very much in earnest to forward the common cause, but I will honestly confess to you, that towards the last, when the danger seemed to be in a great measure over, and when they began to appoint ministers of finance, and ministers of one thing and ministers of another, I did not think so well of them. Near the end of the war, I sold a pair of as good fat cattle as any in the parts, to one of our commissaries, for thirty-pounds, which was cheap, and not more than they would have sold for before the war—he, indeed, appeared very generous, and did not seem to wish to bait me of the price—our bargain was for hard money, then pretty currently going in the country—but, instead of this, he gave me paper, that he called Morris's Notes,[1] which, he said, was every bit as good, and I took them at his word; but, he was hardly gone from my house, before another man came, who said, he was immediately from Philadelphia, and told me a quite different story, and said, that they were much depreciated, and this made me very uneasy, you may be sure, as I did not like to throw away my cattle for nothing—however, he offered to take them from me, if I would make him an allowance, so I let him have them for five and twenty pounds, which, if I remember rightly, he called the discount—now, I thought this very strange, but my neighbour ———'s son, who, you know, was a serjeant in the standing forces, came home to see his parents a few days after, and he told me, there was nothing more common, for, whenever the soldiers got any pay it was in that way, and that they were often obliged to sell, at the rate of ten shillings for the pound, and that they must either do it or starve, for they could not do without some money; but, that I was very wrong, for I could have laid out of my money a little while, and sent the notes to Philadelphia and got the cash, for that some of these notes issued, but when there was money at command to pay them off.—I told him, I thought this was very strange, since at that rate, they might send the money at once, as well as the notes—he said, I knew nothing of the matter, for, that there was a number of people always following the commissaries, quarter-masters, and pay masters, who bought these notes up in the manner they did from me, and who were concerned with great men, among them they made a great deal of money by it—whereas, if the money was sent at once, they would not have an opportunity of filling their pockets. Now, as I said before,

I confess to you, worthy sir, this gave me a bad opinion of some of our great men; but to return to the new constitution, I really have not had much time to read it, or the papers about it, being much behind hand in my business this year, owing to one disappointment or another—I remember well that our first or second Congress, I do not know which, and I believe they were both made up of as wise and as good men as any ever we have had since, wrote letters to the people of England and Ireland, and to our neighbours in Canada, endeavouring to convince them, that we were right to oppose the late government, which they clearly proved was unjustly oppressing and injuring us. In their letter to the people of Canada, they complained grievously of the conduct of the rulers of our former government, and told them, that a certain Mr. Beccaria (who I suppose must have been a countryman of theirs, and, of course, more likely to be believed by them) says, "that there is an effort continually tending to confer on one part the heighth of power and happiness, and to reduce the other to the extreme of weakness and misery;"[2] I believe these are the very words. Now, I am really very much afraid, that this is the case with the new constitution men, for it appears to me, that this president-general will have a great deal of power, and I think the chance is as ten to one when he gets a standing army, and has the command of all the militia, that he may not make the best use of them, and I should not wonder at all (unless he should happen to be a very good tempered man) that the backs of some, of our militia men, would pay for it, as the tories did during the war— besides the senate seem to have a vast deal of power too, and from the manner they are appointed and continued in their places, I dont see how we are to set about to turn them out if they behave badly; indeed, good sir, the president looks to me very much like a king, and the senate like a house of lords, and, I suppose, the supreme judiciaries that are spoke of, will be like the lord justices of the assizes, or the twelve great judges in the old countries, where, they tell me, a man need to have a deep pocket if he goes to law, and that a poor man stands but very little chance, at any rate, to get justice done him, especially if he has to contend with a rich one—besides, it seems to me, that the president and senate will have a great deal of business to do together, and it is so jumbled and contrived, that if they do wrong, we can hardly find out who to lay the blame to—and, I think it wont be a hard matter, as they have a great many good things to give, to get the assembly-men too on their side of the question, and I believe, we may pretty certainly expect, that if they once get fairly a going they will do as this Mr. Beccaria says, keep down the common people and encrease their own power, especially, as I see they are to have a common treasury, out of which they can pay themselves what they please, without asking any body, and I suppose they will make us sweat in taxes to keep it full.

There is another thing, our Congress told the people of Canada, in their letter, and I believe they were in earnest, "That the trial by jury, was one of the best securities in the world, for the life, liberty and property of the people."[3]—Now to be sure, I am very much of their opinion in this; for I would rather trust my life, liberty and property to a verdict of twelve of my honest neighbours, than to the opinion of any great man in the world, for great men are not always honest men, and they may be too proud, and not care to give themselves the trouble to enquire very narrowly into common people's disputes; and if an honest farmer should happen to say any thing against a great man, tho' it was ever so true, it would be in the power of the Judge to punish him for it very severely—and I don't doubt, but what he would do it; but I am sure a good honest jury of his neighbours would never punish him for speaking the truth; I know it is said that truth is not to be spoken at all times, but the best of us may be guilty of little acts of imprudence, for which however, we should not be too severely handled: I find the writers disagree about this matter; the one says this right of trial by jury is taken away by the new constitution, and the other says it is not.— Now, as they differ, I have been trying to find out the truth myself, and, it appears to me middling clear, that if it is not absolutely taken away; yet that this new General Congress, that we read of, may take it away whenever they please—now, if it is so good a thing that it never ought to be taken away, I think we ought not to give them power to do it; for I can't see the reason of giving them power, which they never can make use of, without doing us a great deal of hurt: Now all parties may mean what is honest at present, but notwithstanding, there may be a time, when we have bad men to rule us, and I think it would be imprudent to give power, which every one allows there is no necessity for, and with which bad men, if so disposed, might do us a great deal of harm, and I am more confirmed in this belief, when I think of what the said Mr. Beccaria says about this desire, which has always prevailed in men of increasing their power. This is all I can say about the matter at present, having, as I mentioned before, little time to attend to it; but, as my neighbour —— ——, whom you know to be a sensible thinking man, and has more learning than I have, has agreed with me to spend some time together to read it more carefully over, now that the evenings are growing long, and the hurry of business is pretty near past, I will write to you again on the subject, if my letters do not prove troublesome.

Before I finish, I will relate to you, however, what has happened in our neighbourhood, since you were here, for although it is an affair of little consequence, it seems to me to be something like this new-government business; you know that we belonged to the —— congregation, and the church was at a great distance from us, and it was often very inconvenient to us, for many who had not horses for all our families to ride to church, were obliged, when it was bad walking, to stay at home, and in truth, we did not like the minister; this made us think of forming ourselves into a separate congregation, which, after taking the proper steps, we did; and we set about a subscription, and raised a little money, and built ourselves a small snug house to worship in, and called a very good kind of a man for a minister, who preached to us for a very moderate stipend, which we made out to pay him pretty punctually, considering the hardness of the times; and we were all very happy and contented, and religion seemed to flourish amongst us, until lately, that some of our young men, who were in the wars, returned home; some of these set about studying, and very soon became lawyers; others got a little goods, and became shop-keepers; and others done no business at all, but lived like gentlemen, expecting to get a living by public employments, as they called it: These young men began to find fault with every thing we did; they said, we were unacquainted with the world, and could not judge properly how matters should be conducted; they said our church was too small, too plain, and not well finished; and, upon this account, that we were despised by all the neighbouring congregations, who had larger and finer churches; and, it is strange to tell, but so it is, by these means they soon worked upon the vanity of some of our more elderly and serious people, and though they could not get them to consent to build a new church, they agreed to enlarge and repair the old one, and make it much more shewy. The next thing they did, was to get themselves with two or three of the elderly men (who were honest men and pretty wise about other matters, but knew little about repairing churches) appointed trustees to manage the business; which being done, they set about and collected a quantity of great heavy strong timber and other materials, and up they set a spacious large new house, as fine as you please, leaving the old one (though a good deal weakened by taking out some of the under-pinning) standing, in the mean time to worship in, 'till the new one can be finished;—but now our difficulties began, the more sober part of the congregation found that this new building was a very expensive one, and was likely to create great divisions in the congregation, many of them liking the old one better than the new one, and thinking that it might have been repaired, so as better to answer all our purposes: these began to say, that they would pay nothing towards it, and have nothing to do with it: and, what greatly added to their dissatisfaction, was, that they found that it was not to end here, for from some hints that were thrown out by those young men, and plans (as they are called) of the building, it was found, that this new building was so contrived, that it was to have a large steeple and galleries added to it, and large high pews in it for the better sort of people to sit in, so that they might not be troubled with the common people, or rabble as they fained to call them; and some even went so far as to say that upon raising the covering of that end of the church, where steeples are usually placed, and peeping in, that they had discovered the mortices and other things, which could only be contrived for adding a steeple to it in good earnest; this as you may judge, increased the discontent, until at length more than one half of the congregation refused to have any thing to do with it; the trustees finding this, brought suits against them to make them pay, what they said they had promised, and as they were chiefly lawyers, they had the advantage, for if judgment was given against them, they certiorared the justices, and put them to such costs and trouble in attending the courts at a great distance, that they are almost fairly tired and worried out; our poor minister too was led astray by these young men; they made him believe that his salary ought to be raised, and by following their advice in trying to get more, he, at last, could get nothing at all, and was obliged to leave us: now in this our disagreeable situation, many of our most zealous and best-disposed people talk of breaking off entirely and joining the old congregation, seeing they cannot worship here peaceably without quarrelling, and too heavy expence for them to support, so that we are brought into a very sad pickle, by following the advice of these young men, and I do not know what will become of us. I heartily wish you could be among us a few days, in hopes, by your good advice, that we might get reconciled and to rights again; for we all place great confidence in you, and your opinion would have great weight among us; indeed, as I said before, I do not know what will become of us, if with our present difficulties and troubles, we should be saddled with more, by the new constitution.

I remain, honored sir, Your real friend, and Humble servant, A COUNTRYMAN.

1. Beginning in 1782, "Morris's Notes" were issued by Robert Morris, the Confederation Superintendent of Finance, in an effort to establish his administration's credit. The notes were used in public business and were directly related to Morris's person and office, being guaranteed in both his public and private capacities. The notes usually passed at par in the Middle States.

2. On 26 October 1774 the First Continental Congress addressed a letter to the inhabitants of Quebec, in which Congress quoted the first two sentences of the introduction to Cesare Bonesana, Marchese di Beccaria's *An Essay on Crimes and Punishments.* As quoted in the letter, the sentences read: "In every human society, there is an *effort, continually*

tending to confer on one part the heighth of power and happiness, and to reduce the other to the extreme of weakness and misery. The intent of good laws is to *oppose this effort,* and to diffuse their influence *universally* and *equally*" (JCC, I, 106). Beccaria's work first appeared in Italian in Livorno (Leghorn) in 1764. Except for the italics inserted by Congress, the text quoted in this letter to Quebec's inhabitants is almost identical to that found in an English edition of Beccaria printed in London in 1770. The letter to Quebec was printed in Philadelphia in both English and French by order of Congress. A German edition, for which Congress made Pennsylvania's delegates responsible, was also printed in Philadelphia. The address was then printed in several other American towns and cities (Evans 13726–36, 13740). "Federal Farmer" quoted the same two sentences from Beccaria in his *Additional Number of Letters to the Republican* which was published on 2 May 1788 (see III below and CC:723, p. 279).

3. The address to Quebec's inhabitants states: "The next great right is that of trial by jury. This provides, that neither life, liberty nor property, can be taken from the possessor, until twelve of his unexceptionable countrymen and peers of his vicinage, who from that neighbourhood may reasonably be supposed to be acquainted with his character, and the characters of the witnesses, upon a fair trial, and full enquiry, face to face, in open Court, before as many of the people as chuse to attend, shall pass their sentence upon oath against him . . ." (JCC, I, 107).

New York Journal, 6 December 1787[1]

Extract of a letter from a merchant in London to his friend in America, dated the 3d Oct. 1787.

"Dear Sir, Your last letters are very discouraging to our farther advances in the American commerce, the precarious state of property under the instability, and I might say —— of the partial state laws, make us fear we have much more abroad than we shall ever recover; however, we would not wish you to be more than decently pressing with our debtors, the present prospect of a war gives us hopes that we shall at last be secured and eventually paid. It is wispered, that should the war be determined on, we shall, with a powerful fleet and army, take possession of Rhode-Island, from which it is expected the following advantage will arise.

1st. It will be in our power to restrain any commerce to or from America, which we may think injurious, and perfectly guard against her taking any secret part contrary to our interests.

2d. It will be an advantageous and safe port for our shipping, and in case any enterprize should be undertaken against the West-Indies, it will be a healthy and well chosen rendezvous for an army.

3d. We shall obtain all the provisions we shall want from America, and secure the carrying of them in our own bottoms.

4th. In case of necessity, we shall be able with our frigates to collect a large quantity of American seamen for manning our navy.

5th. By granting commissions for privateers to the Americans (if they retain their spirit of enterprize) we shall employ the greatest part of their naval strength against their good friend and ally, and perhaps eventually draw them into the war, in defiance of all the requisitions of their Congress.

6th. By the sale of prizes at that port, we shall necessarily draw there the principal merchants of America, and from the quantity of money that will necessarily be in circulation there, we shall not only have the means of collecting our arrears, but the Americans may be brought to wish for a return to their ancient government; we have no doubt of the Rhode-Islanders. And should this not be the case at the close of the war, a few of our frigates could lay your sea-port towns under contribution, to reimburse us some of those guineas we have trusted you with; and to convince the Americans of the insignificance of their Fœderal Government.—These, and many other substantial reasons, it is said, are urged in the cabinet for the measure. I should not have been so explicit with you upon this subject, but the circumstances being duly considered, it becomes necessary for you to determine, whether it would not be proper for you to secure a house at New-Port: if the event takes place, I make no doubt I shall have the necessary intelligence, so as to be able to send you out a proper cargo to answer our mutual interest, I shall proportion it to the embarkation from 2000 to 5000, and abide your future orders for further shipments."

1. This letter extract was reprinted in the *Country Journal*, 19 December, and in whole or in part in fifteen newspapers outside New York by 8 March 1788: N.H. (2), Mass. (3), R.I. (1), Conn. (3), N.J. (1), Pa. (2), Va. (3).

Publius: The Federalist 18 (James Madison assisted by Hamilton) New York Packet, 7 December 1787

Inadequacies of ancient Greek confederacies. For text, see CC:330. For reprintings, see Appendix IV, below.

James Kent to Nathaniel Lawrence Poughkeepsie, 8 December 1787[1]

I have only a moment to do our Friendship the compliment of a Line—I have nothing to inform you from this Quarter that deserves much Attention—The Minds of our better Sort of People are engrossed & much animated by the great political question—As you appear by your last Letter not to have absolutely made up your Mind I am in hopes you will embark at last fervently with me in the federal faith—If you should not I shall think the same of your political Discernment & Virtue & probably with some little additional Diffidence of the Strength & Justice of my own Opinion—As yet Sir all I can read & reflect serves but to convince me of the high expediency of adopting the Government & that it is take it *all in all* about as good & perfect a System as the various Interests & Prejudices & Opinions of this Continent will permit us to form—I recommend Publius to you as the best thing I have seen hitherto in print on the federal side[2]—I hope with my Knowledge of your Candor & firmness I may say it will silence some of the Difficulties which may have been presented to your Eye—I have also read Webster & with the most friendly Submission I think it *spirited & sensible* except a few Paragraphs wherein he undertakes to refute the Objections which have been raised & there he deserves the Epithets you have conferred on his publication[3]—I was the more disappointed & grieved at such a Refutation since I am fully persuaded as I observed before of the Goodness of his Cause & have so long since entertained I conceive much well grounded Respect for his discerning & independent Mind & his various & extensive erudition—excuse my Haste & Confusion & believe me to be with the highest Respect & Friendship—

1. RC, L. W. Smith Collection, Morristown National Historical Park, Morristown, N.J.

2. For more on Kent's thoughts about "Publius," see his 21 December letter to Lawrence (below). For Kent's role in getting the essays of "Publius" reprinted in the *Country Journal,* see the headnote to *The Federalist* 1, *Independent Journal,* 27 October (above).

3. The reference is to Noah Webster's pamphlet *An Examination into the Leading Principles of the Federal Constitution,* . . . which was printed in Philadelphia on 17 October under the pseudonym, "A Citizen of America." In one part of the pamphlet, Webster gives specific answers to nine Antifederalist objections to the Constitution. (For the text of the pamphlet, see Mfm:Pa. 142; and for a discussion of its publication, circulation, and impact, see CC:173.)

Robert R. Livingston to John Stevens, Sr.
New York, 8 December 1787 (excerpt)[1]

. . . I am very glad to hear the choice your county[2] has made of members for the convention, & hope from the general complection of your state that you will have the honour of being the first in acceeding to the new constitution In saying this I answer your question, & let you know that it meets with my sincere concurrence, & indeed I shd. censure a constitution which I had no small agency in framing, if I were not to approve it. It is expressly formed upon the model of our state government. My vanity is not a little flattered to find that the only *new idea* in government which has been started in America, where so many have thought on the subject, owes its birth to me & has been adopted by such respectable bodies as Massachusetts New York & the general convention I mean the council of revision.[3] Tho the alteration they have made in vesting this power of revision in the executive magistrate *alone*, rather than as with us in the *Executive* & *Judicial* the Latter of whom are independent is a material defect, since the legislative have always been equaly solicitous to encroach on both. I have not leisure to enter in to a minute discussion of the federal constitution. It is not without its defects, but these are abundantly over ballanced by its advantages. A perfect governmt. is hardly to be expected till angels make it, & perhaps not even then, for we find the Jews dissatisfied & rebellious under a theocracy (or the government of god himself.) In all popular assemblies the wise & the weak, the ignorant & the experienced, will divide the influence, & each must be gratified, their favorite child, like the son of the patr[i]arch, will wear a coat of many colours[4]—tho this may excite the censure of envious brothers yet I fondly hope that the parallel will still hold in this instance and our community like the house of Israel owe its ~~safty~~ prosperity to this reviled brother. . . .

1. RC, Stevens Family Papers, NjHi. Livingston was a son-in-law of Stevens.

2. Stevens was one of three Hunterdon County delegates elected to the New Jersey Convention, which unanimously ratified the Constitution on 18 December.

3. On 1 April 1777 Livingston, who sat on the committee of the state constitutional convention to draft a constitution, proposed an amendment to the draft constitution calling for the Council of Revision which he thought was an improvement upon the governor's veto power. As state chancellor, Livingston himself sat on the Council of Revision. Throughout his life, Livingston maintained that this proposal was his greatest contribution to the new government.

4. The reference is to Joseph, the favorite son of the patriarch Jacob. See Genesis, chapters 37 through 50; see especially Genesis 37:3, 23, and 32, for the coat of many colors that Jacob gave to Joseph.

Publius: The Federalist 19 (James Madison assisted by Hamilton) New York Independent Journal, 8 December 1787

Inadequacies of medieval and modern confederacies. For text, see CC:333. For reprintings, see Appendix IV, below.

William Constable to William Chambers New York, 10 December 1787 (excerpt)[1]

. . . We are in hopes of getting the duties considerably augmented on China Goods not imported direct from the place of their growth— Which is at present the Case in several of the States—Shoud the New Confederation take place, one uniform Code of Commercial Laws will be adopted which must be attended with very great Advantages to the Union at large, indeed this appears to be One of the principal points aimed at by the New Constitution, as it is the only *real* inconvenience which We labour under; the others complained of being either in Idea or Apprehension. . . .

1. FC, Constable-Pierrepont Collection, Letterbook, 1782–1790, NN. Constable (1752–1803), a wealthy merchant and land speculator, was a native of Ireland who, after the Revolution, was a merchant in Philadelphia. He moved to New York City in 1784, establishing the firm of Constable, Rucker, and Company. After the death of Constable's partner, Robert and Gouverneur Morris invested in the firm (now Constable and Company) which traded with India and China. From a part of the letter not printed here, it appears that William Chalmers was a merchant or a merchant-agent stationed in the Far East. Constable refers to a letter from Chalmers that he received in May 1787, when the *Empress of China* returned from the Far East. Constable's own mercantile firm had sent that vessel on its second voyage to the Far East.

Roderick Razor
New York Daily Advertiser, 11 December 1787[1]

Mr. PRINTER, I am a worthy and deserving citizen, which has supported or underwent as you may say, several important and fruitless State offices; but being now out of place, I would be willing to undergo, or be located to some snug birth in one of the *street Sovereignties*, which is like to be soon erected and accommodated in and about this city, as I am informed.

I beg therefore humbly to put *myself up* (as we do some times for Semblymen) for Norotor General, to any pretty large and populatious street that is going. Thank Heaven I have good lungs, and I have kept company so long, with our most learned and most virtuous, and most wisest men; that I can say off about standing armies, and juries without trial, and the extinguishing the liberty of speaking and printing, and excise, and all them things, as well as my betters; whose betters I expect one of these days to be. Turn and turn about, Mr. Printer, is fair play. In all well manufactured free Governments, there is a lively and pleasant kind of a circum rotation as it were, like unto the whirling of a squirrel's cage; the top goes quick to the bottom, and the bottom to the top; which is a much seemlier and juster comparison, than that of the boiling of a pot and the scum's rising up, which is only a kind of a jumblification; whereas your circum rotation is a much pleasanter motion, and gives a chance to all to come in for a cut of what is going; bottoms, tops and middles. Some say there a'nt to be such a place as what I am asking for; that is all a hum; and they are only bamboozling us; but I know better. MR. LATNER is one of our family, and he is certainly *of our side;* for he has got *our* watch word or counter-sign, which is STOCRACY; and there is MONTESQUE[2] in another mightily used by us. I asked *Squire Sour Crout* (who was one of our head men) what this same *Stocracy* was? And he told me "it meant the same as tho' you should say, such a one is *not of our side.* He said it was a marvellously useful word; he took the first notion of it from *Domine*[3] *Van Wrangletext,* who calls all that come to hear him, and that are willing to contribute *to the support of the gospel, Our-to-dox, or our side*; and those that go to hear other Domines, *and squander their money upon them,* he calls *Etterodox,* or *otherwise*; which *means t'other side.* When Domine Van Wrangletext find his parish following after *strange Domines, and wasting their substance,* he cries lustily, Etterodox! Etterodox! the Etterodox will all be damned! eternally damned! The Church is in danger! and maybe sometimes he will throw THE STATE too into the bargain to make an alarm, and scare away them who would overthrow *the Christian religion.*" Sometimes it is good policy to bring in politics with religion; and sometimes religion into politics. Now there is your *Centry,*[4] the great Philadelphia writer *in our cause*; he has found out more than our ninny's here. They have made a noise about there being no security in the new fangled Government, for the liberty of the press; but he has found out, that the liberty of religion is in danger; which is a most excellent discovery, because it will larum[5] and terrify a great many who know nothing about politics, and strengthen the *true cause.* Squire Sour Crout says, "that there is a deep laid scheme to establish unfidelity, which is the wickedest of all religions, because it has no religion at all in it. He says there is to be no tests under the new Government. No man is to be obliged to say his prayers, or his creed, and tell whether he believes in the Devil, or the doctrine of chance. This is the work of the haughty Southern Nabobs, who have no religion, and want to spend all the public money on Barbers to powder their hair, and for silk stockings and fineries. Says he yarn ones are good enough for me or any body. They are warm in winter, and in summer *they soak up the sweat,* at which I suppose your Southern Dilly Daiseys would be ready to faint, and say it should be called *upsorping the pusfiration,* but I am for the plain humspun neighbor Razor. I hope to see the day when trade will be at an end, and there will be no foreign luxuries imported but striped blankets—when ancient simple manners will prevail, and he that can't make his own moccasons may go barefoot, and he that wont build his own wigwam, why let him set out of doors."

These Nabobs are so monstrous proud, because they command a heap of negroes. That is one thing makes them so much for Slavery and Stocracy. Now if you can find in Duchess and Albany counties, any *of our friends and the opposers of the new tyranny,* who have half a dozen big negro slaves, I will believe that his Honor Squire CLIP PURSE VAN CLINK de GELT[6] loves money, and made a snatch at the *Congress Treasury.* He has been very ill used, good and worthy man! He stood stout against voting away the public money, for a heap of useless offices in the new *Hio lands.*[7] He buffed or bucked at the *katteract* of corruption as long as he could, for there was no Loan-offices made for honest men to encourage them; but at last, some how or other his strength failed him. "This worthy Patriot was not, neighbour Razor (says the Squire) pleasantly paddling his canoe between the Over-Slaugh and Albany, against the freshes of the Hudson, in the delightsome sport of taking its favorite fish the Sturgeon: but it was the mighty Southern torrent of luxury and boundless profusion; deep, wide and rapid as the Ohio, whose lofty and tossing billows he buffeted, until he became faint and weary, and drowsiness began to steal upon him." I says to the Squire not to interrupt you, I suppose sir, that he leaned poor man a little upon one side; and so did the canoe; and then he nodded, and so off went his hat, and *that fine new wig.* For the Albany canoes are many of them very narrow and tottlish. "I wish that had been all my friend, but to proceed says the Squire, the paddle with which he has so long and dextrously steered both his canoe, and OUR STATE, dropped out of his hands; and souze went he into the mighty waters, which to him will be ever waters of bitterness and affliction. A huge wave struck him on the head, stunned him, and canted him round; and he drove senseless down the stream *only a little way;* and the Southern Lords, what should they do out of spite, but whip abroad, and call every body to see the poor old gentlemen catched as it were —— but I shall not use the expressions unlucky boys are wont to do when they *suddenly surprize* some profound Philosopher or great Statesman, like our patriot in his *most retired place of meditation;* suffice it to say he was shamefully exposed in an unlucky moment; and in a posture not only unseemly, but comical, and most melancholy withal.

"The moment he waked, *he cut and run for it;* and while he stays at home drying himself, I hope he won't be idle; but will stir his stumps against *our enemies and their schemes;* and that no infernal plots will be hatched *by those he has run from,* while this *our honest and sharp sighted* State pilot and watchman, *is absent:* and that we shall shortly see him here again, with a new paddle, and *a better pair of spectacles.*" Ah, Mr. Printer, it is melancholy, very melancholy indeed! when the righteous stumbleth, the wicked always rejoice and laughs them to scorn. We think it is the work of some of the party of that little D—l who deserves to be hanged for signing, and *that alone too,* the dead warrant of our

State Sovereignty.[8] We shall never do cleverly while he lives. I wish he was put out of the way. It would be as good a deed as to drink, to do it. I am sure I should not stick at either a rope or a razor, if I had a chance. He tossicated the heads of our staunchest men last winter, and staggered them so confoundedly, he almost made them believe, there was *one* honest man *of that side,* that did not mean to ruin the State. Ifackins if *our side had not cunningly taken to the bush,* where his business wont so well let him follow us, it might have gone hard with us. He may be as knowing as a sarpent, but I'll be hanged if he is as harmless as a sucking dove, for he stings most consumedly. If he should find out *the right way to get in* (and we know how the trick is done) and set his cap that way. Egad I am afraid we should all *be in the suds;* the Philistines would be upon us. *Squire Sour Crout* says, "it was meant at first to have tried and hanged him for high treason *against the State,* and all the rest who spoke or wrote for overturning *the State Constitution.* For tho' it gives liberty of speech and the press, yet it is meant he says *only on such matters, and at such times, as the best men in the State think proper and for the good of the State:* and if we could have been sure of a pretty large majority, we should have tucked up all who were enemies to its Sovereignty; and might have done it under the Constitution, just as handily as we voted out the general impost by it. But as matters now look, the Squire says he is sorry the cat was unluckily let out of the bag—that it was unwarily mentioned by some of our side, that signing the Convention was treason against the State; because our adversaries may take handle against us, and say mere declarations are not a full security; for a prevailing State or national faction, having both inclination and power, will not suffer *words* (which they can construe as they like) to defend those they have marked out as victims.

"A Bill of Rights or Constitution, *in suitable hands and properly managed,* is a very useful and pliable convenience, said he. That of Pennsylvania, when in the hands of the true friends to *equal* liberty was most excellent; but now it has got into other hands, it is abominable. That a *majority of bad men* should govern, is contrary to all sound *republican* doctrine; which teaches that when an *impious majority* bear sway, the *virtuous minority,* when they cannot seize the reins of Government into their own hands, should like Sampson pull down its pillars, and bury themselves and their enemies under its ruins; as was bravely attempted by the Sixteen *true and virtuous Republicans* in Pennsylvania:[9] and it would have been done too, had it not been for the villainous Philadelphia populace. If," says the Squire, "the *new scheme* goes down, it will be the confoundedest bite that ever happened; he and the rest of our side laughed, he says, heartily, at the notion of a number of grave noddles getting together to alter and mend *the old thing*. Let them have turned it, or altered the cape, or the cuffs, or have cut the skirts shorter, it would make it no better; and if they had put two or three good new strong patches into it, the stitches would not hold in the old cloth, but it would tear the more and the faster for the new pieces; but as to making an entire new coat, they never dreamt the plaguy fellows would attempt it. Zounds! if the people wear it now it is made, neighbour Razor," says he, "it will be the most infernal take-in that ever we were bamboozled with."

A fig, and a fiddle-stick's end, Mr. Printer, for your fidderal or fodderal nonsensikalities. "*Every tub stand on its own bottom;*[10] *every dog shake his own paw; the hardest send off; let him laugh that wins;*[11] and the like, his honor Squire *Clip Purse Van Clink de Gelt* says, "these is the maxums and axums of TRUE STATE POLICY." A good night's rest to his pious soul, whenever we must lose him. A customer of mine, a young Lawyer, who writes politics, and makes poetry too, says, "He is sure the Angel in Heaven that keeps the Records, or is Clerk of the Court of Oyer and Terminer there, will drop a tear on the word Felony, in the indictment which the Treasury Board Nabobs have sent up against him, and blot it out for ever. So that it will be squashed, and he never be called upon to plead to this one, if he can but keep his fingers still, and will go and do so no more."

Mr. Printer, I speak it with reverence and submission, I humbly conceive I can smell a rat as quick, and see as far into a mill-stone as some others. I do now smell a plot; nay, I smell two plots. The southern bashaws are for establishing unfidelity; the eastern saints, double stilled high wine piritanism. Every body knows they once punished a sea-captain just come home, for kissing his wife on a sabbaday, as he met her in the street. Now the squire, who is "as deep as Chelsea," as the saying is, "says that all men love power; that the supreme Fedderal court may go from one step to another, until they get to try justice cases; and may in time set here in the room of our magistrates, and send any one they call antifederal to bridewell.[12] In like manner the saints will proceed, as you may say, progressively; and tho' from the time, place, and other circumstances, the squire says it is presumed the kissing aforesaid was not more, or other, than simple *osculation*, or lip salutation upon the *sabbath*; yet it may in process of time be artfully extended to kissing in every manner and form, and of every kind, degree, grade, and species; upon any day, or hour of the day in the whole week; nay, even to the night, and not only to the night, but to every hour in the night: And what then, says he, neighbour Razor, in the name of procreation! is to become of the human specie? The world will be at an end! it will become *destinct!"*

I do declare and affirm, and avow, that it is a crying sin, that there is no Bill of Rights to the new Scheme—I have heard that there was once a bloody war between the big Endians and little Endians, because their Bill of Rights did not say they might break their eggs at which end they pleased. I have heard it said, and that too by *credulous* men, that by a jury of Cockneys, a sort of people that live in Lunnon,[13] a man would be hanged that boiled a leg of mutton without turnips: but there is no security in the new Constitution, that in their own free country a Lunnoner may either eat potatoes or carrots with his mutton if he chuses, or let them alone. Another monstrous danger has been mentioned by some *interested* friends, who are not one bit affected by the trade or malufacture. I shall briefly discourse of some who are aboveboard, and doing very well for themselves. Thank Heaven, they have good snug births *for themselves;* I say, for they have been unfortunately *separated from their wives and children, ever since they were born.* Every one must allow, that *the trade of Dungarvan,*[14] which is the malufactory of feet for children's stockings, of all trades ought certainly to be free. No imposts, duty, or excise on it; yet they shake their heads, and have great jealously on this business: "First, says they, neighbour Razor, perhaps comes a small duty *on stockings;* then if the people will bear it, a stout import *on legs;* and last of all brings up the rear, a swinging excise, or impost or some accursed prohibition, on the malufactures themselves. They have declared they will oppose every infringement on this business, tho' they never have followed it; nor ever expect to follow it;" which I think is very generous *in them* indeed.

Should a standing army be raised in time of peace, and under pretence of guarding the frontiers, be marched to stop this trade; I'll be hanged if your old continentals would not quit the ranks the minute they smoaked the business; and if we wanted help (which I don't think we should) why I dare say the volunteers of Ireland, who took up arms, they say, for liberty and *a fair and free trade,*[15] would come over to help us, and their countrymen here would, every man and mother's son, join them; so that the new Constitution won't be able to take away our dearest rights and privileges. Let them set it to work then if they will, Mr. Printer, as Kecksey says in the Play, "who's afraid?"[16] and so Mr Printer, I am your humble sarvant, RODERICK RAZOR.

1. On 28 November the *Daily Advertiser* announced that "Roderick Razor" was received and would appear as soon as possible.

2. A reference to political thinker Montesquieu, the author of *Spirit of Laws.*

3. Lord or master, a term of address for the clergy or a member of the professions.

4. A reference to "Centinel," the Philadelphia Antifederalist writer. See "New York Reprinting of the Centinel Essays," 17 October 1787–12 April 1788 (above).

5. Archaic for "alarm."

6. Probably Abraham Yates, Jr., of Albany, a delegate to Congress. "Gelt" refers to money.

7. In July 1787 Yates was the only delegate in Congress to vote against the Northwest Ordinance. Nathan Dane, the Ordinance's principal author, noted that "All agreed finally to the inclosed [ordinance] except A. Yates" (Smith, *Delegates*, XXIV, 358. See also JCC, XXXII, 343.).

8. Alexander Hamilton was the only New York delegate to sign the Constitution in the Constitutional Convention.

9. See "New York Reprinting of the Address of the Seceding Members of the Pennsylvania Assembly," 9–18 October (above).

10. Charles Macklin, *The Man of the World* (1781), Act I, scene 2.

11. An English proverb that is "Spoken when persons laugh at our losses or misfortunes" (John Ettlinger and Ruby Day, eds., *Old English Proverbs: Collected by Nathan Bailey, 1736, Edited from His Dictionarium Britannicum or a More Compleat Universal Etymological English Dictionary* [Metuchen, N.J., and London, 1992], 77). Also "They laugh that wins," William Shakespeare, *Othello*, Act IV, scene 1, line 122.

12. For the meaning of "bridewell," see "Examiner" IV, *New York Journal*, 24 December, note 2 (below).

13. London.

14. A seaport town in southern Ireland.

15. Because the American War for Independence disrupted Ireland's profitable trade with Bourbon France and Spain, the Irish economy was in dire straits. Consequently, the Irish sought the relaxation of trade restrictions within the British Empire. Because money was not available to pay the militia, bodies of Volunteers were raised to combat the threat of a Bourbon invasion. These Volunteers, who were mostly Irish Protestants and who numbered about 40,000 in 1779, became a potent political force and a rallying point for patriotic feeling. Irish Protestants, unlike their Roman Catholic counterparts, were hostile to British policy in the thirteen mainland colonies of North America. The Volunteers were successful in opening trade within the Empire and in challenging the authority of Parliament over the Irish Parliament.

16. The reference is to Old Kecksy, a comedic character in English actor-playwright David Garrick's farce, *The Irish Widow* (1772). On several occasions, Kecksy ended his lines with the question: "Who's Afraid?"

Examiner I
New York Journal, 11 December 1787[1]

The Antifederalist *New York Journal* printed five numbered Federalist essays signed "Examiner" between 11 December 1787 and 4 January 1788. The *New York Journal* followed with several attacks upon "Examiner." On 14 December the *Journal* printed the first of three attacks on "Examiner" by "Democritus" who criticized "Examiner" for attacking "republican writers," such as "Cato" and "Brutus," who were on the side of liberty (below). Five days later, "A Friend to Common Sense," noted that Anglo-Irish novelist and polemicist Jonathan Swift had used the pseudonym "Examiner," while defending the Tory ministry of Queen Anne. "Examiner" was accused of being a member of an aristocratic party and of maliciously criticizing opponents of the Constitution. "Examiner's" malice, continued "A Friend to Common Sense," would defeat its intended effect; "like a *wounded* viper, he ["Examiner"] only darts his venom into himself" (*New York Journal*, 19 December, below).

On 21 December "Democritus" voiced his suspicions about the authorship of "Examiner" in the *New York Journal*, when he noted that "Examiner" was "a most renowned physician" who was "deeply versed in both surgery and physic," as attested by "Examiner's" use of "technical terms" (below). A week later, "Democritus" was more explicit when he referred to "Examiner" as "Dr. Sawney M'Foolish" (*New York Journal*, 28 December, below. "Sawney" was a derisive term for a Scotsman.). It remained, however, for "Observer," writing in the *New York Journal* on 1 January 1788 in defense of "Examiner," to be even more explicit (below). "Observer" identified "Examiner" as "my friend Dr. M'K——," a more direct reference to Charles McKnight, an eminent New York City surgeon and physician.

McKnight (1750–1791), a native of New Jersey and a 1771 graduate of the College of New Jersey (Princeton), was the son of a Scotch-Irish Presbyterian clergyman. During the Revolution, he was surgeon of the Pennsylvania battalion of the Flying Camp; senior surgeon, Flying Hospital, Middle Department, 1777–78; surgeon general of Hospital, Middle Department, 1778–80; and chief hospital surgeon, 1780–82. After the Revolution, McKnight moved to New York City and became a member of the New York Society of the Cincinnati. He was port physician for New York City, 1784–91; and professor of surgery and anatomy at Columbia College, 1785–91.

MR. GREENLEAF, Some of your enemies have been so uncandid as to traduce you with the appellation of a partial Printer; a stigma to the injustice of which I shall always stand ready to bear testimony, from the attention you have generally paid to the pieces I have sent you against the party whose cause you are supposed warmly to espouse: I therefore make choice of your Daily Patriotic Register for the publication of my sentiments concerning some of the late Anti-Fœderal pieces, in preference to any other.

The Anti-Fœderal scriblers have indeed made a great deal of bustle and noise against the new constitution, which, I am persuaded, most of them are convinced in their hearts, is the best that ever was framed. Instead of all this clamor, why does not some one of them model a better one, if he can?—No, that cannot be done—No system of government can be perfect, and if all the Anti-Fœderal wisdom was collected together to hodge podge a constitution suitable to their taste and turn, it would bear no comparison with the beauty of that which they now affect to hold in so much abhorrence.

The sophistry of these dissatisfied gentry puts me in mind of a man who once wanted to persuade, that light was darkness, for which purpose he used the following arguments:

"Is not light changed into obscurity when a man keeps his eyes fixed for any time on the sun? Doth not an owl see clearly in the dark and not in the light. If therefore you had owls eyes, what would you call light, and what darkness? What then is light but a state of the eye? and if it be only a state of the eye, is not light darkness and darkness light?"

I thought, at first, he was only joking, but finding him serious, I replied, sir, you do not possess a single grain of understanding, inasmuch as all that region is closed upon you which is above the sphere of rationality, and that only is open to you which is below the rational sphere: at which he turned from me in a furious passion, and went to retail his nonsense elsewhere.

Now, your Cato, your Brutus, your Sidney, your Republican, your Timolean, your Cincinnatus, your Citizen, your Querist, and all that black train of sophists, who have been striving, through the channel of your paper, to turn this happy land into fields of blood and carnage, have talents exactly similar to the gentleman I have mentioned. They have no character they deserve less than that of being accounted wise politicians, because all their conceptions are entangled in doubts, and arguments, about evils that cannot possibly exist but in their own depraved imaginations. They may indeed be compared to so many owls; their minds being illuminated by a false light, by which they are enabled to give falshood the semblance of truth.

1. On 10 December the *New York Journal* announced that "Examiner" was received too late to be included in that day's issue, but that it would appear the next day.

Publius: The Federalist 20 (James Madison assisted by Hamilton) New York Packet, 11 December 1787

Inadequacy of The Netherlands Confederacy. For text, see CC:340. For reprintings, see Appendix IV, below.

One of Your Constant Readers Lansingburgh Northern Centinel, 11 December 1787

WASHINGTON COUNTY, *Dec.* 7, 1787.
To the Printers of the Northern Centinel.

Messrs. *Claxton* & *Babcock*, I am a plain countryman, and have received but a very moderate education, yet it is sufficient to enable me to read your papers, with which I am much pleased; and am happy to find that the good people of the states in general, are anxious to have the new federal constitution adopted as speedily as possible.

I do not pretend to be much of a politician; but it appears to me that the adoption of the proposed constitution for our new states, will be the most certain means of enabling us to pay off our debts, both at home and abroad—by a general union, add strength to our young empire—and greatly increase the foreign trade of our country, which will make our produce in much more demand; and cause us to get a quicker sale, and better price, than we now do—to the great advantage of us farmers.

I think the general government proposed, will, if adopted, be a means of uniting us firmly together, and make us one GREAT PEOPLE, instead of our continuing to be a number of petty insignificant, jarring states, whose interests will be ever clashing, and cause jealousies and innumerable quarrels; of which our enemies will be ever ready to take the advantage—keep us disputing with each other, ruin our trade, take our produce at their own prices, and finally reduce us to so distracted and divided a situation, that we shall at last be obliged to submit to their government, and become in reality their hewers of wood and drawers of water.

How melancholy is the tale, that the treasure and even the blood of so many thousands of our most valuable citizens should be expended, to procure our independence, and we should then neglect to reap the benefits of it, by establishing a government which must excite the envy and admiration of the world.

I hope the eyes of every one may be speedily opened, and that we may all see the necessity of uniting ourselves under a general government, which appears to me so well calculated to preserve our freedom, and make us a great, a happy and powerful people.

There are among us, in our country, some men of influence, who are doing all in their power to prejudice us against the constitution proposed; but I believe their conduct proceeds from interested motives. Some few of them have pretty well feathered their nests already, to the injury of the public and addition of our taxes, and I am fully persuaded that some of them are fearful, if an alteration of government should take place, they may lose the privilege or opportunity they have long enjoyed of picking our pockets.

They tell us dreadful stories of the danger we are in from establishing the union proposed; but I have, by the assistance of a friend of mine near New-York, seen, I believe, nearly all the publications that have been made both for and against the excellent federal constitution, now under consideration; and after fully examining the frame of government in question, and with the most serious attention weighed the arguments for and against it,—I can, with the greatest truth, tell you, my countrymen, that I fully believe that no mode of government was ever yet established so well calculated to preserve equal liberty to every individual member of the community, and render a people powerful and reputable among the nations. I really believe the opposition it meets with, does not arise from an anxiety to serve the country, but from the fears of many, that should a good efficient government take place, they would no longer have it in their power to hoard up wealth at the expence of the poor industrious people of the state. Many of those who make the loudest clamours, appear to be fearful their accounts and charges may be examined into, and that they may, e're long, be so *Hewed, Planed*, &c. as will reduce them to the size of their honest neighbours, and possibly less, even in point of purse and consequence—That it may be the fate of every peculator, I most seriously wish with as much anxiety as I am satisfied some of them fear it.

I wish the good people of our country in general may avoid being misled by these designing *Skinners of the Public*, and in time fix their minds on proper, impartial men, of sense, abilities, honesty, and judgment, to represent them in the expected convention of the state, in order to approve, or disapprove the new federal government, which is recommended to us by the late august convention. I think its being graced with the names, and having the approbation of a WASHINGTON and a FRANKLIN, will give it much weight with my countrymen, and make those, who from a want of knowledge themselves to judge rightly, give more freely their approbation to it, as, from the known characters, and good judgment of those *two worthies*, there is not the least room to suppose they would recommend a government that they did not think well calculated to render great, powerful and happy, that country they have taken such unwearied pains to establish free and independent.

If you think these, my observations, will have a tendency to remove the scruples of even one honest, well-meaning man, and consequently add one more to the number of those who are anxious for the glory and happiness of North-America, you will please to correct my spelling, and give them a place in your useful Centinel.

I am, gentlemen, One of your CONSTANT READERS.

Lansingburgh Northern Centinel, 11 December 1787[1]

THE SYREN's SONGS,
As sung by the celebrated modern CATO,
And set to music by his X—L—N—C.
To the tune of the Hypocrite: *a new tune very much in vogue.*

SONG FIRST.

Halloo, halloo Americans, who sail
The sea of life with passion's driving gale;
Bring to,—heave in the wind—alas, the waves
Scarce hide the rocks, that cause ten thousand graves.—
Behold yon breakers—see the surges beat!
Your dangers past arc small to those you'll meet:
Whirlpools all round display impending fate—
Bring to, my friends, and leisurely debate.—
Here on these rocks, from lofty thrones of mud,
I stretch my lungs across the raging flood;
The hollow sound re-echo's in the gales,
Distroys the sharks and frights approaching whales;—
Taught by experience all the coast around,
Fears when I yell, and trembles at the sound;—
Aw'd by my howling, storms and whirlwinds cease,
And leave reluctantly the waves at peace.
Then hear attentive, and with rage pursue,
A plan for safety—lengthy, weak and new:
Your ship is leaky, has been long confest,
But leaky ships in storms are much the best;
For when o'erwhelm'd by seas on every side,
The gaping chinks discharge the briny tide,
You cry, *we sink*; I grant it's even so,
But then, my friends, it's lamentably slow;
You may with care some hours preserve your breath,
But yon new ship is fraught with snares and death.
Step not on board, first view her well all round,
('Tis safer sinking where with ease we drown)
See if her stern new constitution wears,
If so, she'll founder in a thousand years.
No ship is fitting o'er the waves to climb
That may impair by age or endless time;—
Search out her faults, nor credit empty fame,
Who'd make immortal ev'ry builder's name.
What of itself should teach ye to dispise her
Is—*they were men, and might, perhaps, be wiser.*
In one like her, where yonder breakers roar,
There ship-wreck'd Holland sinks to rise no more.
A ship like her, while yet upon the strand,
Made Shays, her builder, quit his native land.
Who would not sooner perish in the flood

Than risque their lives on such delusive wood?
Then search her well, nor quit your crazy float,
Some may escape with nothing but the boat;
But if no faults your searching eyes explore,
In future I shall lamentably roar;
I'll make her flaws in ev'ry dismal howl
Plain to the night hawk and the hooting owl.
Here I'll remain and grope about my cave—
From hence my future comments you shall have.
            (*The remaining Songs to appear in future papers.*)[2]

1. This satirical verse attacks his Excellency ("X—L—N—C") Governor George Clinton, the alleged author of the Antifederalist "Cato" essays. For a second "Syren's Song," see Lansingburgh *Northern Centinel*, 18 December (below). For an allusion to these satirical verses, see *Northern Centinel*, 1 January 1788, at note 3 (below).
2. See *Northern Centinel*, 18 December (below).

Cato
Poughkeepsie Country Journal, 12 December 1787[1]

To the PUBLIC,

Friends and Fellow-Citizens, In my address to you in the spring of 1786,[2] on the subject of our political concerns, I promised at a future period to continue my observations; but was happy to find, that the general voice of the nation superseded the necessity of them. The radical defects in the constitution of the confederate government, was too obvious to escape the notice of a sensible, enlightned people—they saw with concern the danger their former caution & jealousy had involved them in; and very wisely called a general Convention of the States to devise a plan to check the mischief of anarchy in its bud—happily for this country many of the wisest men and most distinguished characters, independent in their principles and circumstances, and disconnected with party influence, were appointed to the important trust; and their unanimity in the business affords a pleasing presage of the happiness that will result from their deliberation.

It is but a groveling business, and commonly ruinous policy, to repair by peace-meal a shattered defective fabric—it is better to raise the disjo[i]nted building to its formation, and begin a new. The confederation was fraught with so many defects, and these so interwoven with its substantial parts, that to have attempted to revise it would have been doing business by the halves, and therefore the Convention with a boldness and decision becoming free-men, wisely carried the remedy to the root of the evil; and have offered a form of government to your consideration on an entire new system—much depends on your present deliberations.—It is easy to foresee that the present crisis will form a principal epoch in the politics of America, from whence we may date our national consequence and dignity, or anarchy, discord and ruin; the arguments made use of by a certain class of political scriblers, I conceive calculated (instead of throwing light on the subject) to deceive the ignorant but perhaps honest part of the community; and to misguide the thoughtless and unweary—in our present enquiry it is of no consequence who are the authors of these inflamatory productions, whether they are the result of the vanity of a northern champion to become the head of a party;[3] the expiring groans of a principal magistrate of a state;[4] or the last effort of the *patriotic hewer* of a Treasury to gain popularity;[5] or all together, I trust will bare equal rights on the minds of the public. It is natural enough to suppose that, when any general plan is proposed, that thwart the private interests or views of a party, that, such party will draw the most unpleasing picture of the plan, and blacken it with all the false colouring that a gloomy imagination can invent: thus are we told by these evil prophets, that the system is impracticable; smallness of territory being essential to a republican government[6]—in support of this doctrine, Montesquieu (who was born and educated under a monarchical government and knew nothing of any other but in theory) is quoted as an uncontrovertable authority, and after all, I presume they have mistaken the meaning of this author, for if I comprehend him right he is speaking of a pure democracy, such as Athens where the people all met in council; to be sure in such a government, extensive territory would be inconvenient, but a remedy to this evil has long since been found out: when the territory of any state became too large for the general assembling of the people, it was thought best to transact the business of the Commonwealth by representation: and thus large states may be governed as well by delegates from twenty districts, as small ones are from two or three; but this is what we are told by the politicians of the day constitutes a *dangerous aristocracy,* for say they in their learned diffinition, it is *a government of the few*; on this shameful quibble they attempt to ketch the attention of the rabble and frighten them into the measure of rejecting the proposed government—if I understand any thing of the meaning of the term, aristocracy signifies a government by a body of Nobles, who derive their power either from hereditary succession or from self appointment; and are no way dependent on the people for their rank in the state. By the plan offered to us, both the legislative and executive, derive their appointments either directly from the people, or from the representatives chosen by the people: how this can be called an aristocracy exceeds the limits of my comprehension; it is true that we are

told that the better sort of people will be appointed to govern; I pray
God the prediction may not be a false one. But should that be the case,
say these political empirics, we shall not have an equal representation.
Why? Because every class of people will not be represented. God knows
that fools and knaves have voice enough in government already; it is
to be hoped these wise prophesiers of evil would not wish to give them
a constitutional privilege to send members in proportion to their numbers. If they mean by classes the different professions in the state, their
plan is totally new, and it is to be feared the system once adopted, there
would be no end to their democratical purity; to take in every profession from the Clergy to the Chimney-sweep, will besides composing a
motley assemblage of heterogeneous particles, enlarge the representation so that it will become burthensome to the Community; had the
representation in Massachusetts been no larger than that in the proposed government of the Union, Shays would never have had a fol-
lower:—I think my judgment will not be impeached when I say that if
our representation in this state was less, we should be better represented, and the public saved a very great expence—to judge of the
future by the past, it is easy to perceive, that small states are as subject
to aristocratic oppression as large ones; witness the small territory of
Venice, at present the purest aristocracy in the world: Geneva, the circumference of which may be traversed in an hour's march is now oppressed by a dangerous aristocracy; while the democratic branch of the
legislature in England retains its primitive purity. Who was it that enslaved the extensive empire of Rome, but an abandoned democracy?
Who defended the republic at the battle of Pharsallia, but the better
sort of people? Cæsar can be considered in no other light than a more
fortunate Cattiline, and the latter in no other than that of an ambitious
demagogue attempting to ruin the Commonwealth, at the head of licentious democracy. In the present crisis of our public affairs I confess
with the frankness [of] a free man and the concern of a patriot, that
I apprehend more danger from a licentious democracy, than from aristocratic oppression.

I clearly perceive there will be no mid-way in the present business;
we must either adopt the advice of these pretended democratical pur-
itans, and then carry their doctrines to the point they evidently lead,
viz. To divide the present union into at least five hundred independent
sovereign states, build a council-house in the centre of each, and by a
general law declare all the servants and apprentices free, and then let
the multitude meet and govern themselves—or on the other hand, fall
to the plain road of common sense, and govern the union by representatives in one collective council; as pointed out in the system offered

to your consideration: In the first you will possess popular liberty with a vengeance, and like a neighbour [(a)]state, no man's property will be secure, but each one defrauding his neighbour under the sanct[i]on of law,—thus subverting every principle of morality and religion.—In the second you will enjoy the blessing of a well balanced government, capable of inspiring credit and respectability abroad, and virtue, confidence, good order and harmony at home.—Should the Author have leisure to attend to it, the dangerous consequences that will inevitably flow from dividing the union, will be the subject of another paper.

(a) Rhode-Island.

1. On 5 December the *Country Journal* announced that "CATO is received and will appear in our next."

2. "Cato" published at least seven articles in the *Country Journal* between 6 April and 26 July 1786, some of which attacked the institution of slavery while others were concerned with a Dutchess County election. The essay printed on 5 July deals with the need to strengthen the Confederation (Mfm:N.Y.).

3. Possibly John Williams of Washington County. Other possibilities are John Lansing, Jr., or Robert Yates, both of Albany County.

4. Probably Governor George Clinton.

5. Probably Abraham Yates, Jr., who sometimes used the pseudonym "Rough Hewer" when writing for newspapers and who was formerly a commissioner for Continental loans.

6. See especially "Cato" III, *New York Journal*, 25 October (above).

Americanus V
New York Daily Advertiser, 12 December 1787

Montesquieu's Spirit of Laws is certainly a work of great merit. The philanthropy and acuteness of observation which every page discloses, are evidences of the excellency of his heart, and the penetrative force of his understanding.—On an attentive perusal, however, of this celebrated performance, it will manifestly appear, that the main object of the author, and what he seems ever to have most at heart, was to mollify the rigors of Monarchy, and render this species of Government in some degree compatible with Liberty. No man ever had a juster claim to the grateful acknowledgments of his countrymen. But tho' his work has been of infinite service to his country, yet the principles he has endeavored to establish will by no means stand the test of the rigid rules of philosophic precision. It ever has been the fate of system mongers to mistake the productions of their own imaginations, for those of nature herself: And their works, instead of advancing the cause of truth, serve only as false guides, who are ever ready to mislead us and impede our progress. Tho' the Spirit of Laws contains a fund of useful and just observations on Government, yet, the systematic part of it is evidently

defective. His general divisions of Government into different species—
his definition of their several natures, and the principles he deduces
from them, do not convey to the mind clear and distinct ideas of different qualities really existing in the nature of things.

To begin with his general divisions, he has divided Government into
three species; Republican, Monarchial, and Despotic. His definitions of
their several natures are as follows: "A Republican Government is that
in which the body, or only a part of the people is possessed of the
supreme power: Monarchy, that in which a single person governs by
fixed and established laws: A Despotic Government, that in which a
single person directs every thing by his own will and caprice."[1]

In the first definition are blended together two species of Government, evidently distinct in their natures. In the one, the supreme
power, or the source of power, is in the body of the people; in the
other, it is in a certain number of persons, be they more or less, who
form a class of men distinct from the people at large. This is a distinction derived from the very nature of things. The one is in its nature a
free Government, the other is in its nature Arbitrary or Despotic. The
two last definitions are only modifications of the same species. It is a
Government in which all power is centered in, or derived from a single
person. In order to elucidate the propriety of this general division, he
has endeavoured to establish certain principles, which are the different
springs of action which set these different species of Government in
motion. The principle of Republican Government is VIRTUE: That of
Monarchy is HONOR: That of Despotic Government is FEAR. This is
certainly a very fanciful piece of business. It is to be sure an ingenious
conceit, by which he would endeavor to establish a distinction between
an Arbitrary Monarch and a Despotic one. Notwithstanding this happy
discovery of Montesquieu in favor of the Government of his native
country, fear, I apprehend, is still the most predominant principle in
this Government. A military establishment, consisting of two or three
hundred thousand men, is a principle of action in Government a thousand times more energetic than this vague sentiment of honor. Is honor
a principle of action sufficiently powerful to make a peasant (for instance) submit with chearfulness to all the grievous impositions by
which the poor are so miserably oppressed?

The theory which Montesquieu has endeavored to establish, is certainly erroneous. His general divisions; his definitions of the natures of
the different species of Government, and the principles which form
the springs of action in each, are unsatisfactory.

The most obvious and natural general division, and which has prevailed universally 'till Montesquieu introduced this new theory, is into
Democracy, Aristocracy and Monarchy.

In Democracy the supreme power is possessed by, or derived from the aggregate body of the people. In Aristocracy, this power is possessed by, or derived from a part only of the people. In Monarchy it is possessed by, or derived from a single person. This general division may be again subdivided. Democracy may be either pure, that is where the people govern themselves, or it may be representative, that is where they delegate the powers of Government to certain persons for a limited time. So too in Aristocracy, the supreme power may be exercised by the whole body of the Nobles, or intrusted to a certain number. Monarchy may be either a pure disposition where every thing depends immediately on the will of the Prince, or assume a milder aspect by the establishment of intermediate, subordinate, and dependent powers.

As to the principles which ensure obedience, and enable the Government to operate, they are universally the same in every species of Government, though compounded in various degrees.

1. Fear, or the dread of punishment. This is the simplest, most powerful, and of course the most universal motive of obedience amongst mankind, and is therefore principally depended upon in all arbitrary Governments.

2. Attachment. This arises from an infinite variety of circumstances, and becomes the more forceable in proportion to the moderation and freedom of the Government. Customs, manners, habits, prejudices, are the ordinary sources of this attachment. But what, among an enlightened people, ought to form the strongest motive of attachment to Government, arises from a conviction of its necessity and utility.

Montesquieu tells us that "ambition is pernicious in a Republic."[2] So far is this from being true, that the fact is, that no Government so much requires the aid of this powerful spring to human actions. By ambition however, I do not mean that insatiate lust of domination and despotic sway, by which the annals of mankind have been so disgraced, but that laudable desire of excelling in whatever we undertake, which is the source of every excellence of which our nature is capable. Without the impulse of this noble passion, where would the people find men, who would cheerfully submit themselves to the toils, cares, and perplexities incident to the management of public affairs? Montesquieu may talk of virtue as the spring of action in a republican Government;[3] but, I trust, its force would be found too feeble to produce great exertions without the aid of ambition. Can any man, who has a tolerable acquaintance of human nature, imagine that men would so eagerly engage in public affairs, from whence they can hope to derive no personal emolument, merely from the impulse of so exalted, so pure, so disinterested a passion as patriotism, or political virtue? No! it is ambition that constitutes the very life and soul of Republican Government. As fear and attachment insure obedience to Government, so does ambition set its wheels in motion.

The necessity of following Cato, naturally led me into an investigation of the nature and principles of Republican Government. Though an enquiry of this kind is not immediately necessary in the business at present agitating, yet it is intimately connected with it, and is certainly a very interesting speculation. I shall now proceed to make some remarks on Cato's fifth number.[4]

The Constitution directs that the members to the House of Representatives be elected biennially. This departure from the good Democratic rule it seems does not meet with Cato's approbation. The question then is, whether this delegation of legislative power for the term of two years can prove any way dangerous to liberty. If Cato will permit us to reason from analogy on this point, I conceive there will not remain the least shadow of apprehension. For if, in the Government of England, such as I have described it, a septennial Parliament, forming so inadequate a representation of the nation, and in which too officers under Government are admitted to have seats, has proved however so firm a barrier in favor of liberty, what reasonable fears can be entertained against a biennial House of Representatives, who are restricted from holding any office under Government, and who form a just and equal representation of the great body of the people. If then there can be no room for apprehensions of danger from the establishment of biennial elections, we must allow at least that it is more convenient, and affords the members more time to acquire a knowledge of public affairs competent to the station they fill.

From the whole tenor of the passage in Cato's fifth number respecting the power given to the State Executives to make temporary appointment of Senators, we are led to suppose that this power has been placed in the executive of the general Government. The executive of the Federal Government, would indeed form a strange depository of a power of this nature. It is unnecessary for me to point out the different consequences resulting from this power being vested in a State or a Federal Executive. They are certainly too important to leave the matter in the least doubtful. Candor therefore required the utmost explicitness.

But what were the views of the Convention in vesting this temporary power in the executive of each State? Was it not evidently from a scrupulous attention to the interests of the States individually. This objection therefore does not come with a good grace from Cato, who is so great an advocate for State sovereignty. It is surely of the highest importance to the States individually that they be fully represented in an

Assembly who have the power of forming treaties and alliances, appointing Ambassadors, and other public ministers and consuls, judges of the Supreme Court, and all other officers of the United States, whose appointments are not otherwise provided for.

But "it is an important objection to this Government, that the representation consists of so few." How "corruption" and "treachery" should ever prevail in an Assembly constituted as this is, I cannot even conjecture. In an Assembly framed on the plan of the present Congress, where the whole of the legislative and executive powers centre in a single body, in such an Assembly there might be some ground for apprehensions of this nature.

But what man could there be in the Government who could form a separate interest of such magnitude, as to induce him to have recourse to such vile means. Surely a President, whose term of office is so short, and whose powers are so limited, could have no object in view sufficiently important to recompence him for the disgrace and ignominy which would inevitably attend an action so atrocious. But admitting that every scruple of this nature was overcome, and that he had so far succeeded in his project as, contrary to all human probability, to corrupt a majority of the Legislature to concur with him, could this business be kept a secret? Would not suspicion set the minority to work, and would there be a possibility of preventing a discovery of the plot? And would not the President and his corrupt majority be hurled from their stations and consigned to everlasting infamy? But experience is the safest guide. Let us on[c]e more appeal to the Government of Great-Britain. We find an hereditary Monarch, who pursues a permanent interest manifestly distinct from the community at large. An house of Peers wholly at his devotion. He possesses an infinite variety of means of influencing a majority of the house of Commons, which can never obtain in a Government upon the plan of that we have now before us. Notwithstanding all these unfavorable circumstances we can find few or no instances in which the general interest of the nation has been betrayed or neglected.

But what would be the consequence of a representation bearing any kind of proportion to that of a State Assembly? In all probability, in half a century more, these States will contain twenty millions of people, which number, according to the rule established by the Constitution, would require a house of representatives, consisting of near seven hundred members.[5] An Assembly much larger than this, could not act with any tolerable convenience as one deliberative body.

"Another thing may be suggested against the small number of representatives is, that the choice will be confined to a very few." And so it would be was this number quadrupled. For what proportion would twenty four[6] bear to the whole number of citizens in this State. But the fact is, that no Government, that has ever yet existed in the world, affords so ample a field, to individuals of all ranks, for the display of political talents and abilities. Here are no Patricians, who engross the offices of State. No man who has real merit, let his situation be what it will, need dispair. He first distinguishes himself amongst his neighbours at township and county meeting; he is next sent to the State Legislature. In this theatre his abilities, whatever they are, are exhibited in their true colors, and displayed to the views of every man in the State: from hence his ascent to a seat in Congress becomes easy and sure. Such a regular uninterrupted gradation from the chief men in a village, to the chair of the President of the United States, which this Government affords to all her citizens without distinction, is a perfection in Republican Government, heretofore unknown and unprecedented.

1. *Spirit of Laws*, I, Book II, chapter II, 11.
2. *Ibid.*, Book III, chapter VII, 36.
3. *Ibid.*, Book V, chapters I–II, 58–59.
4. See "Cato" V, *New York Journal*, 22 November (above).
5. "Americanus" incorrectly interprets the Constitution's ratio of representation, which is not to *exceed* one representative for every 30,000 inhabitants.
6. Under Article I, section 2 of the Constitution, New York was allotted six representatives in the first House of Representatives. "Americanus" arrived at the number 24 by quadrupling that figure.

D——
New York Daily Advertiser, 12 December 1787

Mr. CHILDS, About a fortnight ago I observed a paragraph in your paper, extracted from Oswald's of Philadelphia, in which it was asserted, that the Hon. John Jay, after due reflection, had pronounced the Federal Government as a system, which, if adopted, would soon destroy the freedom of commerce, and the liberties of the people.[1]

Now, Sir, tho' I am persuaded the impudent paragraph alluded to, was inserted to answer some base purposes of the Antifederal party, and·tho' I am convinced Mr. Jay's opinion is very different in fact; yet, designedly as it has been misrepresented, and hitherto unrefuted, it may—nay it unquestionably will have such influence in society, as the Hon. Gentleman, I am sure, would by no means wish to establish. The character of Mr. Jay stands too high throughout the States, to have his authority trifled with, especially on a subject the most important ever agitated in this Western world. I have no doubt but that his particular friends know, that his sentiments on this great subject have been grosly misstated, yet it is proper that the people (who are intended to be misled) should also be made acquainted with them. The report, if false, ought certainly to be contradicted:—this appears to be the more necessary, since it is now industriously circulating by Antifederalists, *as a truth which Mr. Jay will not deny.*[2]

I have been induced to offer this *hint,* in consequence of a conversation I entered into this morning with a gentleman of some consideration, who loves his country, and is warmly attached to the New Government. This honest American candidly acknowledged, that he would distrust and abandon the good opinion he had formed of the Federal System, if it was reprobated in such terms by Mr. Jay; whom he considered as a gentleman learned in the science of legislation, and much conversant with modern politics:—an American too, of tried integrity, who aimed at the real happiness, aggrandizement and glory of his country.

Monday.

1. The reference is to an item that appeared in the Philadelphia *Independent Gazetteer* on 24 November and that was reprinted in the *Daily Advertiser* on 29 November. See "John Jay and the Constitution," 24 November–7 December (above).

2. On 7 December the Philadelphia *Independent Gazetteer* printed Jay's 1 December letter to John Vaughan, in which Jay indicated that he supported the Constitution. The *Daily Advertiser* reprinted Jay's letter on 13 December. See "John Jay and the Constitution," 24 November–7 December (above).

Publius: The Federalist 21 (Alexander Hamilton)
New York Independent Journal, 12 December 1787

Confederation Congress lacks powers of enforcement and taxation. For text, see CC:341. For reprintings, see Appendix IV, below.

One of the Nobility
New York Journal, 12 December 1787[1]

MR. GREENLEAF, I request you to publish the following political creed of every patriotic Fœderalist. Every person that peruses it, must instantaneously acknowledge its liberality, reasonableness, and regard for the rights of the people. I have the vanity to think, that, like an axiom, it must no sooner be read, than agreed to—and that it is, in itself, sufficient to overthrow all the objections alledged against our new liberal constitution, by Brutus, Cato, the Centinel, Old Whig, and other ragamuffin, reprobate, impudent, and rascally quill-driving scribblers. Contractedness in sentiment, is reprehensible in an individual, and highly disgraceful to a people. My fellow citizens, consequently, cannot shew greater prudence, generosity, and benevolence, than in freely trusting, without any restrictions, to their rulers, liberties which they are themselves incapable of protecting; their governors will then be so pierced with gratitude for such generous favors, that they will strain every nerve to promote the felicity of their benefactors. Who would wish to restrain the powers of his friend? and what people in their senses, would curb the authority of their greatest friends—the administrators of their government? Venice was formerly a democracy, but the people acted very wisely, in committing the management of their affairs, without the least controul, to the hands of the *well-born* and opulent—they, by this excellent and truly prudential conduct, became very formidable and powerful, and are, at this day, in the actual possession of more freedom and happiness than any nation whatever.

Although, sir, I am *well-born*, and expect to be honored with a considerable office, when the new establishment takes place, yet you may rest assured of my real disinterestedness when I assert, that the proposed government ought to be universally adopted without the least hesitation, examination, alteration, or amendment. Horace, was unquestionably a wise man, and he observes—

Odi profanum vulgus, & arces.[2]

Have not our patriotic conventioneers imitated his example, in constructing a constitution, which effectually expels the *nobility* from public offices? Let the *farmer,* the *merchant,* and the *mechanic,* reflect, if they are chosen to any dignified stations, that their farms and stores must suffer, and their tools grow rusty.

The great mass of the people are in a state of brutal ignorance, incapable of forming a rational idea—guided wholly by instinct—destitute of sensibility, and all the exalted virtues—mere *orang outangs*—blockheads, numskulls, asses, monkeys, sheep, owls, and lobsters—and only created to be subservient to the pleasures and interest of their superiors—they have no business to intermeddle with politics—if they can scrape together money enough to pay their taxes, they ought to be satisfied: all the offices of government are, by the laws of nature, appropriated to *men of family, fortune and genius.* I have ten thousand more equally as incontestible arguments to add, but an impudent taylor has interrupted my further writing, by his impertinent solicitations. When I am appointed under the new government, the scoundrel shall repent his insolence. However, I cannot conclude, sir, without giving you a word of advice, as I am disposed to befriend you. I have observed several Republican or Anti-Fœderal pieces in your paper, which, certainly, exposes you to danger, and, if the new constitution takes place, your ears are in a very precarious situation. Follow my advice, and refrain for the future, and I promise you the office of PRINTER TO THE CONGRESS.

I have the honor to be, Sir, Your most obedient servant, One of the Nobility.

———

Political Creed of every Fœderalist.

I believe in the infallibility, all sufficient wisdom, and infinite goodness of the late convention; or, in other words, I believe that some men are of so perfect a nature, that it is absolutely impossible for them to commit error, or design villainy.

I believe that the great body of the people are incapable of judging in their nearest concerns, and that, therefore, they ought to be guided by the opinions of their superiors.

I believe that it is totally unnecessary to secure the rights of mankind in the formation of a constitution.

I believe that aristocracy is the best form of government.

I believe that the people of America are cowards and unable to defend themselves, and that, consequently, standing armies are absolutely necessary.

I believe that the trial by jury, and the freedom of the press ought to be exploded from every wise government.

I believe that the new constitution will not affect the state constitutions, yet that the state officers will oppose it, because it will abridge their power.

I believe that the new constitution will prove the bulwark of liberty— the balm of misery—the essence of justice, and the astonishment of all mankind. In short, I believe (in the words of that inimitable reasoner, Attorney Wilson) that it is the best form of government which has ever been offered to the world.[3]

I believe, that to speak, write, read, think, or bear any thing against the proposed government, is damnable heresy, execrable rebellion, and high treason against the sovereign majesty of the convention—And lastly, I believe that every person, who differs from me in belief, is an infernal villain. AMEN.

1. On 11 December the *New York Journal* announced that "ONE OF THE NOBILITY, with the POLITICAL CREED OF EVERY FEDERALIST annexed, is received; but as it came late yesterday could not be inserted this day. The Editor has given it a cursory review, and conceives some few alterations indispensible before it can make its appearance in the Daily Patriotic Register; for which reason an interview with the author is requested."

2. Actually "Odi profanum vulgus et arceo" (Latin). "I hate the common or vulgar herd and keep them off" (Horace, *Odes*, Book 3, Ode 1, line 1).

3. Commenting on the Constitution in a 6 October speech, James Wilson stated that "I am bold to assert, that it is the best form of government which has ever been offered

to the world" (CC:134, p. 344). See also "New York Reprinting of James Wilson's 6 October Speech Before a Philadelphia Public Meeting," 13–25 October (above).

A Countryman II (DeWitt Clinton) New York Journal, 13 December 1787[1]

Honored and good Sir, Your kind letter of the 10th of this month gave me great relief, for I was sore afraid that my very long epistle to you, had wearied and offended you, which I am very glad to find is not the case, as you ask me to write to you again, which I shant fail doing: my neighbour ——, and myself, as I mentioned to you in my last[2] we intended, have since spent several evenings together, and sat up late, reading the new constitution, and papers, in hopes to come to a thorough knowledge of them, which to be sure, is not an easy matter; one thing, and it would appear but a trifling matter, puzzled us exceedingly, that is, the names the different writers have fixed upon one another; for we found that those who are for abiding by the confederation and strengthening it, so as to make it lasting, are called antifederalists; and the other party who are for throwing it aside, and having nothing farther to do with it, but are for making of us into one solid government, are called federalists: now I did not know the meaning of the high-flown words, but my neighbour told me, that antifederalists were people, that were against the confederation; and that federalists were those that were for it: now, as I said before, this puzzled us very much, and often prevented our understanding what we were reading—at length we both agreed, that either the writers themselves or the printers had made a mistake; so to hinder our being bothered any more, it was agreed, that my neighbour should take pen and ink, and strike out anti, where it was used, and put it to the other word, so as to make it read right all through, and this, I can assure you, was a great help to us, and well paid for the time it took, for we could understand what we read with much greater ease afterwards. The day after, our old neighbour ——, who, you heard me tell, had just before the war, moved down to Pennsylvania, and had come up to see his friends here, and spent the next evening with us, and we mentioned the matter to him, and he told us there was nothing at all strange in it, for it was the way some great men had to deceive the common people, and prevent their knowing what they were about; he said it was just so down with them, for there was a party of grand men in Philadelphia, who had made a great deal of money during the war, and lived like princes, had been trying all their might to overset their constitution this several years, and he did not doubt, but they wished to have a king, that they might be lords, or something else still greater themselves and make more money again, yet they called themselves republicans, because they knew it was a name that is very pleasing to the people, when, in truth, they are no more republicans than the pope, or the pretender himself; this you may judge, worthy sir, cleared up the matter to us at once; however we did not repent that we made the alterations, for they will be useful to our neighbours, when we lend the papers to them to read. But to go on, after we thought we understood the new constitution, nearly as well as it can be understood, I thought to myself, I would shew my neighbour the last letter I wrote to you, for I kept a copy of it, which I did, and he read it over and over again, and it pleased me a good deal, to find, that he thinks, what I said there, was very right; but he said at the same time, that though my letter was very long, I had not been quite plain enough about one thing, for, he said, we should be careful not to give a bit more power to our rulers than we could well help; for they would always find a way to get more fast enough, and they knew how to keep it when they once had it, so that we could never get any part of it back again; and to prove what he said, he put me in mind, that the convention was only sent to amend the old constitution, yet they sat about making a new one, though they had no power to do that at all; besides he made some other remarks which I will now mention to you, for we think very much alike about the business; he agrees with me, that very little dependence can be put on the president-general, and the senate, that they are to be appointed in a very odd manner, and would be so far above the common people, that they will care little about them, and when they get themselves fairly fixed in the saddle, there will be no such thing as to get them out again; but he seems to think, that the assemblymen, if there was enough of them, and if we could be sure that they would be honest and faithful, might give the others a deal of trouble, and hinder them from doing much mischief for a good while; but there are so very few of them, and the chance of getting good ones so little, from the manner which may be contrived by this new government, for making choice of them, that we cannot have much dependence from this quarter. We do not see but that they may order the election to be held in New-York city; I am sure, if they do, there is not one in a hundred of us country people, will be at the expence and trouble of attending there, to give our votes, except it should happen in the fall, just when we take our truck to market, and then a few of us might by chance, if we could get time [to] give a vote, so that your mayor, and other great folks, may put in who they please, and, I believe, there is little doubt, but they will put in such folks as Mr. Beccaria speaks of,[3] that will love to increase their own power, and keep down the common people; besides, if the election should be or-

dered to be held at any other place, lords of manors, and other great
folks will attend, and be able to divide these places among themselves,
in spite of all the common people can do; indeed, my neighbour tells
me, he has often heard some of these great people say (for you know
many of them think a good deal of him, and tell their minds very freely
to him) that we were very wrong to send to our present congress, some
people that we sent there, that although they were honest, and men of
good enough sense, yet they could do us little or no good there, for
they were unacquainted with the world; and that no man could be of
service, if he was not very rich, and had large family connections, and
knew how to dance, and dress well. Now, I suppose it will be the same
case in this new government; and if so, I am sure, we would lean upon
a broken reed, if we rely upon the assemblymen a bit more than upon
the others.

There is another thing, in this new constitution, that my neighbour
and me, have talked a good deal about; it is what is called in the writings you sent me, article 9th, section 1st [i.e., Article I, section 9].
Indeed, we hardly know what they will be at by this; for fear you should
mistake me, I believe I had better write it down; they say, "the migration, or importation of such persons, as any of the states now existing
shall think proper to admit, shall not be prohibited by the congress,
prior to the year 1808, but a tax, or duty may be imposed on such
importation, not exceeding ten dollars for each person."

Now we think it very hard, if that is their meaning, that they should
make every man, that comes from the old countries here, pay ten dollars to the new government. A great many of us, have our relations in
the North of Ireland, and other places, that were very good friends to
us all the war, and gave a great deal of trouble to the British, and I
believe, partly upon our accounts, who might wish to come and settle
here, among us; and I am sure they would be of great service to us,
but do not you think it would be a hard matter for them to pay for
their passages, besides their other expences, ten hard dollars for themselves, and each person in their families, when they get to this country.
But our old neighbour from Pennsylvania, says, that it is thought among
them, to mean worse than this, that its true meaning, is to give leave to
import negroes from Guinea, for slaves, to work upon the rich men's
plantations, to the southward; but that it is not mentioned plainly on
purpose, because the quakers, and a great many other good religious
people, are very much against making slaves of our fellow-creatures, and
especially, against suffering any more to be brought into the country,
and this, if it was known, might make them all against the new govern-

ment: now, if this is really the case, it is to be sure, much worse than my neighbour and me first thought it to be; for all good christians must agree, that this trade is an abomination to the Lord, and must, if continued, bring down a heavy judgment upon our land. It does not seem to be justice, that one man should take another from his own country, and make a slave of him; and yet we are told by this new constitution, that one of its great ends, is to establish justice; alas! my worthy friend, it is a serious thing to trifle with the great God; his punishments are slow, but always sure; and the cunning of men, however deep, cannot escape them. I well remember, that our congress (and I believe, as I mentioned before, that they were honest, good men who meant as they said) when they declared independence, solemnly said, that "all men were created equal; and that they were endowed by their creator with certain unalienable rights; and that among them, are these, life, liberty, and the pursuit of happiness." They also talked much about the sacredness of a trial by jury;[4] and complained loudly, that the old government tried to hinder the peopleing of this country, by discourageing people to come here from the old countries;[5] and for these, and other causes, they went to war, after making a solemn appeal to God, for the rectitude of their intentions; and even the infidel must confess, that God was remarkably with us, watched over us in the hour of danger, fought our battles, and subdued our enemies, and finally gave us success. Alas! my good friend, it is a terrible thing to mock the almighty, for how can we expect to merit his favor, or escape his vengeance; if it should appear, that we were not serious in our professions, and that they were mere devices to gratify our pride and ambition, we ought to remember, he sees into the secret recesses of our hearts, and knows what is passing there. It becomes us then to bear testimony against every thing which may be displeasing in his sight, and be careful that we incur not the charge mentioned by the prophet Hosea, "ye have plowed wickedness, ye have reaped iniquity; ye have eaten the fruit of lies, because thou didst trust in thy ways, in the multitude of thy mighty men."[6] Here I shall finish this present letter; and when I find a little more leisure, I will continue to write to you again.

I remain, Honoured Sir, Your real friend, And humble servant. A COUNTRYMAN.

1. On 6 December the *New York Journal* announced that "A Countryman" II and "Cato" VI were received and that they would be printed "as soon as possible." Along with "Brutus" V, both of these essays were printed on Thursday, 13 December. (The Thursday issue of the *Journal* was more widely circulated than any other issue of that newspaper.)

2. See "A Countryman" I, *New York Journal*, 6 December (above).

3. See *ibid.*, note 2 (above).

4. The Declaration of Independence charged the King and Parliament with passing legislation "For depriving us in many cases, of the benefits of Trial by Jury:—For transporting us beyond the Seas to be tried for pretended offences." The King and Parliament also used "a mock Trial" to protect British troops quartered in America (CDR, 74).

5. The Declaration of Independence charged that the king "has endeavoured to prevent the population of these States; for that purpose obstructing the Laws for Naturalization of Foreigners; refusing to pass others to encourage their migrations hither, and raising the conditions of new Appropriations of Lands" (CDR, 74).

6. Hosea 10:13.

Brutus V
New York Journal, 13 December 1787[1]

To the PEOPLE of the State of NEW-YORK.

It was intended in this Number to have prosecuted the enquiry into the organization of this new system; particularly to have considered the dangerous and premature union of the President and Senate, and the mixture of legislative, executive, and judicial powers in the Senate.

But there is such an intimate connection between the several branches in whom the different species of authority is lodged, and the powers with which they are invested, that on reflection it seems necessary first to proceed to examine the nature and extent of the powers granted to the legislature.

This enquiry will assist us the better to determine, whether the legislature is so constituted, as to provide proper checks and restrictions for the security of our rights, and to guard against the abuse of power—For the means should be suited to the end; a government should be framed with a view to the objects to which it extends: if these be few in number, and of such a nature as to give but small occasion or opportunity to work oppression in the exercise of authority, there will be less need of a numerous representation, and special guards against abuse, than if the powers of the government are very extensive, and include a great variety of cases. It will also be found necessary to examine the extent of these powers, in order to form a just opinion how far this system can be considered as a confederation, or a consolidation of the states. Many of the advocates for, and most of the opponents to this system, agree that the form of government most suitable for the United States, is that of a confederation. The idea of a confederated government is that of a number of independent states entering into a compact, for the conducting certain general concerns, in which they have a common interest, leaving the management of their internal and local affairs to their separate governments. But whether the system proposed is of this nature cannot be determined without a strict enquiry into the powers proposed to be granted.

This constitution considers the people of the several states as one body corporate, and is intended as an original compact, it will therefore dissolve all contracts which may be inconsistent with it. This not only results from its nature, but is expressly declared in the 6*th article* of it.[2] The design of the constitution is expressed in the preamble, to be, "in order to form a more perfect union, to establish justice, insure domestic tranquility, provide for the common defence, promote the general welfare, and secure the blessings of liberty to ourselves and posterity." These are the ends this government is to accomplish, and for which it is invested with certain powers, among these is the power "to make all laws which are *necessary and proper* for carrying into execution the foregoing powers, and *all other* powers vested by this constitution in the government of the United States, or in any department or officer thereof." It is a rule in construing a law to consider the objects the legislature had in view in passing it, and to give it such an explanation as to promote their intention. The same rule will apply in explaining a constitution. The great objects then are declared in this preamble in general and indefinite terms to be to provide for the common defence, promote the general welfare, and an express power being vested in the legislature to make all laws which shall be necessary and proper for carrying into execution all the powers vested in the general government. The inference is natural that the legislature will have an authority to make all laws which they shall judge necessary for the common safety, and to promote the general welfare. This amounts to a power to make laws at discretion: No terms can be found more indefinite than these, and it is obvious, that the legislature alone must judge what laws are proper and necessary for the purpose. It may be said, that this way of explaining the constitution, is torturing and making it speak what it never intended. This is far from my intention, and I shall not even insist upon this implied power, but join issue with those who say we are to collect the idea of the powers given from the express words of the clauses granting them; and it will not be difficult to shew that the same authority is expressly given which is supposed to be implied in the forgoing paragraphs.

In the 1st article, 8th section, it is declared, "that Congress shall have power to lay and collect taxes, duties, imposts and excises, to pay the debts, and provide for the common defence, and general welfare of the United States." In the preamble, the intent of the constitution,

among other things, is declared to be to provide for the common defence, and promote the general welfare, and in this clause the power
is in express words given to Congress "to provide for the common
defence, and general welfare."—And in the last paragraph of the same
section there is an express authority to make all laws which shall be
necessary and proper for carrying into execution this power. It is therefore evident, that the legislature under this constitution may pass any
law which they may think proper. It is true the 9th section restrains
their power with respect to certain objects. But these restrictions are
very limited, some of them improper, some unimportant, and others
not easily understood, as I shall hereafter shew. It has been urged that
the meaning I give to this part of the constitution is not the true one,
that the intent of it is to confer on the legislature the power to lay and
collect taxes, &c. in order to provide for the common defence and
general welfare. To this I would reply, that the meaning and intent of
the constitution is to be collected from the words of it, and I submit
to the public, whether the construction I have given it is not the most
natural and easy. But admitting the contrary opinion to prevail, I shall
nevertheless, be able to shew, that the same powers are substantially
vested in the general government, by several other articles in the constitution. It invests the legislature with authority to lay and collect taxes,
duties, imposts and excises, in order to provide for the common defence, and promote the general welfare, and to pass all laws which may
be necessary and proper for carrying this power into effect. To comprehend the extent of this authority, it will be requisite to examine 1st.
what is included in this power to lay and collect taxes, duties, imposts
and excises.

2d. What is implied in the authority, to pass all laws which shall be
necessary and proper for carrying this power into execution.

3d. What limitation, if any, is set to the exercise of this power by the
constitution.

1st. To detail the particulars comprehended in the general terms,
taxes, duties, imposts and excises, would require a volume, instead of
a single piece in a news-paper. Indeed it would be a task far beyond
my ability, and to which no one can be competent, unless possessed of
a mind capable of comprehending every possible source of revenue;
for they extend to every possible way of raising money, whether by
direct or indirect taxation. Under this clause may be imposed a poll-
tax, a land-tax, a tax on houses and buildings, on windows and fire
places, on cattle and on all kinds of personal property:—It extends to
duties on all kinds of goods to any amount, to tonnage and poundage
on vessels, to duties on written instruments, news-papers, almanacks,

and books:—It comprehends an excise on all kinds of liquors, spirits, wines, cyder, beer, &c. and indeed takes in duty or excise on every necessary or conveniency of life; whether of foreign or home growth or manufactory. In short, we can have no conception of any way in which a government can raise money from the people, but what is included in one or other of these general terms. We may say then that this clause commits to the hands of the general legislature every conceivable source of revenue within the United States. Not only are these terms very comprehensive, and extend to a vast number of objects, but the power to lay and collect has great latitude; it will lead to the passing a vast number of laws, which may affect the personal rights of the citizens of the states, expose their property to fines and confiscation, and put their lives in jeopardy: it opens a door to the appointment of a swarm of revenue and excise officers to prey upon the honest and industrious part of the community, eat up their substance, and riot on the spoils of the country.

2d. We will next enquire into what is implied in the authority to pass all laws which shall be necessary and proper to carry this power into execution.

It is, perhaps, utterly impossible fully to define this power. The authority granted in the first clause can only be understood in its full extent, by descending to all the particular cases in which a revenue can be raised; the number and variety of these cases are so endless, and as it were infinite, that no man living has, as yet, been able to reckon them up. The greatest geniuses in the world have been for ages employed in the research, and when mankind had supposed that the subject was exhausted they have been astonished with the refined improvements that have been made in modern times, and especially in the English nation on the subject—If then the objects of this power cannot be comprehended, how is it possible to understand the extent of that power which can pass all laws which shall be necessary and proper for carrying it into execution? It is truly incomprehensible. A case cannot be conceived of, which is not included in this power. It is well known that the subject of revenue is the most difficult and extensive in the science of government. It requires the greatest talents of a statesman, and the most numerous and exact provisions of the legislature. The command of the revenues of a state gives the command of every thing in it.—He that has the purse will have the sword, and they that have both, have every thing; so that the legislature having every source from which money can be drawn under their direction, with a right to make all laws necessary and proper for drawing forth all the resource[s] of the country, would have, in fact, all power.

Were I to enter into the detail, it would be easy to shew how this power in its operation, would totally destroy all the powers of the individual states. But this is not necessary for those who will think for themselves, and it will be useless to such as take things upon trust, nothing will awaken them to reflection, until the iron hand of oppression compel them to it.

I shall only remark, that this power, given to the federal legislature, directly annihilates all the powers of the state legislatures. There cannot be a greater solecism in politics than to talk of power in a government, without the command of any revenue. It is as absurd as to talk of an animal without blood, or the subsistence of one without food. Now the general government having in their controul every possible source of revenue, and authority to pass any law they may deem necessary to draw them forth, or to facilitate their collection; no source of revenue is therefore left in the hands of any state. Should any state attempt to raise money by law, the general government may repeal or arrest it in the execution, for all their laws will be the supreme law of the land: If then any one can be weak enough to believe that a government can exist without having the authority to raise money to pay a door-keeper to their assembly, he may believe that the state government can exist, should this new constitution take place.

It is agreed by most of the advocates of this new system, that the government which is proper for the United States should be a confederated one; that the respective states ought to retain a portion of their sovereignty, and that they should preserve not only the forms of their legislatures, but also the power to conduct certain internal concerns. How far the powers to be retained by the states shall extend, is the question; we need not spend much time on this subject, as it respects this constitution, for a government without the power to raise money is one only in name. It is clear that the legislatures of the respective states must be altogether dependent on the will of the general legislature, for the means of supporting their government. The legislature of the United States will have a right to exhaust every source of revenue in every state, and to annul all laws of the states which may stand in the way of effecting it; unless therefore we can suppose the state governments can exist without money to support the officers who execute them, we must conclude they will exist no longer than the general legislatures choose they should. Indeed the idea of any government existing, in any respect, as an independent one, without any means of support in their own hands, is an absurdity. If therefore, this constitution has in view, what many of its framers and advocates say it has, to

secure and guarantee to the separate states the exercise of certain powers of government it certainly ought to have left in their hands some
sources of revenue. It should have marked the line in which the general
government should have raised money, and set bounds over which they
should not pass, leaving to the separate states other means to raise
supplies for the support of their governments, and to discharge their
respective debts. To this it is objected, that the general government
ought to have power competent to the purposes of the union; they are
to provide for the common defence, to pay the debts of the United
States, support foreign ministers, and the civil establishment of the union, and to do these they ought to have authority to raise money adequate to the purpose. On this I observe, that the state governments
have also contracted debts, they require money to support their civil
officers, and how this is to be done, if they give to the general government a power to raise money in every way in which it can possibly be
raised, with such a controul over the state legislatures as to prohibit
them, whenever the general legislature may think proper, from raising
any money. It is again objected that it is very difficult, if not impossible,
to draw the line of distinction between the powers of the general and
state governments on this subject. The first, it is said, must have the
power of raising the money necessary for the purposes of the union, if
they are limited to certain objects the revenue may fall short of a sufficiency for the public exigencies, they must therefore have discretionary power. The line may be easily and accurately drawn between the
powers of the two governments on this head. The distinction between
external and internal taxes, is not a novel one in this country, it is a
plain one, and easily understood. The first includes impost duties on
all imported goods; this species of taxes it is proper should be laid by
the general government; many reasons might be urged to shew that no
danger is to be apprehended from their exercise of it. They may be
collected in few places, and from few hands with certainty and expe-
dition. But few officers are necessary to be imployed in collecting them,
and there is no danger of oppression in laying them, because, if they
are laid higher than trade will bear, the merchants will cease importing,
or smuggle their goods. We have therefore sufficient security, arising
from the nature of the thing, against burdensome, and intolerable impositions from this kind of tax. But the case is far otherwise with regard
to direct taxes; these include poll taxes, land taxes, excises, duties on
written instruments, on every thing we eat, drink, or wear; they take
hold of every species of property, and come home to every man's house
and packet. These are often so oppressive, as to grind the face of the

poor, and render the lives of the common people a burden to them. The great and only security the people can have against oppression from this kind of taxes, must rest in their representatives. If they are sufficiently numerous to be well informed of the circumstances, and ability of those who send them, and have a proper regard for the people, they will be secure. The general legislature, as I have shewn in a former paper,[3] will not be thus qualified, and therefore, on this account, ought not to exercise the power of direct taxation. If the power of laying imposts will not be sufficient, some other specific mode of raising a revenue should have been assigned the general government; many may be suggested in which their power may be accurately defined and limited, and it would be much better to give them authority to lay and collect a duty on exports, not to exceed a certain rate per cent, than to have surrendered every kind of resource that the country has, to the complete abolition of the state governments, and which will introduce such an infinite number of laws and ordinances, fines and penalties, courts, and judges, collectors, and excisemen, that when a man can number them, he may enumerate the stars of Heaven.

I shall resume this subject in my next,[4] and by an induction of particulars shew, that this power, in its exercise, will subvert all state authority, and will work to the oppression of the people, and that there are no restrictions in the constitution that will soften its rigour, but rather the contrary.

1. On 27 November the *New York Journal* announced that "Brutus" V was received and that it would "be attended to as soon as possible." "Brutus" V was reprinted in the Boston *American Herald*, 31 December, and the Boston *Independent Chronicle*, 3 January 1788.

2. See the supremacy clause, Article VI, clause 2.

3. See "Brutus" III–IV, *New York Journal*, 15 and 29 November (both above).

4. See "Brutus" VI, *ibid.*, 27 December (below).

Cato VI
New York Journal, 13 December 1787

On 6 December the printer of the *New York Journal* announced that "Cato" VI was "received, and shall be attended to as soon as possible.—The AUTHOR of Cato will doubtless excuse the Editor for having neglected to acknowledge his sixth number, four days since, if he reflects upon the multiplicity of business at this office." "Cato" VI was reprinted in the *Daily Advertiser* on 15 December.

To the PEOPLE *of the State of* NEW-YORK.

The next objection that arises against this proffered constitution is, that the apportionment of representatives and direct taxes are unjust.—The words as expressed in this article are, "representatives and direct taxes shall be apportioned among the several states, which may be included in this union, according to their respective numbers, which shall be determined by adding to the whole number of free persons, including those bound to service for a term of years, and excluding Indians not taxed three fifths of all other persons." In order to elucidate this, it will be necessary to repeat the remark in my last number,[1] that the mode of legislation in the infancy of free communities was by the collective body, and this consisted of free persons, or those whose age admitted them to the rights of mankind and citizenship—whose sex made them capable of protecting the state, and whose birth may be denominated Free Born, and no traces can be found that even women, children, and slaves, or those who were not sui juris,[2] in the early days of legislation, meeting with the free members of the community to deliberate on public measures; hence is derived this maxim in free governments, that representation ought to bear a proportion to the number of free inhabitants in a community; this principle your own state constitution, and others, have observed in the establishment of a future census, in order to apportion the representatives, and to increase or diminish the representation to the ratio of the increase or diminution of electors.[3] But, what aid can the community derive from the assistance of women, infants, and slaves, in their deliberation, or in their defence? and what motive therefore could the convention have in departing from the just and rational principle of representation, which is the governing principle of this state and of all America.

The doctrine of taxation is a very important one, and nothing requires more wisdom and prudence than the regulation of that portion, which is taken from, and of that which is left to, the subject—and if you anticipate, what will be the enormous expence of this new government added also to your own, little will that portion be which will be left to you. I know there are politicians who believe, that you should be loaded with taxes, in order to make you industrious, and, perhaps, there were some of this opinion in the convention, but it is an erroneous principle—For, what can inspire you with industry, if the greatest measures of your labours are to be swallowed up in taxes? The advocates for this new system hold out an idea, that you will have but little to pay, for, that the revenues will be so managed as to be almost wholly drawn from the source of trade or duties on imports, but this is delusive—for this government to discharge all its incidental expences, besides paying the interests on the home and foreign debts, will require more money than its commerce can afford; and if you reflect one moment, you will find, that if heavy duties are laid on merchandize, as must be the case, if government intend to make this the prime medium to lighten the people of taxes, that the price of the commodities, useful as well as luxurious, must be increased; the consumers will be fewer; the merchants must import less; trade will languish, and this source of revenue in a great measure be dried up; but if you examine this a little further, you will find, that this revenue, managed in this way, will come out of you and be a very heavy and ruinous one, at least—The merchant no more than advances the money for you to the public, and will not, nor cannot pay any part of it himself, and if he pays more duties, he will sell his commodities at a price portionably raised—thus the laborer, mechanic, and farmer, must feel it in the purchase of their utensils and clothing—wages, &c. must rise with the price of things, or they must be ruined, and that must be the case with the farmer, whose produce will not increase, in the ratio, with labour, utensils, and clothing; for that he must sell at the usual price or lower, perhaps, caused by the decrease of trade; the consequence will be, that he must mortgage his farm, and then comes inevitable bankruptcy.

In what manner then will you be eased, if the expences of government are to be raised solely out of the commerce of this country; do you not readily apprehend the fallacy of this argument. But government will find, that to press so heavily on commerce will not do, and therefore must have recourse to other objects; these will be a capitation or poll-tax, window lights, &c. &c. and a long train of impositions which their ingenuity will suggest; but will you submit to be numbered like the slaves of an arbitrary despot; and what will be your reflections when the tax-master thunders at your door for the duty on that light which is the bounty of heaven. It will be the policy of the great landholders who will chiefly compose this senate, and perhaps a majority of this house of representatives, to keep their lands free from taxes; and this is confirmed by the failure of every attempt to lay a land-tax in this state; hence recourse must and will be had to the sources I mentioned before. The burdens on you will be insupportable—your complaints will be inefficacious—this will beget public disturbances, and I will venture to predict, without the spirit of prophecy, that you and the government, if it is adopted, will one day be at issue on this point. The force of government will be exerted, this will call for an increase of revenue, and will add fuel to the fire. The result will be, that either you will revolve to some other form, or that government will give peace to the country, by destroying the opposition. If government therefore can, notwithstanding every opposition, raise a revenue on such things as are odious and burdensome to you, they can do any thing.

But why should the number of individuals be the principle to apportion the taxes in each state, and to include in that number, women, children and slaves. The most natural and equitable principle of apportioning taxes, would be in a ratio to their property, and a reasonable impost in a ratio to their trade; but you are told to look for the reason of these things in accommodation; but this much admired principle, when striped of its mistery, will in this case appear to be no less than a basis for an odious poll-tax—the offspring of despotic governments, a thing so detestable, that the state of Maryland, in their bill of rights, declares, "that the levying taxes by the poll, is grievous and oppressive, and ought to be abolished."[4]—A poll-tax is at all times oppressive to the poor, and their greatest misfortune will consist in having more prolific wives than the rich.

In every civilized community, even in those of the most democratic kind, there are principles which lead to an aristocracy—these are superior talents, fortunes, and public employments. But in free governments, the influence of the two former is resisted by the equality of the laws, and the latter by the frequency of elections, and the chance that every one has in sharing in public business; but when this natural and artificial eminence is assisted by principles interwoven in this government—when the senate, so important a branch of the legislature, is so far removed from the people, as to have little or no connexion with them; when their duration in office is such as to have the resemblance to perpetuity, when they are connected with the executive, by the appointment of all officers, and also, to become a judiciary for the trial of officers of their own appointments: added to all this, when none but men of oppulence will hold a seat, what is there left to resist and repel this host of influence and power. Will the feeble efforts of the house of representatives, in whom your security ought to subsist, consisting of about seventy-three, be able to hold the balance against them, when, from the fewness of the number in this house, the senate will have in their power to poison even a majority of that body by douceurs of office for themselves or friends. From causes like this both Montesquieu and Hume have predicted the decline of the British government into that of an absolute one;[5] but the liberties of this country, it is probable if this system is adopted, will be strangled in their birth; for whenever the executive and senate can destroy the independence of the majority in the house of representatives then where is your security?—They are so intimately connected, that their interests will be one and the same; and will the slow increase of numbers be able to afford a repelling principle? but you are told to adopt this government first, and you will always be able to alter it afterwards; this would be first submitting to be slaves and then taking care of your liberty; and when your chains are on, then to act like freemen.

Complete acts of legislation, which are to become the supreme law of the land, ought to be the united act of all the branches of government; but there is one of the most important duties may be managed by the senate and executive alone, and to have all the force of the law paramount without the aid or interference of the house of representatives; that is the power of making treaties. This power is a very important one, and may be exercised in various ways, so as to affect your person and property, and even the domain of the nation. By treaties you may defalcate part of the empire; engagements may be made to raise an army, and you may be transported to Europe, to fight the wars of ambitious princes; money may be contracted for, and you must pay it; and a thousand other obligations may be entered into; all which will become the supreme law of the land, and you are bound by it. If treaties are erroneously or wickedly made who is there to punish—the executive can always cover himself with the plea, that he was advised by the senate, and the senate being a collective body are not easily made accountable for mal-administration. On this account we are in a worse situation than Great-Britain, where they have secured by a ridiculous fiction, the King from accountability, by declaring; that he can do no wrong; by which means the nation can have redress against his minister; but with us infalibility pervades every part of the system, and neither the executive nor his council, who are a collective body, and his advisers, can be brought to punishment for mal-administration.

1. See "Cato" V, *New York Journal*, 22 November (above).

2. "Sui juris" is a Latin legal term for "of his own right; possessing full social and civil rights; not under any legal disability, or the power of another, or guardianship."

3. The New York constitution of 1777 provided that a census of the electors and inhabitants be taken seven years after the war ended and that the representation be reapportioned in the Assembly among the counties and in the Senate among the districts on the basis of the number of electors. A census of the electors was then to be taken every seven years thereafter and the Assembly and Senate were to be reapportioned accordingly (Thorpe, V, 2629–30). The constitutions of New Hampshire, Massachusetts, Pennsylvania, South Carolina, and Georgia also provided for legislative reapportionment based on population.

4. Thorpe, III, 1687.

5. See Montesquieu, *Spirit of Laws*, I, Book XI, chap. VI, 237. David Hume discusses the British monarchy in an essay entitled "Whether the British Government Inclines More to Absolute Monarchy, or to a Republic," in *Essays: Moral, Political, and Literary*, ed., Eugene F. Miller (rev. ed., Indianapolis, 1987), 47–53. Hume's essay first appeared in 1741.

New York Daily Advertiser, 14 December 1787

A distant correspondent observes, that the author of the Federalist, No. 6, need not have gone even so far as Massachusetts for a *reference tending to illustrate* the principle he had been asserting, viz. that the ENMITY, *interest, hopes and fears of leading individuals, in the communities of which they are members, tend to disturb the peace and tranquility of a nation.*[1]

If we had had no *Shays* among ourselves, that is, *desperate debtors,* &c. &c. it is not to be supposed that our code of laws since the revolution would have been so *disgraceful,* as they are said to be in a former No. of the Federalist[2]—and as the laws of a country, especially of Republics, are supposed to be characteristic of the people, what an insult is this on the community at large? And every abuse of that kind must *tend* to disturb the peace and tranquility of a country as much as one or two riots, and indeed are most frequently the occasion of such riots.—The remedying this evil (and no small one it is) will be among the happy effects expected from the adoption of the proposed Constitution.

1. While discussing "the causes of hostility among nations," *The Federalist* 6 stated that some of these causes take their "origin intirely in private passions; in the attachments, enmities, interests, hopes and fears of leading individuals in the communities of which they are members. Men of this class, whether the favourites of a king or of a people, have in too many instances abused the confidence they possessed; and assuming the pretext of some public motive, have not scrupled to sacrifice the national tranquility to personal advantage, or personal gratification." *The Federalist* 6 maintained that Daniel Shays would not have plunged Massachusetts into civil war had he not been "a *desperate debtor*" (*Independent Journal,* 14 November, CC:257).

2. See *The Federalist* 7, *Independent Journal,* 17 November (CC:269, p. 135).

Democritus
New York Journal, 14 December 1787[1]

To the EXAMINER, in [the] REGISTER of 11th inst.

I really pity you, sir, I pity you when I consider the herculean task which you have undertaken; a task infinitely above your abilities; a task which all the aristocratics in America cannot execute: I allude to your promise of refuting the republican writers; it shews great vanity, but little sense.

You say "the antifederalists have made a great deal of bustle and noise against the new constitution," that republicans have condemned it, I grant; that they have condemned it without reason, has not been proved; and that they will continue to point out its defects, and oppose its adoption, aristocratics will experience to their great mortification. The able writers, on the side of liberty, have opened the eyes of the deluded votaries of tyranny, have convinced every reflecting man, that the proposed government will blast the rights of mankind, will annihilate those inestimable liberties, for which we have suffered, for which we have bled; and for which, many of our brave countrymen, have sacrificed their lives.

You proceed in that style of candor, which so eminently distinguishes your party, to assert, that the republicans are convinced that the government, which they oppose, is the best that ever was framed; this is as much as saying, because you think like a blockhead, every other person must be of your opinion.

While, sir, I disapprove of your sentiments, I admire the elegance of your language, and the acrimony of your wit; *hodge podge*, is a polite, a happy expression; how fortunate are some people in possessing brilliant talents, and great knowledge? hodge-podge is alone sufficient to immortalize your name; I suppose it is a word of your own coining; O the force of genius! hodge-podge!

What a severe stroke you gave the fellow, who attempted to prove that light was darkness; it is so good that it cannot be too often repeated; here I set it down, as one of the most extraordinary effusions of wit, with which the world ever was gratified; "I replied, sir, you do not possess a single grain of understanding, inasmuch as all that region is closed upon you which is above the sphere of rationality, and that only is open to you which is below the rational sphere." Mr. Examiner, this was too sarcastic; no wonder the poor man "turned from you in a furious passion." it might have metamorphased him into a statue.

You are, sir, unmercifully severe upon these republican writers; how angry must they have been when they read that bitter simile, wherein you compared them to owls: I, however, cannot perceive any similarity between a writer and an owl, unless, indeed, the former, like yourself, be destitute of every particle of good sense, and consequently resemble the latter in irrationality.

I cannot take my leave of you, sir, without giving you credit for the only candid observation in your work. You deny the partiality, attributed to the editor of this paper, by persons who endeavour to palliate their own, in fixing a similar imputation upon him. I will not (like the boyish Cæsar) promise to follow you,[2] least your future productions (as is very probable from a consideration of the present one) should be so excessively foolish and weak, that it would be highly disgraceful to honor them with notice; indeed I should not have noticed you at all, if I had not accidentally felt an inclination to be merry at the expence of your absurdities.

1. "Democritus" attacks "Examiner" I, *New York Journal*, 11 December (above). He also criticized him in the *New York Journal* on 21 and 28 December (both below). These last two essays also implied strongly that "Examiner" was Charles McKnight. For a defense of "Examiner," see "Observer," *New York Journal*, 1 January 1788 (below).

2. Probably a reference to the last paragraph of "Caesar" I, *Daily Advertiser*, 1 October (above), in which "Caesar" ended his criticism of "Cato" I, *New York Journal*, 27 September (above), with this statement: "Cato, it appears, intends to adventure on perilous ground; it will therefore become him to be cautious on what terms he takes the field. 'He advises us to attach ourselves to measures, and not to men.' In this instance he advises well; and I heartily recommend to *himself*, not to forget the force of that important admonition: for Cato, in his future *marches*, will very probably be *followed* by CÆSAR." The

phrase "the boyish Cæsar" is possibly a reference to Alexander Hamilton, the alleged author of the "Caesar" essays.

Examiner II
New York Journal, 14 December 1787

MR. GREENLEAF, When a man is predetermined in any cause, he will seldom listen to arguments against his system, but when they are produced and read to him, his organs of hearing are not more deeply impressed, than by the whispers of the wind, or the sound of a drum.

I am therefore convinced, that I shall never be able to make a convert of such a character as Cato, who declared against the new constitution before ever he saw it.[1] It is evident however, that he has promised much more than he has abilities to perform. I expected, from what he observed in his second number,[2] that his succeeding ones would contain something more than bare assertions of his own. I expected to have seen numberless quotations from the most sensible and approved political writers in favor of what he advanced, this being the method he promised to pursue; instead of which he has totally neglected Grotius, Puffendorf, Sydney, Locke, Hume, and others equally celebrated, confining himself to one or two thread-bare quotations from Baron Montesquieu which have appeared before in several recent publications.

Now Sir, I think it is ten to one that Cato has never read the works of either of those great men I have mentioned, and it is more than probable he has never seen any more of Montesquieu's works, than a few scraps, picked out of some late mi[s]cellaneous pieces. If he knows any thing of the Baron, he has certainly used him very scurvilly by mutilating and tearing in pieces his spirit of laws, in the manner he has done; especially as he is cautioned by the Baron himself "not to judge of the labor of twenty years by a few hours reading; that his design can only be completely found in the book entire, and not in particular phrases."[3]

Cato has cast a net, which I believe will catch very few fish. He affects the appearance of a true son of liberty, but he is an hypocrite, and may be compared to a carved image with a double head one within the other; the inner head cohering with the trunk or body, and the outer being moveable about the inner, and painted in front the colour of an human face, not unlike the wooden heads exposed to view in a barber's shop.

1. The reference is to Governor George Clinton, the alleged author of the "Cato" essays who was accused by Alexander Hamilton of attacking the work of the Constitutional Convention while it was still in session. See "Alexander Hamilton Attacks Governor George Clinton," 21 July–30 October (above).
2. "Cato" II, *New York Journal,* 11 October (above).

3. Montesquieu made this statement in the second paragraph of the preface to his *Spirit of Laws.*

Publius: The Federalist 22 (Alexander Hamilton)
New York Packet, 14 December 1787

Confederation Congress lacks powers to regulate commerce and enforce treaties. Equal representation of states in Congress criticized. For text, see CC:347. For reprintings, see Appendix IV, below.

Antoine de La Forest to Comte de Montmorin
New York, 15 December 1787 (excerpts)[1]

. . . It is not yet known what the Special assemblies of Rhode island, Newyork, North Carolina, Maryland and virginia will decide. . . .

As for the State of Newyork, My Lord, it has no interest which is able to thwart the adoption of the new Government. But the preponderance of its civil officers until now have prevailed over the *federalist* party and the former have personal motives for preserving the complete and full direction of the affairs of the state for as long as possible. The application of money arising from [state] import duties to the funding of public securities on which they Speculate is of major importance for their fortunes. . . .

1. RC (Tr), Affaires Étrangères, Correspondance Consulaires, BI 909, New York, ff. 294–97, Archives Nationales, Paris, France. Printed: CC:349. Antoine René Charles Mathurin de la Forest (b. 1756) was French vice consul for the United States stationed in New York City.

A Countryman IV (Hugh Hughes)
New York Journal, 15 December 1787[1]

⟨LETTERS from a Gentleman in DUTCHESS-COUNTY,
to his Friend in NEW-YORK.
(Continued from this Register of the 3d. inst.)[2]
December 8th 1787.
DEAR SIR, When I closed my third letter, I wished to be more explicit on some things which I had mentioned in that, as well as to make several observations on the new constitution, as it is called; but the conveyance waited, and time would not admit of saying any further.

I will now resume the affair of calling a convention.⟩ When I said, that I could not see the propriety, or necessity, of the legislatures calling a convention, it was merely on the principle of calling one in consequence of the resolve or recommendation of the late convention, at Philadelphia;[3] lest the people should infer, that the legislature, by recommending a state convention, considered the proceedings and re-

solve of the Philadelphia convention in some measure obligatory on
them so to do. When, as the latter rejected the authority of those by
whom they were appointed (at least, that appears to me to have been
the case with the delegate of this state, as well as with the delegates of
several other states) and renounced all allegiance to the present United
States, I cannot admit to be binding on the legislature, in any manner
whatever, even had the late convention really offered a good constitution. But, as it is, I cannot help being of opinion, that the resolve or
recommendation is an aggravation, if possible, of the crime and insult.—Should the legislature, when they meet, think that the calling of
a convention will be the best means of restoring public tranquility, I
shall acquiesce. But then, I wish them not to do it from a sense of any
obligation which they are under to the act of their delegate,[4] or that
of the delegates of any other state, in the late convention; as the exorbitant act of that body, has, in my opinion, cancelled all obligation,
on the part of this state, for considering their proceedings as binding.
I should therefore be glad to see them very explicit on such a most
extraordinary emergency; for surely such it must appear to all unprejudiced minds. It is to be hoped, that they will ascribe the effects to their
true causes, which were, an evident want of duty, and an inordinate
desire for unlimited power, in some of the members who composed
the convention; at the same time, pointing out to the people, in the
plainest manner, the snare which is laid for them, and, that the adopting of it, will be their *last sovereign act,* unless it should be a violent
resumption, by arms.

I imagine, that the faction were rather apprehensive of a reprimand,
when they referred their plot to conventions of the people, "for their
assent and ratification," in preference to the legislatures, by whom they
had been appointed, and from whom they derived all the authority
which they had to assemble for a very different purpose. Though, in
their reference of it to conventions of the people; they have not been
much more polite to those bodies, than they have to the legislatures,
and that you must have observed; as it is not submitted to the former
for their consideration, improvement, or rejection; but expressly "for
their assent and ratification;" which seems to exclude all manner of
choice! Was ever self-sufficiency more evident in man?

The legislatures are advised to call conventions of the people for
*registering the revolt of their citizens and deputies, as the supreme law of the
land!*—Could any thing be more humiliating to sovereign and independent states?—Would this junto have dared to offer such an indig-
nity to any sovereign prince in Europe, had they been appointed by
one?—I know that your answer must be in the negative. Why then thus

presumptuously attempt to prostrate thirteen sovereignties?—But the answer is obvious, and therefore not requisite at this time.

If the legislature should not be pointedly clear on such an open attempt to dissolve the present confederacy, may we not, in a little time, expect a Shays, or, perhaps, a much more formidable insurgent in this state?

Have you considered the tendency of the 2d paragraph of the 6th article of the NEW EDICT?—It does not appear to me, that either the Centinel, Federal Farmer, or any other writer that I have seen, has sufficiently attended to that clause, and all the consequences which it may involve. I am sensible, that the Centinel calls it a "sweeping clause;"[5] but, I imagine, not on account of what I am going to observe, or he would have been more explicit. These are the words:—"This constitution, and the laws of the United States which shall be made in pursuance thereof; and all treaties made, or which shall be made, under the authority of the United States, shall be the *supreme* law of the land, &c." You well know that I am not fond of disputing about words, unless they have an evident tendency to deceive or lead to error, in which case, I think, they ought to be thoroughly canvassed, and well understood, especially in an affair of such vast importance as the present. The word "supreme" is, I believe, generally received, in law and divinity, as an adjective of the superlative degree, and implies the highest in dignity or authority, &c. Now, if we analyze this clause, we shall see how it will appear.

The constitution is to be the *high-authority*—the laws made in pursuance of the constitution are to be the *highest authority*, and *all treaties made, or to be made* are to be the *highest authority*; and yet there is to be *but one highest authority!* However easy it may be for the contrivers of this, to reconcile it to their own views, I confess to you, that it appears to me something like creed-making.

If all the laws and treaties which may be made, in pursuance of this constitution (provided it be adopted) are to be of *as high authority*, as the constitution, I should be glad to know what security we can have for any one right, however sacred or essential, when there is no explicit proviso, that the laws and treaties which may be made, shall not be repugnant to the constitution?

It is true, that they are to be made in *pursuance* of the constitution; but, *pursuance* is a vague term, and, I presume, generally implies little more than "in consequence, &c."—I have always understood, that the laws derived all their just authority from the constitution, or social compact, as it is sometimes called; and that the latter receives its whole authority, in free governments, from the common consent of the people, and recognizes or acknowledges all their essential rights and liberties, as well as ascertains the reciprocal duties or relations between the governed and their governors, or, perhaps, more properly, their principal public servants, who undertake to manage or conduct the affairs of the community agreeable to certain fixed stipulations, which are mentioned in the original compact or constitution, and not otherwise, but at the risk of being disobeyed, or opposed, as the case may require.

If these ideas of a free government are just, ought there not to have been a positive distinction between the authority of the constitution and that of the laws, treaties, &c. The constitution, when once government is organized, will be mostly passive, but the laws, treaties, &c. of Congress, will be active and voluminous; whence it is easy to foresee what will become of the passive supremacy of it, when it happens to come in competition with two active supremacies, which are coeval and coequal with it, besides several others which will be added, you may rely: For there must be the supreme Lex Parliamentaria of a meagre, biennial representation of the people, and another of an encroaching lordly sexennial Senate, with the supreme prerogatives of a poor, greedy, quadrennial monarch, who must ever be ready to concur in any measures for fleecing the people, provided he is but allowed to participate of the spoil. And, to crown the whole, there must, of course, be a most supreme standing army *for us to feed, clothe and pay, if you will pardon the redundancy of the phrase.*

Does it not appear to you, as if the framers of this clause had profited by the embarrassments which the British ministry frequently met with in their attempts to render acts of parliament, paramount to magna charta, or the great charter of the peoples essential rights, which is acknowleged, by the 43d. of Edward the 3d. not to be in the power of parliament to alter, change, or destroy; as all statutes made or to be made, against, or contrary to that constitution, or bill of rights, are, immediately, to be considered as null and void?[6] *I have many more observations to make on this political phenomenon, as well as its origination; but domestic affairs require my attention, and I must bid you adieu until another opportunity.*

       I am, dear sir, Very respectfully, Your's &c. A COUNTRYMAN.
To a Citizen.

1. This essay is part of the "Countryman" series written by Hugh Hughes. On 28 February 1788 the Philadelphia *Independent Gazetteer* reprinted this essay, except for the text in angle brackets at the beginning. The *Gazetteer's* version was reprinted in the *New York Morning Post,* 5 March; and the Baltimore *Maryland Gazette,* 11 March. On 1 May the *Gazetteer* reprinted the complete essay. A manuscript draft of "A Countryman" IV is in the Hugh Hughes Papers at the Library of Congress. For a facsimile of Hughes's manuscript, see Mfm:N.Y. The draft is filled with many unreadable cross-outs, as well as numerous insertions.

2. "A Countryman" III, *New York Journal,* 3 December (above).

3. For the 17 September 1787 resolution of the Constitutional Convention, see Appendix III (below).

4. Alexander Hamilton was the only New York delegate to sign the Constitution.

5. See "Centinel" II, Philadelphia *Freeman's Journal*, 24 October (CC:190, p. 460). After quoting the supremacy clause, "Centinel" stated "Does not the sweeping clause subject every thing to the controul of Congress?"

6. The reference is to 42 Edward III, chapter 1 (1369), which commands that "the Great Charter and the Charter of the Forest be holden and kept in all points, and if any statute be made to the contrary that shall be holden for none."

New York Journal, 17 December 1787

A correspondent observes, that he cannot refrain from exclaiming, with ejaculatory gratitude, notwithstanding the real and fabulous evils America groans under, that we have a goodly heritage, that our lands teem with fatness, that the tillars of our soil do not labour in vain, neither are we cursed with locusts, blasts, or mildews; that the *season* is propitious to the industrious poor, who, however paradoxical it may seem, are the riches of the land, and at whose ease, and domestic enjoyment, the republican fathers will ever rejoice.—This is the 17th day of December, and none of the distressing severities of winter have yet been felt; it is supposed, upon calculation, that not more than one third of the quantity of wood has been expended, as was the last fall to this date. We have had no cold until last week, and that not severe; no snow has yet appeared.

Not a news-paper arrived from Philadelphia by Saturday's southern mail; a circumstance which it is wished our brother Types at the southward would attend to, as the printers in this city depend much upon the SATURDAY MAILS.[1]

Notwithstanding no papers are come to hand of a later date than Wednesday last from Philadelphia, we are assured, from good authority, "THAT THE STATE CONVENTION OF PENNSYLVANIA ADOPTED THE NEW CONSTITUTION ON THURSDAY LAST." Yeas FORTY-SIX, noes TWENTY-THREE; being the 13th instant, December, 1787.[2]

1. This paragraph was reprinted in the Philadelphia *Independent Gazetteer*, 26 December.

2. The Pennsylvania Convention voted to ratify the Constitution on Wednesday, 12 December. The Form of Ratification was adopted on Thursday, 13 December (RCS:Pa., 590–92, 603).

Publius: The Federalist 23 (Alexander Hamilton)
New York Packet, 18 December 1787

Confederation Congress lacks authority to raise military forces. For text, see CC:352. For reprintings, see Appendix IV, below.

Lansingburgh Northern Centinel, 18 December 1787

THE SYREN's SONGS,

As sung by the celebrated modern CATO,
and set to music by his X—L—N—C.
To the tune of the Hypocrite: *a new tune very much in vogue.*

SONG SECOND.[1]

View, O! my friends, the laws the rights, the plan
Of gen'rous pow'r, prepar'd for ev'ry man;
By our grandfathers, in the days of yore,
The price of toil, of wounds, and clotted gore;
Ere fancy form'd us, ev'n in embrio,
They gain'd our freedom from the British foe:
Then be't not said, that in your hands decay'd
What to your offspring should have been convey'd.

In the last sound that stun'd your aking ears,
I bawl'd to fill each doubtful soul with fears;
To make you loiter on the brink of fate,
And while a sinking leisurely debate:
To hint how yon new ship, with as much ease,
Can steer on rocks, as sail upon the seas;
To warn you all that no one take a part,
Or *pro* or *con*, till I beguile his heart;
I promis'd to convince, in future howls,
The screaming night-birds and the greater owls.
Here had I stay'd, and rested on my mud,
An introduction fraudulent but good;
Had CÆSAR[2] slept—who treats you all—or me,
With ev'ry insult, short of calumny;
All I would say, unluckily he prates,
And what I fain would hide, anticipates.
And since, my friends, you cannot hear nor see,
Nor think aright without the help of me:
In me 'tis criminal to hesitate
A moment to appear your advocate;
You've none so fitting for a chief as I,
Therefore, unask'd, your combat mean to try;
For if I keep you in your present line,
Altho' you drown, your property is mine:
I mind not Caesar (tho' I grope in dust)

Who knows my actions always gave distrust;
And tho' he threats—he jeers—he ridicules,
Yet I'll with blanney try to make ye fools:
I'm slow of foot, but let me mount your backs,
I'd fight his shadow and destroy his tracks;
I'd chase him through the fields from side to side
And for my service ever after ride:—
Yon group of builders sent to overhall,
Have built a new ship, rudder, keel and all,
With the same cost, and of a better mould,
But I am still for patching up the old.
To build a new was more than they'd a right,
Therefore I'd even burn her in their sight:
Then think my friends deliberate and free,
And censure Caesar while you honor me;
None shall henceforth make me my plan give o'er
While I've a cave along the dreary shore:
I mean to view, and view her o'er agen,
And find some fault about her if I can:
Then be prepar'd ye senseless drowning throng,
And you shall hear a lamentable song.

1. For "song first" of "The Syren's Songs," see Lansingburgh *Northern Centinel,* 11 December (above). Like the first song, the song printed here continues the attack on Governor George Clinton, the alleged author of the "Cato" essays. For an allusion to these satirical verses, see *Northern Centinel,* 1 January 1788, at note 3 (below).

2. Probably a reference to Alexander Hamilton, the alleged author of the "Caesar" essays. Hamilton had attacked Clinton as early as July 1787 for criticizing the then sitting Constitutional Convention. See "Alexander Hamilton Attacks Governor George Clinton," 21 July–30 October (above).

A Country Federalist
Poughkeepsie Country Journal, 19 December 1787 (supplement)

"A Country Federalist" was written by lawyer James Kent of Poughkeepsie. The praise of *The Federalist* essays of "Publius" voiced in the last paragraph echoes that found in Kent's 8 and 21 December letters to Nathaniel Lawrence (above and below). In this paragraph and in his memoirs Kent revealed that he sent some of *The Federalist* essays to the editor of the *Country Journal* for republication. (See the headnote to *The Federalist* 1, *Independent Journal,* 27 October, above.)

To all Rational and Independent Citizens.

While the most incessant attempts are made by parties in this and the other states to defeat the progress of the new constitution;—while every exertion and ingenuity are put in practice to terrify the imagi-

nations of the people, and propagate jealousy and delusion; I shall
presume with the honest freedom resulting from the persuasion of a
good cause to deliver my independent sentiments in favor of a system
which so essentially involves in its fate the happiness or the misery of
America. Every man it is admitted must and will think on all public
matters for himself, and after having formed his opinion from the most
ardent reflection and the most deliberate and unprejudiced research
it is his duty to declare that opinion and the reasons of it, candidly and
firmly.

The question submitted to the public, most assuredly deserves to
command and animate their whole attention. It is one of those great
and comprehensive ones which rarely in centuries falls under political
contemplation. In my apprehension of it when searched to the bottom,
and traced to its consequences it amounts substantially to this—shall
we and shall the fate of future generations be submitted to a government which has been deliberately planned and recommended by our
best and wisest men, chosen specially for the purpose, or shall we as
all other nations have been obliged to do, leave those matters to be
dictated by the sword? The alternative is awfully serious. It touches
every consideration in life, and awakens most deeply the active and
ardent sensations of the human breast.

Without meaning to dwell on circumstances which are a mere retort,
I cannot, however, but observe, that the adversaries of the new government have availed themselves of some adventitious advantages in their
addresses to the temper of the people. I allude not to their artfully
diverting the attention from the leading principles of the institution,
as I shall fully and fairly demonstrate; but they endeavour to poison
the whole plan by insinuations against the integrity of its authors. From
the circumstance that the Convention conducted their deliberations in
private, for the purpose of a more free and liberal discussion, they
assert that it originated in the absolute conspiracy of a set of *false detestable* patriots (for these are their epithets) to erect a despotic government over this country; and by sacrificing their pens with apparent
devotion to the genius of liberty, they appeal with a winning address to
the most powerful passions of the heart. But I trust there is too much
good sense in this country to be deceived, and too much public spirit
not to resent such gross artifices—such malevolent slander. I know it
is no solid argument in itself, and yet for my part, I cannot but consider
it as a circumstance highly favorable to the character of a free people,
and to the momentous importance of the object, that the Convention
was composed of some of the brightest, the most vigorous, and the
most faithful patriots of our country. Not only of those whose rich

understandings were known to the accurate observer, but of some whom I shall ever regard with reverence as the Fathers of the revolution—whose republican faith and elevated minds had been tried and purified in the hour of peril and distress, and whose memories will live forever in the gratitude of a more generous posterity.

I will not undertake to say, that the federal constitution is the most perfect system of continental government which could be devised. I know it is not since it was acknowledged to result from a spirit of mutual concession.[1] Nor will I descend by refinement to unfold imperfections. I know that frailty is the natural and inevitable attendant on every human institution. If we seek to satisfy every wish of our minds, we must dispense with every gift of humanity. But what is to the purpose, I believe the new constitution to be the best practicable system which the people of America can unite in—that it is perfectly safe and honorable, and necessary for them to adopt; and that it is reared in the true spirit and founded on the true principles of liberty.

By the first article it says, that all legislative power granted by the constitution shall be vested in a congress consisting of a Senate and House of Representatives—that the house of Representatives shall be composed of members chosen every second year, by the people of the several states; and the electors in each state shall have the qualifications requisite for electors, of the most numerous branch of the state legislature—That the number of representatives shall be appointed among the several states according to their numbers, not exceeding one for every 30,000; and in the mean time, that New-York shall have six &c.— That the senate shall be composed of two senators from each state, chosen by the legislature thereof for six years—that they shall be divided as equally as may be into three classes, so that one third may be chosen every second year &c.

These clauses which I have selected, form the only requisite magna charta for the citizens of America.

The right of the people to a free and frequent election of the legislative power will be found I trust after all other theories and refinements are exploded, to be the great and strong ground of freedom in a republican government. Where this is the case, and the people exercise the right with judgment and firmness, government will always be in perfect subordination to their interests and happiness. But where this right is not the leading principle or is not properly and duly exercised, government will certainly be abused, notwithstanding there may be a volume of written limitations to its authority, or however numerous or just the declaration of rights may be which is prefixed to the constitution.

In the first place we may be certain that when people have a free vote they will elect such men to govern as think, feel and act as they do, or in other words men who can completely represent, and therefore are willing to supply the wants and wishes of the community. We may be equally certain that the administration of such rulers will be such as is most likely to please their constituents by promoting their interests and maintaining their security. There is a possibility indeed that rulers when seated in the government by the hands of the people, may turn tyrants and abuse their trust. This cannot absolutely be provided against in any constitution, but we may safely and indeed must necessarily infer the contrary practice from every strong principle which governs human nature. If rulers will not endeavour to do what is right from the feeble sentiment of gratitude to their benefactors, they will from the interested or ambitious wish to prolong their elevation. Where this principle fails them they are restrained by a dread of the contempt, or the resentment, and possibly the violence of the public: They are further restrained by the striking consideration that they must shortly descend into their former private life, and feel themselves the pressure of that rod which they had established for others. We might presume also another inducement, even from the natural dictates of benevolence and the love of order and of justice, which are most likely to be found in men best qualified for the business of government, I mean in those whose minds are enlightened by the habits of education and harmonized by the precepts of philosophy. We can with difficulty suppose a government hardy enough to proceed in opposition to such a strong chain of attraction. If however it should still be the case, even then the evils which it may create can be of no long duration, as the people will have it in their power by a new election to effect a total change in the administration, and that too within the very short limits prescribed by the constitution.

If we examine history and experience, they will confirm the justness and solidity of this reasoning.

WE have no bill of rights annexed to the constitution of this state, nor any provision made in favor of the liberty of the press, or against the establishment of armies, the unlimited powers of taxation, and many other formidable prerogatives of government. Experience however teaches us that we run no hazard in conferring "supreme legislative power" to our senate and assembly as long as the same constitution provides that those bodies shall be elected by the people, and responsible to them for their administration.

In Connecticut, one of the freest states possibly recorded in history, there is no original compact at all between the government and the people defining the rights of the one, or circumscribing the jurisdiction of the other. Their government originated in a charter from King

Charles 2d. incorporating all the freemen into one body politic under
the name of the *Governor and Company,* &c. and giving them the rights
incident to all other corporate bodies, and directing a deputation from
the whole society, of not more than two from each town, to meet twice
every year and make "*wholesome*" byelaws, not contrary to the laws of
England, for the establishment of courts of justice, settling the forms
of government and defining the powers of officers, or in other words,
to exercise full powers of legislation.[2] The first thing their general assembly did after it had met with this plenitude of power, was to pass
an act for securing certain privileges of the people, and declaring that
none of those privileges which were enumerated in the act should be
taken away without a law of their general court, and where there was
no such law *without express authority from the word of God.*[3] It is needless
to make any comment on the supremacy of their general court. The
same power that creates can at any time dissipate a right, but this power
never has been nor never will be exercised contrary to the wishes of
the people, because it was provided by their charter, that the assembly
was to be a deputation sent twice a year by the majority of the freemen.

In England it is their house of commons the representative body of
the nation, and not their magna charta [or?] their bill of rights, which
is the palladium of liberty, the tutelary goddess [who?] protects the
state. "Many securities to liberty (says a celebrated writer and by far the
boldest and most splended patriot of his age[(a)]) are provided in the
british constitution, but the integrity which depends on the freedom
and the independency of parliament is the keystone that keeps the
whole together. If that be shaken the constitution totters. If it be quite
removed the constitution falls into ruin."[4] These observations appear
to have been founded on an accurate and philosophical attention to
facts. Notwithstanding considerable improvements had been made by
the dim light of science and of commerce in the inaccurate genius of
the old English constitution, yet the people even under Henry the 8th
were insensible to the importance of their voice in parliament, and the
members for the most part esteemed their attendance as an useless and
troublesome ceremony of state. The whole influence and terror of the
crown facilitated by the amazing insensibility of the people, could procure a House of Commons entirely devoted to its will. This appears to
have been the fact, and the House was composed of a most abject set
of slaves, who by a single act the most extraordinary that ever was recorded, conferred on the King's proclamations the force of law.[5] Here
was at once a formal and total surrender by the representatives of the
people of all the boasted rights of Englishmen—the securities of
magna-charta and the fabric of the constitution into the hands of the
crown.

Even in a much later period when political rights were more accurately defined, and the powers of government had been deeply investigated and thoroughly understood, we find parliament sporting with the great duties of their trust. At the accession of George the 1st. a statute was passed in the hurry of a faction which infected the House of Commons, and spread its inauspicious influence throughout the nation, declaring that the same house which was chosen for three, should sit for seven years.[6] This was the act for changing triennial into septennial elections, [and?] struck at the very foundation of their constitution. So feeble and idle indeed were the checks introduced into government by two such important and recent æras as the revolution and the accession when set in opposition to the inconsiderate heat and violence of a triumphant party.

I believe no man of the virtuous minority in Rhode-Island believes that constitutional declarations can check the legislative power. The trial by jury was ever considered as a fundamental right in that state. But the better to enforce their depreciated currency, the trial by jury is denied to the subject. Their judges pronounce that law unconstitutional and refuse to enforce it. Those judges are dismissed and others placed in their stead. We may fairly infer that the majority of the people in that state are corrupted, for their rulers must have been immediately changed had they not acted in compliance with the wishes of their constituents.

In short the uniform experience of history demonstrates that government founded on elective principles or on the broad basis of the people, never will violate the laws of justice and good order, unless the people are so stupid as to neglect their rights, or so corrupt as to countenance the conduct of a wicked administration. When this is the case experience further demonstrates that none of the checks provided in the national compact are of any avail. When the spirit of liberty and justice has forsaken the great body of the people, then indeed no form of government in the universe can preserve that people free. The constitution becomes according to a well known allusion like a cumbersome Gothic Castle, venerable perhaps for its ramparts and walls, but neither susceptible of conveniency or defence.

The right of election then residing in the great body of the people, and exercised with spirit and discernment forms the simplest but most efficacious limitation to the excesses of the sovereign power. That right and the distribution of the powers of legislation into two branches, in order to form a check upon the impetuous sensations of either of them singly, are in my opinion the true secrets, the great desiderata in republican politics. By these we can always assemble the wisdom of the state, and make that wisdom subservient to public security abroad and to private happiness at home. When I find such a source and such a distribution of the legislative power in any political fabric, I pronounce the main pillars of that fabric to be good, and to be laid on the solid and durable foundations of freedom. I grow pretty indifferent as to the ornaments or ascent of the superstructure because I know they can at any time be modified to the public good. I can resign my personal rights and all that is dear to me as an individual, with pleasure and confidence into the hands of such a political system.

And now my fellow citizens, permit me to ask you, have any of the publications you have read against the federal constitution invited your attention to this principal part? They have not—they have only dwelt on those branches which are immaterial to the great question, and which were they as imperfectly organized as they pretend them to be, might still be confided, as we and Connecticut have done in our state governments, to the future wisdom of the representative body. Have they painted, I mean not in the glow of eloquence, but with the colours of sincerity, the importance of a federal union to our justice, our honor, our freedom and our happiness; or have they shewn from reasoning and history the great difficulty of ever preserving a federal union between independent communities? Have they awakened your fears and called your exertions to that side of the question, and taught you the imminent hazard the people of this continent are now in through jealousy and opposition of having their national union rescinded forever? Have they reminded you of the beginning of the late war, when the hearts of all true patriots beat [in] unison with each other to the sentiment *"Unite or die."*—When the people of this country made a common cause of the injuries of their brethren in Massachusetts, and associated in one voluntary league of affection[7] to break loose their oppressive ties with the eastern continent, and to erect a free and independent empire over this fairest portion of the globe? Finally, have they reminded you of the momentary triumphs and cruel devastations of a people shaken with civil dissention? No my fellow citizens, they have done just the reverse—they have depreciated the blessings of the union to the utmost of their abilities—they have endeavoured to shew, that this continent is so extensive, that no federal government can be organized on principles favorable to liberty. I believe such doctrines as they advance to be the most dangerous heresy to the citizens of these United States.

I confess with them that the patronage of genuine liberty is worthy of the noblest minds, and ought to be the sole [end?] and spirit of every political institution. But that attractive goddess surely dwells not in the tempest of national distress, nor is she alluring us with Syren song from the course of order and obedience. Where there is no law, says Mr. Locke, there can be no liberty.[8] This was the case in a state of nature, and this led men to society and to the erection of civil government in order to purchase the blessings of freedom and security by a rational submision to the laws of the whole. The American states are now nearly in the same situation as thirteen individuals would be in a state of nature. They are each of them in their public capacity as so many moral persons capable of doing good and evil, and susceptible of laws and obligations. They must therefore resort to a firm and durable union by government, if they mean that the strong shall not give law to the weak—If they mean to procure the blessings of political life, and to avoid all the distresses incidental to the wild state of nature.

This whole subject is illustrated in a Series of publications in the New-York Papers under the signature of *Publius*. They treat on the necessity of the union in every point of view, and in all its consequences in such an able manner, and with such strong and animated painting, that they denote the hand of a Master. They not only abound in my candid judgment with new and brilliant thoughts, but they carry along with them the most irresistable conviction. Those pieces I warmly recommend to the perusal of the public. I have sent them to the Printer of this Paper for republication, but they are so lengthy, that I am informed they cannot be admitted in a regular series. For the benefit of such as cannot procure the originals, I may possibly hereafter make an abridgment of some of their principal arguments and extracts from some of their most striking parts, and occasionally hand them for Publication.[9]

(a) *See dissertation on parties.*[10]

1. See George Washington, the President of the Constitutional Convention, to the President of Congress, 17 September (Appendix III, below), in which Washington stated that "the Constitution, which we now present, is the result of a spirit of amity, and of that mutual deference and concession which the peculiarity of our political situation rendered indispensible."

2. For the Connecticut charter, granted in 1662, see Thorpe, I, 529–36.

3. The Connecticut charter was publicly read in the Connecticut General Assembly on 9 October 1662 and on the same day the Assembly ordered and declared that "all the Lawes and orders of this Colony to stand in full force and vertue, unles any be cross to the Tenour of o[u]r Charter." In 1650 the General Assembly adopted a code of laws, prefaced by a bill of rights, parts of which are similar to what "A Country Federalist" describes here.

4. Henry St. John, Viscount Bolingbroke, *A Dissertation upon Parties: In Several Letters to Caleb D'Anvers, Esq.* (9th ed., London, 1771), Letter X, 151. The *Dissertation upon Parties* first appeared in 1733–34 in *The Craftsman*, a weekly newspaper in opposition to the ministry of Sir Robert Walpole. It was published in book form in 1735. In 1749 Bolingbroke published together two works on patriotism—*The Idea of a Patriot King* and *A Letter on the Spirit of Patriotism*. (The latter work had actually been written first in 1736.)

5. The reference is to an act passed in 1539, called the *Lex Regia* of England, which gave the King (Henry VIII) the power, with the advice of his council or a majority of that body, to make proclamations that would have the force of statutes. The punishment for

disobeying such a proclamation was a fine or unlimited imprisonment, although punishment did not extend to life, limb, or forfeiture. The act was repealed in the first year of the reign of Edward VI, Henry VIII's successor.

6. The Septennial Act was adopted in 1716.

7. Probably a reference to the Articles of Association adopted by the First Continental Congress on 20 October 1774 which were, in part, a response to Parliament's restrictive acts concerning Massachusetts (JCC, I, 75–80).

8. Locke, *Two Treatises*, Book II, chapter VI, section 57, p. 324.

9. For more on the publication of *The Federalist* in the *Country Journal*, see "Country Federalist," *Country Journal*, 9 January 1788 (below). See also "Printings and Reprintings of *The Federalist*" (Appendix IV).

10. See note 4 (above).

Cato
Poughkeepsie Country Journal, 19 December 1787 (supplement)

To the PUBLIC.

It does not require the spirit of prophecy to foretell, that should the people be so regardless of their own safety, as to reject the proposed constitution, a dissolution of the union will follow; an event that a junto in this State has long since endeavoured to bring about. I have often reflected on their conduct with astonishment, and been lost in my attempts to discover their motive to so dangerous an undertaking. The wretches that were seen plundering the city of Lisbon during the convulsions of the earthquake, pursued a much more rational business; for should they escape the present calamity they might enjoy their ill-got wealth, but with these they must sink in the general ruin: The conduct of the mariner who abandoned the helm in the midst of a dangerous storm, with a view of plundering the ship under the general confusion, was not unsimilar to the infatuated policy of these popular leaders; yet is there not one among them, so lost to all sense of shame, so regardless of his own reputation, as to attempt to point out a single blessing that can in the nature of things flow from the disunion of the States. Why then do they wish to plunge us into a situation of *all against all?* They well know that mutual jealousies, clashing interests, private views of factions yet in embryo, and ambitious designs of ascendency of one State over the other, will rush us headlong into all the horrors of a civil war; that domestic dissentions would invite foreign invasion; *divide and command* would be the operating maxim of our enemies. Thus should we fall unlamented victims to our own imbecility, our want of virtue to govern ourselves, and firmness enough to guard against the designs of evil counsellors. Perhaps there is not a State in the union more wretchedly situated for so perilous an undertaking as our own. In the south five or six of our counties are exposed to maritime depredations; a single ship of war could lay our capital under contribution; turn our eyes to the north, we shall find ourselves in the neighbourhood of an extensive military province of our most inveterate enemies, who are in close friendship and alliance with numerous tribes of warlike savages, whose hatchets are yet stained with the blood of our women and children; on the east we are bound by a numerous, enterprising, restless and warlike people; on the west we shall not find ourselves very happily circumstanced from New-Jersey and Pennsylvania, particularly the former, who views us already with an evil eye on account of the advantage taken of her local situation, in our unrighteous impost. Thus hopefully circumstanced, ought it not to be considered as the heighth of madness in us, to carry our democratic quixotism so far in the pursuit of a false construed maxim of Montesquieu's, as to set the world at defiance; yet to the astonishment of all wise men, do these pretended patriots, mislead the vulgar by their inflamatory publications, replete with the most inconsistent declamation; and what they dare not write, (for they yet pretend to some share of reputation) they privately disseminate through the medium of their minions. Stories (of plots formed against the liberties of the people) that can find no parallel but in the records of ancient superstition, of witchcraft, hobgoblins and fairies: in one county we are told that General Washington is to be appointed King; in another, that the inhabitants of the east end of Long-Island are to be called to the German Flatts to give their votes; in a third, that Prince William Henry[1] is expected from Canada to assume regal government in the name of his father; in a fourth, that the militia is to be embodied, and sent to France to pay off the congressional debt. Thus my fellow citizens, do they add to the cruelty of embarrassing your public affairs, a barbarous mockery of your understandings. Is it not a proof of a bad cause, when such shameful measures are practised for its support. But perhaps I shall be told that this is not the language of the *Federal Farmer*—we should do well to beware of the sophistry of this writer; he sets out with much seeming candor, tells us that the present confederacy is inadequate to the purposes of it; that a reform is necessary, but finally comes back to the old tract of his coadjutors, and attempts to frighten us with the impracticability of bringing it about; and this favourite doctrine he would wish to support by drawing an inference from a part of the constitution, which I humbly conceive does not follow. The large States while in convention (we are told by this well-informed gentleman) could not obtain an equal representation in the Senate; and therefore the union is impracticable:[2] So far is this part of the constitution from operating against the union, that I think it a proof of the moderation and federal disposition of the large States. The proposed constitution cannot be considered any thing more or less than a well organized confederacy, with powers adequate to the execution of it. If a union is necessary, a government is also necessary for that union; for to make general laws without having power of executing them, would be idle and nugatory. In short, there is no law without a remedy: but we are told that the constitution abridges the state sovereignties; this is a self evident truth, no body denies it; the present confederacy feeble, and unequal to the purposes of government, as it is, does the same; the power of negotiation, of making treaties of peace, and declarations of war, are acts of sovereignty, and were never in the hands of the state governments. I am disposed to believe that the constitution under consideration will be found in its operation to partake of both species, that the powers necessary to be given to a confederated government, for the purposes of executing the general laws of the union, will carry with them some of the qualities of a consolidation; and I firmly believe that this form of government is the only one calculated for the United States.—The idea of a confederate government on the general principles that its power extends not over individual persons, but individual States, constitutes a monster in politics. For suppose a few individual persons should violate the general laws of the union, the federal government has no remedy but to carry its arms into the State of which the aggressors are members, and thus punish the innocent with the guilty. To return to the point in question, if the proposed constitution partakes of any of the qualities of a confederacy, (and that it does must appear obvious to every unprejudiced observer) so far individual States are component parts of the government, and so far ought they to be separately represented. Hence that part of the constitution which gives to each State an equal voice in the Senate; now admitting that the constitution partakes of some of the qualities of a consolidated government, the house of representatives is elected upon the principles of it, so that instead of drawing this part of the constitution into disgrace, it will be found a proof not only of the harmony and accommodating temper of the States in convention; but of the profound wisdom of the venerable sages that composed it. Then may the unsubstantial building of the enemies of the union, smitten by the rays of truth, totter to pieces, and crush the authors under their ruins.

1. For Prince William Henry of Great Britain, see "A Parody of the News-Mongers' Song," *Northern Centinel*, 27 November, note 6 (above).
2. See "Federal Farmer," *Letters to the Republican*, 8 November (above).

Publius: The Federalist 24 (Alexander Hamilton) New York Independent Journal, 19 December 1787

Standing army defended. Navy needed. For text, see CC:355. For reprintings, see Appendix IV, below.

Examiner III
New York Journal, 19 December 1787[1]

MR. GREENLEAF, I shall not waste yours or my own time much longer upon the wretched cavillings of so trifling an advocate, for anarchy, as Cato. In my subsequent numbers, Brutus and some others will be considered, who have happier talents for giving sophistry, the air of logical justness and argumentative precision.

In the mean time, however, I would ask the antifœderal junto, why the new constitution should be reprobated, because it is not infinitely perfect, which is an evil inseperable from every production of finite beings? must not the man who condems it, purely because bounds may be set to its perfections, give up all reason, philosophy, proportion, and analogy, and run into downright scepticism, blind fate, witchcraft and inchantment?

As to that sniviling blockhead, Democritus, his drunken performance does not indeed merit a reply, but as he came a long journey from Utica, overcharged with abuse, I shall for once, out of real pity and compassion, vouchsafe him one.

That identi[c]al Hodge-Podge, which has given so much offence to his delicate organs, is the very thing that has so long remained indigested, in the foul stomach of Cato, and has made him so very costive, that in four months he has had but six discharges. The poor man must have died but for the kindly injections of the scientific Brutus, and other good friends of his party.

When a writer is destitute of both genius and information, his works must of necessity be very dull and insipid, for without the former, his researches cannot extend to the possible and aparent analogy of things, and without the latter he is liable to many blunders.

I would advise Democritus, who cannot relish the Hodge-Podge, or see the analogy between an antifederal writer, and an owl, to have his eyes annointed with something to cure the Gutta Serena[2] which obstructs his optic nerves, when he will clearly see, that a constitution framed on the principles of his party, would be like a Solomon Gundy, composed of raw fish and flesh,[3] calculated to throw the person who eats it into a fever. He will then also discern the difference between the nocturnal glare of the antifederal owl, and the bright sun of the federal dove.

It is this cursed disorder, called the gutta serena, that has also infected Brutus, and other antifederal writers. While it remains uncured, truth and argument offered to them, I fear, will be but fixing a pearl into a swine's snout, or, like a diamond thrown into mud, will remain absorbed, or be rejected, and rebound like an elastic ball thrown against the side of a house.

1. Reprinted: Boston *American Herald*, 31 December.
2. Gutta serena or amaurosis is a loss or decay of sight, from the loss of power in the optic nerve.
3. Solomon Gundy is a Jamaican specialty blending smoked herring, hot peppers, and seasoning to create a paté.

A Friend to Common Sense
New York Journal, 19 December 1787[1]

Mr. GREENLEAF, As it is the duty of men, who reverence religion, to discountenance impiety and vice, so it is incumbent on those, who respect good sense, to express their disapprobation of folly, and to use their utmost endeavors to shame its votaries into a course of conduct more consistent with the dignity of rational beings: this consideration induces me, to animadvert upon the Examiner in your paper of the 14th inst. Nothing can make a man more ridiculous, than the affectation of qualities, which he does not possess. The celebrated Dean Swift wrote periodical papers, in support of the Tory ministry of queen Anne, under the signature of the Examiner:[2] a writer in New-York undertakes to imitate the Dean, in wit and ingenuity, styles his foolish productions, the Examiner, and, in the importance of self-sufficiency, dogmatizes with the air of ability, lashes his opponents with all the severity of dullness, and resembles his predecessor in nothing, except in his attachment to tyranny. Our second Swift is evidently unfortunate in the use of his wit—his observations are designed to be satirical, but they amount to nothing more than general censure and railing; he [Examiner] calls Cato an owl and an hypocrite, and taxes him with want of abilities; if the preservation of my life depended upon the issue, I could not discover any wit in these remarks; the person, who ascribes wit to the Examiner, must also allow, that every scavenger and chimney-sweeper in the city, possesses it in the most consummate perfection; for they are, in my very humble opinion, even superior to him in the excellent qualification of blackguardism.

What a farrago of nonsense is the following:—"Cato may be compared to a carved image with a double head, one within the other; the inner head cohering with the trunk or body, and the outer being moveable about the inner, and painted in front the colour of an human face, not unlike the wooden heads, exposed to view in a barber's shop;"—would an intelligent man ever publish such a ridiculous simile and palm it upon the world as a stroke of genuine wit? such a chaos of words procures the confused, unthinking head of the author. A monkey has more unexceptionable claims to reason, than the Examiner to elegance or satire.

The presumption of the imitator of Swift, in supposing his capability of refuting Cato, I consider one of the most remarkable instances of self-conceit, to be met with in the history of mankind; as well might a parrot attempt to correct the language of an able rhetorician.

The Examiner asserts, that Cato has promised much more than he is able to perform; this is the judgment of a partial, and I may say, injudicious writer. Every man of penetration would, independently of any other consideration, conclude that Cato wrote with great force and ability: and why?—because he is attacked by a whole swarm of dunces.

Our American Swift further observes, that Cato's pieces contain nothing but bare assertions, and that he has neglected to quote the most approved writers on government, excepting one or two thread bare quotations from Montesquieu, which have appeared before, in several recent publications; one would, from these remarks, be led to suppose, that he had never read any of Cato's productions—we must either believe this or something worse. Let him point out those recent publications which, he insinuates, are copied by Cato; with what propriety can he censure assertions, when his performance is composed of nothing but assertions; but Cato acts directly the reverse; when he gives his opinions, he at the same time, gives the reasons upon which they are founded.

The Examiner, however inconsistent with common sense, acts perfectly consistent with the practices of his party; a party, chiefly made up of aristocratics, who, unable to answer the cogent reasonings of their adversaries, have recourse, as their dernier resort, to scurrility and wilful misrepresentation; who solace themselves, for the weakness of their argumentation, by the plaudits and huzzas of mercenaries and ignoramuses; who circulate falsehoods, which, without any hyperbole, would fill volumes; and, who calumniate their antagonists, with all the virulence of malignity. I advise the Examiner to reflect, that the palpability of his malice will defeat its intended effect; and that, like a *wounded* viper, he only darts his venom into himself.

As a person, who wishes well to every individual, I would advise the Examiner to desist: As a republican, I say—proceed, sir!—Nothing can be better calculated to bring your party into contempt, than such contemptible productions.

December 16th, 1787.

1. "A Friend to Common Sense," responds to "Examiner" II, *New York Journal*, 14 December (above).

2. In 1710 Jonathan Swift, an Anglo-Irish Anglican priest, satirist, and propagandist, was approached by Tory minister Robert Harley, the chancellor of the exchequer, who wanted Swift's support for the new Tory ministry of Queen Anne. Harley hoped that Swift's contributions to *The Examiner: Or, Remarks upon Papers and Occurrences*, a weekly periodical and organ of the ministry, would gain popular approval for the ministry. It was not difficult to convince Swift, who approved of the new ministry and wanted to obtain the remission of certain ancient fees that the Irish clergy paid to the Crown. Swift contributed (anonymously) about thirty-five numbers to the *Examiner* between 1710 and 1712.

Pennsylvania Journal, 19 December 1787[1]

By a gentleman from New-York and New-Jersey, we are informed that it is reported, in those states, that a Governor not one hundred miles from the seat of Congress, still sets his face against the new Constitution of the United States; and has gone so far, it is said, as to proffer thro' a person of considerable weight in Jersey,[2] one half of the impost of his state, to Jersey, if they would reject the new Constitution.

1. Reprinted: *New York Journal,* 24 December; *Maryland Journal,* 25 December. Immediately below this item the *New York Journal* printed this bracketed statement: "How useful, says the *spirit* of this New-York and New-Jersey *gentleman,* would a 'LYING GAZETTE' be at this juncture."
2. The reference is to Abraham Clark, a New Jersey delegate to Congress, who was suspected of opposing the Constitution. For other attacks on Clark and for his criticism of the Constitution, see Mfm:N.J. 37 A–D, and DHFFE, III, *passim.*

Albany Gazette, 20 December 1787[1]

We cannot (says a correspondent) affirm, that "that those who have turned the world upside down, are come hither also"; but we can with safety say this much, that they have *troubled* this part of the country with *false* alarms (viz. George Bryan's Centinels)[2] in abundance.—The paper on which these things are printed, however, is of a *soft* texture, and answers the good people a very *necessary* purpose.

1. Reprinted: Hartford *American Mercury,* 31 December.
2. George Bryan, a leading Pennsylvania Antifederalist, was thought to be the author of the "Centinel" essays that were actually written by his son Samuel (CC:133).

Albany Gazette, 20 December 1787

☞ A correspondent presents his compliments to the Antifederalists, begs that in their future publications they would pay a *little* regard to TRUTH. Their compliance in this particular, will give much satisfaction to the honest part of the community.

Albany Gazette, 20 December 1787[1]

A correspondent observes, that those great men, who have given proofs of their superior abilities in discussing the weighty state topics, at present before us, may be aptly compared to the most famed actors in a theatre, who are intent only on performing their respective parts, so as to obtain applause from the discerning part of their auditors, without heeding the noise, hisses and dirt from the rabble of the gallery. Publius, Brutus and Cato are, at present, the foremost figures on the stage. They merit the plaudits of all, but such as have their senses poisoned by the rage of party, and are incapable of perceiving truths, unless they strike in unison with their passions. While all sincere friends to their country, with anxious earnestness, behold the political balance, poised by those geniuses, the offspring, and ornament, of an infant nation, who rival, as statesmen, the boasted characters of Europe; a few, unable to mount to the same conspicuous eminence, have their spirits blasted by envy, and outswell the frog in the fable,[2] till their croaking is put to an end by a ridiculous burst. A scribbling poetaster, who has several times made an appearance in the Lansingburgh Advertiser, with *Impromtu's*,[3] *Conundrums* and *XLNC's*,[4] seems to vie only with himself in the profundity of his art; and cannot be compared to any thing, more properly, than to a certain animal, described in Gulliver's Travels, whose delight was, after hiding himself among the branches of a tree, to surprise the unwary passenger with a discharge of his excrements. It is therefore proposed, that such characters be in future distinguished by the appellation of a creature they so much resemble, and be called YAHOOS.[5]

1. Reprinted: *Northern Centinel*, 25 December.
2. See Aesop's fable of "The Frog and the Ox," the moral of which is "self-conceit may lead to self-destruction."
3. See "Impromptu," *Massachusetts Centinel*, 18 August, an attack on Governor George Clinton (above). "Impromptu" was reprinted in the *Northern Centinel* on 3 September.
4. See "The Syren's Songs," *Northern Centinel*, 11, 18 December, that attack His Excellency (i.e., "X—L—N—C'") Governor George Clinton (both above).
5. For a full description of the "Yahoos," see Lemuel Gulliver [Jonathan Swift], *Travels into Several Remote Nations of the World* (London, 1726), Part IV, chapter I, "A Voyage to the Country of the Houyhnhnms."

A Lunarian
New York Daily Advertiser, 20 December 1787

Mr. CHILDS, *Please to insert in your paper the following extract of a letter, lately received from a correspondent in the Moon, and you will greatly oblige yours, &c.* A Speculator.

DEAR SIR, As I take it for granted that you understand the laws of gravitation, you must know, that those bodies which contain the greatest quantity of matter in the smallest dimensions, are said to possess the greatest specific gravity, and are therefore entitled to the first place amongst solid bodies; and that those productions both of nature and art, which have but little substance in their composition, and are of huge dimensions, must acquire qualities similar to a Balloon, being easily buoyed up, and wafted into the æreal regions. Know then, that it is by means of this modification of matter, that we Lunarians, are furnished with the weekly productions of Brutus, Cato, Cincinnatus, Timoleon, &c. against the proposed Federal Constitution; I have perused the whole of their voluminous conscriblations, and think it clear beyond a doubt, that they have been inspired by the benign influences of our planet, otherwise it would have been impossible for sublunary beings to have created, and exposed so many defects, horrid blunders, and wicked designs in that iniquitous system of Government, fabricated by the late Convention, to enslave the people of the thirteen dis-united States.

The inhabitants of our planet are greatly concerned for the welfare of those worthy patriots, and wish them success in their opposition to the proposed Constitution; they are the first Statesmen in your lower world, who have discovered the true principles of our Lunarian mode of Legislation and Finance, which is an acquisition of more importance, than the discovery of the philosopher's stone. It is a God-like art, to create a circulating medium, almost out of nothing, and to annihilate it again at pleasure. We have our wars as well as you, and large tracts of public land beyond the mountains in the moon. When a war happens, with a neighbouring nation, which renders it necessary to raise an army, for the defence of the State, we create a paper currency to pay them, and purchase necessaries for their support; as long as this medium will answer, we deal it out liberally, and pledge the faith of the people to redeem it with gold and silver, when it fails in credit, we give large bounties in lands, in fine we *promise* every thing in the time of *danger*, but when the danger is over, and peace established, we reason thus: as it was dire *necessity* which compelled us to enter into these engagements, and make these solemn *promises*, certainly the obligation should cease with the *necessity* which compelled us to make them, for what person of common sense ever expected that effects should continue, after the cause which produced them was removed, or had ceased to act.

Besides, in these cases, the public debtors are far more numerous than the public creditors; it is therefore plain that it is for the interest of the majority to annul the public debt, and all good Representatives know, that the interests of the majority of their Constituents, should be preferred to that of the minority.

After having thus demonstrated the propriety of the measure (for *justice* you know should never be permitted to interfere in politics) we proceed to repeal the grants of bounty lands that have been made during the war, and annihilate all the public securities, that we cannot conveniently get into our own hands. By this prudent method of conducting affairs, many of us are much more opulent at the termination of a war, than we were at its commencement. It is true that busy meddling people are apt to raise the cry of justice, conscience, public faith, and the support of public credit: but however well such puritannic nonsense may sound, when coming from the mouth of whining, canting Priests, such language would render a politician ridiculous indeed.

But even amongst the disturbers of the peace, with all their whining sanctified cants, where is the man to be found that would not purchase a public security from his neighbour for two shillings and six-pence per pound, and realize it in the purchase of a landed estate, rather than be taxed in his full proportion, to pay his said neighbour the full amount of such security, both principal and interest?

But even supposing that there may be some individuals who have no talents for speculation, where is the man that would not wish to avoid taxation?

And how is it possible to do this without adhering strictly to the present plan?

And depend upon it, if you are ever so foolish as to adopt the new Constitution, you will be obliged to pay the national debt, the annual interest of which, as Cincinnatus has demonstrated, (by saying so) amounts to 4,800,000 dollars; to which we may add, 1,200,000 for the expence of collecting it; It will then amount to six millions of dollars annually.[1] Allowing 3,000,000 of inhabitants in the Thirteen United States, it will amount to the enormous sum of two dollars per man, which, if they pay their tax monthly, (which is probably the best mode) it will amount to the sum of one shilling and four-pence per month. If this is not sufficient to frighten you into a rejection of the new Constitution, the Lord have mercy on you, poor miserable bankrupts.

1. See "Cincinnatus" V, *New York Journal*, 29 November, at note 14 (above).

A Countryman III (DeWitt Clinton)
New York Journal, 20 December 1787[1]

WORTHY SIR, My neighbour and me have been busy almost every evening, since I wrote to you last, and sometimes we set up very late,

still trying all we could to find out the real meaning of this new constitution; but really, as I said before, we find it a hard matter to come
at it. We cannot be reconciled to it, that people who may wish to come
here from the old countries, to get clear of the oppression of great
folks there, should be obliged to pay ten dollars, besides their passage
and other expences, for leave to do it—and we cannot help still thinking it a very pitiful thing, in this new government, to give leave to make
slaves of our fellow creatures, for the sake of a triffling sum of money:—
these things set very heavy upon our mind, for we believe, that they
are establishing wickedness instead of justice, let some folks pretend to
what they will. We see that this new government will have power to levy
and collect taxes, duties, imposts and excises upon us; now, with respect
to the duties and imposts, we suppose that is money that is to be raised
upon goods and liquors, that may be brought from abroad to this country, and we are very easy about it, for we are sure the less that is
brought, the better it will be for us, for the less we will have to pay for;
but as to excises, some of our neighbours from the old countries, where
they say, they are as common as Mayweed—tell us that they will go to
almost every thing—and, that if they set to work at this, they will make
us pay more for the small beer and cyder we drink, than they would
fetch, if we were to sell them and drink water in their stead. As for
taxes, I will warrant you, we are at no loss about the meaning of that
word, for we have learned by experience to understand it pretty well—
indeed many of us have been driven to our last shifts, to pay what has
been demanded of us already by our own state—and, I am sure, if this
new government sets about this work too, between both, we shall be
sadly hampered, and ten to one, if not only our stocks, but our farms
too, will be sold to satisfy the collectors: but this is not all, it seems
there is to be a new sort of tax, which we have not before heard of,
called a capitation-tax; I should never have found out what was meant
by it, if it had not been for my neighbour, who tells me, it is a tax upon
the head, and that a poor man's head, though he is not worth a groat
in the world, must pay as much, as a rich man's head, let him be ever
so wealthy;—now this appears to me very little more like justice, than
the affair about the poor blacks, though it may not be quite so wicked;
for, although a poor man may have as good a head and as much brains
in it, as a rich man, and be as honest and as wise a man; yet, where
there are any good things a going (such as any place, by which there
is a deal of money or honor to be had) the rich man's head is always
best then, and, by one means or another, he finds out ways to get these
things to himself; so that I think his head ought to be taxed more than
the poor man's, for it is an old and true saying, pay alike share alike:

besides, he has more of the good things of this world, and is better able to pay.

There is one thing, worthy Sir, that has given us a deal of trouble; we have seen on reading the constitution through the first time, that there were some things mentioned which, it is said, this new government should not do—and, we thought it very right, that they should not, for to be sure they were such things, as we would not like to see done; but upon reading it over and over again, and attending to it still more carefully, we began to think between ourselves, what could be the reason of saying they should not do these things, because, as we had understood matters at first, there was no power given to this new government to do them; one of these matters I mean, is, where they say, "No title of nobility shall be granted by the United States," now it is very plain to me, if there was no power given to this new government to grant titles of nobility, (I suppose what it means is to make lords) then there was no occasion to say that they should not do it, because it would be very foolish to say, that they should not do a thing which they could not do; this, as I said before, made us examine it again, and that very closely, and to be sure, to our great surprise, we found out some clauses, and some big words that we had not before taken notice of, appear to carry with them a very broad meaning, and though they did not just mention any thing about making lords, or (as it is called) granting titles of nobility, yet it very well may be, that these clauses give them power to do every thing, only, what it is said, they should not do—and my neighbour who understands what he reads better than me, thinks this must be the case, for he can't believe that such wise men, as they say, the convention was made up of, and a great many of them judges and lawyers too, would have ever taken so much pains to guard against this new government's doing things, which they would have had no power to do. But, as this seemed to us a matter of no little consequence, and we did not like to be in a mistake about it—my neighbour, who stands well with the young lawyers, and lads who are looking out for public employments, asked me to come over the next evening to his house, for he would have a parcel of them there, and we would try whether we could not find out their opinion about this matter; I accordingly went the next evening to my neighbour's, and there, as he promised, he had a number of them—he soon began to talk with them about the new constitution, and mentioned several of the difficulties we had met with to understand it, and some things in it which appeared to us not to be right; such as the taking away the trial by jury, head-tax business, and encouraging the making slaves of our fellow-creatures; but we found they did not like to speak much about it, and that they were very loth to say a word against it, they seemed indeed, to think there might be some small things in it which might have been as well left out; but, upon the whole, they said it would do very well, and that when we once got it agoing, we could mend it; and that something must be done, or we will all git into anarchy (as they called it) and confusion; my neighbour asked them, whether it would not be the best and safest way to mend it first, for fear if we once parted with so much power, as was given to this new government, we could never git it back again, and put them in mind of what Mr. Beccaria[2] and other great men (whose names I do not remember) had said about giving more powers than were necessary to rulers; but, they did not like this and said, if we once began to alter, we should never agree about it, and get a quarrelling with one another. Indeed, good sir, I have but very indifferent thoughts (to say no worse) about these young men, for though I hear that in other places many of their cloth are very honest, and think very right about matters, yet those among us appear to be guided entirely by their own interest; they hold themselves above their neighbours, and seem to think themselves better and wiser than every body else, and I have heard that they do not scruple saying in private, that this new government would be a fine thing for them; that it will make a great deal more law business; that they will git higher costs; and that it will not be in the power of the country-members to keep lowering them as they have done lately, for the state legislatures will have nothing to do with these grand courts or any thing else of consequence, for which, they say, they are not fit. It is even said, that some of the young men who are looking for places, are so taken in with the notion of a standing army, that they have already bespoke cloth at the shop-keepers for regimentals. Now for my share, I am fully of my neighbours opinion, that it would be best to mend this new government before we agree to take it, for if we cannot agree to make it good now without quarrelling, I do not see how we will agree to do it afterwards—indeed, I think, it will be much harder; for those that have once got the power, I am afraid, will be very unwilling to part with it—they tell me it is no common thing, nay, some go so far as to say, it has never been known to happen. I should think it a very unwise thing to pull down an old house, in which I lived very comfortably for many years, and which had sheltered me and my family, and move into a new house, just to gratify the pride and vanity of the children, because it was larger and appeared finer, on the outside, when I knew at the same time, that it was not well finished within, that the foundation was bad, the chimnies smoky, the roof leaky, and many of the posts rotten, so as to make it dangerous to go in it, and that it would cost me more than I was worth in the world to furnish and keep it in repair, and I am apt to believe if I got ruined by it, I should meet with few to pity me; and yet it is strange, we are told if we do not do something as foolish as this about the new government, we shall get a quarrelling; but let them quarrel that will, I am for continuing peaceably in the old house, and for mending it now and then, as it stands in need of it. I observe from the papers you sent me, that those who are warmly in favor of this new government, say, that it will make us able to pay our debts, establish our credit, and make us respectable abroad; but I cannot see how it is to do all these good things, and they have not undertaken to tell us; I think it but a poor way to pay debts, by getting a more costly government, and I cannot see that it will establish our credit, by being fickle and changing every day from one thing to another; I am sure an unsteady whimsical man, is but illy trusted by his neighbors, for few will put any dependence upon him; and I believe it will be pretty much the case with a government, that is always changing, for though it might be something this year, that we liked very well, and were very fond of, next year it might be changed into something else that we did not like at all, and could not bear to live under; and I can hardly think, it would make us very respectable abroad, when the people in the old countries found out, that we could not be contented, neither with the one thing or the other, and did not know what we would be at ourselves; besides, for my own part, I think we ought first to make ourselves happy at home, and I believe that will be found the best way to make people abroad think well of us. O my good friend, we ought carefully to guard against the pride and vanity of our hearts, which are always taking us from the good old way, and leading of us into new schemes and devices, and are dangerous enemies to our happiness both here, and hereafter; if our great men were oftener to read their bibles, they would find many lessons on this head, which might be of great service to them, and fit them better for the high places to which they are called; they might profit much on the present occasion by attending to the history of the Children of Israel, as recorded in that holy book; they did not trust in the promises, which were made them by their heavenly father through his holy prophets; they were restless under the government, which was appointed over them by the Almighty; they were fickle and fond of changing; they were ambitious, and wanted to appear respectable abroad; they must be like all the nations, have a king to judge them, and to go out before them, and fight their battles; notwithstanding, that good prophet Samuel protested solemnly against it, by the command of our maker, and shewed them the manner of the king that should reign over them, yet they would have a new government, and they got Saul the son of kish for a king;[3] the history of whose wicked reign I need not relate to you.[4] O my dear sir, we ought to be much in prayer with God, least the same temper which seems to prevail too much at this day among many of us, should bring down upon our land also some heavy judgment; for to me it appears as if there was a rod in soak for us.

I remain, Honoured Sir, Your real friend, And humble servant. A COUNTRYMAN.

1. On 19 December the editor of the *New York Journal* noted that "A Countryman" IV [III] "was received yesterday, but could not be inserted this day; it shall appear to-morrow."

2. See "A Countryman" I, *New York Journal,* 6 December, note 2 (above).

3. 1 Samuel 8:10–18; 9:1–27; 10:1; 11:15.

4. For Saul's failure to carry out God's instructions as given him by Samuel, see especially 1 Samuel 8–11; 13:7–14; 15:1–35; and for the last years of Saul's reign and Samuel's anointing of David to replace Saul as king, see especially 1 Samuel 16:1–31.

New York Journal, 20 December 1787[1]

FROM A CORRESPONDENT.

It has been reiterated, Oh! my countrymen, that the freedom, and consequent happiness, of a country, diminishes in an exact proportion to the diminution of its public virtue. In the years 74, 5, 6, 7, &c. how frequently were ye reminded of this truth; and the glorious success of our arms greatly demonstrates, how rigidly ye then adhered to this fundamental principle of patriotism. But, alas! how is the scene changed!—The consequences of this change, if not guarded against, by a re-adoption of moral, as well as political, virtue, will be, RULE BY A ROD OF IRON!—Remember the emphatical exclamation of that old republican veteran, CATO—Oh! liberty: Oh! virtue: Oh! my country[2]— and let the moral be zealously attended to—Explain it to your children, ye hoary fathers of America; and, ye children, inculcate it among your brethren. The precepts of your God, the conjures of the sullen ghosts of stern forefathers, the soil you tread on, all combine to impress upon your minds the duty you owe *yourselves*—you owe *posterity*. Pin not your faith upon another's sleeve; act for yourselves, and be forever independent and happy.

1. Reprinted in the *Country Journal,* 2 January 1788, and in six newspapers outside New York by 17 January: N.H. (1), Mass. (1), N.J. (1), Pa. (1), Md. (1), S.C. (1).

2. From Joseph Addison's play, *Cato. A Tragedy* (1713), Act IV, scene 4.

James Kent to Nathaniel Lawrence
Poughkeepsie, 21 December 1787[1]

My Dear Friend,

As Jemmy Cooper makes the last trip tomorrow & our communications will of course be more doubtful & oftner interrupted hereafter, I send you a faithful line notwithstanding you are already in my debt.

Gilbert[2] who came up this week with Capt. North[3] says he saw you & that you are so firmly fixed on the side of *his darling* anti-federal cause that I am to expect ⟨a long and severe letter⟩[4] from you in support of your Principles & to my own confusion. He hints it in a way that leads me to suppose you said something expressive of your intention to write to me ⟨copiously⟩[5] on the subject. I own I stand in need of hearing some abler advocate than Gilbert for he has so much of the fanatic & so much of the boy about him that he is enough to ruin the best cause even if it is the amiable Religion of our Saviour. But I believe it is best for me to anticipate your political Letter by telling you that if it is against me it had better be omitted for as I said before in some letter I am unwilling to ⟨sever our friendly and affectionate⟩[6] & respectful correspondence with the acrimony of political dispute. For my part I only tell my mind *I am decided—I believe as firmly as I believe my existence that every thing which is dear & valuable to America depends on the Success of the new federal Constitution.*

I know my Friend you will do me the Justice to believe that *I think* I have cogent Reasons for my Sentiments & further that I have firmness enough to persevere. I believe all this of you whatever side you espouse & in the present ⟨cause⟩[7] I esteem & like you just as well tho you are against me. notwithstanding permit me to say I never was more disappointed in my calculations of a Gentleman's Opinion in my Life. From my knowledge of your habits of thinking & your temper I felt when I discovered your political sentiments, a little of *the Surprise* tho none of the confusion or despair which Caesar felt in finding Brutus among the number of the Conspirators.

You may praise who you please & I will presume to say that I think *Publius* is a most admirable writer & wields the sword of Party dispute with justness, energy, & inconceivable dexterity. The Author *must be* Hamilton who I think in Genius & political Research is not inferior to Gibbon, Hume or Montesquieu.

Please to instruct me whenever you are kind enough to favor me with a reply, on Some of those law subjects which remain (& not a little to our discredit as ⟨lawyers⟩[8]) quite unexhausted & unnoticed between us.

1. Typescript, Law Library, DLC. Another transcription of this letter is in the Bodley Book Shop Catalogue No. 18, *General Literature* . . . (New York, c. 1941), Kent Family Papers, Columbia University Libraries, Rare Book and Manuscript Library. The typescript, which is transcribed literally, seems to be defective in several cases. The Bodley transcription, while also defective in a few instances and modernized, seems to be a more accurate transcription of the words. Whenever the Bodley transcription seems to be more accurate, we have inserted it here within angle brackets, with a footnote to describe the transcription in the typescript.

2. Antifederalist Gilbert Livingston was Kent's law partner.

3. Captain North was master of a Hudson River sloop.

4. In the typescript this phrase is: "along & several letters."

5. In the typescript this word is "expressly."

6. In the typescript this phrase is "fire our friendly our affectionate."

7. In the typescript this word is "case."

8. In the typescript this word is "Lawyer."

Constitutional Convention Delegates Robert Yates and John Lansing to Governor George Clinton, Albany, 21 December 1787

Robert Yates and John Lansing, Jr., along with Alexander Hamilton, were New York's delegates to the Constitutional Convention which was called to revise the Articles of Confederation. The New York legislature had appointed the state's delegates on 6 March 1787, instructing them to meet in May "for the sole and express purpose of revising the Articles of Confederation, and reporting to Congress and the several legislatures such alterations and provisions therein, as shall, when agreed to in Congress and confirmed by the several states, render the federal constitution adequate to the exigencies of government and the preservation of the Union" (Appendix II, below). The language of this resolution was borrowed from the congressional resolution of 21 February 1787 calling for the Convention (CDR, 187; CC:1).

In the Constitutional Convention, Yates and Lansing opposed the Virginia Resolutions which called for a total abandonment of the Articles and the establishment of a strong central government. Instead, Yates and Lansing favored a revision of the Articles of Confederation, as exemplified by the New Jersey Amendments to the Articles (CDR, 250–53). On 19 June the Convention rejected the New Jersey Amendments and approved the Amended Virginia Resolutions (CDR, 247–50), thereby committing itself to the creation of a strong central government. Increasingly disenchanted, Yates and Lansing left the Convention on 10 July, more than two months before the Convention adjourned. They never returned. (Alexander Hamilton had already left the Convention. He returned and attended from time to time, eventually signing the Constitution for New York on 17 September. See "Introduction," above.)

Various reasons were given for Yates and Lansing's early departure and their refusal to return. Virginia Convention delegate George Mason noted that they left because "the season for courts came on" (Farrand, III, 367). The New York Supreme Court met in Albany from 31 July until 8 August and the circuit courts through the end of September. Yates was a Supreme Court justice, while Lansing practiced before it. On 26 August Abraham G. Lansing, John Lansing's brother, reported that both men attended the circuit court in Montgomery

County and that Yates was on his way "to hold a Court" in Washington County. "I find," Abraham G. Lansing continued, "but Little Inclination in either of them to repair again to Philadelphia, and from their General Observations I believe they will not go—early in the Commencement of the Business at Philadelphia, my Brother informed me that he was in sentiment with a respectable *Minority* of that Body, but that they had no prospect of succeeding in the measures proposed, and that he was at a Stand whether it would not be proper for him to Leave them. this Circumstance convinces me the more that they will not again attend" (to Abraham Yates, Jr., Mfm:N.Y.). Maryland Convention delegate Luther Martin, like Yates and Lansing a part of the Convention's minority, essentially agreed with Abraham G. Lansing. Martin declared that Yates and Lansing "had uniformly opposed the system, and I *believe*, despairing of getting a *proper one* brought forward, or of *rendering any real service*, they returned no more" (*Genuine Information* III, Baltimore *Maryland Gazette*, 4 January 1788, CC:414, p. 255). Daniel of St. Thomas Jenifer, another Maryland Convention delegate, contradicted Martin's assertion, stating that Martin told him that Yates and Lansing intended to return to the Convention ("Extract of a letter from Annapolis," *Pennsylvania Packet*, 14 February, CC:414, p. 256, note 7).

On 23 September the Spanish encargado de negocios, writing from New York City, charged that Yates and Lansing left the Convention early "in order not to ratify" the Constitution (Don Diego de Gardoqui to Conde de Floridablanca, CC:89). Several days later, the French vice consul in New York City asserted that Yates, Lansing, and three other delegates "abstained from Signing under various pretexts" (Antoine de la Forest to Comte de Montmorin, 28 September, CC:105). A brief item in the *Massachusetts Gazette*, 20 November, implied that eight Convention delegates, including Yates and Lansing, left the Convention because they opposed the Constitution. The next day a respondent in the *Massachusetts Centinel* wrote that Yates and Lansing probably were "obliged by domestick concerns to return home" before the Constitution was signed. (For both newspaper items, see CC:Vol. 2, Appendix I.)

Yates and Lansing waited several months before publicly declaring their objections to the Constitution. On 21 December, ten days before the scheduled meeting of the New York legislature, they wrote Governor George Clinton, giving their reasons for opposing the Constitution. New York City merchant Walter Rutherfurd saw Clinton's hand in the letter (to John Rutherfurd, 8, 15 January 1788, below). "A Dutchess County Farmer" believed that Yates and Lansing were "inspired by Cato" (i.e., Clinton), when they noted that they opposed the Constitution because of their instructions "and a conviction of the impracticability [of] establishing a beneficial general Government" (*Country Journal*, 26 February, III below). When the legislature attained a quorum on 11 January 1788, Clinton gave the legislature the report of the Constitutional Convention (Appendix III, below), the congressional resolution of 28 September 1787 forwarding the report to the states, and the Yates-Lansing letter. (For Clinton's speech, see II below.)

The Yates-Lansing letter was printed in the *Daily Advertiser* and *New York Journal* on 14 January. The *Daily Advertiser* included it with the legislative proceedings for 11 January, even though the journals of neither house of the legislature include the text of the letter. The *New York Journal* published the letter separately under the heading "REASONS of DISSENT," preceded by this preface: "Late yesterday evening we were favored, by a correspondent, with the following COPY *of a* LETTER from the Hon. ROBERT YATES, jun. [*sic*] and JOHN LANSING, Esquires, members of the general convention, lately held in the city of Philadelphia, assigning their reasons for giving their dissent to the constitution, agreed upon by that body, and which was laid before the legislature by his excellency the Governor, at the opening of the session, on Friday last.—From a consideration of the *very interesting nature* of this LETTER to the public, notwithstanding the late hour of its receipt, the editor thus expeditiously presents it to the public view." The *Journal* also printed the letter in its Thursday issue (17 January), which "had *a more general Circulation in the Country.*"

In New York, the Yates-Lansing letter was also reprinted in the *New York Packet* and *New York Morning Post*, 15 January; *Independent Journal*, 16 January; *Albany Gazette*, 17 January (evening supplement); *Country Journal*, 22 January (supplement); and *Hudson Weekly Gazette*, 31 January. By 10 March the letter was reprinted outside New York in the February issue of the nationally circulated Philadelphia *American Museum* and in eleven newspapers: N.H. (1), Mass. (1), Pa. (5), Md. (1), Va. (1), S.C. (1), Ga. (1).

The Yates-Lansing letter generated little public response in New York. "A Citizen" complained that the two men should have remained in the Constitutional Convention and explained their reasons of dissent to that body. The power to revise and amend the Articles, continued "A Citizen," had given the Convention latitude to amend them in toto, not just in parts (*Daily Advertiser*, 6 February, III below. This item was reprinted from a non-extant issue—either 22 or 29 January—of the *Northern Centinel*.). "A Dutchess County Farmer" charged that Yates and Lansing left early because they "did not find so many gaping blockheads to swallow down" their "antifederal jargon at the Convention." They were intent on opposing any government formed by the Convention (*Country Journal*, 26 February, III below). For the response to the letter outside New York, see CC:447, p. 368.

The text of the Yates-Lansing letter printed below is transcribed from the *Daily Advertiser* of 14 January. The punctuation and capitalization in the *New York Journal* printing of the same date varies slightly from the *Advertiser's* version. No manuscript of this letter has been located; a manuscript was once part of the George Clinton Papers at the New York State Library, but it was probably destroyed in the great fire of 1911 which devastated some of the library's collections. As stated above, the letter does not appear in the journal of either house of the legislature.

SIR, We do ourselves the honor to advise your Excellency, that, in pursuance of concurrent resolutions of the Honorable Senate and Assembly, we have, together with Mr. Hamilton, attended the Convention appointed for revising the articles of Confederation, and reporting amendments to the same.

It is with the sincerest concern we observe, that in the prosecution of the important objects of our mission, we have been reduced to the disagreeable alternative of either exceeding the powers delegated to us, and giving our assent to measures which we conceived destructive of the political happiness of the citizens of the United States; or opposing our opinion to that of a body of respectable men, to whom those citizens had given the most unequivocal proofs of confidence. Thus circumstanced, under these impressions, to have hesitated would have been to be culpable. We therefore gave the principles of the Constitution, which has received the sanction of a majority of the Convention, our decided and unreserved dissent; but we must candidly confess, that we should have been equally opposed to any system, however modified, which had in object the consolidation of the United States into one Government.

We beg leave briefly to state some cogent reasons which, among others, influenced us to decide against a consolidation of the States. These are reducible into two heads.

First. The limited and well defined powers under which we acted, and which could not, on any possible construction, embrace an idea of such magnitude as to assent to a general Constitution in subversion of that of the State.

Secondly. A conviction of the impracticability of establishing a general Government, pervading every part of the United States, and extending essential benefits to all.

Our powers were explicit, and confined to the *sole and express purpose of revising the articles of Confederation*, and reporting such alterations and provisions therein, as should render the Federal Constitution adequate to the exigencies of Government, and the preservation of the Union.

From these expressions, we were led to believe that a system of consolidated Government, could not, in the remotest degree, have been in contemplation of the Legislature of this State, for that so important a trust, as the adopting measures which tended to deprive the State Government of its most essential rights of Sovereignty, and to place it in a dependent situation, could not have been confided, by implication, and the circumstance, that the acts of the Convention were to receive a State approbation, in the last resort, forcibly corroborated the opinion, that our powers could not involve the subversion of a Constitution, which being immediately derived from the people, could only be abolished by their express consent, and not by a Legislature, possessing authority vested in them for its preservation. Nor could we suppose, that if it had been the intention of the Legislature to abrogate the existing Confederation, they would, in such pointed terms, have directed the attention of their delegates to the revision and amendment of it, in total exclusion of every other idea.

Reasoning in this manner, we were of opinion, that the leading feature of every amendment ought to be the preservation of the individual States, in their uncontroled constitutional rights; and that, in reserving these, a mode might have been devised, of granting to the Confederacy, the monies arising from a general system of revenue, the power of regulating commerce, and enforcing the observance of Foreign treaties, and other necessary matters of less moment.

Exclusive of our objections, originating from the want of power, we entertained an opinion that a general Government, however guarded by declarations of rights or cautionary provisions, must unavoidably, in a short time, be productive of the destruction of the civil liberty of such citizens who could be effectually coerced by it; by reason of the extensive territory of the United States; the dispersed situation of its inhabitants, and the insuperable difficulty of controling or counteracting the views of a set of men (however unconstitutional and oppressive their acts might be) possessed of all the powers of Government, and who, from their remoteness from their constituents, and necessary permanency of office, could not be supposed to be uniformly actuated by an attention to their welfare and happiness; that however wise and energetic the principles of the general Government might be, the extremities of the United States could not be kept in due submission and obedience to its laws at the distance of many hundred miles from the seat of Government; that if the general Legislature was composed of so numerous a body of men as to represent the interest of all the inhabitants of the United States in the usual and true ideas of representation, the expence of supporting it would become intolerably burthensome, and that if a few only were invested with a power of legislation, the interests of a great majority of the inhabitants of the United States must necessarily be unknown, or if known even in the first stages of the operations of the new Government, unattended to.

These reasons were in our opinion conclusive against any system of consolidated Government: to that recommended by the Convention we suppose most of them forcibly apply.

It is not our intention to pursue this subject further than merely to explain our conduct in the discharge of the trust which the Honorable the Legislature reposed in us—interested however, as we are in common with our fellow citizens in the result, we cannot forbear to declare that we have the strongest apprehensions that a Government so organized as that recommended by the Convention, cannot afford that security to equal and permanent liberty, which we wished to make an invariable object of our pursuit.

We were not present at the completion of the New Constitution; but before we left the Convention, its principles were so well established as to convince us that no alteration was to be expected, to conform it to our ideas of expediency and safety. A persuasion that our further attendance would be fruitless and unavailing, rendered us less solicitous to return.

We have thus explained our motives for opposing the adoption of the National Constitution, which we conceived it our duty to communicate to your Excellency, to be submitted to the consideration of the Hon. Legislature.

We have the Honor to be, with the greatest Respect, your Excellency's most obedient and very humble Servants,

Democritus
New York Journal, 21 December 1787[1]

Most sublime, most witty, and most elegant EXAMINER! !
I bow down before you; I am vanquished by the ascendency, which your all-powerful, transcendant abilities, have over your obedient, abject slave. Although you have thought fit, in the majesty of your justice, to scourge me with your august displeasure, and severe sarcasms, for presuming to differ from you in opinion; yet, I have such great confidence in your benevolence and compassion, that I hope to be admitted into your favor; which is most earnestly desired by me, when I consider that you are not only an *eminent* writer, but also a most renowned physician, and consequently able to remove the drunkeness, which you say, has attacked your servant.

That you are deeply versed in both surgery and physic, I observe, from the technical terms, with which you have interlarded your third lecture; and which, I cannot read, without praying, that you would, as you profess pity and compassion for me, take away "the *serene gut* which obstructs my optic nerves," so that I may thoroughly understand your *Solomon Gundy* and other high-flown and learned words.[2]

That I may do something to merit your patronage and favor, I will here inform you of divers plans, which (if I enjoy health and live long enough) I intend to execute; and humbly request your sublimity to acquaint me, whether they engage your approbation.

I purpose to collect from your judicious works, a book of similies, and metaphors; as a specimen take the following:

Like Solomon Gundy.
Noctural glare of the antifederal owl.
Bright sun of the federal dove.
Fixing a pearl into a swine's snout.
Like a diamond thrown into the mud.
Like an elastic ball thrown against the side of a house.

I also purpose to compile a dictionary of Medical terms, from your learned writings; by what follows, you will observe, I have a large stock of them already.

Delicate organs.	Gutta serena.
Indigested.	Optic nerves.
Foul Stomach.	Fever.
Very costive.	Uncured.
Six discharges.	Infected.
Kindly injections.	Disorder.
Eyes anointed.	

I furthermore intend, to compose a book of medical observation, and receipt, from your works. For instance,

"Solomon Gundy, composed of raw fish and flesh, is calculated to throw the person who eats it into a fever."

A man of your extensive reading, must well know, that it is the practice in England, to comprise, the beautiful reflections, and striking excellencies of eminent writers, into small volumes, and style them the Beauties of Shakespear, Blair,[3] Johnson, &c. Now as your performances contain many rare, elegant, and uncommon observations, I mean to publish a book, and entitle it—*The Beauties of the Examiner.*   e. g.

Perfection.

The works of a finite being cannot be perfect.

EXAMINER, No. III.

Composition.

The works of a writer,[4] destitute of both genius and information, must be very dull and insipid, because he has no genius and information.

Idem, something abbreviated.

I hope you will accept these my intentions in good part, and forgive my late impudence, as I have forgiven your severity.

When I revolve in my mind the merits of your writings, I am astonished at your universal knowledge. This is the only exception I have ever known to your profound remark—*that the works of a finite being cannot be perfect;* for you seem to be a complete master of the whole circle of human learning.

Your works shew that you are

—A chymist; for you speak of the *absorption of mud.*[5]

—A natural philosopher; for you speak of the *elastic ball.*

—A logician; for you speak of *analogy, logical justness, argumentative precision,* and *sophistry.*

—A metaphysician; for you speak of *evil, infinity, scepticism, perfection,* and *blind fate.*

—A mathematician; for you speak of *proportion.*

—A soothsayer; for you speak of *enchantment* and *witch craft.*

—A rhetorician; for you speak of *hodge-podge.*

—A cook; for you speak of *Solomon Gundy, composed of raw fish and flesh.*

—A swine-keeper; for you speak of *ringing hogs snouts.*

In short, your productions evince your intimate knowledge of all arts and sciences.

I hope, sir, you will acknowledge I am not so much of a *block head,* but I can perceive your great abilities; your accurate discernment; your exact judgment; your comprehensive understanding; your refined taste; your retentive memory; your vigorous fancy; your lively genius; your noble invention; your elegant wit; your &c. &c.

I have the honor to be,

Most mighty,

Most tremendous writer,

With the utmost devotion, respect,

esteem, gratitude, and affection,

Your most obedient, most humble,

most devoted, and most

profound servant,

DEMOCRITUS.

19th December, 1787.

P. S. *Pardon my presumption, in suggesting, that you might* cool *the fire of Brutus, Cato, &c, by the application of* Clysters. *I were on the point of knocking a fellow down, for asserting, that you are better qualified to handle a clyster-pipe than a pen.*

I am, as above, DEMOCRITUS.

1. On 20 December the *New York Journal* announced that it would print the reply to "Examiner" by "Democritus" the next day. This essay by "Democritus" was the second of three that he wrote attacking "Examiner." (See headnote to "Examiner" I, *New York Journal,* 11 December, above.) "Democritus" gives some hints as to the identity of the "Examiner"; also he is more explicit in his third essay that is printed in the *New York Journal* on 28 December (below).

2. For the terms "gutta serena" and "Solomon Gundy," see "Examiner" III, *New York Journal*, 19 December, notes 2 and 3 (above).

3. A reference to Hugh Blair (1718–1800), a Presbyterian minister and Regius Professor of Rhetoric and Belles-Lettres at the University of Edinburgh, whose sermons and lectures on rhetoric and belles lettres were widely published. Some of Blair's writings were published in a series of "small volumes," *The Beauties of. . . .* See *Sentimental Beauties and Moral Delineations from the Writings of the Celebrated Dr. Blair . . .* (London, 1782).

4. On 22 December, the printer of the *New York Journal* informed his readers that for "winter" they should read "writer." (See *New York Journal*, 22 December, Mfm:N.Y.)

5. On 22 December, the printer of the *New York Journal* informed his readers that for "mind" they should read "mud." (See *New York Journal*, 22 December, Mfm:N.Y.)

Publius: The Federalist 25 (Alexander Hamilton)
New York Packet, 21 December 1787

Standing army needed. For text, see CC:364. For reprintings, see Appendix IV, below.

Publius: The Federalist 26 (Alexander Hamilton)
New York Independent Journal, 22 December 1787

U.S. under new Constitution will effectively control army. For text, see CC:366. For reprintings, see Appendix IV, below.

Editors' Note
New York Reprinting of Richard Henry Lee's
Proposed Amendments to the Constitution
22 December 1787–24 January 1788

The Constitutional Convention adjourned on 17 September and on the same day Governor Edmund Randolph, a delegate, wrote fellow Virginian Richard Henry Lee (then attending Congress in New York City), explaining why he had not signed the Constitution. The next day George Mason, another Virginia delegate, also wrote Lee explaining why he had not signed the Constitution. (Neither letter is extant.) On 20 September the Constitution was read in Congress and a few days later it was reported that Lee was "forming propositions for essential alterations in the Constitution, which will, in effect, be to oppose it" (Edward Carrington to James Madison, 23 September, RCS:Va., 14).

On 26 and 27 September Congress debated the manner in which it should send the Constitution to the states. Opponents of the Constitution, including Lee, wanted it forwarded to the states with Congress indicating that the Convention had violated the Articles of Confederation and the congressional resolution of 21 February 1787 (CC:1). Supporters of the Constitution wanted it transmitted with Congress' approbation. Toward the end of the debate on 27 September, Lee proposed amendments to the Constitution including a bill of rights, but Congress did not consider them or place them on the journal. The next day Congress, as a compromise, voted unanimously to send the Constitution to the states without approbation or disapproval, but with the recommendation that the state legislatures call ratifying conventions. (See "The Confederation Congress and the Constitution," 26–28 September, above.)

Between 29 September and 5 October Lee sent copies of his amendments to George Mason and to Elbridge Gerry of Massachusetts, who also had refused to sign the Constitution. (Gerry was in New York City at this time.) Lee also forwarded copies to William Shippen, Jr., his brother-in-law living in Philadelphia, and to Samuel Adams, Lee's old revolutionary compatriot from Massachusetts (RCS:Va., 25, 28–30, 32–33, 36–39). While still in New York City on 16 October, Lee wrote to Governor Randolph expressing his opinion on the Constitution and enclosing a copy of his amendments (RCS:Va., 59–67). Lee probably distributed copies among some of the city's Antifederalists, although there is no record that the amendments circulated there in manuscript as they did in Virginia. Lee had no intention of keeping his opposition to the Constitution a secret and he encouraged both Shippen and Randolph to make the amendments public.

On 16 November Lee's amendments appeared in the Winchester *Virginia Gazette*, but this printing went largely unnoticed. Lee's 16 October letter and the accompanying amendments were printed in the Petersburg *Virginia Gazette* on 6 December and then reprinted throughout America. In New York, the letter and amendments were reprinted in the *New York Journal* on 22 and 24 December and in the *Albany Gazette* on 10 and 24 January 1788.

Throughout the United States, especially in Virginia, the responses to Lee's letter and amendments were voluminous. He was criticized in about a dozen major essays, although none of these was original to any New York newspaper. In fact, Lee's letter and amendments appear to have been mostly ignored in New York's newspapers and in the private letters of New Yorkers. One of the major responses to Lee was Philadelphia merchant Tench Coxe's "An American," which appeared in the Philadelphia *Independent Gazetteer* on 28 December (CC:392–A). On the same day Coxe wrote Virginia congressman James Madison in New York City, requesting that Madison get the essay reprinted in, among other places, "some of the country News Papers of New York and New England" (CC:392–B). On 3 January 1788 Madison replied to Coxe, informing him that he had shown the essay to Alexander Hamilton who read it "with equal pleasure & approbation with myself." According to Madison, Hamilton "seems to think that the Farmers of New York are in no danger of being infected with an improper jealousy of a sacrifice of their interests to a partiality for commerce or navigation" (CC:392–C). (In his letter, Lee had complained that navigation acts could pass Congress by a simple majority, whereby the seven Northern States could "by law create the most oppressive monopoly upon the five southern states.")

For the text of Lee's letter and amendments and for a full discussion of their circulation and the responses to them outside New York, see CC:325.

Examiner IV
New York Journal, 24 December 1787[1]

MR. GREENLEAF, Candour obliges me to allow, that Brutus possesses a genius something above mediocrity, for he writes in a plain, perspicuous, and, indeed, elegant manner. To an uncommon share of natural sagacity, he adds an extraordinary degree of industry, perseverance, and precision, in the prosecution of his researches: but, alas! the sight of his political eye is very defective. The component parts of the new constitution, appear to him like a confused image; and he forms his reasonings and conclusions from this imperfect vision. The constitution therefore remains invulnerable from his attacks, as he has not brought a single charge against it that has not already been solidly refuted. This long-winded anti-federal champion entertains his readers, with a tedious rhodomantade, upon the impossibility of a republic's long subsisting, over a country so widely extended as the United States: but what argument has he produced in support of his position? None, indeed, of the least weight or significance: for as there never existed a nation since the world was made, who were circumstanced as we are, so it is impossible for us to derive any information or advantage from the sources of former experience.

He next finds fault with the representation, and observes, that two thousand representatives would not, at the present day, be too large a number for the security of liberty.

In the name of wonder and all the sciences! what idea does he mean to convey, by such a random shot as this, to the ignorant and uninformed? What would be the effect of a representation, according to this rule, when our numbers increase to fifty millions? The legislative body would then consist of at least thirty thousand members. From such a legislative mob, gracious heaven defend us and our posterity.

It is needless for me to follow Brutus through all his windings, twistings, turnings, flackings, wearings, and tearings. His political knowledge, which is the basis or lowest region of his intellects, appears as a vail sparkling with infernal fire, in some cases black as smoke, and in others pale and livid as a corpse.

I really pity the situation of that poor devil Democritus, who is stark staring mad. My advice is, that he be sent in the next packet to England, and confined in Tothill-field's Bridewell,[2] along with his literary brother the love-distracted John Stone.

1. "Examiner" responds to "Brutus" I (size of a republic), *New York Journal*, 18 October and "Brutus" III–IV (representation), *ibid.*, 15, 29 November (all above).
2. Bridewell was a prison located in the Tothill Fields area of Westminster in England.

Publius: The Federalist 27 (Alexander Hamilton) New York Packet, 25 December 1787

Laws will be better enforced under new Constitution. For text, see CC:378. For reprintings, see Appendix IV, below.

Lansingburgh Northern Centinel, 25 December 1787[1]

A correspondent remarks, that the vile, dirty arts certain great characters in this state have had recourse to, and are still making use of, to prejudice the honest uninformed part of the community against the new federal system of government, by circulating, in a private manner, an antifederal piece signed *The Centinel*,[2] and other productions of our enemies, containing falshoods and sophistical arguments, of which even *they* themselves are ashamed, is a species of villainy beneath our avowed enemies. It is by no means extraordinary they should endeavour to conceal themselves in this low business, as in future elections they may, and most probably will, wish to make the electors believe they have ever had the good of their country more at heart, than their own private interest and aggrandizement: But in spite of all their cunning, the discerning part of the citizens are well convinced from what quarter, and with what views, those scarecrow tales are privately circulated, consequently they will not have the effect these propagators intend, as the freemen of this country feel too great a degree of independence to be guided in point of judgment by any one, unless it be where truth, reason, justice, and the good of their country direct; especially in a matter so momentous as that of their very existance as a United Nation.—Did those distributors believe themselves to be doing their country a service, they would not be ashamed to avow their conduct and let their names be publicly known, that the citizens at large might applaud or censure them as justice determined—*Dark designs require secret, cautious conduct.*

1. Reprinted: *New York Morning Post*, 4 January 1788; *Pennsylvania Journal*, 19 January. The *Morning Post* omitted the last sentence.
2. For "Centinel," see "New York Reprinting of the Centinel Essays," 17 October 1787–12 April 1788 (above).

Publius: The Federalist 28 (Alexander Hamilton)
New York Independent Journal, 26 December 1787

Domestic insurrections and usurpation of authority will be less of a danger under new Constitution. For text, see CC:381. For reprintings, see Appendix IV, below.

Brutus VI
New York Journal, 27 December 1787[1]

It is an important question, whether the general government of the United States should be so framed, as to absorb and swallow up the state governments? or whether, on the contrary, the former ought not to be confined to certain defined national objects, while the latter should retain all the powers which concern the internal police of the states?

I have, in my former papers, offered a variety of arguments to prove, that a simple free government could not be exercised over this whole continent, and that therefore we must either give up our liberties and submit to an arbitrary one, or frame a constitution on the plan of confederation. Further reasons might be urged to prove this point— but it seems unnecessary, because the principal advocates of the new constitution admit of the position. The question therefore between us, this being admitted, is, whether or not this system is so formed as either directly to annihilate the state governments, or that in its operation it will certainly effect it. If this is answered in the affirmative, then the system ought not to be adopted, without such amendments as will avoid this consequence. If on the contrary it can be shewn, that the state governments are secured in their rights to manage the internal police of the respective states, we must confine ourselves in our enquiries to the organization of the government and the guards and provisions it contains to prevent a misuse or abuse of power. To determine this question, it is requisite, that we fully investigate the nature, and the extent of the powers intended to be granted by this constitution to the rulers.

In my last number[2] I called your attention to this subject, and proved, as I think, uncontrovertibly, that the powers given the legislature under the 8th section of the 1st article, had no other limitation than the discretion of the Congress. It was shewn, that even if the most favorable construction was given to this paragraph, that the advocates for the new constitution could wish, it will convey a power to lay and collect taxes, imposts, duties, and excises, according to the discretion of the legislature, and to make all laws which they shall judge proper and necessary to carry this power into execution. This I shewed would totally destroy all the power of the state governments. To confirm this, it is worth while to trace the operation of the government in some particular instances.

The general government is to be vested with authority to levy and collect taxes, duties, and excises; the separate states have also power to impose taxes, duties, and excises, except that they cannot lay duties on exports and imports without the consent of Congress. Here then the two governments have concurrent jurisdiction; both may lay impositions of this kind. But then the general government have supperadded to this power, authority to make all laws which shall be necessary and proper for carrying the foregoing power into execution. Suppose then that both governments should lay taxes, duties, and excises, and it should fall so heavy on the people that they would be unable, or be so burdensome that they would refuse to pay them both—would it not be necessary that the general legislature should suspend the collection of the state tax? It certainly would. For, if the people could not, or would not pay both, they must be discharged from the tax to the state, or the tax to the general government could not be collected.—The conclusion therefore is inevitable, that the respective state governments will not have the power to raise one shilling in any way, but by the permission of the Congress. I presume no one will pretend, that the states can exercise legislative authority, or administer justice among their citizens for any length of time, without being able to raise a sufficiency to pay those who administer their governments.

If this be true, and if the states can raise money only by permission of the general government, it follows that the state governments will be dependent on the will of the general government for their existence.

What will render this power in Congress effectual and sure in its operation is, that the government will have complete judicial and executive authority to carry all their laws into effect, which will be paramount to the judicial and executive authority of the individual states: in vain therefore will be all interference of the legislatures, courts, or magistrates of any of the states on the subject; for they will be subordinate to the general government, and engaged by oath to support it, and will be constitutionally bound to submit to their decisions.

The general legislature will be empowered to lay any tax they chuse, to annex any penalties they please to the breach of their revenue laws; and to appoint as many officers as they may think proper to collect the taxes. They will have authority to farm the revenues and to vest the farmer general, with his subalterns, with plenary powers to collect them, in any way which to them may appear eligible. And the courts of law, which they will be authorized to institute, will have cognizance of every case arising under the revenue laws, the conduct of all the officers employed in collecting them; and the officers of these courts will execute their judgments. There is no way, therefore, of avoiding the destruction of the state governments, whenever the Congress please to do it, unless the people rise up, and, with a strong hand, resist and prevent the execution of constitutional laws. The fear of this, will, it is presumed, restrain the general government, for some time, within proper bounds; but it will not be many years before they will have a revenue, and force, at their command, which will place them above any apprehensions on that score.

How far the power to lay and collect duties and excises, may operate to dissolve the state governments, and oppress the people, it is impossible to say. It would assist us much in forming a just opinion on this head, to consider the various objects to which this kind of taxes extend, in European nations, and the infinity of laws they have passed respecting them. Perhaps, if leisure will permit, this may be essayed in some future paper.

It was observed in my last number,[3] that the power to lay and collect duties and excises, would invest the Congress with authority to impose a duty and excise on every necessary and convenience of life. As the principal object of the government, in laying a duty or excise, will be, to raise money, it is obvious, that they will fix on such articles as are of the most general use and consumption; because, unless great quantities of the article, on which the duty is laid, is used, the revenue cannot be considerable. We may therefore presume, that the articles which will be the object of this species of taxes will be either the real necessaries of life; or if not these, such as from custom and habit are esteemed so. I will single out a few of the productions of our own country, which may, and probably will, be of the number.

Cider is an article that most probably will be one of those on which an excise will be laid, because it is one, which this country produces in great abundance, which is in very general use, is consumed in great quantities, and which may be said too not to be a real necessary of life.

An excise on this would raise a large sum of money in the United States. How would the power, to lay and collect an excise on cider, and to pass all laws proper and necessary to carry it into execution, operate in its exercise? It might be necessary, in order to collect the excise on cider, to grant to one man, in each county, an exclusive right of building and keeping cider-mills, and oblige him to give bonds and security for payment of the excise; or, if this was not done, it might be necessary to license the mills, which are to make this liquor, and to take from them security, to account for the excise; or, if otherwise, a great number of officers must be employed, to take account of the cider made, and to collect the duties on it.

Porter, ale, and all kinds of malt-liquors, are articles that would probably be subject also to an excise. It would be necessary, in order to collect such an excise, to regulate the manufactory of these, that the quantity made might be ascertained, or otherwise security could not be had for the payment of the excise. Every brewery must then be licensed, and officers appointed, to take account of its product, and to secure the payment of the duty, or excise, before it is sold. Many other articles might be named, which would be objects of this species of taxation, but I refrain from enumerating them. It will probably be said, by those who advocate this system, that the observations already made on this head, are calculated only to inflame the minds of the people, with the apprehension of dangers merely imaginary. That there is not the least reason to apprehend, the general legislature will exercise their power in this manner. To this I would only say, that these kinds of taxes exist in Great Britain, and are severely felt. The excise on cider and perry, was imposed in that nation a few years ago, and it is in the memory of every one, who read the history of the transaction, what great tumults it occasioned.[4]

This power, exercised without limitation, will introduce itself into every corner of the city, and country—It will wait upon the ladies at their toilett, and will not leave them in any of their domestic concerns; it will accompany them to the ball, the play, and the assembly; it will go with them when they visit, and will, on all occasions, sit beside them in their carriages, nor will it desert them even at church; it will enter the house of every gentleman, watch over his cellar, wait upon his cook in the kitchen, follow the servants into the parlour, preside over the table, and note down all he eats or drinks; it will attend him to his bed-chamber, and watch him while he sleeps; it will take cognizance of the professional man in his office, or his study; it will watch the merchant in the counting-house, or in his store; it will follow the mechanic to his shop, and in his work, and will haunt him in his family, and in his bed;

it will be a constant companion of the industrious farmer in all his labour, it will be with him in the house, and in the field, observe the toil of his hands, and the sweat of his brow; it will penetrate into the most obscure cottage; and finally, it will light upon the head of every person in the United States. To all these different classes of people, and in all these circumstances, in which it will attend them, the language in which it will address them, will be GIVE! GIVE!

A power that has such latitude, which reaches every person in the community in every conceivable circumstance, and lays hold of every species of property they possess, and which has no bounds set to it, but the discretion of those who exercise it. I say, such a power must necessarily, from its very nature, swallow up all the power of the state governments.

I shall add but one other observation on this head, which is this— It appears to me a solecism, for two men, or bodies of men, to have unlimited power respecting the same object. It contradicts the scripture maxim, which saith, "no man can serve two masters,"[5] the one power or the other must prevail, or else they will destroy each other, and neither of them effect their purpose. It may be compared to two mechanic powers, acting upon the same body in opposite directions, the consequence would be, if the powers were equal, the body would remain in a state of rest, or if the force of the one was superior to that of the other, the stronger would prevail, and overcome the resistance of the weaker.

But it is said, by some of the advocates of this system, "That the idea that Congress can levy taxes at pleasure, is false, and the suggestion wholly unsupported: that the preamble to the constitution is declaratory of the purposes of the union, and the assumption of any power not necessary to establish justice, &c. to provide for the common defence, &c. will be unconstitutional. Besides, in the very clause which gives the power of levying duties and taxes, the purposes to which the money shall be appropriated, are specified, viz. to pay the debts, and provide for the common defence and general welfare."[(a)] I would ask those, who reason thus, to define what ideas are included under the terms, to provide for the common defence and general welfare? Are these terms definite, and will they be understood in the same manner, and to apply to the same cases by every one? No one will pretend they will. It will then be matter of opinion, what tends to the general welfare; and the Congress will be the only judges in the matter. To provide for the general welfare, is an abstract proposition, which mankind differ in the explanation of, as much as they do on any political or moral proposition that can be proposed; the most opposite measures may be pursued by different parties, and both may profess, that they have in view the general welfare; and both sides may be honest in their professions, or both may have sinister views. Those who advocate this new constitution declare, they are influenced by a regard to the general welfare; those who oppose it, declare they are moved by the same principles; and I have no doubt but a number on both sides are honest in their professions; and yet nothing is more certain than this, that to adopt this constitution, and not to adopt it, cannot both of them be promotive of the general welfare.

It is as absurd to say, that the power of Congress is limited by these general expressions, "to provide for the common safety, and general welfare," as it would be to say, that it would be limited, had the constitution said they should have power to lay taxes, &c. at will and pleasure. Were this authority given, it might be said, that under it the legislature could not do injustice, or pursue any measures, but such as were calculated to promote the public good, and happiness. For every man, rulers as well as others, are bound by the immutable laws of God and reason, always to will what is right. It is certainly right and fit, that the governors of every people should provide for the common defence and general welfare; every government, therefore, in the world, even the greatest despot, is limited in the exercise of his power. But however just this reasoning may be, it would be found, in practice, a most pitiful restriction. The government would always say, their measures were designed and calculated to promote the public good; and there being no judge between them and the people, the rulers themselves must, and would always, judge for themselves.

There are others of the favourers of this system, who admit, that the power of the Congress under it, with respect to revenue, will exist without limitation, and contend, that so it ought to be.

It is said, "The power to raise armies, to build and equip fleets, and to provide for their support, ought to exist without limitation, because it is impossible to foresee, or to define, the extent and variety of national exigencies, or the correspondent extent and variety of the means which may be necessary to satisfy them."

This, it is said, "is one of those truths which, to correct and unprejudiced minds, carries its own evidence along with it. It rests upon axioms as simple as they are universal: the means ought to be proportioned to the end; the person, from whose agency the attainment of any end is expected, ought to possess the means by which it is to be attained."[b]

This same writer insinuates, that the opponents to the plan promulgated by the convention, manifests a want of candor, in objecting to the extent of the powers proposed to be vested in this government; because he asserts, with an air of confidence, that the powers ought to be unlimited as to the object to which they extend; and that this position, if not self-evident, is at least clearly demonstrated by the foregoing mode of reasoning. But with submission to this author's better judgment, I humbly conceive his reasoning will appear, upon examination, more specious than solid. The means, says the gentleman, ought to be proportioned to the end: admit the proposition to be true it is then necessary to enquire, what is the end of the government of the United States, in order to draw any just conclusions from it. Is this end simply to preserve the general government, and to provide for the common defence and general welfare of the union only? certainly not: for beside this, the state governments are to be supported, and provision made for the managing such of their internal concerns as are allotted to them. It is admitted, "that the circumstances of our country are such, as to demand a compound, instead of a simple, a confederate, instead of a sole government," that the objects of each ought to be pointed out, and that each ought to possess ample authority to execute the powers committed to them. The government then, being complex in its nature, the end it has in view is so also; and it is as necessary, that the state governments should possess the means to attain the ends expected from them, as for the general government. Neither the general government, nor the state governments, ought to be vested with all the powers proper to be exercised for promoting the ends of government. The powers are divided between them—certain ends are to be attained by the one, and other certain ends by the other; and these, taken together, include all the ends of good government. This being the case, the conclusion follows, that each should be furnished with the means, to attain the ends, to which they are designed.

To apply this reasoning to the case of revenue; the general government is charged with the care of providing for the payment of the debts of the United States; supporting the general government, and providing for the defence of the union. To obtain these ends, they should be furnished with means. But does it thence follow, that they should command all the revenues of the United States! Most certainly it does not. For if so, it will follow, that no means will be left to attain other ends, as necessary to the happiness of the country, as those committed to their care. The individual states have debts to discharge; their legislatures and executives are to be supported, and provision is to be made for the administration of justice in the respective states. For these objects the general government has no authority to provide; nor is it proper it should. It is clear then, that the states should have the command of such revenues, as to answer the ends they have to obtain. To say, "that the circumstances that endanger the safety of nations are infinite," and from hence to infer, that all the sources of revenue in the states should be yielded to the general government, is not conclusive reasoning: for the Congress are authorized only to controul in general concerns, and not regulate local and internal ones; and these are as essentially requisite to be provided for as those. The peace and happiness of a community is as intimately connected with the prudent direction of their domestic affairs, and the due administration of justice among themselves, as with a competent provision for their defence against foreign invaders, and indeed more so.

Upon the whole, I conceive, that there cannot be a clearer position than this, that the state governments ought to have an uncontroulable power to raise a revenue, adequate to the exigencies of their governments; and, I presume, no such power is left them by this constitution.

(a) Vide an examination into the leading principles of the federal constitution, printed in Philadelphia, Page 34.[6]

(b) Vide the Federalist, No. 23.[7]

1. On 26 December the *New York Journal* announced that "Brutus" VI would be published "To-Morrow." Unlike the first five numbers of "Brutus," numbers VI–IX, XI–XVI are not addressed to the citizens or people of the state of New York. "Brutus" VI was not reprinted.

2. See "Brutus" V, *New York Journal*, 13 December (above).

3. *Ibid.*

4. A reference to the excise tax on cider adopted in 1763 by Parliament, upon the recommendation of Lord Bute's administration. This unpopular tax touched off several riots. Eight days after the act levying the tax received the royal assent, Lord Bute resigned as first lord of the treasury.

5. Matthew 6:24.

6. "A Citizen of America" (Noah Webster), 17 October (Mfm:Pa. 142; and CC:173).

7. Publius, *The Federalist* 23, *New York Packet*, 18 December (CC:352).

A Republican
New York Journal, 27 December 1787[1]

To the PEOPLE of the UNITED STATES.

FRIENDS, *and* FELLOW CITIZENS, As the press has teemed with productions respecting the new constitution, it is to be presumed, that most of you have already formed an opinion, as to its general principles; it is, therefore not my intention to trouble you with any remarks on those parts, which have been discussed; but, to call your attention to a point, which has been entirely unnoticed, and which appears to be sufficiently interesting and important to demand the most serious consideration.

It is necessary to premise, that the proposed constitution, if adopted, must be considered, as an original compact, deriving its sanction from the concurrence of the people, totally abolishing the existing federal system, and establishing a government, different in style, construction, and principles:—And as there is no provision made, for continuing in force the acts and ordinances of the present confederation, they, of course, will be abrogated.

The convention that formed our state constitution acted upon this principle, when they ordained, that the common and statute laws of England, together with the acts of the colonial legislature, and the resolutions of the convention, should continue to be the law of the state;[2] but even if this should be an erroneous position, yet by the dissolution of the present system and its different offices, it is obvious that the acts and ordinances made under it, will become inapplicable and inefficient. Now, as it is declared by the new constitution, that no ex post facto laws shall be passed, will not all responsibility in those, who have been entrusted with the management of our monied concerns, be destroyed by this absolute and unqualified prohibition? Will not all laws, enacted by the general legislature, to oblige delinquents to account for the public treasure in their hands, come under the description of ex post facto laws, and as repugnant to the constitution, be nugatory and void?

The 1st paragraph of the 6th article, directs, that ["]all debts contracted, and engagements entered into, before the adoption of this constitution, shall be as valid against[3] the United States, under this constitution as under the confederation."—It was highly proper to give this security to our national creditors; the provision however, evinces it to have been the sense of the framers of the new constitution, that the acts and ordinances, by which the federal debts were contracted, and engagements entered into, would become void by the establishment of this new government—for, upon this principle only, it could have been deemed necessary. There is something very remarkable in the language of this clause—it provides, that all debts contracted, and engagements entered into, before the adoption of the constitution, should be valid against the United States.—But there is nothing which ordains, that debts due to the United States, or contracts in their favor, shall be valid—although such a provision, it is evident, was equally essential and necessary.

That the secret committees of Congress, who, for a long time, possessed the uncontrouled command of the key of the continental treasury—drew from thence immense sums of money—and that large sums, have also, from time to time, been issued by resolutions of Congress, to the different officers of the various staff departments, are uncontrovertible facts, and that a great proportion of those monies, to the amount of some millions of dollars, remains to this day unaccounted for, cannot be denied, and if it should, I presume a recurrence to the treasury, and other public offices, will establish it beyond the possibility of dispute.[4]

The people of America are impoverished by a long and ruinous war, borne down with taxes; and it requires their utmost exertions to pay their foreign and domestic debts. In this situation, my fellow citizens, would it be prudent, would it be justifiable, like a neighbouring state, to commence a jubilee, kindle up bonfires, set your bells ringing, and execute a general release to the public debtors[5]—debtors who have sported away your substance[6] in the hour of your distress, and who now wantonly riot on the spoils of your bleeding count[r]y?—it certainly would not. You ought therefore seriously to consider, before you give your fiat to an instrument, which will inevitably annihilate the debts due to the United States. I am sensible, ex post facto laws are generally deemed dangerous and iniquitous—and, in this point of view, their prohibition has been held out, by the advocates of the new constitution, as a lure for its adoption. History, and daily experience however, evince their necessity in some cases, particularly for the purpose of bringing those, concerned in the management of public monies, to justice. It is well worthy of observation, my friends and fellow citizens, that by the new constitution, our most[7] inestimable rights, the trial by jury, and the freedom of the press; nay, even the liberty of conscience, are committed to the mercy of the general government, without a single stipulation for their security, and you are told by its advocates, that these important privileges are safely deposited. That the dangers apprehended from their abuse are imaginary and idle—and that from the nature of the government, a bill of rights would have been superfluous and ridiculous. How then are we to reconcile this restriction of power, in the representatives of the people, as to ex post facto laws, with the assertion that all power may be safely entrusted to them. Is it not a solecism in politics, through fear of the abuse of a power, which is in some instances absolutely necessary, totally to prohibit a government from the exercise of it—and yet commit our most important rights (which can never be necessary to promote the public good) into their hand, without the least limitation; you have been informed, in a speech made in favour of the new constitution, by one of its framers, and who (if credit can be given to common fame) took a principal lead in the business, that "it is the nature of man to pursue his own interest in preference to the public good."[8]—and as it is well known, that there were gentlemen in the convention of great weight and influence, who have, in divers characters, been most largely concerned in the monied transactions of the United States, and whose accounts remain unsettled,[9] is it uncharitable to conclude, that they were influenced by the above sentiment of their friend and colleague, and consequently solicitous to establish a principle which would effectually preclude a settlement of their accounts; and is this not rendered the more probable, by the consideration, that their agents and connections throughout the states, are the warmest advocates, for its precipitate adoption even before the people could have time to understand its principles and reflect upon the resulting consequences.

It is, however, immaterial to the public, whether the clause against ex post facto laws, proceeded from corruption or inattention; its effects will be the same.[10]

1. On 26 December the *New York Journal* and the *Daily Advertiser* both announced that they had received "A Republican" and that it would be printed the next day, when both newspapers did indeed publish "A Republican." The text printed here is taken from the *Journal*. The *Journal* and *Advertiser* versions differ in punctuation, capitalization, spelling, and in the use of italics. (See notes 3, 6, and 7.) "A Republican" was reprinted in the *New York Packet*, 1 January 1788, and in the Philadelphia *Freeman's Journal*, 9 January.

2. The reference is to Article XXXV of the New York state constitution of 1777. See Appendix I (below).

3. "Against" is italicized in the *Daily Advertiser.*

4. Beginning early in the Revolution, Congress appointed secret committees, on such matters as commerce and foreign affairs, that became standing committees. The activities of these committees were kept secret even from Congress, although Congress could require that the committees produce documents when called upon to do so. Congress supplied the committees with funds, sometimes in large amounts. The agents of the committees were given considerable discretionary powers to act on their own initiatives. Sometimes, the committees made contracts with their own members or former members, giving rise to charges of corruption. During the Revolution, Philadelphia merchant Robert Morris controlled two of the most important committees, those on commerce and foreign affairs.

5. Probably the state of Rhode Island, the legislature of which often adopted legislation favorable to debtors.

6. "Substance" is italicized in the *Daily Advertiser.*

7. "Most" is italicized in the *Daily Advertiser.*

8. See James Wilson's 6 October speech before a Philadelphia public meeting (CC:134, p. 343). See also "New York Reprinting of James Wilson's 6 October Speech Before a Philadelphia Public Meeting," 13–25 October (above).

9. Among the members of the Constitutional Convention whose Revolutionary accounts were still unsettled were Pennsylvanians Thomas Mifflin and Robert Morris. (See "Centinel" XVI and XVII, Philadelphia *Independent Gazetteer*, 26 February and 24 March 1788, for the harsh criticism directed at these two men in Pennsylvania [CC:565, 642].)

10. Directly below this item the *New York Journal* reprinted "The Dissent of the Minority of the Pennsylvania Convention" (CC:353. See also the Editors' Note immediately below for the reception of the "Dissent" in New York.).

Editors' Note
New York Reprinting of the Dissent of the Minority of
the Pennsylvania Convention, 27 December 1787–April 1788

The Pennsylvania Convention convened on 20 November, attained a quorum on 21 November, and debated the Constitution until 12 December, when it was ratified. Early in the debates the Convention defeated an Antifederalist motion to allow any member to enter on the journal his reasons for dissenting to any vote. (Such a privilege was accorded to members of the state Assembly by the state constitution of 1776.) When an earlier motion to ratify the Constitution was reintroduced on 12 December, Antifederalist Robert Whitehill presented petitions, praying that the Constitution should not be ratified without amendments, especially not without a bill of rights. After the petitions were tabled, Whitehill read fifteen proposed amendments and then moved that the Convention adjourn to allow Pennsylvanians to consider these amendments and any amendments that might be recommended by other states. Whitehill's motion was rejected. The Constitution was then ratified by a vote of 46 to 23. On 13 December Whitehill and fellow Antifederalist John Smilie protested that Whitehill's amendments were not inserted in the Convention Journal as they should have been. Recognizing that the opponents of the Constitution would lose a vote to insert the amendments on the Journal, Smilie withdrew his motion requesting that the amendments be so inserted.

The *Pennsylvania Herald* printed Whitehill's amendments on 15 December and soon after the Convention's minority published its formal objections and the amendments. On 18 December the "Dissent of the Minority" appeared in the *Pennsylvania Packet* and in a broadside struck by Eleazer Oswald of the Philadelphia *Independent Gazetteer*. Dated Philadelphia, 12 December, the dissent was signed by twenty-one of the twenty-three Convention members who voted against ratification of the Constitution.

The "Dissent" was probably written by Samuel Bryan. Bryan also wrote the "Centinel" essays. The "Dissent" summarized the arguments made against the Constitution in the Convention and the public debate preceding and during the Convention. It attacked the authority of the Constitutional Convention to draft a new constitution and its secret proceedings. It denounced the force used to secure a quorum of the state Assembly in calling the state Convention and the procedures employed by the Convention's majority. Most important, the "Dissent," as the formal statement of the Convention's minority, provided the public with Whitehill's amendments.

Antifederalists attempted to circulate the "Dissent" throughout much of America in newspapers, pamphlets, and broadsides. The "Dissent" was reprinted in three New York City daily newspapers—the *New York Morning Post*, 24, 25, 26, 27, and 28 December; the *Daily Advertiser*, 25, 26, and 27 December; and the *New York Journal*, 27, 29, and 31 December. The *Daily Advertiser* obtained the "Dissent" as early as 24 December, when it revealed that the "Dissent" was received "by the last Southern Mail." The *New York Journal* announced on 26 December that it would print the "Dissent" on the 27th. On 4 January 1788 the *Journal* informed its readers that "A few Copies" of the "Dissent" were still available for sale at the newspaper's office. Ashbel Stoddard of the *Hudson Weekly Gazette* published an abbreviated edition of the "Dissent" in a four-page broadside (Evans 20620). Stoddard omitted the first four paragraphs. Beginning in the second week of April 1788, the "Dissent" also began to circulate throughout the state as part of an Antifederalist pamphlet anthology which the New York Federal Republican Committee distributed to local county committees. (See III below for a full discussion of this anthology.) A correspondent of the *Hudson Weekly Gazette*, 10 April, was so distressed by the "Dissent's" assiduous circulation in Columbia County that he asked Federalists to circulate "an antidote against this artful and designing piece." (See Columbia County election, IV below.)

The "Dissent" elicited considerable response throughout America, although in New York only a few people commented upon it. On 30 December Robert R. Livingston noted that "I am fearful that violence of party in Pennsylvania will excite new troubles there, & the address of the minority is evidently calculated for very dangerous purposes, & may possibly be the means of effecting them" (to John Stevens, Sr., Mfm:N.Y.). Noah Webster—writing as "America"—published a major criticism of the "Dissent" in the *Daily Advertiser* on 31 December (below). Brief criticisms followed in "Americanus" VI and "Curtiopolis," *Daily Advertiser*, 12 and 18 January 1788 (both below). The "Dissent" was praised briefly by "A Plebeian" (Melancton Smith?) in a pamphlet entitled *An Address to the People of the State of New York* published on 17 April (III below).

For the text of the "Dissent of the Minority of the Pennsylvania Convention," its background and authorship, and its national circulation and the national response to it, see CC:353.

Henrietta Maria Colden to Frances Bland Tucker
New York, 28 December 1787 (excerpt)[1]

. . . There seems little disposition towards Gaiety at present in this City—The Theatre is open, and we have an Assembly, as usual but

Public Places are thinly attended, and fewer private Parties than I ever saw in this Place—The Minds of all ranks of People appear affected with the Situation of this Country, a general anxiety for the Event, suspends the love of pleasure. All the Men are immers'd in Politicks—; And the Women say "Life, is not Life without them." I tell them 'tis all a Mistake, but they won't believe me. . . .

1. RC, Tucker-Coleman Papers, Swem Library, College of William and Mary. This letter was carried to Tucker in Matoax, Va., by Edward Carrington, a Virginia delegate to Congress. Colden was the widow of Richard Nicolls Colden of New York City, a former officer in the British army and surveyor of customs at the time of his death in 1777. She was a prominent member of New York society; in this letter she sent Tucker the regards of Alexander Hamilton and William Duer. Frances Bland Tucker (1752–1788), the widow of John Randolph of Matoax, was married to St. George Tucker (1752–1827), a prominent Virginia lawyer.

Democritus
New York Journal, 28 December 1787[1]

MR. GREENLEAF, I was until lately a most violent enemy to the new Constitution; I considered it as a damnable design to reduce my countrymen to a state of vassallage; I viewed it with abhorrence and detestation; but my sentiments are totally altered. I now esteem it a perfect production, and will here unfold the reasons for my political regeneration, and hope, they will convert my deluded countrymen from their errors, and render their concurrence universal.—Know then, sir, I once thought Dr. Rushlight's assertion in the convention of Pennsylvania, *that the proposed government descended from heaven,*[2] little better than blasphemy and impiety; I supposed it was, in other words, saying, that the devil had made a fresh eruption from hell, and became Lord Paramount of the celestial regions. But, when I reflected upon the Doctor's learning and genius, and upon the rationality of all his remarks, I concluded, that he must have some good reasons for his observation, which he did not think proper to divulge. This subject employed my greatest attention, and the more I revolved it in my mind, the more I was involved in doubt and uncertainty. Until at length, sir, I got happily extricated from the difficulty, and now am convinced of the truth of the Doctor's position.

That some people of Scotland have supernatural and prophetic visions is a fact as true as it is notorious. Might not then Mr. W—n[3] have perceived the proposed form of government, by the power of second sight, and have known its excellent tendency to promote the public good, by his prognostic faculty? certainly he might—and, no doubt, this circumstance induced the assent of the Fœderal Convention, when he recommended it to their adoption.—This hypothesis, I will establish upon uncontrovertible grounds.

1st. Mr. W—n's conduct demonstrates the reality of his inspiration: he was previously a man of worldly knowledge, and versed in profane studies—but his behavior in the convention of Pennsylvania shews a wonderful change for the better; he speaks of the heathenish Homer and his commentators with contempt, and hints that no plan of a fœderal government was to be found in his works, though by profession a lawyer; yet he forgets a remarkable passage in Blackstone, about the trial by jury in Sweden[4]—while he recollects two whole lines in Sternhold and Hopkins's psalms:[5] this behavior evinces, that he neglected and despised his former studies, and betook himself to the perusal of pious and holy books—and, this could never have happened, unless he were under the influence of some extraordinary occurrence.

2d. The unanimity of the fœderal convention, is infallible evidence of the truth of the Doctor's position; how is it possible, that thirty-nine men should be unanimous in favor of a government, unless they were convinced of its descention from heaven.

3d. Some priests are strongly in favor of the new constitution, and not only pray, but preach for its adoption; it is conjectured, that some of them have a design to excommunicate the bible, and introduce it as a system of faith—and would it not be a solecism in language to say, that divines prize politics more than divinity?

4th. The infinite perfection of the government demonstrates its heavenly source. After having thus established, with irresistable arguments, an important fact—it behoves me to answer two objections against its certainty.

1st. It may be alledged, if it were true that Mr. W—n was, by inspiration, directed to compose the new constitution, this momentous circumstance would never have been concealed from the people: I answer, that the great modesty of the seer prevented its promulgation—and the ambition of the conventioneers, which stimulated them to arrogate to themselves—a production too perfect for the work of man.

2d. It may be further remarked—that the inspiration of an attorney is extremely improbable, and too miraculous for belief—but, did not Balaam's ass see the angel of the Lord, and save his master's life by disobeying him?[6] Why then might not Mr. W—n, though an attorney, have a government revealed to him? and by disobeying the instructions of his constituents, he has very probably preserved their liberty and property. So the ass and he acted precisely alike, being both influenced by preternatural causes.

O ye people of America, rest satisfied and rejoice—for ye are greatly favored—like the children of Israel—ye are blessed with a government from heaven. In imitation of the Jews, blend physician and priest together in the high-priest; place the great Doctor in the shoes of Aaron, with this single restriction, that he never set up a golden calf for the people to worship.[7] Appoint the great attorney seer, generalissimo of the United States, and agree to the celestial constitution.

I am conscious, Mr. Greenleaf, that I shall be derided by sceptics, but I despise their derision. I have established my creed upon the rock of truth, and the man who disbelieves it, must be a disciple of Pyrrho.[8]

DEMOCRITUS.

P. S. I hope my good friend Dr. Sawney M'Foolish, the Examiner, will not be angry with me, for employing another physician, to cure me of my madness. I am sure, he must ken vary weele, that I know he is mickle learned in quackery, and of the twa, is the stoutest fighter for the constitution, whilk the convention did tak upon themselves to make. I am glad to see him gie baith the brute and cat a bonny downset. He needna think otherwise, but I was free frae jocularity, when I tauld him, I wud make a set of buiks from his writings, whilk wud shaw him a bennisun to the bairns of Adam; and I donna doubt, but he will be sick mickle thought of in Europe, that he will be mad— a doctor of Medicine, since he has found out so important a thing, that Solomon Gundy[9] will throw a man into a fever; and I trust the good people of America, will be grateful, and reward him with the office of man-midwife to her sacred majesty, the lady Presidentess, under the new government, for his able performances in defence of it.

1. In the postscript to this essay, "Democritus" criticizes "Examiner" for the third time, the first two times having occurred in the *New York Journal* on 14 and 21 December (both above). "Democritus" also comes very close to naming Dr. Charles McKnight as "Examiner," when he refers to "Dr. Sawney M'Foolish." See "Examiner" I, *New York Journal*, 11 December (above).

2. The reference is to Philadelphia physician Benjamin Rush's speech of 12 December in the Pennsylvania Convention in which he declared that Divine Providence was employed in drafting the Constitution. Two different summary versions of Rush's speech appeared in the *Pennsylvania Herald*, 15 December; and in the *Pennsylvania Gazette*, Philadelphia *Independent Gazetteer*, and *Pennsylvania Packet*, 19 December. The *Herald's* version was reprinted in both the *New York Journal* and *Daily Advertiser* on 22 December; while the other version was reprinted in the *Daily Advertiser*, 28 December; *New York Morning Post*, 31 December; and *Albany Gazette*, 7 February 1788.

The republication of the latter version in New York City was perhaps the result of Rush's own efforts. On 21 December Rush wrote to William Irvine, a Pennsylvania delegate to Congress, that "I am reduced to the necessity of doing myself justice from a late attack upon me in the news paper, by requesting you to publish the enclosed extract from One of my Speeches in convention in *all* the news papers in New York.—I am concerned more for the honor of the cause committed to me by fellow citizens, than for my own reputation—for as a fool & a madman I am you know *Scandal proof* in Pennsylvania." (See RCS:Pa., 592–96; and CC:357.)

Rush was also criticized by "A Countryman" VI, *New York Journal*, 14 February 1788; and "A Plebeian," *An Address to the People of the State of New York*, 17 April (both III below).

3. James Wilson, a member of the Pennsylvania Convention and a strong proponent
of the Constitution. See "New York Reprinting of James Wilson's 6 October Speech Before a Philadelphia Public Meeting," 13–25 October (above).

4. On 8 December, in the Pennsylvania Convention, James Wilson and Thomas Mc-
Kean, another supporter of the Constitution, challenged Antifederalist William Findley's
assertion that jury trial existed in Sweden. Two days later Findley produced his sources,
one of which was the third volume of William Blackstone's *Commentaries on the Laws of
England.* On 11 December Wilson acknowledged that Findley was correct. (See RCS:Pa.,
527–28, 532, 550–51.) This three-day exchange was reported in the *Pennsylvania Herald*
on 12 December, but the only New York newspaper to reprint this exchange was the *Daily
Advertiser* of 17 December.

5. On 3 December Wilson quoted several lines that he said were from Thomas Sternhold and John Hopkins' book of psalms (RCS:Pa., 460–61). The first edition of the psalms
by Sternhold alone appeared before 1549. The third edition, the first with Hopkins,
appeared in 1551. The complete book of psalms appeared in 1562 and numerous editions
(with additional contributors) under different titles followed.

Printed in the *Pennsylvania Herald,* 5 December, Wilson's speech was reprinted in the
Daily Advertiser, 10 December, *New York Journal,* 11 December, and *Hudson Weekly Gazette,*
20 December. "Squib" reported in the *New York Journal,* 18 December, that the "lines"
quoted by Wilson were "not in that version of the psalms, nor, I believe in any other"
(Mfm:Pa. 272).

6. Numbers 22:21–35.

7. For the episode of the golden calf, see Exodus 32.

8. Pyrrhon (c. 365–c. 275 B.C.), a philosopher, was the founder of Greek skepticism.

9. See "Examiner" III, *New York Journal,* 19 December, at note 3 and note 3 (above).

Publius: The Federalist 30 (Alexander Hamilton)
New York Packet, 28 December 1787

U.S. Congress will have power to levy and collect taxes, power lacking in
Confederation Congress. For text, see CC:391. For reprintings, see Appendix
IV, below.

Timothy Pickering to John Pickering
Philadelphia, 29 December 1787 (excerpt)[1]

Dear Brother

. . . Much opposition is expected in New-York. That state has long
been acting a disingenuous part. They refused the impost to Congress[2]—because half of New-Jersey, a great part of Connecticut, the
western part of Massachusetts, & Vermont, received their imported
goods thro' New-York, who put into her *own* treasury all the duties
arising on the goods consumed in the states above enumerated: and
the same selfish spirit seems still to actuate too many in that state: but
the federalists in it appear pretty confident that the new constitution
will be adopted, tho' not without a severe struggle. . . .

1. RC, Timothy Pickering Papers, MHi. Printed: CC:393 (longer excerpt). John Pickering of Salem (1740–1811), elder brother of Timothy, was justice of the peace, justice of the Common Pleas, and register of deeds for Essex County, Mass.

2. For New York and the federal Impost of 1783, see "Introduction" (above).

New York Journal, 29 December 1787[1]

Dr. PRICE observes, in his essay on the importance of the American revolution, ["]that the United States are now setting out; and all depends on the care and foresight with which a plan is begun, which hereafter will require only to be strenghtened and ripened. But that in America abuses have not gained sacredness by time—that there the way is open to social dignity and happiness, and reason may utter her voice with confidence and success. But that there is danger a society so happy will not be of long duration—that simplicity and virtue, will give way to depravity—that equality will in time, be lost—the cursed lust of domineering shew itself—liberty languish—and civil government gradually degenerate into an instrument, in the hands *of a few to oppress and plunder the many.*"[2]

1. Reprinted: *New Jersey Journal,* 2 January 1788.

2. Richard Price, *Observations on the Importance of the American Revolution, and the Means of Making It a Benefit to the World* . . . (London, 1785), in Bernard Peach, ed., *Richard Price and the Ethical Foundations of the American Revolution* . . . (Durham, N.C., 1979), 206, 207, 208. *Observations* first appeared in London in 1784. The first American edition was printed in Boston the same year (Evans 18739). Seven more American editions were published in 1785 and 1786. The italics were inserted by the *New York Journal.*

Roger Alden to Samuel William Johnson
New York, 31 December 1787 (excerpts)[1]

I thank You for the letter of 30th Sept. and in return will give a general Statement of the politics on the Continent—the report of the Convention affords a fruitful subject for wits, politicians and Law-makers—the presses, which conceived by the incubation of the Convention are delivered from the pangs of travail, & have become prolific indeed—the offspring is so numerous, that the public ear has become deaf to the cries of the distressed, and grow impatient for the christning of the first born—

The opposition have many Characters of extensive knowledge and great influence—but their efforts have failed in some of the States. . . . It is not expected that New York will be among the number of the federalists—the Assembly meets in a few days—we shall be able to form a more accurate Judgment, when the Sentiments of the Legislature are known. . . .

[P.S.] You will receive with this some of the papers of this city—I have not been able to procure all which contain the pieces against the constitution—a writer under the signature of Publius takes up the matter upon the best grounds—and is a very fair candid, sensible advocate upon the federal side—there is nothing personal or scurrilous in his writings—he only means to convince by plain reasoning—by arguments drawn from facts & experience.[2] . . .

1. RC, William Samuel Johnson Papers, DLC. Printed: CC:396. From Stratford, Conn., Alden (1754–1836) was a former major in the Continental Army, a deputy secretary of Congress, and a son-in-law of William Samuel Johnson, a Connecticut signer of the Constitution. Samuel William Johnson (1761–1846), a son of William Samuel Johnson, was living at this time in St. George's, Bermuda.

2. This postscript, written on a separate piece of paper, was docketed by Samuel William Johnson "Major Alden Decr. 31st. 87."

America
New York Daily Advertiser, 31 December 1787

On 24, 25, and 27 December three New York City newspapers—the *New York Morning Post, Daily Advertiser*, and *New York Journal*, respectively—began printing installments of the "Dissent of the Minority of the Pennsylvania Convention," one of the most substantial criticisms of the Constitutional Convention and the Constitution (CC:353. See also "New York Reprinting of the Dissent of the Minority of the Pennsylvania Convention," 27 December 1787–April 1788, above.). On 28 December Noah Webster, an active Federalist polemicist, noted in his diary that he was "Busy answering the address of the dissenting members of Pensylvania" (NN). Webster sent his response, signed "America," to the editor of the *Daily Advertiser*, thinking that the editors of the *New York Morning Post* and the *New York Journal* would reprint it. When the latter editors did not, Webster placed the following item in the *Advertiser* on 5 January 1788: "The Writer of the Address, under the signature of AMERICA, expected that the Printers, who published the *Address* and *Dissent* of the *Minority* in Pennsylvania, would insert the Answer, without any particular request. He flatters himself that they will still notice it, as soon as possible." Despite this challenge, only one paragraph of "America" was ever reprinted. (See note 16 below.) Webster included excerpts of this essay in *A Collection of Essays and Fugitiv Writings. On Moral, Historical, Political and Literary Subjects* (Boston, 1790), 142–50 (Evans 23053). (See notes 1 and 4–11, below.)

Noah Webster (1758–1843)—Connecticut native, graduate of Yale College (1778), teacher, grammarian, lexicographer, and author of textbooks—had recently moved from Philadelphia to New York City, where he was preparing to launch the first issue of the monthly *American Magazine*. He edited this magazine throughout most of 1788. A proponent of a strong central government, Webster published a tract in 1785 advocating such a government (Evans 19366). As "A Citizen of America," he published in Philadelphia on 17 October 1787 a pamphlet entitled *An Examination into the Leading Principles of the Federal Constitution Proposed by the Late Convention Held at Philadelphia. With Answers to the Principal Objections that Have Been Raised Against the System* (Evans 20865), which was advertised for sale in the *Daily Advertiser* on 22 October. (For the text of the pamphlet, see Mfm:Pa. 142, and for its background and circulation and the response to it, see CC:173.) In 1806 Webster published *A Compendious Dictionary of the English Language* and in 1828 he followed with the majesterial two-volume *An American Dictionary of the English Language.*

To the DISSENTING MEMBERS of the late CONVENTION of PENNSYLVANIA.

Gentlemen, Your long and elaborate publication, assigning the reasons for your refusing to subscribe the ratification of the NEW FEDERAL CONSTITUTION, has made its appearance in the public papers, and, I flatter myself, will be read throughout the United States. It will feed the flame of opposition among the weak, the wicked, the designing, and the factious; but it will make many new converts to the proposed Government, and furnish the old friends of it with new weapons of defence. The very attempt to excite uneasiness and disturbance in a State, about a measure legally and constitutionally adopted, after a long and ample discussion in a Convention of the people's Delegates, ⟨marks a disposition, beyond all conception, obstinate, base, and politically wicked. But *obstinacy* is the leading trait in your public characters, and, as it serves to give *consistency* to your actions, even in error, it cannot fail to procure you that share of respect which is paid to the *firmness* of Satan and his fellow apostates, who, after their expulsion from Heaven, had too much pride to *repent* and *ask for a re-admission.*⟩[1] My address to you will not be so lengthy as your publication; your arguments are *few,* altho' your harangue is *long* and *insidious.*

You begin with telling the world, that *no defect was discovered in the present Confederation, till after the war.* Why did you not publish the truth? You know, Gentlemen, that during six years of the war, we had *no Confederation at all.* You know that the war commenced in April, 1775, and that we had *no Confederation* till March, 1781. You know (for some of you are men of abilities and reading) or ought to know, a principle of *fear,* in time of war, operates more powerfully in binding together the States which have a common interest, than all the parchment compacts on earth. Could we, then, discover the defects of our present Confederation, with *two years'* experience only, and an enemy in our country? You know we could not.

I will not undertake to detect the falshood of every assertion, or the fallacy of all your reasoning on each article. In the most of them the public will anticipate any thing I could say, and confute your arguments as fast as they read them. But I must tell you, Gentlemen, that your reasoning against the *New Constitution* resembles that of Mr. Hume on

miracles.[2] You begin with some *gratis dicta*, which are denied; you assume *premises* which are *totally false*, and then reason on them with great
address. Your whole reasoning, and that of all the opposers of the Federal Government, is built on this *false principle*, that the *Federal Legislature*
will be a body *distinct from* and *independent* of the people. Unless your
opposition is grounded on *that principle*, it stands on *nothing*; and on
any *other* supposition, your arguments are but *declamatory nonsense*.

But the principle is false. The Congress, under the proposed Constitution, will have the *same interest* as the people—they are a *part* of
the people—their interest is *inseparable* from that of the people; and
this union of interest will eternally remain, while the right of election
shall continue in the people. Over this right Congress will have no
control: the time and manner of exercising that right are very wisely
vested in Congress, otherwise a delinquent State might embarrass the
measures of the Union. The safety of the public requires that the Federal body should prevent any particular delinquency;[3] but the *right of
election* is above their control: it *must* remain in the people, and be
exercised once in two, four or six years. A body thus organized, with
thirteen Legislatures watching their measures, and several millions of
jealous eyes inspecting their conduct, would not be apt to betray their
constituents. Yet this is not the best ground of safety. The first and
almost only principle that governs men, is *interest*. *Love of our country* is
a powerful auxiliary motive to patriotic actions; but rarely or never
operates against[4] *interest*. The only requisite to secure liberty, is to con-
nect the *interest* of the *Governors* with that of the *governed*. Blend these
interests—make them inseparable—and both are safe from voluntary
invasion. How shall this union be formed? This question is answered.
The union is formed by the equal principles on which the people of
these States hold their property and their rights. But how shall this
union of interests be perpetuated? The answer is easy—bar all perpe-
tuities of estates—prevent any exclusive rights—preserve all prefer-
ment dependent on the choice of the people—suffer no power to exist
independent of the people or their Representatives. While there exists
no power in a State, which is independent on the will of the electors,
the rights of the people are secure. The only barrier against tyranny,
that is necessary in any State, is *the election of Legislators* by the yeomanry
of that State. Preserve *that*, and every privilege is safe. The Legislators
thus chosen to represent the people, should have all the power that
the people would have, were they assembled in one body to deliberate
upon public measures. The distinction between the powers of the *people*
and of their *Representatives* in the Legislature, is as absurd in *theory*, as

it proves pernicious in *practice*. A distinction, which has already countenanced and supported *one rebellion* in America; has prevented many *good* measures; has produced many *bad*; has created animosities in many States, and embarrassments in all.[5] It has taught the people a lesson, which, if they continue to practise, will bring laws into contempt, and frequently mark our country with blood.

You object, Gentlemen, to the powers vested in Congress. Permit me, to ask you, where will you limit their powers? What bounds will you prescribe? You will reply, *we will reserve certain rights, which we deem invaluable, and restrain our rulers from abridging them.* But, Gentlemen, let me ask you, how will you define these rights? would you say, *the liberty of the Press shall not be restrained*? Well, what is this liberty of the Press? Is it an unlimited licence to publish *any thing and every thing* with impunity? If so, the Author, and Printer of any treatise, however obscene and blasphemous, will be screened from punishment. You know, Gentlemen, that there are books extant, so shockingly and infamously obscene and so daringly blasphemous, that no society on earth, would be vindicable in suffering the publishers to pass unpunished. You certainly know that such cases *have* happened, and *may* happen again—nay, you know that they are *probable*. Would not that indefinite expression, *the liberty of the Press*, extend to the justification of every *possible publication*? Yes, Gentlemen, you know, that under such a general licence, a man who should publish a treatise to *prove his maker a knave*, must be screened from legal punishment. I shudder at the thought!—But the truth must not be concealed. The Constitutions of several States *guarantee that very licence.*

But if you attempt to define the *liberty of the Press*, and ascertain what cases shall fall within that privilege, during the course of centuries, where will you *begin*? Or rather, where will you *end*? Here, Gentlemen, you will be puzzled. Some publications certainly *may* be a breach of civil law: You will not have the effrontery to deny a truth so obvious and intuitively evident. Admit that principle; and unless you can define precisely the cases, which are, and are not a breach of law, you have no right to say, the liberty of the Press shall not be restrained; for such a license would warrant *any breach of law*. Rather than hazard such an abuse of privilege, is it not better to leave the right altogether with your rulers and your posterity? No attempts have ever been made by a Legislative body in America, to abridge that privilege; and in this free enlightened country, no attempts could succeed, unless the public should be convinced that an abuse of it would warrant the restriction. Should this ever be the case, you have no right to say, that a future Legislature, or that posterity shall not abridge the privilege, or punish its abuses. ⟨The very attempt to establish a permanent, unalterable Constitution, is an act of consummate arrogance. It is a presumption that we have all possible wisdom—that we can foresee all possible circumstances— and judge for future generations, better than they can for themselves.⟩[6]

But you will say, that trial by jury, is an unalienable right, that ought not to be trusted with our rulers. Why not? If it is such a darling privi- lege, will not Congress be as fond of it, as their constituents? An ele- vation into that Council, does not render a man insensible to his privi- leges, nor place him beyond the necessity of securing them. A member of Congress is liable to all the operations of law, except during his attendance on public business; and should he consent to a law, anni- hilating any right whatever, he deprives himself, his family and estate, of the benefit resulting from that right, as well as his constituents. This circumstance alone, is a sufficient security.

But, why this outcry about juries? If the people esteem them so highly, why do they ever neglect them, and suffer the trial by them to go into disuse? In some States, *Courts of Admiralty* have no juries—nor Courts of Chancery at all. In the City-Courts of some States, juries are rarely or never called, altho' the parties may demand them; and one State, at least, has lately passed an act, empowering the parties to submit both *law* and *fact* to the Court. It is found, that the judgment of a Court, gives as much satisfaction, as the verdict of a jury, as the Court are as good judges of fact, as juries, and much better judges of law. I have no desire to abolish trials by jury, although the original design and excellence of them, is in many cases superseded.—While the peo- ple remain attached to this mode of deciding causes, I am confident, that no Congress can wrest the privilege from them.

But, Gentlemen, our legal proceedings want a reform. Involved in all the mazes of perplexity, which the chicanery of lawyers could invent, in the course of 500 years,[7] our road to justice and redress is tedious, fatiguing and expensive. Our Judicial proceedings are capable of being simplified, and improved in almost every particular. For God's sake,[8] Gentlemen, do not shut the door against improvement. If the people of America, should ever spurn the shackles of opinion, and venture to leave the road, which is so overgrown with briers and thorns, as to strip a man's cloaths from his back as he passes, I am certain they can devise a more easy, safe, and expeditious mode of administering the laws, than that which harrasses every poor mortal, that is wretched enough to want *legal* justice. In Pennsylvania,[9] where very respectable merchants, have repeatedly told me, they had rather lose a debt of fifty pounds, than attempt to recover it by a legal process, one would think that men, who value liberty and property, would not restrain any Government from suggesting a remedy for such disorders.

Another right, which you would place beyond the reach of Congress, is the writ of *habeas corpus*. Will you say that this right may not be suspended in *any* case? You dare not. If it may be suspended in any case, and the Congress are to judge of the necessity, what security have you in a declaration in its favor? You had much better say nothing upon the subject.

But you are frightened at a standing army. I beg you, Gentlemen, to define a *standing army*. If you would refuse to give Congress power to raise troops, to guard our frontiers, and garrison forts, or in short, to enlist men for any purpose, then we understand you—you tie the hands of your rulers so that they cannot defend you against any invasion. This is protection indeed! But if Congress can raise a body of troops for a year, they can raise them for a *hundred years*, and your declaration against *standing armies* can have no other effect, than to prevent Congress from denominating their troops, a *standing army*. You would only introduce into this country, the English farce of mechanically passing an annual bill for the support of troops which are never disbanded.

You object to the indefinite power of taxation in Congress. You must then limit the exercise of that power by the sums of money to be raised; or leaving the sums indefinite, must prescribe the *particular mode* in which, and the *articles* on which the money is to be raised. But the sums cannot be ascertained, because the necessities of the States cannot be foreseen nor defined. It is beyond even *your* wisdom and profound knowledge, Gentlemen, to ascertain the public exigencies, and reduce them to the provisions of a Constitution. And if you would prescribe the mode of raising money, you will meet with equal difficulty. The different States have different modes of taxation, and I question much whether even *your* skill, Gentlemen, could invent a uniform system that should sit easy upon every State. It must therefore be left to experiment, with a power that can correct the errors of a system, and suit it to the habits of the people. And if no uniform mode will answer this purpose, it will be in the power of Congress to lay taxes in each State, according to its particular practice. ⟨But you know, Gentlemen, that an efficient Federal Government will render taxes unnecessary—*that it will ease the people of their burdens*, and *remove their complaints*, and therefore when you raise a clamor about the right of taxation, you must be guilty of the *basest design*—your hearts must be as *malignant* as your actions have been *insidious*.⟩[10] You know that requisitions on the States are ineffectual—That they cannot be rendered effectual, but by a compulsory power in Congress—You know that without an efficient power to raise money, Government cannot secure person, property or justice— Nay, you know further, that such power is as safely lodged in your *Representatives* in Congress, as it is in your *Representatives* in your distinct Legislatures.

You would likewise restrain Congress from requiring *excessive bail,* or imposing *excessive fines* and *unusual punishment.* But unless you can, in every possible instance, previously define the words *excessive* and *unusual*—if you leave the discretion of Congress to define them on occasion, any restriction of their power by a general indefinite expression, is a nullity—mere *formal nonsense.* What consummate arrogance must you possess, to presume you can *now* make *better* provision for the Government of these States, during the course of ages and centuries, than the future Legislatures can, on the spur of the occasion! Yet your whole reasoning on the subject implies this arrogance, and a presumption that you have a right to legislate for posterity!

But to complete the list of unalienable rights, you would insert a clause in your declaration, *that every body shall, in good weather, hunt on his own land, and catch fish in rivers that are public property.* Here, Gentlemen, you must have exerted the whole force of your genius! Not even the *all-important* subject of *legislating for a world* can restrain my laughter at this clause! As a supplement to that article of your bill of rights, I would suggest the following restriction:—"That Congress shall never restrain any inhabitant of America from eating and drinking, *at seasonable times,* or prevent his lying on his *left side,* in a long winter's night, or even on his back, when he is fatigued by lying on his *right.*"—This article is of just as much consequence as the 8th clause of your proposed bill of rights.

But to be more serious, Gentlemen, you must have had in idea the forest-laws in Europe, when you inserted that article; for no circumstance that ever took place in America, could have suggested the thought of a declaration in favor of hunting and fishing. Will you forever persist in error? Do you not reflect that the state of property in America, is directly the reverse of what it is in Europe? Do you not consider, that the forest-laws in Europe originated in *feudal tyranny,* of which not a trace is to be found in America? Do you not know that in this country almost every farmer is Lord of his own soil? That instead of suffering under the oppression of a Monarch and Nobles, a class of haughty masters, totally independent of the people, almost every man in America is a *Lord himself*—enjoying his property in fee? Where then the necessity of laws to secure hunting and fishing? You may just as well ask for a clause, giving licence for every man to till *his own land*, or milk *his own cows*. The Barons in Europe procured forest-laws to secure the right of hunting on *their own land*, from the intrusion of those who had no property in lands. But the distribution of land in America, not only supersedes the necessity of any laws upon this subject, but renders them absolutely trifling. The same laws which secure the property in land, secure to the owner the right of using it as he pleases.

But you are frightened at the prospect of a *consolidation of the States*. I differ from you very widely. I am afraid, after all our attempts to unite the States, that contending interests, and the pride of State-Sovereignties, will either prevent our union, or render our Federal Government weak, slow and inefficient. The danger is all on this side. If any thing under Heaven now endangers our liberties and independence, it is that single circumstance.

You harp upon that clause of the New Constitution, which declares, that the laws of the United States, &c. shall be the supreme law of the land; when you know that the powers of the Congress are defined, to extend only to those matters which are in their nature and effects, *general*. You know, the Congress cannot meddle with the internal police of any State, or abridge its Sovereignty. And you know, at the same time, that in all general concerns, the laws of Congress must be *supreme*, or they must be *nothing*.[11]

⟨But the public will ask, who are these men that so violently oppose the New Constitution? I will tell them. You are the heads of that party, Gentlemen, which, on the celebration of a very glorious event in Philadelphia, at the close of the war, collected in a mob, and broke the windows of the Quakers, and committed the most detestable outrages, because their religion would not suffer them to illuminate their windows, and join in the rejoicings.[12] You are the men, Gentlemen, that wrested the Charter from the Bank, without the least justifiable pretence; sporting with a grant which *you* had made, and which had never been forfeited.[13] You are the men, that, without a show of right, took away the Charter of the University, and vested it in the hands of your own tools.[14] Yes, Gentlemen, you are the men, who prescribed a test law and oath of abjuration in Pennsylvania,[15] which excluded more than half the Citizens of the State from all Civil Offices.⟩[16] A law, which, had it not been altered by the efforts of more reasonable men, would have established you, and your adherents, as an Aristocratic junto, in all the offices and emoluments of the State. Could your base designs have been accomplished, *you* would have rioted in all the benefits of Government, and Pennsylvania would now, have been subject to as tyrannical an Aristocracy, as ever cursed Society. Such has been the uniformly infamous conduct of the men, who now oppose the best Constitution of Government, ever devised by human wisdom.

But the most bare-faced act of tyranny and wickedness, which has distinguished your political characters, remains to be mentioned. You are the men, Gentlemen, who have abandoned your parts of duty, and betrayed the constitutional rights of the State of Pennsylvania, by *seceding from the Legislature*, with the design of defeating the measures of a constitutional quorum of the House.[17] Yes, Gentlemen, and to add to the infamy of your conduct, you have the audacity to *avow the intention*. Will you then attempt to palliate the crime, by saying it was *necessary*? Good Heavens! *necessary* that a State should be *ruled by a minority! necessary* that the sense of a legislature should be defeated by a junto, which had labored incessantly, for four years, to establish an *Aristocracy* in the State! The same principle which will vindicate you, will justify any *one* man in defeating the sense of the *whole* State. If a minority may prevent a law, one man may do it; but is this liberty? Is this your concern for the rights of the State? Dare you talk of rights, which you have so flagrantly invaded? Will the world expect *you* to be the guardians of privileges? No, Gentlemen, they will sooner expect lessons of morality from the wheel-barrowed criminals, that clank their chains along your streets.[18]

Do you know, Gentlemen, that you are treading in the steps of the Governors before the revolution? Do you know that from the first settlement of Pennsylvania, there was a contest between the people and the deputies of the proprietaries? And that when a Governor could not bring the Assembly to resign their rights, he would *prevail on certain members to leave the House*, and prevent their measures. Yes, Gentlemen, you are but following the precedents of your tyrannical Governors.[(a)] You have begun, and pursued, with unwearied perseverance, the same plan of Despotism which wrought the late revolution; and, with a calm, hypocritical phiz, pretend to be *anxious for the liberties of the people.*

These facts stare you in the face! They are *felt* in Pennsylvania—and *known* to the world! There is not a spot in the United States, where the solemnity of contracts and grants, has been so sacrilegiously violated—and the rights of men so wantonly and perseveringly abused, as by you and your junto in Pennsylvania[19]—except only, in the little detestable corner of the Continent, called *Rhode-Island*. Thanks be to the Sovereign Ruler of events, you are checked in your career of tyranny—your power is dwindling into impotence—and your abuse of the respectable Convention, and of the friends of our Federal Union, will shroud you in oblivion, or accelerate your progress to merited contempt.

(a) *See, a Review of the Constitution and Government of Pennsylvania, Page* 24.[20]

1. This text in angle brackets was replaced in *A Collection of Essays and Fugitiv Writings* with the following: "will create suspicions of the goodness of your cause."

2. David Hume believed that no reasonable man could accept the miracles of the New Testament because miracles were contrary to the laws of nature and could not be proven. See L. A. Selby-Bigge, ed., *Enquiries Concerning the Human Understanding and Concerning the Principles of Morals by David Hume* . . . (2nd ed., 1902; reprint ed., London, 1966), 109–31. The *Enquiry Concerning Human Understanding* was first published in London in 1748 as *Philosophical Essays Concerning Human Understanding.*

3. In the pamphlet Webster published in October 1787 (see headnote above), he objected to Congress' power over the election of its own members: "I see no occasion for any power in Congress to interfere with the choice of their own body. . . . [it] gives *needless* and *dangerous* powers" (Mfm:Pa. 142, p. 26).

4. In *A Collection of Essays and Fugitiv Writings*, Webster added the word "*private*" after "against" and before "*interest.*"

5. When Webster reprinted "America" in *A Collection of Essays and Fugitiv Writings* in 1790 (see headnote above), he added this footnote here: "Some of the bills of rights in America declare, that the people have a right to meet together, and consult for the public safety; that their legislators are responsible to them; that they are servants, &c. Such declarations give people an idea, that as individuals, or in town meetings, they have a power paramount to that of the Legislature. No wonder, that with such ideas, they attempt to resist law."

6. This text in angle brackets was omitted in *A Collection of Essays and Fugitiv Writings.*

7. This number was changed to "five thousand" years in *A Collection of Essays and Fugitiv Writings.*

8. "For God's sake" was changed to "For mercy's sake" in *A Collection of Essays and Fugitiv Writings.*

9. "Pennsylvania" was changed to "States" in *A Collection of Essays and Fugitiv Writings.*

10. This text in angle brackets was omitted in *A Collection of Essays and Fugitiv Writings.*

11. The reprint of "America" in *A Collection of Essays and Fugitiv Writings* ends at this point.

12. In 1777 the Constitutionalist-dominated Supreme Executive Council tried to protect Quakers who would not illuminate their houses during the celebrations of important events. Magistrates were ordered to terminate festivities by eleven o'clock at night and soldiers were ordered to patrol the streets. Despite these efforts, some people still damaged the houses of Quakers.

13. The Republican-controlled Bank of North America was chartered by Congress on 31 December 1781 and by the Pennsylvania legislature early in 1782. Constitutionalists tried unsuccessfully to limit the Bank's powers. In September 1785 the Constitutionalist-controlled Assembly revoked the Bank's charter, but in March 1787 a Republican Assembly restored it.

14. In November 1779 a Constitutionalist legislature reorganized the College of Philadelphia under the name of the University of the State of Pennsylvania and placed Constitutionalists in the important offices. After a long and bitter fight, Republicans restored the old college in 1789.

15. In September 1776 the Pennsylvania Convention, which adopted a new constitution, required voters to take oaths upholding the constitution and required officeholders to declare their belief in one God and in the divine inspiration of the Scriptures. In June 1777 the legislature ordered that all white male inhabitants take an oath of allegiance to

the state. In April 1778 a man in a profession or a trade was not permitted to carry on business unless he took an oath of allegiance, and in September 1778 no one could vote in an election unless he produced a certificate stating that he had taken the oath of allegiance before 1 June 1778. After much effort, Republicans managed to get all of these laws repealed by 1789.

16. The text within brackets in this paragraph, with minor variations, was reprinted in the *New Haven Gazette* on 10 January 1788.

17. For the secession of Pennsylvania assemblymen in September 1787, see "New York Reprinting of the Address of the Seceding Members of the Pennsylvania Assembly," 9–18 October (above).

18. Prisoners, who were required to work on public improvements, were given wheelbarrows to use.

19. Possibly a reference to Pennsylvania's paper money policies enacted during the spring of 1785 that established a loan office and funded the interest due on state and federal securities owned by Pennsylvanians. By mid-1787 Pennsylvania currency had depreciated to two-thirds of its face value.

20. In 1688 the deputy governor of Pennsylvania, acting for proprietor William Penn, dismissed the Provincial Council because of "Animosities and Dissentions" among the members. The Provincial Assembly answered: "As for the Charge of Animosities and Dissentions amongst us before thy coming here, it is so general, that we can make no other Answer than that in Matters of Government, our Apprehensions were otherwise, the End of good Government being answered, in that Power was supported in Reverence with the People, and the People were secured from the Abuse of Power; but for what thou mentions to have been renewed since amongst the Members of Council, we leave them to answer" ([Richard Jackson], *An Historical Review of the Constitution and Government of Pennsylvania, From Its Origin* . . . [London, 1759], 22, 24).

Biographical Gazetteer

The following sketches outline the political careers of the principal New York leaders. Their political positions are indicated (1) on the Constitution in 1787–1788; (2) in national politics after 1789.

BENSON, EGBERT (1746–1833)
Federalist/Federalist
   Born New York City. Graduated King's College (Columbia), 1765. Read law with John Morin Scott; admitted to bar, 1769; and began practice in Red Hook, Dutchess County, 1772. Member, Provincial Convention, 1775, and second Council of Safety, 1777–78. Represented Dutchess County in Assembly, 1777–81, 1787–88. State attorney general, 1777–87. Member, Hartford Convention, 1780; Confederation Congress, 1784, 1787–88; and Annapolis Convention, 1786. N.Y. commissioner to settle western lands dispute with Mass., 1786. Member, U.S. House of Representatives, 1789–93, 1813. Justice, N.Y. Supreme Court, 1794–1801. Member, commission to set boundary between Maine and New Brunswick, Canada, 1796. One of President John Adams's "midnight" judicial appointments, 1801. A founder of New-York Historical Society, 1804, and its first president, 1805–15.

CLINTON, GEORGE (1739–1812)
Antifederalist/Republican
   Born Little Britain, Ulster County. Served on privateer and in militia during French and Indian War. Studied law in New York City with William Smith, Jr. (who had defended John Peter Zenger); admitted to bar, 1764; and began practice in Ulster County. Clerk, Ulster County Court of Common Pleas, 1759–1812. Member, colonial Assembly, 1768–75; Continental Congress, 1775–76 (left for military duty before Declaration of Independence was signed); Provincial Convention, 1775; and Third and Fourth Provincial congresses, 1776–77. Brigadier general in both militia, 1775–77, and Continental Army, 1777–83; brevet major general, Continental Army, 1783. Governor, 1777–95, 1801–4. Vice President, N.Y. Society for the Manumission of Slaves, 1785. Member, state convention (Ulster Co.), 1788, and as president did not vote. Unsuccessful candidate for U.S. Vice President, 1788, 1792. Member, state Assembly, 1800–1801. U.S. Vice President from 1805 until his death. Candidate for U.S. President, 1808. Alleged to have written "Cato" essays during ratification debate.

DUANE, JAMES (1733–1797)
Federalist/Federalist
   Born New York City. Studied law with James Alexander (who had defended John Peter Zenger); admitted to bar, 1754. Practiced in New York City. Married Mary Livingston, daughter of Robert Livingston, Jr., third lord of Livingston Manor, 1759. Land speculator in upstate N.Y. and Vt. King's Attorney, 1767. Member, Continental and Confederation congresses, 1774–84; Provincial Convention, 1775; Third and Fourth Provincial congresses, 1776–77; and state Senate, 1782–85, 1788–90. Active role in drafting state constitution, 1777. Mayor, New York City, 1784–89. In Mayor's Court, presides over *Rutgers* v. *Waddington*, 1784. Chosen delegate to Annapolis Convention, but did not attend, 1786. Member, state Convention, 1788; voted to ratify Constitution. U.S. District Judge for N.Y., 1789–94.

495

HAMILTON, ALEXANDER (1757–1804)
Federalist/Federalist

Born Nevis, Leeward Islands, British West Indies. Came to America in 1772. Entered King's College (Columbia), 1773. Wrote pamphlets and newspaper essays favoring independence, 1774–75. Commissioned by Second Provincial Congress to command artillery company, 1776. George Washington's aide-de-camp with rank of lieutenant colonel, 1777–81. Married Elizabeth Schuyler, daughter of Philip Schuyler, 1780. Led attack on redoubt at Yorktown, 1781. Settled in Albany, studied law, and admitted to bar, 1782. Member, Confederation Congress, 1782–83, 1788. Opened law office in New York City, 1783. Argued case of *Rutgers* v. *Waddington*, 1784. A founder of Bank of N.Y., 1784. Delegate to Annapolis Convention, 1786; drafted report of Convention. Member, state Assembly, 1787. Delegate to Constitutional Convention, 1787; signed Constitution as only N.Y. delegate. Published attack on Gov. George Clinton, 21 July 1787. Possible author of "Cæsar" essays, 1787. Co-author of "Publius": *The Federalist*, 1787–88. Member, state Convention, 1788; voted to ratify Constitution. U.S. Secretary of the Treasury, 1789–95. Leader of Federalist Party. After retirement from Treasury, returned to New York City to practice law; remained active in politics. Major General (second in command) of Provisional Army raised to meet potential threat from France, 1798. Opposed Aaron Burr's election as U.S. Senator, 1797, as President, 1800–1801, and as governor of N.Y., 1804. Killed in duel with Burr.

HOBART, JOHN SLOSS (1738–1805)
Federalist/Federalist

Born Fairfield, Conn. Graduated from Yale College, 1757. Resided in New York City before moving to Huntington, Suffolk County, where he owned inherited property. Member, New York City Sons of Liberty, 1765. Member, Suffolk County committee of correspondence, 1774. Member, Provincial Convention, 1775; all four Provincial congresses, 1775–77; and first Council of Safety, 1777. Justice, N.Y. Supreme Court, 1777–98. Member, Hartford Convention, 1780. Member, state Convention, 1788; voted to ratify Constitution. U.S. Senator, 1798; U.S. District Judge for N.Y., 1798–1805.

HUGHES, HUGH (1727–1802)
Antifederalist/Republican

Born Upper Merion, Pa. Moved to New York City by 1752, where he was a currier and tanner. Suffered severe financial reverses in 1765; thereafter kept school for a time. Member, Sons of Liberty and a strong supporter of independence. In 1775–76 corresponded with Samuel and John Adams concerning state of politics in New York City and surrounding area. Appointed commissary of military stores for N.Y. by Second Provincial Congress, 1776. Deputy quartermaster general, Continental Army, with rank of colonel, 1777–78, 1780–83. Moved to Yonkers, Westchester County, c. 1785, where he rented a farm from John Lamb and tutored Lamb's sons and others. Wrote "A Countryman" and "Expositor" newspaper essays opposing ratification of Constitution, 1787–88.

JAY, JOHN (1745–1829)
Federalist/Federalist

Born New York City. Graduated King's College (Columbia), 1764. Studied law with Benjamin Kissam in New York City; admitted to bar, 1768. Secretary of royal commission to fix boundary between N.Y. and N.J., 1773. Married Sarah Livingston, daughter of William Livingston, 1774. Member, N.Y. committee of correspondence, 1774. Delegate to Continental and Confederation congresses, 1774–76 (but absent and did not sign Declaration of Independence), 1778–79 (president), 1784. Member, Provincial Convention, 1775; Third and Fourth Provincial congresses, 1776–77, where he favored agreeing to Declaration of Independence and played major role in drafting and adoption of state constitution of 1777. Member, First Council of Safety, 1777. First chief justice, N.Y. Supreme Court, 1777–79. Appointed minister plenipotentiary to Spain, 1779. Joint commissioner for negotiating peace with Great Britain, 1782–83. Returned to U.S., July 1784. Confederation Secretary for Foreign Affairs, 1784–90. President, N.Y. Society for the Manumission of Slaves, 1785–90. Co-author, "Publius": *The Federalist*, 1787–88; author, *An Address to the People of the State of New-York*, under signature of "A Citizen of New-York," 1788. Injured in "Doctor's Riot" in New York City, April 1788. Member, state Convention, 1788; voted to ratify Constitution. Chief Justice, U.S., 1789–95. Unsuccessful Federalist candidate for governor, 1792. As special envoy to Great Britain, negotiated Jay Treaty, 1794. Returned to U.S., 1795. Governor, 1795–1801. Declined appointment as Chief Justice of U.S., Dec. 1800. Retired from public life to estate in Bedford, Westchester County, 1801.

JONES, SAMUEL (1734–1819)
Antifederalist/Federalist
    Born Fort Hill, Queens County. Attended school in Hempstead and worked as merchant sailor. Studied law in New York City with William Smith, Jr. (who had defended John Peter Zenger); admitted to bar, 1760. Member, New York City committee of correspondence, 1774; Committee of One Hundred, 1775. But did not take up arms against British during Revolution; moved to Conn., then to Orange County, and finally, in 1776, to West Neck, Queens County, where he practiced law. Took oath of allegiance to state, 1786. In 1786 appointed (with Richard Varick) to codify New York laws under N.Y. constitution of 1777 (published in 1789). By end of 1786 opened a law office in New York City. Member, state Assembly, 1786–90 (Queens County); state Convention, 1788 (Queens County), where he voted to ratify Constitution; and state Senate, 1791–97. Recorder, New York City, 1789–96. State comptroller, 1797–1807. Unsuccessful candidate for state Senate, 1800, 1806. Retired from public life to his farm at Oyster Bay.

LAMB, JOHN (1735–1800)
Antifederalist/Republican
    Born New York City; son of former English criminal who had been transported to America. Manufactured mathematical instruments and then became a wine merchant. Leader, N.Y. Sons of Liberty, 1765; continued active opposition to British policy for next decade. Called before colonial Assembly in 1769 for libeling the house, but charges dismissed for lack of evidence. In response to battles of Lexington and Concord, joined Isaac Sears to seize custom house to prevent vessels from leaving N.Y. harbor. Seized military stores at Turtle Bay (in mid-Manhattan on East River), 1775. Commissioned captain in N.Y. Artillery; joined General Richard Montgomery in invasion of Canada, 1775. Wounded (lost an eye) and captured at Quebec; paroled, 1775–76. Exchanged for British prisoners; appointed colonel in Continental Artillery, 1777. Wounded again at Compo Hill, Conn., 1777. Commander of artillery at West Point, 1779–80. Brevet brigadier general, 1783. Member, state Assembly, 1784. Collector of customs for Port of N.Y., 1784–89. Actively opposed Constitution, 1787–88; chairman, N.Y. Federal Republican Committee, 1788. U.S. collector of Port of N.Y., 1789–97.

LANSING, JOHN, JR. (1754–1829)
Antifederalist/Republican
    Born Albany. Brother of Abraham G. Lansing. Studied law in Albany with Robert Yates and in New York City with James Duane; admitted to bar in Albany, 1775, and began practice there. Military secretary to Gen. Philip Schuyler, 1776–77. Member, state Assembly, 1780–84, 1786, 1788 (speaker, 1786, 1788); Confederation Congress, 1785; and commission to settle western land disputes with Mass., 1786. Mayor, Albany, 1786–90. Delegate, Constitutional Convention, 1787; left early and did not sign Constitution. Member,

state Convention, 1788; voted against ratification of Constitution. Justice, N.Y. Supreme
Court, 1790–1801 (chief justice, 1798–1801). Commissioner to settle boundary between
N.Y. and Vt., 1790. Chancellor, 1801–14. Resumed law practice. Disappeared on 12 December 1829.

LIVINGSTON, ROBERT R. (1746–1813)
Federalist/Republican
   Born New York City. Graduated King's College (Columbia), 1765. Studied law with
William Livingston and William Smith, Jr. (who had defended John Peter Zenger); admitted to bar in 1770; and began practice in New York City in partnership with John Jay.
Recorder, New York City, 1773–75. Delegate, Continental and Confederation congresses,
1775–76, 1779–80, 1784–85 (on committee to draft Declaration of Independence). Member, Provincial Convention, 1775; Third and Fourth Provincial congresses, 1776–77
(where he helped draft state constitution); and first Council of Safety, 1777. Chancellor,
1777–1801. First Confederation Secretary for Foreign Affairs, 1781–83. Member commissions to fix boundary with Mass., 1784, and Vt., 1790. Commissioner to settle western
lands dispute with Mass., 1786. Appointed delegate to Annapolis Convention, 1786, but
did not attend. Member, state Convention, 1788; voted to ratify Constitution. Administers
oath of office to President George Washington, 30 April 1789. Unsuccessful candidate
for governor, 1798. U.S. Minister to France, 1801–4 (negotiates Louisiana Purchase,
1803). Retired to his estate, Clermont, Columbia County.

MCKESSON, JOHN (1734–1798)
Antifederalist/Republican
   Born Chester County, Pa. Graduate, College of New Jersey (Princeton), 1753. Studied
law and practiced in New York City. Secretary to: Provincial Convention, 1775; all four
Provincial congresses, 1775–77; and first and second Councils of Safety, 1777–78. Clerk
of: state Assembly, 1777–94; and state Convention, 1788.

MORRIS, RICHARD (1730–1810)
Federalist/Federalist
   Born Morrisania, Westchester County (now in Bronx County). Entered Yale College
in 1746, remained there briefly, but did not receive a degree until 1787. Studied law in
New York City; admitted to bar, 1752. Judge, Court of Admiralty for N.Y., N.J., and Conn.,
1762–75. State senator, 1778–79. Chief justice, N.Y. Supreme Court, 1779–90. Member,
state Convention, 1788; absent for vote on Constitution. Upon reaching mandatory retirement age of 60, retired from Supreme Court to his estate in Scarsdale, Westchester
County. Gouverneur Morris was his younger half brother.

OOTHOUDT, HENRY (1742–1818)
Antifederalist/Republican
   Member, Second Provincial Congress, 1775–76; state Assembly, 1779–80; Council of
Appointment, 1781–82; and state Senate, 1781–84. Appointed surrogate, Albany County,
1782. Member, state Convention, 1788; chairman of committee of the whole; and voted
against ratification of Constitution.

SCHOONMAKER, CORNELIUS C. (1745–1796)
Antifederalist/Republican
   Born Shawangunk (now Wallkill), Ulster County. Surveyor and farmer. Member, state
Assembly, 1777–90, 1795; state Convention, 1788, where he voted against ratification of
Constitution; and U.S. House of Representatives, 1791–93.

SCHUYLER, PHILIP (1733–1804)
Federalist/Federalist
  Born Albany. Studied with private tutor. Wealthy landowner and investor in banking, manufacturing, and transportation. Officer in British army during French and Indian War. Member, colonial Assembly, 1768–75; Provincial Convention, 1775; and Continental Congress, 1775, 1777, 1778–80. Major General, Continental Army, 1775–79. Defeated for governor, 1777, 1783. Member, state Senate, 1780–84, 1786–90, 1792–97. State surveyor general, 1781–84. Member, Council of Appointment, 1786, 1788, 1790, 1794. U.S. Senator, 1789–91, 1797–98. Father-in-law of Alexander Hamilton and Stephen Van Rensselaer.

SMITH, MELANCTON (1744–1798)
Antifederalist/Republican
  Born Jamaica, Queens County. As youth clerked in store in Poughkeepsie; then became merchant and land speculator in same city. Member, First Provincial Congress, 1775. Militia captain and officer to detect Loyalist conspiracies. Sheriff, Dutchess County, 1778–81. Appointed commissioner to settle disputes between Continental Army and contractors at West Point and elsewhere, 1782. Moved to New York City about 1785, where he was a wealthy merchant and lawyer. Delegate, Confederation Congress, 1785–87; state Convention (Dutchess Co.), 1788, where he voted to ratify Constitution; and state Assembly, 1792. Close political ally and adviser of Gov. George Clinton. Supports Aaron Burr for U.S. Vice President, 1792.

TILLINGHAST, CHARLES (1748–1795)
Antifederalist/Republican
  Born New York City. Distiller in New York City. Assistant Deputy Quartermaster General, Middle Department, Continental Army, during Revolution (under Hugh Hughes and Timothy Pickering). Secretary, N.Y. Federal Republican Committee, 1788. Deputy collector of customs, Port of N.Y., when he died of yellow fever. John Lamb's son-in-law.

VAN CORTLANDT, PIERRE (1721–1814)
Federalist/Federalist
  Born New York City. Large landholder. Moved to Croton Manor, Westchester County, 1749, where he managed his farms and mills. Member, colonial Assembly, 1768–75; and Second, Third, and Fourth Provincial congresses, 1775–77 (presided over drafting the state constitution, 1777). Militia colonel, 1775. President, first Council of Safety, 1777. Lieutenant Governor, 1777–95. Unsuccessful candidate for governor, 1789. Retired from public life in 1795.

VAN GAASBEEK, PETER (1754–1797)
Antifederalist/Republican/Federalist
  Born Kingston, Ulster County. Kingston merchant. Militia major during Revolution. County supervisor, 1787–93. Leader of Clintonians in Ulster County, but supports Burr in 1792, and then becomes Federalist leader in Ulster County, 1792. Member, U.S. House of Representatives, 1793–95.

VAN RENSSELEAR, JEREMIAH (1740–1810)
Antifederalist/Republican
  Landholder, surveyor, and businessman. Lived in Albany. Rose to the rank of lieutenant in Continental Army during Revolution. Chair, Albany Antifederalist Committee and head

of mob that burned Constitution, 1788. Member, state Assembly, 1788–89; and U.S. House of Representatives, 1789–91. President, Bank of Albany, 1798–1806. Presidential elector, 1800. Lieutenant governor, 1801–4. Brother-in-law of Philip Schuyler.

VAN RENSSELAER, STEPHEN (1764–1839)
Federalist/Federalist

Born New York City. Studied at College of New Jersey (Princeton), 1779–81; graduate, Harvard College, 1782. Married daughter of Philip Schuyler, 1783. Eighth patroon of Manor of Rensselaers; known as "The Patroon." Moved to manor house "Watervliet" located in Albany, 1785. Militia officer, rising to rank of major general in 1801. Member, state Assembly, 1789–90, 1808–10, 1818; state Senate, 1791–95; and Council of Appointment, 1792. Unsuccessful candidate for lieutenant governor, 1792. Lieutenant governor, 1795–1801. Unsuccessful candidate for governor, 1801, 1813. Member, canal commissions, 1810–1839; state constitutional conventions, 1801, 1821; and U.S. House of Representatives, 1822–29. Founded Rensselaer Polytechnic Institute at Troy, 1824.

WILLIAMS, JOHN (1752–1806)
Antifederalist/Republican/Federalist

Born Barnstable, Devonshire, England. Studied medicine and surgery. Served one year as surgeon's mate on British warship. Emigrated to America, 1773. Settled at New Perth, Charlotte County (now Salem, Washington County). Practiced medicine. Active in protecting frontier as militia colonel during Revolution. Member, all four Provincial congresses, 1775–77; state Senate, 1777–78, 1782–95; state Assembly, 1781–82; state Convention, 1788, where he voted against ratification of Constitution; Council of Appointment, 1789; and U.S. House of Representatives, 1795–99. Militia brigadier general, 1786. Married into wealth. Purchaser of confiscated Loyalist estates; large landowner and land speculator; country merchant and wholesaler; and promoter of economic development in northeastern New York. Became Federalist chiefly over Jay Treaty, 1795.

YATES, ABRAHAM, JR. (1724–1796)
Antifederalist/Republican

Born Albany. Apprenticed to shoemaker; became lawyer and wine seller. Sheriff, Albany County, 1754–59. Member, Albany Common Council, 1754–73; Provincial Convention, 1775; all four Provincial congresses, 1775–77; first and second Councils of Safety, 1777–78; Council of Appointment, 1777–78, 1784; state Senate, 1777–78, 1779–90; and Confederation Congress, 1787–88. Continental loan officer, 1777–81. Receiver, City of Albany, 1778–79. Leader of public opposition to Impost of 1783. Postmaster of Albany, 1783. Mayor, City of Albany, 1790, until his death. Presidential elector, 1792. Author of many essays signed "Rough Hewer," "Sidney," and "Sydney."

YATES, ROBERT (1738–1801)
Antifederalist/Republican

Born Schenectady. Studied law with William Livingston; admitted to bar, 1760; and began practice in Albany. Albany alderman, 1771–75. Member, all four Provincial congresses, 1775–77. Justice, N.Y. Supreme Court, 1777–98 (chief justice, 1790–98). Delegate, Constitutional Convention, 1787, which he left early; and state Convention, 1788, where he voted against ratification of Constitution. Unsuccessful Federalist candidate for governor, 1789; unsuccessful Republican candidate for governor, 1795.

Appendix I
The New York Constitution, 20 April 1777, and
Act Concerning the Rights of the Citizens, 27 January 1787

The New York Constitution (excerpts)[1]

. . . III. And whereas, Laws inconsistent with the spirit of this constitution, or with the public good, may be hastily and unadvisedly passed; BE IT ORDAINED, that the Governor for the time being, the Chancellor and the Judges of the Supreme Court, or any two of them, together with the Governor, shall be, and hereby are, constituted a Council to revise all bills about to be passed into laws by the legislature. And for that purpose shall assemble themselves, from time to time, when the legislature shall be convened; for which nevertheless, they shall not receive any salary or consideration under any pretence whatever. And that all bills which have passed the Senate and Assembly, shall, before they become laws, be presented to the said Council for their revisal and consideration; and if upon such revision and consideration, it should appear improper to the said Council, or a majority of them, that the said bill should become a law of this State, that they return the same, together with their objections thereto, in writing, to the Senate, or House of Assembly, in whichsoever the same shall have originated, who shall enter the objections sent down by the Council, at large, in their minutes, and proceed to reconsider the said bill. But if after such reconsideration, two thirds of the said Senate or House of Assembly, shall, notwithstanding the said objections, agree to pass the same, it shall, together with the objections, be sent to the other branch of the legislature, where it shall also be reconsidered, and if approved by two thirds of the members present, shall be a law.

And in order to prevent any unnecessary delays, BE IT FURTHER ORDAINED, that if any bill shall not be returned by the Council, within ten days after it shall have been presented, the same shall be a law, unless the legislature shall, by their adjournment render a return of the said bill within ten days impracticable; in which case the bill shall be returned on the first day of the meeting of the legislature, after the expiration of the said ten days. . . .

XXIII. That all officers, other than those, who by this constitution are directed to be otherwise appointed, shall be appointed in the manner following, *to wit*, The assembly shall, once in every year, openly nominate and appoint one of the Senators from each great district, which Senators shall form a council for the appointment of the said officers, of which the Governor for the time being, or the Lieutenant-Governor, or the President of the Senate, when they shall respectively administer the government, shall be President, and have a casting voice, *but no other vote*; and with the advice and consent of the said council, shall appoint all the said officers; and that a majority of the said council be a quorum. And further, the said Senators shall not be eligible to the said council for two years successively. . . .

XXX. That Delegates to represent this State, in the General Congress of the United States of America, be annually appointed as follows, *to wit*, The Senate and Assembly shall each openly nominate as many persons as shall be equal to the whole number of Delegates to be appointed; after which nomination, they shall meet together, and those persons named in both lists shall be Delegates; and out of those persons whose names are not in both lists, one half shall be chosen by the joint ballot of the Senators and Members of Assembly, so met together as aforesaid. . . .

XXXV. And this Convention doth further, in the name and by the authority of the good people of this State, ORDAIN, DETERMINE and DECLARE, that such parts of the common law of England, and of the statute law of England and Great-Britain, and of the acts of the legislature of the colony of New-York, as together did form the law of the said colony on the 19th day of April, in the year of our Lord one thousand seven hundred and seventy-five, shall be and continue the law of this State; subject to such alterations and provisions, as the legislature of this State shall, from time to time, make concerning the same. That such of the said acts as are temporary, shall expire at the times limited for their duration respectively. That all such parts of the said common law, and all such of the said statutes, and acts aforesaid, or parts thereof, as may be construed to establish or maintain any particular denomination of Christians, or their ministers, or concern the allegiance heretofore yielded to, and the supremacy sovereignty, government or prerogatives, claimed or exercised by the King of Great-Britain and his predecessors, over the colony of New-York and its inhabitants, or are repugnant to this constitution, be, and they hereby are, abrogated and rejected. And this convention doth farther ordain, that the resolves or resolutions of the Congresses of the colony of New-York, and of the Convention of the State of New-York, now in force, and not repugnant to the government established by this Constitution, shall be considered as making part of the laws of this State; subject, nevertheless to such alterations and provisions, as the legislature of this State may from time to time make concerning the same. . . .

XXXVIII. And whereas we are required by the benevolent principles of rational liberty, not only to expel civil tyranny, but also to guard against that spiritual oppression and intolerance, wherewith the bigotry and ambition of weak and wicked priests and princes, have scourged mankind: This Convention doth further, in the name and by the authority of the good people of this State, ORDAIN, DETERMINE and DECLARE, that the free exercise and enjoyment of religious profession and worship, without discrimination or preference, shall for ever hereafter be allowed within this State to all mankind. Provided that the liberty of conscience hereby granted, shall not be so construed, as to excuse acts of licentiousness, or justify practices inconsistent with the peace or safety of this State.

XXXIX. And whereas the ministers of the gospel, are by their profession, dedicated to the service of God and the cure of souls, and ought not to be diverted from the great duties of their function; therefore no minister of the gospel, or priest of any denomination whatsoever, shall at any time hereafter, under any pretence or description whatever, be eligible to, or capable of holding any civil or military office or place, within this State.

XL. And whereas it is of the utmost importance to the safety of every State, that it should always be in a condition of defence; and it is the duty of every man, who enjoys the protection of society, to be prepared and willing to defend it; this Convention therefore, in the name and by the authority of the good people of this State, doth ORDAIN, DETERMINE and DECLARE, that the militia of this State, at all times hereafter, as well in peace as in war, shall be armed and disciplined, and in readiness for service. That all such of the inhabitants of this State, being of the people called Quakers, as from scruples of conscience, may be averse to the bearing of arms, be therefrom excused by the legislature; and do pay to the State such sums of money in lieu of their personal service, as the same may, in the judgment of the legislature, be worth: And that a proper magazine of warlike stores, proportionate to the number of inhabitants, be, for ever hereafter, at the expence of this State, and by acts of the legislature, established, maintained, and continued in every county in this State.

XLI. And this Convention doth further ORDAIN, DETERMINE and DECLARE, in the name and by the authority of the good people of this State, that trial by jury, in all cases in which it hath heretofore been used in the colony of New-York, shall be established, and remain inviolate forever. And that no acts of attainder shall be passed by the legislature of this State for crimes, other than those committed before the termination of the present war; and that such acts shall not work a corruption of blood. And further, that the legislature of this State shall, at no time hereafter, institute any new court or courts, but such as shall proceed according to the course of the common law.

XLII. And this Convention doth further, in the name and by the authority of the good people of this State, ORDAIN, DETERMINE and DECLARE, that it shall be in the discretion of the legislature to naturalize all such persons, and in such manner as they shall think proper; provided all such of the persons, so to be by them naturalized, as being born in parts beyond sea, and out of the United States of America, shall come to settle in, and become subjects of this State, shall take an oath of allegiance to this State, and abjure and renounce all allegiance and subjection to all and every foreign King, Prince, Potentate and State, in all matters ecclesiastical as well as civil.

1. *The Constitution of the State of New-York* (Fishkill, 1777), 14–15, 24, 26–27, 28–29, 31–33 (Evans 15473). For the complete text of the constitution, see also Thorpe, V, 2623–38.

An Act Concerning the Rights of the Citizens of this State 26 January 1787[1]

Be it Enacted by the People of the State of New-York, represented in Senate and Assembly and it is hereby enacted and declared by the Authority of the same:

First: That no authority shall, on any pretence whatsoever, be exercised over the Citizens of this State, but such as is or shall be derived from and granted by the People of this State.

Second: That no Citizen of this State shall be taken or imprisoned, or be disseised of his or her freehold or liberties, or free customs, or outlawed, or exiled, or condemned, or otherwise destroyed, but by lawful judgment of his or her Peers, or by due process of law.

Third: That no Citizen of this State shall be taken or imprisoned for any offence, upon petition or suggestion, unless it be by indictment or presentment of good and lawful men of the same neighbourhood, where such deeds be done, in due manner, or by due process of law.

Fourth: That no person shall be put to answer without presentment before Justices, or matter of record, or due process of law, according to the law of the land, and if any thing be done to the contrary, it shall be void in law, and holden for error.

Fifth: That no person, of what estate or condition socver, shall be taken, or imprisoned, or disinherited, or put to death without being brought to answer by due process of law, and that no person shall be put out of his or her franchise or freehold, or lose his or her life or limb, or goods and chattels, unless he or she be duly brought to answer, and before-judged of the same by due course of law; and if any thing be done contrary to the same, it shall be void in law and holden for none.

Sixth: That neither justice nor right shall be sold to any person, nor denied, nor deferred, and that writs and process shall be granted freely and without delay, to all persons requiring the same; and nothing from henceforth shall be paid or taken for any writ or process, but the accustomed fees for writing, and for the seal of the same writ or process; and all fines, duties and impositions whatsoever, heretofore taken or demanded, under what name or description soever, for, or upon granting any writs, inquests, commissions, or process to suitors in their causes, shall be, and hereby are abolished.

Seventh: That no Citizens of this State shall be fined or amerced without reasonable cause, and such fine or amerciament, shall always be according to the quantity of his or her trespass or offence, and saving to him or her his or her contenement; that is to say, every freeholder saving his freehold, a merchant saving his merchandize, and a mechanic saving the implements of his trade.

Eighth: That excessive bail ought not to be required, nor excessive fines imposed, nor cruel and unusual punishments inflicted.

Ninth: That all elections shall be free, and that no person by force of arms, nor by malice or menacing, or otherwise, presume to disturb or hinder any Citizen of this State to make free election, upon pain of fine and imprisonment, and treble damages to the party grieved.

Tenth: That it is the right of the Citizens of this State to petition the Person administering the Government of this State for the time being, or either House of the Legislature, and all commitments and prosecutions for such petitioning are illegal.

Eleventh: That the freedom of speech and debates, and proceedings in the Senate and Assembly, shall not be impeached or questioned in any Court or place out of the Senate or Assembly.

Twelfth: That no tax, duty, aid, or imposition whatsoever, shall be taken or levied within this State, without the grant and assent of the People of this State, by their Representatives in Senate and Assembly; and that no Citizen of this State shall be by any means compelled to contribute to any gift, loan, tax, or other like charge, not set, laid, or imposed by the Legislature of this State; and further, that no Citizen of this State shall be constrained to arm himself, or to go out of this State, or to find soldiers, or men of arms, either horsemen or footmen, if it be not by assent and grant of the People of this State, by their Representatives in Senate and Assembly.

Thirteenth: That by the laws and customs of this State, the Citizens and Inhabitants thereof cannot be compelled, against their wills, to receive soldiers into their houses, and to sojourn them there, and therefore no Officer military or civil, nor any other person whatsoever, shall, from henceforth, presume to place, quarter, or billet any soldier or soldiers, upon any Citizen or Inhabitant of this State, of any degree or profession whatever, without his or her consent, and that it shall and may be lawful for every such Citizen and Inhabitant to refuse to sojourn or quarter any soldier or soldiers, notwithstanding any command, order, warrant, or billeting whatever.

1. *Laws of the State of New-York, Passed by the Legislature of said State, at their Tenth Session* (New York, 1787), Chapter I, 5–6 (Evans 20578).

Appendix II
New York Appoints
Delegates to the Constitutional Convention
13 January–18 April 1787

On 13 January 1787 Governor George Clinton addressed the opening session of the New York legislature meeting in New York City and transmitted to both houses several papers, including the report of the Annapolis Convention of September 1786 and a Virginia act dated 23 November 1786. The Annapolis Convention report recommended that the states appoint commissioners (or delegates) to meet in convention in Philadelphia on the second Monday in May 1787 "to devise such further provisions as shall appear to them necessary to render the constitution of the Foederal Government adequate to the exigencies of the Union; and to report" these provisions to the Confederation Congress (CDR, 182–85). The Virginia act, recognizing that a "crisis" was at hand, authorized the election of delegates to attend the convention in Philadelphia for the purpose described in the Annapolis Convention report (CDR, 196–98; and RCS:Va., 540–41).

The Assembly immediately considered the governor's message and accompanying documents in the committee of the whole and gave the committee permission to sit again. On 15 January the Assembly, upon a recommendation of the committee of the whole, appointed a committee of five to consider and report on the Annapolis Convention report and the Virginia act. The matter languished until 15 February, when the Assembly rejected an unconditional ratification of the Impost of 1783 despite Alexander Hamilton's impassioned speech favoring ratification. (See the section entitled "The Impost of 1783" in the "Introduction" [above].) On 17 February William Malcolm of New York County, "agreeable to the notice he had given" the previous day to the Assembly, introduced a motion authorizing the appointment of a committee to draft instructions to New York's congressional delegation to call for a convention to revise the Articles of Confederation and to report such alterations and amendments to Congress and to the states. After some debate, this motion, was amended and adopted. As amended, the motion provided for actual instructions to the state's congressional delegation. According to Senator Philip Schuyler of Albany County, the resolution was "violently opposed by the ——s [i.e., the governor's] friends," but some felt compelled to support the resolution to demonstrate that they were not entirely antifederal (to Henry Van Schaack, 13 March, below).

The resolution was sent to the Senate, where Abraham Yates, Jr., of Albany County led the opposition with charges of "Aristocracy King, Despot, unlimited power, sword and purse . . . in all the confusion of unintelligible Jargon. in short he was outrageous. He had the Mortification to fail of Success" (Schuyler to Van Schaack, 13 March, below). On 20 February the Senate concurred with the resolution by a vote of 10 to 9.

On 21 February, when Congress considered the report of its grand committee on the report of the Annapolis Convention, New York's congressional delegates (Egbert Benson and Melancton Smith) laid before Congress the instructions that they had received from the New York legislature and moved to postpone consideration of the report of the grand committee in order to take up New York's proposition for calling a constitutional convention which they presented. New York's motion to postpone—which ignored the convention recommended by the report of the Annapolis Convention and the acts already passed by six states appointing delegates to a convention—was defeated. Instead, Congress considered, amended, and adopted a resolution introduced by Massachusetts' delegates. As adopted, Congress' resolution called for a convention to meet in Philadelphia on the second Monday in May "for the sole and express purpose of revising the Articles of Confederation and reporting to Congress and the several legislatures such alterations and provisions therein as shall when agreed to in Congress and confirmed by the states render the federal constitution adequate to the exigencies of government and the preservation of the Union." (For a full discussion of the actions of Congress and for the significance of the defeat of New York's proposition in Congress, see CDR, 176–90; and the section entitled "The Constitutional Convention" in the "Introduction" [above].)

On 23 February Governor Clinton, acting through his private secretary, sent to the Assembly Congress' resolution calling a constitutional convention, which the Assembly submitted to a committee of the whole house. Three days later, the Assembly committee of the whole house considered Congress' resolution. After some time, the Assembly adopted a resolution proposed by Alexander Hamilton that provided for the election, "by joint ballot," of five delegates to meet in convention in Philadelphia on the second Monday in May "for the sole and express purpose of revising the Articles of Confederation, and reporting to Congress, and to the several Legislatures, such alterations and provisions therein, as shall, when agreed to in Congress, and confirmed by the several States, render the Fœderal Constitution adequate to the exigencies of Government and the preservation of the Union." On the same day this resolution was sent for concurrence to the Senate.

On 27 February, after a heated debate, the Senate refused to concur in the resolution and sent its resolution of non-concurrence to the Assembly. Philip Schuyler led the opposition to this motion that had been presented by his son-in-law because it called for the appointment of convention delegates by joint ballot of the two houses. Schuyler explained that "this would have afforded the opponents [i.e. Clintonians] an Opportunity to commit the delegation to creatures of their own complexion. I moved a rejection of the resolution on the specious, and well founded reason, that the senate would be deprived of Its proper share of influence in the appointment. Yates soon perceived the true cause of my Objection, but durst not avow it,—he stickled however most stren[u]ously for adopting the resolution as It stood. my motion, however prevailed by a small majority" (to Henry Van Schaack, 13 March, below).

On 28 February Senator Schuyler proposed a substitute resolution to elect five delegates to the proposed constitutional convention in the same manner as delegates to Congress were elected (i.e., by comparing lists of men separately nominated by each house of the legislature). Abraham Yates, Jr., "attempted to shackle this, but without success" (Schuyler to Henry Van Schaack, 13

March, below). On a motion of John Haring of Orange County, the Senate, by a vote of 11 to 7, reduced the number of delegates from five to three. (In his 13 March letter to Van Schaack, Schuyler identified the maker of this motion as Yates.) Yates, then moved several amendments "to the powers to be exercised by the delegates, which, If carried, would have rendered their Mission absolutely useless" (Schuyler to Van Schaack, 13 March, below). One of Yates's amendments stated that the proposed constitutional convention should limit its proposals to alterations and amendments "not repugnant to or inconsistent with the constitution of this State." (For other Clintonian attempts to protect the state constitution, see the editorial note to "The New York Legislature Calls a Convention," 11 January–1 February 1788, II below.) After some "long conversations," Yates's motion was defeated when a 9 to 9 tie was broken by the Senate's president, Lieutenant Governor Pierre Van Cortlandt. On the same day, the Assembly concurred in the Senate's version of the resolution.

On 6 March the Assembly nominated Robert Yates, Alexander Hamilton, and John Lansing, Jr., as delegates to the Constitutional Convention. The Senate nominated the same three men. In a joint session, the two houses compared their nominees, and then adjourned to their separate chambers, where each adopted resolutions appointing these three men delegates. (For a fuller discussion of this election and its significance, see the section entitled "The Constitutional Convention" in the "Introduction" [above].)

On 16 April the Assembly, by a vote of 26 to 21, adopted a resolution introduced by Alexander Hamilton that authorized the adoption of two additional delegates to the proposed constitutional convention. Hamilton argued that the two additional delegates could be either Robert R. Livingston, Egbert Benson, James Duane, or John Jay. (Of these four men, only Livingston and Duane had received votes in the Assembly on 6 March.) The Senate received the resolution for its concurrence on 17 April and on 18 April—three days before the legislative session ended—it defeated the resolution by a vote of 12 to 5, sending its non-concurrence to the Assembly.

The resolutions appointing delegates to the Constitutional Convention did not provide for the pay of the delegates. Not until 21 March 1788 did the legislature, in an act for the payment of salaries of government officials, authorize thirty-two shillings per day (including the time traveling to and from the Convention) for each of the three delegates.

For the official legislative proceedings of the two houses mentioned in this editorial note but not printed below, see Mfm:N.Y., under "New York Appoints Delegates to the Constitutional Convention," 13 January–18 April 1787. This grouping of documents also includes the *Daily Advertiser's* reports of the Assembly's proceedings that are not printed below. These reports are useful, in part, because they identify motion makers that the Assembly's journal failed to identify. The *Advertiser* also published extensive notes of debates in the Assembly for this session, although its reports on the appointment of Constitutional Convention delegates was minimal.

Assembly Proceedings, Friday, 23 February 1787 (excerpts)[1]

. . . A Message from his Excellency the Governor, delivered by his Private Secretary, was read, and is in the words following, *viz.*

"GENTLEMEN, By this Message I have the honor of laying before you, a resolution of the United States in Congress assembled, of the 21st instant. . . .

GEO. CLINTON."

New-York, February 23, 1787.

The resolution . . . which accompanied the said Message of his Excellency the Governor, were also read.

Resolved, That the said Message of his Excellency the Governor, and the papers which accompanied the same, be committed to a Committee of the whole House. . . .

Assembly Proceedings, Monday, 26 February 1787 (excerpt)[2]

. . . *Resolved* (If the Honorable the Senate concur herein) that five Delegates be appointed on the part of this State, to meet such Delegates as may be appointed on the part of the other States respectively, on the second Monday in May next, at Philadelphia, for the sole and express purpose of revising the Articles of Confederation, and reporting to Congress, and to the several Legislatures, such alterations and provisions therein, as shall, when agreed to in Congress, and confirmed by the several States, render the Fœderal Constitution adequate to the exigencies of Government and the preservation of the Union; and that in case of such concurrence, the two Houses of the Legislature will meet, on Thursday next, at such place as the Honorable the Senate shall think proper, for the purpose of electing the said Delegates, by joint ballot.

Ordered, That Mr. John Livingston deliver a copy of the last preceding resolution, to the Honorable the Senate. . . .

Newspaper Report of Assembly Proceedings
Monday, 26 February 1787 (excerpt)[3]

. . . On motion of Mr. J. Livingston.

The house resolved itself into a committee of the whole on the message from his excellency the governor, together with the resolution of Congress of the 21st instant for calling a convention to revise and amend the federal constitution.

Mr. Clarke in the chair.

After some time spent thereon, the committee rose, when

On motion of Mr. Hamilton, it was resolved, that on Thursday next, the 1st day of March, both houses by joint ballot would proceed to the election of five commissioners, in conformity to the recommendations of Congress, to meet at Philadelphia in May next for the sole purpose of revising and amending the federal constitution, and to report the same to the United States in Congress assembled, for their approbation; and which when agreed to will be adequate to the preservation and protection of the union. . . .

Senate Proceedings, Monday, 26 February 1787 (excerpts)[4]

. . . A Message from his Excellency the Governor transmitted by the Honorable the Assembly[5] was read as follows, *viz.*

Gentlemen, By this Message I have the honor of laying before you a resolution of the United States in Congress assembled, of the 21st instant. . . .

GEO. CLINTON.

New-York, 23d February, 1787.

The resolution of the United States in Congress assembled was also read.

The following resolution of the Honorable assembly, accompanying the above Message and delivered by Mr. John Livingston, was read, *viz.*

Resolved, (if the Honorable the Senate concur herein,) That five delegates be appointed on the part of this State, to meet such delegates as may be appointed on the part of the other States respectively, on the second Monday in May next at Philadelphia, for the sole and express purpose of revising the articles of confederation and reporting to Congress and to the several Legislatures, such alterations and provisions therein as shall, when agreed to in Congress and confirmed by the several States, render the Fœderal constitution adequate to the exigencies of government and the perservation of the Union; and that in case of such concurrence, the two houses of the Legislature will meet on Thursday next, at such place as the Honorable the Senate shall think proper for the purpose of electing the said delegates by joint ballot.

Ordered, That the consideration of the said resolution, be postponed until to-morrow.

Then the Senate adjourned until ten of the clock to-morrow morning.

Senate Proceedings, Tuesday, 27 February 1787 (excerpt)[6]

. . . The Senate proceeded to the consideration of the resolution received from the Honorable the Assembly yesterday, proposing that five delegates be appointed by the two houses of the Legislature by joint ballot, on the part of this State, to meet delegates on the part of the other States respectively at Philadelphia for the purpose of revising the confederation, which resolution was read and the President having put the question, whether the Senate do concur with the Honorable the Assembly in their said resolution, it was carried in the Negative. Thereupon,

Resolved, That the Senate do not concur with the Honorable the Assembly in their said resolution.

Ordered, That Mr. Williams deliver a copy of the preceding resolution of nonconcurrence to the honorable the Assembly. . . .

Senate Proceedings, Wednesday, 28 February 1787 (excerpt)[7]

. . . Mr. Philip Schuyler moved, that the Senate adopt the following resolution, viz.

Resolved, (if the Honorable the Assembly concur herein) that five delegates be appointed on the part of this State to meet such delegates as may be appointed on the part of the other States respectively, on the second Monday in May next, at Philadelphia, for the sole and express purpose of revising the Articles of Confederation, and reporting to Congress and to the several Legislatures, such alterations and provisions therein as shall, when agreed to in Congress, and confirmed by the several States render the Fœderal Constitution adequate to the exigencies of government and the preservation of the Union; and that in case of such concurrence the two houses of the Legislature will on Tuesday next, proceed to nominate and appoint the said delegates in like manner as is directed by the constitution of this State for nominating and appointing delegates to Congress, which resolution having been read.

Mr. [John] Haring moved that instead of five, that three delegates be appointed for the purposes set forth in the said resolution. Debates arose, and the question being put thereon, it was carried in the affirmative, in manner following, viz.

FOR THE AFFIRMATIVE [11].

Mr. Yates,	Mr. Ward,	Mr. Swartwout,	Mr. Parks,
Mr. Tredwell,	Mr. Russell,	Mr. Hathorn,	Mr. Williams.
Mr. Haring,	Mr. Hopkins,	Mr. Humfrey,	

FOR THE NEGATIVE [7].

Mr. Stoutenburgh,	Mr. Townsend,	Mr. Peter Schuyler,	Mr. Philip Schuyler.
Mr. Vanderbilt,	Mr. Morris,	Mr. L'Hommedieu,	

Mr. Haring then moved to expunge, after the words Tuesday next to the end of the resolution, and to substitute the following, viz. Meet at such place as the Honorable the Assembly shall think proper for the purpose of electing the said delegates by joint ballot. Debates arose, and the question being put thereon, it was carried in the negative, in manner following, *viz.*

FOR THE NEGATIVE [12].

Mr. Stoutenburgh,	Townsend,	Mr. Swartwout,	Mr. Parks,
Mr. Tredwell,	Mr. Morris,	Mr. L'Hommedieu,	Mr. Williams,
Mr. Vanderbilt,	Mr. Peter Schuyler,	Mr. Humfrey,	Mr. Philip Schuyler,

FOR THE AFFIRMATIVE [6].

Mr. Yates,	Mr. Ward,	Mr. Hopkins,	Mr. Hathorn,
Mr. Haring,	Mr. Russell,		

Mr. Yates then moved to insert in the said resolution, after the words *and provisions therein*, the following, *viz.* not repugnant to or inconsistent with the constitution of this State. Debates arose, and the question being put thereon, it was carried in the negative, in manner following, *viz.*

FOR THE NEGATIVE [9].

Mr. Stoutenburgh,	Mr. Townsend,	Mr. Peter Schuyler,	Mr. Williams,
Mr. Tredwell,	Mr. Morris,	Mr. L'Hommedieu,	Mr. Philip Schuyler,
Mr. Vanderbilt,			

FOR THE AFFIRMATIVE [9].

Mr. Yates,	Mr. Russell,	Mr. Swartwout,	Mr. Humfrey,
Mr. Haring,	Mr. Hopkins,	Mr. Hathorn,	Mr. Parks,
Mr. Ward,			

The Senate being equally divided upon the question, his honor the President [Pierre Van Cortlandt] voted in the negative. Thereupon,

Resolved, (if the Honorable the Assembly concur herein) that three Delegates be appointed on the part of this State, to meet such delegates as may be appointed on the part of the other States respectively, on the second Monday in May next at Philadelphia for the sole and express purpose of revising the articles of confederation, and reporting to Congress and to the several Legislatures such alterations and provisions therein as shall when agreed to in Congress and confirmed by the several States, render the Fœderal constitution adequate, to the exigencies of government and the preservation of the Union; and that in case of such concurrence the two houses of the Legislature will on Tuesday next, proceed to nominate and appoint the said delegates in like manner as is directed by the constitution of this State, for nominating and appointing Delegates to Congress.

Ordered, That Mr. Williams deliver a copy of the preceding resolution to the Honorable the Assembly. . . .

Assembly Proceedings, Wednesday, 28 February 1787 (excerpt)[8]

. . . A copy of a resolution of the Honorable the Senate, delivered by Mr. Williams, was read, that the Senate do not concur with this House in their resolution of the 26th instant, relative to the appointment of five delegates, to attend at Philadelphia, on the second Monday in May next.

A copy of a resolution of the Honorable the Senate, delivered by Mr. Williams, was read, and is in the words following, *viz.*

"*Resolved,* (if the Honorable the Assembly concur herein) that three Delegates be appointed on the part of this State, to meet such Delegates as may be appointed on the part of the other States respectively, on the second Monday in May next, at Philadelphia, for the sole and express purpose of revising the Articles of Confederation, and reporting to Congress, and to the several Legislatures, such alterations and provisions therein, as shall, when agreed to in Congress, and confirmed by the several States, render the Fœderal Constitution adequate to the exigencies of government, and the preservation of the Union; and that in case of such concurrence, the two Houses of the Legislature, will, on Tuesday next, proceed to nominate and appoint the said Delegates, in like manner as is directed by the Constitution of this State, for nominating and appointing Delegates to Congress.["]

Resolved, That the House do concur with the Honorable the Senate, in the said Resolution.

Ordered, That Mr. Dongan deliver a copy of the last preceding resolution of concurrence, to the Honorable the Senate. . . .

Senate Proceedings, Thursday, 1 March 1787 (excerpt)[9]

. . . A Message from the Honorable the Assembly by Mr. Dongan, was received, with a resolution of concurrence with the Senate in their resolution of yesterday, for appointing Delegates on Tuesday next, on the part of this State, to meet with Delegates on the part of the other States respectively, for the sole and express purpose of revising the Articles of Confederation, and reporting thereon to Congress and the Legislatures of the respective States. . . .

Assembly Proceedings, Tuesday, 6 March 1787 (excerpt)[10]

. . . The order for the day, for the nomination and appointment of three Delegates on the part of this State, to meet such Delegates as may be appointed on the part of the other States respectively, on the second Monday in May next, at Philadelphia, for the sole and express purpose of revising the articles of Confederation, pursuant to concurrent resolutions of both Houses of the Legislature, on the 28th ultimo, having been read; the House proceeded openly to nominate three Delegates for that purpose; and each of the Members present nominated three persons, as follows, *viz.*

	Robert Yates, Esq. [52]	James Duane, Esq. [23]	Alexander Hamilton, Esq. [49]	Robert R. Livingston, Esq. [4]	John Lansing, jun. Esq. [26]	Melancton Smith, Esq. [1]	John Tayler, Esq. [1]
Mr. Vrooman,	1	1	1				
Mr. C. Livingston,	1	1	1				
Mr. Malcom,	1	1	1				
Mr. Hamilton,	1	1		1			
Mr. Bayard,	1	1	1				
Mr. Ray,	1		1		1		
Mr. Bancker,	1	1	1				
Mr. Denning,	1	1	1				
Mr. Brooks,	1	1	1				
Mr. Doughty,	1		1		1		
Mr. Clark,	1		1	1			
Mr. Harper,	1		1		1		
Mr. Parker,	1		1		1		
Mr. Jones,	1				1		1
Mr. Wyckoff,	1		1		1		
Mr. E. Clark,	1	1	1				
Mr. Strang,	1		1		1		
Mr. Paine,	1		1		1		
Mr. Frey,	1		1		1		
Mr. Crane,	1	1	1				
Mr. Savage,	1	1	1				
Mr. Martin,	1		1		1		
Mr. Griffen,	1		1		1		
Mr. Lockwood,	1		1		1		
Mr. Purdy,	1		1		1		

	Robert Yates, Esq. [52]	James Duane, Esq. [23]	Alexander Hamilton, Esq. [49]	Robert R. Livingston, Esq. [4]	John Lansing, jun. Esq. [26]	Melancton Smith, Esq. [1]	John Tayler, Esq. [1]
Mr. James Livingston,	1	1	1				
Mr. Thorne,	1		1		1		
Mr. Schenck,	1	1	1				
Mr. Taulman,	1		1		1		
Mr. Frost,	1	1	1				
Mr. C. Smith,	1	1	1				
Mr. Patterson,	1			1	1		
Mr. Hedges,	1		1		1		
Mr. Sickles,	1	1	1				
Mr. Duboys,	1		1	1			
Mr. Cooper,	1	1	1				
Mr. Townsend,	1		1		1		
Mr. Havens,	1	1	1				
Mr. Dongan,	1	1	1				
Mr. D'Witt,	1		1		1		
Mr. Batcheller,	1		1		1		
Mr. N. Smith,	1		1		1		
Mr. Snyder,	1		1		1		
Mr. Tierce,	1		1				1
Mr. Tayler,	1	1	1				
Mr. Glen,	1	1	1				
Mr. John Livingston,	1	1	1				
Mr. Osborn,	1		1		1		
Mr. Ludenton,	1		1		1		
Mr. Brinckerhoff,	1		1		1		
Mr. Bronck,	1	1	1				
Mr. Tompkins	1		1		1		

Thereupon, on motion of Mr. Denning,

Resolved, That the Honorable Robert Yates, Esquire, be, and he is hereby nominated by this House, a Delegate on the part of this State, to meet such Delegates as may be appointed on the part of the other States respectively, on the second Monday in May next, at Philadelphia, for the purpose mentioned in the Resolution of the United States of America in Congress assembled, on the 21st ultimo.

On motion of Mr. Malcom,

Resolved, That Alexander Hamilton Esquire, be, and he is hereby nominated by this House, a Delegate on the part of this State, to meet such Delegates as may be appointed on the part of the other States respectively, on the second Monday in May next, at Philadelphia, for the purpose mentioned in the resolution of the United States of America in Congress Assembled, on the 21st ultimo.

On motion of Mr. Paine,

Resolved, That John Lansing, junior, Esquire, be, and he is hereby nominated by this House, a Delegate on the part of this State, to meet such Delegates as may be appointed on the part of the other States respectively, on the second Monday in May next, at Philadelphia, for the purpose mentioned in the resolution of the United States of America in Congress Assembled, on the 21st ultimo. Thereupon,

Resolved, That the Honorable Robert Yates, Esquire, and Alexander Hamilton and John Lansing, junior, Esquires, be, and they are hereby nominated by this House, Delegates on the part of this State, to meet such Delegates as may be appointed on the part of the other States respectively, on the second Monday in May next, at Philadelphia, pursuant to concurrent resolutions of both Houses of the Legislature, on the 28th ultimo.

Resolved, That this House will meet the Honorable the Senate immediately, at such place as they shall appoint, to compare the lists of persons nominated by the Senate and Assembly respectively, as Delegates on the part of this State, to meet such Delegates as may be appointed on the part of the other States respectively, on the second Monday in May next, at Philadelphia, pursuant to concurrent resolutions of both Houses of the Legislature, on the 28th ultimo.

Ordered, That Mr. N. Smith deliver a copy of the last preceding resolution, to the Honorable the Senate.

A copy of a resolution of the Honorable the Senate, was delivered by Mr. Vanderbilt, that the Senate will immediately meet this House in the Assembly-Chamber, to compare the lists of persons nominated by the Senate and Assembly respectively, as Delegates, pursuant to the resolutions before mentioned.

The Honorable the Senate accordingly attended in the Assembly Chamber, to compare the lists of persons nominated for Delegates as above mentioned.

The list of persons nominated by the Honorable the Senate, were the Honorable Robert Yates, Esquire, and John Lansing, junior, and Alexander Hamilton, Esquires; and on comparing the lists of the persons nominated by the Senate and Assembly respectively, it appeared that the same persons were nominated in both lists. Thereupon,

Resolved, That the Honorable Robert Yates, John Lansing, junior, and Alexander Hamilton, Esquires, be, and they are hereby declared duly nominated and appointed Delegates on the part of this State, to meet such Delegates as may be appointed on the part of the other States respectively, on the second Tuesday in May next, at Philadelphia, for the sole and express purpose of revising the Articles of Confederation, and reporting to Congress, and to the several Legislatures, such alterations and provisions therein, as shall when agreed to in Congress, and confirmed by the several States, render the fœderal Constitution adequate to the exigencies of government, and the preservation of the Union. . . .

Senate Proceedings, Tuesday, 6 March 1787 (excerpt)[11]

. . . The Senate proceeded pursuant to the concurrent resolutions of the Senate and Assembly of the 28th of February last past, to nominate three Delegates on the part of this State to meet such Delegates as may be appointed on the part of the other States respectively, on the second Monday in May next, at Philadelphia, when *the Honorable Robert Yates, Esquire, John Lansing, junior, and Alexander Hamilton, Esquires,* were openly nominated. Thereupon,

Resolved, That *the Honorable Robert Yates, Esquire, John Lansing, junior, and Alexander Hamilton, Esquires,* are nominated Delegates on the part of this State to meet such Delegates as may be appointed on the part of the other States respectively, on the second Monday in May next, at Philadelphia, pursuant to the concurrent resolutions of both Houses of the Legislature of the 28th of February last past.

A Message from the Honorable the Assembly by Mr. N. Smith, was received with a resolution, that they would immediately meet the Senate at such place as they shall appoint, to compare the lists of persons nominated by the Senate and Assembly respectively, as Delegates on the part of this State, to meet such Delegates as may be appointed on the part of the other States respectively, on the second Monday in May next, at Philadelphia, pursuant to the concurrent resolutions of both Houses of the Legislature of the 28 February last.

Resolved, That the Senate will immediately meet the Honorable the Assembly in the Assembly Chamber, to compare the lists of persons nominated by the Senate and Assembly respectively, as Delegates on the part of this State to meet such Delegates as may be appointed on the part of the other States respectively, on the second Monday in May next, at Philadelphia, pursuant to the concurrent resolutions of both Houses of the Legislature of the 28th of February last past.

Ordered, That Mr. Vanderbilt deliver a copy of the preceding resolution to the Honorable the Assembly.

The Senate accordingly met the Honorable the Assembly in the Assembly Chamber, and being returned, the president reassumed the chair and informed the Senate that on comparing the respective lists of the Senate and Assembly, they were found to agree in the nomination of *the Honorable Robert Yates, Esquire, John Lansing junior, and Alexander Hamilton, Esquires.*

Thereupon,

Resolved, That *the Honorable Robert Yates, John Lansing, junior, and Alexander Hamilton, Esquires,* are duly nominated and appointed delegates on the part of this State, to meet such delegates as may be appointed on the part of the other States respectively on the second Monday in May next at Philadelphia, for the sole and express purpose of revising the articles of confederation, and reporting to Congress and the several Legislatures such alterations and provisions therein, as shall, when agreed to in Congress and confirmed by the several States, render the Fœderal constitution, adequate to the exigencies of Government and the preservation of the union. . . .

Philip Schuyler to Henry Van Schaack
New York, 13 March 1787 (excerpt)[12]

. . . Previous to the recommendation of Congress to the states, to appoint delegates to meet in convention, for the purpose of revising and amending the confederation, and reporting thereon, Several members of Congress expressed an anxious wish, that some state should instruct its delegates, to move in Congress, for such a recommendation as now exists, those of our legislature who have ever held in abhorance, the Interested policy of this state, so injurious to and so justly reprehended by Its neighbours, embraced the Idea with Alacrity, a favorable opportunity offered to propose It. Colo: Hamiltons Speech on the impost bill,[13] altho It carried no conviction to minds, determined not to be convinced, had such an effect on a numerous and respectable audience, that indignation was strongly marked on their countenances, when a Majority, without a single Sylable haveing been said In answer to Hamilton, rejected the bill.[14] severe animadversions were made on the conduct of the majority, in every company, and such of them, as had been led to vote against the bill, by promises, and the influence of a certain great man, were ashamed of their conduct, and wished an opportunity to make some atonement, whilst this impression agitated influenced these people, It was concieved the proper time to bring the proposition for instructions, forward, and it was accordingly introduced into the Assembly, violently opposed by the ——s [i.e., governor's] friends, but as many of those, who are at his beck, had committed themselves too far in private conversation, they voted (tho perhaps) reluctantly, for It.—In senate Mr Abraham Yates took the lead in opposition to it. Aristocracy King, Despot, unlimited power, sword and purse, fell from him in all the confusion of unintelligible Jargon. in short he was outrageous. He had the Mortification to fail of Success, the resolution was carried and transmitted to our delegates—The recommendatory resolve to the states was then moved in Congress carried, and without delay communicated to this state. It was too late to retract, and they Acquised with chagrin in a resolution for the appointment of delegates to the convention. Inadvertently the friends to the measure had acceeded to a resolution, so worded, as that the appointment should be by Joint ballot of both houses. this would have afforded the opponents an Opportunity to commit the delegation to creatures of their own complexion. I moved a rejection of the resolution on the specious,[15] and well founded reason, that the senate would be deprived of Its proper share of influence in the appointment. Yates soon perceived the true cause of my Objection, but durst not avow it,—he stickled however most stren[u]ously for adopting the resolution as It stood. my motion, however prevailed by a small majority. I then moved a resolution in substance as to the powers of, and number of the delegates, the same as that which came from the Assembly, but directing the like mode of appointment, as is used in the nominating delegates to Congress. Abraham attempted to shackle this, but without success, he then moved a reduction of the number of delegates from five, to three, in this he prevailed.—this was followed by proposed amendments on his part, to the powers to be exercised by the delegates, which, If carried, would have rendered their Mission absolutely useless, long conversations ensued in support of, and against the amendments, the latter were successful, and the resolution was sent to the Assembly, concurred in, and delegates were appointed Judge Yates, Colo: Hamilton and John Lansingh Jun Esqr are the men.—

"What will our state do, will they prefer temporary advantages to lasting good"? this is your question, it is almost decidedly Answered by the rejection of the impost bill,—but we have decided for a convention to amend the Confederation! And this you may think augers well. It will doubtless appear so, to those who are unacquainted with the political system which prevails with a certain Junto.—the principles of which are, a state impost, no direct taxation, keep all power in the hands of the legislature, give none to Congress which may destroy our influence, and cast a shade over that plenitude of power which we now enjoy,—since we could not prevent a Convention,—let it meet, alterations will be proposed, confering additional powers on Congress, we will propagate that every additional power conferred on that body, will be destructive of Liberty, may [induce?] a King, an Aristocracy, or a despot, the people will be alarmed, and their representatives will be deterred, from affording their assent, besides a variety of pretences may turn up for not Acceeding!—this I am fully persuaded is the reasoning of this selfish Junto, which under the present distracted state of the foedral goverment is increasing Its influence, an Influence which there is too much reason to believe will soon become as extensive as that of the british minister in the house of commons, but directed to infinitely [less laudable?] and honest purposes. . . .

Assembly Proceedings, Monday, 16 April 1787 (excerpts)[16]

. . . Mr. Hamilton made a motion that the House would agree to a resolution in the words following, *viz.*

Resolved, (if the Honorable the Senate concur herein) That two Delegates be appointed, in addition to those already appointed to represent this State at the Convention proposed to be holden at Philadelphia, on the second Monday of May next; and that any three of the persons heretofore appointed and of those now to be appointed, shall be sufficient to represent this State at the said Convention; and that this House will be ready on Wednesday next to proceed to the appointment of the said two Delegates, in the manner in which Delegates are appointed to Congress.

The question being put, whether the House would agree to the said resolution, it was carried in the affirmative, in the manner following, *viz.*

FOR THE AFFIRMATIVE [26].

Mr. C. Livingston,	Mr. Doughty,	Mr. Gordon,	Mr. Schenck,	Mr. Powers,
Mr. Malcom,	Mr. Harper,	Mr. Frey,	Mr. Frost,	Mr. Tayler,
Mr. Hamilton,	Mr. Wykoff,	Mr. Crane,	Mr. C. Smith,	Mr. Glen,
Mr. Bayard,	Mr. E. Clark,	Mr. Rockwell,	Mr. Sickels,	Mr. Osborn,
Mr. Bancker,	Mr. Strang,	Mr. Thorne,	Mr. Dongan,	Mr. Broanck,
Mr. Denning,				

FOR THE NEGATIVE [21].

Mr. Ray,	Mr. Savage,	Mr. Patterson,	Mr. D'Witt,	Mr. Snyder,
Mr. Clark,	Mr. Martin,	Mr. Armstrong,	Mr. Batcheller,	Mr. J. Smith,
Mr. Parker,	Mr. Griffen,	Mr. Duboys,	Mr. N. Smith,	Mr. Ludenton,
Mr. Jones,	Mr. Taulman,	Mr. Cooper,	Mr. Cantine,	Mr. Tompkins.
Mr. Paine,				

Thereupon,

Resolved, (if the Honorable the Senate concur herein) That two Delegates be appointed in addition to those already appointed, to represent this State at the Convention proposed to be holden at Philadelphia, on the second Monday of May next; and that any three of the persons heretofore appointed, and of those now to be appointed, shall be sufficient to represent this State at the said Convention; and that this House will be ready on Wednesday next, to proceed to the appointment of the said two Delegates, in the manner in which Delegates are appointed to Congress.

Ordered, That Mr. Duboys, deliver a copy of the preceding resolution to the Honorable the Senate. . . .

Newspaper Reports of Assembly Proceedings and Debates
Monday, 16 April 1787 (excerpt)

Daily Advertiser, 19 April

. . . Mr. Hamilton moved for a resolution to appoint two additional delegates, to represent this state in the convention.

He mentioned the great benefits that would arise from sending, either Mr. Chancellor Livingston, Mr. Benson, Mr. Duane, or Mr. Jay, particularly the latter. These were names he threw out for the consideration of the members.

On the question, this resolution was agreed to, and sent up to the senate for concurrence, when, if it meets their opinion, two additional delegates will be chosen. . . .

———

Daily Advertiser, 24 April

In our paper of the 19th inst. we gave the following account of Mr. Hamilton's motion for a resolution to send additional delegates to the convention.

"*Mr. Hamilton moved for a resolution to appoint two additional delegates, to represent this state in convention.*

"*He mentioned the great benefits that would result from sending, either Mr. Chancellor Livingston, Mr. Benson, Mr. Duane, or Mr. Jay, particularly the latter. These were names he threw out for the consideration of the members.*"

On a review of our notes we find that there is an idea conveyed in the above short account of the matter which does not correspond with what was said.

Mr. Hamilton after several introductory observations went on thus.—
I think it proper to apprise the house of the gentlemen on some of whom I wish their choice to fall, and with a view to which I bring forward the present motion. Their abilities and experience in the general affairs of this country cannot but be useful upon such an occasion.—I mean Mr. Chancellor Livingston, Mr. Duane, Mr. Benson, and Mr. Jay. The particular situation of the latter may require an observation or two. His being a servant of Congress might seem an objection to his appointment, but surely this objection if it had any weight would have applied with equal force to the appointment of a member of that body. In the case of Mr. Lansing the two houses appear to have thought there was no force in it; and I am persuaded there can be no reason to apply a different rule to Mr. Jay.[17] His acknowledged abilities, tried integrity, and abundant experience in the affairs of this country, foreign and domestic will not permit us to allow any weight to any objection which would imply a want of confidence in a character that has every title to the fullest confidence.

Senate Proceedings, Tuesday, 17 April 1787 (excerpts)[18]

. . . A Message from the Honorable the Assembly, by Mr. Dubois, was received, with the following resolutions for concurrence, *viz.*

Resolved, (if the Honorable the Senate concur herein) That two Delegates be appointed in addition to those already appointed to represent this State at the Convention proposed to be holden at Philadelphia, on the second Monday of May next; and that any three of the persons heretofore appointed, and of those now to be appointed, shall be sufficient to represent this State at the said Convention: And that this House will be ready on Wednesday next, to proceed to the appointment of the said two Delegates, in the manner in which Delegates are appointed to Congress. . . .

Ordered, That the consideration of the said resolutions be postponed. . . .

Senate Proceedings, Wednesday, 18 April 1787 (excerpt)[19]

. . . The Senate proceeded to the consideration of the resolution of the Honorable the Assembly, received yesterday, proposing that two additional Delegates be appointed to meet in Convention at Philadelphia, in May next, which being read, debates arose, and the question being put for concurring with the Honorable the Assembly in their said resolution, it was carried in the negative in manner following, *viz.*

F O R   T H E   N E G A T I V E [12].

Mr. Yates,	Mr. Peter Schuyler,	Mr. Hathorn,	Mr. Floyd,
Mr. Tredwell,	Mr. Russell,	Mr. Humfrey,	Mr. Williams.
Mr. Ward,	Mr. Swartwout,	Mr. Parks,	Mr. Van Ness.

F O R   T H E   A F F I R M A T I V E [5].

Mr. Stoutenburgh,	Mr. Townsend,	Mr. Morris,	Mr. L'Hommedieu.
Mr. Vanderbilt,			

Thereupon,

Resolved, That the Senate do not concur with the Honorable the Assembly in their said resolution.

Ordered, That Mr. Russell deliver a copy of the preceding resolution of non-concurrence to the Honorable the Assembly. . . .

Assembly Proceedings, Wednesday, 18 April 1787 (excerpt)[20]

. . . A copy of a resolution of the Honorable the Senate, also delivered by Mr. Russell, was read, that the Senate do not concur with this House, in their resolution of the 16th instant, for appointing two additional Delegates to represent this State at the Convention proposed to be holden at Philadelphia, on the second Monday of May next. . . .

1. *Assembly Journal* [12 January–21 April 1787] (New York, 1787), 63 (Evans 20576). These proceedings were printed in the *Daily Advertiser* on 28 February (Mfm:N.Y.).

2. *Assembly Journal*, 68. The *Daily Advertiser*, 1 March (immediately below), identified Alexander Hamilton as the maker of this motion.

3. *Daily Advertiser*, 1 March.

4. *Senate Journal* [12 January–21 April 1787] (New York,1787), 42–43 (Evans 20577).

5. The Assembly had received this message on 23 February (above).

6. *Senate Journal*, 43. On 27 February Lewis Morris, Sr., reported that "warm disputes" were taking place in the Senate on whether to appoint delegates to the proposed constitutional convention (to Lewis Morris, Jr., 27 February, Mfm:N.Y.).

7. *Senate Journal*, 44–45. In a supplementary issue on 10 May 1788, the *Albany Gazette* printed (without editorial comment) these Senate proceedings through the paragraph indicating that the Senate's president broke a tie vote.

8. *Assembly Journal*, 70–71. These proceedings were printed in the *Daily Advertiser* on 3 March (Mfm:N.Y.).

9. *Senate Journal*, 46.

10. *Assembly Journal*, 82–84. On 8 March the Assembly's proceedings were printed in the *Daily Advertiser* which gave the vote totals for each of the seven men who received votes to be delegates to the proposed constitutional convention (Mfm:N.Y.). Unlike the *Assembly Journal*, the *Advertiser* did not reveal how each of the fifty-two assemblymen voted. On 7 March the *Advertiser* had printed a squib that was widely circulated, indicating that Robert Yates, Alexander Hamilton, and John Lansing, Jr., had been elected convention delegates.

11. *Senate Journal*, 50–51.

12. RC, Henry Van Schaack Scrapbook, Newberry Library, Chicago. Printed: Henry Cruger Van Schaack, *Memoirs of the Life of Henry Van Schaack* . . . (Chicago, 1892), 149–55. Van Schaack (1733–1823), a native of Kinderhook, N.Y., had become wealthy in the fur trade before the Revolution. During that war he was a Loyalist who tried to remain

neutral. Nevertheless, he was banished to Hartford, Conn., and then allowed to go to Massachusetts. After the war he settled first in the Berkshire County town of Richmond and then in Pittsfield, where he lived for more than twenty years before returning to Kinderhook.

13. For the text of Alexander Hamilton's 15 February speech on the Impost of 1783, see Syrett, IV, 71–92. See also "Introduction" (above).

14. After Hamilton finished speaking, the Assembly voted 36 to 21 against removing New York's restrictions on Congress' power to levy the impost.

15. In the eighteenth century, "specious" meant "plausible" or "pleasing."

16. *Assembly Journal*, 165–66.

17. John Jay was Confederation Secretary for Foreign Affairs, while John Lansing, Jr., was a delegate to Congress, having been elected on 26 January 1787.

18. *Senate Journal*, 93.

19. *Senate Journal*, 95.

20. *Assembly Journal*, 170.

Appendix III
The Report of the Constitutional Convention
17 September 1787

The President of the Convention to the President of Congress[1]

In Convention, September 17, 1787.

SIR, We have now the honor to submit to the consideration of the United States in Congress assembled, that Constitution which has appeared to us the most adviseable.

The friends of our country have long seen and desired, that the power of making war, peace and treaties, that of levying money and regulating commerce, and the correspondent executive and judicial authorities should be fully and effectually vested in the general government of the Union: but the impropriety of delegating such extensive trust to one body of men is evident—Hence results the necessity of a different organization.

It is obviously impracticable in the fœderal government of these States, to secure all rights of independent sovereignty to each, and yet provide for the interest and safety of all—Individuals entering into society, must give up a share of liberty to preserve the rest. The magnitude of the sacrifice must depend as well on situation and circumstance, as on the object to be obtained. It is at all times difficult to draw with precision the line between those rights which must be surrendered, and those which may be reserved; and on the present occasion this difficulty was encreased by a difference among the several States as to their situation, extent, habits, and particular interests.

In all our deliberations on this subject we kept steadily in our view, that which appears to us the greatest interest of every true American, the consolidation of our Union, in which is involved our prosperity, felicity, safety, perhaps our national existence. This important consideration, seriously and deeply impressed on our minds, led each State in the Convention to be less rigid on points of inferior magnitude, than might have been otherwise expected; and thus the Constitution, which we now present, is the result of a spirit of amity, and of that mutual deference and concession which the peculiarity of our political situation rendered indispensible.

That it will meet the full and entire approbation of every State is not perhaps to be expected; but each will doubtless consider, that had her interests been alone consulted, the consequences might have been particularly disagreeable or injurious to others; that it is liable to as few exceptions as could reasonably have been expected, we hope and believe; that it may promote the lasting welfare of that country so dear to us all, and secure her freedom and happiness, is our most ardent wish.

With great respect, We have the honor to be SIR, Your Excellency's most Obedient and humble servants.

George Washington, President.
By unanimous Order of the Convention,

HIS EXCELLENCY
The President of Congress.

1. Broadside, PCC, Item 122, Resolve Book of the Office of Foreign Affairs, 1785–89, tipped in between pages 98–99, DNA. The original letter has been lost. The above is transcribed from the official copy of the Convention Report, printed by John McLean and attested by Charles Thomson.

The Constitution of the United States[1]

We the People of the United States, in Order to form a more perfect Union, establish Justice, insure domestic Tranquility, provide for the common defence, promote the general Welfare, and secure the Blessings of Liberty to ourselves and our Posterity, do ordain and establish this Constitution for the United States of America.

Article. I.

Section. 1. All legislative Powers herein granted shall be vested in a Congress of the United States, which shall consist of a Senate and House of Representatives.

Section. 2. The House of Representatives shall be composed of Members chosen every second Year by the People of the several States, and the Electors in each State shall have the Qualifications requisite for Electors of the most numerous Branch of the State Legislature.

No Person shall be a Representative who shall not have attained to the Age of twenty five Years, and been seven Years a Citizen of the United States, and who shall not, when elected, be an Inhabitant of that State in which he shall be chosen.

Representatives and direct Taxes shall be apportioned among the several States which may be included within this Union, according to their respective Numbers, which shall be determined by adding to the whole Number of free Persons, including those bound to Service for a Term of Years, and excluding Indians not taxed, three fifths of all other

Persons. The actual Enumeration shall be made within three Years after the first Meeting of the Congress of the United States, and within every subsequent Term of ten Years, in such Manner as they shall by Law direct. The Number of Representatives shall not exceed one for every thirty Thousand, but each State shall have at Least one Representative; and until such enumeration shall be made, the State of New Hampshire shall be entitled to chuse three, Massachusetts eight, Rhode-Island and Providence Plantations one, Connecticut five, New-York six, New Jersey four, Pennsylvania eight, Delaware one, Maryland six, Virginia ten, North Carolina five, South Carolina five, and Georgia three.

When vacancies happen in the Representation from any State, the Executive Authority thereof shall issue Writs of Election to fill such Vacancies.

The House of Representatives shall chuse their Speaker and other Officers; and shall have the sole Power of Impeachment.

Section. 3. The Senate of the United States shall be composed of two Senators from each State, chosen by the Legislature thereof, for six Years; and each Senator shall have one Vote.

Immediately after they shall be assembled in Consequence of the first Election, they shall be divided as equally as may be into three Classes. The Seats of the Senators of the first Class shall be vacated at the Expiration of the second Year, of the second Class at the Expiration of the fourth Year, and of the third Class at the Expiration of the sixth Year, so that one third may be chosen every second Year; and if Vacancies happen by Resignation, or otherwise, during the Recess of the Legislature of any State, the Executive thereof may make temporary Appointments until the next Meeting of the Legislature, which shall then fill such Vacancies.

No Person shall be a Senator who shall not have attained to the Age of thirty Years, and been nine Years a Citizen of the United States, and who shall not, when elected, be an Inhabitant of that State for which he shall be chosen.

The Vice President of the United States shall be President of the Senate, but shall have no Vote, unless they be equally divided.

The Senate shall chuse their other Officers, and also a President pro tempore, in the Absence of the Vice President, or when he shall exercise the Office of President of the United States.

The Senate shall have the sole Power to try all Impeachments. When sitting for that Purpose, they shall be on Oath or Affirmation. When the President of the United States is tried, the Chief Justice shall preside: And no Person shall be convicted without the Concurrence of two thirds of the Members present.

Judgment in Cases of Impeachment shall not extend further than to removal from Office, and disqualification to hold and enjoy any Office of honor, Trust or Profit under the United States: but the Party convicted shall nevertheless be liable and subject to Indictment, Trial, Judgment and Punishment, according to Law.

Section. 4. The Times, Places and Manner of holding Elections for Senators and Representatives, shall be prescribed in each State by the Legislature thereof; but the Congress may at any time by Law make or alter such Regulations, except as to the Places of chusing Senators.

The Congress shall assemble at least once in every Year, and such Meeting shall be on the first Monday in December, unless they shall by Law appoint a different Day.

Section. 5. Each House shall be the Judge of the Elections, Returns and Qualifications of its own Members, and a Majority of each shall constitute a Quorum to do Business; but a smaller Number may adjourn from day to day, and may be authorized to compel the Attendance of absent Members, in such Manner, and under such Penalties as each House may provide.

Each House may determine the Rules of its Proceedings, punish its members for disorderly Behaviour, and, with the Concurrence of two thirds, expel a Member.

Each House shall keep a Journal of its Proceedings, and from time to time publish the same, excepting such Parts as may in their Judgment require Secrecy; and the Yeas and Nays of the Members of either House on any question shall, at the Desire of one fifth of those Present, be entered on the Journal.

Neither House, during the Session of Congress, shall, without the Consent of the other, adjourn for more than three days, nor to any other Place than that in which the two Houses shall be sitting.

Section. 6. The Senators and Representatives shall receive a Compensation for their Services, to be ascertained by Law, and paid out of the Treasury of the United States. They shall in all Cases, except Treason, Felony and Breach of the Peace, be privileged from Arrest during their Attendance at the Session of their respective Houses, and in going to and returning from the same; and for any Speech or Debate in either House, they shall not be questioned in any other Place.

No Senator or Representative shall, during the Time for which he was elected, be appointed to any civil Office under the Authority of the United States which shall have been created, or the Emoluments whereof shall have been encreased during such time; and no Person holding any Office under the United States, shall be a Member of either House during his Continuance in Office.

Section. 7. All Bills for raising Revenue shall originate in the House of Representatives; but the Senate may propose or concur with Amendments as on other Bills.

Every Bill which shall have passed the House of Representatives and the Senate shall, before it become a Law, be presented to the President of the United States; If he approve he shall sign it, but if not he shall return it, with his Objections to that House in which it shall have originated, who shall enter the Objections at large on their Journal, and proceed to reconsider it. If after such Reconsideration two thirds of that House shall agree to pass the Bill, it shall be sent, together with the Objections, to the other House, by which it shall likewise be reconsidered, and if approved by two thirds of that House, it shall become a Law. But in all such Cases the Votes of both Houses shall be determined by yeas and Nays, and the Names of the Persons voting for and against the Bill shall be entered on the Journal of each House respectively. If any Bill shall not be returned by the President within ten Days (Sundays excepted) after it shall have been presented to him, the Same shall be a Law, in like Manner as if he had signed it, unless the Congress by their Adjournment prevent its Return, in which Case it shall not be a Law.

Every Order, Resolution, or Vote to which the Concurrence of the Senate and House of Representatives may be necessary (except on a question of Adjournment) shall be presented to the President of the United States; and before the Same shall take Effect, shall be approved by him, or being disapproved by him, shall be repassed by two thirds of the Senate and House of Representatives, according to the Rules and Limitations prescribed in the Case of a Bill.

Section. 8. The Congress shall have Power To lay and collect Taxes, Duties, Imposts and Excises, to pay the Debts and provide for the common Defence and general Welfare of the United States; but all Duties, Imposts and Excises shall be uniform throughout the United States;

To borrow Money on the credit of the United States;

To regulate Commerce with foreign Nations, and among the several States, and with the Indian Tribes;

To establish an uniform Rule of Naturalization, and uniform Laws on the subject of Bankruptcies throughout the United States;

To coin Money, regulate the Value thereof, and of foreign Coin, and fix the Standard of Weights and Measures;

To provide for the Punishment of counterfeiting the Securities and current Coin of the United States;

To establish Post Offices and post Roads;

To promote the Progress of Science and useful Arts, by securing for limited Times to Authors and Inventors the exclusive Right to their respective Writings and Discoveries;

To constitute Tribunals inferior to the supreme Court;

To define and punish Piracies and Felonies committed on the high Seas, and Offences against the Law of Nations;

To declare War, grant Letters of Marque and Reprisal, and make Rules concerning Captures on Land and Water;

To raise and support Armies, but no Appropriation of Money to that Use shall be for a longer Term than two Years;

To provide and maintain a Navy;

To make Rules for the Government and Regulation of the land and naval Forces;

To provide for calling forth the Militia to execute the Laws of the Union, suppress Insurrections and repel Invasions;

To provide for organizing, arming, and disciplining, the Militia, and for governing such Part of them as may be employed in the Service of the United States, reserving to the States respectively, the Appointment of the Officers, and the Authority of training the Militia according to the discipline prescribed by Congress;

To exercise exclusive Legislation in all Cases whatsoever, over such District (not exceeding ten Miles square) as may, by Cession of particular States, and the Acceptance of Congress, become the Seat of the Government of the United States, and to exercise like Authority over all Places purchased by the Consent of the Legislature of the State in which the same shall be, for the Erection of Forts, Magazines, Arsenals, dock-Yards, and other needful Buildings;—And

To make all Laws which shall be necessary and proper for carrying into Execution the foregoing Powers, and all other Powers vested by this Constitution in the Government of the United States, or in any Department or Officer thereof.

Section. 9. The Migration or Importation of such Persons as any of the States now existing shall think proper to admit, shall not be prohibited by the Congress prior to the Year one thousand eight hundred and eight, but a Tax or duty may be imposed on such Importation, not exceeding ten dollars for each Person.

The Privilege of the Writ of Habeas Corpus shall not be suspended, unless when in Cases of Rebellion or Invasion the public Safety may require it.

No Bill of Attainder or ex post facto Law shall be passed.

No Capitation, or other direct, Tax shall be laid, unless in Proportion to the Census or Enumeration herein before directed to be taken.

No Tax or Duty shall be laid on Articles exported from any State.

No Preference shall be given by any Regulation of Commerce or Revenue to the Ports of one State over those of another: nor shall Vessels bound to, or from, one State, be obliged to enter, clear, or pay Duties in another.

No Money shall be drawn from the Treasury, but in Consequence of Appropriations made by Law; and a regular Statement and Account of the Receipts and Expenditures of all public Money shall be published from time to time.

No Title of Nobility shall be granted by the United States: And no Person holding any Office of Profit or Trust under them, shall, without the Consent of the Congress, accept of any present, Emolument, Office, or Title, of any kind whatever, from any King, Prince, or foreign State.

Section. 10. No State shall enter into any Treaty, Alliance, or Confederation; grant Letters of Marque and Reprisal; coin Money; emit Bills of Credit; make any Thing but gold and silver Coin a Tender in Payment of Debts; pass any Bill of Attainder, ex post facto Law, or Law impairing the Obligation of Contracts, or grant any Title of Nobility.

No State shall, without the Consent of the Congress, lay any Imposts or Duties on Imports or Exports, except what may be absolutely necessary for executing it's inspection Laws: and the net Produce of all Duties and Imposts, laid by any State on Imports or Exports, shall be for the Use of the Treasury of the United States; and all such Laws shall be subject to the Revision and Controul of the Congress.

No State shall, without the Consent of Congress, lay any Duty of Tonnage, keep Troops, or Ships of War in time of Peace, enter into any Agreement or Compact with another State, or with a foreign Power, or engage in War, unless actually invaded, or in such imminent Danger as will not admit of delay.

Article. II.

Section. 1. The executive Power shall be vested in a President of the United States of America. He shall hold his Office during the Term of four Years, and, together with the Vice President, chosen for the same Term, be elected, as follows

Each State shall appoint, in such Manner as the Legislature thereof may direct, a Number of Electors, equal to the whole Number of Senators and Representatives to which the state may be entitled in the Congress: but no Senator or Representative, or Person holding an Office of Trust or Profit under the United States, shall be appointed an Elector.

The Electors shall meet in their respective States and vote by Ballot for two Persons, of whom one at least shall not be an Inhabitant of the same State with themselves. And they shall make a List of all the Persons voted for, and of the Number of Votes for each; which List they shall sign and certify, and transmit sealed to the Seat of the Government of the United States, directed to the President of the Senate. The President of the Senate shall, in the Presence of the Senate and House of Representatives, open all the Certificates, and the Votes shall then be counted. The Person having the greatest Number of Votes shall be the President, if such Number be a Majority of the whole Number of Electors appointed; and if there be more than one who have such Majority, and have an equal Number of Votes, then the House of Representatives shall immediately chuse by Ballot one of them for President; and if no Person have a Majority, then from the five highest on the List the said House shall in like Manner chuse the President. But in chusing the President, the Votes shall be taken by States, the Representation from each State having one Vote; A quorum for this Purpose shall consist of a Member or Members from two thirds of the States, and a Majority of all the States shall be necessary to a Choice. In every Case, after the Choice of the President, the Person having the greatest Number of Votes of the Electors shall be the Vice President. But if there should remain two or more who have equal Votes, the Senate shall chuse from them by Ballot the Vice President.

The Congress may determine the Time of chusing the Electors, and the Day on which they shall give their Votes; which Day shall be the same throughout the United States.

No Person except a natural born Citizen, or a Citizen of the United States, at the time of the Adoption of this Constitution, shall be eligible to the Office of President; neither shall any Person be eligible to that Office who shall not have attained to the Age of thirty five Years, and been fourteen Years a Resident within the United States.

In Case of the Removal of the President from Office, or of his Death, Resignation, or Inability to discharge the Powers and Duties of the said Office, the Same shall devolve on the Vice President, and the Congress may by Law provide for the Case of Removal, Death, Resignation or Inability, both of the President and Vice President, declaring what Officer shall then act as President, and such Officer shall act accordingly, until the Disability be removed, or a President shall be elected.

The President shall, at stated Times, receive for his Services, a Compensation, which shall neither be increased nor diminished during the Period for which he shall have been elected, and he shall not receive within that Period any other Emolument from the United States, or any of them.

Before he enter on the Execution of his Office, he shall take the following Oath or Affirmation:—"I do solemnly swear (or affirm) that I will faithfully execute the Office of President of the United States, and will to the best of my Ability, preserve, protect and defend the Constitution of the United States."

Section. 2. The President shall be Commander in Chief of the Army and Navy of the United States, and of the Militia of the several States, when called into the actual Service of the United States; he may require the Opinion, in writing, of the principal Officer in each of the executive Departments, upon any Subject relating to the Duties of their respective Offices, and he shall have Power to grant Reprieves and Pardons for Offences against the United States, except in Cases of Impeachment.

He shall have Power, by and with the Advice and Consent of the Senate, to make Treaties, provided two thirds of the Senators present concur; and he shall nominate, and by and with the Advice and Consent of the Senate, shall appoint Ambassadors, other public Ministers and Consuls, Judges of the supreme Court, and all other Officers of the United States, whose Appointments are not herein otherwise provided for, and which shall be established by Law: but the Congress may by Law vest the Appointment of such inferior Officers, as they think proper, in the President alone, in the Courts of Law, or in the Heads of Departments.

The President shall have Power to fill up all Vacancies that may happen during the Recess of the Senate, by granting Commissions which shall expire at the End of their next Session.

Section. 3. He shall from time to time give to the Congress Information of the State of the Union, and recommend to their Consideration such Measures as he shall judge necessary and expedient; he may, on extraordinary Occasions, convene both Houses, or either of them, and in Case of Disagreement between them, with Respect to the Time of Adjournment, he may adjourn them to such Time as he shall think proper; he shall receive Ambassadors and other public Ministers; he shall take Care that the Laws be faithfully executed, and shall Commission all the Officers of the United States.

Section. 4. The President, Vice President and all civil Officers of the United States, shall be removed from Office on Impeachment for, and Conviction of Treason, Bribery, or other high Crimes and Misdemeanors.

Article III.

Section. 1. The judicial Power of the United States, shall be vested in one supreme Court, and in such inferior Courts as the Congress may from time to time ordain and establish. The Judges, both of the supreme and inferior Courts, shall hold their Offices during good Behaviour, and shall, at stated Times, receive for their Services, a Compensation, which shall not be diminished during their Continuance in Office.

Section. 2. The judicial Power shall extend to all Cases, in Law and Equity, arising under this Constitution, the Laws of the United States, and Treaties made, or which shall be made, under their Authority;—to all Cases affecting Ambassadors, other public Ministers and Consuls;—to all Cases of admiralty and maritime Jurisdiction;—to Controversies to which the United States shall be a Party;—to Controversies between two or more States;—between a State and Citizens of another State;—between Citizens of different States,—between Citizens of the same State claiming Lands under Grants of different States, and between a State, or the Citizens thereof, and foreign States, Citizens or Subjects.

In all Cases affecting Ambassadors, other public Ministers and Consuls, and those in which a State shall be Party, the supreme Court shall have original Jurisdiction. In all the other Cases before mentioned, the supreme Court shall have appellate Jurisdiction, both as to Law and Fact, with such Exceptions, and under such Regulations as the Congress shall make.

The Trial of all Crimes, except in Cases of Impeachment, shall be by Jury; and such Trial shall be held in the State where the said Crimes shall have been committed; but when not committed within any State, the Trial shall be at such Place or Places as the Congress may by Law have directed.

Section. 3. Treason against the United States, shall consist only in levying War against them, or in adhering to their Enemies, giving them Aid and Comfort. No Person shall be convicted of Treason unless on the Testimony of two Witnesses to the same overt Act, or on Confession in open Court.

The Congress shall have Power to declare the Punishment of Treason, but no Attainder of Treason shall work Corruption of Blood, or Forfeiture except during the Life of the Person attainted.

Article. IV.

Section. 1. Full Faith and Credit shall be given in each State to the public Acts, Records, and judicial Proceedings of every other State. And the Congress may by general Laws prescribe the Manner in which such Acts, Records and Proceedings shall be proved, and the Effect thereof.

Section. 2. The Citizens of each State shall be entitled to all privileges and Immunities of Citizens in the several States.

A Person charged in any State with Treason, Felony, or other Crime, who shall flee from Justice, and be found in another State, shall on Demand of the executive Authority of the State from which he fled, be delivered up, to be removed to the State having Jurisdiction of the Crime.

No Person held to Service or Labour in one State, under the Laws thereof, escaping into another, shall, in Consequence of any Law or Regulation therein, be discharged from such Service or Labour, but shall be delivered up on Claim of the Party to whom such Service or Labour may be due.

Section. 3. New States may be admitted by the Congress into this Union; but no new State shall be formed or erected within the Jurisdiction of any other State; nor any State be formed by the Junction of two or more States, or Parts of States, without the Consent of the Legislatures of the States concerned as well as of the Congress.

The Congress shall have Power to dispose of and make all needful Rules and Regulations respecting the Territory or other Property belonging to the United States; and nothing in this Constitution shall be so construed as to Prejudice any Claims of the United States, or of any particular State.

Section. 4. The United States shall guarantee to every State in this Union a Republican Form of Government, and shall protect each of them against Invasion; and on Application of the Legislature, or of the Executive (when the Legislature cannot be convened) against domestic Violence.

Article. V.

The Congress, whenever two thirds of both Houses shall deem it necessary, shall propose Amendments to this Constitution, or, on the Application of the Legislatures of two thirds of the several States, shall call a Convention for proposing Amendments, which, in either Case, shall be valid to all Intents and Purposes, as Part of this Constitution, when ratified by the Legislatures of three fourths of the several States, or by Conventions in three fourths thereof, as the one or the other Mode of Ratification may be proposed by the Congress; Provided that no Amendment which may be made prior to the Year One thousand eight hundred and eight shall in any Manner affect the first and fourth Clauses in the Ninth Section of the first Article; and that no State, without its Consent, shall be deprived of it's equal Suffrage in the Senate.

Article. VI.

All Debts contracted and Engagements entered into, before the Adoption of this Constitution, shall be as valid against the United States under this Constitution, as under the Confederation.

This Constitution, and the Laws of the United States which shall be made in Pursuance thereof; and all Treaties made, or which shall be made, under the Authority of the United States, shall be the supreme Law of the Land; and the Judges in every State shall be bound thereby, any Thing in the Constitution or Laws of any State to the Contrary notwithstanding.

The Senators and Representatives before mentioned, and the Members of the several State Legislatures, and all executive and judicial Officers; both of the United States and of the several States, shall be bound by Oath or Affirmation, to support this Constitution; but no religious Test shall ever be required as a Qualification to any Office or public Trust under the United States.

Article. VII.

The Ratification of the Conventions of nine States, shall be sufficient for the Establishment of this Constitution between the States so ratifying the Same.

The Word, "the," being interlined between the seventh and eighth Lines of the first Page, The Word "Thirty" being partly written on an Erazure in the fifteenth Line of the first Page, The Words "is tried" being interlined between the thirty second and thirty third Lines of the first Page and the Word "the" being interlined between the forty third and forty fourth Lines of the second Page.

done in Convention by the Unanimous Consent of the States present the Seventeenth Day of September in the Year of our Lord one thousand seven hundred and Eighty seven and of the Independance of the United States of America the Twelfth In Witness whereof We have hereunto subscribed our Names,

Attest William Jackson Secretary

Go: Washington—Presidt.
and deputy from Virginia

Delaware {	Geo: Read Gunning Bedford junr John Dickinson Richard Bassett Jaco: Broom	

New Hampshire { John Langdon / Nicholas Gilman

Massachusetts { Nathaniel Gorham / Rufus King

Maryland { James McHenry / Dan of St Thos. Jenifer / Danl Carroll

Connecticut { Wm: Saml. Johnson / Roger Sherman

New York . . . Alexander Hamilton

Virginia { John Blair— / James Madison Jr.

North Carolina { Wm. Blount / Richd. Dobbs Spaight. / Hu Williamson

New Jersey { Wil: Livingston / David Brearley / Wm. Paterson / Jona: Dayton

South Carolina { J. Rutledge / Charles Cotesworth Pinckney / Charles Pinckney / Pierce Butler

Pensylvania { B Franklin / Thomas Mifflin / Robt Morris / Geo. Clymer / Thos. FitzSimons / Jared Ingersoll / James Wilson / Gouv. Morris

Georgia { William Few / Abr Baldwin

1. Engrossed MS, RG 11, DNA.

Resolutions of the Convention Recommending the Procedures for Ratification and for the Establishment of Government under the Constitution by the Confederation Congress[1]

In Convention Monday September 17th. 1787.

Present The States of New Hampshire, Massachusetts, Connecticut, Mr. Hamilton from New York, New Jersey, Pennsylvania, Delaware, Maryland, Virginia, North Carolina, South Carolina and Georgia.

RESOLVED, That the preceeding Constitution be laid before the United States in Congress assembled, and that it is the Opinion of this Convention, that it should afterwards be submitted to a Convention of Delegates, chosen in each State by the People thereof, under the Recommendation of its Legislature, for their Assent and Ratification; and that each Convention assenting to, and ratifying the Same, should give Notice thereof to the United States in Congress assembled.

Resolved, That it is the Opinion of this Convention, that as soon as the Conventions of nine States shall have ratified this Constitution, the

United States in Congress assembled should fix a Day on which Electors should be appointed by the States which shall have ratified the same, and a Day on which the Electors should assemble to vote for the President, and the Time and Place for commencing Proceedings under this Constitution. That after such Publication the Electors should be appointed, and the Senators and Representatives elected: That the Electors should meet on the Day fixed for the Election of the President, and should transmit their Votes certified, signed, sealed and directed, as the Constitution requires, to the Secretary of the United States in Congress assembled, that the Senators and Representatives should convene at the Time and Place assigned; that the Senators should appoint a President of the Senate, for the sole Purpose of receiving, opening and counting the Votes for President; and, that after he shall be chosen, the Congress, together with the President, should, without Delay, proceed to execute this Constitution.

By the Unanimous Order of the Convention

W. Jackson Secretary.   Go: Washington Presidt.

1. Engrossed MS, RG 11, DNA.

Appendix IV
Printings and Reprintings of *The Federalist*

Between 27 October 1787 and 28 May 1788 eighty-five essays—entitled *The Federalist* and signed "Publius"—were published in New York City newspapers and in two volumes, totalling more than 600 pages. Published by New York City printers John and Archibald M'Lean, the first volume which appeared on 22 March 1788 contained thirty-six essays and the second which appeared on 28 May 1788 had forty-nine. The last eight essays were published for the first time in the second volume and subsequently were reprinted in two New York City newspapers.

This table shows the original printings and reprintings of all the essays. The essays are assigned the numbers used in the volumes. The author of each essay is identified as either Alexander Hamilton, John Jay, or James Madison. The first printing of each essay is followed by its identifying number in the *Commentaries on the Constitution* series.

No.1 (Hamilton)
New York *Independent Journal*, 27 October 1787 (CC:201)
    New York *Daily Advertiser*, 30 October
    New York Packet, 30 October
    Salem Mercury, 6 November (excerpt)
    Pennsylvania Journal, 7 November
    Boston *Independent Chronicle*, 8 November (excerpt, RCS:Mass., 208)
    Worcester Magazine, 8 November (excerpt)
    New Hampshire Mercury, 9 November (excerpt)
    Boston *American Herald*, 12 November
    Lansingburgh *Northern Centinel*, 13 November
    Northampton, Mass., *Hampshire Gazette*, 14 November (excerpt)
    Albany Gazette, 15 November
    Pennsylvania Packet, 20 November (excerpt)
    Pennsylvania Gazette, 21 November (excerpt)
    Hudson Weekly Gazette, 22 November
    Providence *United States Chronicle*, 22 November
    Philadelphia *American Museum*, November
    Charleston *Columbian Herald*, 6 December (excerpt)
    Virginia Independent Chronicle, 12 December
    Richmond Pamphlet Anthology, c. 15 December (CC:350)

No. 2 (Jay)
New York *Independent Journal*, 31 October 1787 (CC:217)
    New York *Daily Advertiser*, 1 November
    New York Packet, 2 November
    Pennsylvania Journal, 10 November
    Pennsylvania Gazette, 14 November

Lansingburgh *Northern Centinel*, 20 November
Albany Gazette, 22 November
Providence *United States Chronicle*, 22 November
Boston *American Herald*, 26 November
Hudson Weekly Gazette, 29 November
Philadelphia *American Museum*, November
Richmond Pamphlet Anthology, c. 15 December (CC:350)
Virginia Independent Chronicle, 19 December

No. 3 (Jay)
New York *Independent Journal*, 3 November 1787 (CC:228)
New York *Daily Advertiser*, 5 November
New York Packet, 6 November
Pennsylvania Journal, 17 November
Pennsylvania Gazette, 21 November
Lansingburgh *Northern Centinel*, 27 November
Albany Gazette, 6, 13 December
Hudson Weekly Gazette, 6 December
Boston *American Herald*, 10 December
Norfolk and Portsmouth Journal, 12 December
Richmond Pamphlet Anthology, c. 15 December (CC:350)
Virginia Independent Chronicle, 26 December
Providence *United States Chronicle*, 27 December
Philadelphia *American Museum*, December

No. 4 (Jay)
New York *Independent Journal*, 7 November 1787 (CC:234)
New York *Daily Advertiser*, 8 November
New York Packet, 9 November
New Haven Gazette, 15 November (excerpt)
Pennsylvania Gazette, 28 November
Albany Gazette, 29 November
Lansingburgh *Northern Centinel*, 4 December
Hudson Weekly Gazette, 13 December
Richmond *Virginia Gazette*, 22 December
Philadelphia *American Museum*, December

No. 5 (Jay)
New York *Independent Journal*, 10 November 1787 (CC:252)
New York *Daily Advertiser*, 12 November
New York Packet, 13 November
New Haven Gazette, 15 November (excerpt)
Pennsylvania Journal, 28 November
Boston *American Herald*, 3 December
Pennsylvania Gazette, 5 December
Lansingburgh *Northern Centinel*, 11 December
Albany Gazette, 13 December
Hudson Weekly Gazette, 13 December
Winchester *Virginia Gazette*, 14 December (excerpt)
Richmond *Virginia Gazette*, 29 December
Philadelphia *American Museum*, December

No. 6 (Hamilton)
New York *Independent Journal*, 14 November 1787 (CC:257)
   New York *Daily Advertiser*, 15 November
   New York Packet, 16 November
   Pennsylvania Gazette, 5 December
   Lansingburgh *Northern Centinel*, 18 December
   Albany Gazette, 20 December
   Hudson Weekly Gazette, 20 December
   Philadelphia *American Magazine*, December
   Norfolk and Portsmouth Journal, 9 January 1788

No. 7 (Hamilton)
New York *Independent Journal*, 17 November 1787 (CC:269)
   New York *Daily Advertiser*, 19 November
   New York Packet, 20 November
   Pennsylvania Gazette, 12 December
   Hudson Weekly Gazette, 20, 27 December
   Lansingburgh *Northern Centinel*, 25 December

No. 8 (Hamilton)
New York Packet, 20 November 1787 (CC:274)
   New York *Daily Advertiser*, 21 November
   New York *Independent Journal*, 21 November
   New Haven Gazette, 29 November (excerpts)
   Pennsylvania Gazette, 19 December
   Hudson Weekly Gazette, 27 December
   Lansingburgh *Northern Centinel*, 1 January 1788
   Albany Gazette, 3 January

No. 9 (Hamilton)
New York *Independent Journal*, 21 November 1787 (CC:277)
   New York *Daily Advertiser*, 21 November
   New York Packet, 23 November
   Salem Mercury, 4 December (excerpt)
   Pennsylvania Gazette, 26 December
   Hudson Weekly Gazette, 3 January 1788
   Lansingburgh *Northern Centinel*, 8 January
   Albany Gazette, 10 January

No. 10 (Madison)
New York *Daily Advertiser*, 22 November 1787 (CC:285)
   New York Packet, 23 November
   New York *Independent Journal*, 24 November
   Pennsylvania Gazette, 2 January 1788
   Hudson Weekly Gazette, 10 January
   Lansingburgh *Northern Centinel*, 15 January
   Albany Gazette, 17 January

No. 11 (Hamilton)
New York *Independent Journal*, 24 November 1787 (CC:291)
   New York Packet, 27 November
   New York *Daily Advertiser*, 27, 28 November
   Salem Mercury, 4 December (excerpt)

Massachusetts Centinel, 8 December (excerpt)
Pennsylvania Packet, 19 December (excerpt)
Baltimore *Maryland Gazette*, 25 December (excerpt)
Charleston *Columbian Herald*, 14 January 1788 (excerpt)
Pennsylvania Gazette, 16 January
Hudson Weekly Gazette, 17 January

No.12 (Hamilton)
New York Packet, 27 November 1787 (CC:297)
New York *Independent Journal*, 28 November
New York *Daily Advertiser*, 29 November
Pennsylvania Gazette, 23 January 1788
Albany Gazette, 31 January

No. 13 (Hamilton)
New York *Independent Journal*, 28 November 1787 (CC:300)
New York *Daily Advertiser*, 29 November
New York Packet, 30 November
Massachusetts Centinel, 8 December
Pennsylvania Gazette, 30 January 1788
Albany Gazette, 7 February

No.14 (Madison)
New York Packet, 30 November 1787 (CC:310)
New York *Daily Advertiser*, 1 December
New York *Independent Journal*, 1 December
Massachusetts Gazette, 11 December (excerpt)
Boston *American Herald*, 17 December
Pennsylvania Packet, 25 December (excerpt)
Maryland Journal, 1 January 1788 (excerpt)
Poughkeepsie *Country Journal*, 9 January (excerpt)
Salem Mercury, 15 January (excerpt)
Pennsylvania Gazette, 13 February

No. 15 (Hamilton)
New York *Independent Journal*, 1 December 1787 (CC:312)
New York Packet, 4 December
New York *Daily Advertiser*, 4, 5 December
Boston *American Herald*, 24 December
Poughkeepsie *Country Journal*, 16 January 1788 (supplement)
Pennsylvania Gazette, 20 February

No. 16 (Hamilton)
New York Packet, 4 December 1787 (CC:317)
New York *Independent Journal*, 5 December
New York *Daily Advertiser*, 6 December
Poughkeepsie *Country Journal*, 16 January 1788 (supplement)
Pennsylvania Gazette, 27 February
Winchester *Virginia Gazette*, 9 April

No. 17 (Hamilton)
New York *Independent Journal*, 5 December 1787 (CC:321)
New York *Daily Advertiser*, 7 December

New York Packet, 7 December
Poughkeepsie *Country Journal*, 22 January 1788 (supplement)
Pennsylvania Gazette, 5 March
Albany Gazette, 13 March

No. 18 (Madison assisted by Hamilton)
New York Packet , 7 December 1787 (CC:330)
    New York *Daily Advertiser*, 7, 8 December
    New York *Independent Journal*, 8 December
    Poughkeepsie *Country Journal*, 22 January 1788 (supplement)
    Pennsylvania Gazette, 12 March

No. 19 (Madison assisted by Hamilton)
New York *Independent Journal*, 8 December 1787 (CC:333)
    New York *Daily Advertiser*, 10 December
    New York Packet, 11 December
    Poughkeepsie *Country Journal*, 29 January 1788 (supplement)
    Pennsylvania Gazette, 19 March

No. 20 (Madison assisted by Hamilton)
New York Packet, 11 December 1787 (CC:340)
    New York *Independent Journal*, 12 December
    New York *Daily Advertiser*, 12, 13 December
    Poughkeepsie *Country Journal*, 29 January, 5 February 1788 (supplements)

No. 21 (Hamilton) .
New York *Independent Journal*, 12 December 1787 (CC:341)
    New York *Daily Advertiser*, 14 December
    New York Packet, 14 December
    Poughkeepsie *Country Journal*, 5 February 1788 (supplement)

No. 22 (Hamilton)
New York Packet, 14 December 1787 (CC:347)
    New York *Independent Journal*, 15 December
    New York *Daily Advertiser*, 17, 18 December

No. 23 (Hamilton)
New York Packet, 18 December 1787 (CC:352)
    New York Journal, 18 December
    New York *Daily Advertiser*, 19 December
    New York *Independent Journal*, 19 December
    Boston *American Herald*, 7 January 1788

No. 24 (Hamilton)
New York *Independent Journal*, 19 December 1787 (CC:355)
    New York *Daily Advertiser*, 19 December
    New York Journal, 19 December
    New York Packet, 21 December

No. 25 (Hamilton)
New York Packet, 21 December 1787 (CC:364)
    New York *Daily Advertiser*, 21 December
    New York Journal, 21 December
    New York *Independent Journal*, 22 December

No. 26 (Hamilton)
New York *Independent Journal*, 22 December 1787 (CC:366)
   New York *Daily Advertiser*, 24 December
   New York Journal, 25 December
   New York Packet, 25 December

No. 27 (Hamilton)
New York Packet, 25 December 1787 (CC:378)
   New York Journal, 25 December
   New York *Daily Advertiser*, 26 December
   New York *Independent Journal*, 26 December

No. 28 (Hamilton)
New York *Independent Journal*, 26 December 1787 (CC:381)
   New York *Daily Advertiser*, 28 December
   New York Packet, 28 December
   New York Journal, 2 January 1788

No. 29 (Hamilton)
New York *Independent Journal*, 9 January 1788 (CC:429)
   New York *Daily Advertiser*, 10 January
   New York Packet, 11 January
   New York Journal, 12 January

No. 30 (Hamilton)
New York Packet, 28 December 1787 (CC:391)
   New York *Daily Advertiser*, 29 December
   New York *Independent Journal*, 29 December
   New York Journal, 2, 4 January 1788

No. 31 (Hamilton)
New York Packet, 1 January 1788 (CC:403)
   New York *Daily Advertiser*, 2 January
   New York *Independent Journal*, 2 January
   New York Journal, 5 January

Nos. 32–33 (Hamilton)
New York *Independent Journal*, 2 January 1788 (CC:405)
   New York *Daily Advertiser*, 3 January
   New York Packet, 4 January
   New York Journal, 8 January

No. 34 (Hamilton)
New York Packet, 4 January 1788 (CC:416)
   New York *Daily Advertiser*, 5 January
   New York *Independent Journal*, 5 January
   New York Journal, 8 January

No. 35 (Hamilton)
New York *Independent Journal*, 5 January 1788 (CC:418)
   New York *Daily Advertiser*, 7 January
   New York Packet, 8 January
   New York Journal, 9 January

No. 36 (Hamilton)
New York Packet, 8 January 1788 (CC:426)

New York *Independent Journal*, 9 January
New York *Daily Advertiser*, 10 January
New York Journal, 11, 12 January

No. 37 (Madison)
New York *Daily Advertiser*, 11 January 1788 (CC:440)
    New York *Independent Journal*, 12 January
    New York Packet, 15 January
    New York Journal, 19 January

No. 38 (Madison)
New York *Independent Journal*, 12 January 1788 (CC:442)
    New York *Daily Advertiser*, 15 January
    New York Packet, 15 January
    New York Journal, 25, 26 January
    Exeter, N.H., *Freeman's Oracle*, 15 February (excerpt)

No. 39 (Madison)
New York *Independent Journal*, 16 January 1788 (CC:452)
    New York *Daily Advertiser*, 16 January
    New York Packet, 18 January
    New York Journal, 30 January

No. 40 (Madison)
New York Packet, 18 January 1788 (CC:458)
    New York *Daily Advertiser*, 19 January
    New York *Independent Journal*, 19 January

No. 41 (Madison)
New York *Independent Journal*, 19 January 1788 (CC:463)
    New York Packet, 22 January
    New York *Daily Advertiser*, 22, 23 January

No. 42 (Madison)
New York Packet, 22 January 1788 (CC:466)
    New York *Independent Journal*, 23 January
    New York *Daily Advertiser*, 24 January

No. 43 (Madison)
New York *Independent Journal*, 23 January 1788 (CC:469)
    New York *Daily Advertiser*, 25 January
    New York Packet, 25 January

No. 44 (Madison)
New York Packet, 25 January 1788 (CC:476)
    New York *Independent Journal*, 26 January
    New York *Daily Advertiser*, 29 January

No. 45 (Madison)
New York *Independent Journal*, 26 January 1788 (CC:478)
    New York Packet, 29 January
    New York *Daily Advertiser*, 30 January

No. 46 (Madison)
New York Packet, 29 January 1788 (CC:483)
    New York *Independent Journal*, 30 January
    New York *Daily Advertiser*, 31 January

No. 47 (Madison)
New York *Independent Journal*, 30 January 1788 (CC:486)
  New York Packet, 1 February
New York *Daily Advertiser*, 1, 2 February

No. 48 (Madison)
New York Packet, 1 February 1788 (CC:492)
  New York *Independent Journal*, 2 February
  New York *Daily Advertiser*, 4 February

No. 49 (Madison)
New York *Independent Journal*, 2 February 1788 (CC:495)
  New York Packet, 5 February
New York *Daily Advertiser*, 6 February

No. 50 (Madison)
New York Packet, 5 February 1788 (CC:500)
  New York *Independent Journal*, 6 February
  New York *Daily Advertiser*, 9 February

No. 51 (Madison)
New York *Independent Journal*, 6 February 1788 (CC:503)
  New York Packet, 8 February
New York *Daily Advertiser*, 11 February

No. 52 (Madison?)
New York Packet, 8 February 1788 (CC:514)
  New York *Independent Journal*, 9 February

No. 53 (Madison or Hamilton)
New York *Independent Journal*, 9 February 1788 (CC:519)
  New York Packet, 12 February

No. 54 (Madison)
New York Packet, 12 February 1788 (CC:521)
  New York *Independent Journal*, 13 February

No. 55 (Madison?)
New York *Independent Journal*, 13 February 1788 (CC:525)
  New York Packet, 15 February

No. 56 (Madison?)
New York *Independent Journal*, 16 February 1788 (CC:533)
  New York Packet, 19 February

No. 57 (Madison?)
New York Packet, 19 February 1788 (CC:542)
  New York *Independent Journal*, 20 February

No. 58 (Madison?)
New York *Independent Journal*, 20 February 1788 (CC:546)
  New York Packet, 22 February

No. 59 (Hamilton)
New York Packet, 22 February 1788 (CC:555)
  New York *Independent Journal*, 23 February

No. 60 (Hamilton)
New York *Independent Journal*, 23 February 1788 (CC:558)
  New York Packet, 26 February

No. 61 (Hamilton)
New York Packet, 26 February 1788 (CC:564)
  New York *Independent Journal*, 27 February

No. 62 (Madison?)
New York *Independent Journal*, 27 February 1788 (CC:569)
  New York Packet, 29 February

No. 63 (Madison?)
New York *Independent Journal*, 1 March 1788 (CC:582)
  New York Packet, 4 March

No. 64 (Jay)
New York *Independent Journal*, 5 March 1788 (CC: 592–A)
  New York Packet, 7 March

No. 65 (Hamilton)
New York Packet, 7 March 1788 (CC:601)
  New York *Independent Journal*, 8 March

No. 66 (Hamilton)
New York *Independent Journal*, 8 March 1788 (CC:607)
  New York Packet, 11 March

No. 67 (Hamilton)
New York Packet, 11 March 1788 (CC:612)
  New York *Independent Journal*, 12 March

No. 68 (Hamilton)
New York *Independent Journal*, 12 March 1788 (CC:615)
  New York Packet, 14 March

No. 69 (Hamilton)
New York Packet, 14 March 1788 (CC:617)
  New York *Independent Journal*, 15 March
  Albany *Federal Herald*, 31 March

No. 70 (Hamilton)
New York *Independent Journal*, 15 March 1788 (CC:619)
  New York Packet, 18 March

No. 71 (Hamilton)
New York Packet, 18 March 1788 (CC:625)
  New York *Independent Journal*, 19 March

No. 72 (Hamilton)
New York *Independent Journal*, 19 March 1788 (CC:628)
  New York Packet, 21 March

No. 73 (Hamilton)
New York Packet, 21 March 1788 (CC:635)
  New York *Independent Journal*, 22 March

No. 74 (Hamilton)
New York Packet, 25 March 1788 (CC:644)
New York *Independent Journal*, 26 March

No. 75 (Hamilton)
New York *Independent Journal*, 26 March 1788 (CC:646)
New York Packet, 28 March

No. 76 (Hamilton)
New York Packet, 1 April 1788 (CC:656)
New York *Independent Journal*, 2 April

No. 77 (Hamilton)
New York *Independent Journal*, 2 April 1788 (CC:657)
New York Packet, 4 April

No. 78 (Hamilton)
Book Edition, Volume II, 28 May 1788 (CC:759)
New York *Independent Journal*, 14 June
New York Packet, 17, 20 June

No. 79 (Hamilton)
Book Edition, Volume II, 28 May 1788 (CC:760)
New York *Independent Journal*, 18 June
New York Packet, 24 June

No. 80 (Hamilton)
Book Edition, Volume II, 28 May 1788 (CC:761)
New York *Independent Journal*, 21 June
New York Packet, 27 June, 1 July

No. 81 (Hamilton)
Book Edition, Volume II, 28 May 1788 (CC:762)
New York *Independent Journal*, 25, 28 June
New York Packet, 4, 8 July

No. 82 (Hamilton)
Book Edition, Volume II, 28 May 1788 (CC:763)
New York *Independent Journal*, 2 July
New York Packet, 11 July

No. 83 (Hamilton)
Book Edition, Volume II, 28 May 1788 (CC:764)
New York *Independent Journal*, 5, 9, 12 July
New York Packet, 15, 18, 22, 25 July

No. 84 (Hamilton)
Book Edition, Volume II, 28 May 1788 (CC:765)
New York *Independent Journal*, 16, 26 July, 9 August
New York Packet, 29 July, 8, 12 August

No. 85 (Hamilton)
Book Edition, Volume II, 28 May 1788 (CC:766)
New York *American Magazine*, June (excerpt quoted in review)
New York *Independent Journal*, 13, 16 August
New York Packet, 15 August

Appendix V
New York Population from the 1790 U.S. Census[1]

County	Slaves	Total
Albany	3,929	75,921
Clinton	17	1,614
Columbia	1,623	27,732
Dutchess	1,856	45,266
Kings	1,432	4,495
Montgomery	599	29,914
New York	2,369	33,131
Orange	966	18,478
Queens	2,309	16,014
Richmond	759	3,835
Suffolk	1,098	16,440
Ulster	2,906	29,397
Washington	47	14,033
Westchester	1,419	23,941
TOTALS	21,329	340,211

1. U.S. Bureau of the Census, *Heads of Families at the First Census of the United States Taken in the Year 1790: New York* (Washington, 1908), 9–10.